COMMUNISM:
The Final Crisis?

COMMUNISM:
The Final Crisis?

An Editorials On File Book

Editor: Oliver Trager

Facts On File

New York • Oxford • Sydney

COMMUNISM:

The Final Crisis?

Published by Facts On File, Inc.
© Copyright 1990 by Facts On File, Inc.

Library of Congress Cataloging-in-Publication Data

Communism : the final crisis? / edited by Oliver Trager.
    p. cm. — (An Editorials on file book)
  Summary: A compilation of newspaper editorials about the social and political changes in the communist world around 1990.
  ISBN 0-8160-2507-X
  1. Communism—1945- 2. Communist countries—Politics and government. 3. Communist countries—Social conditions. 4. American newspapers—Sections, columns, etc.—Editorials.
[1. Communism—1945- 2. Communist countries—Politics and government.] I. Trager, Oliver. II. Series.
HX44.C6424 1990
909'.09717'0828—dc20   90-3229

                                                              CIP
                                                              AC

Printed in the United States of America
9 8 7 6 5 4 3 2 1

Contents

COMMUNISM:
The Final Crisis?

Preface

The communist world is undergoing a dramatic transformation. The toppling of the Berlin Wall, the peaceful transition of Poland, the violent overthrow of Romania's totalitarian regime, and pro- democracy movements in Bulgaria, Hungary and Czechoslovakia have all loosened the Soviet Union's control role in Eastern Europe. Soviet internal affairs, political, social and economic, are also in a state of flux. Secessionist movements in the Baltic states combined with ethnic and religious unrest in Azerbaijan pose major challeneges to Soviet President Mikhail Gorbachev's visions of restructuring the U.S.S.R.

But the reshuffling of communism and the issues this raises are not confined to the Soviet realm. The 1989 prodemocracy student movement in China and its bloody suppression called into question the morality and political will of that nation's government as well as its future.

Attendant upon these developments is the course the U.S. and the rest of the developed Western world should steer as a consequence of communism's changing face. *COMMUNISM: The Final Crisis?* explores the events and issues that have dominated the news in the last year and the questions that have come to the fore: Will Gorbachev be able to hold on to power in the U.S.S.R.? How successful will democratic elections be in once closed societies? What effect will self-determination have on the geopolitics of the Baltic states? Should Germany be reunified in the wake of the dismantling of the Berlin Wall? How will Solidarity fare in Poland's political arena? Is there still a need for an arms race in view of communism's apparent demise? How will the expanding of political rights and the opening of borders change the economies of the U.S.S.R., its satellites and Western Europe? What effect will changes in communism have on the cold war and the presence of U.S. troops in Western Europe? How should U.S. relations with China proceed post – Tiananmen Square?

As the Communist world reevaluates its political ideology and direction, *COMMUNISM: The Final Crisis?* explores the crucial decisions facing both East and West.

May 1990

Oliver Trager

Part I:
The Union of Soviet
Socialist Republics

Virtually from the moment he became the youngest Soviet Communist Party leader since Joseph Stalin, it was clear that Mikhail S. Gorbachev was bent on transforming the Soviet Union. But few people would have predicted the sweeping change that has taken place in the ensuing five years. His policies have not only altered the U.S.S.R., but the communist world as well.

Gorbachev faced his country's many serious problems head-on when he assumed power. His main challenge was to open on several levels what had long been a closed society. He forced out the party's old guard, a creaky bureaucracy that was resistant to change, clearing the way for a younger, more flexible Soviet leadership. He allowed the introduction of Western-style free-market economic reforms to revive the stagnant economic system unable to meet the demands of the Soviet populace. He instituted democratic reforms leading to elections that not only demonstrated the population's frustration with the Communist Party but began rectifying the nation's woeful human rights record. He put an end to the expensive and unpopular war in Afghanistan, muted tensions between the superpowers and arrested the escalating arms race with deft diplomatic and arms-control maneuvers.

Now that the Russian terms *glasnost* (openness) and *perestroika* (restructuring), the cornerstones of Gorbachev's domestic policies, have become household words in the West, Gorbachev himself has become one of the world's most charismatic and dynamic leaders.

However, it is still too early to determine how successful Gorbachev's alchemization of Soviet-style communism will be. The many troubling questions that arose as he introduced his dramatic initiatives remain unanswered. Will an infusion of capitalism improve the living standard of the Soviet people? How far will the U.S.S.R. go to implement human-rights and democratic reforms? How much independence will the Kremlin allow Soviet ethnic minorities and the countries of the Eastern bloc?

Gorbachev has entered a critical and precarious phase in the realization of his grand design for the Soviet Union. When the Congress of People's Deputies installed Gorbachev in an enhanced executive presidency, he earnestly undertook to reform Soviet Communist Party autocracy and promise democracy. Soviet-watchers say that this is nothing less than the demolition of communist ideology as the ruling force of Soviet political life.

In a recent interview, Gorbachev himself said that he was bound during the first five years of his leadership to espouse the virtues of Leninism because his power flowed from the Communist Party. He claimed that his reforms, criticized within and outside the Soviet Union as being "halfway," were limited because more drastic measures such as privatization and a multiparty political system are antithetical to communist ideology.

Though the notion that Gorbachev was only pretending to be a Leninist may sound revisionist, there is no denying that increasingly he behaves more

2

like a man freed from ideological constraints. A draft of new party rules published in March 1990 confirmed the party's plan to eliminate the job of general secretary, the post from which Soviet leaders since Stalin have run both party and country.

This is a vulnerable time for Gorbachev. An ongoing worry is that those who stand to lose most in the transfer of power will panic and take one last opportunity to strike out at him. Since Gorbachev initiated *perestroika*, the foremost nightmare of Soviet liberals has been an alliance of hard-line Communist Party opponents of Gorbachev with the military or the KGB, the country's internal security intelligence apparatus.

Soviet watchers suggest that the spectacle of Communist Party hard-liners in league with the military, as was seen in the spring 1990 occupation of Lithuania, is a chilling reminder that the Soviet military and the KGB remain among the most politicized of institutions, permeated by Communist Party cells and indoctrinated in the defense of Leninism. Though Gorbachev may have this operation in motion when he tried to frighten Lithuania into backing away from its claim to independence, his apparent solicitousness of the military may be greater than it would be in stable times. It is also apparent that in this period when the party is being stripped of power, the military may not yet stripped of the party.

Many other factors threatening Gorbachev's grip on power must be addressed: ethnic disturbances in the Transcaucasus, growing labor unrest in the country's key industries, and moves toward religious freedom. The varied and changing circumstances of Soviet communism raise a fundamental query: Can the the natural structures in the state, in family, in religion be recreated once they have been dismantled?

Soviet Party Regulars Humbled in Nationwide Parliamentary Elections

The Soviet Union March 26, 1989 held its first nationwide multi-candidate parliamentary elections since 1917. The step toward Western-style democracy produced unexpectedly embarrassing results for the Communist Party (CP) leadership.

Voters across the country chose among candidates to fill 1,500 seats in the new 2,250 seat Congress of People's Deputies. The remaining 750 seats of the restructured parliament had been reserved for deputies picked by the party and by labor, social and youth organizations.

Voter turnout was reported to be heavy, even in some districts where there was only one candidate on the ballot. Candidates ran with no opposition in about 25% of the districts. In other districts, there were as many as 12 candidates on the ballot. An election was not valid unless a minimum of 30% of the eligible voters in a district cast ballots.

Preliminary results disclosed by government and party officials gave a broad picture of the outcome. It was evident from the official reaction that the voting did not go as the leadership had anticipated. Where Soviet leader Mikhail S. Gorbachev had intended the election to result in a vote of confidence for his reformist policies, the result instead appeared to show deep dissatisfaction with the status quo and a desire for even more sweeping change.

Populists, liberals, radicals, reformists and ethnic nationalists defeated party regulars in many districts. In other districts, some party loyalists won seats with a bare minimum of the necessary votes.

Party bosses were not exempt from the humiliation. In the most noteworthy defeat, Yuri F. Solovyev, the CP first secretary of the Leningrad region, and a nonvoting member of the Central Committee Politburo, failed to win a seat even though he was the only candidate on the ballot in his district. Under the rules of the election, an unopposed candidate had to receive at least 50% of votes cast in his or her district. Voters in Solovyev's district were reported to have crossed his name off their ballots en masse.

Pravda, the Communist Party newspaper, March 28 omitted mention of Solovyev's defeat in a summary of election results. The official news agency Tass mentioned it in passing. Local media coverage in Leningrad of the results simply named those who had won seats.

Leningrad city CP boss Anatoly Gerasimov was soundly defeated by shipbuilder Yuri Boldyrev. Leningrad Mayor Vladimir Khodyrev, running unopposed, was a victim of a "cross-out" campaign.

Five Ukrainian regional party leaders ran unopposed in their districts and each failed to reach the 50% mark. Kiev party leader Konstantin I. Masik and the city's mayor, Valentin A. Zgursky, were defeated.

Nationalist candidates in the Baltic regions trampled predominantly nonnationalist party regulars. In Lithuania, 31 of the 42 seats went to nationalists.

In another hotbed of nationalist tensions, the Transcaucasus region, Armenian activists charged the elections had been rigged in favor of antinationalist candidates.

The second secretary of the Moscow region, Yuri Prokofyev, failed in his bid. Moscow Mayor Valery Saikin also failed, in spite of a vigorous campaign that had included Gorbachev style "walkabouts." Some Western observers viewed the defeats of Prokofyev and Saikin as a spillover from the triumph of Boris N. Yeltsin, the populist former party boss of Moscow. Yeltsin won Moscow's at-large seat in the new parliament with 89% of the vote over Yevgeny A. Brakov, the managing director of the Zil automobile works. *Pravda* March 28 announced Yeltsin's victory but did not say it was a landslide. The item was buried on page two.

St. Petersburg Times

St. Petersburg, FL, March 28, 1989

It was the Soviet people's first taste of democracy in 70 years, and they devoured it so voraciously that their appetite for it is no longer in serious doubt, if indeed it ever was. Now Mikhail Gorbachev and the rest of the Soviet leadership must prove that they have the stomach to allow their democratic experiment to run its course once the implications of Sunday's startling results have been fully digested.

The Soviets have shown themselves to be a relatively well educated and politically astute people who have not allowed their democratic spirit to be extinguished even by a lifetime of the most suffocating form of totalitarian rule. Sunday's election may have been messy — as elections tend to be when the results aren't known before the balloting begins — but the Soviets generally behaved as though they had been doing this all their lives. In particular, Boris Yeltsin's emotional victory in the election to represent his city in the new Soviet congress was the culmination of an old-fashioned reform-*vs.*-machine contest that might have looked more in place in Chicago than Moscow.

Yeltsin almost certainly will continue to irritate the party hierarchy in his expanded role as progressive gadfly, but his political rehabilitation is far from the most serious challenge to the Communist Party's control that emerged from Sunday's election. The real test of democratic reform will come with the official response to what appears to have been the overwhelming repudiation of the party's chosen candidates, particularly in the Baltic republics and other regions controlled by ethnic minorities. For example, in Lithuania, the independent Sajudis movement, which demands a new degree of sovereignty and identity for all 15 Soviet republics, defeated the Communist Party's chosen candidates in almost all of the region's 42 contested seats. Other high-ranking party officials were trounced by political outsiders even in Russian strongholds such as Leningrad.

Many older and more conservative party officials of the central government fear that the encouragement of new political organizations in the Baltic republics, as well as other troubled regions such as Azerbaijan, will only fuel ethnic tensions and separatist sentiments that had been effectively submerged for decades. The party's controlling faction, led by Gorbachev, continues to insist that the democratic reforms of *glasnost* offer the best hope of giving voice to the grievances of political and ethnic minorities without threatening the Soviet Union's very structure. The tensions between those two views will re-emerge when the newly elected congress convenes to choose a legislature to work with the person (presumably Gorbachev) chosen to serve in the newly created office of president.

In the meantime, Gorbachev's balancing act enters a new stage. He must convince skeptical Soviet citizens that his new political system will evolve into a genuine vehicle of democratic reform. At the same time, he must convince an increasingly nervous power structure that his changes ultimately serve its interests as well.

Gorbachev's audacious revolution-from-within is still far from ultimate success, but the rest of the world can no longer doubt the seriousness or the sincerity of his intent. Whether it succeeds or fails, the Soviet Union's political experiment, unthinkable only a few years ago, creates new challenges for the United States and the traditional Western alliance. For now, though, our government should simply join the rest of the world in congratulating the Soviet people, and the Soviet leadership, on having shown the courage to take this first step along a road untraveled for more than 70 years.

Omaha World-Herald
Omaha, NE, March 29, 1989

Commentators who pointed out that the elections in the Soviet Union didn't live up to Western standards of democracy may have missed the point. As in the story of the talking dog, the important thing is not what the dog said but that it talked at all.

The give-and-take in the Soviet Union in the past few weeks has been astonishing. So has the independence of Soviet voters. Populist maverick Boris Yeltsin received nearly 90 percent of the approximately 3 million votes that were cast in his Moscow district. Nationwide, more than 190 million voters turned out, and some longtime bureaucrats lost their bids to be members of the new assembly.

Soviet voters sent the party a message.

Almost 80 percent of the 1,500 parliamentary seats in Sunday's balloting were contested — a breakthrough in a nation that had not had a free, open, contested election since 1917. In the 1917 election, which featured multiple parties, the Communists received only 25 percent of the vote.

The party didn't do particularly well Sunday. Yeltsin, for all practical purposes, was running against the establishment — even against President Mikhail Gorbachev, whom Yeltsin has accused of going too slow in initiating reforms.

The degree of general discontent was evident also in the losses suffered by Communist Party officials in the Ukraine, Latvia, Estonia, Lithuania and Armenia, where nationalist movements have emerged as a counterforce to the party.

Some people believe that a kind of two-party system may be developing within the Communist umbrella, with liberals, reformers and some nationalists congregating around Yeltsin and conservatives forming an opposing bloc. In some cases, conservatives chose to campaign on a reform platform and were successful.

The 2,250-member Congress of People's Deputies will choose the nation's president for a five-year term and will select, from among its members, a smaller body to serve as a law-making body for eight months of each year. Gorbachev has indicated that all members of the new assembly will eventually serve in the smaller body.

These developments, embracing a degree of pluralism unheard of since the time of Lenin, reflect the profound changes that are occurring. The steps that have been taken still leave the Soviet system far from Western-style democracy. But the progress from what prevailed just a few years ago is dramatic.

THE SAGINAW NEWS
Saginaw, MI, March 30, 1989

After 72 years, the Soviets must have forgotten all they ever knew about rigging an election.

In old Chicago, for sure, a Boris Yeltsin who had been bounced from the Moscow machine 18 months ago would not now win an 89 percent landslide. In Lithuania, the president, the prime minister and the minister of justice would not be dumped. In Latvia, the premier would survive.

Well, maybe no one ever told Mikhail Gorbachev about Richard Daley. But even that embattled leader must be stunned by the rebellious mood that came out of the first elections since the Bolshevik revolution that meant anything.

And he might also be secretly pleased.

Across the Soviet Union, voters selecting parliamentary delegates rejected kingpins of the old regime. Lithuanian nationalists took 31 of the 42 seats. In the Ukraine, five regional party chairmen lost.

The results were not simply a show of regional nationalist feeling. The Communist chief in Leningrad lost, too. One top official in that city failed to win even though he ran unopposed. Voters crossed out his name to deny him the required majority. Just like that, the Russians moved ahead of us; our system has not yet devised a way to actually choose "none of the above."

Internal Soviet analysts may be new to their game, but it does not take a sophisticated politico to sense the surge against the status quo. But if the old party lost, the new Soviet man — Gorbachev — should be the winner. Above all, the election confirmed that his drive for reform and fundamental change is heading, however haltingly, in the right direction as far as the people are concerned.

Even to Gorbachev, the results in the restive republics may be an excess of perestroika. Elections or not, it is doubtful he can survive his Politburo opposition by presiding over the dismantling of the Soviet empire. This is a time when two sets of reformers need to understand each other.

Unless Gorbachev prevails, this may be the last opportunity for Soviets, as a whole, to tell the bosses what they think of them — not much, in all honesty. But whatever happens, the election should leave a lasting impression. And having tasted some real power, Soviet citizens may not surrender it too readily. The party has learned what power to the people really means, and that is revolutionary indeed.

The Washington Post
Washington, DC, March 28, 1989

A SEVERE CONTRADICTION lies at the heart of the Soviet Union's second contested elections. On one side, there was an exceptionally live process, notably in maverick Boris Yeltsin's Moscow blitz and in anti-establishment campaigns in the Baltics and elsewhere. The elections may not have approached Western standards: a third of the members of the new Congress of People's Deputies, including Mikhail Gorbachev himself, had already been picked by the Communist Party, and one of four seats up on Sunday went uncontested. The Soviet Union remains a one-party state, and more candidates were party members this time than in previous no-choice elections. Still, for a society having its first taste of democracy, there was some real excitement in the air.

But this is not the whole of it. Mikhail Gorbachev remains a son of the Lenin who cancelled the unwelcome results of the first Soviet contested elections, right after the 1917 Revolution. Nothing about him suggests he is a closet democrat—certainly not his carefully qualified championing of political competition or his government's arrest of the whole Armenian counter-slate. Rather, he is shrewdly using democratic forms to diminish the entrenched party core and other bureaucratic and conservative elements that impede his reform. He is creating—in the Congress, in the smaller first standing national legislature it is to appoint and in the coming new local governing bodies—an alternate structure apart from the party with which to push the party and conceivably even to supplant it. He is also creating, atop the Congress, an executive position of tremendous power which he will occupy in addition to the posts (head of party and government) he already holds. To appoint an executive president "with such powers in a country that does not have a multiparty system," says Andrei Sakharov, "is just insanity."

It seems that many Soviet people voted more from the habit of discipline than from genuine faith in a new era. The Western press located the springs of enthusiasm among newly unleashed democrats, but it found reservoirs of popular apathy and skepticism as well. How could it be otherwise? No one can know where these first small steps will take the Soviet Union. That may turn out to be the major point of the exercise. Something new was being tested. The results are not so much unknown as undeveloped, not yet there to be seen and measured. Give Mikhail Gorbachev credit for that.

"TELL YOU HOW I VOTED?? WHY, I THOUGHT THAT SORT OF INTRUSIVE MEDDLING WITH THE DEMOCRATIC PROCESS ONLY HAPPENED IN AMERICA!"

The Burlington Free Press

Burlington, VT, March 29, 1989

Wallflowers for 70 years, the Soviet people finally got asked to dance at their revolution.

They did an ecstatic boogie to the ballot box on Sunday, where millions refused to let their Communist Party partner do the leading. Wherever voters were given a choice they embraced populists and non-conformists. They rejected party chiefs and Army generals, a member of the Politburo and at least one mayor.

One election doesn't mean the collapse of the Soviet system — the new Congress of People's Deputies will meet only once a year and will have limited power. It will elect a full-time Legislature, the Supreme Soviet, but the Party can probably ensure that the reformers get token, if any, representation.

The Party will have a harder time telling its people the party's over.

By all reports, most Russians took to elections and campaigning — to *choice* — with the enthusiasm of, well, Americans. Mass rallies and candidates' harangues against the privileged elite blew away Mikhail Gorbachev's cautious definition of *glasnost*. *Glasnost*, openness, isn't hedged speeches and between-the-lines criticism in Pravda. *Glasnost* is an Army lieutenant colonel, a candidate for the Congress, calling for an end to the draft. *Glasnost* is a deputy editor telling a rally how his newspaper manipulated the news to damage populist Boris Yeltsin. *Glasnost* is Yeltsin calling for study of a multi-party system.

Soviet citizens, new to the dance, may have unreasonable expectations of electoral politics. Even with the best will in the world, the Congress of Deputies can not quickly shorten food lines, build millions of new apartments or improve the quality of manufactured goods. Elections, like *glasnost*, are the technically easiest parts of fundamental change.

Nevertheless, Gorbachev seemed to recognize the bolt of energy that Sunday's dance shot through his people — it's that energy he needs to change his country. More elections, more choices, more citizen involvement are the only way to harness it.

Boris Yeltsin seems an unlikely Patrick Swayze, but he's proof Russians, too, swoon for the dirty dancing of democracy.

Toronto, Ont., March 28, 1989

A funny thing happened on the way to the Congress of People's Deputies. Instead of automatic elevation, there was an election, said to be historic.

It was an election too. But it was one-dimensional, not to be confused with what happens here.

It was an election only in the sense that Soviet citizens had a choice of personalities, almost all from the *one* party that only a comparatively few citizens belong to.

Nearly all of the attention focused on Boris Yeltsin, the so-called Kremlin rebel, running in Moscow.

Yeltsin came to power because of Mikhail Gorbachev. When he was bounced from the ranks of the mighty because of a fight with the conservative old guard, he didn't fall that far, again because of Gorby.

He had a soft landing as a deputy minister in the construction industry. And he used that post to lash out as a populist against the perks lavished on top Communists.

Yet there was a certain measure of hypocrisy — something not unknown in western politics — in his public repudiation of privileges. His wife lined up for food with the other housewives but he didn't give up his official car, dacha or special health services.

At the same time, his bid at a political comeback — unheard of in Soviet life — in the Moscow constituency that is the largest in the country, made him the focal figure of the campaign in the western media.

He won by a landslide. And we suspect that's also good for Gorbachev. Yeltsin is a useful safety valve in Gorbachev's programs of *glasnost* and *perestroika*, the reforms of openness and restructuring that even feature elections in a "democratization" of Soviet society.

Yeltsin's a way of letting the people blow off steam if they're unhappy with how the reforms are going. He's called for different paces and approaches.

It's another brilliant move by Gorbachev as he plays chess to capture popular support both within and without. We can say this election wasn't really democratic but it was certainly better than what they did. So we continue to applaud Gorbachev while warning that his manipulation still places perception ahead of reality.

You would think he was running North America.

THE CHRISTIAN SCIENCE MONITOR

Boston, MA, March 16, 1989

LITHUANIAN nationalists are calling for independence. They aren't likely to prevail anytime soon, but their call shows how far the reforms initiated by Mikhail Gorbachev have come.

The question for Lithuanians, Latvians, Estonians, Ukrainians, and others is how far they can go before Moscow reacts. Mr. Gorbachev faces plenty of pressing issues: a new round of arms talks with the West; a battle over the direction of Soviet agriculture; growing popular concern about environmental damage in the country. He may be willing to bear with activists in the Baltics and elsewhere, letting the process of political evolution take its course. But pressures to act have to be mounting.

The leaders of the Lithuanian popular front, Sajudis, recognize this and caution against premature calls for separation from the Soviet Union. Economic independence, a real possibility under Gorbachev, should be the immediate goal, in their view.

The Baltic nationalists have seized on the March 26 Soviet parliamentary elections as a vehicle for their political aspirations. Lithianian, Latvian, and Estonian popular-front candidates are likely to trounce Communist Party regulars at the polls.

Ukrainian nationalism, though off to a slower start, has its own popular movement. called the Ruk. Given the Ukraine's 50 million people and economic clout, nationalist activism there could have a profound impact. But there are also built-in brakes: a more authoritarian Communist Party and a cultural divide between the western part of the republic and the more Russified east.

And nationalism in the Soviet Union isn't just an activity for minorities. Pamyat, a Russian nationalist group dedicated to glorifying the Stalinist past, decries current reforms and any move toward democracy.

That kind of nationalism could prove at least as worrisome to Gorbachev and his lieutenants as Baltic separatism.

MILWAUKEE SENTINEL

Milwaukee, WI, March 22, 1989

A telling test of how Soviet political reform works when the loyal opposition is a high-profile figure with a base of ardent supporters could take place if Boris Yeltsin stays on the ballot for the March 26 elections to the Soviet Union's new national parliament.

Yeltsin is the former party chief of Moscow who was dumped by Soviet leader Mikhail S. Gorbachev, apparently for being too outspoken. It's important to note that Yeltsin is not opposed to Gorbachev's reforms. He wants them to move faster and to be applied more broadly.

Now Yeltsin is gathering huge crowds in Red Square in what sounds like an American-type campaign, complete with signs and banners. "Yes to Yeltsin, no to the bureaucratic system," reads one banner.

In what otherwise would have been accepted as standard practice, the Communist Party's Central Committee has undertaken a secret investigation of charges that Yeltsin, who is still a member of the Central Committee, is opposing party policies. But his supporters reportedly are openly angered by this.

Some analysts say Yeltsin could be hoist on his own petard because a lot of bureaucrats live in Moscow.

But as a former big man in the big city, Yeltsin must have his hand on the pulse of the people. His call for limiting work permits for temporary employes who stretch the housing capability of Moscow suggests he does.

Unless his candidacy is quashed, the Kremlin chiefs could learn what it was like to deal with somebody like the late Mayor Richard J. Daley of Chicago.

Herald News

Fall River, MA, March 29, 1989

"A brisk to heavy voter turnout, nationwide," reported the Soviet News Agency Tass.

When a people's capacity to choose has been routinely suppressed for 70 years, a phenomenon like Sunday's parliamentary election in the Soviet Union is an experiment worth watching.

Secretary Mikhail Gorbachev, in an attempt to restructure a political and economic system in which the hard-line centralization of Communist machinery proved to have diminishing returns, has introduced the limited system of electoral choice as an aspect of the sweeping internal reforms known as 'perestroika' (restructuring).

Today's citizens of the USSR have never experienced a change of government leaders that is neither a rubber-stamp, single candidate-per-post assent, imposed by the Communist party; nor, as in the days of of V.I. Lenin, a bloody revolution against the vested aristocracy of the Tsars. A revolution, though it may express 'the will of the people,' is not primarily a matter of individual choice.

Even Gorbachev might be somewhat confounded by the apparent victory of his former protege, populist reformer Boris N. Yeltsin, the Moscow Communist party boss whom Gorbachev ousted for nonconformism in 1987. Yeltsin racked up an overwhelming popular vote over party stalwart Yevgeny Brakov, director of a factory that makes luxury cars for high-ranking officials. Yeltsin campaigned against privileges in high party echelons, and called for a better standard of living for the people.

The 2,250-member Congress of People's Deputies, created last year, is also an aspect of the new electoral reforms. About 190 million of the 280 million Soviet citizens over 18 years old were eligible to cast ballots in the free, secret election. About 1,500 seats were subject to the voting process. About 82 per cent of the candidates were Communist party members. Some 750 members were previously elected by the Communist Party, labor unions, and professional and social organizations.

Therefore, the election has certainly not broken the hold of the Communist party. No one ever expected it would. Within two months, the unwieldy new congress will elect 400 of its members to the Supreme Soviet, a working legislature; and name a president, presumably Gorbachev. His power will be thereby consolidated, and independent of the the party's policy-making Central Committee.

Presidential power will also expand: As president, Gorbachev would administer the nation, lead the Defense Counsel, make recommendations to the Supreme Soviet, and conduct foreign negotiations.

The 15 constituent Soviet Republics also elected deputies. In these provincial races, the radical movement toward ethnic autonomy was asserted, notably in Estonia, Latvia, and Lithuania. Eastern Europe is rife with nationalistic rumblings.

The Soviet elections are hardly what western observers would call full-scale and free. But they have allowed for much more public confrontation and dissent than could have been imagined in the pre-Gorbachev years. The new electoral system, though limited, is good practice for an inexperienced populace.

To survive, all institutions must change. After 70 years of monolithic statism, even the USSR must bend a little to the will of the people.

Soviet Congress Opens;
Gorbachev Wins Presidency

The Congress of People's Deputies, the new Soviet parliament, opened May 25, 1989 in the Kremlin's Palace of Congresses. Some 2,250 deputies were in attendance, most of them chosen for the parliament through direct elections. The majority of deputies were workers and academicians, not professional politicians.

The opening day, and the ensuing days, of the parliamentary session were televised live in the U.S.S.R. Soviet citizens were given an uncensored, unscripted look at their government in action: Radical statements, blunt criticisms directed at the regime and tedious debates over parliamentary procedure.

The highlight of the first day was the election of Communist Party (CP) General Secretary Mikhail S. Gorbachev to the revamped Soviet presidency. Gorbachev had held the post under the old parliament. The new post – an executive presidency in the French mold – carried broad powers over foreign and domestic policy and budget matters.

Gorbachev thus held not only the top party post but supplanted Premier Nikolai I. Ryzhkov as the government's top official. The Council of Ministers, the supercabinet headed by the premier, would chiefly serve to carry out the mandates of the president and the parliament.

About 85% of the deputies were Communist Party loyalists. Some 400 of the legislators – mainly from Moscow, Leningrad and the Baltic states – made up a loose opposition faction of radical reformists, liberals and ethnic nationalists.

Early in the initial session, the opposition faction lost a vote on the rules of order handed down by a panel of party loyalists.

Prior to the presidency vote, a parade of deputies made two hours of brief speeches at the rostrum. While pledging support for Gorbachev, many complained about the troubled economy and the poor results of *perestroika* (restructuring). Valentin A. Logunov, the deputy editor of the Moscow edition of *Pravda*, the CP newspaper, called on Gorbachev to resign as general secretary before assuming the presidency.

An Estonian nationalist leader, Marju Lauristen, demanded to know if Gorbachev had been involved in the decision to use soldiers against the demonstrators in the Soviet Georgian capital of Tibilsi, which resulted in the deaths of 20 protesters.

Gorbachev spoke before the vote, saying, "Many questions have been raised: There have been grave miscalculations and there have been tragedies. And some of these could have been avoided. I suffer, just like you do. I don't think you suspect me of wanting things to get worse. I think we are still at the stage when we're taking the situation into hand, but it's struggling to get away from us. The reform is trying to break loose, so is the political process..."

The presidency vote was conducted in secret. Gorbachev, unopposed, captured 95.6% of the vote. A total of 87 deputies voted against him.

The deputies May 26 voted in secret to choose the 542 members from among their number who would serve on the Supreme Soviet, the nation's new standing legislature. The election results were announced May 27.

Members of the new Supreme Soviet had been chosen in district caucuses before the opening of the congress. The major exception was Moscow, where 55 candidates had been nominated for a total of 29 seats.

In the vote May 26, only one leading Moscow reformist – dissident historian Roy A. Medvedev – was elected to the Supreme Soviet. Prominent reformists defeated included: Boris N. Yeltsin, the maverick former CP chief of Moscow; Tatyana I. Zaslavskaya, a radical sociologist; liberal economist Gavril K. Popov; agriculture expert Vladimir A. Tikhonov; and foreign affairs specialist Sergei Stankevitch.

The widespread defeat of reformists left the Supreme Soviet with an overwhelming majority of party loyalists, most of them professional politicians, including members of the top party leadership. In disgust, Yuri N. Afanasyev, a deputy and liberal historian, May 27 described the newly chosen legislature as a "Brezhnevite-Stalinist" body.

Lincoln Journal

Lincoln, NE, June 9, 1989

Meanwhile, back in Moscow... the new, awkward and somewhat combative 2,250-member Congress of People's Deputies continues to stay in session, feeling its way, making news. It also may have a more important if unanticipated function.

Because the congress is being televised live across the nation's 11 time zones, and because a number of elected deputies have been unaccountably brave in critical remarks, the Soviet people are being provided a kind of rare political catharsis. And they love it. Their access to consumer goods remains maddeningly blocked but at least they gain internal satisfaction knowing that leading government figures are catching deserved hell — and right in their face, too, on the congressional floor.

Some of the stinging, sarcastic remarks are as choice and filling as Russian rye bread.

The Associated Press reported a deputy from Siberia named Yuri Komarov lit into Gosagroprom, a central government agricultural superministry created only several years ago and abolished last March. How bad was Gosagroprom? So bad, the deputy cracked, that "people were saying it was the most successful action by the CIA against the Soviet economy."

Earlier, a national sports hero and a deputy from Moscow, Yuri Vlasov, ripped into the KGB as an uncontrolled underground empire. He bitterly cited Lubyanka prison as a place where "the cream of our nation" has been tortured.

The deputies' only real duty was to elect a president and a new, smaller legislature. Putting aside jokes and gibes, time will demonstrate whether this interesting representative body has any substantive impact beyond letting off steam.

Of course, that in itself has value, as any observer of Nebraska legislative life knows. Not a legislative session goes by around here without unintimidated citizens appearing before committees, sometimes lecturing state senators on their deficiencies, other times raging against government bureaucracy. Those outbursts only occasionally do practical good. They may not change things. But they do allow citizens to return home feeling psychologically pepped up and able to report "I told 'em a thing or two in Lincoln."

Just by itself, that release helps.

San Francisco Chronicle

San Francisco, CA, June 12, 1989

SEVERAL GENERATIONS of Americans have an image of a mighty and menacing USSR glowering and presiding over captive minions unfortunately within the immediate grasp of huge bear paws.

That image is rather ingrained and wants to persist. It suffered perhaps lasting damage, however, in last week's proceedings of the Congress of the People's Deputies in Moscow. The entire USSR, from the Pacific to the Baltic, reportedly sat transfixed before television tubes as the new deputies unburdened themselves with the wrongs which had been bottled up ever since the Communists came to power more than seven decades ago.

What has emerged, very generally, is the picture not of a marauding grizzly but more of a scraggly bear, showing ribs and trying to squeeze out a living in a third-rate carnival. It is not a pleasant picture but we are convinced it is a truer one. The congress, we believe, has stripped the Soviet image bare and has not done much for its soul either.

THE MOST ASTONISHING development — even after several years of Mikhail Gorbachev's new candor — came at the congress when economist and congress member Nikolai Shmelyov warned his colleagues that the country was headed for inevitable collapse within the next few years. To avoid this, he said, the country should cut off economic and military aid to Cuba and Nicaragua, sell land to the farmers of the nation and cut back on imports of American wheat.

For those of us who remember when the West faced the very real threat of "wars of national liberation" encouraged and armed by the Soviet Union, the change is a dramatic one indeed. We do not want to be lulled by the words coming out of a nation still armed to the nuclear teeth while confessing poverty, but the change is simply astonishing.

Times~Colonist

Victoria, B.C., June 7, 1989

For diehard, dyed-in-the-wool Communists, these are not happy days. Wherever a self-respecting comrade looks, he finds his system assailed, shaken by tremors, criticized or rejected.

In Moscow, at the inaugural session of the new Congress of People's Deputies, speaker after speaker dares to stand up and unleash devastating condemnations of previously sacred cows, including the Politburo, the KGB and the Soviet military.

In Beijing, thousands of Chinese citizens have the nerve to walk the streets, uncowed by last weekend's slaughter of protesting students. They seem disinclined to believe the government line, that the troops were simply suppressing thugs and counter-revolutionaries.

And in Poland . . well, the actors fail to follow the script in the country's first elections (or reasonable facsimile thereof) since it came into the Russian bear's embrace. A neat little numbers game had been cooked up by Solidarity leaders and Communist officials, not only to rig the overall results but allow the ruling party to emerge with a modicum of dignity. (Solidarity's motive was purely pragmatic: too lopsided a result might provoke a Communist backlash.)

But the voters, bless 'em, wanted no part in this intricate charade. At every ballot box opportunity, they just voted no to the Communist candidates. In the history of humiliating electoral messages, this result stands apart. Lenin must be turning in his tomb.

Rockford Register Star

Rockford, IL, June 5, 1989

The creature that Mikhail Gorbachev fathered has growled and hissed at him a couple times lately — and the Soviet leader doesn't seem to mind a bit. The occasions have been sessions of the Congress of People's Deputies, which represents an experiment in democratic government. A good time is being had by all.

"This is unheard of," exclaimed a Radio Moscow political analyst as newly elected deputies took turns grilling and criticizing Gorbachev. "This is truly democracy."

Well, yeah, sort of. Though most members of the Congress were chosen in competitive elections, the Communist Party still holds controlling power. And for all their gibes at Gorbachev, members still voted him to the post of president.

To be sure, this new democracy in the Soviet Union is crawling before it can walk. "It's like dancing lessons for legless people," said one deputy. Yes, but it sure beats the totalitarian tradition of forced marches.

Here is a Soviet political body where members feel free to vote against the programs of the prevailing leadership, and free to demand attention from leaders to their concerns, and free even to denounce the leaders. And all of this is shown to the general populace over television.

These are heady developments. Democratic practices seem likely to establish themselves in short order as durable Soviet traditions, formidable safeguards against backsliding toward the dark ages of Stalinism and such.

Gorbachev's campaigns of *glasnost* and *perestroika* have given rise to countless everyday tableaus, any one of which would have stunned the world as recently as five years ago. Today, open and democratic debate among citizen-politicians in the Soviet Union is met in the western world by mere smiles of approval rather than gasps of incredulity.

The pace of Gorbachev's revolution has become that swift.

The Seattle Times

Seattle, WA, June 5, 1989

THE hope is that Yuri P. Vlasov, who won a gold medal in weightlifting for the U.S.S.R. at the 1960 Olympics, has kept himself in shape.

Vlasov may need his strength in the days ahead.

He had the courage — some might say audacity — to take on the most powerful strongmen in the Soviet Union: the KGB.

In a stunning speech to the Congress of People's Deputies in Moscow, he called the KGB "a threat to democracy," "practically uncontrollable" and an "underground empire."

"When coming in conflict with the KGB, it is impossible to find the truth, and it is dangerous to seek it," he added. "The democratic renewal in the country has not changed the position of the KGB in the political system. This agency exercises all-embracing control over society, over each individual."

All those things are true. Yet to speak them aloud in the U.S.S.R. in years past would have guaranteed a one-way ticket to the Gulag — or worse.

In 1953, when Vlasov was 17, his father, a devoted Communist and Soviet diplomat, was summoned to a KGB office — and never again seen by his family.

The fact that Vlasov was able to criticize the KGB in a public forum — and earn a standing ovation from hundreds of deputies — is a sign of how dramatically the Soviet Union has changed under Mikhail Gorbachev. However, ruling Politburo and KGB officials reportedly remained seated with frozen stares, and Gorbachev applauded only briefly.

If Vlasov plans to bench press any heavy weights in the near future, he'd better make sure his spotters aren't KGB.

©1989 THE PITTSBURGH PRESS
UNITED FEATURE SYNDICATE ROGERS

I'M QUITE PLEASED WITH GORBACHEV'S EFFORTS TO IMPLEMENT ECONOMIC AND POLITICAL REFORM IN RUSSIA...

WE BEGIN BOMBING IN FIVE MINUTES.

CHENEY

The London Free Press

London, Ont., June 1, 1989

If anyone symbolizes the changing face of Soviet communism under Mikhail Gorbachev, it is Boris Yeltsin.

Yeltsin was voted overwhelmingly to the Soviet Congress during the country's first contested elections in 70 years last March. However, his maverick ideas haven't made him popular with his fellow deputies, who initially refused him a seat in last weekend's elections for the Supreme Soviet — the country's smaller, full-time legislature.

After tens of thousands of Muscovites rallied to protest Yeltsin's exclusion from the legislature, however, a place was made for him. In a parliamentary manoeuvre that had Gorbachev's blessing, another legislator resigned on condition that Yeltsin take his place.

The decision defused a tense situation and demonstrated that the Soviet leadership is paying some attention to public attitudes.

Yeltsin also symbolizes a growing Soviet tendency to admit differences within the party. In October, 1987, he was stripped of his Moscow and Politburo posts after a speech criticizing the slow place of Gorbachev's reforms. That setback doesn't appear to have tamed him.

In his first address before the new Congress, he said that Gorbachev's reforms have failed to improve people's lives and instead have given the Soviet president so much power they could lead to a "new dictatorship."

That Gorbachev allows such criticism may also be a measure of his strength, and his confidence in the security of his position.

Just how much power the new Congress will exert is clearly in the hands of Gorbachev himself. But the openness with which his authority is being questioned and the broadening scope of domestic political debate and participation are further positive signs of dramatic change in a country where, until recently, unyielding state oppression was the rule.

The Burlington Free Press

Burlington, VT, June 9, 1989

If the Politburo's gray old men ever seize glasnost by the neck, the death of a freer Soviet Union will be instantly apparent to 200 million Russians. The television cameras will go off.

What happened in Moscow last week was not democracy but the fertilizer of democracy — open debate and a ringing challenge to absolute authority. Live television was its essential tool.

As 200 million Soviet people watched, the new Congress of People's Deputies listened to one unbuttoned indictment of the Soviet system after another. Deputies took a verbal bullwhip to the Communist Party, the military, the secret police and even Mikhail Gorbachev. Andrei Sakharov looked into the faces of the generals who invaded Afghanistan and denounced their "criminal adventure." To a standing ovation, Deputy Yuri Vlasov delivered the first all-out public attack, ever, on the KGB, "This service (that) sowed grief, cries, torture on its native land." to a standing ovation.

It was not the charges themselves that stunned watchers. The general truth of them is acknowledged in the privacy of most Soviet households. But for the accusations to be hurled in the faces of the men accused and in a public forum — the foundations of absolutism still tremble with the aftershocks. Ten thousand Muscovites took to the streets after they watched their delegate (and political folk hero) Boris Yeltsin denied a seat on the Supreme Soviet. The next day, Yeltsin got his seat.

The system won't tumble, yet. As democracy, the Congress of People's Deputies is all smoke and mirrors. Party loyalists wrote the election laws to guarantee themselves a decisive majority. They will continue to control the pace and direction of change in the Soviet Union, and undoubtedly will try to keep that pace as slow as possible.

Liberals and dissidents will remain a vocal minority dependent on Gorbachev, not the secret ballot, to force fundamental economic, political and social changes. As long as the television cameras remain on, their intoxicating rhetoric constitutes a kind of nectar that feeds the hunger for freedom while leaving the diner famished.

If the cameras continue to roll, the gray old men in their inner sanctum may find themselves with a populace no longer satisfied with just the rhetoric of deomcracy.

The Philadelphia Inquirer

Philadelphia, PA, June 12, 1989

For those who are weary of Congress' petty scandals in Washington, a look at the parliaments-aborning in Moscow and Warsaw is a good antidote.

Over there, where one-person-one-meaningful-vote is still a concept that makes people shake their heads, it is possible to feel in the gut the significance of having the freedom to choose one's government.

In Moscow, intellectuals carry on about how Soviets have no political traditions to help them understand how a parliament should work. They point to centuries of authoritarian rule under the czars, followed by the dead weight of communist rule.

But given the chance, the new members in the Soviet Congress of People's Deputies are setting about learning the process with a vengeance. They talk about issues, heaven help them. And they can't stop talking (not surprising when one reckons that 70 years of communist misrule has hitherto gone unchallenged). No one there has time to worry about a deputy's sex life; the problems of political and economic reform are much too pressing. Like those on Capitol Hill, the smarter deputies have figured out that power lies with him who controls the budget, and Moscow's new pols are already challenging the regime to let them see the books.

And what is one to make of Poland, where a trade union with no practical political experience managed in a few weeks' time to organize a campaign that routed the ruling communist party? At the polls, voters wielded their pens like guns, shooting down nearly every communist candidate on the ballot. Overnight, dissidents became skilled politicians. People who hadn't voted in 40 years — or had merely filed like sheep to *pro forma* communist balloting — learned how to maneuver through a very complicated ballot.

To watch democratic politics come alive in Moscow and Poland, in spite of the limitations that still exist on real pluralist politics, is a humbling experience — and an excellent civics lesson for those Americans cannot remember back 200 years. In viewing the passion with which Poles and Soviets seize the chance to have a say in how they are governed — a privilege most Americans take for granted but citizens of communist countries look on as nirvana — one can appreciate anew the significance of the free ballot.

The Salt Lake Tribune

Salt Lake City, UT, June 5, 1989

The Soviet Union's new Congress of People's Deputies is getting the hang of representative democracy. Members launched their first ethics probe right away, forcing their new president to defend his perks and accusing the government of foot-dragging in its investigations of official corruption. That should play well for the voters back home in Rostov-on-Don.

The nation has been stunned by the blunt oratory. John Tower, Jim Wright and Tony Coelho should have warned the Soviets about the righteous indignation of congressmen in high dudgeon.

The inaugural session of the congress, the first national assembly chosen mostly by competitive elections since the revolution of 1917, has been a curious mixture of populism and machine politics. Mikhail Gorbachev's election as president was never in doubt, but no one could have predicted the grilling he got from the deputies prior to the balloting. Several complained of the concentration of power in the person of Mr. Gorbachev, who now heads both the party apparatus and the government. His choice for vice president, Anatoly I. Lukyanov, suffered the same vigorous vetting before he was elected.

The so-called radicals have spoken boldly, yet most of them were defeated for membership in the new Supreme Soviet, the standing legislature, by the Communist Party machine. As often happens in legislatures, the reformers, many of them academics, won a symbolic victory, but they failed to pay enough attention to practical politics and suffered a drubbing at the hands of the Old Pols when the ballots were counted.

Now they know what communists — Republicans and Democrats, for that matter — mean when they talk about organization and party discipline.

On the other hand, the powers that be moved swiftly to accommodate the popular will when Boris Yeltsin's defeat prompted a public outcry. Another deputy who had been elected to the Supreme Soviet offered to give up his seat to Mr. Yeltsin, and the congress quickly found a way to make the compromise legal.

Legality itself has been a major theme of the congress. Mr. Gorbachev's reforms have nudged the nation away from arbitrary rule based on absolute power toward constitutional government. Other reformers, and Mr. Gorbachev himself, want to proceed much farther. The major debate seems to be over the pace of change.

One deputy, an Estonian nationalist, questioned Mr. Gorbachev about how he intends to alter the Soviet constitution to guarantee the sovereignty of constituent republics and how a democracy can justify use of the military against the civilian population. The obscure deputy who ran against Mr. Gorbachev as a token opposition candidate for the presidency argued for stripping the government bureaucracy of lawmaking powers and creating an independent judiciary.

This congress represents the first steps toward a truly independent, democratic legislature. By Western standards, the Soviets still have a long way to go. By the measure of the Soviet past, however, these first steps have been momentous.

Rockford Register Star

Rockford, IL, June 4, 1989

Here's another Soviet name to learn: Boris N. Yeltsin. It's one the Soviets know well. They probably will get to know him even better.

To begin with, he was an ally of Soviet leader Mikhail Gorbachev. But he lost his job as Moscow party chief when he criticized his boss for not moving faster to straighten out Soviet ills, including its flagging economy and its inability to feed itself (hence the hefty wheat purchases from the United States).

Now he's back on the same soap-box, charging that Gorbachev holds too much power and could become a dictator, charging that with all that power goes responsibility for failing Soviet citizens generally. He also wants Gorbachev subjected to an annual referendum reviewing how successful his reforms have worked. Such views seldom lead to power in the Soviet Union.

Thus Yeltsin was viewed as an outsider, the equivalent of being sent to Siberia, when he was fired from his Moscow post.

But then reforms allowed for popular elections. Yeltsin received 90 percent of Moscow's vote, higher than any other deputy elected to the Congress of People's Deputies consisting of 2,250 members. Yeltsin believes this Congress, not the 20-million members of the Communist Party, should run the Soviets' political show. He has said as much from public forums.

Then came the slight that put a new cloud over Yeltsin's political future. Members of Congress bypassed Yeltsin to sit on its 542-member legislature, the Supreme Soviet. That wasn't unexpected; what came next was. What came next was a public outcry throughout Moscow. Because television now covers the sessions of Congress, members began to feel the heat from Russians who want Yeltsin to represent them.

Then one man on the legislature said he would resign if the vacancy were conferred on Yeltsin. By secret ballot, the Congress reversed itself and accepted Yeltsin, more from resignation than joy. The Soviet public had won an unusual victory.

Yeltsin's a fighter. He wants special privileges of the party elite reviewed and eliminated. He also wants rides on mass transit and the costs of medicines to be free for tens of millions who are the Soviet poor, a condition not publicly discussed until *glasnost* and *perestroika* became pillars of the Gorbachev regime.

As for Gorbachev himself, Yeltsin said the two had a 90-minute talk recently about Yeltsin's future. "I think we have had a rapprochement ... I think there is a warming without a doubt. I always supported the strategic line of Comrade Gorbachev, and moreover I fought for it."

Yeltsin, a name to remember.

'88 Soviet Economic Report Gloomy; Poor Grain Harvest Reported

A government economic report, made public Jan. 21, 1989, painted a gloomy portrait of 1988 Soviet economic performance. The report was published by *Izvestia*, the government newspaper. The report projected a budget deficit of at least $100 billion rubles (US$160 billion at the official exchange rate) by 1990. In October 1988, when Moscow had first revealed a budget shortfall, the figure used by officials had been 36.3 billion rubles (US$58 billion).

The study cited the accumulated cost of the Chernobyl nuclear accident clean-up, the anticipated costs of of solving severe shortages in food and housing, and the anticipated cost of rebuilding after the Armenian earthquake as factors in its deficit projection. It said that the deficit could amount to 11% of the U.S.S.R.'s national income (a measure similar to gross national product in the West).

In 1988, the report said, Soviet national income had risen 4.4%, compared with the target of 6.6%. Similarly, the production of consumer goods had increased 5.1%, compared with the target of 7%, and the agricultural production had grown 0.7%, compared with the target of 6.3%.

The study noted that overall productivity had increased 4.7% in 1988, but reduced costs resulting from that gain had been offset by a nearly 7% increase in wages. The average monthly wage of workers in state industries had been US$347. But the report disclosed that the three million workers had earned less than US$132 a month.

Some 1.1 million workers had lost their jobs in the state sector in 1988, according to the report. (The study placed the number of state workers and civil servants at 117.5 million in 1988. It said that two million people had worked in cooperatives or had been self- employed.)

The report disclosed that one in 10 state industries had lost money in 1988, but that the number of unprofitable farms had fallen to 2,100 in 1988 from 6,500 in 1987. However, the study noted that the total farm profit of US$54 billion amounted to little more than half of the total state subsidies directed to the agricultural sector.

Leonid I. Abalkin, a leading Soviet economist, Jan. 25 confirmed that the nation's budget deficit was at least US$160 billion. Speaking to reporters in Moscow, Abalkin complained that the deficit was ruining the economy and disrupting the course of economic reform. Abalkin suggested that planned radical price reform, one of the cornerstones of *perestroika* (restructuring), be postponed until the deficit was brought down.

The economist said that the government wanted to eliminate the shortfall within three years through a series of measures, including spending curbs, reductions in capital investment and the issuing of bonds to raise revenues.

Separately, the State Planning Committee (Gosplan) Jan. 16 announced that the 1988 grain harvest had been the smallest since 1985. Stephen Sitaryan, Gosplan's first deputy chairman, told reporters that the harvest had yielded 195 million tons, some 40 million tons below the production target and 16 million tons less than the harvest of 1987.

Western analysts surmised that the disappointing 1988 harvest had been a key factor in compelling Moscow to sign a new grain agreement with the U.S. in 1988.

THE COMMERCIAL APPEAL

Nashville, TN, February 23, 1989

IMAGINE a top Washington official admitting that the government has been deceiving the public about the size of our federal deficit — that the true figure is triple the usual estimate.

That is essentially what has happened in the Soviet Union.

Leonid Abalkin, director of the Economics Institute at the Soviet Academy of Sciences, told a Moscow news conference that the government is running a budget deficit of 100 billion rubles — about 11 percent of gross national product. He said the regime is preparing severe spending cuts.

Even if those cuts work, the country's near-term prospects remain bleak. The key question, Abalkin acknowledged, is how long it will take for perestroika to bring material benefits to the average Soviet family. His brutally candid answer: "only by 1995."

The dilemma for Soviet reformers is that the economy can't move toward long-term prosperity without radical changes, such as the abolition of government controls on wages and prices. In the short run, some of those changes threaten to make life worse.

Gorbachev planned to repeal ceilings on consumer prices by 1991; he now has postponed that move because of popular opposition. But the longer such reforms are deferred, the longer the economy remains a caricature of bureaucratic inefficiency — a system in which peasants use bread as cattle feed because price controls make it cheaper than raw grain.

The Kremlin recently admitted that last year's grain harvest fell short of the target by nearly 17 percent. This means Moscow will have to buy 40 million tons abroad, further straining its foreign currency reserves.

So time is not on Gorbachev's side. His staunchest ally in the ruling Politburo, Alexander Yakovlev, said in a speech that the reform faction probably has only two or three years left to prove that socialism can work.

Twenty-five years ago a backlash within the Soviet leadership stunned Western optimists by ousting reform leader Nikita Khrushchev and elevating hardliner Leonid Brezhnev. Unless he quickens his reforms, Gorbachev may suffer Khrushchev's fate.

The Hartford Courant

Hartford, CT, March 20, 1989

It is not an earth-shattering note, but it does illustrate the extent to which the United States has not absorbed its new relationship with the Soviet Union: the Bush administration does not want to let the U.S.S.R. into GATT.

GATT is the General Agreement on Tariffs and Trade, an organization of mostly Western industrialized nations built around the principle of free trade. It provides the world's only forum for settling trade disputes. The Soviets, who shunned GATT for decades, now want to join, but the U.S. government says that they ought not to be allowed because theirs is not a market economy.

The Soviets are unlikely to become capitalists, not in any true sense, any time soon. But they are moving in that direction and joining GATT might push them further along.

Of course one Washington worry might be that the Soviets want to move closer culturally to Western Europe, and their joining GATT could be another means to that end. But closeness to Western Europe is not a zero-sum game, certainly not if we really believe the Cold War is over. The U.S. government can take diplomatic and economic initiatives on its own, regardless of what the Soviets are doing.

If anything, U.S. foreign policy has suffered from the fact that Soviet intentions, often misread or downright unreadable, have been treated as the chief component of almost any foreign-policy problem. The matter of whether the U.S.S.R. should be encouraged to trade with the major economic players of the world should be considered on its own merits.

If the Soviets are serious about modernizing and rationalizing their economy and we are serious about encouraging them, then it makes sense for the U.S.S.R. to be admitted to GATT. Let them try to make a ruble the old-fashioned way, and let the world share what they generate via trade. In the realm of economic expansion, the Soviets should be the least of our worries for the next generation or two.

Los Angeles Times

Los Angeles, CA, April 19, 1989

The shopping list is much like what an American consumer would take to the market: toothpaste, razor blades, detergent, shoes, panty hose, among other items. The quantities, though, are on a scale that manufacturers dream of. The Soviet Union plans to increase its imports of Western consumer goods this year by $8 billion, on top of the more than $51 billion already budgeted. Included are new funds to buy 300 million razor blades, 10 million compact cassette recorders, 15 million pairs of leather shoes, 10,000 tons of toothpaste. It is indicative of the growing climate of Soviet consumer discontent that orders for these products have gone out, as a deputy trade minister acknowledges, with "uncharacteristic urgency." Soviet shops are supposed to start receiving this bounty within a few weeks.

And then? And then, so Soviet President Mikhail S. Gorbachev and other advocates of economic reform hope, the idea should begin to percolate through the labor force that the regime's repeated promises of a higher living standard have some credibility after all, and that harder work can bring greater material rewards. A contented worker, so the argument runs, will be a more productive worker, and increased output and productivity are vital if Soviet economic stagnation is to be overcome.

The interest in making consumer products more available doesn't mean that the Soviet Union's traditional spending priorities, with their emphasis on heavy industry and the military, have been abandoned. But clearly the emphasis has shifted somewhat, toward a greater willingness to spend more hard currency to try to reduce some of the chronic and, lately, worsening shortages in the consumer sector.

One of the considerations that helped to spur this long-debated change was the defeat suffered in last month's national elections by a number of senior Communist Party officials, in many cases after they—and the party—were criticized in public forums for the growing scarcity and shoddy quality of most consumer products. Even before then, the seriousness and urgency of the problem were a matter of public discussion. As a columnist in the increasingly outspoken Moscow News wrote earlier this year, "It is clear to everyone that if the country is not supplied in the next few years with foodstuffs, and people with clothing, shoes, furniture, electric appliances and so on . . . all faith in *perestroika* will evaporate and the party will be deprived of the people's confidence."

High-level opposition to spending more on consumer imports remains, however. Traditionalists prefer to see the billions of dollars in credits the Soviet Union has obtained from the West used for machinery and other capital goods. The reformers counter that unless purchasing patterns are changed to provide a broader flow of consumer products the labor force will have no motivation to work harder. The decision to spend more on imports this year doesn't mean the argument has been finally settled.

Conservatives can be expected to insist that a bigger budget for consumer imports must show a prompt return in the form of higher productivity and expanded output. Otherwise, presumably, they will try to have the experiment branded a failure and insist that the old spending priorities be restored. Demanding such a regressive step may be a lot easier than taking it; any attempt to snatch back from consumers the little more that they have been given could surely be expected to deepen popular resistance, cynicism and resentment, making things worse than they were before. The opponents of reform may think that the spigot of high-quality consumer goods that is being opened can simply be turned off if things don't go the way they would like. It can be, if that is what the regime wills, but perhaps only at the cost of inviting a political explosion.

DESERET NEWS

Salt Lake City, UT, February 2/3, 1989

Will the real Soviet budget please stand up?

Last August, in a prospectus for its first foreign bond issue, the Russian government claimed to be running a budget surplus, putting the figure at 3 billion rubles or $1.8 billion.

Only two months later, the Kremlin admitted it actually was running a deficit — something that outside observers had suspected for years but were unable to prove — and claimed the red ink amounted to 35 billion rubles, about $58 billion at current exchange rates.

But now Soviet economist Leonid I. Abalkin, director of the National Institute of the Economy, says the deficit is nearly three times bigger than the Kremlin first admitted. That would put the Soviet deficit at about $165 billion, or 11% of Russia's gross national product. By comparison, the U.S. federal deficit amounts to about 4% of GNP.

What conclusions should be drawn from this unaccustomed exercise in Soviet candor, with its resulting contradictions and confusion?

For one thing, the rest of the world ought to go slow on approving Russia's applications to join the International Monetary Fund, the World Bank, and the General Agreement on Trade and Tariff. These organizations require "transparent" reporting of financial conditions in which no numbers are hidden. At this point, it isn't clear if Russia really knows how bad off it is, let alone how far Moscow is willing to go in admitting its difficulties.

For another, individual nations also should be cautious about making loans to Russia as long as there are such serious questions about the Soviets' willingness as well as their ability to pay them off.

Why question Russia's willingness on this score? Because Soviet prices remain under government control, enabling the Kremlin to disguise or at least delay an inflationary spiral. And because Soviet leader Mikhail Gorbachev has yet to follow through on a price reform that would reduce red ink by eliminating subsidies on many commodities. Yet this reform is supposed to be a key part of Gorbachev's "perestroika" campaigns to restructure the Soviet economy.

By all means, the Soviets should be encouraged to keep publishing previously secret economic statistics. But it would pay to view those figures with some skepticism. After all, there's no reason to think the Soviet statisticians are more competent and reliable than are the economic planners who gave Russia its chronic shortages of crops and consumer products.

Chicago Tribune

Chicago, IL, March 22, 1989

Mikhail Gorbachev has forced the leaders of the Communist Party to choose between food and socialism, and for now food has won the day.

Heeding the Soviet leader's call for an overhaul of the agricultural system, the party's Central Committee approved letting farmers lease state-owned land for life and pass the land on to their children. While it's not the same as possessing the deed to the south 40 in America, it's the closest thing to property rights that Soviet farmers have had in decades.

In addition, farmers will have more leeway in what they grow and in the prices they can charge to distributors, although retail prices still will be set by the state. And the giant agricultural bureaucracy that Gorbachev created in 1985 to streamline food production will be dismantled.

Even Yegor Ligachev, the Soviet Union's top agricultural official and a staunch conservative and defender of the status quo, seemed to buy into the program. Gorbachev's plan, he said, will produce "a feast on our street" and an end to food shortages by 1995.

But Ligachev also emphasized that Moscow remains committed to the collective and state farm system. That's the same inefficient system that allows one-third of a Soviet harvest to rot before reaching market, that has brought food rationing to many parts of the country and that requires billions of rubles in government subsidies.

Has Gorbachev begun an irreversible process of change in rural Russia? Or, in agreeing to keep the collective farms, has Gorbachev settled on an unsatisfactory compromise that sets him up for another failed attempt to alter the farming system?

The answers to those questions, and to Gorbachev's political future, may depend largely on those Russian farmers who haven't fled to the cities and are working the nation's 50,000 farms. They must display "independence, enterprise and initiative," says Gorbachev, if reform is to succeed and Russians are to be fed.

But opinion polls in the Soviet press taken before Gorbachev's new farm program was announced last week indicate that only 5 percent of the farmers are willing to try leasing land and equipment and making their own decisions on what to grow and sell. Some of their reluctance stems from history.

In the 1920s, Stalin took away free food production by shooting successful peasants or sending them to prison camps. Some hesitancy comes from anxiety over being the leaders of rural change in a society that distrusts wealth and fears that Moscow could still abandon *perestroika*. Some remember that, after Gorbachev encouraged competition through private cooperatives more than a year ago, the government clamped down on such ventures this year by slapping on price controls and banning some outright.

Marx must be spinning in his grave at the thought of putting the means of production into the private hands of Russian farmers. But, if the farmers step forward as they should and Gorbachev's reforms end up putting more food on Russian tables, even conservative ideologues in the Kremlin won't care. For now, the choice between food and socialism is an easy one.

The Providence Journal

Providence, RI, March 30, 1989

Mikhail Gorbachev hopes to energize Soviet farmers with market incentives, but before we congratulate them on their good fortune, let us wait to see whether the plan takes effect, and how the farmers themselves react to it.

The plan would allow them to lease land from collectives until they die, and pass leases on to their children — the nearest the Kremlin has ever come to recognizing property rights. Supply and demand would gradually replace state quotas and price-setting. Farmers who choose to leave state farms would have new rights protecting their enterprise, while those who seek to remain under the state's aegis could do so.

Will the plan succeed? We shall see. Americans tend to assume that the Soviet farmer is frustrated by life on the collectives, and eager to throw off the yoke of the state. That is not necessarily so. While few consider their lot a paradise, Soviet farmers know they will be paid whether they work or not. Despite scarcity and long lines, many prefer security to risking their livelihoods on their abilities.

It may be that Mr. Gorbachev's refusal to force farmers off the collectives, as they were forced to join them in the 1930s, will undermine his policy. He himself seems to recognize that possibility. "No fool is going to work on a lease contract as long as he can have a salary without earning it," he said last October, after disclosing that changes in Soviet agriculture were afoot. He has placed his chief Politburo opponent, Yegor K. Ligachev, in charge.

Still, entrepreneurial spirit remains among Soviet citizens: the black market flourishes, and the output of the nation's farmers has long been dominated by a limited number of plots leased outside the collective under an experimental program. The new agricultural policy should encourage that spirit to flourish, wherever it exists.

It exists most profusely in Lithuania, Latvia, Estonia and the Ukraine, where the reforms are expected to proceed more swiftly. The first three were annexed into the Soviet Union only in 1940, and Ukrainians still resent the famine perpetrated by Stalin to force its farmers onto the collectives.

Whether swift or slow, a further restriction of state power over the individual can only improve Soviet life, in part by encouraging more change. This poses risks to Mr. Gorbachev and his economic restructuring policies, which could be reversed if he is deposed, or if the Communist Party sees its power being undermined. We await with interest the results of this new approach.

If the Soviet Union becomes a freer, more prosperous nation, it is likely to become less ideological and more concerned with internal affairs. The world could perhaps then sleep easier.

The Charlotte Observer

Charlotte, NC, March 19, 1989

The agricultural reform program pushed through the Soviet Communist Party's Central Committee last week shows again the boldness — and power — of Soviet President Mikhail Gorbachev. But if boldness and power in Moscow were enough to make the crops grow, Soviet agriculture would not be such a desperate failure.

President Gorbachev has power, as he demonstrated by winning approval for a program that is heretical in its reliance on privatization — including allowing farmers to lease state land for life and pass it on to their heirs. His conservative rival Yegor Ligachev, who had been campaigning for a traditional bolstering of the failed state farms, was sent out after the vote to explain that of course everyone now agrees with the Gorbachev plan.

But commanding the country can be more difficult than commanding the Central Committee. President Gorbachev has already been forced to backpedal on his anti-drinking campaign, for example. While some of the outlying republics are more ready for private-sector initiatives, there is deep resistance in the Soviet system. Farmers trying to respond to earlier opportunities have sometimes faced hostility from their disapproving neighbors. The essential support systems are not set up to serve private efforts, and probably not inclined to.

Even if there were no political resistance, reform would be extraordinarily difficult. Soviet agricultural society was ravaged by Stalin's brutal collectivization drives — which murdered, starved or exiled millions of the most capable farmers. The new reforms depend on a culture that the government has spent decades trying to hammer out of the Soviet people.

While the Soviet leader wants to make use of market principles, he dares not go all the way to free markets and free prices — a shock that the Soviet system, and maybe the Soviet leader, could not withstand.

That is the direction that President Gorbachev and his country must move. But while we in the West may admire his boldness, and applaud the additional freedom that comes with each new bit of individual economic self-determination, the questions asked in the Soviet Union are likely to be simpler and blunter: Does it put food on the table? Does it produce results worth the turmoil and strife it will bring even if successful?

Omaha World-Herald

Omaha, NE, March 22, 1989

The Soviet Union has been saying for years that it couldn't feed itself because of its unfavorable climate. Admittedly, poor growing conditions have been part of the problem. But as outsiders could see — and the Soviets have belatedly come to admit — the Communist system was a big part of the problem. Now, finally, the government seems about to face that fact.

President Mikhail Gorbachev has asked the Communist Central Committee to junk the decades-old centralized farming system. This was a system in which prices and quotas were set by a central administration. Layer upon layer of bureaucracy were added to the system as it staggered along, unable to produce and deliver enough meat, vegetables and fruit for the Soviet people. Farm workers, with no land ownership and few incentives, lost enthusiasm for their work and apathetically followed orders from above.

The collectivization of farming was a keystone of the Stalinist system. In the 1930s, the government, through its secret police, waged war on private farming and destroyed the system of prosperous, family-owned farms that existed at the time. The most successful farmers were treated as enemies of the state. Their farms were seized, and many of the farmers were murdered as the government, in effect, waged class warfare.

When farmers in the rich agricultural regions of the Ukraine responded by killing their farm animals, Stalin ordered the region cut off from the outside so that the protesters would starve. Some historians estimate now that as many as 5 million Russians and Ukrainians died as a result of this policy.

The Soviet people paid an extraordinarily high price for the system of agriculture imposed on them by the Communists. The results have been a disaster, as speaker after speaker readily admitted during the Central Committee's recent deliberations. After considering the issue, the committee moved to adopt Gorbachev's proposals to dismantle the agricultural bureaucracy, end centralized direction of farming and lease the collective farmlands to the farmers for from five years to life.

Lifetime leases could be inherited, making the arrangement one of ownership in everything but name.

Solving the agricultural problem could lead to solutions to some of the Soviet Union's other problems. Health, for one. The average Soviet citizen's diet contains only half the meat and fruit that are present in the average American's diet but has twice as many potatoes and half again as much sugar.

In addition, rural areas have been strikingly backward in terms of roads, schools, housing and health care. Despite strict controls, tens of thousands of rural Soviet citizens have left the collective farms and small towns and moved to cities seeking better jobs. This puts more strain on the already overburdened Soviet economy and helps create an unemployment problem.

Leasing the land to farmers to grow what they want and allowing them to sell as they can is risky for an authoritarian system that once did its best to destroy initiative, incentive and ownership. The fact that it arose as an option illustrates how badly the old system has failed.

The Seattle Times

Seattle, WA, March 19, 1989

CHRONIC food shortages forced Soviet President Mikhail Gorbachev to admit failure; his own and that of the central government.

A key element of Gorbachev's overhaul of his country's network of state-run farms is the dismantling of a massive bureaucracy he created in 1985.

Gorbachev organized a superministry, Gosagroprom, to pump life into a moribund farming system. All that grew was the bureaucracy, and queues for imported foodstuffs.

Decades of rigid agricultural policies only nurtured long lines for scarce basic commodities. Meat, vegetables, fruits, sugar and grain products are strangers to the market basket.

In an act of political desperation, Gorbachev hopes to entice farmers with two inducements that are rare in the Soviet economic culture: choice and risk.

Farmers would be lured from the stolid security of state farms with the lure of long-term leases that would keep land in a family. Farmers, not bureaucrats, would decide what to plant, when to sow and harvest crops, and how to market them.

These are radical notions in a country hobbled by agricultural paper-shufflers, jealous of their authority, and farmers who have swapped independence for security.

Gorbachev must risk offending Communist Party ideologues because the current system is bankrupting the treasury, and not feeding the nation. Billions of rubles are spent on agricultural and consumer subsidies.

Success might be spoiled by another weak link. Tons of produce and grain rot each year because they cannot get from remote farms to processors and markets.

Policymakers are fearful the changes will be mistaken for what they are: a wholesale indictment of a failed experiment. "Radical changes in rural life and production relations should be carried out on a purely voluntary basis ... without any kind of force or repressive methods," a Politburo member told reporters.

Such sentiments mock the brutality used to bind productive farms into state-run collectives in the 1920s and 1930s.

Gorbachev is bucking history, ideology, culture and an old joke that says there are only four things wrong with Soviet agriculture: spring, summer, fall and winter.

Cultivating political change in the Soviet Union may be the only undertaking more risky than farming.

Communists Disavow One-Party Rule

The Soviet Communist Party (CP) Central Committee Feb. 7, 1990 voted to renounce the party's constitutionally guaranteed monopoly on political power. It was a historic victory for President Mikhail S. Gorbachev and his program of "democratization."

The move came at the end of a stormy three-day Central Committee plenum in Moscow at which the party officials debated a draft platform for sweeping change. The meeting was held behind closed doors, although some details were revealed by the Soviet press.

A crumbling Soviet economy, along with mounting ethnic and nationalist unrest, had pushed Gorbachev to seek a multiparty system. As well, the political upheavals in Eastern Europe had left the U.S.S.R. behind in the area of democratic reform. (The U.S.S.R. was the only one of the seven Warsaw Pact states that retained a "leading role" for its Communist Party.)

Rival parties had been banned officially in the U.S.S.R. since the 10th Communist Party Congress, in 1921. Article Six of the Soviet constitution, added to the document in 1977, made the Communist Party the only legal political party in the country.

The notion of a multiparty system was at variance with the orthodox interpretation of the ideas of V.I. Lenin, the revered father of Soviet communism. One of Lenin's key contributions to Marxist theory had been the concept of a "dictatorship of the proletariat [exploited working class]," as embodied in a single, all-powerful political organization.

One event prior to the plenum had indicated that Lenin's ideas were no longer sacrosanct. *Pravda*, the Soviet CP newspaper, Feb. 1 had published parts of a discussion by the party's commission on ideology. Vadim A. Medvedev, the chief ideologist, pointedly stressed the need to reevaluate Leninism in light of the Stalinist "deformation" in the years following Lenin's death. Other participants called for an end to the notion of "Lenin as icon."

The plenum was only the first step in a process that could lead to a multiparty system in the U.S.S.R. The Supreme Soviet (the standing legislature) and the Congress of People's Deputies (parliament) had to revise Article Six or remove it altogether. Final party action on the question was scheduled for a Central Committee meeting in March and a party congress in the summer.

Tens of thousands of people participated in a massive pro-democracy parade in the heart of Moscow Feb. 4. It was believed to be the largest unofficial demonstration since the 1917 Bolshevik Revolution.

President Gorbachev Feb. 5 opened the Central Committee meeting with an endorsement of the draft platform, which called for "humane, democratic socialism...relying on the great legacy of Marx, Engels and Lenin."

The exact details of the platform were not made public, but it was apparently worded in a manner so as to sanction an introduction of a multiparty system, a loosening of the restrictions on the private ownership of property and a wholesale reorganization of the party's structure.

Gorbachev told the plenum, "We should abandon the ideological dogmatism that became ingrained during the past decades, outmoded stereotypes in domestic policy and outmoded views on the world revolution process and world development as a whole."

The president continued: "The party is a renewing society and can play its role as vanguard only as a democratically recognized force. This means that its status should not be imposed through constitutional endorsement. The Soviet Communist Party, it goes without saying, intends to struggle for the status of the ruling party. But it will do so strictly within the framework of the democratic process."

Gorbachev used the speech to lobby for a revamping of the Soviet presidency into a U.S. style executive office with broader authority than he now exercised. (The draft platform raised the possibility of direct popular elections for president, and presidential powers that would encompass those of the Soviet premier.)

THE INDIANAPOLIS STAR
Indianapolis, IL, February 9, 1990

In Moscow, Dr. Svyatoslav Fydorov called it "fantastic" — and it is.

The Soviet Union appears to be taking its first big step toward freedom and democracy since the people's revolution of 1917 that toppled Czar Nicholas.

That revolution was captured in a coup by the communists. They broke up the constituent assembly elected to establish representative government. They created a dictatorship that tightened its monopoly of power with secret police, mass killing and imprisonment.

Freedom and democracy were derailed for more than seven decades. During most of that time communism's leaders used deception and force to spread the Red tide worldwide.

When captive nations tried to break away, they sent in troops and tanks to crush them.

Their monopoly of power in the USSR was guaranteed by the Soviet Constitution's Article 6. President Mikhail S. Gorbachev led the drive to repeal the article. By a nearly unanimous vote, the party's 249-member central committee agreed Wednesday to let other parties share power, barring only those that foment ethnic violence or advocate the violent overthrow of the government.

The platform also calls for direct election of the president.

Constitutional changes must be approved by the Supreme Soviet legislature, which meets next Wednesday, and the Congress of People's Deputies, to meet in the spring.

"There will be a multiparty system; there will be a normal democracy," said Dr. Fydorov, an eye surgeon and participant in Wednesday's session. He called the change "fantastic."

At best the transition is likely to be slow and difficult. The party will retain an overwhelming advantage in finances, authority, influence and control of the media.

The party has 20 million members of whom 750,000 are members of the *nomenklatura*, the party elite. These authoritarian leaders, accustomed to privilege and the exercise of power, may yet try to stop or slow any populist movements that threaten to displace them.

The countries along the Soviet border, where the current changes began, had long-standing opposition movements and a tradition of alternate parties. These are lacking in the USSR, where the seven-decade monopoly of the Communist Party replaced the centuries-old monopoly of the czars and nobility.

Even so, strong impulses toward freedom, human rights guarantees and democratization have been evident among the people since the Soviet state was established. The word *svoboda* — freedom — was heard often during Wednesday's historic session. Freedom has many champions inside the USSR.

No matter what the obstacles, the road to freedom and democracy is worth traveling. If Wednesday's decision has put the Soviet Union on that road, and the time of its joining the community of free societies is drawing closer, it was a historic turning-point, not only for the Soviet Union but for the world.

THE SACRAMENTO BEE

Sacramento, CA, February 7, 1990

Mikhail Gorbachev's proposal that the Soviet Communist Party give up its monopoly on power is breathtaking and historic, further testimony to his ability to keep riding the tiger without, so far, losing his balance. It envisions far more than just a restructuring of an apparatus that has ruled the Soviet Union since 1917, because it would remove the Communist Party from the central policy-making function, which is precisely what party conservatives fear.

Under Gorbachev's plan, all crucial political and economic decisions would no longer be made by the party as such. The government, headed by Gorbachev as president, would assume that role, and the increasingly independent-minded Supreme Soviet would make the laws. Ideological dogma, as Gorbachev said in his landmark speech to the Communist Party Central Committee on Monday, would be replaced by a pragmatic approach not only to the exercise of power but to setting the goals of Soviet society.

Revolutionary as this is, it is no more than a reflection of what has already happened in Eastern Europe and is being demanded by an ever more outspoken Soviet populace. Sunday's demonstration in Moscow, in which more than 200,000 took part, may have looked ordinary on Western television screens, but in the Soviet context it was unprecedented — in its magnitude, its peacefulness and in the fact that it took place at all.

Gorbachev is aware that, while glasnost (openness) has produced astonishing results, perestroika (restructuring) has failed to bring the benefits promised. The economy has worsened, and the standard of living has fallen, in large part because the leadership has been trying to have it both ways — to allow reforms here and there while still keeping central control over the economy gener-

ally and of the political system. That won't work, as Gorbachev has recognized in proposing the most fundamental change of course in Soviet history.

"The crux of the party's renewal," Gorbachev told the Central Committee, "is the need to get rid of everything that tied it to the authoritarian, bureaucratic system. . . ." That means that the party "can exist and play its role as vanguard only as a democratically recognized force. . . . Its status should not be imposed through constitutional endorsement."

That was a reference to an article in the Soviet constitution that guarantees the party's leading role. Gorbachev wants that removed, and wants to purge resisters from the Central Committee. And by moving a crucial party congress forward from autumn to early summer, he hopes to get these changes ratified quickly. Whether he will get all that may become evident today, when the Central Committee considers revisions of his plan demanded by radicals and conservatives who complain that it's too vague.

The next few months could be the most crucial for the Soviet Union since its violent birth and its first turbulent decade, during which a popular revolution was transformed into totalitarian rule under Stalin. In the meantime, Gorbachev must cope with the Baltic independence movement, ethnic and separatist conflicts in the country's southern republics, pressure from Eastern Europe for withdrawal of Soviet troops, the rush toward German unification and negotiations with the West to shrink both nuclear and conventional arsenals. That seems an impossible task, but so far Gorbachev has shown that if any world leader today is up to it, he's the one.

The Houston Post

Houston, TX, February 8, 1990

MIKHAIL GORBACHEV has won again. But the blistering debate that preceded the vote by the Communist Party Central Committee to give up its constitutional lock on power exposed deep fissures within the leadership over the Soviet president's reforms.

Though the maverick reformer, Boris Yeltsin, was the only committee member to vote against Gorbachev's new platform, what had been planned as a two-day meeting had to be extended an extra day to thresh out differences. The key item in the platform was the abolishment of Article 6 of the Soviet Constitution guaranteeing the Communist Party a monopoly on power. Its removal is to be recommended to the Soviet Parliament next week. This will open the way for a multiparty system, though there are now no other parties.

Gorbachev's proposal to remove Article 6 is a 180-degree turn for him. Only last December he persuaded the Soviet Congress of People's Deputies to defeat reformers' efforts to kill it.

The prospect of the party's having to compete for power for the first time since 1917 deeply disturbs Gorbachev's hard-line opponents. They remember the drubbing some party candidates took in last year's national elections and fear it will happen again in local and republic elections later this month and next.

A great deal of rhetorical blood was spilled in the closed-door meeting. Gorbachev's chief conservative opponent, Yegor Ligachev, charged that his reforms had cost Communist regimes control of Eastern Europe and ignited ethnic and nationalist strife at home.

U.S. Secretary of State James Baker arrived in Moscow Wednesday. He picked a good time to assess Gorbachev's ability not only to survive but to negotiate for his country on arms control, regional conflicts involving the superpowers, and other issues.

Having emerged victorious from the bruising Central Committee meeting, the Soviet leader now appears to be in a significantly stronger position to stay the course.

Omaha World-Herald

Omaha, NE, February 8, 1990

Soviet President Mikhail Gorbachev has made progress in steering his country off the cruel, repressive and belligerent path of his predecessors. Even as Gorbachev promotes more reforms in Moscow, however, the question grows stronger: Can he go far enough in time to prevent the Soviet Union from collapsing or disintegrating?

Vasily Selyunin, who writes for influential Soviet journals, recently predicted that the Soviet economy will quit functioning this summer and that the political system will fall apart soon afterward. Gorbachev, the journalist contends, might be able to save himself politically by moving away from the Communist Party and allying himself with radical reformers. Or he might not save himself.

Within a few days of Selyunin's predictions, Gorbachev seemed to be moving to broaden his base. Among other things, he won the approval of his colleagues to end the constitutional ruling mandate of the Communist Party, which some people said could lead to a multiparty system. Reports in the Soviet press indicated that Gorbachev now supports a system of private property rights.

But that may not be enough. Decades of privation, of persecution and of repressed nationalistic pride have built up a reservoir of impatience that seems unlikely to be contained by anything less than swift and fundamental reform.

Lithuania is in open defiance of Moscow. Latvia, Estonia, Armenia and Azerbaijan aren't far behind. Ethnic and religious pride is resurfacing in the Ukraine and in Russia itself.

Sunday, when 100,000 people demonstrated in Moscow for reform, it wasn't hard to think about similar demonstrations in Prague, Warsaw and Leipzig in recent months.

If Selyunin is right, Gorbachev doesn't have much time. Selyunin, who is one of his country's leading commentators on economics, predicts quadruple-digit inflation and a declining standard of living for the Soviet people. People will simply stop working soon, probably by summer, he said. After that, nearly anything is possible. Riots, perhaps. Revolution.

There are still apologists for Karl Marx who contend that the system that has performed so badly wasn't a true Marxist state, or even a Leninist state. They say that it was a mutant, distorted by the likes of Josef Stalin and Leonid Brezhnev and that its failure doesn't say anything about Marxism as a theory.

Selyunin disagrees. He says his people have been failed by the classic tenets of Marx and Lenin. The only solution, he says, is a non-totalitarian form of government.

A lot of Americans have been saying much the same thing for years. Now the tides of history are too powerful to be ignored. Not by Americans. Certainly not by the people of what were once referred to as the satellite nations. And now, it appears, not even by the worried circle of men who hold court in the Kremlin.

The Boston Globe

Boston, MA, February 7, 1990

Citizens throughout the Soviet Union sense their country disintegrating politically, economically and geographically. The program Mikhail Gorbachev defended before the Communist Party Central Committee was the effort of a realistic statesman to channel the flood tide already overwhelming the sand castles of established power.

"Anarchy" was a word heard often during the deliberations of the Central Committee – a prospect evoked by hardliners who abhor Gorbachev's vision of pluralism, and also by communist reformers who complain that he is retreating into the future. Both sides recognize the imminent peril of a descent into disorder. The 20th century has taught all Soviet citizens the horrors of violent revolution and civil war.

The suspense that attends Gorbachev's call for democracy – in the country and in the party – is the suspense proper to matters of life and death. His proposal to eliminate the party's constitutional monopoly on power, his call for a party congress this summer to "renew" the membership of the Central Committee, his projection of a decentralized, democratic federation of Soviet republics – all were attempts to make possible the peaceful transformation of an imploding system.

The drama enacted by Gorbachev is no longer the struggle of a lifelong communist to preserve the power and privileges of his ruling class. He is a realist. It was he who warned Erich Honecker of East Germany that those who do not learn from life are doomed to be swept away.

A telling sign of Gorbachev's own determination to adapt to events is that he recognized the inevitability of a multiparty system a scant two months after he scorned Andrei Sakharov's plea to annul Article Six of the Soviet Constitution, the legal basis for the party's "leading role."

Gorbachev's struggle is now to prevent chaos. Implicit in his speech to the Central Committee is a recognition of impending calamities: economic collapse, the melting of communist authority, the dissolution of the union.

In the past few weeks, indignant citizens have tossed out local party bosses in the Soviet heartland – a domestic replay of what happened in East Berlin, Prague and Sofia, where the sudden coalescing of "civil society" caused the abdication of communist regimes that had ruled in the name of the people. Popular fronts have sprung into existence throughout the Soviet Union, forming a political opposition in the streets, making pluralism a fait accompli.

Gorbachev told the Central Committee he sent troops to Azerbaijan to prevent "a coup attempt, nothing more, nothing less."

To prevent anarchy, Gorbachev has appealed for a peaceful and legal transition to pluralist democracy, private property and a new federation of Soviet republics. It is an appeal to reason, made in the shadow of irrational forces.

The Oregonian

Portland, OR, February 8, 1990

Mikhail Gorbachev continues to confound the skeptics.

Despite the speculation on how far he can go and how long he can survive, Gorbachev continues to ride the reform wave. The latest remarkable event was the decision by the Soviet Communist Party's Central Committee to give up the party's monopoly control of the Soviet Union's government.

Surprise follows surprise, shock after shock.

Only a few weeks ago this was the move Gorbachev wouldn't accept. But Gorbachev has been remarkably able to adapt to the pressures he himself unleashed after he assumed the Soviet leadership in March 1985. Clearly, rigid, entrenched and unpopular functionaries of the Communist Party have become liabilities more than allies in his effort to restructure the Soviet economy. Thus, he will restructure the political system, too. He will force the party to compete for power.

We don't know yet, of course, how this potentially revolutionary move will play out, what limits yet will be placed on competition for control. Gorbachev's initiative could make it easier for him to hold the Soviet Union intact against the various republics' cries for autonomy. But it also flies against 70 years' experience with Lenin's system of single-party control of every facet of government.

Maybe Lenin would understand, though. In 1913, he wrote, "Political institutions are a superstructure resting on an economic foundation." Economic disasters drive the Soviet reforms today.

For now, the United States and its allies can only watch developments. Secretary of State James Baker III is in Moscow hoping for insights.

Fortunately, developments in Moscow, like those in other Warsaw Pact nations, pose no threat requiring an immediate U.S. response. Quite the contrary. The trend toward democracy encourages all our hopes for a more stable, peaceful world, even as we nervously wonder just how far Gorbachev will or can go.

But the Gorbachev course raises fascinating considerations about what should be a historic foreign policy debate. The Cold War was not over some historic animosity between the United States and Russia; it was over communism. It was over whether that ideology should spread throughout the world or be contained by democratic, capitalist nations.

This seeming collapse of communism calls containment into question. The United States has to be prepared to respond appropriately. To do that, it needs to develop the intellectual foundations of a new view of its own interests and how to pursue them.

This rethinking doesn't have to happen overnight. It would be hard to get ahead of developments in Eastern Europe in any event. But we must be as adaptable as Gorbachev, or old views of the world could hamstring new beginnings.

The Tennessean

Nashville, TN, February 9, 1990

THE Soviet leader, Mr. Mikhail Gorbachev, has gambled and won in the powerful Central Committee for a restructuring of the political system and, perhaps, multiparty politics.

But the results of all this hardly mean, as a British newspaper put it, "the end of the party," meaning the Communist Party. The party has its troubles, from shortages to ethnic violence, it has its divisions and it has its critical public. But that doesn't mean it will fold its tents in the face of any vanguard of democratic horsemen.

In the first place, the Soviet Union has no history of democratic institutions that lasted very long. After the czars there was Bolshevism and the ways of Marx and Lenin. Russian citizens who were not born before 1917 have known little else. Decades of indoctrination and the squelching of all dissent have stamped on the people a psychosis that is much different from most socialist societies. And the party is one vast patronage machine.

Soviet discontent with the party runs deep, but it is not so much from an ideological point of view as it is for its misrule, its inability to manage the economy and for decades of its broken promises — and particularly the way things have gone on for the last five years.

There seems to be no similar national yearning for democracy per se. There is a national frustration over lack of change. Even in the restive republics, the thrust is for self-determination in their own affairs, divorced from Moscow's heavy hand.

Mr. Gorbachev's strengths, obviously, are his ability with the political maneuver and the fact there is no single person in the wings to match his vision. His weakness is not from political opponents but from having things begin to disintegrate into uncontrollable chaos.

Should the political events go into fast forward, the Communist Party might lose a few candidates in elections, but it has the money, the infrastructure, the media and other forces to survive. Mr. Gorbachev doesn't want to be its pall bearer, no matter what the West perceives, but rather the architect who remakes and redesigns it and finally, presides as a powerful president over it and the Soviet Union. ∎

Rockford Register Star

Rockford, IL, February 9, 1990

"We will have a normal democracy."

Such was the astonishing observation of a participant at this week's plenum of the Soviet Communist Party's Central Committee in the wake of that body's nearly unanimous vote to surrender its historic monopoly of power in the Soviet Union. This latest of triumphs for Mikhail Gorbachev stands as one of the most remarkable world events of this waning 20th century.

The birth of a multi-party political system awaits only the pro forma ratification of the new platform at the forthcoming Communist Party Congress. And thus will the process of reform set in motion by Gorbachev some five years ago have reached a point that probably even he never imagined.

In fact, it was just last year that Gorbachev himself labeled as "rubbish" the notion of abandoning his Communist Party's constitutional control of the Soviet system.

In short order, however, he recognized the volatility of forces that had been unleashed by *glasnost* and *perestroika* and saw that Communist retrenchment was a hopeless cause; with astounding political adroitness, then, he engineered this week's historic shift toward Western-style democracy.

The world can now smile wryly at its own fears of just days ago that Gorbachev faced a tough selling job at the party plenum, indeed, that he even faced the risk of being ousted from power.

As it turned out, however, Gorbachev ended up squarely in the middle of the current political spectrum, the target of criticism from conservatives that he has been going too far with his reforms and from radicals that he hasn't gone far enough. He parried the thrusts from both sides, called for a vote on his platform, and won the assent of all but two of the 249 members of the committee. Just another day at the office.

None of this means that the Soviet Union will tomorrow resemble a quaint democracy from some Frank Capra movie. No, the country faces formidable obstacles by way of severe economic woes and growing ethnic unrest. Even a magician like Gorbachev will be hard-pressed to keep the proverbial lid on long enough for democratic reforms to take root.

But the seeds have been sown. The Soviet peoples soon will have it within their powers to forge a future that is, for better or worse, of their own making.

The world is now a much different place.

Chicago Sun-Times

Chicago, IL, February 9, 1990

The Communist Party leadership in Moscow agreed Wednesday to end 72 years of monopoly power in the Soviet Union and turn to creation of a democratically styled presidency and cabinet.

No one we know ever thought they'd see the day. And no one we know can say now with assurance what will come next, and when. But nothing can diminish Wednesday's outcome as a historic event of epochal proportion.

Of course the Communist Party did not agree to go out of business. It and its adherents will remain, at minimum, a powerful force in Soviet and international affairs. Yet the party's opening of the door to other parties pursuing their own visions, its acceptance of a pluralistic system rooted in popular approval instead of dictatorship, is a startling shift.

A people accustomed to taking orders from the top may have difficulty at first adjusting to self-government. But that cannot blur the reality that the Soviet Union has renounced the omniscience and omnipotence of party doctrine. The world does turn.

Las Vegas Review-Journal

Las Vegas, NV, February 14, 1990

Call it the great reawakening of the democratic ideal — the phenomenon of recent months and years marked by the emergence or rebirth of democracy in many of the great nations of the world, from Brazil to Czechoslovakia, from Argentina to Poland.

We are not talking about Third World backwaters here. The countries that have embraced the democratic ideal in recent times are major nations, once and future regional powers — the sprawling, potentially wealthy republics of South America and the ancient, industrialized, culturally rich nations of Eastern Europe.

And now the bear, with an envious glance in its eye, turns west too.

Mikhail Gorbachev and the Soviet leadership know what works and what does not: The obvious, dismal, universal failure of the communist "experiment" stands in stark contrast to the success of liberal, market-oriented democracy. It has emerged as an undeniable fact: The democratic, market-driven societies of the West are inherently superior to Marxist nations by almost all important measures. They are vastly more free, vastly more productive, vastly more creative and far wealthier. As Winston Churchill put it so succinctly in 1952:

"The inherent vice of capitalism is the unequal sharing of blessings; the inherent virtue of socialism is the equal sharing of miseries."

If the Soviet Union had been able to provide its people with a modicum of wealth, perhaps they would have resented less the loss of freedom under successive communist dictatorships. But all they got was a share of the misery.

Churchill's comment about democratic capitalism was also correct: It is not a perfect system, just the best one yet devised by mankind.

The Soviet "communist" party is now prepared to admit that an "unequal share of blessings" is preferable to the "equal sharing of miseries."

We put "communist" party in quotes here because, after this week's startling announcement of a new party platform in Moscow, the "Communist" Party of the Soviet Union is no longer communist by even the mostly wildly stretched definition.

The party cast aside all the basic tenets that define both the practice and the theory of communism. Indeed, the new party platform contains language that seems derivative of Thomas Jefferson, if not Milton Friedman.

Incredibly, the party's statement of principles on human rights seems to have been distilled directly from the U.S. Bill of Rights. It includes guarantees of freedom of religion, the press and assembly, just as in the First Amendment. While not as detailed as the Bill of Rights, the Soviet document is, in certain respects, more expansive, calling for guarantees of "freedom of conscience" and "protection of a citizen's personality and honor, the immunity of his home and property, the secrecy of correspondence."

At the same time that the Communist Party of the Soviet Union was advancing the principles of basic human rights, it also embraced the idea of private property, saying: "The Communist Party of the Soviet Union believes the existence of individual property, including ownership of the means of production, does not contradict the modern stage in the country's economic development."

The party platform constituted nothing less than a blanket disavowal of Marxist theory.

There survive some true believers in the religion of Marxism, but they are to be found mostly in Hollywood, on American university faculties and inside the "liberation theology" movement. The people who have actually lived with Marxism know it to be a cruel fraud. That recognition has now been formalized within the Communist Party of the Soviet Union, which now appears to be bereft of communists.

Soviet CP Monopoly Revoked; President's Role Revamped

The Soviet Congress of People's Deputies, the national parliament, March 12-15, 1990 repealed the Communist Party's (CP) political monopoly, revamped and strengthened the presidency and elected Mikhail S. Gorbachev to a five-year term as a new-style executive president.

At Gorbachev's behest, the congress had been convened in a special session to consider a package of constitutional amendments to revise the Soviet political system. The 2,250-member congress normally met only twice a year.

The amendments were an outgrowth of the CP Central Committee plenum Feb. 5-7 at which the party heirarchy had endorsed a platform of sweeping changes. The platform had been published by the party Feb. 13. Western analysts viewed the document as a broad attempt to satisfy the reformist and conservative wings of the party. They said that the platform appeared to be full of contradictions.

Among its provisions, the document:

■ Played down the role of dogma in party policies. But the platform also stated that the party would continue to be guided by the "dialectical methadology of Marx, Engels and Lenin."

■ Stated that the Communist Party did not "claim a monopoly" and did not "preclude the possibility" of a multiparty system in the U.S.S.R. But the platform implied that the only legal parties should be those that embraced "democratic socialism."

■ Committed the party to the "creation of a full-fledged market economy." But it also stated, "Modern production is impossible without a centralized planned economy."

■ Called for a separation of executive, legislative and judicial powers. But it also urged that the head of state be given powers that would encompass all three branches of government.

■ Supported the right of "self-determination, including secession," of the Soviet republics. But it also opposed "separtist slogans and movements that would lead to the destruction of the great, multiethnic democratic state."

The Congress deputies March 13 repealed Article Six of the Soviet constitution, which guaranteed the Communist Party political monopoly. The repeal was accomplished by a vote of 1,771 to 24, with 74 abstentions.

The Congress March 13 voted to revamp the presidency. The vote was preceded by heated debate and behind-the-scenes deals. It was a major victory for Gorbachev at a time when he was marking the fifth anniversary of his ascension to the CP leadership. The measure passed, 1,817 to 133, with 61 abstentions.

The Soviet leader's plan, mainly left intact, had been to create a presidency with broad executive powers, essentially combining the posts of head of state and head of government. For the first time the word *prezident* would appear in the Soviet constitution.

Under the old system, the president's official title had been chairman of the Supreme Soviet, the standing national legislature. The constitutional revision made the presidency and the parliamentary chairmanship separate posts.

Gorbachev envisioned a president who would be the U.S.S.R.'s chief official in international affairs; would be the commander in chief of the military; have the authority to appoint or dismiss all of the top officials in executive, legislative and judicial branches; could make significant political and economic decisions by decree; could unilaterally override parliament votes; and could unilaterally declare marshal law in any part of the country.

Gorbachev linked the plan to an end of the Communist Party's political monopoly and the likelihood of a multiparty system. He argued that only a powerful central figure – one not tied to partisan politics or special interests – could guide *perestroika* (restructuring) to a successful conclusion.

Many lawmakers – radicals, conservatives and nationalists – were wary of the plan inpart or as a whole. Some argued that it would give dictatorial powers to whoever held the presidency.

Chicago Tribune

Chicago, IL, March 16, 1990

The latest of the recurring reports of Mikhail Gorbachev's imminent political demise—as Mark Twain once said of his own prematurely reported death—obviously were greatly exaggerated.

The more the doomsayers, a persistent and highly vocal minority in the Soviet Union and abroad, sound their dirges, it seems, the broader is Gorbachev's smile as he emerges victorious from the latest test.

This week the grin got wider and wider as the Congress of People's Deputies debated bitterly changes that will transform the Soviet Union beyond recognition—then handed him one win after another.

The first approved his plan for a strengthened presidency. The second revoked the constitutional guarantee of dominance by the Communist Party, setting the stage for multiparty elections. The third granted his wish that the congress elect the president for the first four years. The fourth gave him the new office.

Most of the victories were by impressive margins. But the final vote to give him the executive powers he sought was relatively close, especially since both his nominated opponents had begged off. He got only about 200 more votes than the majority he needed. A cynic might suspect he had borrowed an old American political trick and thrown a few votes to mollify critics who wanted an immediate popular election. With no opposition, any more of a steamroller would have been embarrassing. As one reformer noted, it was "a good thing it wasn't 100 percent."

While it may not have been 'Western-style democracy, it was a sharp break from the Soviet tradition that prevailed until very recently.

It is easy to understand in the current atmosphere of economic and political crisis why Gorbachev was eager for the power to press reform without having to tailor every proposal to the conservative tastes of the Communist Party's Central Committee and the Politburo. And he has seen what's happened to party leaders at home and in Eastern Europe who were forced to put their popularity to electoral tests. But he should have agreed to face the voters in a year or two instead of taking a four-year pass.

Responding to fears he'll become a dictator, Gorbachev promised he would use his new muscle only to make *perestroika* work better. A successor might have quite another agenda, so his most ardent critics wish him good health. Just as Americans must.

Actually, Gorbachev's new powers are akin to those of American presidents. He can propose legislation, veto bills, conduct foreign policy, name cabinet members, declare emergencies and under some conditions impose presidential rule. There are provisions for legislative restraint on most of those and a veto override.

What awaits the test of time is whether the Soviet people, who've known no history of democratic rule, will have the instinctive intolerance for abuses that provides that important extra measure of restraint imbedded in the American system.

ST. LOUIS POST-DISPATCH

St. Louis, MO, March 16, 1990

For five years, the predictions of Soviet President Mikhail Gorbachev's eminent demise have been made as regularly as clockwork. Yet during each crisis, Mr. Gorbachev has displayed an uncanny knack for consolidating and expanding his power. Now as Lithuania prepares for independence and the Soviet Union embarks on a new path of evolution or devolution, Mr. Gorbachev has once again strengthened his power. The vote by the Soviet Parliament to create a strong presidency, while a double-edged sword, gives Mr. Gorbachev the autonomy he wants to push perestroika along and the flexibility to respond to the swirl of events.

It is no accident that the decision to institute a strong presidency came at the same session that the Communist Party's governmental monopoly was abolished. They are, indeed, two sides of the same coin. Traditionally, the Communist Party was the state. Parliamentary reforms, multiparty elections and now the end of the party's monopoly have driven a wedge between the Communist Party and the state. They are no longer identical. In light of these reforms, the creation of a strong president undercuts and diminishes the power of the general secretary of the Communist Party, once the most powerful position in the Soviet Union. Indeed, Mr. Gorbachev, once securely ensconced in this enhanced presidency, may, it is rumored, resign his position as party chairman.

The danger of a strong executive is, of course, that the powers can be exercised for dictatorial ends. An institutional corrective is, however, possible: a new constitution that also creates an independent judiciary and legislature.

Mr. Gorbachev's latest triumph hammers yet another nail into the Communist Party's coffin at a most opportune time. The single biggest item on the Soviet agenda is now the Soviet Union itself: its size and structure. New thinking, not old chestnuts, must be applied to this dilemma — and fast.

The Miami Herald

Miami, FL, March 17, 1990

MIKHAIL Gorbachev, who has been one of Stalinism's fiercest critics, has just succeeded in turning Stalin on his head. By a remarkable combination of persuasion, Machiavellian bullying, and crafty bargaining in the Soviet parliament, Mr. Gorbachev has transformed his country's totalitarian system into an authoritarian arrangement that has some of the elements of czarist Russia.

Thus the new powers of the Soviet presidency, approved this week in Moscow, introduce an important qualitative change in the politics of the USSR. But the concentration of power in the office of a chief executive preserves some of the traits that led to Stalinist dictatorship in the first place.

Henceforth, the Soviet president can rule autocratically without the consent of any political party. In the Soviet system, checks and balances are scarce. Moreover, as the parliament has shown in its recent dealings with Mr. Gorbachev, as a body it is not yet sufficiently experienced to counterbalance a clever and determined chief executive. A cleverer, more-determined chief executive than he is hard to imagine.

The potential for a Gorbachev dictatorship exists, but not the threat — at least not yet. Mr. Gorbachev's credentials as a reformer and as a Russian democrat are not in question. Indeed, he claims that a powerful presidency is needed to accelerate economic and political reforms. Mr. Gorbachev says his new authority is also needed if he's to act decisively in times of crisis, as now, when the Kremlin is trying to bring orderly change to its empire in the face of powerful, centrifugal secessionist forces.

The Soviet parliament also approved constitutional reforms that legalize political pluralism and multiparty democracy. These reforms are not unrelated to Mr. Gorbachev's desire for a "czarist presidency." The Soviet Communist Party's demise makes it impracticable for him to rely on the Politburo and Central Committee to govern. And it will be increasingly difficult for Mr. Gorbachev to govern — or to win elections — if he is regarded as the chief of a discredited Communist Party and not as an impartial president who embodies the will of all Soviet voters.

Marx has once again been proven wrong: Even in some post-Communist countries, the state does not wither away. It grows more powerful as the *party* withers away.

The Hartford Courant

Hartford, CT, March 18, 1990

It's hard to think of Mikhail S. Gorbachev, the toast of the West, as an anachronism.

But, at the beginning of Mr. Gorbachev's sixth year in power, more and more Soviet citizens regard him as losing touch, no longer leading the parade toward change but perhaps being overtaken by it.

As always, he got his way last week when the Congress of People's Deputies ratified his plan for an executive presidency with sweeping powers and then — somewhat grudgingly — gave him the job for the next five years. It was not a love feast: Critics among the delegates almost succeeded in making him face a nationwide election for the post. But popular election of the president will have to wait until 1995.

His opponents claim that Mr. Gorbachev has not delivered what he promised on the economy and that he is too authoritarian. They worry that the structure built at his insistence could be abused by a dictator, and Russian history gives them no comfort. He survives, apparently, because there is no credible alternative.

The criticism seems misplaced, on the surface. The Soviet leader is seen, especially in the United States and Europe, as the father of democratic and capitalistic development in the East, a liberator and the catalyst for change.

His first five years made exciting history. Change came slowly at first and then accelerated with such speed and force that it's not surprising the paramount changemaker himself is at risk:

The unmuzzling of Soviet society. Withdrawal from Afghanistan. Virtual repeal of the doctrine that said arms would be used to crush challenges to Soviet authority in Eastern Europe. Breathtaking concessions to the United States on arms control. Plans for a market economy and the ownership of private property. Greater autonomy for the republics. Free elections for some posts and a semblance of opposition parties. Surrender of the Communist Party's leading role and its gradual decoupling from the government.

But now Mr. Gorbachev has turned cautious while many of his subjects have become impatient for even greater change. The threat to him is not so much from the old-guard Communists, whom he has boxed around pretty much at will, but from those who are hooked on the first tastes of democracy he has given them.

The deputies acceded to his wishes for a super-presidency, but many of them didn't like it. Mr. Gorbachev, the liberator, can rule by emergency decree, declare war and dismiss the legislature. He says he needs strong executive power to effect further reforms and to keep order in a vast country where ethnic rivalries are always at a flashpoint. But he didn't trust his people enough to ask them for the power.

In that, he is not a great deal different from the Soviet leaders he followed, including Leonid I. Brezhnev and the successor fossils whose names most people have already forgotten.

Those who wish him well hope that Mr. Gorbachev's instincts are correct, and that somehow he will have managed to bring about enough stability and prosperity in the next five years so that true democracy can have a chance.

It's a pity that he has chosen to impose democracy by autocratic means. Such a course breeds despair and cynicism. Listen to Ilya I. Zaslavsky, a liberal deputy: "When people are elected in non-democratic ways, and then play the democrats, as Gorbachev has done, then that's not democracy either. It is just another form of the same old thing."

Mr. Gorbachev could dispel some of the gloom settling in over his reforms by quickly giving up the top job he now holds in the Communist Party, which is rapidly losing public favor anyway. He might also devise some way to submit his plans for further reform to popular vote, so that his people can buy into the program.

The last thing the Soviet Union needs now is another form of the same old thing.

The Atlanta Journal
THE ATLANTA CONSTITUTION
Atlanta, GA, March 19, 1990

Mikhail Gorbachev's long string of domestic political victories are coming harder and harder. Last year, for instance, he ran for chairman of the Congress of People's Deputies and won 95 percent of the votes. Last week, in the up-or-down vote for his country's newly empowered presidency, he got only 59 percent.

The falloff stems in part from regional separatists who abstained as a statement of alienation from Moscow and from complainers wondering, and maybe justifiably so, "Where's the beef?", the economic payoff from perestroika.

There was significant new element to the opposition this time: widely expressed unease that Mr. Gorbachev is going too far in his drive to jump-start the economic and political apparatus, especially that he is grasping for too much power, a gut concern in a land of czars and commissars.

Passage last week by the Soviet Parliament of most of Mr. Gorbachev's proposed constitutional changes was just a formality. Deinstitutionalizing the Communist Party, approving multiparty contests for political office, even guaranteeing private property rights — all these had been tentatively approved by the Supreme Soviet last month.

The issues in some doubt involved (a) a new model of chief executive, a presidency likened to America's or France's and (b) whether Mr. Gorbachev should be the first person to occupy the position, especially since he tailored it to his specifications.

Mr. Gorbachev makes a good argument for a strong presidency, and not just because he needs the authority during the current paralysis to overcome bureaucratic and societal inertia and push through reforms — though that's a point in his favor.

A better reason yet is to snap the heretofore inextricable link between the Communist Party and the government. No longer should the Soviet leader, whoever he or she may be, derive power by reason of rising to the top of the Politburo heap. Legitimacy will be conferred upon the leader elected by the people and unburdened, theoretically, of party imperatives.

Granted, Mr. Gorbachev didn't submit himself to his people's judgment, not this time, and his excuse is flimsy — that the Soviets' crises demand remedy now and can't wait for a long election campaign. Say this for him, though: His elevation and empowerment were approved by the most representative body of the Soviet people since the Bolshevik takeover.

The system is still wildly out of balance, however, with the executive branch grotesquely overmuscled. An aficionado of the law, Mr. Gorbachev shows signs of nurturing the adoption of a new, fairer legal code and a Heimlich hug for the Soviets' moribund judiciary. Without these changes, the new structure he is trying to fashion will always be on the verge of toppling.

THE CHRISTIAN SCIENCE MONITOR
Boston, MA, March 19, 1990

THE greatly expanded powers of Mikhail Gorbachev, the new "prezident" of the Soviet Union, are cause for both hope and worry. The people of the Soviet Union are being asked to take a leap of faith in the hope that a much stronger central leadership position will help Mr. Gorbachev bring about successful economic reforms and further democracy.

Certainly there has been a need in the Soviet Union for executive decisions, and, yes, order – that old Russian demand. The January uprising in Azerbaijan, along with confusion in the chain-of-command regarding the use of force in Tbilisi last spring, make this clear. Russians don't have a high threshold for anarchy and chaos. There's a lot of it today. Somebody has to take charge.

The creation of a Soviet presidency, a position theoretically more akin to democratic presidencies in the West, is positive. It has diminished the role of the Communist Party and the Politburo, and set forth a multiparty Soviet future.

Yet there are disturbing elements in Gorbachev's new role. He can now dismiss ministers, presumably those who oppose liberalization. He commands the armed forces. He has a new and vague "power of decree" – which may or may not be used as a private steering mechanism for change.

By themselves, these are not extravagant powers for Gorbachev at a time of historic change and instability in Russia. It would, however, be regrettable to see central authority slowly become institutionalized in the presidency. Russia does not need a new czar. Direct elections are five years off. That is a long time. (It's only been five years since Gorbachev came to power.) So far, there's no sign that Gorbachev would abuse his powers. But then the man remains something of a mystery. Too much central power could stifle democratization.

That said, one must again marvel at Gorbachev's political abilities. The Soviet Congress of People's Deputies did not give him a sweeping mandate. But he managed to stay ahead of the conservatives and behind the liberals, thus occupying a strong middle ground. If he can get through the crisis over Lithuania, now Latvia, and eventually Estonia, in the same way, he may be aptly described as a wizard.

DAYTON DAILY NEWS
Dayton, OH, March 18, 1990

Mikhail Gorbachev got his presidency the old-fashioned way — by having it handed to him. That cheapens it, weakens his moral authority. The idea in creating a Soviet presidency was to create a strong leader, albeit one with checks on his power. Some checks are there. Whether sufficient strength is there now is not clear.

In deciding — on a close vote — not to hold a presidential election for another five years, the Soviet politicians apparently took to heart the insistence by some that things are just too fragile in that country right now. Independence movements are arising here and there; the disintegration of the Communist Party is creating a power vacuum; the always awful economy is getting worse; extremist, anti-Semitic and other unattractive thoughts are being heard more all the time. An election might be too volatile.

But to put off an election while trying to create a national commitment to democracy is to weaken the long-term effort.

Moreover, the notion that democracy itself is a threat to domestic peace is dubious. Democracy is not a cure-all, not a solution that always works. Democracy can be said to have created Hitler, after all.

The only real case against an election now, though, is that democracy can be said to have created the problems that Hitler fed on, specifically directionlessness, the atmosphere of chaos, a feeling that what was needed was a strong hand. Some modern Soviets may be worrying about the possibility of chaos in the Soviet Union leading to calls for a return to dictatorship.

However, chaos seems unlikely if Mr. Gorbachev were to win a 1990 or 1991 election. Of course, few Soviet observers are assuming that he could. Most say there is intense public dissatisfaction with him.

That fact seems odd to many Westerners, because Mr. Gorbachev's impact on the world seems so obviously positive. But public discontent is probably inevitable in a country with a declining economy and growing civic unrest. Many Soviets may be happy about the future they see for their country (many are not, of course), but it must be difficult to be happy about current circumstances. And unhappiness about current circumstances always hurts incumbents.

Today, Americans and British alike think of Winston Churchill as the greatest figure in the modern history of his country, because of his efforts to prepare his country for World War II and because of his leadership in victory. But immediately after the war, he was turned out of office in an election. The economy was doing badly. That, in the short term, was what mattered.

At any rate, for Mr. Gorbachev to lose an election now would probably require the opposition to unite around somebody. That it could do that seems doubtful, because the criticism of the incumbent comes from every philosophical direction. If critics could settle on another person, then that person should be president, and probably could be effective.

Still, all things considered, the movement toward democracy in the Soviet Union looks real; and Mikhail Gorbachev does not seem like the kind of guy who will look for some pretext five years hence not to hold another election. The American concern about how things are going in the Soviet Union must be not with whether democracy is taking hold and working, but with whether capitalism is.

The Boston Globe

Boston, MA, March 17, 1990

Mikhail Gorbachev this week abolished the Communist system in the Soviet Union. In its stead he instituted a multi-party democracy with a strong presidency modeled after the French and American systems. Despite flaws in its form and sequence, this legal and peaceful revolution is a momentous achievement.

Independent and radical deputies in the Soviet Parliament had sound reasons for objecting to the haste and improvisation of the changes they were asked to approve. They argued that before there is a president with the power to send troops into the 15 republics, or to annul decisions made by their legislatures, there should be a constitutional definition of the powers that belong to the central government and those that are retained by the republics.

This is, in the abstract, a persuasive argument. Proof that it may be invalid for the particular circumstances now prevailing in the Soviet Union may be found in the political behavior of parliamentary deputies from the Baltics. Though they are the legislators most immediately concerned with the rights and powers of independent republics, they struck a back-room deal with Gorbachev. They voted to have parliament elect him president in return for his promise to enter into discussions with them on the secession of their republics from the Soviet Union.

The deal suggests two instructive lessons about the enormous changes ushered in by Gorbachev. One is that he has already conceded the principle of a republic's right to secession, and needs to command a strong executive branch in order to negotiate the terms and methods of Baltic independence. The Baltic deputies recognize that a peaceful separation from Moscow cannot be negotiated with the old center of power – the barons of a discredited and fast-dissolving Communist Party. A strong president is needed immediately, so that he can preside over the decolonization of the internal Soviet empire.

The second lesson is that the mercantile essence of democracy – the need of accountable politicians to barter favors and votes – has already transformed political life in the Soviet Union. Gorbachev may never match Lyndon Johnson as a wheeler-dealer, but his readiness to trade concessions to Baltic secessionists in exchange for their votes augurs well for future relations between the legislative and executive branches of the new Soviet government.

It is precisely on this question of checks and balances that the radical deputies made their strongest case against Gorbachev's hasty effort to institutionalize a presidential system. They had logic on their side when they contended that a strong presidency could be a temptation to authoritarian abuse if it were not balanced, constitutionally, by a "fully authoritative Supreme Soviet." Not only did these skeptics have the experience of watching Gorbachev manipulate the Congress of People's Deputies while he chaired its sessions, they also feared that a more authoritarian successor might one day exploit his constitutional prerogatives to run roughshod over a weak legislative branch.

Understandable as this anxiety may be, it ignores the immediate need to create a new balance of power in the Soviet polity. The powers that must be checked immediately are those of the party bosses in the Central Committee and the politburo. And the revolutionary purpose of the constitutional amendments Gorbachev shepherded through the full Congress this week was precisely to eradicate all legal justification for the Leninist system. As one of Gorbachev's loyalists, Segei Alexeyev, told the deputies, they were voting for a "peaceful passage from a totalitarian system to a democratic and humane system."

The goal of this new system is to separate the state from the party. Hence the state should no longer be seen as "the instrument of dictatorship," but as the "guarantor of legality, of freedom, the defender of peoples' rights."

In his acceptance speech Gorbachev acknowledged "fears about the president being able to usurp power." To prove his devotion to "carefully designed checks and balances," he has granted parliament a constitutional right to override a presidential veto and also the power to annul a state of emergency declared by the president.

Gorbachev has plucked a democratic rabbit from a totalitarian hat. Now he must conjure up a prosperous market economy and a stable confederation of autonomous republics.

THE RICHMOND NEWS LEADER
Richmond, VA, March 21, 1990

Now he really is President Gorbachev. After approving Mikhail Gorbachev's proposal to move toward a Western-style presidency, the Soviet legislature "elected" him to the first five-year term. Popular votes presumably will elect subsequent presidents.

An honest-to-goodness elected president would solve one of the USSR's historic problems: leadership succession. No Soviet maximum leader ever has retired. The General Secretaries have either died (at the hands of assassins, perhaps), or they have been purged. Dangerous (to the losers, that is) power struggles have accompanied every change of guard. Orderly transitions have not occurred.

A presidential system would change all that. Candidates would run for office and, when elected, would assume power peacefully. The losers presumably would receive tickets to the swearing-in parties — not to the Gulag.

Some of Gorbachev's critics fear that he could exploit his presidential powers for dictatorial purposes. They have a point. Gorbachev may be a force for positive change, but no country — least of all the USSR — needs a personality cult. True democracy depends on a regular rotation of officeholders. Individuals come and go, but the constitutional structure endures.

Dostoyevsky knew that it was Russia's curse always to depend on the will — good or ill — of one man. A presidential system will allow the Soviets to move beyond the commissars and czars. Ultimately, however, the pressure will be on Gorbachev himself. For democracy will triumph only if he voluntarily steps aside when voted out of office, yielding with good grace the reins to his freely elected successor.

The Pittsburgh PRESS
Pittsburgh, PA, March 18, 1990

Mikhail Gorbachev has secured for himself five years in which to make good the promise of "perestroika" before he must face the Soviet voters in an election.

If he succeeds in delivering to his people and the world the benefit of a reformed, democratic Soviet Union, he will have justified the gamble the Soviet Congress has taken by further centralizing power in one man.

On the face of it, Gorbachev's course is contradictory. He says he seeks democracy -- yet he refuses to accede to the strong new presidency by popular election. He claims to be "laying the groundwork for building a rule-of-law country" — but rewrites the constitution as it suits his purpose.

Many touted reforms, such as the law on religious freedom, are promised over and over but haven't appeared.

Gorbachev's own ideas have evolved, but his direction has been steady. Soon after coming to power in 1985, he wrote "Perestroika," describing the "revolution" he sought for the Soviet Union. Since then, he has been tested repeatedly, in Eastern Europe, in arms talks and at home. The movement away from coercion, toward consent has been reaffirmed at almost every turn.

Today, no course open to the Soviet Union is without peril. Its economy has sunk into permanent crisis, ancient ethnic hatreds are fueling chronic violence, half a dozen constituent republics are moving to secede from the empire assembled by the czars.

In this pass, if Gorbachev should die or be killed or otherwise removed from office, his successor would inherit exceptionally strong executive powers but not necessarily Gorbachev's humane intent or political skill.

In the past five years, Gorbachev has brought his people into a wilderness of uncertainty. He himself is groping on every front: for some form of federalism that will satisfy restive republics but save the union; for a strong economy compatible with socialism.

Why trust him, despite the risks? Because of what he has delivered so far: He led the Soviet people out of their prison of lies and fear.

ST. LOUIS POST-DISPATCH

St. Louis, MO, March 16, 1990

For five years, the predictions of Soviet President Mikhail Gorbachev's eminent demise have been made as regularly as clockwork. Yet during each crisis, Mr. Gorbachev has displayed an uncanny knack for consolidating and expanding his power. Now as Lithuania prepares for independence and the Soviet Union embarks on a new path of evolution or devolution, Mr. Gorbachev has once again strengthened his power. The vote by the Soviet Parliament to create a strong presidency, while a double-edged sword, gives Mr. Gorbachev the autonomy he wants to push perestroika along and the flexibility to respond to the swirl of events.

It is no accident that the decision to institute a strong presidency came at the same session that the Communist Party's governmental monopoly was abolished. They are, indeed, two sides of the same coin. Traditionally, the Communist Party was the state. Parliamentary reforms, multiparty elections and now the end of the party's monopoly have driven a wedge between the Communist Party and the state. They are no longer identical. In light of these reforms, the creation of a strong president undercuts and diminishes the power of the general secretary of the Communist Party, once the most powerful position in the Soviet Union. Indeed, Mr. Gorbachev, once securely ensconced in this enhanced presidency, may, it is rumored, resign his position as party chairman.

The danger of a strong executive is, of course, that the powers can be exercised for dictatorial ends. An institutional corrective is, however, possible: a new constitution that also creates an independent judiciary and legislature.

Mr. Gorbachev's latest triumph hammers yet another nail into the Communist Party's coffin at a most opportune time. The single biggest item on the Soviet agenda is now the Soviet Union itself: its size and structure. New thinking, not old chestnuts, must be applied to this dilemma — and fast.

The Hartford Courant

Hartford, CT, March 18, 1990

It's hard to think of Mikhail S. Gorbachev, the toast of the West, as an anachronism.

But, at the beginning of Mr. Gorbachev's sixth year in power, more and more Soviet citizens regard him as losing touch, no longer leading the parade toward change but perhaps being overtaken by it.

As always, he got his way last week when the Congress of People's Deputies ratified his plan for an executive presidency with sweeping powers and then — somewhat grudgingly — gave him the job for the next five years. It was not a love feast: Critics among the delegates almost succeeded in making him face a nationwide election for the post. But popular election of the president will have to wait until 1995.

His opponents claim that Mr. Gorbachev has not delivered what he promised on the economy and that he is too authoritarian. They worry that the structure built at his insistence could be abused by a dictator, and Russian history gives them no comfort. He survives, apparently, because there is no credible alternative.

The criticism seems misplaced, on the surface. The Soviet leader is seen, especially in the United States and Europe, as the father of democratic and capitalistic development in the East, a liberator and the catalyst for change.

His first five years made exciting history. Change came slowly at first and then accelerated with such speed and force that it's not surprising the paramount changemaker himself is at risk:

The unmuzzling of Soviet society. Withdrawal from Afghanistan. Virtual repeal of the doctrine that said arms would be used to crush challenges to Soviet authority in Eastern Europe. Breathtaking concessions to the United States on arms control. Plans for a market economy and the ownership of private property. Greater autonomy for the republics. Free elections for some posts and a semblance of opposition parties. Surrender of the Communist Party's leading role and its gradual decoupling from the government.

But now Mr. Gorbachev has turned cautious while many of his subjects have become impatient for even greater change. The threat to him is not so much from the old-guard Communists, whom he has boxed around pretty much at will, but from those who are hooked on the first tastes of democracy he has given them.

The deputies acceded to his wishes for a super-presidency, but many of them didn't like it. Mr. Gorbachev, the liberator, can rule by emergency decree, declare war and dismiss the legislature. He says he needs strong executive power to effect further reforms and to keep order in a vast country where ethnic rivalaries are always at a flashpoint. But he didn't trust his people enough to ask them for the power.

In that, he is not a great deal different from the Soviet leaders he followed, including Leonid I. Brezhnev and the successor fossils whose names most people have already forgotten.

Those who wish him well hope that Mr. Gorbachev's instincts are correct, and that somehow he will have managed to bring about enough stability and prosperity in the next five years so that true democracy can have a chance.

It's a pity that he has chosen to impose democracy by autocratic means. Such a course breeds despair and cynicism. Listen to Ilya I. Zaslavsky, a liberal deputy: "When people are elected in nondemocratic ways, and then play the democrats, as Gorbachev has done, then that's not democracy either. It is just another form of the same old thing."

Mr. Gorbachev could dispel some of the gloom settling in over his reforms by quickly giving up the top job he now holds in the Communist Party, which is rapidly losing public favor anyway. He might also devise some way to submit his plans for further reform to popular vote, so that his people can buy into the program.

The last thing the Soviet Union needs now is another form of the same old thing.

The Miami Herald

Miami, FL, March 17, 1990

MIKHAIL Gorbachev, who has been one of Stalinism's fiercest critics, has just succeeded in turning Stalin on his head. By a remarkable combination of persuasion, Machiavellian bullying, and crafty bargaining in the Soviet parliament, Mr. Gorbachev has transformed his country's totalitarian system into an authoritarian arrangement that has some of the elements of czarist Russia.

Thus the new powers of the Soviet presidency, approved this week in Moscow, introduce an important qualitative change in the politics of the USSR. But the concentration of power in the office of a chief executive preserves some of the traits that led to Stalinist dictatorship in the first place.

Henceforth, the Soviet president can rule autocratically without the consent of any political party. In the Soviet system, checks and balances are scarce. Moreover, as the parliament has shown in its recent dealings with Mr. Gorbachev, as a body it is not yet sufficiently experienced to counterbalance a clever and determined chief executive. A cleverer, more-determined chief executive than he is hard to imagine.

The potential for a Gorbachev dictatorship exists, but not the threat — at least not yet. Mr. Gorbachev's credentials as a reformer and as a Russian democrat are not in question. Indeed, he claims that a powerful presidency is needed to accelerate economic and political reforms. Mr. Gorbachev says his new authority is also needed if he's to act decisively in times of crisis, as now, when the Kremlin is trying to bring orderly change to its empire in the face of powerful, centrifugal secessionist forces.

The Soviet parliament also approved constitutional reforms that legalize political pluralism and multiparty democracy. These reforms are not unrelated to Mr. Gorbachev's desire for a "czarist presidency." The Soviet Communist Party's demise makes it impracticable for him to rely on the Politburo and Central Committee to govern. And it will be increasingly difficult for Mr. Gorbachev to govern — or to win elections — if he is regarded as the chief of a discredited Communist Party and not as an impartial president who embodies the will of all Soviet voters.

Marx has once again been proven wrong: Even in some post-Communist countries, the state does not wither away. It grows more powerful as the *party* withers away.

Strikes by Soviet Coal Miners Shake Kremlin

The Soviet Union was hit by nationwide wildcat strikes by coal miners July 10-26, 1989. The strikes further weakened the Soviet economy and forced the leadership to pledge major concessions to end the walkouts. At their peak, the strikes idled nearly 500,000 coal miners and cost the nation an estimated $60 million in lost production. The U.S.S.R. was the world's third-largest coal producer, after China and the U.S. Most of its annual output, over 700 million tons, was for domestic consumption rather than export.

The walkouts, coupled with continuing ethnic violence, caused divisions in the Kremlin over the direction of *perestroika* (restructuring), the program of liberal reforms initiated by President Mikhail S. Gorbachev. The events prompted Gorbachev to threaten a purge of unresponsive Communist Party (CP) officials at all levels of the party.

The strikes began July 10 with a walkout of coal miners in Mezhdurechensk, a town in western Siberia. The town was located in the Kuznetsky Basin, one of the nation's two most important coal regions. The Mezhdurechensk miners issued a list of complaints that, in one form or another, was duplicated in the strikes that followed. The grievances included: low general wages, with little or no compensation for night shifts; unsafe working conditions, inadequate housing and medical care; a badly polluted environment; and shortages of food and such consumer items as soap and shoes.

As negotiations began in Siberia on July 17, workers at eight coal mines in the Donestsk Basin of the Ukraine, the nation's main coal region, walked off their jobs.

But as the Siberian strikers reached a settlement with the government July 19, the Ukraine strikes by July 20 had expanded as far east as northern Kazakhstan and as far north as the Russian Arctic Circle.

Amid the crisis, Gorbachev addressed the CP Central Committee July 18. The debate confirmed Western speculation that Kremlin conservatives, and some Gorbachev allies, were using the crisis to question the president's policies.

The coal strikes waned by July 26, after the government offered the regional strike committees concessions on the order of the Siberian settlement. The Council of Trade Unions July 27 presented the Supreme Soviet with a draft law that would outlaw strikes not approved by the council's local units.

THE CHRISTIAN SCIENCE MONITOR
Baltimore, MD, July 23, 1989

COMPLAINTS from Soviet coal miners have piled up for years, by the government's own admission. But extreme shortages of basics like sugar and soap have now combined with longstanding unhappiness over working and living conditions to spark widespread strikes.

In the age of *perestroika*, the miners want more than attention to physical needs. Demands include self-management of their mines, an end to privileges for Communist Party and government bureaucrats, and even a stop to Soviet development aid for the third world.

Some conservatives in the party doubtless view the strikers' militancy as intolerable in a system that glorifies the "worker." They may push for force to put down the strikes. But Mikhail Gorbachev is likely to see the strikes as another opportunity to get *perestroika* – his retooling of the Soviet economy – off dead center.

The government has made some concessions on wages, and it has shipped off extra sugar and soap to the coal regions. But there are clear limits to what can be done along these lines. Transferring scarce commodities, after all, amounts to shifting shortages from one place to another.

Gorbachev is probably more than willing, however, to address strikers' political demands, shake up local bureaucracies, and put management decisions in new hands. Intransigent mid-level bureaucrats have been road blocks to *perestroika* right along.

Striking miners, recognizing that the government can't do much economically and appreciating political changes, may thus be mollified. Or they may not. The economic discontent runs deep.

Every Gorbachev move is a high-wire act of sorts. And the suspense is only heightened when one sensitive move – resolving the strikes – has to be combined with another, perhaps even more demanding maneuver – quelling continued ethnic strife in the Caucasus region.

THE ⬛ SUN
Boston, MA, July 21, 1989

The dichotomy of what Mikhail S. Gorbachev has called the "pre-crisis situation" in the Soviet Union is becoming sharper day by day. Cultural freedoms keep passing new mileposts, but the Communist giant's industrial infrastructure is squeaking and grinding to a halt. Inexplicable shortages of gasoline throughout the world's biggest oil-producing nation have led to some of the worst deficits of food and consumer staples since World War II. They are now threatening to unsettle the season's harvesting.

Even more ominous is the current wave of mining strikes. Even as neighboring Poland is moving toward reconciliation after a decade of chronic political and labor struggle, the Solidarity fever of free unions seems to be infecting the Soviet Union. Labor stoppages on this scale have not been seen there since the discontent and economic chaos that enabled the Bolsheviks to grab power in 1917. If they continue and extend to other industries, these stoppages — along with renewed ethnic clashes — may prove to be the catalyst to propel the Soviet Union into a crisis of existence that because of the country's larger scope and importance in world affairs could be far worse than Poland's. Such a crisis, in turn, could endanger the very essence of the Gorbachev reforms and return the country to methods of its Stalinist past.

These are unsettling prospects. It is in the West's interests to have an enlightened Kremlin leader ushering the Soviet Union steadily toward liberalization and a full partnership in the world community. Yet, as Soviet workers now are learning that strikes are an effective weapon to force concessions from the party and government, there is little the West can do to help. Accumulated grievances are the result of seven decades of Communist misrule. They probably cannot be ended until the Communist Party agrees to relinquish its monopoly on political power and permits privatization of such crucial sectors of the economy as agriculture. This it is not willing to do.

A potent example of mindless Communist mismanagement comes from Ukraine's Donetsk Basin (Donbass) region, where tens of thousands of coal miners have been joining strikes in recent days. While authorities claim the strikes threaten the country's economy, *Radyanska Ukraina* reports that some 35 million tons of extracted coal has piled up around the coal fields because of the state railroad's failure to transport it. There have been several instances of the coal self-combusting. Witnessing such incompetence and the bare shelves of their food stores, it is no wonder that the idea of blackmailing concessions through strikes is suddenly so appealing to Soviet workers.

Rockford Register Star

Rockford, IL, July 28, 1989

You can almost feel the disorientation of the Russian Bear. Communism hasn't worked, and the Soviet Union is facing great disarray with nationalist movements sprouting and disaffected workers striking.

Some 100,000 coal miners recently went on strike for better hours, better pay, more food, more clothing. Mikhail Gorbachev, the Soviet leader, said they'd get these if they would go back to work. He said the ranks of communism should be stripped of those who hadn't paid the miners any prior attention.

Troubling questions are rippling through the ruling ranks. Of the recently elected officials, 85 percent are Communist — but a different breed of Communist. This breed has questions about their party's dogma.

In a recent meeting of the Communist Party, Gorbachev urged a purge of conservative officials at all levels of the party up to the Politboro, until leaders reflecting the public's mood of today emerge. This must be done soon, he exclaimed.

But some party stalwarts feel events are moving so fast that the party can't keep up. Some even seem to be hoping for a return to "the old days" when the press was controlled, when thoughts were controlled, when ideologues ruled over the disbelieving.

That is not Gorbachev's itinerary, however. He says, "If perestroika is a revolution — and we agreed that it is — and if it means profound changes in attitudes toward property, the status of the individual, the basics of the political system and the spiritual realm, and if it transforms the people into a real force of change in society, then how can all of this take place quietly and smoothly?"

That is the ferment he presides over. Will he be able to tame it to his desires? Unless that develops soon, he may become engulfed in the very flood that emerged when he opened the floodgates.

The TENNESSEAN

Nashville, TN, July 22, 1989

THIS is labor's summer of discontent, not only in the U.S., but in the Soviet Union and Great Britain. The reasons are not all similar, but the common thread is dissatisfaction.

Soviet coal strikes idled thousands of workers in Siberia earlier this week. Some miners reportedly began to return to work after being promised better food, housing and working conditions.

But now the strike has spread to other regions of the Soviet Union, idling thousands of additional strikers and threatening fuel supplies to many of the nation's industries. The strikes are the most severe challenge so far to President Mikhail Gorbachev's reforms.

The United States has been having its own coal strike. Wildcat stoppages, at one point, closed virtually all United Mine Workers-organized mines east of the Mississippi. Most of the mine closings came as a result of a single mine operator, Pittston Co., where a union-sanctioned strike has stopped work for three months.

Pittston had demanded a cut in workers' benefits, notably in pension and health areas. The miners went on strike. The walkouts in other coal fields seemed to stem from fears that if Pittston got away with its aims, other coal operators might try the same thing. Most of the wildcat strikers have gone back to work.

Members of the Bituminous Coal Operators Association, the industry group which has a national contract with the UMW, are understandably distressed that their agreement was violated and didn't protect them from the backlash of Pittston, which isn't a member of the BCOA. Some companies are so irritated at the lack of union discipline, they are talking of dropping out of the BCOA.

That would be a severe blow to the UMW's collective bargaining process and to the union itself. Whether the union and Pittston can reach some agreement, a great deal of damage has already been done to both sides.

In Britain, hundreds of thousands of strikers have closed down the railway system, the London subways, and at least 37 ports. It is the strongest challenge to Prime Minister Margaret Thatcher, who in the past has pretty much had her own way with the unions.

In Britain the issue is money, and union workers want more. By and large, British transportation workers are among the lowest paid of most sectors.

Mrs. Thatcher is, of course, trying to control inflation. But a wave of strikes is bound to hurt the economy even more than a pay increase for some workers.

In time, all these work stoppages may be ironed out, both in the U.S. and abroad. In Britain and the Soviet Union at least, they will have tested severely the leadership of both countries. ∎

The Houston Post

Houston, TX, July 20, 1989

ALREADY PLAGUED by bloody ethnic clashes, Soviet leader Mikhail Gorbachev is faced with another threat to his *perestroika* reform program — labor unrest.

Gorbachev warned the new parliament, the Supreme Soviet, Wednesday that strikes by coal miners in Siberia and the Ukraine could severely damage the communist superpower's already stagnant economy. He also raised the possibility that "extreme measures" would have to be taken if the trouble escalates.

Not many days ago, he issued a similar warning that his economic revitalization plans were endangered by continuing violent ethnic confrontations in the Soviet Central Asian republics. Miners in western Siberia, who walked out last week, were reported to be returning to work late Wednesday, but there was no apparent end to the strikes in the Ukrainian mines, where the strikes spread this week. This is the worst labor unrest Gorbachev has encountered since he came to power in 1985.

Prolonged disruption of production in the nation's richest coal fields would force a greater domestic use of oil and gas. The Kremlin relies on the export of these resources as its main earner of scarce hard currency.

To Gorbachev's credit, he has used a conciliatory approach so far, sending a Politburo delegation and Communist Party officials to offer concessions to the miners. This is a welcome departure from the heavy-handed suppression of strikes in the Stalin and Brezhnev eras.

Another Gorbachev reform — *glasnost,* or openness — is also evident in the reporting on the miners' grievances, which point up the failure of the Soviet leader's economic changes to improve productivity or living conditions. Miners complain of critical shortages of such basic consumer items as soap. And they want greater autonomy and more of the profits from mining operations to remain in their areas.

The shortcomings of *perestroika* have also helped fuel the lethal ethnic strife in the southern Soviet republics. Fresh outbreaks of violence in the Georgia republic, where 20 people were killed in April, has claimed 18 more lives. Rioters shot up two trains, attacked a hydroelectric dam, and fought police for weapons.

As he has before, the canny Soviet leader may be able to turn these disturbances and the coal miners' strikes to his advantage by arguing that they show the need to speed up his reforms. But he also wants help from the West, as indicated by his letter to the seven-nation Economic Summit in Paris last week.

The letter calling for closer East-West economic ties was greeted cautiously by President Bush and the leaders of the other affluent Western summit nations, who don't think his reforms go far enough. The irony for the architect of *perestroika* is that he hasn't been able to make his program work to the satisfaction of his own people or the leading practitioners of democracy and free-market economics. Back to the drawing board, Mikhail.

The Record

Hackensack, NJ, July 25, 1989

The Soviet economy is a disaster. Mikhail Gorbachev knows it and is willing to admit it. The question is whether he can fix it.

The reason the Soviet economy is in such sorry shape is no secret. Communism simply doesn't work. Power is concentrated in the hands of a centralized bureaucracy. The result is the crippling of initiative and an economy where supply and demand never meet. Shortages are one of the few things produced with certainty. Sugar and soap, staples taken for granted in the United States, are precious commodities in the Soviet Union.

Shortages are at the center of the recent labor unrest among coal miners. What began as a wildcat strike in a single mine in Siberia quickly spread to most of the nation's coal fields. Among the complaints: Miners can't clean up after a dirty day's work because soap is in such short supply.

Mr. Gorbachev has tried to coax the miners back to work by making concessions and embracing their grievances as his own. Shipments of food, clothing, and scarce consumer goods like soap have been promised to workers in Siberia. Discussions are under way to give the miners a greater say in management and a share of profits. Instead of criticizing the miners, Mr. Gorbachev has applauded them for "taking matters into their own hands." He has blasted local bureaucrats for letting the problems fester so long. In a country where dissent has long been synonymous with treason, Mr. Gorbachev's actions are a bold departure from the past.

So far the Gorbachev gambit seems to be working. Miners have begun returning to work. But the strategy is risky. If it fails, and the chances are good that it will, a crackdown is almost sure to follow. If it succeeds, other workers are likely to follow the miners' lead and stage strikes of their own.

By taking up the cause of the miners, Mr. Gorbachev hopes to move the bureaucracy enough to bring about the kinds of institutional changes needed to make the Soviet economy more productive. His instincts are right on target. Mr. Gorbachev knows that reforms, even those delivered from the highest level of the government, will remain meaningless rhetoric as long as mid- and low-level apparatchiks have the power to thwart them.

•

Breaking up the bureaucracy, however, is no simple matter. Reforms will be resisted both inside and outside the party. Communist hardliners, already aghast by how far criticism of the government has been allowed to go, fear the party's power will be undermined if it veers from the path of a centralized economy. One has only to look to China to see what happens when communist hardliners feel their power is ebbing.

Bureaucrats certainly won't be any help to Mr. Gorbachev. Few will give up their power, perquisites, and privileges without a fight. And Mr. Gorbachev probably won't get a lot of support from workers either. They are likely to remain on the sidelines as skeptical observers. They've heard promises before.

That brings the problem full circle. Productivity must be improved. But how can productivity improve as long as the forces of stagnation remain in place? Mr. Gorbachev is a man on a tightrope. If he cannot bring reforms about, worker unrest will grow. If he moves too swiftly, he may find himself pushed aside by hardliners. In both cases, some sort of crackdown is likely.

The problems are enormous. Communism doesn't work. But more to the point. It probably can't be fixed.

Omaha World-Herald

Omaha, NE, July 25, 1989

Strikes in the Soviet coal mines have given Mikhail Gorbachev another opportunity to demonstrate his adroitness as a politician. More than a few governments over the years have been brought down by a strike such as the one that has paralyzed Soviet coal mines. Gorbachev's ability to bend events to his advantage has again been evident.

The Soviet president used the occasion to adopt a populist tone, sympathizing with the strikers and suggesting that their goal is to hasten the pace of reform. By identifying himself with the strikers, some analysts said, Gorbachev maneuvered himself into position to purge anti-reform officials who remain in the government.

Gorbachev said Monday that almost all the miners had returned to work. "We are coming out of a very serious crisis, the biggest test during the four years of perestroika," he told members of the Supreme Soviet.

It's hard to imagine any of his predecessors using anything resembling diplomacy to halt a strike, but Gorbachev long ago indicated that he is a different kind of Kremlin leader. Now the Soviet Union, under his leadership, is becoming a different kind of nation — one in which workers can strike, at least for now, and have their grievances heard and sympathized with.

Gorbachev has a few things working in his favor. He is benefiting from the legislative reforms that were made under his direction. The Supreme Soviet has become the focal point for discussion of national emergencies. Thus, as the rising expectations of glasnost and perestroika cause disruptions and expressions of dissatisfaction, the new parliamentary system provides a safety valve.

Gorbachev also is benefiting from a reservoir of international good will that, considering the position he holds, is virtually unprecedented. Demonstrators in Tiananmen Square held up posters identifying him as a hero of democracy. Western Europeans cheer him wildly during his trips beyond the Iron Curtain. More than a few Americans consider him the best hope for reasonableness in the Kremlin.

The fact that Gorbachev has maintained his balance during a series of natural, economic and political misfortunes contributes to the impression that he is a master politician.

Certainly, fancy political footwork won't solve the problems of the average Soviet citizen — for that, fundamental economic and political reform will be required. But Gorbachev seems unusually adept at buying the time he will need to bring about genuine reform. How unfortunate it would be if he failed and were replaced by forces who believe that reform has already gone too far.

The ⬥ State

Columbia, SC, July 25, 1989

THE STRIKES in the Soviet Union offer a stunning illustration of the dilemma *perestroika* has thrust on President Mikhail S. Gorbachev and others who champion his policy of restructuring Soviet economic and political life.

The walkouts, which swept Siberia and the Ukraine, not only have threatened the Soviet economy but the wisdom of *perestroika* which made such protests possible.

As *The Washington Post* noted, "Suddenly, the coal miners in the Soviet Union, who in theory have long represented the proletarian vanguard, are actually acting as a revolutionary element."

And the government, which a few years ago would have come down hard on such disgraceful behavior, has actually granted concessions, and some miners have returned to work.

How long this labor unrest — the worst in 60 years — will continue remains to be seen, but, as one writer noted, the Soviet Union is now tasting some of the fruits of capitalism, including strikes.

Herald ⬥ News

Fall River, MA, July 26, 1989

Widespread strikes by Russian coal miners over the past two weeks have created discord among the balalaikas of perestroika. Director Mikhail Gorbachev admits he is being put to the biggest test his leadership has faced in four years.

Are the musicians of the revolutionary ensemble straying from the score? Have they forgotten the programmed sequences of the symphony of restructuring?

At the height of last week's unrest, half of the Soviet coal industry's one million workers were off the job, endangering the national economy. Yet Gorbachev blamed the coal ministry and local officials, rather than the workers. In the USSR, unions are instruments of government, doling out benefits rather than advocating the rights of workers.

Addressing the Central Committee of the Communist Party, Gorbachev warned that perestroika is in itself a revolution, requiring "profound changes in attitude" toward property, the individual, the political system, and the spiritual realm. Therefore, tension, surprises and difficulties must be expected, he said, keeping his cool as the coal miners kept vigil in town squares.

Apparently, old guard Communist leaders are discouraged by the party's loss of influence. Some blame Gorbachev for dallying with dangerous experiments in freedom.

However, Gorbachev, using a western phrase, called, not for a purge, but for a "renewal in the ranks, an influx of fresh forces" at every level, from the work collective to the Politburo. He wants a new breed of popular leaders to emerge. To this effect, he has kept public communications open, even when they convey news of ethnic and labor troubles.

On July 11, more that 100,000 coal miners in Siberia began the unexpected wildcat action, which soon spread westward to the Ukraine, and even to the Arctic Circle and Central Asia. The government feared that iron and steel workers might follow on the trails of 300,000 miners in the Ukraine's Donetz coalfields, the nation's largest. Here, strikers were, according to government reports, going back to work in large numbers by Monday.

The strikers gave an example of courage and discipline, demanding better living conditions, especially housing. Siberian workers are crowded into crumbling, communal, three-story, cold-water flats with minimal sanitary and kitchen facilities. Actually, the buildings are almost as unsafe as the mines.

Consumer goods are at a premium in the USSR. Salaries in Siberia are, by Soviet standards, good — about $480 a month. But the state stores have long run out of meat. Mining families clamor for clothing, sewing machines, medical supplies, and, of course, higher pay and more control of the industry.

In the long run, the strikes may be seen as underscoring — even assisting — Gorbachev's vison of universal change. He praised the workers' initiative as "inspiring," while decrying the disruptive tactics of strike action as such.

On television Sunday, the Soviet president said he understood the miners' distrust of a government that has long ignored them. Thus, Gorbachev has adopted a position of conciliation to human needs.

The practical problem, feared by party regulars and glossed over by Gorbachev, is how quickly the Soviet economy can be transformed to supply consumer goods to match the extraordinary social change.

The Cincinnati Post

Cincinnati, OH, July 26, 1989

Opponents of change in the Soviet Union have said all along that glasnost and perestroika would bring chaos.

Now, four years after the easing of censorship and the talk of economic restructuring began, widespread strikes, ethnic violence and calls for secession bear the critics out.

But Mikhail Gorbachev, who led his country into these treacherous waters, presses forward.

He has promised striking miners five billion rubles' worth of improvements in their pay and miserable living conditions. That's $8 billion at the depressed official exchange rate. His political concessions could be even more far reaching.

Responding to one of the miners' demands, the Soviet president Monday reversed a decision to postpone local elections until 1990. Instead, the country's 15 republics will decide for themselves how soon to hold the vote.

Gorbachev's strategy is to harness popular unrest behind perestroika by unleashing workers' rage at unresponsive bureaucrats and party officials. The president wants not only elections for local government councils, but also "renewal" of personnel and policies at every level of the Communist Party, with workers given a voice.

Already in the Soviet Union's first competitive national elections this spring, the party suffered humiliating routs. Wherever the coming elections are fair and free, the diehard enemies of change can expect defeat.

Gorbachev's move is an expedient, rather than an affirmation of popular rule. But his choice reverberates.

His words — "We won't succeed commanding things from here" — have implications he cannot stifle.

Like Gen. Wojciech Jaruzelski in Poland, Gorbachev has reached a point where he must enlist his sullen, desperate people — or restore order by force.

So far, social turmoil has not deflected him from his course of reform. But devotees of order, waiting in the wings, no doubt would be willing to let the tanks roll.

Whether Gorbachev can keep them at bay remains to be seen.

Baltic Republics Protest '39 Hitler-Stalin

The Soviet Baltic republics of Estonia, Latvia and Lithuania Aug. 23, 1989 marked the 50th anniversary of the signing of the 1939 Hitler-Stalin pact with massive demonstrations and calls for independence from the U.S.S.R. The pact was a nonaggression treaty between Adolf Hitler's Nazi Germany and Joseph Stalin's Soviet Union. Secret protocols to the pact divided Eastern Europe into German and Soviet spheres of influence, provided for the partition of Poland and gave the U.S.S.R. a free hand in the then-independent Baltic states.

The Soviets annexed Estonia, Latvia and Lithuania in 1940 under the pretext that those nations sought to be part of the U.S.S.R. in order to be protected from the Nazi menace. The Kremlin for 50 years denied the existence of the secret provisions.

In protests on the 50th anniversary, the popular fronts of the three republics Aug. 23 issued a joint statement from Tallinn, the capital of Estonia. Some government and Communist Party officials of the republics also joined the declaration.

The statement said that the U.S.S.R. had "infringed on the historical right of the Baltic nations to self-determination, presented ruthless ultimatums to the Baltic republics, occupied them with overwhelming military force, and – under conditions of military occupation and heavy political terror – carried out their violent annexations."

Large-scale nationalist demonstrations were held in each of the republics Aug. 23, culminating with as many as one million people joining hands to form a human chain to show the solidarity of the Baltic region. The chain ran about 400 miles from Tallinn in the north, through the Latvian capital of Riga, and south to Vilnius, the capital of Lithuania.

The Soviet Politburo Aug. 17 had issued a long-awaited statement of policy on the decentralization of power in the Soviet Union. The document was carried in *Pravda*, the Communist Party newspaper.

The statement supported the concept of limited economic autonomy at the regional level. It said that each of the U.S.S.R.'s 15 republics should be allowed to decide its own system of economic management, with the approval of the central government. The document also said that each republic should be permitted to challenge national laws that affected it. The Politburo proposed the creation of a special court to adjudicate conflicts between the republics and the central government. The statement called for a strengthening of the powers of the autonomous regions, making them more independent of the control of the republics.

The Oregonian

Portland, OR, August 21, 1989

In the 20th century, August has been the cruelest month.

With all the attention that has been directed lately to anniversaries — the 200th of the French Revolution, the 20th of the Woodstock festival, the 12th of Elvis Presley's death — some ought to be reserved for the most devastating events of modern times, the two world wars. Both of them broke out in August, 75 and 50 years ago.

To remember how Europe bumbled into World War I someone would have to be nearly 90 years old. But many who are in their 60s today can recall living through the sickening march of Nazi Germany and its allies in the late 1930s.

Hitler sent his troops in 1936 into the Rhineland, territory along Germany's western border that the Versailles Treaty had directed should remain demilitarized. In the next three years, piece by piece, Germany swallowed all of Austria, two gulps of Czechoslovakia and a bite of Lithuania, and claimed parts of Poland. Meanwhile, Hungary also occupied part of Czechoslovakia, and Italy invaded Ethiopia and Albania.

The major European democracies, France and Britain, let these things happen with the passive fascination of chickens watching a snake. The United States paralyzed itself with the belief that it must not again become entangled in Europe's wars.

Only in August 1939 did Britain and France realize that to stop the Nazis they would have to fight again, disastrously unprepared though they were. The convincing event was a non-aggression treaty that Germany and the Soviet Union signed 50 years ago this Wednesday. It had the effect of assuring Hitler he could invade Poland without worrying about being attacked by the Soviets. He launched the invasion Sept. 1, and the war was on.

Stalin gained from the treaty a share of Poland and a free hand to absorb the Baltic states and part of Finland, but he outsmarted himself. Hitler invaded the Soviet Union two years later.

This is not dusty history; it is the basis of today's news. The Soviet Union still backs communist governments and stations tanks in the countries along its western border to guard against another invasion. Poland and the Baltic states are struggling to increase their independence from Moscow. From prewar isolationism, the United States has swung to fundamental commitment to its military alliance with the European democracies.

And August is the month to remember why.

The Boston Globe

Boston, MA, August 23, 1989

If cynicism were to seek an anniversary date, Aug. 23 would be a leading candidate. Fifty years ago today, Adolf Hitler and Joseph Stalin engaged in an act of cynical villainy that led to World War II and its rivers of blood. The nonaggression pact signed in Moscow that day, and the secret protocol accompanying it, scorned the legitimate interests of mankind. Only this month did Stalin's successors acknowledge its underlying character.

Its cynicism was captured by Low's cartoon, "Rendevous," reprinted here. Hitler, for whom communism was anathema and Russia a prize to be sought greedily, courted Stalin's own ambitions by offering an agreement carving up Poland and the Baltic states. Hitler's haste in seeking the agreement, to clear the way for a Sept. 1 invasion of Poland, lured the Russians into a pact some may have thought was buying them time and space.

Instead, it horrified a world that had regarded the Soviet Union as an implacable enemy of surging Naziism, and widened the breach between the Western democracies and Moscow – a breach that would close only with Hitler's deadly lurch into Soviet territory less than two years later.

In the absence of the agreement, Britain, France and the Soviet Union might have given Hitler second thoughts about launching blitzkrieg attacks across Europe, and given more sober forces in Germany the opportunity to contain his megalomania.

Whatever might have been, the reality became terror beyond belief after the pact was signed to the accompaniment of mutual praise and obscene toasts to peace and cooperation.

Now, Moscow and the Gorbachev regime have acknowledged the secret protocol that gave Stalin a free hand in eastern Poland and the Baltic states. Those acts will not be undone easily, soon or perhaps ever. Even without the protocol, postwar Europe might have been redrawn in its present format. The pact, though, stands as a monument to man's inhumanity to man. It should not be forgotten.

THE SACRAMENTO BEE

Sacramento, CA, August 20, 1989

When Hitler and Stalin concluded their non-aggression pact 50 years ago this week, no one had to read the fine print to know that there would be war within days. And so there was. On Sept. 1, 1939, just as Hitler had planned for months, the Germans, secure in the knowledge that they wouldn't have to worry about the Russians, invaded Poland. The French, who, like the British, had committed themselves by treaty to come to the aid of Poland if she were attacked, dragged their feet for a couple of days, but by Sept. 3 they, too, had come in, and World War II had begun.

Although we are now further from those days than they were from the death of Bismarck, the issues and configuration of much of the world we inhabit are still fatefully, in some cases tragically, shaped by the events and arrangements of that war. The fate of Eastern Europe and the Baltic republics, which were delivered to the Russians by secret protocol in the Hitler-Stalin pact, is once again uncertain. The lesson of Munich — no appeasement of dictators — was learned too well, if belatedly with respect to the consequences for Russia's neighbors, yet has still not been learned well enough in the West with respect to terrorists.

And yet a great deal more has changed, in large measure because some other lessons were learned. One can travel these days through a peaceful, prosperous Western Europe, from Lisbon to Vienna, from Stockholm to Naples, without seeing a pillbox or a string of barbed wire, in some instances without even seeing a customs agent. There is no longer a colonial system, and if the problems of some of the former colonies often seem overwhelming, there are also a growing number — among them India, South Korea, Zimbabwe — that seem to be gaining in stability and economic strength. Meanwhile, the Japanese seem to have learned that power and influence come more surely from economic than military initiatives — a lesson not yet fully learned in this country.

Because it's the 50th anniversary of the outbreak of World War II, the next six years will bring a series of semicentennials — Pearl Harbor, Midway, Guadalcanal, D-day, V-E Day, Yalta, Hiroshima, V-J Day. Among the many conclusions we draw from the remembrance of those events, surely the most pervasive will be the recognition that never have we as Americans been as together — and therefore as successful — as we were then.

In the last eight years there has been an attempt to recreate that sense of unity, in part by pretending that our most serious problems — economic, environmental, social, moral — don't exist; in part by building internal walls of isolation that make that cherished unity even more elusive. The United States tried something very much like that in the global arena during the two years after the European war began in 1939 — but that, as we discovered in 1941, was the pursuit of an illusion.

The unity and sense of community that the attack on Pearl Harbor helped to forge were relatively easy to achieve. This time, absent a clearly identifiable foreign antagonist, we will have to disenthrall ourselves of our illusions, some of them still lingering from World War II, and forge those qualities within ourselves. In that effort, we will get little help from others.

The Providence Journal

Providence, RI, August 23, 1989

In between Woodstock (20) and World War II (50), there is another anniversary worth remembering. It was fifty years ago today that the Nazi-Soviet nonaggression pact, the infamous alliance that set the Second World War in motion, was concluded and burst upon an unsuspecting world. One week after Hitler and Stalin affixed their signatures to the mutual division of Europe, German troops crossed the Polish frontier on the west while Soviet troops prepared to move into Poland from Russia. The rest, as they say, is history.

If observances in Moscow are a little restrained this season, there is good reason, for the consequences of the pact are still very much with us. The blunt fact is that it was Hitler who wanted a free hand on the continent, and it was Stalin who gave it to him. Moreover, unlike the French and British, who were at least motivated by political concerns about their military prowess, the Kremlin was largely interested in sharing the spoils of a conquered Europe with the Nazis. The SS and Gestapo met gleefully with their counterparts in the NKVD (precursor of the KGB) and exchanged useful information. They also exchanged humans: German Communists and Jews who had fled Hitler to serve Stalin were shipped home for liquidation, and Moscow and Berlin united to wipe out the Polish resistance.

History is most useful when it teaches us a lesson, and the lessons of the Hitler-Stalin pact are both fresh and compelling. Appeasement did not mollify Hitler but whetted his appetite, and national aspirations will transcend even the most belligerent ideologies.

Of course, Mikhail Gorbachev was only eight years old when the pact was signed, but his working day is spent wrestling with its consequences. The struggles for freedom in Eastern Europe, in the Baltic states, and in the Ukraine, Moldavia and Byelorussia within the USSR, all began on this day in 1939. What's past is prologue.

THE SUN

Baltimore, MD, August 23, 1989

There is a specter haunting Eastern Europe — the specter of the notorious Hitler-Stalin pact. The treaty, signed 50 years ago today, continues to be an explosive issue in Poland, which was invaded and carved up by the two dictators. The once-independent nations of Estonia, Lithuania and Latvia were dragooned into the Soviet Union as a result of secret clauses incorporated into the agreement, which raised the curtain on World War II.

The Russians have always insisted that these nations joined the Soviet Union "voluntarily" but the people of the Baltic republics have never swallowed the official line. Only lately have the Russians started to concede what the rest of the world knows. This is of more than academic interest, for the Baltic states are growing ever more daring in trying to work their way out from under the Soviet thumb. The dramatic events unfolding in Poland are also likely to add to the tension.

Just the other day, the Estonians approved a law that denied some Russian residents the right to vote. Estonians called the law a necessity to maintain political control in their homeland, where ethnic Russians are flocking because of better economic conditions. Kremlin leaders rejected the measure as unconstitutional but are considering easing up on central control over the various local governments.

Soviet officials justify the embarrassing nonaggression agreement signed with Nazi Germany by saying it was aimed at gaining time to prepare for an eventual attack by Hitler — an attack which came nearly two years later. But Western historians, who have examined the original documents found after the war in the files of the German Foreign Office, contend that acquisition of part of Poland and Romania, as well as the Baltic states — all territories that Russia had lost after its revolution — was the overriding factor.

The world was shocked by the treaty. Russia had been regarded as the standard-bearer of anti-fascism. Only a few weeks before, the Soviets had talked with Britain and France regarding the defense of Poland, earmarked by the Nazis as their next target. Bewildered, horrified and furious at this cynical betrayal, fellow travelers and dedicated Communists in Europe and America abandoned the various Communist parties in droves.

Fifty years later, Europe is still haunted by the Hitler-Stalin pact and its aftermath.

Los Angeles Times

Los Angeles, CA, August 28, 1989

History is a remorseless creditor. Eventually, it demands that all accounts be settled in full, sometimes in a currency harder than anyone could have imagined.

Half a century ago, the leaders of Nazi Germany and the Soviet Union conspired to deprive three tiny countries on the Baltic of their freedom. Their conspiracy succeeded. Estonia, Latvia and Lithuania now are among the most discontented constituents of the Union of Soviet Socialist Republics, and those who govern from the Kremlin today are being called upon to settle their debt to history and its victims.

Last week, nearly a million Balts marked the anniversary of the secret Hitler-Stalin pact by joining hands in a human chain of protest extending 400 miles from the Estonian capital of Tallinn to Vilnius in Lithuania. In conjunction with the protest, members of the popular fronts that now dominate the region's politics issued a statement demanding that Moscow "restore their independent statehood."

The historical due bill the protesters presented was compelling and indisputable. The Soviet Union, they said, had "infringed on the historical right of the Baltic nations to self-determination, presented ruthless ultimatums to the Baltic republics, occupied them with overwhelming military force, and under conditions of military occupation and heavy political terror carried out their violent annexations."

How the government of Soviet President Mikhail S. Gorbachev—whose policies of openness and reconstruction have made possible the resurgence of Baltic nationalism—will respond to all this remains an open question. The possibility of new repression cannot be excluded; on the other hand, a desire to accommodate the Balts, a dynamic and developed people, may help nudge the Soviet system toward some gentler form of socialist federalism that will allow for a fuller expression of national identities.

How the West, particularly the United States, will respond to the nationalist turmoil in the Baltic and elsewhere in the Soviet Union and its bloc also is an open question. A part of us, of all Americans—a romantic part, perhaps—yearns to share in that assertion of human freedom that was expressed so eloquently more than a century ago by the popular leader of another of Europe's "little" peoples. "No man has a right to put a stop to the forward march of a nation," said the Irishman Charles Stewart Parnell. "No man has a right to say to a people, 'This far shall you go, and no further.' " At the same time, the principled but prudent voice of a great American statesman who confronted similar situations in his own day counsels caution: "We are the friend of liberty everywhere," said John Quincy Adams, "but the custodian of none but our own."

The Courier-Journal & TIMES

Louisville, KY, August 23, 1989

THIS WEEK'S meeting in Latvia of a group formed to discuss the dissolution of the "Soviet Empire" is as timely as it is astounding.

Fifty years ago, Adolf Hitler and Josef Stalin agreed to a "non-aggression" pact that for a time made the monsters of 20th Century history allies and collaborators.

Their representatives, Joachim von Ribbentrop and Vyacheslav Molotov, also agreed secretly to divide the territory between the two countries into "spheres of influence." The Nazis got much of Poland, which they invaded a week later, starting World War II. The Russians got the rest, most of which remains part of the Soviet Union, and a green light to annex the three Baltic states that had

INTERNATIONAL NEWS PHOTO

Von Ribbentrop prepares to board a plane for Moscow to sign the Hitler-Stalin pact.

become free of Russian rule just 20 years earlier.

Moscow has long denied that a secret protocol existed, just as it has insisted that Latvia, Estonia and Lithuania were willing, even eager, to be incorporated into the Soviet Union. But the same spirit of *glasnost* that apparently tolerates the demands of Baltic firebrands for total independence has moved Moscow finally to acknowledge its complicity in one of modern history's biggest lies.

Yes, the Soviets finally admit, Nazi and Communist emissaries did draw a line through Eastern Europe. Can it be more than a matter of time before they are also shamed into repudiating the other fiction — that Baltic parliaments, their countries already occupied by the Red Army, voted *voluntarily* to merge with the Soviet Union?

The World War II anniversaries that crowd the calendar until 1995 will force many Europeans to confront the "unresolved past."

The trauma may be greatest for the Russians as they grapple with evidence that the leader of their great patriotic war shared the blame for the savagery inflicted on them and others. The treaty of Aug. 23, 1939, among other things, gave Hitler time to consolidate his conquests in the West before invading Russia.

And the emerging truth about how Stalin built his now shaky empire can't help but give new impetus to the separatists. The theme of the Riga conference, if breathtaking, is by no means preposterous.

The Union Leader

Manchester, NH, August 31, 1989

It's ironic.

For years, liberals have scarcely acknowledged the existence of the Captive Nations, while conservatives fought a lonely battle to keep their memory alive. President Jimmy Carter was the first and only President not to issue the annual Captive Nations Week proclamation "authorized and requested" by Congress in Public Law 86-90, approved by President Eisenhower in July 1959.

But now it is considered chic in liberal circles to suggest that freedom is right around the corner in Poland and the Baltic states, while conservatives, although ever hopeful, warn realistically that the Russian bear will not return freedom to her captive "cubs" without a fight.

President Bush gushed last Monday: "I think that Mr. Gorbachev's reactions to the changes in Poland were extraordinarily understanding and certainly not militant in any way, and I hope that would be the tone as the rapid change that's taking place in Eastern Europe goes forward, not just in Poland, but in other countries as well. I must say the way Mr. Gorbachev has handled this and reacted to it has been very positive."

But, simultaneously, good old "extraordinarily understanding" Gorbachev was warning the Baltic states, especially Lithuania, that their initial tentative moves toward independence had gone too far. The Soviet Communist Party Central Committee in Moscow 48 hours earlier issue a stinging warning that separatists were leading Lithuania, Latvia and Estonia into any abyss, and the Soviet government newspaper Izvestia went so far as to deny the historical finding of a Lithuanian commission that the incorporation of the Baltic nations into the Soviet Union in the 1939 Hitler-Stalin pact was an "international crime."

Granted, some will attribute President Bush's fatuous effulgence to "diplomacy." But by what measure then do they judge Gorbachev's bluntness?

©1989 THE PITTSBURGH PRESS
UNITED FEATURE SYNDICATE
ROGERS

BALTIC STATES

DESERET NEWS
Salt Lake City, UT, August 19, 1989

Although the Kremlin has accepted a demand by restless Baltic states to rewrite the 1922 "unification agreement" that created the modern Soviet Union, this does not mean that the 15 republics that make up the country are going to become independent.

The little Baltic states of Latvia, Lithuania and Estonia were forcibly annexed into the Soviet Union at the end of World War II. Encouraged by changes in Moscow, those states are seeking to regain their former independence. But while the strings may be loosened a bit, independence does not appear possible.

A willingness to consider more autonomy for the various Soviet republics probably arises out of ethnic unrest that has bubbled all across the Soviet Union this year, affecting not only the Baltic states but such states as the Ukraine and Georgia. Bitterness against Moscow has been especially deep in the latter region where ethnic groups have called for outright secession.

The Communist Party, in agreeing to a rewrite of the unification laws, appears willing to let the republics "question" national laws that they oppose but is not willing to allow the states to reject them.

In addition, the party wants to outlaw "nationalist" organizations. More than 100 such groups have sprung into being to agitate for changes rang-

ing from restoration of their native languages to secession.

The party's Central Committee has planned a major meeting in the fall to discuss what it concedes is the "acute" question of dealing with the many nationalities that make up the Soviet Union.

Even if radical reformers manage to push through major changes — as some in the Communist Party fear — the mere existence of a document guaranteeing certain rights is not really any guarantee at all.

One has to look no further than the Soviet constitution, adopted after the 1917 revolution. That constitution, on paper, outlines a remarkably open, democratic society. Yet in actual practice, the Soviet Union has been a harsh, totalitarian society.

The ethnic issue poses a real problem for Soviet leader Mikhail Gorbachev. If Moscow gives too much latitude to the republics, the entire Soviet Union could begin to disintegrate into small, fiercely independent states. Failure to give more autonomy to the republics could feed a growing unrest and even revolt.

Either way, it could lead to a power struggle and a repressive backlash such as the world has seen in China. There is clearly a great deal riding on the outcome of those distant ethnic struggles in the Soviet Union.

Chicago Tribune
Chicago, IL, August 24, 1989

No one is watching developments in Poland more anxiously than the people of the Baltics, who've been testing the limits of Mikhail Gorbachev's good intentions like no one else in the Soviet Union.

In a demonstration unlike any in memory in a communist country, tens of thousands of Baltic residents joined hands Wednesday to form a human chain across their lands in protest on the 50th anniversary of the hated Nazi-Soviet pact that consigned Lithuania, Latvia and Estonia to Stalin's domination.

While Moscow has at long last acknowledged the existence of secret protocols to the 1939 nonaggression treaty that divided Eastern Europe into spheres of influence, it hasn't admitted the Baltic countries didn't voluntarily join the Soviet Union.

A study for the Soviet parliament that said the pact

leading to the takeover of the Baltic states should be "null and void" was published Tuesday in Estonia, adding fuel to nationalistic fires being stoked by vocal advocates of independence in the three republics.

The dramatic protest that found Lithuanians, Latvians and Estonians taking up positions along a 370-mile route from the Gulf of Finland south to Vilnius, the capital of Lithuania, also served as a rally for those seeking freedom. "We are proclaiming to each other and to the whole world that we in the Baltic nations have never given up our freedom," said a leader of the Estonian People's Front.

Most Baltic leaders believe more autonomy is the most they can hope for, but some still dream of independence. That, of course, is as crazy as the idea of a Solidarity government in Poland.

Lithuanian Communist Party Breaks with Moscow

The Lithuanian Communist Party, in an unprecedented move, Dec. 20, 1989 declared itself independent of the Soviet national Communist Party (CP). It was the first regional branch of the ruling party ever to proclaim independence. The move confirmed Lithuania's status as the most radical of the Baltic republics, where powerful nationalist movements were pressing the party leadership.

The declaration came in the form of a resolution voted at the Lithuanian party congress in the republic's capital of Vilnius. In the voting, a total of 855 delegates supported an "independent Communist Party of Lithuania, with its own statutes and programs." Another 160 delegates favored limited independence. Twelve delegates abstained.

After the resolution was voted, the party declared that its goal was the creation of an "independent democratic Lithuanian state."

In earlier developments:

■ The Lithuanian party Sept. 23 published a draft of the plan to break with the national CP.

■ The full Lithuanian Supreme Soviet (parliament) Sept. 23 voted, 274-0, to declare as an illegal act the republic's 1940 annexation by the U.S.S.R.

■ The republic's parliament Nov. 3 approved legislation that would allow Lithuanians to decide on secession from the U.S.S.R. through a referendum.

Lithuanian CP leader Algirdis Brazauskas was summoned to Moscow Nov. 16, where he had 10 hours of talks with President Mikhail S. Gorbachev. Brazauskas apparently refused to alter the party plan or referendum law, and was reported to have turned down a Gorbachev request that the Lithuanian party congress be delayed until 1990.

At the opening of the Congress, Dec. 19, Brazauskas had called on the republic's Communists to form a "united front" with the Lithuanian nationalist movement Sajudis "to counterbalance any attempts from outside to limit our achievements."

Lithuania had defied the central government Dec. 7 by becoming the first Soviet republic to adopt a multiparty political system.

The Lithuanian Supreme Soviet voted 243-1, with 39 abstentions, to remove Article Six of the republic's constitution. The provision guaranteed the Communist Party's monopoly on power in Lithuania. All 15 Soviet republics had an Article Six in their constitutions. Article Six of the Soviet national constitution made the Communist Party the only legitimate political party in the country. On Dec. 6, a move in the Lithuanian parliament to remove Article Six had been defeated by nine votes.

Gorbachev Dec. 26 condemned the decision of the Lithuanian CP to break with the national party. But he agreed to go to Lithuania to consult with Lithuanian CP members.

At a two-day Central Committee emergency meeting in Moscow that ended Dec. 26, Gorbachev and other leaders of the national Communist Party were highly critical of the Lithuanian move. Gorbachev called the action "illegitimate," and he pointedly ruled out any secession of any of the nation's 15 constituent republics.

Gorbachev, who was the leader of the national party, attacked Brazauskas, the Lithuanian CP leader, who was present at the meeting. Gorbachev said Brazauskas had followed "a line chosen for appeasement" and had made many concessions to demands from Sajudis, a vocal and powerful Lithuanian nationalist group.

But moderates on the Central Committee proposed that Gorbachev and other national party leaders meet with rank-and-file members of the Lithuanian party to survey the political damage. No firm date was set for the trip.

Lithuanian authorities Dec. 28 formally registered the 2,000-member Party of Democrats, the first non-Communist political party to be legally sanctioned anywhere in the Soviet Union. The newly independent Lithuanian Communist Party was also registered that day for local elections scheduled for early 1990.

THE
SAGINAW NEWS
Saginaw, MI,
December 28, 1989

Mikhail Gorbachev is taking a stern message to the Soviet republic of Lithuania: You should stay a Soviet republic.

In view of the source, the Lithuanians should and will listen.

They will hear his criticism of the decision of their Communist Party to cut loose from Moscow.

They will consider his warnings that moving toward secession "means to blow up the union, set the people against each other and sow conflict and blood and death."

They will watch for the "or else."

And they might give him a message of their own: To prepare for a slightly shrunken Soviet Union.

If Gorbachev truly is Time magazine's wise "man of the decade," he will respond not with tanks, but with overdue justice.

No less than Eastern Europe, the northern Baltic States of Lithuania, Latvia and Estonia are part of the movement of oppressed nations to regain their freedom. That their peaceful but heartfelt revolution takes place within the borders of the Soviet Union itself is an accident — no, a crime — of history.

The Soviets themselves have conceded that the annexation of the independent Baltic States resulted from a secret, illegal deal between Hitler and Stalin. The Baltics never wanted to join. Why is it any surprise that, in self-determination, they might want to leave?

Gorbachev can handle the admittedly touchy question of a chain reaction elsewhere in his shaky union by emphasizing that the Baltics are a special case, victims of an evil pact between evil men. The message Gorbachev should take to Lithuania and, by extension, to Latvia and Estonia is that he is not a man to perpetuate such evil.

Unlike the invaders of 1940, the Baltic people have no desire to fire a single shot in pursuit of their purpose. If their rightful quest brings "conflict and blood and death," as Gorbachev says, he will be the bearer.

The Atlanta Journal
THE ATLANTA CONSTITUTION
Atlanta, GA, December 28, 1989

Two categorical statements out of Moscow this past week have Lithuanians pondering so hard one might get the impression their lives depended upon it.

What are they to think? First, in response to the Lithuanian Communist Party's decision to break away from the national party as a first step toward an independent Lithuania, Soviet President Mikhail S. Gorbachev said emphatically: "Actions to preserve the federal state and safeguard its unity are a strict necessity, and on this there should be no illusions about the intentions and capabilities of the center."

No sooner had Lithuanians finished shuddering over that frostily understated admonition than the chief party ideologist, Vadim A. Medvedev, piped up with a softening addendum, obviously with Mr. Gorbachev's blessing, to the effect that "the party is fighting for preservation of the union with political means, not military means; we're against a military solution to problems inside the country in principle."

But Lithuanians have grounds to wonder if what Moscow opposes in principle, it might still implement in practice — that is, if force was the only way to prevent the breakup of the Soviet Union.

In fact, Mr. Gorbachev understands full well the conflicting dynamics that have set Communist against Communist in his patchwork of a country. Understanding them, though, doesn't mean he can control them.

He and his reformist colleagues must maintain order and unity, not only to protect their political hides from the remaining orthodox Marxist backbiters but in order to get perestroika (restructuring) in motion. Further, in the case of Lithuania and its sister Baltic republics, Moscow is eager to use their relatively advanced economies as laboratories and showcases for the essential changes to be emulated in the vast backward regions of the U.S.S.R.

Survival is no less an issue with the Lithuanian Communists. A contested regional election is coming up on Feb. 24, and their candidates probably don't stand a chance against nationalist-minded opponents unless they themselves show their own fearlessness and autonomy from Moscow.

It is a hard thing to contemplate — the hope that Lithuanians choose a less rash course for themselves in the near term than the total independence that the free world has wished for them ever since the end of World War II. They are in the sad position, it seems, where they must postpone their dream so as not to set off a chain reaction that would produce a political Chernobyl.

By way of consolation, Mr. Gorbachev will be traveling to Lithuania next week more than willing to offer up accommodations that are to its inhabitants' liking — short, that is, of a complete break.

He has given them ample signals he neither expects nor wants them to knuckle under. The same day he warned them how seriously Moscow viewed the prospect of secession, he also said the Lithuanian problem (and by extension, that of the other Baltic republics) can be settled only "on the basis of civil peace, not civil war, when the two sides are ready to listen to each other, to make mutual concessions, to understand the high value of reasonable compromises."

Chances are, this isn't just talk. Mr. Gorbachev is poised to make his very best offer, and the Lithuanians, regardless of their gut instincts, had better be prepared to listen attentively.

The New York Times
New York, NY, December 26, 1989

The news yesterday of Nicolae Ceausescu's execution shows what can happen to brutal dictators who prefer to go on killing and denying freedom to people in Eastern Europe. Fortunately for the people of the Soviet Union, Mikhail Gorbachev is a leader who prefers to bargain peacefully with those who rightly seek more freedom and autonomy.

Mr. Gorbachev opposes the Lithuanian Communist Party's declaration of independence from Moscow. But while he angrily warns of dark consequences, he has not uttered a final no and still searches for compromise.

The Soviet leader can sidestep a showdown by recalling what he told the United Nations a year ago: "Freedom of choice is a universal principle which allows no exceptions." He's put that principle into practice in much of Eastern Europe. Why not in Lithuania and other Baltic republics?

Mr. Gorbachev's reforms encourage greater independence. But little holds his vast country together except the army, which he is loath to use, and the party. If others follow the Lithuanian lead and form independent Communist parties or vote non-Communists into power, the party would cease to be a unifying force, and armed force alone would remain to hold his nation together.

Mr. Gorbachev needs time for economic restructuring to pay political dividends and renew party support. In the meantime he needs a semblance of party unity. That's why he's not yet prepared to end the party's leading role in politics and policy-making, and expose it to opposition parties in free and fair elections.

But Lithuania's Communist Party cannot wait. It has been losing support rapidly. To salvage its tattered mandate, it voted overwhelmingly to renounce its leading role and face avowedly nationalist opposition parties in elections set for Feb. 24. To survive those elections as a political force, it now declares independence from the Soviet Communist Party and also urges eventual independence for Lithuania.

Old-line Communists say this amounts to destroying the party in order to save it. Since they still hold a sizable bloc of seats in the Moscow party's Supreme Soviet, Mr. Gorbachev wants to postpone the issue. In the meantime, he may try to round up Communist loyalists to run in the Lithuanian elections. If, as expected, they fare poorly, that could advance the cause of party reform.

With the conspicuous exception of Rumania, Communists across Eastern Europe have conceded freedoms to try to hold onto some power. Lithuania should not become another exception.

DESERET·NEWS
Salt Lake City, UT, December 28, 1989

"Freedom of choice is a universal principle which allows no exceptions."

Guess who made that ringing declaration.

Some Free World leader extolling the fresh wind of freedom that has been sweeping through communist-dominated Eastern Europe lately?

Or maybe just some enthusiastic orator celebrating the individual liberties long enjoyed by much of the Western world?

Guess again.

Instead, that sweeping endorsement of freedom was made a year ago before the United Nations by none other than Soviet leader Mikhail Gorbachev.

And now Gorbachev's words are being put to perhaps the severest test yet as a result of the break-away spirit manifested in the Soviet Baltic state of Lithuania. Indeed, it could be a test not just of Gorbachev's sincerity but of his ability to keep holding on to power.

A few days ago, Lithuania's Communist Party voted overwhelmingly to split from the national party and form the first independent republican party in Soviet history.

In response, the Soviet Communist Party has authorized Gorbachev and other senior leaders to undertake a peace mission to Lithuania in an effort to talk their fellow communists there out of their independent leanings.

What a remarkable change from those not-so-distant days when even the mildest leanings within the Soviet empire toward independence would have provoked a bloody purge and mass deportations.

And what a dilemma this development in Lithuania poses for Gorbachev.

If he puts down the secession movement with force, it would mean the end of the reform movement for which he has won international acclaim — and the end of the economic cooperation with the West that is essential to Soviet progress.

But if Lithuania is able to defy the Kremlin with impunity, it would be bound to inspire similar efforts at breaking ties with Moscow on the part of Estonia, Latvia and possibly other parts of the Soviet Union. Down that path lies a Russia that would be much weaker than it is now. It's hard to believe that the coterie in the Kremlin would treat kindly a Gorbachev who in effect presided over the dissolution of the Soviet empire.

Whatever happens in Lithuania, the moment of truth seems to be at hand for Mikhail Gorbachev.

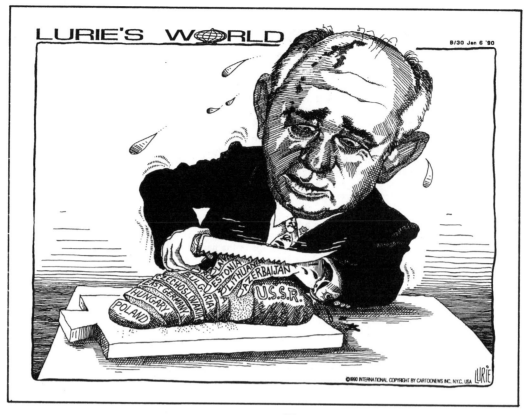

LURIE'S WORLD

8/30 Jan 6 '90

©1990 INTERNATIONAL COPYRIGHT BY CARTOONEWS INC. N.Y.C. USA   LURIE

Newsday

New York, NY, December 28, 1989

The moment of truth approaches for Mikhail Gorbachev in the form of Lithuania.

Will he be able to apply in the Baltic republics the same principles of non-interference with radical reform that he has used in Eastern Europe — and not start the dominoes falling in the Soviet Union? Will he have to use force to thwart the independence movement in Lithuania? Or will he once again pull the rabbit from the hat and find a way out?

This week the Communist Party Central Committee announced that Gorbachev and other high party officials would go to Lithuania to try to convince Communist Party leaders there to repudiate their recent vote to make their party independent of the Communist Party of the Soviet Union. The central committee won't decide what to do about Lithuania until after Gorbachev's visit.

Undoubtedly Gorbachev will go to Vilnius with carrots and sticks. But he has an almost impossible task. He is himself the architect of the elections to be held Feb. 24 to elect new party leaders. The only way Lithuanian communists stand any chance of winning the elections is by staying out in front of the reform movement. To repudiate the vote to separate themselves from the party would cost them the election. What carrots can he offer to persuade them to commit political suicide? And what sticks can Gorbachev use without destroying perestroika and his ties to the West?

The other major option — allowing reform to proceed — might not be acceptable to the central committee because of fear it will lead to the step-by-step dismemberment of the Soviet Union. Are the Ukraine and Georgia next?

Gorbachev is now having to contend with the forces his reform has turned loose. His nation's economy continues to spiral downward even as political events spin out of control. Whether he can stay atop events or will be consumed by them is the difference between being an historic statesman and just another courageous but unsuccessful Soviet reformer.

Pittsburgh Post-Gazette

Pittsburgh, PA, December 29, 1989

Paraphrasing a Frank Sinatra song, a spokesman for the Soviet Foreign Ministry said recently that the nations of Eastern Europe must manage their affairs "their way" — a tolerant attitude that underlies this year's democratic revolutions in Poland, East Germany, Hungary and Czechoslovakia.

Now, however, the architect of that non-interventionist policy, Mikhail Gorbachev, is being asked to extend the same dispensation to a constituent republic of the Soviet Union, the Baltic state of Lithuania, and Mr. Gorbachev is balking. This week he warned that to let Lithuanians do it "their way" would invite the disintegration of the Soviet Union and the ruination of perestroika.

Mr. Gorbachev's apprehensions are understandable, and are even shared by some Western strategists. But where Lithuania and the other Baltic States, Estonia and Latvia, are concerned, Mr. Gorbachev's best hope of peacefully keeping them in the fold may be to acknowledge their special grievances and their special histories.

The Soviet leader will have that opportunity soon when he visits Lithuania for consultations about two recent initiatives: the separation of the Lithuanian party from that of the U.S.S.R. and a vote by the Lithuanian Parliament to abolish the Communist Party's monopoly on power. (The latter action was emulated yesterday by the Latvian Parliament.)

Mr. Gorbachev's decision to discuss these matters with the Lithuanians reflects a compromise between members of the party's Central Committee who would ignore the Lithuanian actions and others who espouse what Mr. Gorbachev has called "harsh positions," including the forcible dissolution of the newly independent Lithuanian party.

One man's nation, it has been said, is another man's province, and there are few nations that aren't willing to make exceptions to the widely venerated principle of self-determination. It is also true that much blood has been shed in this century in attempts to make political boundaries perfectly reflect ethnic or linguistic configurations.

Still, the Baltic states, part of the Soviet Union since 1940, have a recent and deeply felt claim to nationhood. Only this week the Soviet Congress of People's Deputies declared that Hitler and Stalin had illegally conspired to divide Eastern Europe in secret protocols to their 1939 non-aggression treaty. Baltic nationalists long have argued that the treaty led to their absorption by the U.S.S.R.

Even if that were not the case, the Soviet Constitution allows constituent republics to secede. That Mr. Gorbachev opposes such a development is understandable; the question is how best to forestall it. If Baltic secessionism threatens perestroika, so would any resort to the "harsh" reprisals Mr. Gorbachev referred to. A wiser course would be to recognize parallels between the Baltic states and the satellite nations, and to devise an arrangement in which the Baltics might remain within a Soviet confederation while enjoying significantly greater autonomy.

Of course, such a solution would beg the question of whether similar concessions shouldn't be made to other Soviet republics. And if the Communist Party can give up its monopoly on power in the constituent republics, why not in the U.S.S.R. as a whole, a step Mr. Gorbachev has resisted mightily?

In the realm of the ideal, the answer is that pluralism and self-determination should know no limits of time or geography. In the real world as described by Mr. Gorbachev, the success of perestroika requires the cohesion provided by one-party rule and a secession-proof Soviet Union. Even if he is right, however, a compromise with the Baltics might be the better part of wisdom.

The Houston Post
Houston, TX, December 28, 1989

MIKHAIL GORBACHEV heads for the restive little Soviet Baltic republic of Lithuania soon to try to resolve a problem for which there can be no totally satisfactory solution. In an unprecedented move, the Lithuanian Communist Party has declared its independence from the national party.

This looms as the first schism in the monolithic Soviet Communist Party since it was formed by Vladimir Lenin more than 70 years ago. How Gorbachev — the party's leader — handles this defiant step could have a profound impact not only on his liberalizing perestroika reforms but on his political future.

The Soviet leader has alternately cajoled and blustered, trying to reverse the Lithuanian Communist Party's decision. At one point he called LCP leaders to Moscow for a lengthy meeting with the Soviet Union's ruling Politburo. At another he sent the Soviet Communist Party's ideological chief to Lithuania for talks with the rebellious LCP.

In a speech to the Soviet Communist Party Central Committee Monday, he accused the LCP leaders of not standing up to the nationalist, secessionist demands of Sajudis, the most popular non-Communist political organization in Lithuania. But he seemed relieved when a Central Committee member proposed yet another meeting between the LCP and the Soviet party hierarchy headed by him.

Though the Soviet leader has not ruled out force to return the maverick Lithuanian Communists to the fold, he clearly wants to avoid such an extreme measure. At the same time, however, he has supported the Soviet Constitution's guarantee of the Communist Party's dominance. He has also warned that he will not permit the dissolution of the Soviet Union.

If that last statement has a Lincolnesque ring, it is a false note. Abraham Lincoln fought the Civil War to preserve an American union that was formed voluntarily. But Lithuania and its Baltic neighbors, Estonia and Latvia, were annexed by Moscow under the terms of the infamous Hitler-Stalin pact of 1939 that heralded the start of World War II. The three little Soviet republics were independent countries between the World Wars, and have not abandoned the hope of being free again.

Small wonder that Lithuanian Communist Party candidates fared so badly in legislative elections earlier this year. Party leaders contend that only by cutting its ties with its parent in Moscow can the LCP survive.

Enter Mikhail Gorbachev, accompanied by a delegation of the Kremlin bigwigs — including party hard-liners who favor tougher treatment of dissidents. One of Gorbachev's persistent themes has been that the Soviet Communist Party is in urgent need of reform. He could cite the Lithuanian party's problems as powerful evidence for that argument.

With a measure of flexibility from the Lithuanian Communists, a shrewd politician like Gorbachev should be able to finesse this potentially explosive situation that, if mishandled, could wreck perestroika and his leadership.

The Courier-Journal
Louisville, KY, December 24, 1989

Crowded off the front pages by the crash of the Communist government in Romania, an event took place last week within the Soviet Union itself that holds potentially far greater significance for that nation. A Communist party congress in Lithuania voted overwhelmingly to split from the Soviet national party and form the first independent Communist party in Soviet history.

Romania's collapse was simply the latest in a now familiar series of rumblings that signal the crumbling of the Soviet Communist empire. Whatever emerges among its erstwhile Eastern Europe satellites — reformed Communist governments, non-Communist governments, westward-looking governments — Moscow apparently feels it can live with.

But the end of empire is one thing (Britain lived through it). The dismantling of a nation is altogether something else. And that, very possibly, is what the Lithuanian action threatens. For the Lithuanians made plain that they are thinking not just of an independent Communist organization but of an "independent Lithuanian government." That means, essentially, an independent Lithuanian nation.

In many eyes, of course, Lithuania never ceased to be a nation. Its incorporation into the Soviet Union is deemed by much of the world to be illegal, the product of a deal between Josef Stalin and Adolf Hitler. But for all practical purposes, Lithuania has been a republic of the Soviet Union since World War II.

If Lithuania is allowed to go its own way — as a Communist party or as a state — Latvia and Estonia are sure to follow. Indeed, all of the Soviet Union is a powder keg of national and ethnic populations, easily ignited by a spark of independence anywhere within the Soviet borders. Ukrainians, Armenians, Georgians, Tatars, Russia's ethnic Germans, the Moslem republics — all have dreams not unlike those of the Baltic peoples, and all will be watching what happens in Lithuania and its neighbors.

Moscow has responded with an urgent call of a plenum of the Communist Party's Central Committee. It may convene at any moment. There is no predicting its reaction. But recent months (in China) and recent days (in Romania) have shown the measures to which a Communist government that feels itself in deadly peril will resort.

A crucial time is at hand for Soviet leader Mikhail Gorbachev and his reforms, for Lithuania, for all the peoples of the Soviet Union.

Minneapolis Star and Tribune
Minneapolis, MN, December 31, 1989

Mikhail Gorbachev is beginning to treat political independence as though it were toxic waste dumped near the Kremlin. The Soviet president was tolerant when yearnings for freedom swept away the Communist dictatorships in Poland, East Germany, Czechoslovakia and, finally, Romania. But its spread to Lithuania was too much. Not In My Back Yard, he bellowed. Yes, Mr. Gorbachev, in your back yard.

The Lithuanian Communist Party's decision to separate itself from the Soviet party poses two challenges to Gorbachev. First, it is a threat to the traditional power monopoly of Soviet Communists, not only in Lithuania, but throughout the Soviet Union. Yet a multiparty system is inevitable for the Soviet Union under the changes Gorbachev has set in motion. Indeed, multiparty rudiments already exist, ratified in Lithuania and Latvia by their parliaments. The Lithuanian Communist Party's separation from Moscow merely takes the evolution the next logical step.

When Gorbachev and other Moscow party leaders make their emergency visit to Vilnius, Lithuanian Communists will tell them that separation was their only choice. Unless Lithuanian Communists stay ahead of events and in tune with their republic's nationalistic aspirations, they are likely to be swept aside in elections scheduled for late February — elections that Gorbachev pushed.

Ironically, development of a multiparty system could help Gorbachev deal with the other challenge from Lithuania — the challenge to the Soviet empire. Lithuanians want national independence, which Moscow cannot grant without beginning the dissolution of the Soviet Union.

But if the Soviet Communist Party gives up its monopoly on power, it also will be freed of the tattered myth that Moscow is the holy see of an expanding dictatorship of the proletariat. With that pretense gone, Moscow would have nothing left but the truth: that it intends to remain an imperial power. The Russian empire bequeathed by the czars has controlled Lithuania for most of the last three centuries.

That imperial truth is less likely than expansionist Communist ideology to provoke trouble with the West — especially since Moscow has already released Eastern Europe from its grip. It also allows greater flexibility in working out new relationships that give Lithuania, Estonia, Latvia and other restive republics a greater sense of self-determination short of total independence.

Gorbachev has few options. The train of events that he has set in motion point toward either the dismemberment of the Soviet Union or affirmation of the Russian imperial impulse that has always formed the base of Moscow's rule. Lithuania has made that hard truth inescapable. Very soon Gorbachev must make his choice.

Gorbachev Confronts Lithuanians in Visit

Soviet President Mikhail S. Gorbachev began a scheduled three-day visit to Soviet Lithuania Jan. 11, 1990 in an effort to convince the Lithuanian Communist Party (CP) to rescind its decision to break with the national Communist Party.

He was the first Soviet leader to visit Lithuania since its annexation by the U.S.S.R. The trip was nationally televised, giving Soviets a firsthand look at how Gorbachev handled the nationalist crisis.

Lithuania's decision was regarded by the Kremlin as the first step in what could lead to an attempt by the Baltic republic to secede from the U.S.S.R. Moscow feared that if Lithuania left the union, other Soviet republics would certainly follow, thus destroying the union.

Two members of the national CP Politburo, Vadim A. Medvedev and Yuri D. Maslyukov, had arrived in Lithuania Jan. 8 in advance of Gorbachev. Medvedev, the party ideologist, warned Lithuanian CP officials Jan. 8 that a party split would do irreparable harm to Gorbachev's program of economic reforms.

On Jan. 10, about 20,000 Lithuanians held a nationalist rally in the republic's capital, Vilnius. On Jan. 11, the day of the president's arrival, an estimated 250,000 people participated in an independence demonstration in Vilnius. Vitautas Landsbergis, the chairman of Sajudis, the leading Lithuanian nationalist group, referred to Gorbachev as the visiting head of state of a foreign country. "What was stolen must be returned," Landsbergis told the crowd. "The time has come for intergovernmental negotiations between Lithuania and the Soviet Union."

Gorbachev's reception in Vilnius was polite, but the Lithuanians – both officials and ordinary citizens – appeared to be united on the matter of independence.

The president did not attend the rally for independence, but he did walk through the streets of the capital and addressed workers at a factory. He repeatedly denounced independence as a dangerous folly and a "dead end."

He told people in Lenin Square that a Lithuanian secession would be a "tragedy,…[For] over 50 years, we have become tied together, whether we like it or not."

Gorbachev said the Soviet Union could not risk losing its Baltic ports. "Our security lies here," he argued.

During his walkabout, the president contended that Lithuania could not survive economically as an independent state. "Let's give you independence, and establish world prices, and you'll bog down in a swamp immediately."

At the factory, Maslyukov, the chairman of Gosplan (the state central-planning agency), told the workers that under the national constitution, Lithuanians could "decide their own fate – to stay in the framework of the U.S.S.R. or leave it." But he cautioned that the republic would have to pay "compensation" to the Soviet loyalists who would feel compelled to migrate from the republic if it separated from the U.S.S.R.

Gorbachev, in his factory address, assured the workers that the Congress of People's Deputies, the national parliament, was drafting a law to create a mechanism "on how a republic can leave the Soviet Union." He did not give any details, but was adamant that secession would have to have some form of national approval.

Sajudis Jan. 12 dismissed Gorbachev's assurance. "This is an absurd deceit," said Landsbergis. "It is an insult. Our people must decide for themselves. It is a propaganda trap because if we accept such a law, it will mean that we are admitting that we are a legal part of the union in the first place."

For the first time since coming to power in 1985, Gorbachev indicated in his address that he was willing to be flexible on the matter of a multiparty system. He had vehemently opposed the Communist Party relinquishing its constitutionally guranteed "leading role" in society.

MILWAUKEE SENTINEL

Milwaukee, WI, January 13, 1990

Although he has charmed heads of state around the world, Mikhail S. Gorbachev does not seem to be making headway against the ardor of the Lithuanians to unleash the shackles that have linked them to the Soviet Union.

Indeed, despite one of the most remarkable demonstrations of grass-roots politicking in history, Gorbachev's visit has been one of frustration.

Enamored with his own powers of persuasion, Gorbachev now appears confounded by his inability to convince the people of this Baltic republic to abandon their quest for independence. And his reported arguments seemed to take on an air of desperation.

For example, at one point Gorbachev implied that without support of the Soviet military, Poland might try to retake former Polish territory now held by Lithuania.

Extending his concessions beyond earlier proposals for Lithuanian self-rule, Gorbachev said he would even agree to secession of Lithuania from the Soviet Union if a legal mechanism for such action were established first. But as one Lithuanian told him, there already is a law permitting secession.

Gorbachev's problem is his optimistic dream that he could manage a transition in the government of the Soviet Union and its satellites that would lead to broad citizen participation under a kinder, gentler brand of communism.

In truth, Lithuanians may be worse off if they reject Gorbachev's half-loaf of freedom. And he may be as concerned about their well-being as he is about his own political scalp, which Kremlin conservatives may have if the secessionist move is not quelled.

But the Lithuanians apparently have not accepted Gorby's choice as their own. That may be an inevitability by which Gorbachev may have to live or die.

DESERET·NEWS
Salt Lake City, UT, January 12, 1990

Keep a close watch on the news coming out of previously obscure Lithuania.

Why? Because what happens there in the next few days could determine whether the wave of freedom and reform keeps sweeping across Eastern Europe or ends in bloody repression.

Soviet Premier Mikhail Gorbachev is in the midst of a three-day visit to Lithuania, where the Baltic state's demand for independence from the communist party poses the toughest challenge yet to his reform program and to his own hold on power.

If Gorbachev can't work out a compromise on Lithuania, he faces the stark alternatives of either the potential breakup of the Soviet Union or a harsh crackdown that would doom his effort to improve the desperately sick Soviet economy by alienating western support for the outside help Moscow needs.

It was Gorbachev's insistence on glasnost or openness and perestroika or restructuring that give rise to demands for independence in Lithuania and the other Baltic states of Latvia and Estonia. If the Lithuanians are allowed to go their own way, it would be bound to give ideas to the Ukrainians, Moldavians, Armenians, Georgians, and Azerbaijanis. And it would leave Gorbachev open to charges that he has gone too far and too fast.

The prospect of such a dismemberment of the Soviet empire horrifies not only the hardline leadership clique in the Kremlin but also increasingly nationalistic Russians.

But it's hard for Gorbachev to object to what's happening in Lithuania since democratic reformers toppled communist governments in half a dozen countries in Eastern Europe with Gorbachev's blessings. What's more, the Soviet constitution allows any republic to leave the Soviet Union.

Though the politics of this situation is complex, the moral principle involved is unmistakably clear. Lithuania, Latvia, and Estonia were independent nations between the world wars but were incorporated into the Soviet Union in 1940 under a secret pact with Nazi Germany. Simple justice requires their return to independence — however gradually or expeditiously that may be accomplished.

The Register
Santa Ana, CA, January 14, 1990

Last week in Lithuania, President Mikhail Gorbachev openly spoke of turning the Soviet Union into a "confederation." These words may mark the beginning of the effective *disunion* of the Soviet Union.

Mr. Gorbachev even linked his own fate to Lithuania's continued presence in the Soviet "Union" (or whatever it will be called). Does this mean that he fears the military will step in to declare martial law and hold the "Union" together?

Lithuania presents a special case. In recent months *Register* editorialists have spoken with several top Lithuanian activists, including a member of the Soviet Congress. All had one goal: independence from Moscow.

They wish to maintain economic ties with the other Soviet "republics." As Mr. Gorbachev has himself noted, Lithuanians know that it will take a while to shift from socialism to a market economy. And they know that for some time this means their goods will be more desired in Russia than in Western Europe.

But whatever the arrangements, the Lithuanians want their country back.

The full implications of Lithuanian independence frighten Mr. Gorbachev. Once declared, it means that within a few hours similar declarations will come from Lithuania's fellow Baltic republics, Latvia and Estonia, and from such other captive nations as Armenia. Within days it may also lead to calls for independence by Azerbaijan, Georgia, Moldavia, Kazakhstan, and others, including the populous Ukraine.

The Baltic republics constitute the Soviet Union's most advanced industrial base. The republics' secession (not to mention secession by the other areas) would thus cut off a key center of military weapons production. So the question now is whether the Red Army would tolerate this.

It may. It has already tolerated the dismemberment of the Eastern European nations from the Soviet Empire. Opposition movements in Czechoslovakia, Poland, East Germany, and Hungary are already calling for the full withdrawal of the Red Army, in particular its 380,000 troops in East Germany. This almost certainly will happen. If Moscow won't use the Red Army to keep the Eastern European nations communist, there's no reason to keep it stationed in those countries at great expense.

What we may see this next year is the complete breakup of the Soviet "Union," with only a quasi-economic "confederation" remaining. Mr. Gorbachev will then become the leader of Russia, constituted along the approximate borders it had circa 1850, with a much reduced military. He then could concentrate on solving Russia's own tremendous problems.

Will he be allowed to do this peaceably? That's the question. Expect events to move as fast in the Soviet Union as they did last fall in Eastern Europe. And expect Mr. Gorbachev, who has a keen sense of what his place in history will be, not to act like Nicolae Ceausescu; he doesn't want to end up drenched in his people's blood. In histories of Russia he wants to be remembered as Mikhail the Great, not Mikhail the Terrible.

THE ARIZONA REPUBLIC
Phoenix, AZ, January 12, 1990

FOR months now Mikhail Gorbachev has been warning Lithuanians that, if they pressed their campaign for independence, their demands could "lead to tragedy." He repeated the warning yesterday in Vilnius, the capital of the rebellious Baltic republic.

And to what tragedy does Mr. Gorbachev refer? The break-up of the Soviet Union? Not everyone, least of all the Lithuanians, would regard that as altogether lamentable. Or does Mr. Gorbachev mean to suggest that force would be exerted to keep the Balts in line?

Despite such dark hints and dire warnings, other Kremlin figures appear to have ruled out force. Gennady Gerasimov, the official spokesman for the Foreign Ministry, said yesterday that political persuasion — dialogue — was the only tool Moscow would use to hold the union together. If that is so, if Moscow indeed has rejected the use of the Red Army, then the Soviet empire is doomed. Mr. Gorbachev may aver that "we have been tied together for these 50 years, whether we like it or not," but the 3.7 million Lithuanians clearly would like to alter the arrangement.

Indeed, the decision has been made already. Given the freedom to decide, Lithuanians would settle for nothing less than the immediate undoing of the secret 1940 Stalin-Hitler pact that ceded Lithuania, Latvia and Estonia to the Soviet Union. In the absence of force, Moscow already has lost the Baltic republics.

By going to Lithuania, Mr. Gorbachev has put his prestige on the line. He had hoped to persuade the Lithuanian Communist Party to reverse its declaration of independence from Moscow and to convince Lithuanians to remain part of the Soviet Union.

Lithuanians, however, sense that the tide of history is running strongly in their favor. Taking their cue from the revolutionary changes engulfing Eastern Europe and Moscow's de facto approval by inaction, Baltic nationalists are prepared to press Mr. Gorbachev to the limit. Both sides — the Balts and President Gorbachev — are taking enormous risks.

Along the entire periphery of the Soviet Union — from Azerbaijan to Georgia, from Moldavia to the Baltic republics — non-Russian nationalism is on the march. Unless Mr. Gorbachev can stop Baltic secession, the ethnic dominos will begin falling — an occurrence he could not survive. If he is forced to crack down in order to save himself, then *glasnost*, *perestroika* and the entire structure of Gorbachevian reform would come crashing down, leaving no one can say what.

The Kansas City Times

Kansas City, MO,
January 11, 1990

Mikhail Gorbachev's scheduled visit to Lithuania this week, already canceled once, sums up his dilemma. If the wrongs of Stalin are to be undone, the Baltic states would be a good place to begin. But a great many others in the Soviet orbit are waiting in line for redress for their own wrongs.

Lithuania, Latvia and Estonia were taken over by the Soviet Union through a secret agreement in the Soviet-German pact of 1939. That treaty also doomed Poland to invasion and partition. Adolf Hitler and Josef Stalin presided.

Gorbachev already has released the East European satellites. Without his promise not to use the Red Army, things could not have gone as they have in Poland, Hungary, Czechoslovakia, Romania and Bulgaria.

But the Baltic states, however they came into the U.S.S.R., are seen (at least by Russians) as integral republics in the Soviet Union. Other Soviet republics and subdivisions have come into "Russia" or the U.S.S.R. through conquest. Some were absorbed with the 1917 Revolution; others in the more distant past. There are strong nationalist movements in the Ukraine, Georgia and Armenia. The urge toward self-determination is compounded in the Islamic regions.

All three Baltic states want varying degrees of independence. Last November the Soviet legislature voted to give them economic autonomy beginning Jan. 1. But now, the Communist Party of Lithuania (CPL) has announced its separation from the Communist Party of the Soviet Union. This is apart from the nationalist independent movement, and inspired Gorbachev's journey to Vilnius.

Lithuanian Communists fear that massive demonstrations could ruin the visit. The CPL leader has said that Gorbachev has a vision of a union of free states retaining "socialism." The constant refrain is that perestroika can be destroyed by nationalist excesses, that Gorbachev could fall, and that the new Stalin would arrive to put the pieces back together.

But "socialism" has come to be a code word for doing things Moscow's way. If Gorbachev is not careful, "perestroika" will begin to have the same connotations. Moreover, those seeking independence will explain that the greatest nationalist force in their lives is Russian nationalism. They will recite overt and subtle means of Russification over many years.

Gorbachev's task is immense. In democratization he has loosed forces now beyond his control. The Baltic states seem to be emerging as the test for the future. If it's Vilnius today, can Kiev, Tbilisi and Yerevan be far behind?

FORT WORTH STAR-TELEGRAM

Fort Worth, TX, January 12, 1990

Because Lithuania, Latvia and Estonia did not ask to be engulfed into the Soviet Union in 1940, it is understandable that the peoples of those small Baltic states, with their fierce pride in their cultural distinctiveness, should now want out.

It is equally understandable, however, that Soviet President Mikhail Gorbachev cannot yield to their "let my people go" entreaties. From the perspective of the Kremlin, the Baltic states are not in the same category as the Eastern European countries that are tossing out their communist regimes and loosening their ties to the Soviet Union.

They are a part of the Soviet Union, and they are talking secession. If they succeed, other ethnic republics will seek to do likewise, and the multiethnic mosaic of the Soviet Union would come apart.

That is why Gorbachev has made his extraordinary trip to Lithuania to try to use his enormous powers of persuasion to dissuade that country's communist party from severing its ties to the federal communist party. Gorbachev is prepared to grant the Lithuanians more control over their own affairs, perhaps virtual autonomy. He has made it clear, however, that independence is out of the question.

He has no choice but to take that stance. When Gorbachev warns that "there will be a tragedy" if the Lithuanians and the federal government are pitted against each other, the message is abundantly clear: He will resort to force.

Indeed, if Gorbachev fails to quell the secessionist drive in the Baltic states, he is likely to be pushed out of power by people who will not hesitate to crush the nationalist movements.

Despite the understandable longings of the Lithuanians, Latvians and Estonians for independence, everyone's best interests may be served by their reaching an accommodation with Gorbachev for more control over their economic, cultural and political affairs.

The Providence Journal

Providence, RI, January 12, 1990

There's a good reason why the leader of the Soviet Union looks worried as he tours Lithuania this week. The spirit that has swept over Central and Eastern Europe in the past several months has crossed the frontier and crept into headquarters. Once again the world is looking at another communist regime determined to maintain the *status quo*; once again the people are confronted and confounded by a handful of masters.

The vital difference, of course, is that Mikhail Gorbachev is not Nicolae Ceausescu. By declining to enforce Soviet military control over onetime Warsaw Pact satellites, Mr. Gorbachev has tacitly endorsed the general principle of self-determination in Europe. The question, however, is whether that notion can be applied at home as well. It is one thing to look kindly on the aspirations of the people of Hungary; it is quite another to undermine the foundations of the Soviet regime.

Complicating matters is the particular status of Lithuania. Along with Latvia and Estonia, it is part of the Soviet Union purely as a consequence of military aggression: The cynical, one might say barbarous, division of Eastern Europe by Hitler and Stalin in 1939-40. This is not the Russian homeland or the Siberian tundra we are talking about; this is Kremlin control of what had once been an independent country. Mr. Gorbachev's general declarations may be music to the ears of his many admirers around the world, but in Lithuania, it is deeds, not words, that count.

Who, after all, can blame those masses of demonstrators in Vilnius who cannot understand why it is that what is good for Germany or Czechoslovakia is not so good for them?

Mr. Gorbachev's problem is a serious one, and potentially calamitous. If he is determined to keep Lithuania firmly within the Soviet empire, he is likely to inspire just the sort of civil disobedience and mass resistance that has transformed the rest of the Eastern bloc. At that point he will have to choose between accommodation and repression. Repression would mean a Baltic version of Tiananmen Square — Lithuania has nothing to match the Red Army — and catastrophic damage to Mr. Gorbachev's prestige.

Accomodation, however, is perilous in itself. Mr. Gorbachev made an odd declaration in Vilnius: He said that the Soviet Union is a "unitary state" — not the federation its laws declare — and Lithuania is another part of the Soviet whole. Well, if he should grant concessions to the Lithuanians in this instance, then the Moldavians, Ukrainians, Uzbeks, Latvians, Armenians, Byelorussians, Georgians, Azerbaijanis — the list goes on — will take notice fairly swiftly.

Sometime, somehow, Lithuania must be free. So must the other Baltic nations. But the challenge for Mr. Gorbachev now is to do the right thing by these hostage republics while maintaining stability — stability he needs to accelerate reform — within the Soviet Union. If Mikhail Gorbachev believes what he says about the "common home of Europe" — and we think that he does — change *must* come to his side of the continent.

The Lithuanian crisis is the real test of Mr. Gorbachev's words, and his skills as a statesman. And the test is yet to come.

The New York Times

New York, NY, January 13, 1990

Three triumphs for peace and freedom:

One was the sight of 250,000 people, a tenth of all ethnic Lithuanians, massed peacefully in Vilnius's main square on behalf of independence.

The second was the performance of Mikhail Gorbachev, the only Soviet party chief to visit Lithuania in a half-century. A forceful leader avoiding forceful means to hold together the *Union* of Soviet Socialist Republics, he argued that independence would be wrong, even self-defeating.

And then he opened the door to the third and most surprising triumph: Lithuanians may negotiate their way out of the union. Whatever the outcome, and Lithuanian nationalists' first response was negative, Westerners can only welcome the will of President Gorbachev and of the Lithuanians to seek a political resolution.

•

Crowds of a quarter-million have become a commonplace across Eastern Europe. But this week's disciplined demonstration was inside the Soviet Union. A year ago Mr. Gorbachev called freedom of choice "a universal principle." Does it apply to one of the Soviet Socialist Republics?

Addressing Lithuanian factory workers, Yuri Maslyukov, Mr. Gorbachev's Politburo colleague, could not have been plainer: "It is only natural that Lithuanians have the right to decide their fate — to be within the Soviet Union or to leave the Soviet Union." And Mr. Gorbachev told a man in the crowd, "Nothing will be decided without you." But he added, "Remember, if someone succeeds in pitting us against each other in a clash, there will be a tragedy. We should not allow this."

Mr. Gorbachev argues that independence would be politically risky and economically impractical. What Lithuania now makes, only the Soviet Union buys; and the materials it uses to make its products come mostly from the Soviet Union. If Lithuanians don't heed his words, he'll negotiate long and hard over the terms of independence.

Without saying so, Mr. Gorbachev may be foreshadowing a move from union to commonwealth, in which the centralized state gives way to a federation of constituent republics freer to associate or dissociate themselves.

Difficult questions remain. The hundreds of thousands of Russians who live in the Baltic Republics are regarded as occupiers; how will their rights be protected? Secession in Lithuania could inspire secession among other restless Soviet republics — or a hard-line reaction against Mr. Gorbachev. He has tried to distinguish the Baltic States, forcibly incorporated under the 1939 Nazi-Soviet pact. Will other republics recognize the distinction?

These questions will have to be answered in coming months. But for the moment, it's enough to marvel at the courage of the people of Lithuania and the Soviet leader for taking the political path.

The Philadelphia Inquirer

Philadelphia, PA, January 12, 1990

Pity poor Mikhail Gorbachev, who is on a risky three-day pilgrimage to Lithuania to try to talk the local communists out of splitting from the Soviet Communist Party. He's fighting to keep his nation intact, but history isn't on his side.

This is much more than an arcane party squabble. The Soviet leader knows that if he fails in Lithuania, local communist parties in some of the other non-Russian republics may follow suit. After that will come declarations of independence. And then the whole Soviet internal empire may start coming apart.

One can sympathize with Mr. Gorbachev's pleading remarks yesterday to a small crowd in Vilnius, the Lithuanian capital. He noted that the multinational Soviet population is all scrambled. Sixty million people live outside their national boundaries. Should the union split, this could lead to civil wars.

It must bemuse the Soviet leader that it was his own decision to give the republics more autonomy that spurred the current secession fever. His supporters argue that such separatism is out of step with an age when Western European nations are giving up sovereignty to create a united Europe.

But Mr. Gorbachev, who yesterday avoided a crowd of 300,000 Lithuanians clamoring for independence, misses the essential point: However difficult the economic future for Soviet republics that do secede, these people cannot be talked out of their determination to right history's wrongs.

The Baltic republics — Lithuania, Latvia and Estonia — were annexed by force after a 1939 pact between Joseph Stalin and Adolf Hitler that even the Soviets now condemn. Other republics are a legacy of the imperial expansion of the czars.

In trying to galvanize his people through *glasnost*, Mr. Gorbachev set in motion a chain reaction that can't be contained. Eastern Europe's rush to freedom has hastened a process that was already well under way.

For Mr. Gorbachev, the choices are dismal. He could crush Baltic separatism by force, but that would undermine his reform program. He could expel Lithuanian communists, but that would only strengthen the drive to secede.

Or he could allow independence-minded republics to chart their own destinies. Eventually, the Soviet Union might become a voluntary federation based on mutual economic needs, without domination from the Russian center. Mr. Gorbachev is not yet ready to accept such a future, but he can't stop the historical forces he has set in motion.

Lithuania Declares Independence from U.S.S.R.

The Supreme Soviet (parliament) of Lithuania March 11, 1990 formally declared a restoration of the republic's independence from the Soviet Union. Lithuania was the first Soviet republic to attempt to secede.

Lithuania had been an independent nation from 1918 to 1940, when it was annexed by the U.S.S.R. along with the neighboring Baltic states of Estonia and Latvia.

The declaration came in the form of a resolution voted on at an emergency session of the legislature in the Lithuanian capital, Vilnius. Due to triumphs in elections Feb. 24 and runoffs March 4, the parliament for the first time had a majority of non-Communist, pro-secession deputies.

The resolution read: "The Supreme Soviet of Lithuania, expressing the will of the people, resolves and proclaims that the sovereign rights of the former Lithuanian state, occupied in 1940, are now reborn...From this moment Lithuania becomes an independent state."

Of the 130 deputies present, 124 voted in favor of the resolution and six – all Communist Party loyalists – abstained. There were no negative votes.

Following the vote, the deputies cheered, replaced the Soviet flag with the yellow, green and red flag of Lithuania, and sang the Lithuanian national anthem.

Outside the parliament building, about 1,000 Lithuanians held a joyous celebration. (One man carried a sign that read, "Bye Bye, U.S.S.R.," with the twin-lightning-bolt symbol of the Nazi Germany SS elite guard substituted for the two S's.)

The deputies then elected Vytautas Landsbergis, the president of Lithuania. Landsbergis, a 57-year-old professor of 20th-century music history, was the head of the Lithuanian nationalist organization Sajudis. He defeated the republic's Communist Party chief, Algirdis Brazauskas, 91-38, in the presidential vote. Brazauskas had voted in favor on the independence resolution.)

"We are not asking anyone's permission whether we should take this step," Landsbergis told the parliament after his election as president. "We are acting on our will, according to the dictates of our consciences. Our duty now is to make a reality of the expectations we have created."

In other actions March 11, the legislature:

■ Proclaimed the birth of the "Republic of Lithuania," dropping the Kremlin designation "Lithuanian Soviet Socialist Republic."

■ Renamed itself the Supreme Council.

■ Voted to temporarily retain Soviet civil and criminal laws.

In Moscow, where the Congress of People's Deputies (national parliament) was about to begin a special session, the initial reaction was restrained. The official press reported the Lithuanian development without comment.

Soviet President Mikhail S. Gorbachev March 12 called the Lithuanian move "alarming," and warned that it could "affect the fundamental interests" of the entire Soviet nation.

Arkansas Gazette

Little Rock, AR, March 13, 1990

As a former Arkansas governor might say, just because Lithuania has declared its independence from the Soviet Union does not necessarily make it so. But the declaration is welcome, nevertheless, by all freedom-loving people around the globe.

All three of the Baltic republics — Lithuania, Estonia and Latvia — have strong and undeniable claims to national independence, which they enjoyed until Joseph Stalin and Adolf Hitler engineered a Soviet takeover in dark dealing on the eve of World War II.

The spirit of freedom and independence has never been far from the surface over the last 50 years, but formidable obstacles still stand in the way of realization. It is one thing to declare independence and quite another to achieve it in the face of Soviet resistance.

But the Lithuanians and perhaps the Estonians and the Latvians, whose parliaments may follow suit, are realists. They know that hard negotiations with Soviet President Mikhail Gorbachev lie ahead if their dream is to be realized. Soviet officials have vowed not to use force to keep Lithuania from breaking away, but the possibility of such a danger lurks in the background.

Moscow views Lithuania much like a cork holding 15 Soviet republics in a bottle. If Lithuania goes easily, other republics, not just the Baltic states, will try to follow. The longer the Soviets can negotiate — their opening position is that Lithuania must pay the Kremlin $34 billion for infrastructure built there by the Soviet Union — the more days will pass until the reckoning. The Lithuanians, for openers, contend that what they have endured over the last 50 years is worth far more than $34 billion.

Through all of this emerges a feeling, in the context of change through Eastern Europe and the Soviet Union itself, that Lithuania, Estonia and Latvia will win back their independence, peacefully and without undue delay. This is an optimistic view, but it no longer seems out of reason.

The Phoenix Gazette

Phoenix, AZ, February 27, 1990

There now is no doubt that Lithuania will press its demands for secession from the Soviet Union. The uncertainty is how Moscow and Washington will react.

The Sajudis Popular Front, a coalition of independence-minded parties, rolled over a newly reformed Communist Party for an easy 72 seat majority out of 90 declared winners in Saturday's parliamentary elections. The Sajudis also are expected to win most of the run-off races scheduled for next month.

The Sajudis want Lithuania to negotiate with Moscow as the independent nation it was before its forcible incorporation into the Soviet Union in 1939. Vytautas Landsbergis, president of the Sajudis since 1988, also rejects the idea of a "federation," championed by the reformed Communist Party. He explained that Lithuania's desire for independence cannot be compared to the secession of the southern states in the American Civil War.

"The difference is that Lithuania is not trying to preserve slavery, it is trying to escape it. It is not seeking to establish independence, it is working to restore it," he wrote recently.

If Moscow attempts to obstruct the elected government, it runs the risk of losing international credibility. But the credibility of the United States is also at stake.

"We are testing Moscow, but we are also testing the West," Landsbergis said after the election. "We want to know: What is the West? Are they mere merchants or do they have Christian, democratic principles — principles that extend to others as well as to themselves? We need clearly expressed support, and so far President Bush's words for us are quite reserved."

In a recent press conference President George Bush said that he viewed instability in Eastern Europe and the Soviet Union as the "enemy." The Lithuanians don't see it that way, nor should we. Instability is only a station on the road to freedom.

The Houston Post

Houston, TX, March 13, 1990

MIKHAIL GORBACHEV marked his fifth anniversary as the Soviet Union's leader this week facing the accelerating erosion of communism at home and abroad. His most serious domestic crisis is the weekend secession vote by Lithuania, one of the U.S.S.R.'s 15 republics.

The Lithuanians are only the latest people to declare their desire to shed Communist rule since the explosion in the Kremlin's East European empire. In the independent Mongolian People's Republic, bordering the Soviet Union and China, a democratic opposition has forced the top Communist leaders to resign.

Meanwhile, Italy's Communist Party, the country's second largest, has voted to change both its name and its ideology. And the French Communist Party's leader has also been under pressure to ease his doctrinaire stance.

The Lithuanian action came on the eve of Monday's opening of the Congress of People's Deputies, the top Soviet legislative body. The main items on its agenda are proposed constitutional amendments to give President Gorbachev broad new authority while revoking the Communist Party's monopoly on power.

Though the constitutional changes would empower the president to dissolve the parliaments of republics like Lithuania, Gorbachev has not indicated he would take such steps. He has, however, described the Lithuanian declaration of independence "alarming" and has not recognized its legality so far.

The Lithuanian action puts the Bush administration in a delicate diplomatic position. The United States and most of its Western allies never have recognized the Soviet annexation of Lithuania and its neighbors, Latvia and Estonia, under the infamous Hitler-Stalin pact of 1939. All three of the little Baltic republics had been independent between the World Wars.

Our initial response has been proper — withholding formal recognition of Lithuanian sovereignty while urging Gorbachev to respect the unanimous 124-0 vote of its parliament for independence.

The Soviet hierarchy has stressed its intention to settle the crisis by political means, with one of the more conservative members of the ruling Politburo, Yegor Ligachev, declaring, "We will not use force."

If that remains the Kremlin's policy, it will be a further welcome indication of maturity on the part of the Soviet leadership. Of course, Gorbachev can apply economic pressure. He has already put a $34 billion price tag on Lithuania's departure from the U.S.S.R.

Lithuanians, however, counter with a much larger bill for decades of Kremlin economic mismanagement and Stalinist repression, during which, they charge, 300,000 people were killed, tortured and sent in mass deportations to Siberia. *Touche!*

THE PLAIN DEALER

Cleveland, OH, March 13, 1990

The declaration was just five sentences long. But its implications were immense.

For the first time in more than 70 years of empire, a Soviet republic simply voted to go its own way. Against all historical precedents, the old communists in the Kremlin seemed to have ruled out force to prevent it.

And in a twist on 1990s independence drives, the big beef turned out to be over money, and who gets to keep what.

Moscow reportedly seeks $33 billion for the factories and modern economy it financed in Lithuania since 1940. Russians who live in the Baltic Sea port of Klaipeda have started a petition drive to have their city join Russia. The Lithuanians, for their part, talk about $500 billion in reparations for arrests and economic disasters after Josef Stalin forcibly annexed their country in 1940.

The United States has never recognized that annexation, and Lithuania formally declared it null and void earlier this year. It was thus just a short step to Sunday's 124-0 vote by the newly elected Lithuanian Parliament to return to the constitution adopted in 1920, when Lithuania was a free country.

The hammer and sickle and the red star are gone, replaced by the old icon of Lithuanian nationhood, a white knight. The medieval symbol recalls when Lithuania, once a Baltic crossroads of East and West, was led by warrior-diplomats who stretched its hegemony nearly to the Black Sea.

Rushing to act before the Soviet Congress of People's Deputies granted sweeping new powers to Soviet leader Mikhail S. Gorbachev, Lithuanian legislators Sunday renounced all political and legal ties with Moscow. They also rejected as president of the new Republic of Lithuania the popular, home-grown, communist reformer, Algirdas Brazauskas.

The mantle instead has fallen to a shy, bespectacled music professor who is about as

> *The U.S. government, meanwhile, has laudably resisted the temptation to crow.*

far from a political firebrand as they come. Vytautas Landsbergis, in Cleveland last summer, then spoke the soothing words of revolution through accommodation and gradualism.

Sunday's declaration was far from that. Many in Lithuania now expect a Soviet embargo to punish the breakaway republic's economy.

Yet, in many ways, the declaration was just another piece of fine rhetoric in the newly liberated land of glasnost. The Soviet Union still supplies much of the republic's energy and resource needs, and Red Army troops remain in Lithuania. Negotiations, perhaps led by Brazauskas, to fine-tune terms of Lithuanian separation are thus expected.

The U.S. government, meanwhile, has laudably resisted the temptation to crow. Without any prodding from this country, the other Baltic states, Latvia and Estonia, are expected to follow Lithuania onto the exposed field of self-determination.

It is still possible Gorbachev will be able to recover this latest political fumble and get Lithuania to agree to a formula that allows independence but also economic federalism within the Soviet system. At this juncture, that seems the best he can hope to achieve.

Short months ago it was said on this page that Gorbachev would never preside over the dismantling of empire; it now looks as if he has no other politically viable choice.

Lithuanians can thus look forward to a heady, new era. Lietuva. Freedom.

Nashville, TN, March 13, 1990

THE Baltic republic of Lithuania has declared its independence from Moscow and as a symbolic gesture that is important, but it does not materially change things immediately.

President Mikhail Gorbachev called it "alarming," but gave no indiction he plans action to prevent the republic from breaking away. He did not acknowledge the legality of the action, however. But if force is out, political negotiation between Moscow and the Lithuanian capital of Vilnius is not, and even Lithuanian lawmakers acknowledge that.

In the first place, Lithuania is fully integrated into the Soviet economic structure. It depends, for instance, on Moscow for 75% of its energy needs, and has even greater dependence on the Soviet for raw materials, particularly metals. Without either, its factories can't produce.

And, President Gorbachev has said Lithuania will have to pay the Kremlin $34 billion for the factories and other infrastructure built by the Soviet during a half century of Moscow's rule.

It has no means of paying that anytime in this century. Even if it could it would have to rely on the Soviet Union as a major market for its goods. There are no other big markets available now.

It has a 1.5 billion ruble trade deficit with the rest of the Soviet Union. It has no reasonable way to lure Western investment. It has no treasury and no currency of its own. Even if it printed money, that would be worthless.

It does have one bargaining chip in terms of economics. It has a major seaport through which the Soviet Union must move supplies to a major chunk of its own territory, which would be more or less cut off without it.

Declaring political independence is one thing, but achieving economic independence is a far more difficult mountain to climb.

Some of the reformers in Lithuania talk vaguely of a Finnish model economy, but again that is no panacea. Finland is short of raw materials, so it imports most of them from the Soviet and in turn sells finished products back to the Soviet and the West.

For Lithuania to contemplate complete economic independence from the Soviet Union would be to look in the face of disaster.

Nevertheless, Lithuania has its own aspirations. It has presented Mr. Gorbachev with a crisis of sorts, since he must think of the other Baltic republics and what the signal is that Lithuania is sending them.

It is hoped that both sides will maintain restraint in dealing with each other while they progress toward new freedoms down the road. ■

The Houston Post

Houston, TX, February 27, 1990

ARE THE SOVIET UNION'S Communist leaders hearing footsteps? If not, they're not keeping an ear to the ground. Over the weekend, large chunks of its populace gave clear signals that they are fed up with an oppressive system that doesn't work.

In Lithuania, voters gave 72 of 90 available parliamentary seats to members of the nationalist Sajudis movement. Only seven seats went to Communist candidates loyal to Moscow, and Sajudis candidates are expected to take even more seats in a March 10 runoff. The message is plain: Lithuanians want out of the U.S.S.R. In point of fact, they don't think they've ever been a legal part of it. They're right. Their republic, at that time a nation, was annexed against its will half a century ago.

In 20 or more cities all across the Soviet Union, hundreds of thousands of peaceful protesters turned out on Sunday to show their disgust with the government. They see its Communist leaders as corrupt and ineffectual. Many of them give grudging but faint praise to President Mikhail Gorbachev. In their view, his reforms are slow and ham-handed.

Is what's good for most of the satellites good for Mother Russia? A lot of its citizens seem to think so. And stay tuned for yet more ballot-box dissent this Sunday, as voters in the three largest republics — Russia, Byelorussia and the Ukraine — go to the polls.

It has been said that no good deed goes unpunished. All of this flows from Gorbachev's decision to allow competition among political parties. Yet there was little else he could do. He was close to being forced to choose, at least in some areas, between multi-party elections and open insurrection. Gorbachev is still the leader the Soviet Union needs at this time — but he may have to learn to share power.

PORTLAND EVENING EXPRESS

Portland, ME, March 27, 1990

The first Soviet republic ever to vote for independence has rocked the Soviet Union with the force of freedom.

The vote decided only a bare majority of the seats — 90 of 141 — for a new parliament in Lithuania, a formerly independent republic on the Baltic Sea bordering Poland.

But candidates pledged to throw off Moscow's control won 72 seats, a majority of the entire parliament, leading inevitably down the road to a clear conflict over secession.

The only questions remaining are, when will Lithuania seek to break away — and what will the response from Moscow be when it does?

Those questions are substantial. Lithuania's experience may become a model for other restive border republics in the Soviet Union which have chafed for decades under rulers imposed by the Communist Party.

There is room for optimism. As winter gives way to spring, a wave of support for pluralism is growing in many places in the Soviet sphere.

Not only have its former satellites in Eastern Europe forged their own paths to independence, but on Sunday, Soviet citizens rallied in at least 20 cities from the Baltic to the Sea of Japan. In numbers ranging from the hundreds to the hundreds of thousands, they peacefully demonstrated against the slow pace of economic and political improvement under Mikhail Gorbachev.

It seems highly unlikely that any Soviet ruler could still consider using military force against peaceful separatists. If that's true, however, Lithuania will only be the first republic to seek independence.

We should be doing all we can to assure that the far different Soviet Union of the 21st century comes into existence without violence and with the maximum political and economic benefit for its citizens.

THE CHRISTIAN SCIENCE MONITOR

Boston, MA, February 28, 1990

ELECTION results in Lithuania surprised no one, least of all Mikhail Gorbachev. Since his trip to the Baltic republic last December, the Soviet leader has known that nationalist sentiment there is virtually unstoppable.

Now that the Lithuanian national front, Sajudis, has won a clear majority in the republic's parliament, a resolution of independence can't be far off. That doesn't mean, of course, that independence itself is a simple step around the corner – despite the predictions of Sajudis leaders that it will be attained this year.

Difficult negotiations lie ahead. A government commission is at work trying to define procedures under the Soviet law of succession. Present drafts of their recommendations indicate a drawn-out process: an initial cooling-off period, followed by a referendum in the republic, followed by further negotiations, perhaps years in length, on such details as economic relationships, dismantling of institutions associated with the present union, and restitution to Moscow for union property.

Nationalists could easily grow impatient, and it's anybody's guess where that impatience could lead. As momentum for independence continues to build in the Baltics – Latvia and Estonia won't be far behind Lithuania – Mr. Gorbachev may find he has little choice but to accede to the popular will. His hope is that the impulse to leave the union can be limited to the Baltics.

Elections in Moldavia showed the strength of the popular front organization in that small republic on the Soviet western flank. Separatist sentiments rage in Azerbaijan. Nationalism is alive in the big republics too, with Russian nationalism, allied to conservative elements in the party and army, adding an ominous tone to Soviet popular politics.

Events elsewhere – notably the Nicaraguans' rejection of the Sandinista brand of Marxism – echo in the communist heartland, too.

Local elections are coming this weekend in the Russian, Byelorussian, and Ukrainian republics, with others to follow. They may knock aside resistant bureaucrats and help perestroika move ahead – or they may hasten a political juggernaut that's leaving *perestroika* far behind.

Minneapolis Star and Tribune

Minneapolis, MN, February 27, 1990

For a people repressed through most of this century, the Lithuanians have shown astonishing sophistication in pushing their campaign to secede from the Soviet Union. That campaign now appears far less quixotic than it seemed just months ago.

The Lithuanian opposition movement has masterfully mixed patience and resolve into a strategy that pushes hard, but never too hard. While always moving toward their goal, the Lithuanians have carefully avoided giving the Soviets an excuse to beat them down. Saturday that strategy paid off in the first free, multiparty elections held in the Soviet Union in more than 60 years. Lithuanian independence trounced Soviet communism.

Next for the Lithuanians comes formation of a coalition government and selection of a new president. Then, the Lithuanians hope, negotiations can begin with Moscow on procedures for making Lithuania an independent state.

The Lithuanians' wisdom in plotting their peaceful, procedurally correct revolution was made more apparent Monday when the Kremlin released the draft of a new state-of-emergency law. The draft law would allow the Presidium of the Supreme Soviet to suspend a republic's parliament and assume administrative control when disorder threatens life or health or "could have heavy consequences." So long as the Lithuanians continue to avoid mass unrest, even this new law won't stop their drive to separate from the Soviet Union.

As if inspired by the Lithuanian example, people across the Soviet Union took to the streets Sunday to demand an end to the Communist Party's monopoly on power. Despite intense campaigns to dissuade people from participating, more than 50,000 Muscovites marched in disciplined, peaceful protest. They refused to be intimidated, they refused to give the state a reason to crack down, and they expressed extraordinary anger at the heroes of the Communist revolution, from Lenin to Gorbachev.

In Lithuania, they're now predicting full independence may be just months away. It will take longer for full-fledged democracy to come to Moscow, but that, too, now seems less fanciful hope than honest expectation.

The Globe and Mail

Toronto, Ont., March 13, 1990

Canada has never accepted the legality of the Soviet Union's annexation of the tiny Baltic republic of Lithuania. While Ottawa acknowledges that Moscow has achieved effective control of the region by invasion and occupation, the Canadian position for 50 years has been that Lithuanians should have the right to determine their own destiny.

However, now that the Lithuanian government has finally demanded the restoration of the republic's sovereignty and freedom, its declaration of independence creates cause for anxiety as well as celebration.

Political chaos in the Soviet Union is in no one's interest. During his five years in office, Soviet President Mikhail Gorbachev has accomplished more to make the world a more peaceful place than any other statesman of his generation. As Czechoslovak President and longtime political dissident Vaclav Havel has told the West, Mr. Gorbachev's success is indispensable to the emergence of a free, undivided Europe.

It is unclear today just what implications the Lithuanian declaration has for political stability in the Soviet Union and for Mr. Gorbachev's future. He himself has called the development "alarming," but has cautiously avoided a fuller response.

The Lithuanian people, of course, deserve the congratulations of all democratic governments for the courageous, peaceful way they have pursued their independence. In free elections to the republic's legislature just two weeks ago, they overwhelmingly supported advocates of independence.

Those new politicians voted 124-0 on Sunday endorsing a resolution that said: "The Supreme Council of the Republic of Lithuania, expressing the will of the nation, resolves and solemnly proclaims that the execution of the sovereign power of the Lithuanian state, heretofore constrained by alien forces in 1940, is restored. Henceforth Lithuania is once again an independent state."

The legislature then demanded that the local KGB and police accept its authority, and laid claim to gas pipelines, rail and power lines and military sites on its territory.

In Poland, senior Solidarity official Adam Michnik expressed immediate enthusiasm for the move: "We believe that the declaration of the Lithuanian parliament will not initiate any nationalist conflicts and will become an element in the democratic rebuilding of our European home."

Canadian MPs were equally supportive but a little more muted. Yesterday theyunanimously endorsed a resolution recognizing the Lithuanian government's right to declare independence.

However, it is already apparent that, at best, there is a long process of difficult negotiation ahead. Mr. Gorbachev has said that the Lithuanians may face a bill of as much as $33-billion in compensation for leaving the union. Lithuanian politicians have replied that they could submit their own bill for $480-billion, including damages for the murder or deportation of 300,000 people during the Stalinist era.

That the issue has already moved to some form of bargaining — no matter how far the sides are apart — is a good thing in itself. It is also heartening that top Communist Party conservative Yegor Ligachev has ruled out the use of force. "Tanks will not help in this matter," he told reporters.

But this is just the first demand for independence in the Soviet Union and will not be the last. The other Baltic republics, Latvia and Estonia, are following the same path as Lithuania. Moldavia has advanced a long way toward demanding change. Even the great republics of Georgia and Ukraine are bubbling with separatist unrest.

Losing the Baltic republics is one thing; presiding over the complete disintegration of the Soviet empire is another. It may be that Mr. Gorbachev can turn the Lithuanian declaration of independence to his advantage; previous manifestations of unrest have strengthened his position within the Communist Party, because they have reminded conservatives that he alone has the clout to face them. He has been able to transform many other apparent political losses into gains.

But it is painfully apparent today that Soviet federalism does not work much better than Soviet central planning. Far-reaching changes are needed just to keep relations on a civil basis between the republics and the centre.

If the Lithuanians' brave initiative creates the necessary impetus for change, it may prove to have been the catalyst for the next, necessary wave of liberalization. It may be, as Mr. Michnik says, a constructive step in the rebuilding of Europe.

Much now depends on the attitude that Mr. Gorbachev and the Lithuanians bring to negotiations. The declaration of independence has come far more swiftly than even many Lithuanians had hoped. Now is the time for patience, determination and tolerance.

THE KANSAS CITY STAR

Kansas City, MO, March 13, 1990

The key to Lithuania's future as an independent country is in the 30,000 Soviet troops stationed there and the status of Lithuanians serving in the Red Army.

It is all very well for the Lithuanian Parliament to declare independence unanimously and for Mikhail Gorbachev to be on record as "willing to negotiate." But if the Soviet troops stay in Lithuania, and if Lithuanians must serve in the Soviet Army, all the declarations under the sun won't amount to much.

And exactly what does Gorbachev mean by "negotiate"? Surely not that he would submit the matter to arbitration, or find a compromise midway between the present and an easy future for free Lithuania.

Consider the situation from Gorbachev's position. The other Baltic states are sure to seek independence. Strong secession noises are coming from Georgia. Even in far-away Mongolia there is talk of leaving the U.S.S.R. What about the Ukraine, an immense region? Moldavia? The list goes on. Can Gorbachev

acquiesce in the dissolution of his country and expect to stay in power?

Virtually the entire history of Russia has been the expansion first, from Kiev, and then, from the Duchy of Muscovy. The creation of buffer states and reliance on defense-in-depth strategy are part of the political and national character. Now the western marches are fading fast with the collapse of the Warsaw Pact bloc.

Entirely aside from the plain merits of the Lithuanian case (the country was, after all, stolen by Stalin in a secret agreement with Hitler), it's difficult to see how Gorbachev can let the country go gently. For his own future and presumably the future of a democratic Soviet Union, he is bound to make the cost to Lithuania stand as an object lesson.

Moscow will try to isolate the contagion of independence. If Gorbachev falls amid the rising din from nationalities, the future for all could turn very dark.

The Wichita Eagle-Beacon

Wichita, KS, March 15, 1990

The dominos continue to fall. Last Sunday, just a week after elections swept the independence movement Sajudis into power, Lithuania became the first state to try to secede from the Soviet Union.

The newly elected Lithuanian parliament declared the country's freedom. Yet the little state on the Baltic Sea has many trials ahead before it is truly free.

Soviet President Mikhail Gorbachev says a show of force is out of the question. Even conservative Soviet leaders agree that a political solution is the only answer to the bold secession move by the Lithuanians.

Although Mr. Gorbachev is huffing and puffing and calling the Lithuanian declaration of independence "illegitimate and invalid," observers say that's only political posturing designed to soothe hard-liners. They say negotiations soon will begin to ensure Lithuania's rebirth.

Yet, after 50 years of Soviet domination, negotiations will be difficult and delicate.

Will the Soviets keep troops and naval installations in Lithuania? Who owns Soviet-built factories, as well as banks, farms and ports? Does Lithuania owe Moscow billions

to pay for the economic enterprises built in the last 50 years, or does Moscow owe Lithuania billions in reparations for economic suffering, and the deportation of thousands of Lithuanians to Siberia.

Perhaps the toughest question of all: Can the economy of Lithuania stand on its own? It's a country that gets virtually all of its fuel from the Soviet Union.

Still, Lithuanians around the world are rejoicing, and they should be.

In Wichita, physician Arnold Grushnys, a Lithuanian native who fled his country during World War II, says he understands the future will be hard for his homeland. Recently, Dr. Grushnys received a letter from a friend in Lithuania who suffered eight years in Siberia. He quotes the letter:

"We know and are prepared for difficult economic times. But we will be free."

Lithuania may be the first state in the Soviet Union to test the heady air of freedom, but it almost certainly won't be the last. Its Baltic neighbors, Estonia and Latvia, shouldn't be far behind. Georgia also has demanded negotiations with Moscow to re-establish independence. The dominos continue to fall.

Lithuania Bends on Independence; Soviet Troops Seize Deserters

In the face of continuing pressures from the Soviet government, leaders in the republic of Lithuania March 28, 1990 indicated a willingness to at least discuss holding a referendum on independence. The statements appeared to be a conciliatory gesture aimed at reducing tensions over Lithuania's move to secede from the U.S.S.R.

The Soviet parliament was drafting a law on the requirements a republic would have to meet if it wished to leave the union. The contemplated steps would include a republic-wide referendum, a five-year waiting period after independence was approved by referendum, the satisfaction of Moscow's economic claims and final approval of the Congress of People's Deputies, the national parliament.

A central tenet of the Kremlin's public opposition to Lithuania's declaration of independence was that the move – voted by the republic's parliament – did not truly reflect the wishes of the Baltic republic as a whole. The independence movement was spearheaded by persons of Lithuanian descent, but 20% of the republic's population was non-Lithuanian. Ethnic Russians, ethnic Poles and ethnic Byelorussians were the largest minorities.

Since the March 11 declaration, the Lithuanian leadership had dismissed the need for a referendum on independence. But on March 28, President Vytautas Landsbergis and Deputy Premier Algridis Brazauskas softened their stand.

Landsbergis called for talks with the Kremlin. "There can be no questions that cannot be discussed [at the talks], except the question of Lithuanian independence. The problem of a referendum could also be discussed," he said.

Brazauskas, who was also the head of Lithuania's breakaway Communist Party, said he favored a republic-wide vote on sovereignty. "I have no doubts about what the results of the referendum would be," he explained. "It would be an additional ace...This perhaps could also strengthen the self-determination of out nation."

The shift came after the Kremlin had increased pressure on Lithuania with a series of controversial moves. Soviet President Mikhail S. Gorbachev March 22 had sent a telegram to Landsbergis giving the republic two days to halt the recruitment of a volunteer Lithuanian security force.

On March 23, the Soviet government curbed the movements of foreign journalists in Lithuania, gave Western diplomats 12 hours to leave the republic and restricted the entry into Lithuania of foreigners.

At about 3:00 a.m. on March 24, a Soviet military convoy disrupted an all-night session of the Lithuanian parliament by rumbling past the parliament building in the capital of Vilnius. The convoy had more than 100 tanks and trucks and an estimated 1,500 soldiers.

The Lithuanian leadership March 24 denounced the actions as "psychological warfare." The republic's parliament the same day passed a resolution approving the formation of a Lithuanian government in exile should the Kremlin overthrow the Vilnius regime. Stasys Lozoraitis, Lithuanian charge d'affaires in the U.S., was authorized to head the exile goverment.

Soviet paratroopers seized the Vilnius headquarters of the renegade Lithuanian Communist Party March 25. The headquarters was empty when the troops arrived. Troops also took over other party property in Vilnius, including the Institutue of Marxism-Leninism and the Higher Party School. All of the facilities were turned over to Communist Party members loyal to the Kremlin.

Soviet paratroopers March 27 raided a psychiatric hospital in Vilnius that had given sanctuary to ethnic Lithuanian military deserters. A total of 23 young men were reported to have been taken away by the soldiers. The paratroopers left in their wake evidence of violent struggles. Bloodstained floors, broken glass and overturned furniture littered the area where the deserters had been staying. There were unconfirmed reports that Soviet troops also raided apartments in Vilnius that were suspected of harboring deserters.

The Chattanooga Times

Chattanooga, TN, March 23, 1990

An impasse that neither the Soviet Union nor Lithuania can want is rapidly approaching. Moscow's latest step, tightening border posts and visa requirements and ordering Lithuanians to turn in their hunting rifles within seven days, has been coolly rejected in Lithuania as an illegal order that can only be enforced by brutal military intervention. The intensifying test of wills must conclude in confrontation or negotiation. Both sides have a responsibility to afford each other an out that can lead to negotiation.

By any democratic standard, Lithuania has a legitimate basis on which to claim independence. The Soviet Union's forcible "annexation" of the small Baltic state in 1940, under a secret accord between Stalin and Hitler, ended a 32-year stretch of independence and has never been forgiven, nor officially recognized in the West. Even Soviet President Mikhail Gorbachev has declared it was illegal and morally wrong.

But that is history entangled with decades of Russian occupation, investment and interdependence, much as is the case with some other republics over which the Soviet Union claims sovereignty. Thus Lithuania's unilateral declaration of independence earlier this month dramatizes an immense political dilemma with far-reaching ramifications. If Moscow succumbs to Lithuania's demand, will that be tantamount to a surrender that will start the Soviet Union unraveling, republic by republic?

Estonia and Latvia, Lithuania's Baltic neighbors annexed along with her, have strong independence movements. Other republics on Russia's southern and eastern rim — Georgia, Moldavia, Azerbaijan and Armenia — are candidates for self-rule. The question of whether the Russian empire will break up under Mr. Gorbachev — and whether he or Soviet hard-liners will try to prevent that — has become increasingly at issue as Mr. Gorbachev has set Eastern European satellites free.

Now, the principle of self-determination he espoused in allowing democratization in the Warsaw Pact emboldens dissident republics. President Gorbachev must contradict himself, use force to hold the Soviet empire together, or work out satisfactory secession and confederation status for various republics.

There can be rational negotiation that lets Mr. Gorbachev set secession-minded states free in an orderly way, and Lithuania must seek negotiation to make this a reality — and an example. President Gorbachev himself has sent contradictory signals, presenting one week a conciliatory posture and the next week a stern front. Indeed, he has straddled the middle as long as he apparently can. He will be pushed increasingly into basic choices as alternatives polarize toward logical conclusions and the middle ground vanishes.

But certainly neither Mr. Gorbachev nor Lithuanian leaders can imagine it is in their best interest to push the other into too tight a corner. Their nervy maneuvering has the world watching closely, and Mr. Gorbachev's great attempt to remake the Soviet Union on the line.

SYRACUSE
HERALD-JOURNAL
Syracuse, NY, March 29, 1990

The Bush administration is acting with characteristic caution in its reaction — or lack of reaction — to escalating tensions between Lithuania and Moscow. This is one case where caution is appropriate.

No one who loves freedom can be anything but supportive of the Lithuanian people's effort to rid themselves of the yoke of Soviet domination. The United States, the role model for freedom movements for more than two centuries, is a natural place for them to look for support.

Still, a strident condemnation of recent Soviet actions in Lithuania could do more harm than good to the cause of freedom there and throughout Europe. The ingredients are there for a great deal of harm.

The human catalyst for the changes that have swept Eastern Europe in the last several months is Mikhail Gorbachev. Without the reforms inspired and encouraged by the Soviet president, there would be no movement toward democracy in East Germany, Poland, Hungary, Czechoslovakia, Romania and, yes, Lithuania. The Berlin Wall would still stand, the Ceausescus of Romania would still hold deadly power, Vaclav Havel would still be languishing in prison instead of leading the Czech people out of totalitarian darkness.

For progress to continue, Gorbachev must stay in power. His clash with Lithuanian secessionists is shaping up as a real test of that power and his personal prestige. If he is perceived as being humiliated, it could give Soviet hardliners a lever with which to pry themselves back into power. With the current state of East European politics so volatile, Gorbachev's ouster is not a far-fetched possibility.

Then what would we have? An old-time Stalinist — perhaps a general — likely would rise to power and set about reversing the reforms Gorbachev has fashioned. There would be a crackdown in the Warsaw Pact countries; democracy would be smothered in its crib. The new Soviet leader would launch military action against reluctant satellites — perhaps even a nuclear missile or two to prove a point. The Doomsday Clock would race toward midnight.

So the United States must be careful not to back Gorbachev into a corner on Lithuania. The Bush administration should support the freedom movement there, but it should not issue ultimatums to Moscow. As a practical matter, U.S. bellicosity will not help Lithuania's cause. In the long run it could prove to be destructive for the future of all of Europe — indeed, the world.

Lithuania's best hope lies in reaching peaceful accommodation with the Kremlin. Having tasted democracy, the impulse is to drink deeply. But the Soviets still hold all the real power, and care must be taken not to invite them to use it. Communication is better than confrontation — for Lithuania and for Moscow.

The way the tide of history is running, Lithuania will get what it seeks. It may not happen as quickly as Lithuanians would like. That's still better than not seeing it happen at all.

The Orlando Sentinel
Orlando, FL, March 28, 1990

As Soviet tanks and troops continue to menace Lithuania, the Bush administration suddenly and disturbingly has muted its criticism.

If the Soviets crack down, does this mean the White House plans a sickening, mild response similar to how it handled the Tiananmen Square massacre in China? That would be unconscionable.

No, a crackdown isn't inevitable. Although the Soviets used force in the republic of Georgia a year ago, they have vowed not to in response to Lithuania's declaration of independence.

And in truth, this matter can be resolved peacefully. Successful negotiations could become a precedent for others that consider loosening their ties to Moscow.

That's why it's vital for the United States and other countries interested in seeing reforms succeed in the Soviet Union to be very vocal in pushing the Kremlin to talk with Lithuania. They also can emphasize the consequences a Soviet crackdown would have.

Besides making a mockery of Soviet leader Mikhail Gorbachev's talk of openness, it would damage U.S.-Soviet relations. Mr. Gorbachev would be shortsighted to sacrifice that progress simply to show Lithuanians that he's in charge.

Yes, Lithuania's decision to secede conjures up the image of a disintegrating empire that is, understandably, frightening to Moscow. But this yearning to be independent also stems logically from the new thinking Mr. Gorbachev prompted.

Besides, the Soviets clearly are prepared to allow Eastern Europe to go its own way. Witness the spate of elections planned this year. Already, East Germany and Hungary have held free and fair votes.

Lithuania presents a touchier situation because it's located within Soviet boundaries, but Lithuanians deserve a similar opportunity to decide their future.

What's more, Lithuanians have given Moscow no pretext to use force. Protests have been peaceful. Lithuania's vote to secede, which has only symbolic value, was done through parliamentary channels. Lithuanians have acknowledged that it may take years to negotiate independence.

The point is that Mr. Gorbachev didn't need a show of force to convince Lithuanians that he would be tough to deal with, although he may have appeased Soviet hard-liners this way.

Now the challenge is to ease the crisis. So far, Soviet troops have occupied a few buildings in the Lithuanian capital and have roughed up some deserters. That's deplorable though not grave.

By ending this aggressive behavior while agreeing to terms for talks with Lithuania, Mr. Gorbachev would defuse a dangerous situation. He would also advance his program of reform, which so far has been admirable.

AKRON
BEACON JOURNAL
Akron, OH,
March 29, 1990

THE BATTLE of wills continues as strong-minded Lithuanian nationalists summon all the resources at their command in an attempt to face down the still-powerful government of the Soviet Union.

Lithuanian police are ignoring orders from the Kremlin to turn in shotguns and rifles given them by citizens. Soviet officials, insisting that they will restore law and order, have kept troops in place guarding the Lithuanian republic's Communist Party headquarters.

Lithuanians who evidently deserted from the Soviet army were dragged from a hospital where they had been hiding and were beaten.

In Washington, officials of the Bush administration seemed to be soft-pedaling any criticism of the Soviet regime, thus bringing, in turn, attacks from Lithuanian leaders and charges that Washington has sold out to Moscow in the dispute over freedom for the Baltic republic.

Obviously, the situation is volatile. But it would be difficult to find fault with President Bush and his advisers for wishing to tread softly.

It is, of course, a fact that Lithuania, along with Estonia and Latvia, was taken illegally by the Soviet Union 50 years ago. U.S. policy in regard to that land grab is plain since it has never recognized Soviet sovereignty.

But it is not enough for the Lithuanians to have right on their side against the Soviets. Secession presents too great a threat to the Kremlin. President Mikhail Gorbachev feels he has no choice but to react with strength. A successful separatist move in the Baltic would be disastrous to the unity of his country.

Allowing Lithuania to go its own way would mean virtually automatic freedom for Estonia and Latvia, with the possibility of further breakaways elsewhere in the Soviet Union.

The leaders in the Kremlin know that they cannot allow themselves to be seen as weak. If secession of some Soviet republics is to take place with the approval of Moscow, it will have to happen under the aegis of a strong regime.

With ethnic turmoil common across the length and breadth of the vast Soviet nation and the economy in a shambles, Gorbachev will do what he has to do to keep Lithuania in line. That concept is a bitter pill for Lithuanians to swallow, but it is also 1990 reality.

The Phoenix Gazette

Phoenix, AZ,
March 23, 1990

Lithuania's bid for independence presents Mikhail Gorbachev with the ultimate challenge. Will the Soviet leader revert to the behavior that has made the Soviet Union an outcast among nations since its inception?

Yuri Afanasyev, historian and deputy member of the Congress of People's Deputies, recently told that body what the world has known for 70 years: "The use of force and violence is our entire history. If our leader and founder (Lenin) laid the foundation of anything, it was the institution of mass violence and state terror."

Moscow's reaction to Lithuania's announcement of secession evokes unhappy memories of that legacy. In 1956, for example, Soviet promises of non-intervention in Hungary's bid for independence from Moscow still were being repeated as Soviet tanks rolled toward Budapest.

Gorbachev has called Lithuania's declaration of independence illegal, but also has promised not to use force to keep it from seceding. But Lithuanian officials are protesting increased Soviet military activity and Gorbachev's decree ordering citizens to turn in their guns.

A column of Soviet armored personnel carriers and army trucks reportedly drove through the center of the Lithuanian capital in the Kremlin's latest show of force.

Lithuanian president Vytautas Landsbergis is no irresponsible firebrand. Landsbergis has been a leading exponent of "peaceful revolution." At every stage he has discouraged violent protest and pushed for step-by-step constitutional measures to restore Lithuanian independence.

The bespectacled former music professor, however, lives with vivid memories of his childhood when, as an 8-year-old boy in 1940, he saw Soviet tanks occupy the former Lithuanian capital of Kaunas.

Landsbergis apparently is gambling that Moscow will not risk the international censure that might result from a Lithuanian bloodbath.

Gorbachev, however, also is playing for high stakes, knowing that, if Lithuania goes, other captive people could follow. And there were no international repercussions when Soviet troops attacked independence-minded civilians in Tiblisi, Georgia, last April, an event subsequently blamed on an overly zealous military commander.

The next move is Gorbachev's.

THE ARIZONA REPUBLIC

Phoenix, AZ,   March 23, 1990

ON March 11 the Lithuanian Soviet Socialist Republic declared its independence, removed the hammer-and-sickle from its flag and became the Republic of Lithuania. Fifty years after the Soviets occupied and annexed the tiny Baltic nation, the courageous Lithuanians had asserted their inalienable rights.

Did President Bush respond by extending diplomatic recognition to the new nation? In view of this country's long-standing defense of Baltic independence, such a response might have been expected.

Instead, Mr. Bush took a cautious approach, disavowing any wish to "to stir up trouble" in the Soviet Union — an uncomfortable reminder of the White House dithering last year when pro-democracy students occupied Beijing's Tiananmen Square.

How last year's restraint was received is well known. China's geriatric leaders, many of them friends from Mr. Bush's days as American envoy to the People's Republic, interpreted Washington's inaction as an all-clear signal. Is the same signal being received in Moscow?

Since the March 11 declaration, Mikhail Gorbachev has tightened the screws on the Lithuanians, using every means of intimidation at his disposal short of overt military force. The Lithuanians have reacted with stoic and courageous determination.

This week Mr. Gorbachev increased the pressure, ordering the KGB to disarm Lithuania's militia, confiscate firearms in private hands and stand guard at Lithuania's borders, customs posts and major industrial facilities.

The White House reacted "with concern." Press Secretary Marlin Fitzwater declined to see the Kremlin's renewed ferocity for what it was — tantamount to the use of force. "We don't have enough information," he said, as if any additional information were required.

This timidity is both unconscionable and dangerous. For 50 years the United States has refused to recognize the legality of Moscow's conquest of the "captive nations" of the Baltic. Yet now that the people of Lithuania, at no small risk, demand the return of their sovereignty, Washington recoils from this historically correct and honorable position.

The Lithuanians have risked their lives and fortunes, and Mr. Bush at least might offer moral support, some gesture that the U.S. stands with them. Instead, knuckling under to the perceived sensibilities of Mr. Gorbachev, Mr. Bush declares his faith in Mr. Gorbachev's disavowal of force — all the more reason for Washington to extend formal recognition to Lithuanian independence.

Once upon a time this country stood for freedom and self-determination for all people. It still does, though its leaders at times appear ignorant of the fact.

THE SACRAMENTO BEE

Sacramento, CA, March 28, 1990

Lithuania's declaration of independence and its refusal to submit to Soviet intimidation poses a serious challenge both to Mikhail Gorbachev and George Bush, committed as they are to improving East-West relations and reducing armaments in a changing Europe. How they act in the days ahead could have important effects on bilateral relations and, of course, on the future of Lithuania itself.

Gorbachev's professed devotion to democracy is being called into question as never before, notwithstanding his assurance to visiting Americans on Monday that his government has renounced "Cold War methods and a reliance on force ..." and supports the "right of peoples to choose and to equal security." As he said that, Soviet armored units were rumbling through the Lithuanian capital of Vilnius as troops occupied public buildings; yesterday, they began rounding up young Lithuanians who had refused to report back to their posts in the Soviet army, which they now regard as a foreign army. Witnesses said some of the young men were beaten up.

Such roughhouse tactics apparently don't fall within the Soviet president's definition of force. Perhaps only tanks firing at unarmed civilians qualifies as "Cold War methods." As the confrontation between Gorbachev and Lithuanian leaders hardens, one can't be sure that that won't happen: Soviet authorities have orchestrated anti-independence demonstrations in Vilnius by ethnic Russians, a time-tested means of stirring up violent clashes that might provide the pretext for stronger measures.

For Bush, the problem is no less challenging. Having finally embraced Gorbachev and his "new thinking," the president is trying, so far with some success, to support Lithuanian self-determination while not appearing to meddle in Soviet internal affairs, a tightrope act complicated by the fact that no U.S. administration has ever recognized Soviet sovereignty in Lithuania. What will Bush say or do if Gorbachev uses military force to suppress the autonomy he has vaguely supported in the past?

So far, Bush has not had to face that dilemma, and if cool heads prevail in Moscow and Vilnius, he may not have to. What's deeply troubling, however, is that neither Gorbachev nor Lithuanian leaders have left much room for flexibility. Both could have moderated their positions; instead, both have adopted policies from which to back down would entail a serious loss of face, if not worse. By defying Moscow in absolute terms, Lithuanians may provoke it into overreaction. But by doing that, Gorbachev would imperil the crumbling Soviet empire even more than he would have done by offering its minority peoples the local autonomy that, at the very least, they deserve. Anything Bush can do to remind Gorbachev of that fact might help.

The Register

Santa Ana, CA, March 25, 1990

Will somebody please tell George Bush that a bloodbath in Lithuania is worse than broccoli? While the president was joking about his distaste for the vegetable, he was being less than direct in his statements about the oppressive actions taken in Lithuania by Soviet President Mikhail Gorbachev.

As we go to press events are still unfolding, but at a minimum Mr. Bush should a) recognize the new, democratically elected government of Lithuania, headed by President Vytautas Landsbergis; b) tell Mr. Gorbachev that the Soviet Union has no right to give orders to Lithuania, an independent country, any more than it does to any other country; and c) if US diplomats and American journalists continue to be expelled from Lithuania, order all Soviet diplomats out of the United States.

Mr. Bush should also remind Mr. Gorbachev that as Soviet president he has done much to improve the lot of humankind, such as allowing freedom in Eastern Europe, and that that record should gain him praise, but that the murderous suppression of free Lithuania would depart from that good work. And that the image of a smiling Mr. Gorbachev the world sees today would, by the shedding of blood in the streets of Vilnius, become the image of Mikhail the Terrible, the Butcher of Lithuania.

Mr. Gorbachev should not think that his good image would survive being drenched in Lithuanians' blood, even though Mr. Bush's pusillanimous attitude toward Mr. Gorbachev's actions in Lithuania resembles the his soft reaction to the Tiananmen Square massacre last June. Mr. Gorbachev should look beyond Mr. Bush to world opinion. Just a year ago Chinese dictator Deng Xiao-ping was continually praised as a major reformer, but after the Tiananmen Square butchery Mr. Deng's image was transformed into that of a bloodthirsty tyrant, clutching at power atop a pile of corpses.

The spilling of blood in Lithuania would immediately cancel the work Mr. Gorbachev has done to get the US Congress to repeal trade sanctions against the Soviet Union. That action, combined with the actions of horror-stricken private Western companies and investors in America, Europe, and Japan, would severely curtail investment in Mr. Gorbachev's economic program, *perestroika*.

Such actions would send the already ailing Soviet economy into a steep downturn, leading to a possible revolt that could topple Mr. Gorbachev himself.

This is what the free world, in the voice of George Bush, should trumpet: Let Lithuania go, Mr. Gorbachev. In doing so you cast off not only Lithuanians' chains, but your own.

Richmond Times-Dispatch

Richmond, VA, March 28, 1990

Is Time's "Man of the Decade" about to become known as the Butcher of Vilnius? It is too soon to tell, but the latest Soviet actions in Lithuania are not encouraging. Mikhail Gorbachev is getting a reality check: There is no "third road" between communism and freedom. The question now is whether he will back down from his threats and let Lithuania (and thus much of the periphery of the Evil Empire) go or if he will maintain by force the long occupation of Lithuania.

The day after the Oscars, when well-known policy expert Jack Lemmon gushed from his post in Moscow about the wonderful things happening in the Soviet Union, capping things off with a smiling plea to call him "comrade," the Soviet occupation force began closing Lithuania to the outside world. Foreigners, including journalists, businessmen and diplomats, have been told to leave, and foreign travel to Lithuania has been stopped altogether. The Red Army is rounding up Lithuanian deserters in the republic, severely beating some of them.

The reaction of the Bush White House to all of this is only slightly less offensive than Comrade Lemmon's ringing endorsement of Kremlin policies. Like Comrade Lemmon, whose leftist proclivities are well-known, the best — and worst — that can be said about President Bush's reaction to the events in Lithuania is that he is being consistent. He declined to denounce Communist Chinese leaders following the bloodbath at Tiananmen Square, and he gave Mikhail Gorbachev successive byes in Soviet Georgia and Azerbaijan. We probably should not expect the president to behave any differently in regard to Lithuania, but one can always hope the White House will come to recognize moral principle.

Polish Solidarity leader Lech Walesa suffers from no such malady. In a strongly worded letter, the man who led the Polish freedom movement through 10 years of despair told Mr. Gorbachev that his actions were "in striking contradiction with the spirit of the policy you have been carrying out for years."

"Violating the sovereignty of Lithuania is an action directed against the process of constructing a new democratic order in Europe," Mr. Walesa wrote. "I turn to you, Mr. [Gorbachev], to abandon the practice of military pressure and undertake political dialogue with the Lithuanian government."

And the Bush White House? "We do not want to inflame the situation," spokesman Marlin Fitzwater told reporters (again) on Tuesday. Mr. Bush in mild terms has expressed publicly his displeasure with Soviet actions, and there are reports that the White House has sent private messages to Moscow as well. What is needed now is a much more forceful and public diplomatic offensive, which we have no doubt would startle the Kremlin. The Kremlin needs startling just now.

At this moment, Mikhail Gorbachev's most valuable asset may be his international reputation as a "reformer," a reputation highlighted by cozy relations with the United States. If he is persuaded that a violent crackdown in Lithuania would come with a large political cost in the form of suspended arms reduction negotiations (which the Kremlin is anxious to conclude) and other diplomatic measures, then perhaps he will let Lithuania go. But the public message coming from the White House in recent days, aside from an observation that it could "backfire," is that a crackdown in Lithuania would be a freebie.

Mr. Bush's dithering over Lithuania is unbecoming of the presidency, and it is far below the human rights standard the world has come to expect the United States to uphold. Mr. Walesa is among the few world leaders who seems to truly understand the perilous nature of the situation, as well as the necessity of waging this war of words in public. Mr. Bush should call him.

The Des Moines Register

Des Moines, IA, March 23, 1990

In a show of force Thursday, 15 Soviet armored personnel carriers and five heavy trucks rumbled through the Lithuanian capital of Vilnius. Will Soviet tanks soon follow? Not likely. Soviet President Mikhail Gorbachev cherishes his relations with the West. He's all too aware that a brutal crackdown on the independent-minded Lithuanians would bring back Cold-War tensions. Soviet officials repeatedly have said that they have no intention of mounting an attack.

Yet there's something unnerving about the growing war of words between Moscow and the Lithuanian capital of Vilnius. The two sides are said to be playing a game of bluff, setting the stage for talks regarding conditions for Lithuania's regaining its independence. But you've got to wonder whether somebody may soon take the posturing too far, resulting in martial-law crackdowns, or violence.

The Lithuanians have been modest with their goals. They've said they don't propose erecting a wall between their country and the Soviet Union. Moscow would have access to Lithuanian seaports. Long-term barter agreements would be proposed. Lithuania would not take over factories currently managed by Moscow.

Yet Gorbachev is pressured from his right and cannot ignore concerns that once Lithuania leaves, so will other Soviet Republics, taking with them economic resources and leaving Mother Russia weakened strategically. The president has taken considerable risk with his latest provocative tactic, ordering Lithuanians to turn in their guns, a move intended to cast Lithuanians as violent people and creating fears within them, aimed at dousing the fire of independence.

For people in the West, it's a troubling show from a leader who, probably too much so, has been regarded as a miracle worker. Is Gorbachev as much a thug as the Soviet leaders who preceded him? The answer, despite what has happened in Eastern Europe this week, still is no. But Gorbachev will need every bit of leadership skill he possesses not only to contain the desires of those in the Kremlin who would rush tanks into the Baltics, but also to recognize the unstoppable rush of Lithuanians toward their freedom.

Soviet Georgia Erupts In Nationalist Unrest

At least 16 people were killed April 9, 1989 in a clash between Soviet troops and nationalist demonstrators in Tbilisi, the capital of the republic of Georgia. Three wounded demonstrators died April 10-12, to raise the official death toll to 19. The bloodletting led to the ouster April 14 of two of the republic's top officials.

Georgia, with a population of 5.5 million, was part of the southern Trancaucasus region of the U.S.S.R., where ethnic tensions ran high. As in other republics of the Soviet Union, strong nationalist sentiments had taken hold in Georgia.

On Feb. 25, local security forces had broken up a protest by 15,000 people in Tbilisi marking the 68th anniversary of the annexation of Georgia by the Soviet Union. (Following the 1917 Bolshevik Revolution in Russia, Georgia – part of the Russian Empire – had declared independence under the Mensheviks, an anti-Bolshevik leftist political faction. The Georgian Mensheviks were overthrown by the Red Army in 1921.)

Some 500 people had been arrested Feb. 25, mainly members of the National Democratic of Georgia, one of the republic's main nationalist groups.

The situation had been complicated March 18 by a demand by a separatist force in Abkhazia, an autonomous republic within Georgian jurisdiction, to establish an independent Abkhazian homeland. Georgian nationalists instead favored total annexation of Abkhazia. Both sides had initiated strikes and mass protests to press their views. Over 100 Georgians launched a hunger strike April 4.

Abkhazia, with 500,000 people, was located on stretch of land on the Black Sea north of Georgia proper. The region had a minority population of predominantly Moslem ethnic Abkhazians and a majority population of predominantly Christian ethnic Georgians.

On April 7, Soviet troops and armored vehicles had taken up positions in Tbilisi to discourage repeated large-scale demonstrations and calls by some nationalists for a Georgian secession from the U.S.S.R. Georgian party leader Dzhumber Patiashvili made a televised appeal for calm.

In the clash April 9, at least 10,000 demonstrators gathered in Tbilisi's Lenin Square. Soldiers fired tear gas at the crowd when it defied orders to disperse. Witnesses said that troops waded into the protesters, beating them with batons and army shovels. Many people were reported to have fallen down and been trampled in the ensuing panic.

The official casualty count as of April 12 was 19 protesters dead and more than 200 people injured, including 75 troops. Nationalists claimed that 36 demonstrators had been killed. Tass, the official Soviet news agency, April 9 blamed the violence on "extremist-minded groups" and "antisocial elements." In the wake of the violence, the military April 10 established a curfew of 11 p.m. to 6 a.m. and closed Tbilisi to foreign journalists.

Separately, a leading Soviet toxicologist, Mikhail Vashakidze, confirmed that troops had used a form of poison gas to subdue a nationalist demonstrators in Tbilisi. Witnesses to the Tbilisi clash had reported the use of gas against demonstrators, but it had been assumed at that time to have been ordinary tear gas.

In a related development, three members of the U.S.-based Physicians for Human Rights May 24 reported their conclusions on the debate surrounding the purported use of poison gas surrounding the Tbilisi protesters. The team had spent a week in Georgia on a fact-finding tour.

According to the physicians, evidence suggested that the troops had used a standard antipersonnel gas (either CS or CN) containing the chemical agent chloropicrin, which was debilitating but not usually fatal. They theorized that at least some of the protesters sprayed at close range had died, not from choloropicrin per se, but from inhaling large doses of freon gas used to propel the chemical agent.

THE 〰 SUN

Baltimore, MD, April 11, 1989

The last time Soviet Georgia experienced explosions of long-latent tensions was 34 years ago. Nikita S. Khrushchev's experiments with decentralizing power led him to condemn Joseph Stalin, Georgia's native son and the man who had sired the whole Soviet colossus of repression. The third anniversary of the dictator's death sparked violent student demonstrations. The Red Army was called in; dozens of young people were killed, hundreds wounded. "Many in Georgia held Khrushchev personally responsible for ordering the army to fire on the unarmed crowd," a historian noted.

The Red Army this time clubbed demonstrators to death. As the toll climbed, Georgia's former Communist boss, foreign minister Eduard A. Shevardnadze, canceled a visit to East Germany so that he go help in restoring calm. This is serious stuff. Mikhail S. Gorbachev ultimately will be called before the party's Central Committee to answer for Georgia. And for the separatist movements in the Baltics. And for the agitation in Moldavia to replace the Cyrillic script with Latin alphabets. And for the nationalist sentiments threatening to spill over in the Ukraine, the largest of the 15 Soviet republics. The list goes on.

The history of the shah of Iran — how he tried to end repression and modernize a backward country only to unleash such uncontrollable forces and passions that they devoured him — has been often used as an argument that totalitarian societies are most vulnerable at their moment of liberalization. The gradual but accelerating spread of nationalism and separatism within the Soviet Union appears to support that theory.

Little else can be easily explained. The Baltic nations' quest for self-rule is an orderly exercise of persuasive arguments and demands. The Armenian and Azerbaijan turmoil turned into a pogrom on minorities. Whatever their ultimate aims, the protesting Georgians also seem to be seeking revenge on a minority, the Abkhazians, who they think have too many rights. All these convulsions are symptoms of a deeper malaise — the crisis of the Soviet system and its ethnic complexities.

This latest emergency in the Soviet Union just days after Mr. Gorbachev's return from his triumphant media tour of Cuba and the Great Britain points to an ironic dichotomy: he may be more popular and effective overseas than he is at home. But it also shows how little foreign countries can do to help him in his reforms and how inconsequential even his boldest international initiatives are when compared to his day-to-day challenges. Mr. Gorbachev wins or loses at home.

The Seattle Times

Seattle, WA, April 11, 1989

THE Soviet submarine that caught fire and broke apart last week could almost serve as a metaphor for the Soviet system itself: Troublesome fires keep bursting out in the Union of Soviet Socialist Republics these days, and the eventual outcome could be the breakup of the Soviet empire.

It won't happen overnight; Moscow's power over that vast and diverse country is still enormous. What's more, the Kremlin has all the guns — and is quite willing to use them even with the relatively benevolent Mikhail Gorbachev in command.

Consider last weekend's events in Tbilisi, the capital of Soviet Georgia. Thousands of demonstrators gathered for a public protest — which itself would have been impossible only a few years ago. They included a hard core of hunger strikers demanding more autonomy from Moscow and establishment of an independent Georgian government.

Troops and tanks were called in to control the demonstration. The Soviets commonly deploy soldiers in each republic whose ethnic backgrounds differ from the local population, so natural animosities often heighten tensions.

A predawn standoff erupted into violence; at least 18 demonstrators were killed and more than 100 wounded. Several dozen soldiers also were injured.

It was reportedly a nasty scene: Those who died were clubbed to death with riot clubs or trampled underfoot by the panicked crowd.

This is only the latest nationalities crisis to confront Gorbachev, whose policies of looser control and political reform threaten to touch off runaway demands that he will find difficult to meet.

From Estonia, Latvia and Lithuania in the north; the Ukraine, Crimea and Moldavia to the West, and to Armenia, Azerbaijan and Uzbekistan in the south, citizens of the non-Russian Soviet republics are increasingly restive and militant.

Sparks of discontent are flaming up throughout the Soviet Union, and the Kremlin's firefighters will be hard-pressed to keep them all under control.

FORT WORTH STAR-TELEGRAM

Fort Worth, TX, April 11, 1989

Give some people a little taste of freedom, and more quickly than you can say *glasnost*, they want the whole platter.

That fundamental truth about the human spirit has been demonstrated dramatically by the current upheaval in the Soviet Union's Georgian republic, where scores of people demonstrating for political independence have been killed or injured in clashes with police and Soviet troops.

The trouble in Tbilisi, Georgia's capital, would be a less troubling matter for the Soviet leadership if it were an isolated phenomenon. After all, the Georgians are a proud people, jealous of their language and traditions, who historically have resisted the rule of many foreign occupiers, including the Greeks, Romans, Mongols, Turks and the Russian czars.

Georgia enjoyed a brief period of independence from 1918 to 1921, after the expulsion of the czar, when the Menshevik government was in power in the Soviet Union. But when Lenin came to power, the Bolsheviks incorporated the small country into their realm.

Joseph Stalin, a native of Georgia, brutally suppressed all resistance to domination from Moscow. A greater percentage of the educated and professional classes was eliminated during the purges of 1936-37 in Georgia than anywhere else in the European part of the Soviet Union. But the Georgians clung to their heightened sense of national consciousness.

It is not surprising, then, that they have seized upon the opening presented to them by *glasnost* to give vent to their perpetual yearning for independence. But Mikhail Gorbachev cannot downplay the Tbilisi uprising as merely a case of Georgians being Georgians, because the problem is far more grave.

A pattern of national and ethnic unrest is straining the seams of the Soviet fabric, reflected in the demands for greater autonomy in the Baltic states, Armenia, Azerbaijan, the Ukraine, Kazakhstan and Moldavia.

That ferment could cause the unraveling of the Soviet Union as presently constituted or the abandonment of much of *glasnost* and perhaps the fall of Gorbachev. In order to satisfy the hardliners in the Soviet leadership, Gorbachev may be forced crack down hard on the rebellious or secessionist elements.

But neither Gorbachev nor his critics should delude themselves into believing the Soviet Union's nationalistic problems can be solved with force and suppression. Glasnost did not cause the problem. It merely allowed the ethnic populations to vent some their frustrations and make their aspirations known. The desire for freedom and independence is strong in many of the Soviet republics and is intensifying.

The Soviet leadership must respond to that movement constructively or face shattering social and political cataclysm.

The Houston Post

Houston, TX, April 24, 1989

MIKHAIL GORBACHEV'S policy of *glasnost*, or openness, faces one of its most critical tests as the Kremlin probes charges that the military used poison gas on peacefully demonstrating Soviet civilians. Possibly spurred by press reports and a secretly filmed video tape, a top-level criminal investigation has begun into the brutal crushing of protests in Soviet Georgia.

The official death toll was 20, with another 200 injured, in the April 9 incident in the southern Soviet republic. But Eduard Gudava, a Soviet dissident and rights activist, has urged President Bush to ask for a U.N. investigation, claiming that the number killed was much higher. And Soviet newspapers, including the official paper, Izvestia, reported that toxic chemical weapons were used to break up the pro-independence rally in the Georgian capital of Tbilisi.

The clandestinely shot video, shown to journalists in Moscow, contained scenes of gas cannisters being fired and people trying to protect themselves. The tape also showed deep wounds on bodies, contradicting the official line that the troops used restraint.

The question is who ordered the brutal assault on 8,000 protesters. And if poison gas was used, who made that decision?

Elder Shengelaya, the Georgian filmmaker who showed the video, and others believe those orders came from Moscow. Is the investigation by the Prosecutor's Office of the Soviet Union a move to discredit opponents of Soviet leader Gorbachev's *perestroika* reforms?

There is already speculation that the vicious crackdown on the Georgian demonstrators was intended to embarrass Gorbachev. The head of the republic's Communist Party and its prime minister have resigned.

The candor with which the press has reported the incident is astonishing, even in the age of *glasnost*. So is the showing of the video by Shengelaya, who was recently elected to the new Soviet parliament.

It is tempting to equate these expressions of openness with Western-style freedom of the press. That would be a mistake. As long as Gorbachev is in control, *glasnost* will go just as far as he wants it to go and no further. Still, it will be interesting to see if the probe confirms that civilians were attacked by troops using poison gas, and, if so, who is blamed.

The Charlotte Observer

*Charlotte, NC,
April 12, 1989*

Americans, who would like to see all the Soviet peoples liberated from the stultifying yoke of communist rule, nonetheless must watch nervously as demonstrators in Soviet Georgia and other national enclaves take to the streets demanding autonomy and even independence. In Washington, this must be a time for steadiness.

Georgia, of course, is not the only Soviet republic in ferment. The winds of national pride have been blowing fiercely all through the Soviet empire, an agglomeration of separate nationalities with their own distinctive culture, history and language. But the name of "Georgia" ought to remind us Americans how our own national government reacted when secessionist fever broke out in our Georgia and the other Southern states some 70 years after the adoption of the U.S. Constitution.

Although the Soviet Constitution grants the right of secession in Article 72, Mikhail Gorbachev is not likely to wish a pleasant "bon voyage" to his empire's unhappy nationalities. If the Soviet government decides it is impossible to have both reform and order, it is likely to decide that it will at least try to have order. That would cement the reign of misery at home for another generation, threaten the nascent liberalization in the satellite states of Eastern Europe and, for the West, dash the hope of finding security at lower cost and less tension.

That is not in anyone's interest, least of all ours. What Washington ought to encourage in the Soviet bloc is liberalization and reform, but not chaos. That should not mean a "new Yalta," an agreement effectively guaranteeing another generation of Soviet hegemony in Eastern Europe — something that is hardly guaranteeable today in any case. But Washington can make clear that we will recognize, and reward, increased political and economic freedom within the Soviet bloc. The Soviets must see that normalization within their own sphere — including humane treatment even of extreme dissidents — is the route to normal and stable relations with the West

THE ARIZONA REPUBLIC

Phoenix, AZ, April 16, 1989

THE day after Mikhail Gorbachev returned to Moscow from his successful visit to Great Britain, a decree was adopted by the Presidium of the Supreme Soviet that introduced sweeping new additions to the criminal code on "anti-state activities."

The decree, published last week in *Pravda*, is aimed squarely at the recent nationalistic uprisings in some of the non-Russian republics, the most recent of which took place in Soviet Georgia where a peaceful demonstration in the capital of Tbilisi was broken up by shovel-wielding police. As many as 50 Georgians may have died in the clash. Tanks and Red Army troops now patrol Tbilisi.

Mr. Gorbachev signed the decree that makes it a crime to criticize the government or the Communist Party, as these excerpts reveal:

"Public appeal for the overthrow of the Soviet political and social order, or its alteration by means which are inconsistent with the Constitution of the USSR, or are inconsistent with the implementation of Soviet laws with the aim to disrupt the political and economic system of the USSR, as well as the preparation and dissemination of materials of this nature — is punishable by the deprivation of freedom for a term of up to three (3) years or a fine of up to 2,000 rubles.

"Such activity, carried on continuously or organized by a group of persons, utilizing technical means adapted for mass publication is punishable by the deprivation of freedom for a term of up to seven (7) years or a fine of up to 5,000 rubles."

The decree does not, however, stop at such subversive activities as appealing for the "alteration" of the Soviet political order. Even criticism of the party bosses is a crime:

"A public defamation or the slander of highest organs of state power and the government of the USSR, other state organs, formed or elected by the Congress of People's Deputies of the USSR, officials appointed, elected or ratified by the Congress ... or the Supreme Soviet of the USSR, as well as social or public organizations and their all-Union organs — is punishable by the deprivation of freedom for a term of up to three (3) years and a fine of up to 2,000 rubles."

Some Western monitors of the Helsinki accords on human rights have dismissed the April 11 decree, alleging that the Soviet Union has always had such laws. Coming as it does, however, in the midst of the nationalistic uprisings in Armenia, the Baltic republics, the Ukraine and now Georgia, the decree clearly signals Moscow's intention to crack down in those ethnic regions forcibly annexed to the Soviet Union in the past.

Unlike Mr. Gorbachev's admirers in the West, the Ukrainian Helsinki Union had no difficulty understanding his intention. The group said the decree "signifies a total reversal to anti-democratic methods" and charged that Mr. Gorbachev's warm welcome in London encouraged him to sign the measure.

"If the West would have been more critical and careful in noting violations of legality and international legal statues, which were effectuated during the period of so-called democratization, *glasnost* and *perestroika* ... then perhaps this decree would not have appeared," the Ukrainian statement said.

The criminal code revisions establish that *glasnost* clearly has its limits, and that Mr. Gorbachev will tolerate greater openness only where as it serves his ends.

The Boston Globe

Boston, MA, April 13, 1989

WHEN Mikhail Gorbachev came to power four years ago he had little background in the Soviet Union's nationalities problem. He's a Russian, and had served primarily in the Russian Republic. But as *glasnost* took hold and political expression crackled to life, Mr. Gorbachev began a crash course in nationalism – the latest lesson of which has come from Soviet Georgia.

Last weekend's violent confrontation between troops and demonstrators in Tbilisi, the Georgian capital, was among the sharpest outbreaks of nationalistic fervor yet. Eighteen people are reported to have died in the melee.

The passions in Georgia, as earlier in Armenia, were stimulated by unrest in an autonomous region – in this case the Black Sea enclave of Abkhazia, which is administered by Georgia. The Abkhazians, a minority even in their own region, want independence from Tbilisi. Their protests sparked Georgian nationalism, which culminated in demands for outright independence from Moscow.

Force has quieted things in Georgia for now, but underlying emotions are far from subdued. The Georgians have always been fiercely independent, maintaining a distinctive culture and language despite long domination by stronger powers.

The same can be said about their neighbors, the Armenians, whose push to absorb the largely Armenian region of Nagorno Karabakh (now part of the Azerbaijan Republic) springs from a historic desire to unify a fragmenting nation. The Baltic peoples want the freedom to pursue progressive economic and political paths unencumbered by Moscow's strings. The Ukrainians want to keep their language from being erased by creeping Russification.

Gorbachev has shown a willingness to discuss such matters and avoid the instant crackdown. But when things have gotten to the point of rebellion, as in Tbilisi, the tanks and troops have moved in. He has to gamble, perhaps, that events like those in Georgia will dampen the plans of nationalists elsewhere who might be tempted to stray too far from the politically acceptable.

Georgians, Estonians, Armenians, and others know, too, that their aspirations – if overplayed – could cause the Russians themselves to rally round the empire.

Risks abound. Gorbachev, by loosening the bureaucratic noose around the Soviet economy, has unloosed ever-simmering nationalisms. He hopes that economic reform can produce results quickly enough to draw the country together around a system that works. The old system was held together by an ideological web that's fraying rapidly, creating an intellectual void. New ways of thinking, including a rebirth of religion – and, of course, a resurgence of nationalism – are helping to fill that void.

The rest of the world can only look on in wonder. No one – most of all the Russians who dominate the Kremlin – knows how it will all turn out.

THE PLAIN DEALER

Cleveland, OH, April 11, 1989

The incredible complexity of the Soviet Union's ethnic makeup, and its potential for unraveling the Marxist-Leninist empire, is fully illustrated by the current disturbances in Georgia, birthplace of Stalin. Not only are nationalistic Georgians demanding independence from the U.S.S.R., but other ethnic groups under Georgian control, complaining about mistreatment, also are threatening to secede. By using the army to crush dissent, the Kremlin risks inflaming the anti-Soviet passions that have surfaced recently in the republic.

Oddly, while Georgians harbor strong nationalistic impulses, they had not been in the vanguard of separationist movements that recently have engaged the Kremlin's concern. Unlike the Baltic states, which Stalin annexed after they had enjoyed decades of independence, Georgia has not seeemed a likely candidate for breakaway. While Stalin conducted one of his bloodiest purges in his homeland, he also helped its economy develop to the point where living standards were the highest in the Soviet Union.

Nonetheless, Georgians retained a degree of economic independence that often clashed with Kremlin policies. Black markets thrived in a region blessed with abundant and prosperous agricultural enterprises. In addition, ethnic consciousness, nurtured by centuries of distinctive language, religious and cultural flourishings, survived in Georgia and appears to have received extra stimulation from Mikhail S. Gorbachev's *glasnost* doctrine. It hardly needs stating that Gorbachev did not intend that his call for more openness in Soviet society should encourage the Soviet republics and possessions to split from Moscow, causing blood to flow in provincial capitals as demonstrators and police collided.

When violence erupted Sunday in Tbilisi, Georgia's capital, troops were pitted against unarmed dissidents who were violating a ban on public gatherings. Details are not clear, but it appears that troops fired in the air, then charged demonstrators with riot sticks. Tass said the dissidents hurled rocks, sticks and pieces of metal. There was a crush, in which at least 16 people died.

Even if the official account is substantially correct and the troops did not fire on the crowd, they appear to have provoked a stampede by their tough tactics. The State Department called on Soviet authorities to use restraint in dealing with peaceful protests, which the United States supports.

A complex ethnic web, indeed. But a Soviet regime that talks of peace and enhanced relations with old enemies abroad endangers new relationships when its principal response to its own restless populations is the big stick. Ironically, in sending Foreign Minister Eduard A. Shevardnadze, former head of the Georgian Communist Party, to help restore calm, the Politburo may be asking him to perform a more important task than almost any he has done overseas.

THE CHRISTIAN SCIENCE MONITOR

Boston, MA, April 11, 1989

A specter is haunting the Kremlin. Ethnic and nationalist passions, suppressed since the Bolshevik Revolution, are erupting in one region after another of the Soviet Union, like premonitions of a political earthquake.

The violence in Georgia this past weekend illustrates the gravity of the danger to Soviet authorities. Their anxiety is evident. They cannot help fearing that the nationalist ardors expressed on the streets of Tbilisi, the Georgian capital, will imperil the cohesion of the Soviet Union, its political and economic unity.

As territorial and administrative quarrels escalate among the disparate peoples of the Kremlin's domestic empire, nationalist resentments against the central government billow into secessionist demands. This is what happened in Georgia, where the course of events somewhat resembles the turmoil in Armenia and Azerbaijan.

Moslems in the Autonomous Republic of Abkhazia staged demonstrations last month to demand an end to Georgia's administrative control of their region. The party chief of Abkhazia was replaced last Thursday because he signed a letter in March requesting the change.

Georgians reacted by staging their own rallies against the secessionist claims of the Moslem Abkhazians. The Georgians, feeling their national prerogatives threatened, called for suppression of Abkhazia's autonomous status. The brief for Georgian control of Abkhazia evokes a 1979 census showing that, even within Abkhazia, Georgians outnumber Moslems by almost three-to-one.

Georgians demanding the suppression of Abkhazian independence translated their indignation against Moslem neighbors into a call for Georgian independence from Soviet central authority.

To preserve his programs and his power, Mikhail Gorbachev may have to become a Soviet equivalent of Abraham Lincoln, a leader who puts the unity of his nation before all else.

Soviet Troops Sent to Azerbaijan in Bid to End Ethnic Civil War

The Soviet government dispatched troops to the southern republic of Azerbaijan Jan. 15, 1990 in an effort to quell a virtual ethnic civil war between Moslem Azerbaijanis and Christian Armenians. Five thousand interior ministry troops were already stationed in the Transcaucasus region.

Sporadic outbreaks of violence between the two ethnic groups had been occurring since 1988, fueled by conflicting claims to Nagorno-Karabakh, a predominantly Armenian enclave under the control of the Azerbaijan republic. At least 120 people had dies in 1988-89.

Azerbaijanis had been conducting a railroad blockade of Armenia since early December 1989. The conflict escalated sharply in 1990. Even as the troops were being dispatched, heavily armed Armenian and Azerbaijani guerrillas were fighting along the Armenia-Azerbaijani border. Both sides were reported to have automatic rifles, machine guns, mortars and hand grenades.

Soviet President Mikhail S. Gorbachev Jan. 15 signed a decree issued by the Presidium (executive council) of the Supreme Soviet (the national standing legislature). The decree declared a state of emergency in Azerbaijan and approved the airlifting of about 11,000 military, KGB (state security) and interior ministry troops to the republic to restore order.

"Extremist groups are organizing mass disorders, provoking strikes, fanning national enmity," the decree said. "They are committing bold criminal acts, mining roads and bridges, shelling settlements, taking hostages."

Accounts of the developments in the southern region were complicated by a Kremlin ban on foreign journalists in Azerbaijan. Moscow-based Western journalists had to rely on the official Soviet media and on telephone interviews with people in the troubled area.

The bloodletting in the Transcaucasus area, coupled with the rebuff of Gorbachev by independence-minded Lithuania, was posed a major nationalist challenge to the president.

Both Azerbaijani nationalists and the Kremlin were upset Jan. 9, when the Armenian Supreme Soviet (parliament) passed legislation incorporating Nagorno-Karabakh into an overall 1990 socioeconomic plan for Armenia.

Among other provisions, the legislation was designed to integrate Nagorno-Karabakh into the Armenian economy and would have allowed citizens of the enclave to vote in elections in the Armenian republic. The presidium of the national Supreme Soviet declared the law unconstitutional Jan. 10

In response to the Kremlin move, Armenia's parliament Jan. 11 adopted a resolution asserting Armenia's right to override national laws that affected the republic.

An anti-Armenian rally in the Azerbaijani capital, Baku, turned ugly Jan. 13, as Azerbaijani youths went on a rampage in the Armenian section of the city. Armenians were beaten, shot and stabbed to death, and burned alive. Their homes and shops were looted. At least 30 people, mostly Armenians, were killed during the violence, which lasted into Jan. 14.

Both sides reacted to the Baku killings by forming so-called volunteer militias and self-defense organizations, which clashed on the Armenian-Azerbaijani border and in and around Nagorno-Karabakh.

The Kremlin Jan. 17 ordered the troops airlifted to the Transcaucasus region to fire on militants in self-defense and to protect civilians. The death toll reached 56 by Jan. 17, including an unspecified number of troops attacked by the warring factions.

The White House and the U.S. State Department Jan. 16 supported the sending of Soviet troops to the Transcaucusus region.

The Chattanooga Times
Chattanooga, TN, January 23, 1990

The Soviet government's military response to turmoil in Azerbaijan is at once understandable and frightening in its potential ramifications. The eruption of inter-ethnic violence there, and particularly the rampaging mobs of Azerbaijanis who murdered innocent Armenian citizens in the capital city of Baku, created an untenable situation. Nevertheless, the loss of scores of lives during the army occupation of the city is a cause of great concern, as is the likelihood that the troubles in Azerbaijan and neighboring Armenia will not be quickly or easily pacified.

Soviet President Mikhail Gorbachev justified the use of Soviet troops on grounds that Azerbaijani extremists had their sights set on a forcible seizure of power and were pushing people "to the madness of fratricidal war." The Bush administration gave qualified support to Moscow, saying any government has the responsibility to maintain order and protect its citizens. But the United States properly tempered its position by warning that the "effort to establish order should not . . . become a cloak for the abridgment of the exercise of political rights."

There were troubling charges that the Soviet military fired indiscriminately on civilian non-combatants during its advance on Baku, but those allegations have not been confirmed. And at least one reporter from the Baltic republic of Estonia who witnessed the operation said he saw no such abusive tactics. Moreover, the Soviet military made no effort Monday to bar mass gatherings of Azerbaijani citizens to bury their dead. Obviously, Soviet restraint is essential if the tragedy of conflict in this region is not to be enlarged.

Moscow appears to have enforced calm, at least in Baku and at least for now; and Armenians and Azerbaijanis took a tentative step toward peace in local truce talks Monday. But the mass demonstrations and a general strike to protest military enforcement of civil order demonstrates the population's deep-seated resistance. And the Azerbaijani parliament threatened to consider secession if Moscow does not withdraw its troops.

Warnings that Azerbaijan could become Mr. Gorbachev's domestic Afghanistan must be taken seriously. Enmity between Moslem Azerbaijanis and Christian Armenians dates back centuries, and a peaceful resolution of conflict there will not come easily.

For Mr. Gorbachev, of course, the turmoil in the southern republics adds to the broader political problem of dealing, on the one hand, with nationalistic movements in other restive republics, and, on the other, with hard-line Communists who blame his reform program for the restiveness. Ironically, as former U.S. ambassador to the Soviet Union George Kennan told Congress recently, Mr. Gorbachev's hold on power may be secured largely by the reluctance of hard-line rivals to take on the problems he now faces.

MILWAUKEE SENTINEL

Milwaukee, WI, January 24, 1990

It is small wonder that Soviet President Mikhail S. Gorbachev reportedly started looking for a compromise with the nationalist front in Azerbaijan after support for secession from the Soviet Union emerged in the Azerbaijani legislature.

The secession threat is aimed at forcing the withdrawal of Soviet troops from Azerbaijan. Ultimately, Gorbachev's choice could be to pull out and leave chaos behind or commit even more troops to suppressing the ethnic and religious strife that has ravaged the West Asian republic.

Such an emergency might keep Gorbachev in power — who would want to take over under such circumstances? It also could be the final blow to grandiose, though unfulfilled, plans for economic restructuring, particularly if the unrest persisted and provoked another Afghanistan-type occupation in Azerbaijan.

In any case, the reported offer to compromise is only the latest indication of Gorbachev's second-guessing himself.

In Lithuania, earlier this month, he conceded that a non-communist government might come to power. In Azerbaijan, more recently, he yielded to the pleas of mothers and retracted an order that reservists go into that republic to quell ethnic and religious disturbances. Regular army troops were sent instead.

But that left an image of Gorbachev with the blood of Soviet citizens on his hands, as estimates of civilian dead in Azerbaijan ranged from fewer than 70 to several thousand. That is strikingly out of character for a man whose strength has been epitomized by his ability to walk into crowds and deal with people, one on one, as the consummate persuader.

Walking into a crowd could be dangerous in Azerbaijan, but his offer to compromise is a similar device. No one can guess, however, whether it will be any less persuasive to the Azerbaijanis than the barrel of a gun.

The Evening Gazette

Worcester, MA, January 23, 1990

The Soviet government had to send army troops and internal security forces to halt the fighting between militant Azerbaijanis and members of the Armenian minority. It had no choice. Atrocities had to be brought to an end to save lives and prevent a civil war in two Soviet republics.

Threats of secession by Azerbaijan are just as intolerable as the bloodshed. The possibility of the Soviet Union's disintegration could lead to the downfall of Mikhail Gorbachev. That in turn would almost certainly bring back hard-line control by Moscow, and the republics would lose whatever independence they have gained.

Kept under check by decades of communist rule, hostilities between the two ethnic groups in the Caucasus erupted after Gorbachev's reforms gave minorities across the Soviet Union limited self-determination.

Animosity between Azerbaijanis — the predominant ethnic group of the southern Soviet republic — and ethnic Armenians has existed for a long time. It grew into violence after Armenia announced its intention to disputed Armenian enclave within the Republic of Azerbaijan.

Barbarism has swept the region, with reports of extreme brutality against individuals and intense fighting between large armed groups.

Thousands of Armenians were forced to flee. Hundreds died on both sides as Soviet troops tried to restore order.

The tragedy is immense: At a time when those oppressed minorities would have a chance to build a better future, Soviet soldiers had to be dispatched to protect them from each other.

The irony in this appalling situation is that, at least on the surface, communist control did provide ethnic, religious and racial stability in the past.

The future of Gorbachev and his democratic reforms, as well as the evolution of pluralistic systems in Eastern Europe, largely depend on the Soviet leader's ability to prevent chaos.

If he fails, not only Armenians and Azerbaijanis will suffer but millions of people across the Soviet

The Houston Post

Houston, TX, January 25, 19

THERE ARE DIFFERENCES betwee Russian troops' shooting down civ ians in Baku and Chinese troop slaughtering students in Beijing. But both inc dents reaffirm the bankruptcy of communis as an ideological or governing force.

China's Communist hard-liners ordered tl Tiananmen Square massacre and its repressiv aftermath to crush peaceful demonstrations f democratic reform. Reformist Soviet lead Mikhail Gorbachev ordered the military in Baku, the capital of his Azerbaijan republic, quell ethnic strife verging on civil war.

This is but the latest episode in a long histo of bloodletting between the Moslem Azerbajani majority and the Christian Armenian nority in the southern Soviet republic borde ing Iran. The animosity has been aggravat by the Kremlin's refusal to put the Armeni enclave of Nogorno Karabakh in Azerbaij under the neighboring republic of Armenia.

In using military force, Gorbachev acted the plausible premise that a government mu maintain order and protect its citizens. But t assault on Baku (Houston's Soviet sister cit has been met with continued violence, an c tanker blockade of the Caspian Sea port anc threat of secession by the republic's parliame if the troops aren't withdrawn.

Though the outside world is getting far mc information than it would have under a Stal coverage of the trouble has been no trium for glasnost, Gorbachev's policy of openness

The official death toll from the Baku assa was put at 83, with a total of 170 killed so far the latest round of Azerbaijani-Armenian figh ing. But there are contradictory reports ar rumors that hundreds, even thousands, ha been killed. So far, no credible evidence su ports the higher figures.

While many details are lacking, it is obviou that the republic's Communist Party leadersh has failed to head off or control the violenc There also are indications that, despite his r sort to force, Gorbachev would like to fir moderates in the outlawed Azerbaijan Peopl Front willing to negotiate. The undergrour group is organizing much of the resistance.

Ethnic hatred is only one of the forces dri ing the unrest. Another and more powerf force is nationalism, as it is in the Soviet Bal republics of Latvia, Estonia and Lithuania. Tl Azerbaijanis have no strong allegiance to et nic-Russian-dominated Moscow. Neither, f that matter, do the people of the republics Georgia, Armenia and Moldavia.

The Bush administration has supported tl "territorial integrity" of the Soviet Union. But has also prudently encouraged a dialogue b tween the Kremlin and its unruly subjects.

Shrewd politician that he is, Gorbachev e tricated his country from its no-win involv ment in Afghanistan. Unless he is pushed to hard by independence-minded militants, l seems more likely to pursue a political rath than a military solution to the Azerbaijan stri

The last thing he needs is an Afghan-sty guerrilla war inside the Soviet Union.

THE INDIANAPOLIS STAR

Indianapolis, IN,
January 19, 1990

"Civil war" is the term a correspondent for *Komsomolskaya Pravda* applied to the fighting in the Caucasus, although tribal war would be more accurate for the centuries-old hostility between the mostly Christian Armenians and mainly Moslem Azerbaijanis.

It flared again when the Armenian Soviet Socialist Republic asked in February 1988 for annexation of Nagorno-Karabakh, a predominantly Armenian territory that was attached to the Azerbaijan SSR in 1923. It has been flashing with varying ferocity for nearly two years. Soviet internal security forces have tried without success to control it during that time.

The latest escalating outbreak is the most violent. Armenians in Azerbaijan seem to be getting the worst of it. Anti-Armenian rioting erupted Saturday in the Caspian Sea port city of Baku, where people were reported burned alive and a witness said women were thrown from windows.

Only a few thousand Armenians remain of the 220,000 who lived in the oil-producing city of 1.7 million population in 1988. Some 2,000 have been evacuated by plane and ferry in the last few days.

The Kremlin this week declared a state of emergency. A Page 1 commentary in *Izvestia* said: "*Perestroika* has been forced to defend itself. And it's not its fault if to defend itself and others, it needs the aid of emergency measures."

The emergency measures include a ban on strikes and demonstrations, imposition of curfews, censorship, confiscation of weapons, the disbanding of unofficial organizations and the detention of people for up to 30 days.

At the same time, 6,000 more internal security troops and 5,000 Red Army troops were sent into the area.

Both Armenian and Azerbaijani militants were capturing weapons and ammunition wherever they could get them, and the hills around Nagorno-Karabakh were thick with guerrilla fighters, some of them manning anti-aircraft guns. Correspondents said the area resembled scenes from World War II.

White House spokesman Marlin Fitzwater said: "We recognize the right of any state to ensure the safety of its citizens, and it looks like that is the primary concern at the moment."

The territory south of the Caucasus Mountains has joined others around the world, including Lebanon, Northern Ireland, Sri Lanka, Nigeria, Burundi and Cyprus, where politics, weapons and long-standing rivalries have exploded into violence and suffering.

However, the escalating conflict over Nagorno-Karabakh could have a far wider geopolitical impact if, along with other upheavals in the Soviet Union and along its borders, it led to a shakeup restoring a hard-line faction to power in the Kremlin.

San Francisco Chronicle

San Francisco, CA,
January 19, 1990

AS THE SITUATION in Azerbaijan deteriorates, Soviet leader Mikhail Gorbachev must deal with a critical pressure point: the long-standing political-religious-ethnic feud that has erupted into widespread violence there. Here is trial by fire at a time of particular vulnerability.

Gorbachev has, so far, made appropriate moves. Troops have been dispatched in a primarily peacekeeping mode to this caldron of dispute — to protect Armenian refugees from the depredations of Azerbaijani nationalists; to separate extremists on both sides, and to demonstrate that Moscow does not intend to sit idly by for bloody insurrection.

Gorbachev has widespread backing at home

At home, Gorbachev is getting considerable support. People interviewed in the streets of Moscow were almost unanimous in their backing of the way he has handled Azerbaijan. The situation had become so dangerous, they said, that he had no choice but to use troops to try to stabilize it.

THAT EXPERT on Soviet-American relations, the so-often prescient George Kennan, told Congress earlier this week that Gorbachev is in "danger," but not likely to be replaced soon because his troubles are so acute that even rivals may not want his job.

The United States has quite properly confirmed American backing for Gorbachev in his efforts to halt fighting between Armenians and Azerbaijanis. It is in our interest and the world's — as well as his — to have the Soviet leader put out this conflagration.

The Seattle Times

Seattle, WA, January 16, 1990

MIKHAIL Gorbachev increasingly resembles a locomotive engineer trapped in a runaway train. He started the huge machine in motion, but now it's rolling out of control and he's not sure how to slow it down.

Gorbachev's latest desperate move: He no longer objects to the legalization of multiple political parties in the Soviet Union.

It's an astonishing reversal of long-established policy in the U.S.S.R., where the Communist Party has held a legal monopoly on power for 72 years. In fact, the party's omnipotence is codified in the Soviet constitution.

But Gorbachev is merely facing up to reality. Lithuania and Latvia already have legalized other political parties, which will run against the Communists in the next elections. Gorbachev made his remarkable declaration in an address to Lithuanian dissidents: "I do not see anything tragic about a multiparty system if it emerges and meets the realistic interests of society."

Still, a multiparty system is "not a cure-all," Gorbachev warned. "Democracy and openness are the main things."

An open, democratic system with competing parties will not solve all of the Soviet Union's problems. Events in the Caucasus, where centuries-old ethnic and religious rivalries between Azerbaijanis and Armenians have burst into a bloody feud, make that depressingly clear.

But as long as the Soviet Union remains a one-party empire with a central, authoritarian government, prospects for genuine political progress and economic improvement are nil.

Gorbachev, embattled engineer, is struggling to keep his reform train on the tracks before he falls, or is pushed, off.

©1990 PITTSBURGH POST GAZETTE TIM MENEES.

ARMENIANS

AZERBAIJANIS

THE LINCOLN STAR

Lincoln, NE,
January 17, 1990

The first requirement of a productive, civilized society is a degree of stability.

The Soviet Union appears to be on the edge of losing it.

Civil war has broken out in the Nagorno-Karabakh region of Azerbaijan. The Baltic republics are dead set on quick independence, which threatens to unravel other territories. Midwinter food shortages are occurring, now even in Moscow. The authority and ability of the Communist Party to respond to multiplying crises is crumbling.

Mikhail Gorbachev, hailed as the man of the decade in the West only last month, may go down in history as a tragic figure. Best judgment predicts he has only weeks or days to find stability or to face ouster.

The disintegration of any society, no matter how repressive its history, is not pretty. Anarchy is never a solution. It terrorizes the weak and innocent and makes a fertile breeding ground for harsh tyrants. In a climate of want and fear, civility is trampled.

A fractured, bleeding Soviet Union will further destabilize Europe. A scenario of Red Army divisions with nuclear capabilities facing off is frightening to everyone.

There was a time for Americans to wish the Soviet Union ill. Now is the time to wish it the courage and wisdom to stabilize, to step back from the brink of chaos.

THE ARIZONA REPUBLIC

Phoenix, AZ, January 24, 1990

MIKHAIL Gorbachev may have had little choice in Azerbaijan, but sending the Red Army into Baku has transformed an inter-ethnic conflict into a revolt against Moscow.

If anything, Mr. Gorbachev, who appears reluctant to use force save *in extremis*, probably waited too long to inject the army into the civil war between Armenians and Azerbaijanis in the Soviet Transcaucasus. Two years ago he was widely criticized for not responding more quickly to ethnic riots in Sumgait, and this time he allowed the fighting to continue for nearly a week before the first troops landed in the capital of Baku.

Mr. Gorbachev deployed the army because that was the lesser evil. To have fiddled while Muslim Azerbaijanis slaughtered Christian Armenians would have signaled ethnic minorities throughout the Soviet Union that Moscow was reluctant to protect them. The invasion, however, transmogrified the communal fighting into a Russian-Azerbaijani conflict, a drive for Azerbaijani independence fueled also by Islamic nationalism in bordering Iran.

Though order was restored in Baku, temporarily at least and at great loss of life, the Azerbaijani uprising underscores Moscow's weaknesses. Roughly 40 percent of the Red Army is composed of conscripts from the predominantly Muslim republics of Central Asia. The loyalty of these troops is highly suspect.

Moscow had to use Russian troops exclusively in the Baku operation — a call-up of reservists was canceled after angry mothers protested — and several Azeri military units revolted in support of the radical Popular Front, the de facto political power in Azerbaijan. It appears that Moscow, faced with a prolonged occupation, now may have an internal Afghanistan on its hands — an ongoing liability for a nation that lost sons enough to Muslim guerrillas in Afghanistan.

The White House winks at Mr. Gorbachev's actions in the Caucasus, but draws the line at the use of force to keep the Baltic republics in line. What is the difference? The Balts have no greater claim on independence than do Azerbaijanis — or Armenians or Georgians for that matter. Some will suspect that Washington feels as it does because Balts are European while Azerbaijanis are Asian. To understand Mr. Gorbachev's behavior is one thing; to give it Washington's benediction is quite another.

Some 70 million restive Muslims live on the Soviet Union's southern tier. The Baltic republics are in a ferment. Nationalism is simmering in the Ukraine. The movement for Moldavia to rejoin Romania is picking up steam. Even Siberia is stirring. The Soviet empire — in Lenin's phrase the "prison house of nations" — is coming unstuck, and it is unclear that Mr. Gorbachev can prevent its final collapse.

Part II: Eastern Europe

In the pitch of a damp November night, thousands of Germans from the West and East danced on top of the Berlin Wall, celebrating the announcement that this symbol of post-war Europe was finally coming down. Of all the images emanating out of Eastern Europe in the fall of 1989, this was undoubtedly the most profound.

To a world caught in the dreary grip of the cold war, the events that swept Eastern Europe in 1989 seemed equally surreal. Who imagined a year before that the nations of Eastern Europe, whose tentative steps toward self-determination were brutally suppressed for more than four decades, would charge into the light of democracy? Who would have predicted that Soviet leader Mikhail S. Gorbachev would not only allow such change but openly encouraged it, sparking a wildfire of reform from Bulgaria to the Baltic?

Eastern Europe's rapid transformation began peacefully in Poland, where the Solidarity trade union, underground for eight years, dominated the nation's first democratic election since World War II. Concurrently, independent political parties appeared in Hungary. Then with probable speed, hard-line governments in East Germany, Bulgaria and Czechoslovakia toppled as demonstrators demanded free speech and an end to the Communist Party's monopoly on power. But the rush toward democratic reform turned bloody in Romania by year's end. When secret police killed protesters in that country a revolt was triggered that resulted in the execution of dictator Nicolae Ceausescu and his wife, Elena Ceausescu.

Since 1948, when the Soviet Union established a buffer of puppet governments from Poland to the edge of Greece, democracy in Eastern Europe has been a dream deferred. Soviet tanks ended the 1956 uprising in Hungary and Warsaw Pact troops squashed the 1968 flowering of a democratic-socialist government in Czechoslovakia. Totalitarian regimes snuffed out free speech, arrested dissidents and turned the press into a mouthpiece of Communist Party propaganda. Words were so feared in Romania that authorities registered typewriters to more easily control the flow of language. Even jazz was too much for the Czechoslovak government, which jailed musicians for trumpeting freedom of expression. There seemed little hope for reform.

Many factors incited the rebellions of 1989. The simmering resentment of the populations within these countries from past brutalities undoubtedly resulted in the tremendous backlash that the rest of the world has witnessed. But largely it was the economic failure of communism – crippled economies and declining living standards – that sparked the calls for change. Poland suffered from a $40 billion debt, high inflation and chronic food shortages. While Romanians ate pigs feet and potatoes, their government exported the country's agricultural bounty. Though East Germany boasted the highest standard of living in the communist world, West German television whetted appetites for the fruits of capitalism.

However, the changes that have occurred in Eastern Europe do not mean that the days of hardship have vanished. As these fledgling democracies rebuild their societies, they face a potential array of obstacles that have to be sensitively and resolutely dealt with: high inflation, unemployment and new social tensions – conditions that can ignite extremist political movements. In addition, situations that have turned them against one another in the past, such as border disputes and ethnic rivalries, must be left behind.

As communism recedes, long-standing ethnic rivalries may emerge to haunt Eastern Europe. The region is dotted with minorities, from the tiny population of Sorbs, a Slavic people, in East Germany to the Turks who make up 10% of the population of Bulgaria. Old hostilities are still being played out, like the rivalry of Hungarians and Romanians for ownership of Transylvania.

Czechoslovakia and Yugoslavia are not homogeneous nations. They are amalgams of various ethnic groups trying to share the same country. In Czechoslovakia, ethnic differences were played down during the four decades of cold war, but in Bulgaria and Romania rigid Communist regimes suppressed ethnic minorities as official policy.

In some cases efforts are being made to heal old wounds, as President Vaclav Havel of Czechoslovakia recently tried to do with conciliatory statements about the expulsion after World War II of 3.25 million ethnic Germans from the Sudetenland.

Now, with the lid lifted in Eastern Europe, the ancient divisions are being given free expression and have become more evident than at any other time since World War II. As the dust clears from the revolts of 1989 even neo-nazism is rearing its ugly head. The reemergence of these destrucitve sentiments poses a challenge to the post-Communist republics: Can they accommodate the rivalries, keep the peace and build democracy?

Eastern Europe's future is uncertain, but one thing seems evident: the Iron Curtain is now a tattered veil.

Hungary Begins Removing Austria Border Fence

Hungary May 2, 1989 began to dismantle the barbed-wire fence along its border with neutral Austria, becoming the first Soviet-bloc country to open a border with Western Europe.

The fence, 150 miles long, had been erected in 1969 to replace minefields set up by Hungary in 1949. The barrier was scheduled to be completely torn down in 1990. Some 150 journalists witnessed Hungarian troops begin the dismantling at the border town of Hegyeshalom, on the main road between Budapest and Vienna.

At a press conference May 2, Andras Kovari, a spokesman for the Hungarian interior ministry, said "Not only do we need the world, but the world needs us. An era will be closed with the removal of this fence, and we hope that such systems will never be needed again."

Kovari noted that under new passport regulations – the most liberal in the Soviet bloc – most Hungarians were free to travel abroad. Therefore, it appeared unlikely that Austria would be flooded with Hungarian refugees. Hungary was to continue armed border patrols because of the prospect of other Eastern Europeans crossing the Austrian frontier.

East Germany, Czechoslovakia and Romania were reported to be irate over the removal of the fence. Western analysts surmised that those regimes feared that their people would flee to Austria while on trips to Hungary. There were thousands of Romanian refugees in Hungary, even though Romania had closed its border with Hungary in 1988.

The Evening Gazette

Worcester, MA, May 8, 1989

The 31 tanks and handful of soldiers that left the provincial town of Kiskunhalas 90 miles south of Budapest the other day for the long trip home to the Soviet Union represented only a mere fraction of the huge army that Moscow keeps in Hungary. But their departure marked a historic event; it was the first withdrawal of Soviet troops from Eastern Europe.

If things go well, more will follow. In December, Mikhail Gorbachev pledged to withdraw 50,000 soldiers from Hungary, East Germany and Czechoslovakia as part of a wider demobilization of Soviet forces. The gesture is largely symbolic, because there are an estimated 70,000 Soviet troops in Hungary alone. But the public relations impact is significant, and the Soviets took full advantage of the opportunity.

Only a few months ago, Hungarians were arrested if they ventured within 10 miles of Soviet bases in that country. This time foreign reporters were invited to witness the departure of the tanks and were escorted around by smiling English-speaking officers. It was a real media event.

It's only fitting that the withdrawal should begin in Hungary where Soviet troops caused major devastation after the 1956 uprising and have been present since.

Gorbachev's disarmamant program, genuine or deceptive, made him increasingly popular in Western Europe and has diminished the resolve of America's allies to keep the North Atlantic Treaty Organization strong.

It may be a false sense of security on their part, but the United States can hardly ignore the rapidly changing situation on the continent. The Cold War has turned into a propaganda war, and Gorbachev's forces are winning.

THE SACRAMENTO BEE

Sacramento, CA, May 6, 1989

Hungary has always been a bit ahead of its Eastern European neighbors, whether in food or fashion, economics or politics. Thus in 1968, Budapest was the first Soviet-bloc country to begin reforming the rigid, centralized Communist economic system; by 1972, it had substituted a barbed-wire fence for the mine field that, since the abortive 1956 uprising, had deterred most Hungarians from trying to flee to the West.

Last year, Hungary's Communist government lifted restrictions on foreign travel; this year, it is permitting the formation of opposition political parties to compete in elections next year. And this week, workers began cutting away strands of the 150-mile fence along the Austrian-Hungarian border; within 18 months, the fence should be gone. Then, what Winston Churchill so aptly dubbed the Iron Curtain in 1946 can truly be said to have been breached.

To the West, that breach is symbolic of the winds of freedom blowing in the once-monolithic Soviet bloc, but it's more than that. Despite serious economic problems and the fact that personal freedoms still fall short of those in the West, Hungarians increasingly have less desire to leave their homeland. Indeed, nearly all of those who now flee from Hungary into Austria are citizens of other, more repressive Communist countries. When the fence is gone, will the regimes in Czechoslovakia, East Germany, Romania and Bulgaria continue to allow their citizens to travel within the Eastern bloc?

Communist leaders are not the only ones concerned about the possible consequences of Hungary's action. Austrian officials privately express the fear that today's trickle of refugees may become a torrent once the barbed wire is down across a wide front. More broadly, there's the danger that the growing clamor for freedom in a region so unaccustomed to it will also generate instability, which, before the advent of communism more than four decades ago, was Eastern Europe's natural state. Peoples of the region obviously believe that risk is worth taking, given the potential prize. To the extent the West can help them achieve their goal, and is asked to do so, it should.

The Wichita
Eagle-Beacon

Wichita, KS, May 15, 1989

THE reality matches the rhetoric in Hungary, which has become the lead horse in the dismantling of communist orthodoxy in the Soviet Union and other Eastern European countries.

A few days ago, Hungary removed the tank traps and barbed wire on its border with Austria, becoming the first East Bloc nation to open its frontier to the West.

That action is part of a fundamental transformation of Hungarian society, and it could be a preview of a revolution in European political thought. The government of General Secretary Karoly Grosz plans to legalize non-communist alternative parties and allow them to run in democratic elections. There even are promises that the Communist Party would join a coalition with other parties and give up its monolithic status.

Further, Hungary is accelerating its move toward capitalist economics by expanding the right of citizens to own private property and businesses.

Listening to Hungarian officials, one immediately thinks of Karl Marx spinning in his grave. There is no difference, says Gyula Horn, a Communist Party official, between "bourgeois and socialist criteria for democracy and human rights."

Indeed, Mr. Horn acknowledged that the Hungarian reforms are a repudiation of traditional communist ideology. "In fact, we discredit the ideas of Marx," he said.

Soviet leader Mikhail Gorbachev frequently has cited Hungary as a pilot program for the kind of changes he would like to see in the rest of Eastern Europe. Mr. Gorbachev has seen that even the limited economic freedoms of the past few years have helped make Hungary the richest, most properous country in the Soviet bloc. If the Hungarian experience can work in other socialist countries, the ideological map of Europe would have to be redrawn.

Hungary's example suggests that freedom is taking deep root in Eastern Europe. If nurtured, the tree of liberty soon could push over the Iron Curtain — from the inside.

THE ARIZONA REPUBLIC

Phoenix, AZ, May 22, 1989

IT may appear to be a small matter, a minor action by a squad of soldiers earlier this month along Hungary's lonely border with Austria, an event that barely caused a ripple.

In purely literal terms, the amount of barbed-wire and electrified fencing that the young communist border guards removed that day — just a few meters or so — may not mean much. Symbolically, however, the small cut they made had significant ramifications.

After 40 years, the Iron Curtain, drawn across the heart of the European continent from the Baltic to the Mediterranean to separate two hostile and incompatible political systems, had been breached. The curtain — at least the portion of it that runs through Hungary — will be torn down by the end of 1990, says the government. Along their shared 220-mile border, citizens of Hungary and Austria, in effect, will be free to come and go as they please in either direction.

Since the Hungarian barrier is the tangible expression of the figurative wall of distrust between East and West, the small opening is a harbinger of larger developments. It represents hard evidence of some new thinking in the Soviet bloc — thinking inspired in part by the more liberal policies of Kremlin boss Mikhail Gorbachev.

Moreover, it is no surprise that the historic opening occurred where it did. Of all the East European nations held under the sway of Soviet hegemony since the end of World War II, Hungary had been more or less going its own way economically and politically even before Mr. Gorbachev rose to power in Moscow. And today Hungary would like nothing better than to become the Austria of Eastern Europe, non-aligned and prosperous.

As welcome as the opening is to most people in the free world, not everyone is happy about it. Some Austrians fear that a flood of economic and political refugees from the East might pour through the Hungarian Gap. Other West Europeans worry that their economic and social welfare systems might not be able to handle the pressure of what could become a massive migration westward through the new gateway.

But as London's *Economist* reports, "Most upset are the conservative communists in Czechoslovakia, East Germany and Romania, who fear that Hungary will become an escape route to the West."

Now there is speculation that new border barriers soon will go up. Only this time, the wall of wire and distrust will be erected between Hungary and its socialist allies in the Eastern bloc, who view Budapest's dramatic break in Iron Curtain uniformity as a breach in the fraternal solidarity of the communist nations.

It was Kipling who said years ago and in another context that "East is East, and West is West, and never the twain shall meet, till earth and sky stand presently at God's great judgment seat."

But judging by the events going on behind another Great Wall, the one in China, the indomitable spirit of freedom, no matter how long imprisoned, may yet escape the constraints of totalitarian rule.

The Register

Sacramento, CA, May 7, 1989

Last week, Hungary's Communist regime took two long strides toward restoring the people's ancient freedoms. Hungarian army troops tore down the wall separating the country from Austria. Pieces of barbed wire were given away as souvenirs. This action further advances the greater freedom to travel to the West that the regime has allowed in recent years. It also encourages psychological links with Austria, the country's old partner in the Austro-Hungarian Empire.

The second development is the replacement of the head of the Communist regime's agency regulating religion. The regime's news agency, MTI, announced that Imre Miklos had retired after "crucial changes" in policy toward religion. It said that state control will now be removed to "finalize the separation of the state and churches."

As it has in Poland, the relaxation could mean a resurgence of religious devotion. Hungary's religions flourished before World War II, but were severely persecuted, first by the Nazis, then by the Communists. Estimates are that the country is 67 percent Roman Catholic and 25 percent Protestant, with a significant number of Jews. But because of the many years of repression, no one can say what the actual figures are, or the depth of the people's faith. Yet the fact that all these faiths have survived indicates something.

The regime's next move must be to shore up its faltering economy. Twenty years ago "Goulash Communism" foreshadowed Soviet boss Mikhail Gorbachev's *perestroika* program. But like *perestroika*, itself faltering, the Hungarian experiment has always been doomed by being strapped to the millstone of socialism. The regime must now find a way to create freer markets while not endangering its own power, yet it may be compelled to do so by a populace emboldened by the other relaxations. Freedom is contagious: Once people have it in one area — religion, economics, politics — they soon demand it in all areas.

One way the Hungarian regime might advance economic reform would be to push for a "Danubian dollar." This proposal has been advanced by economist Andrew Erdely, a Hungarian immigrant who now lives in Orange County but maintains ties with people in Hungary. This would be a common currency between the countries along the Danube river, Hungary, Austria, Czechoslovakia, Yugoslavia, and Romania, which have strong historical ties; Poland also might be invited to join.

Erdely said the Danubian dollar would ideally be based on gold, providing "a constant basis for the economy." Such a solid currency would prevent "the constant coming and going of inflation," and would facilitate easy trade between the countries using the Danubian dollar, and trade with Western Europe, the United States, and elsewhere. The biggest hurdle is that some of these countries retain socialist economies, while some already have market economies. Yet with freedom rapidly expanding across the region, the proposal could become a reality.

The Miami Herald

Miami, FL, May 7, 1989

'FROM STETTIN in the Baltic to Trieste in the Adriatic, an iron curtain has descended across the continent." When Winston Churchill fired this first salvo of the Cold War in a speech in Fulton, Mo., in 1946, he did more than warn the West about the growing dangers of Soviet expansionism. He also coined a powerful metaphor for Communist oppression. Within less than a decade, his metaphor became literal as the East-bloc nations laid barbed wire along their borders with Western Europe.

Thus Churchill would have been surprised to see the Iron Curtain being torn down in Communist Hungary this week. No other single act better symbolizes the end — or the beginning of the end — of an era.

Some scholars of communism have argued that the Iron Curtain serves more than just a repressive purpose — though that too, of course. In his book *The Closest of Enemies*, former U.S. diplomat Wayne Smith argues that nascent Communist governments erected the fence much as a young United States adopted the Monroe Doctrine in the 19th Century: "to shield a new and insecure political system from an outside world intent on influencing" it.

If that was the case, then tearing down the fence would seem to indicate that Hungary, at least, no longer feels threatened by the capitalist West. That's a plausible conclusion given the dramatic political and economic reforms taking place in Hungary.

Whatever else it means, an ugly symbol is finally coming down. Ironically, it is now neighboring Austria that has mixed feelings about neighboring Hungary dismantling the fence. The Austrian government is said to fear being flooded by refugees from Eastern European countries who might decide to flee via the Austro-Hungarian border.

That's regrettable. Because even though inarguably there is a world of difference between the attitude of a country that says "Immigrants not welcome" and one that states "Emigration not allowed," physical barriers really have no place along neighboring nations' borders.

Given Hungary's historic decision to remove its Iron Curtain, dare one hope that one day soon the rest of the East bloc's curtain — especially the particularly odious Berlin Wall — will be dismantled too?

THE SAGINAW NEWS

Saginaw, MI, May 9, 1989

Last week Hungary started tearing down the Iron Curtain. Along the 220-mile border with Austria, guards took away the barbed wire, disconnected alarms and removed fenceposts. Hungarians, the government noted, now hold passports allowing them to travel freely as often as they can afford to do so.

It may be Gorbachev's glasnost that gets the credit for opening wide the windows to the West. But it was the courage of the Freedom Fighters of long-ago 1956 that first gave Hungary a taste of the fresh air of freedom. Finally, their revolution has triumphed over the tanks.

THE CHRISTIAN SCIENCE MONITOR

Boston, MA, May 8, 1989

HUNGARY's dismantling of a barbed-wire fence separating it from Austria takes a little more iron out of a corroding "Iron Curtain." It's a symbolic act, but the symbolism is poignant.

Budapest is lurching toward political change. Its once-monolithic Communist Party shows signs of splitting into factions (long a Marxist-Leninist no-no), with the most liberal reformers wielding the bulk of power. A new constitution is on the horizon, incorporating checks and balances and doing away with the Communists' "leading role." Free elections are promised for next year.

Hungarians look West for their role models these days. The social democracy of Sweden, Finland, and Austria — not Soviet-style socialism — is the object of emulation. It was only logical that the fence come down.

Ironically, the highest partitions in Eastern Europe now are those between the reformist socialist states, Hungary and Poland, and their hard-line communist neighbors. Hungary's relations with Romania are particularly tense. Romanian refugees flow its way.

In July, George Bush will recognize the new openness in the East, with stops in Hungary and Poland as part of his first European tour as President. Leaders in both countries will doubtless use the occasion to ask for greater US help with their economic reforms.

Poland is almost as gung-ho for change as Hungary is. Party leader Wojciech Jaruzelski admits that aspects of socialism haven't worked in Poland. Arm in arm with Lech Walesa, head of the Solidarity trade union he once banned, General Jaruzelski is striding into a new era of elections and multipolar politics. The country's redesigned parliament — with all seats in the new upper house and a third of those in the lower chamber freely elected — will have a decisive say in crucial economic reforms.

Jacek Kuron, a Polish activist and political theorist, has said the goal is "an entirely new political geography," with new alignments and new antagonists. Both the Communist Party and Solidarity could be transformed, he says.

The Soviet Union, for now, appears willing to let things proceed. The Poles may be encouraged that *perestroika* has now embraced a limited right to strike for Soviet unionists. Not long ago, that would have been considered an ideological absurdity in the "workers' state." But wildcat strikes have been occurring anyway under Mikhail Gorbachev; the shift favors reality over ideology.

Hungarians busily redefining their politics retain memories of 1956 and the Soviet invasion — triggered, they'll recall, by talk of leaving the Warsaw Pact. Still, Mr. Gorbachev has given his blessing to reform in Hungary and Poland. But even he could be shocked by what the future holds.

Just as important as the Soviet response is the response of average Hungarians and Poles. Can a somewhat cynical, economically strapped populace be rallied behind reform? The coming election campaigns will provide at least a partial answer to that important question.

The Providence Journal

Providence, RI, May 8, 1989

Should historians of the future search for a date by which to mark the demise of the Iron Curtain, chances are they will *not* settle on May 2, 1989. The infamous "curtain" — so baptized by Sir Winston Churchill in his famous address at Westminster College in Missouri in 1946 — has always been more ideological than physical — and, accordingly, its true dismantling has more to do with institutional reforms than literal removal.

Nevertheless, the process begun this week in Hungary to take down the barbed-wire fence that separates that country from Austria is to be welcomed. It provides tangible evidence of the erosion of Communist convictions in that part of the world, and powerfully illustrates that the unnatural divisions of Europe are far from permanent.

For some time now, Hungarians have been flocking to Vienna to buy the goods that are unavailable to them at home. The only restrictions on their travel there — or anywhere, for that matter — are financial, not political. If the absence of an actual physical barrier in getting to the West is of benefit to anyone, it is to other Eastern Europeans who come to Hungary. Prominent among these are Romanians, who are granted automatic status as political refugees, but who have a difficult time because of the far-from-robust Hungarian economy.

Yet throughout Eastern Europe, governmental processes have pretty much replaced daredevil escapes as the preferred means of departure. Add to this the fact that the climate of change is, in a few countries, so tantalizing that it provides an incentive for many people to stay, and you have obviated the need for border-long walls. Today Hungary; tomorrow Berlin.

What will not be so easily dismissed — if, indeed, the Hungarians can set a precedent — is the gap in the quality of life. For while the curtain has symbolized an ideological division of Europe, it has fostered a very real economic division as well. And long after the curtain disappears, these discrepancies will be appallingly clear.

But it is only with its disappearance that they can be corrected.

Calgary Herald

Calgary, Alta., May 9, 1989

In bits and pieces and scraps of old barbed wire, Eastern Europe's Iron Curtain is coming down.

Hungarian soldiers are out with wire-cutters, post removers and, fittingly, television cameras, tearing down major sections of the barbed barrier on the border with Austria.

Hungary has vowed to remove all 240 kilometres of wire on its western border by the end of 1990.

Perhaps by then other Warsaw Pact countries will have begun unbricking, mothballing, stripping and bulldozing their sections of the barricade which has divided Europe for the past four decades.

If glasnost is the Soviet word for "openness" then there is no more fitting example of glasnost in action than the opening of the Iron Curtain.

The Houston Post

Houston, TX, May 15, 1989

THERE IS SOMETHING ironic about a prisoner who is given a key to his cell but is unable to use it.

That is the situation in Hungary. The government has decided to tear down the Iron Curtain, but can't afford to and can't find anyone else willing to do the job.

The barbed wire fence and electronic barriers run for 150 miles along Hungary's border with Austria. On May 2, the Hungarian government announced it was dismantling the barrier. But since no money was budgeted for the project — estimated to cost upwards of $700,000 — it offered companies and farm cooperatives the opportunity to do the job in exchange for the materials. Most of them showed no interest, which is understandable. Others more politely said they didn't have the proper equipment.

So the barrier stands until someone can figure out what to do.

There are several possible solutions. Perhaps Hungary can sell it to another, less-enlightened government. Or maybe some West Texas rancher needs a new stretch of barbed wire. The Hungarian government could establish a De-fence Department. Or, taking a page from the American Way, Hungary could simply borrow the money from the next generation.

But until a solution is found, Hungarians will continue to live behind an Iron Curtain — a curtain that won't go up, or come down.

Arkansas Gazette

Little Rock, AR, May 5, 1989

Hungary's unilateral decision to dismantle the barbed wire fence along its frontier with neutral Austria is rich in symbolism and reality. Most of all it is welcome among freedom-loving people.

As a part of what Winston Churchill dubbed the Iron Curtain, the border fortifications have seen better (or worse, depending on your point of view) days. The fence on the Austro-Hungarian border went up in 1949, but after the Vienna agreement in the mid-1950s brought withdrawal of Allied and Soviet troops and neutral status for Austria the border seemed gradually less menacing.

Strong historical ties exist between the people of Hungary and Austria, and travel between the two countries has become common in recent years. The second language of choice for many Hungarians is German, not the Russian that is ordered in the schools. Hungarians regularly travel to Vienna to shop when they have accumulated enough hard currency. In recent months, some shops in Vienna have even been quietly accepting Forints, the Hungarian currency that is not supposed to be taken out of Hungary.

If there has been a weak spot in the Iron Curtain it has been and is the 225-mile border separating Austria and Hungary. Many Hungarians long for a similar neutral status, in an Eastern mode, but whether this is possible in the near future remains problematical.

In any case, there is no good reason for Hungary to maintain border fortifications. Democratization is well on its way, thanks mostly to the loosening of the reins in Moscow. Western investment has been encouraged and it has made a small dent for capitalism. Hungary clearly wants a full opening to the West, and the way to vault forward toward this goal is to scrap the ugly physical barriers that scar the Danube plain.

Hungary's action may be unsettling to regimes in the Eastern Bloc that have not taken the liberalizing steps that the Budapest government has. Czechoslovakia and East Germany, especially, will be uncomfortable.

Of Hungary's 16 million visitors each year, perhaps half or more are from Eastern countries. Some at least will now visit either for discovering a model of what their countries could become or as an easier route to freedom in the West.

For the people — not the governments — of these nations, Hungary's opening toward the West must be especially sweet.

ST. LOUIS POST-DISPATCH

St. Louis, MO, May 13, 1989

The sentence is one of Sir Winston Churchill's most famous lines, containing the most enduring metaphor of the Cold War: "From Stettin in the Baltic to Trieste in the Adriatic, an iron curtain has descended across the continent."

The "iron curtain speech" that the former British prime minister gave at Westminster College in Fulton, Mo., in 1946 was the call to arms that helped mobilize the American and Western response to Josef Stalin's takeover of Eastern Europe after the fall of Nazi Germany. How fitting it is that 43 years later, with fresh democratic winds sweeping the communist bloc, part of the iron curtain is coming down.

The decision by Hungary to remove the 150-mile-long barbed wire fence along its border with neutral Austria is more than a symbolic gesture. For the first time in decades, people will be able to walk freely across the East-West frontier.

Ironically, those who are most concerned about this development are the Austrians. While officially welcoming the move, Vienna fears a flood of non-Hungarian refugees will come from the more restrictive communist states in Eastern Europe. Hungary already has a liberal border crossing policy for its citizens. Such an influx could be a problem, but one that can be managed.

Of greater importance is the precedent that this sets for the rest of Eastern Europe. While it is unlikely that the hard-line communist regimes in either East Germany or Czechoslovakia will quickly follow Hungary's lead, perhaps some day, the iron curtain will completely rust away.

East Germans Leave Prague, Warsaw for West Germany

More than 17,000 East German refugees emigrated to West Germany from Czechoslovakia and Poland Sept. 30 to Oct. 4, 1989 with the permission of the East German government. But, as the refugee crisis deepened, East Germany moved to curb the flow of its citizens to the West. The crisis was a major embarrassment to East Germany as that nation prepared to celebrate its 40th anniversary on Oct. 7. Not only were East Germans fleeing by the thousands, but new internal opposition had surfaced.

The newest flood of emigrants had been encamped at the West German embassies in Prague and Warsaw. Most of them were vacationing young adults and young families who had refused to return to East Germany. Bonn had closed its Prague embassy to visitors on Aug. 23, but East Germans continued to crowd onto the grounds of the facility. (About 100 refugees left the embassy Sept. 26 in a deal negotiated by East German lawyer Wolfgang Vogel. They were promised emigration if they returned to East Germany. As of Oct. 1, there had been approximately 5,500 East Germans at the Prague embassy, many living in an unsanitary makeshift tent city on the embassy's grounds.

In Poland, only a handful of East Germans had sought refuge at the West German embassy as of the beginning of September. But that number swelled to more than 100 by the middle of the month, forcing Bonn to shut the facility Sept. 20. By Oct. 1, some 800 East Germans had arrived at the facility. Poland, ruled by a new noncommunist coalition government, was generally more sympathetic to the plight of the refugees than was hard-line Czechoslovakia. Both countries wanted the problem resolved by the two Germanys.

The emigration was arranged in talks between West German Foreign Minister Hans-Dietrich Genscher and East German authorities. In an agreement announced Sept. 30, East Germany provided special trains to transport the 5,500 refugees in Prague and the 800 refugees in Warsaw through East Germany to the West German border cities of Hof and Helmstadt, respectively.

The East German official press characterized the emigration as an expulsion of "irresponsible antisocial traitors and criminals," and continued to accuse West Germany of precipitating the crisis.

As the refugee trains began arriving in West Germany Oct. 1, thousands more East Germans in Czechoslovakia began flocking to the West German embassy in Prague in hopes of reaching West Germany. In Poland, about 200 more East Germans sought refuge at the West German embassy in Warsaw Oct. 2.

More than 5,000 new refugees were in the Prague embassy on Oct. 2, with an estimated 1,000 milling outside the gates and clashing with Czechoslovak police, who unsuccessfully attempted to keep them from climbing the fences surrounding the embassy grounds. (In a widely reported incident Oct. 2, a West German diplomat answered a cry for help from a young East German being pulled from atop a fence by two policemen. The policemen relented when the diplomat helped the refugee down and took him inside the embassy.)

As many as 5,000 East Germans crossed the border into Czechoslovakia by car Oct. 2, presenting the East Berlin regime with another challenge. East Germany Oct. 3 announced that it would permit a second wave of emigration to West Germany from Prague.

About 11,000 refugees boarded special trains Oct. 4 for the trip to Hof from Prague. During the journey through East Germany, it was reported that some East Germans attempted to halt the trains in order to get aboard themselves.

In Warsaw, the number of new refugees at the West German embassy hit about 400 as of Oct. 4. No arrangements were made for them to emigrate.

THE RICHMOND NEWS LEADER
Richmond, VA,
August 28, 1989

The Soviets should have known better.

Not long ago, the Kremlin opened the Hungarian border to Soviets living nearby. The action ostensibly was taken to allow Hungarians living in the Soviet Union to visit with their relatives in Hungary. Instead, Soviets have crossed the border by the thousands to buy goods in short supply back home. In only one month, according to reports, 1.5 million Soviet shoppers crossed the border, and each day an average 100,000 visitors swamp the small border towns.

The thriving border commerce that immediately developed to meet the demands of Soviet visitors would delight any capitalist heart. Small shops are expanding, and new ones are opening that will offer any consumer goods shoppers may want. One market operates 24 hours a day, seven days a week. Soviets snap up everything in sight, from food to electronics, from merchants who have flocked to the area.

Not even harsh currency regulations dampen the Soviets' enthusiasm. Each Soviet is permitted to bring 30 rubles across the border, which he changes into Hungarian forints. He spends half his forints, then exchanges the rest for rubles that are worth less than half their official value on the black market. He then returns home with as many rubles as he had when he came, plus the merchandise he bought.

Naturally, this commercial phenomenon has attracted merchants from outside Hungary. Polish merchants have arrived by the hundreds, and West Germany soon will build a department store. An international market is in the making, and it promises to be a lucrative one. The Soviets, who pay only nominal rents and taxes, have few products to buy with their accumulating cash, and their pent-up hunger for goods is explosive.

Once they have satisfied their immediate needs, they will start buying goods to ship to Cousin Anya in Moscow and Uncle Yuri in Gorky. If the Kremlin is embarrassed now by this epidemic of consumerism, then it had better brace itself for even more embarrassment when Soviets far from the Hungarian border demand the necessary internal passports to travel there to get in on the action. Word gets around: Chickens. VCRs. Down parkas. Fresh veggies. Refrigerators.

To the Soviets, the Hungarian opening must be akin to clearance day at Harrod's or Filene's. Deprived for so long of even the most fundamental consumer goods, they give a whole new definition to the motto, "Born to Shop."

The Atlanta Journal
THE ATLANTA CONSTITUTION
Atlanta, GA, October 7, 1989

Didja hear the one about party leaders Erich Honecker and Mikhail Gorbachev getting together in the German Democratic Republic to celebrate the 40th anniversary of the establishment of that utopia on Earth and no other East Germans showed up?

Indeed, there is something darkly funny about today's commemoration, but most East Germans can no longer console themselves with the unintended humor that leavens such staged exercises in hypocrisy.

East Germany is by all measures the most advanced of the East bloc economies, the most favorable laboratory for Marxism. Yet the stark reality is that its inhabitants by the thousands are throwing themselves at police lines, swimming rivers, leaping on moving trains, leaving all behind but the clothing on their backs to flee their homeland and begin a new life in West Germany.

Nothing points up the failure of communism quite so vividly as the contrast between these two countries, a disparity that East Germans themselves became all too familiar with from the time they were allowed to view West German television.

Ever since, their TV sets have been a window into a beckoning land that was at once next door and yet verboten. A deadly barrier had been erected, after all, to discourage an earlier generation of East Germany's best and brightest from leaving.

What has happened over the last year — the departure of 110,000 East Germans since January, accelerating incredibly these past two weeks — is the culmination of these pent-up yearnings, let loose oh-so-grudgingly by the Honecker regime at the gentle suggestion of Mr. Gorbachev.

Lest we in the West take too much pleasure in Mr. Honacker's discomfiture today, it would be well for us to contemplate this:

Many East Germans will have been unable to avail themselves of the brief open door to freedom. Many more who have chosen to stay behind are no less disaffected and nursing grievances — 20,000 of them gathered in Leipzig last Monday singing "We Shall Overcome." The situation cries for leadership but, alas, Mr. Honecker and his cronies are old, tired and unbending.

On this, East Germany's 40th birthday, the truculent Honecker regime is having more than just a mid-life crisis. It is growing unstable to the point of being a danger.

FORT WORTH STAR-TELEGRAM
Forth Worth, TX, October 3, 1989

Thousands of East Germans have a special reason for celebrating the 40th anniversary of the founding of the German Democratic Republic. They left it last weekend to start new lives in a truly democratic country.

They had actually defected months ago and sought refuge in West German embassies in Czechoslovakia and Poland. In an extraordinary accommodation aimed at removing a cloud hovering over the anniversary observance, the East German government permitted them to travel on special trains through East Germany to West Germany.

Despite that uncharacteristic display of flexibility by East Germany, the cloud lingers over the anniversary celebration. Scores of other East Germans are taking their places in the embassies, seeking to emigrate to the West.

Like the mass defections through Hungary, the exodus through Czechoslovakia and Poland speaks volumes about the quality of life in East Germany and the unquenchable desire of most people for political and economic freedom.

The regime of Erich Honecker faces two alternatives to try to stem the tide of emigrations. It can wall in and isolate East Germany or pursue the reformist road that some of its Eastern European neighbors have embarked upon.

Attempting to keep East Germans at home by repression would only exacerbate the regime's growing economic and political problems. Only meaningful reforms that give East Germans hope for a better life will stop them from fleeing.

Honecker could save face and put a better face on the anniversary commemoration by indicating that he now supports Soviet President Mikhail Gorbachev's reformist policies. Otherwise, East Germans by the score will continue to celebrate daily by saying "*auf Wiedersehen.*"

THE CHRONICLE-HERALD
Halifax, N.S., October 3, 1989

THE TWO COMMUNIST states most determined to resist the winds of political and economic change are turning middle-aged a week apart.

China, which was the cutting edge of reforming communism until things went violently "back to normal" with the massacre of student demonstrators last June, marked the 40th anniversary of Mao's assumption of power with an army-supervised gala in Tienanmen Square on Sunday.

Held on the very stones which ran with students' blood last spring, the dance-and-fireworks show was a testament to the contempt the new old-look regime has for liberal ideas and their exponents at home and abroad.

But, with Western representatives boycotting the celebrations, and with only politically reliable Chinese allowed to attend (others were temporarily kicked out of Peking or ordered to stay indoors), there was no one to rain on the comfortable old-men's fantasy that counter-revolution has been heroically resisted and that things are now going fine.

The birthday was marked by the re-emergence of 84-year-old Chen Yun, architect of the unproductive planning system that kept China poor for 30 years, and other signs of nostalgia. Paramount leader Deng Xiaoping (who backed reform until students challenged him) was dishing out pablum about the bracing effects of the crackdown on party ideology, for-

getting his famous aphorism that a cat's colour doesn't matter so long as it catches mice.

Appropriately, the highest-ranking foreign delegation at this re-consecration of Mao — and surely the most approving — came from the German Democratic Republic (GDR), which marks its own fourth decade under communism next Sunday. East Germany, which has never even tried to come in from the cold, is having its failure-to-let-people-grow pains, too. Some 37,000 of its citizens have fled to West Germany this summer.

The most embarrassing trek took place on the weekend, as some 6,000 East Germans, camped out in West German embassies in Prague and Warsaw and refusing to return home, were taken to the West. East Germany provided the trains, to support the official fiction that these people were being expelled. But, like China, its main concern was clearly to be rid of any damning evidence of discontent with stick-in-the-mud communism.

In East Germany's case, the self-deception has so far had better results: people are getting free rather than getting shot or locked up.

But, as in China, what gets you through the anniversary weekend is not going to go on working forever. The GDR can't go on losing people; China cannot modernize under rule by terror and circuses. Unhappily, though, both seem ready to go on trying.

The Honolulu Advertiser

Honolulu, HI,
October 9, 1989

Although East Germany has moved to close its border with Czechoslovakia and stem the tide of refugees, its crisis is far from ended.

Some 140,000 have fled that country of 16 million in the last year, threatening its stability as a nation. Although there is talk of German reunification, that's opposed both by the Soviet Union and Western Europe. It won't be a quick cure for East Germany's problems.

Once before, in 1961, there was a similar exodus of the youngest and brightest to the West. The response was the Berlin Wall. Since other Soviet bloc countries are no longer helping East Germany keep its people home, a much longer wall would be needed today.

East Germany has the strongest economy among Soviet satellites, but it's still a scarecrow next to the prosperity of the West, which also offers political freedom.

The rub is that East Germans think of themselves as Germans. Unlike people in Poland or Hungary, they have little sense of national identity with the East and many have little esteem for communism, even as the country celebrates its 40th anniversary as a communist state.

East Germany's only alternative (short of bloody repression) is economic, social and political reform like that under way in the Soviet Union. But *glasnost* and *perestroika* look risky enough for Gorbachev, who faces re-emerging nationalism and economic quandaries of his own.

So East Germany's communist leadership is paralyzed, with an aging, ailing party chief who clings to the hard line, much like it was in Moscow at the end of the Brezhnev era. What's worse, none of the younger East German leaders now looks like a reformer, his own country's new Gorbachev.

For West Germany, the refugees are a joy, but also a worry. It can certainly absorb the 400,000 ethnic Germans leaving various East bloc nations this year, but would be overwhelmed by ten times more, the number that might leave if East Germany opened its border.

The Houston Post

Houston, TX, October 4, 1989

COMMUNIST EAST GERMANY was trying to avoid embarrassment when it agreed to let thousands of its citizens flee to West Germany. It didn't want to observe its 40th anniversary next Saturday with the refugees conspicuously camped at the West German embassies in Czechoslovakia and Poland, demanding the right to emigrate.

Soviet leader Mikhail Gorbachev should seize on this latest mass exodus of East Germans to make a fresh pitch for his liberalizing reforms when he attends East Germany's birthday celebration Friday and Saturday. Soviet Foreign Minister Eduard Shevardnadze has already been credited by West German officials with intervening in support of last Sunday's refugee release.

East Germany's ailing leader, Erich Honecker, and his hard-line cohorts have resisted Gorbachev's *glasnost*, or openness, and *perestroika*, or restructuring, for their "worker's paradise." Now they are paying the price.

More than 40,000 East Germans — most of them young skilled workers and their families — have escaped to the West in the past few months. Some 25,000 departed through Hungary, most of them since Sept. 11, when that reform-minded communist state let them cross its now-open border into Austria.

Another 7,000 who took refuge in West German embassies in Prague and Warsaw, some as long as three months ago, were then allowed to go West last weekend, after the Honecker regime accepted a face-saving device proposed by West Germany. The refugees had to travel through East Germany, technically satisfying their government's demand that they return home. East Berlin also contended that it was "expelling," not freeing, the refugees.

This subterfuge — intended to spare East Germany further embarrassment — didn't work. Even as the first embassy refugees were being transported to the West Sunday, more battled Czechoslovak police to gain entry to Bonn's Prague embassy. Another 300 flocked to its Warsaw embassy.

The beleaguered Honecker government again relented, reportedly agreeing Tuesday to let these refugees, estimated at more than 10,000, go to West Germany. But East Berlin also clamped controls on travel to Czechoslovakia, requiring East Germans to have visas.

East Germany's communist bosses have so far chosen to enforce the orthodox party line. But unless they loosen their repressive grip, they are destined to see more of their best and brightest choose the West and freedom over a dismal life in their Marxist-Leninist state.

THE SACRAMENTO BEE

Sacramento, CA, October 13, 1989

After years of condemning dissidents as hooligans and those who flee to the West as traitors to socialism, East Germany's ruling Politburo seems to have begun, albeit very tentatively, to concede that perhaps not everything is as it should be in the "workers' paradise" from which some 50,000 people have fled within the past month. Whether party chief Erich Honecker is part of this new thinking, however, is doubtful, which raises the question of how long he can survive in the post he has held for 18 years.

Honecker, who is 77, ailing and seemingly lost in the Stalinist past, still mouths the rhetoric of repression and just this week decried "imperialist" plots to undermine East Germany's Communist system. Yet collectively, the Politburo now concedes the internal origins of dissent, the need "to discuss all basic questions of our society." One key member has called for more openness, more popular participation in solving the country's problems, even for reforming the state-controlled press. What that really means is anyone's guess, yet the language is straight from Mikhail Gorbachev's reformist lexicon, which until now has been strictly *verboten* in East Germany.

Another apparent sign of change is the decision by authorities in Leipzig, Dresden and other cities, after a weekend during which police beat and arrested demonstrators, to change tactics — to permit a peaceful procession that drew 70,000 people in Leipzig and to begin a dialogue with pro-democracy activists. Such unprecedented concessions would hardly have been made without the assent of someone within the Politburo.

It's unclear whether this apparent relaxation results from the pro-reform pep talk that Gorbachev gave Honecker during a visit to Berlin last weekend, from shifting alliances within the party hierarchy or, as some skeptics suggest, simply from a desire to buy time. Nor is there any evidence yet that reforms, if they come, will go very far. Yet it's hard to see how East German leaders can maintain the status quo while so much is changing around them.

It's ironic that so many East Germans, who are materially much better off than their East European neighbors, are leaving in far greater numbers than Poles and Hungarians, who have more freedom of movement. It's also misleading: Despite the attraction of a free, affluent West Germany next door, the great majority of East Germans don't want to leave home so much as they want it to be a better place. Therein lies the opportunity that Honecker and his aging colleagues have, if they will seize it, to stop the drain of talent and the resultant damage to the economy and to national morale, by responding to the widespread demand for reform. If they fail to do that, if they cling stubbornly to their dogma, East Germans will continue to vote with their feet, and today's disorder may come to seem benign by comparison with what follows.

DAILY🔳NEWS

New York, NY, October 4, 1989

IT'S NOT A VERY HAPPY 40TH BIRTHDAY for communism. China and East Germany, for example, planned major celebrations. But the atmosphere just isn't right for partying. If Marxism isn't dead as a doornail, it's on the precipice.

In China, there remains a feeling of revulsion from the Tiananmen Square massacre. Western diplomats were right in refusing to attend 40th anniversary ceremonies in the square. How could anyone with a conscience celebrate a murderous government in the exact place where the carnage took place? The Chinese government may think it got away with the lie that nothing happened, but it hasn't. The whole world *was* watching and knows the truth.

The East German government's party may play to an empty hall. The mass exodus from this Eastern Bloc country couldn't come at a better time. Soviet President Mikhail Gorbachev is due this week for a visit. East German leaders wanted to show him that the old, iron-fisted way of ruling still works. It doesn't. And the East German people are showing their displeasure the only way they can. They are leaving. In droves.

Wimps. That's what East German leaders thought about other Soviet bloc countries that accommodated internal reform movements. Political and economic changes would not occur there, they insisted. Well, the East German government may not be able to read the writing on the wall, but the people can. They see *glasnost* and *perestroika* developing in Russia, Poland, Hungary and other Eastern nations — but not in their homeland.

That's the reason for the mass migration. It is the reaction of people who have been told that when it comes to democracy and prosperity, they're going to be left behind their neighbors.

When most folks reach 40, it's a time for reflection. Now that their governments have reached 40, the leaders of China and East Germany must reflect on the futures of their countries. Change is coming. Either the Chinese and East German leaders are going to help it along, or they will be exchanged.

THE SPOKESMAN-REVIEW

Spokane, WA, October 6, 1989

East Germany, where the Berlin Wall marks a political dividing line that has defined global politics ever since World War II, plans a 40th birthday party on Saturday.

But the party began ahead of schedule. And instead of coming to the party the guests were leaving — by the tens of thousands, in one of the most dramatic repudiations of the socialist-communist system that this century has seen.

In the space of less than four weeks, more than 50,000 East Germans have fled their homeland, driven out by oppression and economic despair, lured to the West by the promise of freedom and economic opportunity.

Swimming rivers, climbing fences, lining railroad tracks to leap aboard passing trains, trudging across country after country often with small children in tow, the refugees made an unforgettable statement, with an eloquence no words could equal, about the utter bankruptcy of Marxist ideology.

Soviet leader Mikhail Gorbachev is expected to speak at the weekend's festivities, but if truth be told, East Germany's leaders consider him a less-than-welcome guest. When thousands of East Germans filled the streets earlier this week and sang "we shall overcome" to protest the current East German regime, they punctuated the familiar freedom song with enthusiastic chants of "Gorby, Gorby, Perestroika, Perestroika."

Gorbachev's historic restructuring grates on East German leader Erich Honecker, who created a symbol of his increasing isolation by closing off East Germany's border with Czechoslovakia in an effort to staunch the hemorrhage in his country's population. A sealed border between East and West is familiar; but a sealed border between communist allies is something else again.

The communist bloc's severe economic woes are what motivate Gorbachev's historic drive to broaden civil rights, open doors to the West and institute the proven practices of free-market capitalism. If Gorbachev is clever as he seems, he may view this week's embarrassing uproar as a means to an end.

West German leaders are waiting eagerly, with rising hopes, for Honecker's fall and a German reunification.

With a non-growing, aging populace, how else can East Germany recover from the exodus of its youngest, boldest workers?

For the 72-year-old Honecker, the only question is how long he can hold out while his country crumbles beneath his stubborn feet.

Government compulsion ultimately fails as a means to economic production and political stability. You cannot keep a whole country in a concentration camp, although Honecker seems to think he can try. Perhaps he'll never learn, but the rest of the world, including some of his allies, can learn from his example.

Chicago Tribune

Chicago, IL, October 10, 1989

Well, in case it's been puzzling you, the East Germans have an explanation for why nearly 50,000 of their own have fled to the West in the last few weeks.

No matter what you may have thought, they want you to know all those folks didn't just pack up by coincidence and go off to Hungary to await their chances to make a run for freedom. No way, according to a commentary from the East German newspaper Neues Deutschland reprinted in English and circulated abroad to set things straight.

What actually happened is obvious to any steadfast East German socialist, but may have escaped you captive readers of the propagandistic American press. Those ugly West German imperialists seduced the refugees in a carefully planned "cloak-and-dagger" operation designed to make the German Democratic Republic look bad in the weeks leading up to last Saturday's 40th anniversary celebration.

If you really want to know what's behind it, the article suggests, remember Hitler's "back-to-the-Reich" movement, which "treats human beings as mere objects of revanchism and chauvinism." And as we mark a half century since the outbreak of World War II, the writer implies, nobody but a greedy capitalist would forget "the devastating consequences and innumerable human tragedies of such politics and practice."

A companion piece from ADN, the East German press service, contends the "orchestrated" effort to "tempt away [East German] citizens in Hungary" had "not even the slightest hint of humanity and love for one's fellow human beings."

The aim, it insists, was to get "cheap labor," providing "an elixir of life" for West Germany to increase its "potential for economic growth." Besides, those who've left for the West have already "experienced a sobering up about their prospects in the labor and housing markets."

So it's easy to understand why East Germany—full of "humanity and love" itself—felt compelled to crack down on pro-democracy demonstrations over the weekend. Just think, if it hadn't arrested and jailed a bunch of misguided protesters, they might have been lured off and enslaved by West German capitalists.

As for those who were only beaten by police or herded down side streets by trucks with steel-mesh cowcatchers, they certainly should be grateful for the lesson in social democracy. After all, as the East German news agency explained, the demonstrators were "troublemakers."

Not that it was all their fault, you understand. The Communist Party's youth newspaper, Junge Welt, also had some explanations. "Wherever the Western reporters went, especially the television crews, certain types showed up seconds later and started trouble," it wrote. So a couple of Western reporters were detained, too, and most were refused renewals of their visas for coverage of the anniversary events.

You can't be too careful. Now if the East German regime could just find some way to hush up that Mikhail Gorbachev fellow with all his talk of *glasnost* and *perestroika*, maybe those "Gorby! Gorby!" protesters would settle down.

The Dallas Morning News

Dallas, TX, August 21, 1989

The recent closing of the West German embassy in Budapest, Hungary, because of an overwhelming number of East German visa requests is a clear reminder that the lower Rio Grande Valley of Texas is not the only area of the Free World currently experiencing immigration overload.

More importantly, the West German decision underscores a contradiction in Western rhetoric about the Iron Curtain that leaders such as President Bush had best resolve quickly. During his trip to Europe last month, Mr. Bush called upon Mikhail Gorbachev to prove his newfound commitment to democratic ideals by tearing down the Berlin Wall. "The passion for freedom cannot be denied forever. The world has waited long enough. The time is right. Let Europe be whole and free," Mr. Bush proclaimed.

Unfortunately, Mr. Bush forgot to ask the West Germans what they thought of his idea. Polls have found that the West German people feel troubled by the prospects of skyrocketing numbers of refugees. According to the *Wall Street Journal*, more than 55,000 East Germans have fled to West Germany so far this year, while the total for 1989 is expected to reach 100,000. This would be more than twice the size of last year's total. Massive numbers of newcomers have intensified competition for jobs, social services and affordable housing.

The impact of the East German population hemorrhage would not be limited to the severe erosion of its labor force. At a time of East-West rapprochement, a precipitate East German economic nose dive can quickly turn into an arctic blast of resentment against West Germany. Regional stability easily could be impaired throughout Western Europe. Already, tensions between the two Germanys are at their highest level since the Berlin Wall went up.

George Bush is no Jack Kennedy, and 1989 is not 1961. Now is not the time to use East German refugees as debating points in an ideological crusade. The consequences of a massive refugee influx into West Germany could easily render that strategy counterproductive. As foreign-affairs writer Stephen Green recently noted in the *Christian Science Monitor*, "The problem is this guy Gorbachev. He has a nasty habit, when challenged in this fashion, of doing exactly what you dare him to do."

The Evening Gazette

Worcester, MA, September 13, 1989

The exodus of thousands of East Germans from Hungary to the West is the greatest escape to freedom in Europe since before the communists erected the Berlin Wall in 1961 to choke off the tide of refugees.

It also is one of the most significant events of the post-World War II era in Eastern Europe, one that is apt to have far-reaching consequences.

In some aspects, today's freedom flight is a replay of the great escape of 1956 when, after the ill-fated Hungarian uprising, an estimated 200,000 people streamed across the Austrian border to seek a new life.

But there is a historic difference: In 1956, the refugees had to climb over barbed wire, cross minefields and duck the bullets of Hungarian border guards. Now the guards wave the East Germans across with a smile.

Hungary has done more than just defy the Brezhnev doctrine of communist solidarity and its alliance with another Warsaw Pact country. For the first time in decades, it has clearly signaled to the world that it is casting its lot with the West. As one Western diplomat put it: "The Hungarians realized that they can't dance in Eastern clothes in a Western party."

As thousands of its jubilant citizens crossed the border that once was known as the Iron Curtain in their puttering, smoky little Trabant automobiles or buses sent from Austria and West Germany, the East German government was reduced to impotent rage.

Incredibly, the Soviet Union has refrained from criticizing Hungary — or Czechoslovakia, which has been part of the escape route — and lamely chose to blame the Western press for "instigating unlawful actions." A few years ago, Moscow would have sent tanks.

No one knows how many of the estimated 60,000 East German "tourists" still in Hungary choose to take advantage of the freedom trail, or how many more may arrive before the gates are closed again. But the exodus already has caused a tremendous brain drain and irreparable loss of prestige to the communist government of Erich Honecker.

Besides Hungary's bold decision to all but cut its ties with the East, the escape of the East Germans has another major significance: It focuses renewed attention on the idea of reunification of the two Germanies. For decades, the Western allies paid lip service to the concept because they knew it was out of the question.

While reunification is not likely to occur any time soon — it still frightens Britain and France — it is being debated again publicly. The flood of Germans from one part of their divided land, coupled with the decline of Soviet influence, keeps the issue alive.

Since Mikhail Gorbachev came to power, there have been astonishing changes in the East, and the results have reshaped international relations.

Those changes have many roots, but there is one overwhelming, great and glorious reason: the determination of people everywhere to move from oppression to freedom.

The TENNESSEAN

Nashville, TN, August 22, 1989

IT is somewhat reminiscent of the days before the Berlin Wall was erected — East Germans are fleeing to the West in growing numbers.

Some have permission. But many are using Hungary and Austria as escape routes since the Hungarians began tearing down the fences that were a part of the "Iron Curtain." While it is difficult for East Germans to get visas to visit the West, there is no particular problem involved in visiting Hungary or Czechoslovakia. So the exodus is on.

More than 55,000 East Germans have fled to West Germany this year. It is expected that 100,000 will have done so by the year's end.

Many of those who flee are young. All are frustrated by widespead deprivation, rigid controls and a lack of any freedom of expression. The East Germans are well aware of changes taking place in the Soviet Union and in Poland. But those who escape maintain that the East German party chief, Mr. Erich Honecker, doesn't contemplate or plan to tolerate the changes going on in other parts of the Communist bloc.

But if the exodus continues, Mr. Honecker may well face a work-force crisis as younger, better educated people flee to the West. He could solve it by giving the East Germans a little more hope for the future. But at 76, the East German chief is too set in the old ways and too afraid of the future to make changes. ∎

The Atlanta Journal
THE ATLANTA CONSTITUTION
Atlanta, GA, September 13, 1989

Even with their increasing familiarity, the remarkable changes in the Soviet Union and most East bloc states retain their power to excite and astound. Now, Hungary has broken with its Warsaw Pact partners, the first nation to do so, letting tens of thousands of East Germans emigrate to West Germany.

Erich Honecker

Its unilateral suspension of the pact's contrary provisions is only temporary, Hungary says, but even if that is so, East Germany and the Soviet Union, sharply disputing the break, are again embarrassed before the world by their inability to hold many of their citizens except by force. Already 10,000 East German "vacationers" in Hungary have used Hungary's extraordinary indulgence to bolt for West Germany. Some 80,000 are expected to make the shift by year's end.

The government of the aged and ailing Erich Honecker complains that West Germany has been enticing the emigrants, but that is universally recognized as a desperate attempt at face-saving. West Germany has observed its unofficial pact with the east to stand mum, taking all comers but seeking none.

Though it has provided better for its people economically than most Soviet bloc nations, East Germany has permitted not even a wisp of the freshening changes that have been blowing, with whatever uncertain future, through the Soviet Union and the East bloc. Its citizens remain in a severe ideological lockdown. As a result, it is losing its well-trained, venturesome young.

For West Germany, the refugees are arriving at a better-than-usual moment. Unemployment has dropped from 9 to 7.6 percent, the lowest in years, and the refugees appear to be a good match overall for the 250,000 job openings that have gone unfilled in a skills shortfall. Even so, Bonn is taking up a heavy if happy resettlement burden.

And with its boldness, Hungary continues to mark itself off from other East bloc nations as the one most willing to take substantial risks for the westward economic ties that it wants, at least partially buying into the Western human rights agenda for its passage.

It is difficult to imagine East Germany permitting this human hemorrhage to continue or, if it does, Hungary wanting to risk all standing in the Warsaw Pact by accommodating it without end. For everyone, the wiser course would be a controlled program negotiated between the Germanies, but a party so fossilized it could not bend to retain its own young is unlikely to bend to accommodate their emigration.

Only the flexibility that the current leadership has rejected could have any chance now of stabilizing the situation, on the one hand allowing enough emigration to let off the social steam while on the other working up reforms that would ease the pressure long run. The Honecker stiffs, neo-Stalinist holdouts, have shown that rigidity can't work without equally rigid accomplices.

THE INDIANAPOLIS NEWS
Indianapolis, IN, August 26, 1989

In spite of the promises of glasnost behind the curtain formerly called "iron," the residents of East Germany are voting no-confidence with their feet.

So far this year, 55,970 East Germans have come to the West, thousands of them without official permission. According to law, West Germany must offer citizenship to East German citizens inasmuch as it does not recognize the division of Germany.

The numbers of the exodus are increasing. For all of 1988, 39,832 emigrated to the West, according to Bonn Govermnent figures. For the month of July alone this year the figure was 11,707, with at least 20 percent having no permission for exit. These numbers do not include the hundreds of East Germans who escaped, for example, by taking vacations in Hungary and subsequently going to other countries.

Every possible avenue of escape is being explored by dissatisfied East Germans. Hundreds are encamped in West German diplomatic missions in East Berlin, Prague and Budapest. The Bonn government estimates that 200,000 East Germans are vacationing in Hungary and that a tenth of them may not plan to return home.

A Bonn government spokesman told The New York Times that "a large majority of East Germans no longer see any hope for the future, including party members up to middle-level functionaries. They do not believe the system or the personalities in their government are going to change any time soon. They are becoming desperate. Many of them now think the only choice is to leave, legally or otherwise."

Most East German observers do not believe there will be an armed revolt, but the mounting exodus is increasingly alarming. East German leaders are somewhat in the same mode as Fidel Castro — still defending their respective brands of socialism. They have not embraced Mikhail Gorbachev's "adaptations" of Marxism, and this is very embarrassing.

Losing an increasing number of its citizens — especially young families — is more than embarrassing for East Germany; it is the worst kind of tragedy. Some long-time analysts are saying that the future of the country is in danger.

If there is a bright side, however, it might provide a beginning for the eventual reunification of Germany.

Omaha World-Herald
Omaha, NE, October 3, 1989

East Germany's leaders continue to live in their dream world, ignoring reality and holding in contempt the articles of the Helsinki Accords that guarantee the right of all people to travel and immigrate. The government, apparently still trapped in the delusion that the way to deal with a dissatisfied populace begins and ends with building a wall, says that all East German problems are made in West Germany.

More than 100,000 East Germans have managed to escape one way or another in the past year. During the weekend, another 6,000 found freedom through Czechoslovakia and Poland after the Soviet government intervened on their behalf.

The agreement that was forced on East Germany allowed the refugees at West German embassies in Prague and Warsaw to proceed to West German soil. Many of the refugees wept with joy at their release.

Some other Eastern bloc leaders are far more realistic. They know that the old ways have failed, that they can no longer keep the populace docile with force, fear and the promise that things will get better in the workers' paradise in the near future.

Just about anyone can see that things are getting worse throughout the Soviet bloc — and that some other countries are responding in a much more rational manner.

The Hungarians have initiated political and economic reforms, including liberal immigration and travel rights, and opened their border with Austria. The Poles have taken dramatic steps toward political reform. President Mikhail Gorbachev has announced a number of reforms in the Soviet system, including a relaxation of emigration barriers for some groups.

No comparable concessions have come from the East German government. Even though East Germany has a higher living standard than any other East bloc country, life in East Germany remains drab and repressive. East Germany lacks the sparks of social and political ferment that have given hope to some Poles, Hungarians and Russians.

Keeping a country's population fenced in is no solution to anything. But neither is the depopulation of East Germany through emigration. The problem will be addressed rationally only when East Germany is governed by people who understand the importance of respecting human rights.

"Hey, what would OKTOBERFEST be without the traditional oompah band ?..."

Richmond Times-Dispatch
Richmond, VA, October 4, 1989

The release of approximately 7,000 East Germans to the West over the weekend, with more to follow, came about as a result of a rather surprising change of heart among various communist governments. The refugees, most of whom who had been holed up in West German diplomatic compounds in Warsaw and Prague for many days, rode trains to the West with stops along the way in East Germany, where still more émigrés joined their number.

This extraordinary passage through the most zealously guarded section of the Iron Curtain came about at least in part as a result of intercession by the Kremlin, which apparently persuaded the aging hard-line East German leadership to relent. With the go-ahead given by Moscow, Warsaw and Prague breathed a collective sigh of relief and allowed the refugees to leave.

The East German government had repeatedly demanded that those who had taken refuge in West Germany's diplomatic compounds return home, and having the freedom trains travel through East Germany on the way to freedom satisfied that requirement. The technical homecoming was not the only face-saving taking place with this latest wave of approved flight to the West; Saturday marks the 40th anniversary of the founding of the East German government, and a continued impasse over refugees would have embarrassed East German leader Eric Honecker during that important celebration.

Unfortunately for Mr. Honecker, this is one problem that just won't seem to go away. Even as the freedom trains made their way west, several thousand more East Germans flooded into West Germany's diplomatic compound in Prague. They, too, will be allowed to escape to the West. It is not clear how long this arrangement will hold up, but at least West Germany is not closing its open door. West Germany's Interior Ministry said in a statement, "Our embassies will not be walled shut."

The real question is how long Eastern Europe can remain walled shut. With the Soviet Union having apparently little desire to stem the flow of refugees, could it only be a matter of time before the Berlin Wall is demolished?

It is easy to get caught in the euphoria of moments such as this. The past few months have seen extraordinary movement on the emigration issue; Hungary has torn down its section of the Iron Curtain, the Soviet Union is allowing tens of thousands of Soviet Jews to emigrate and now even East Germany is relenting. However, one need only note that the Berlin Wall still stands, that travel papers are still required throughout the Soviet Bloc and that most borders remain heavily guarded to see that the current exodus is an exception to the rule.

Ironically, just as the communist bloc is showing signs of liberalizing emigration policies, the United States seems prepared to turn away many of the same people for whom the U.S. government has pleaded for decades. Due to budget constraints, the Bush administration has proposed setting a cap of 50,000 Soviet and 6,500 East European émigrés who can receive government resettlement assistance of approximately $5,000 each (paid over two years) in fiscal year 1990. But at least that many people already have applied for refugee status and as many as 200,000 people are set to leave the Soviet Union alone, many of them hoping to resettle in the United States.

If these deserving people are turned away, their communist masters will be able to claim that the United States has only been bluffing about emigration all of these years. Diplomatic embarrassments aside, such a cold policy could further undermine waning U.S. credibility abroad. This is no time for the Bush administration to play Scrooge. On the scale of government spending, the funds needed to help resettle refugees in the United States are small; surely spending in other areas can be trimmed a bit to make up the shortfall. Making whatever tough choices that would be necessary requires presidential leadership, something we have unfortunately seen very little of in regard to the refugee issue.

THE SACRAMENTO BEE
Sacramento, CA, September 12, 1989

By opening its border with the West to thousands of vacationing East Germans who refuse to return home, Hungary has delivered an unprecedented slap in the face of another Communist government. It has also added to growing uncertainty about the future of the once-solid Eastern bloc of Communist countries allied to Moscow. And because nearly all the refugees are likely to resettle in West Germany, this newest end run around the Berlin Wall threatens what had been, until recently, a gradually improving relationship between Bonn and East Berlin.

How long this new route to the West will stay open — Hungarian officials set no time limit in announcing their decision — and how many will seek to take advantage of it is unclear, although at least 60,000 East Germans are said to be on vacation in Hungary. What's clear is that the symbolic dismantling of the Iron Curtain that began earlier this year with the cutting away of the barbed wire fences along Hungary's border with Austria has become a genuine exodus. As more of the best and brightest seek to leave, it could have ominous consequences for East Germany's economy.

Hungary's refusal to go along with East Germany's demand that thousands seeking a new life in the West be stopped also sharpens the contrast between the liberalizing policies of Hungary and Poland on the one hand and the hard-line Communist regimes of East Germany, Czechoslovakia and Romania on the other. That Hungary's leaders were willing to incur East Berlin's wrath by "temporarily" abrogating an agreement not to allow their territory to be used as a transit route to the West is further evidence of a deepening rift, and of Budapest's deter-

mination to improve ties with the West, in particular with West Germany, in order to secure aid to reform its economy along capitalist lines.

East German reaction has been harsh, and hypocritical. An official statement accusing Hungary of "organized trade of human beings" is ironic, to say the least, in light of East Germany's long-standing practice of allowing some of its citizens to emigrate only upon payment by Bonn of thousands of dollars each in what amounts to ransom.

In the changed, non-interventionist atmosphere within the Soviet-led Warsaw Pact, Hungary's action presumably cannot be undone, and one must hope it won't be, and unless the East German regime closes its own border with Hungary, the exodus could continue. East Berlin might slow it down by instituting reforms like those in progress in the Soviet Union, Poland and Hungary and sought by many in East Germany itself. But its aging, Stalin-era leadership, personified by the ailing, 77-year-old Erich Honecker — ironically the man who supervised the building of the Wall in 1961 — shows no sign of yielding to demands for change.

For the West, including the Bush administration, satisfaction that a new gateway to freedom has been opened is certainly in order; but so, too, is a caution born of the knowledge that Eastern Europe, historically unstable, is in ferment again. As if free-market economic reforms and a dismantling of the Iron Curtain weren't enough evidence of that, Hungary's Communist Party chief is proposing a military accord with neutralist neighbors Austria and Yugoslavia, to include the removal of Soviet tanks from a buffer zone. That's bold, and heartening.

Portland Press Herald
Portland, ME, September 12, 1989

Deprived of freedom, thousands of East Germans are voting with their feet, pouring out of their country through neighboring Hungary to new lives in the West. For many it's been a long wait.

The migration marks the largest exodus of East Germans since the Berlin Wall was hurled up 28 years ago to hold them captive to a repressive communist system.

How they feel about that system isn't in doubt.

Since Hungary opened its border to the West, East Germans in recent weeks have been flocking there looking for a way out. Finally, after talks on their status between Hungary and East Germany broke down this week, they found it.

Hungary gave the green light and, within hours, East Germans, singing,

shouting and cheering, boarded trains, buses and cars for a noisy parade across the border into Austria. Then it was on to West Germany where new citizenship, homes and jobs await them.

Their loss represents more than public humiliation for East Germany, one of the most rigid communist bloc countries. It also marks a painful loss of productive young workers and their families.

Beyond that, however, the mass outpouring testifies to the deprivation and individual hopelessness at the heart of communist societies that Soviet leader Mikhail Gorbachev, risking much, seems determined to change.

So far, East Germany has chosen not to heed him. For that it is paying a heavy price in tickets west.

THE DENVER POST
Denver, CO, September 7, 1989

PRESIDENT George Bush was overly optimistic in his prediction that the Berlin wall will be torn down during his term in office. The wall probably will be dismantled at some point. But convincing the East Germans to do so may take a few more years than Bush is figuring.

This summer, between 3,000 and 6,000 East Germans took advantage of the newly opened Hungarian border to flee to West Germany. Another 5,000 are waiting in refugee camps for permission to continue their journey. And 200,000 others have applied for official permission to immigrate.

Those numbers represent only 1.2 percent of East Germany's population. But most of these immigrants are young, well-educated workers — the very people East Germany's moribund economy can least afford to lose.

Meantime, the already healthy economy of western Europe is expected to soar after 1992, when the European Economic Community consolidates into a unified market. Even neutral Austria has applied for membership in the Common Market, recognizing the tremendous economic and political benefits the consolidation will offer.

East Germany cannot continue to survive as an isolated entity, defying the flow of current events. The Berlin Wall survives only as a stark symbol of the country's backward isolationism.

But if the wall were dismantled, East German's communist leaders would have to surrender their political power and admit that they lost the ideological struggle of the past three decades. That's why the wall likely will remain standing until East Germany's current leaders die or are booted out of office.

Either scenario is possible if events in Europe continue their current course. The pressures on East Germany to demolish the wall and all it signifies are tremendous. The real question is whether that dramatic decision will take place in the next three to seven years as Bush predicted.

The chances are that it will not. Nonetheless, Bush and other free world leaders should continue to work toward getting the East Germans to tear down this most hated symbol of the waning Cold War.

Honecker Ousted as East German Leader

The Central Committee of East Germany's Socialist Unity (Communist) Party Oct. 18, 1989 removed Erich Honecker as the nation's leader and replaced him with Politburo member Egon Krenz. Honecker, 77, had ruled East Germany for 18 years. The Central Committee said that Honecker had decided to step down because of poor health. But Western analysts believed he was forced out.

Honecker's removal had been preceded by a week of rumors in East Germany that a majority of the Politburo no longer supported his uncompromising resistance to change. Pro-democracy protests and the recent refugee mass immigration to West Germany had shaken the leadership.

In addition to Honecker, the Central Committee ousted economy chief Guenter Mittag, 63, and propaganda chief Joachim Herrmann, 60.

Krenz, 52, was the youngest member of the Politburo. His party duties had included oversight of internal security and youth affairs. Krenz assumed all three of the posts held by Honecker: party chief, chairman of the national Defense Council and head of state.

The new leader's position on meaningful reform was in question Oct. 18. Western observers noted that Krenz was a Honecker protege, that he had a reputation for conservatism and that he had controlled East Germany's security forces.

In a nationally televised address Oct. 18, the new leader reaffirmed the party's policies of "continuity and renewal" and stressed its leading role in society. But, he added, "The door is wide open for earnest political dialogue...It is clear that we have not realistically appraised the social developments in our country in recent months, and have not drawn the right conclusions quickly enough."

Krenz called the exodus to West Germany "a great loss of blood." He spoke candidly of problems in the economy, including declining productivity and a shortage of housing.

West German Chancellor Helmut Kohl and U.S. President George Bush Oct. 18 each took a cautious attitude on the East German leadership change.

In Bonn, Kohl said that Krenz would be judged on whether "he takes the path of long-overdue reforms or sticks to a defense of their monopoly of power."

President Bush, speaking with reporters in Washington, doubted that Honecker's replacement meant a significant shift in East German policies. "Mr. Krenz was very much in accord with policies of Mr. Honecker," he noted.

An estimated 100,000 people took part in a pro-democracy protest in Leipzig Oct. 16. It was believed to be the largest unauthorized demonstration in East Germany since 1953.

The demonstration came three days after the regime released hundreds of protesters arrested Oct. 3-9. On the same day the protesters were freed, Oct. 13, Honecker had made a speech at a political gathering in East Berlin expressing the leadership's willingness to confer with "all citizens." The speech was taken by Western observers to be a sign that the party had compelled Honecker to accept a more conciliatory approach.

The Leipzig was march free of violence. Participants chanted "We want new leaders!" and called for wholesale reforms. As in a big Leipzig protest on Oct. 9, security forces did not attempt to stop the demonstration. An estimated 30,000 people staged peaceful protests in parts of Dresden Oct. 16.

THE SACRAMENTO BEE
*Sacramento, CA,
October 21, 1989*

Egon Krenz, who replaced Erich Honecker this week as East Germany's supreme leader, is at 52 the youngest member of the ruling Communist Party Politburo, but also one of its most orthodox. There would be greater cause for reformist hope if Krenz were not a Honecker protege with a hardline record as chief of security and, most recently, as an admirer of the way Chinese leaders put down their people's rebellion in Tiananmen Square.

In his first day on the job, Krenz made some gestures to critics of the regime by visiting a factory, meeting with church leaders, allowing something approximating a live televised news conference and hinting that East Germans may soon have greater freedom to travel abroad. And in an oblique reference to the mass public protests of recent weeks, he conceded that the Politburo had "not realistically enough appraised social developments ... and not drawn the right conclusions quickly enough." Yet he also insisted that "our society already has enough democratic forums ... ," which seems to rule out recognition of popular new opposition groups like New Forum, or reforms with anything like the scope of those now under way in Poland, Hungary and the Soviet Union.

As if to underline what sets East Germany apart from its neighbors, Hungary took a major step toward democracy on the same day that Krenz took over in East Berlin. Having already turned the Communist Party into the Socialist Party, parliament changed the country's name from People's (meaning Communist) Republic to simply Republic of Hungary, created the office of president to replace a 21-member collective ruling body, declared a multiparty democracy, and set the stage for free elections next year.

Such reforms are bound to intensify East Germans' dissatisfaction with their own stifling bureaucracy, an ideologically retrograde leadership and tight controls on free expression. The Politburo replaced its economics minister and the head of the state-run media, but a Cabinet reshuffle, a half-confession of failure and a superficial openness are hardly enough to defuse popular discontent. Perhaps Krenz realizes that; perhaps, like Mikhail Gorbachev, he's simply biding his time until the moment is right for reform.

Against that slim likelihood, however, it's important to recall that East Germany's party elite has long been the most hard-line in the Communist world, not only because of its commitment to a Marxist-Leninist system, but also because it knows, and openly admits, that without that system, East Germany would have no reason to exist as an independent state. In that context, it's hard to see how Krenz can resolve a crisis that, so far, he is only vaguely willing to admit even exists. In ousting the aging and ailing Erich Honecker, his colleagues have replaced an unyielding old Bolshevik with a younger one who looks so far very much the same.

BUFFALO EVENING NEWS
Buffalo, NY, October 29, 1989

EAST GERMANY observed its 40th anniversary this month, but it had little to celebrate. The failures of the rigid Marxist regime were eloquently shown by the flight of thousands of its citizens to the West and by mass public demonstrations for freedom.

These failures helped to topple the aging Communist leader, Erich Honecker, from power last week, but his successor, Egon Krenz, has long been groomed to succeed him and appears unlikely to make fundamental changes.

In switching to Krenz, the East German hard-liners have gone from the man who supervised the building of the Berlin Wall to the man who recently praised China for its suppression of freedom in Beijing.

Krenz seems to be aiming at a more appealing style than Honecker, visiting factories and appearing on television, but the hard-line policies appear unchanged. In a national TV address, he talked of change and promised a dialogue with all segments of society, but he also said that "our society already has enough democratic forums."

In another innovation, top party officials answered phone-in questions on television. The format was encouraging, but the answers were the same old party line.

The accession of Krenz does not signal substantive change. But though democratization is not imminent, there is good reason to think the East German leadership will not be able to hold it off forever. With striking democratic gains being made in Poland, Hungary and the Soviet Union, pressure for reform in East Germany will grow.

When East Germans held demonstrations for freedom in 1953, they were suppressed by Soviet troops. But on a recent visit to East Berlin, Soviet leader Mikhail Gorbachev said East German policies were an internal matter, suggesting that Krenz could expect no help from Moscow if he resorted to force.

Despite his Stalinist leanings, Krenz may gradually have to yield to the yearnings for freedom.

The possibility raises a set of international questions. If all Germans were free, the issue of German reunification would naturally arise — with far-reaching implications. East Germany is the anchor of the Warsaw Pact, and West Germany is the anchor of NATO. What would a reunited Germany do to these alliances?

If not accomplished with care, reunification of Germany might threaten the present equilibrium in Europe and the cordial ties between Washington and Moscow. The United States recognizes this and is now studying where East Germany might fit into the European jigsaw puzzle if it does eventually achieve freedom.

In his talks with the Soviet foreign minister, Secretary of State James Baker has properly stressed that the United States seeks not only freedom in Europe, but stability.

It is impossible to know how many years the larger powers will have to work out their policy on a reunited Germany. The pace of events in Eastern Europe has become dizzyingly unpredictable as the Soviets have loosened control of their satellites.

In the years of adjustment ahead, it is important for the United States to work closely with the Soviet Union, as well as with West Germany, in preparing for a new kind of Europe.

Richmond Times-Dispatch
Richmond, VA, October 23, 1989

In a time of great change behind the Iron Curtain, East Germany has stood as one of a few holdouts against reform. Erich Honecker, who last Wednesday resigned as head of East Germany's Communist Party, was to a large degree responsible for his government's intransigence. But his replacement, Egon Krenz, appears to be no revolutionary, and may continue East Germany's hard-line policies.

Mr. Krenz made his way to the top via the same route taken by Mr. Honecker years ago; he is a past head of the communist youth organization and directed East Germany's vast secret police apparatus for six years. One indication of Mr. Krenz's lack of sympathy toward reform is his recent official visit to the People's Republic of China — after Tiananmen Square. On a visit to West Germany this past summer, Mr. Krenz vigorously supported the bloody crackdown.

Krenz

Brigitte Schulte, a Social Democrat member of West Germany's parliament who accompanied Mr. Krenz on his West German visit, told The New York Times: "He did not voice one original idea. I don't see any chance for him to bring reforms. He is part of a small clique that has all the privileges. And the people don't trust him."

Mr. Honecker was reportedly ousted at least in part for allowing mass demonstrations to take place. The West would do well to apply the lessons of Tiananmen Square now that Mr. Honecker is gone. Few analysts doubt that Mr. Krenz would use force to crush demonstrations. While the West should send signals to Mr. Krenz that any liberalization measures would be well-received, Western leaders must be careful not to encourage protests that could result in massive bloodshed.

It must be kept in mind that East Germany is the key to the Warsaw Pact's military strategy. Thus, East Germany's leadership cannot be expected to tolerate anything that might create instability. We hope we are wrong, but it seems highly unlikely that Mr. Krenz would orchestrate anything remotely resembling the kind of radical reform taking place in Hungary and Poland.

PORTLAND EVENING EXPRESS
Portland, ME, October 28, 1989

East Germany's new leader, Egon Krenz, is actually behaving as though he would welcome political change in his country. He spoke this week about a public debate on reforms, opening a "dialogue" with pro-democracy groups and letting East Germans travel abroad more freely.

At the same time, however, Krenz said the Berlin Wall will not come down anytime soon.

Too bad. There could be no stronger signal to the world at large of a sincere commitment to reform than the demolition of The Wall.

As it is, it stands as a durable emblem of shame for the impoverished political system it encases and the people it attempts to imprison.

The wholesale exodus of East Germans to the West in recent weeks via neighboring countries only serves to remind us of the reason the Berlin Wall was erected in the first place. The government these people have voted against with their feet remains the only regime in history to construct a walled city for the purpose of keep its citizens in rather than strangers out.

So long as East Germany holds on to this symbol of its failure as a government, it will continue to embrace the mechanics of its failure.

And true reform of the sort needed to revive this stagnant nation — economic, social and cultural reform — will remain elusive.

Again we are reminded of poet Robert Frost's line: "Before I built a wall I'd ask to know what I was walling in or walling out."

The new leaders of East Germany ought to put that question to themselves once more.

A candid, pragmatic answer could rescue them.

LE SOLEIL

Quebec, Que., October 20, 1989

Les dirigeants est-allemands ont remplacé un chef dur et dépassé par un jeune leader tout aussi dur, et à la réputation passablement amochée. Egon Krenz succède à Erich Honecker au milieu de l'incrédulité générale: le nouveau chef du parti communiste dirigeait déjà les forces de répression.

Le maquillage politique de Berlin-Est trompe fort peu de gens. À partir du principe de qui se ressemble, se rassemble, M. Krenz a déjà reçu les félicitations de son homologue chinois, Jiang Zemin. À bon entendeur, salut! La République démocratique allemande avait été une des rares nations au monde à féliciter Beijing pour avoir ramené « l'ordre » sur la place Tien An Men, en juin dernier.

À sa première allocution télévisée, le nouveau secrétaire du parti communiste a montré sa volonté de résister au mouvement de changement. Le pays dispose de suffisamment de forums démocratiques pour le moment, a-t-il lancé à une population qui exige sa liberté.

Cinquante-trois mille habitants de la RDA ont quitté le pays ces dernières semaines, et 130,000 depuis le début de l'année. Un économiste est-allemand évalue la perte financière à quelque $500 millions, un dur coup même pour le pays le plus prospère du bloc communiste.

Mais si les Hongrois et les Polonais ont réussi la première étape de leur libération, qu'est-ce qui empêche les 16 millions d'Allemands de l'Est de les imiter? Simplement, la nature même du pouvoir. Ouverte, la RDA disparaîtrait dans les poubelles de l'histoire.

Sans rideau de fer, sans mur de Berlin, les Honecker, Krenz et consorts n'auraient aucun pouvoir. Les Allemands, dans leur ensemble, refusent de légitimer la partition de leur pays en deux.

Le gouvernement cherche en vain des interlocuteurs valables. Les églises protestantes tentent de diriger le mouvement de protestation, comme en Pologne, et le pouvoir leur tend une main bien timide.

Il espère sans doute dépolitiser l'opposition en négociant avec elle un modus vivendi particulier. Les foules de Leipzig et d'ailleurs réclament plus qu'un compromis élitiste. Elles exigent une vraie démocratie, et ce avant de tomber dans le désordre économique à la polonaise.

Edmonton Journal

Edmonton, Alta., October 20, 1989

Erich Honecker's departure from the leadership of the German Democratic Republic may not have been voluntary.

Even so, there's no reason yet to think that the change in leadership will signal a substantial change in East Germany.

Honecker's leadership was under siege as tens of thousands of people took to the streets to demand democratic reforms, and tens of thousands more voted with their feet by fleeing.

New leader Egon Krenz, at 52, is a quarter-century younger than Honecker, but he has been a loyal Communist throughout his career. His does not look very much like the background of a reformer, and it would be premature to think that he will readily take the path of change.

Still, his appointment may indicate that East Germany's leaders are ready to be more flexible than Honecker, the man who put up the Berlin Wall. If nothing else, the change is a generational one, and the younger leaders may be more willing than Honecker to respond to pressures from both the Soviet Union and the Federal Republic of Germany.

The Soviet pressure was made clear during President Mikhail Gorbachev's recent visit, when he urged Honecker to respond to the people's demand for reform.

It may be that Soviet pressure led to Honecker's ouster, even though Gorbachev said that East Germany's future would be decided not in Moscow, but in Berlin.

The new leadership, if nothing else, will listen to what the Soviets have to say. But they are not under the same economic pressures that have forced the U.S.S.R. and other East bloc countries to restructure socialism. They are being asked to add political rights to a fairly affluent economy.

Whatever the future holds, Honecker's departure is the end of an era. He was part of the German Communist movement that flourished before the Second World War, and was later crushed by the Nazis. Honecker spent a decade in a Nazi prison. After the war, he dedicated his career to building an orthodox Communist state that delivered the highest standard of living in the Soviet bloc.

Until the day of his departure, Honecker insisted that his was the correct model for the development of Germany; he was a pure Marxist in Karl Marx's native land.

His successors may not subscribe to so unbending an ideological line. The stunning scale of change in Eastern Europe cannot bypass East Germany forever.

Even as Honecker was being replaced, the Hungarian parliament voted a series of constitutional amendments that opened the way to a multiparty democracy.

Krenz and the new leadership show no inclination to follow suit, but perhaps they realize, as Honecker did not, that some degree of change is inevitable. The civil unrest can be quelled by force, the flight of people is not so easy to contain.

The pressures for change come not just from the people, but from East Germany's allies in the Warsaw Pact — that combination may prove difficult to resist.

THE INDIANAPOLIS STAR

Indianapolis, IN, October 23, 1989

Of all Erich Honecker's lifetime accomplishments, he was proudest of the Berlin Wall. He said it helped preserve peace.

Actually, the 102-mile wall, built in 1961, helped preserve the East German state. If it had not been for the wall, much of the population might have escaped from the dismal, regimented communist paradise.

In 1971 Honecker became East German chief of state and Communist Party leader. East Germans kept escaping. Many died trying. The workers' paradise was not for them. Since the recent relaxation of travel restrictions, some 60,000 East Germans have gone West, looking for the change they could not find at home.

Demonstrating in the streets, East Germans have been calling for free speech and other reforms. Honecker would not budge.

Last week hard-liner Honecker resigned, supposedly for reasons of health. He turned his office over to his hand-picked successor, hard-liner Egon Krenz, who promised a "turning point" in the country's policies.

What kind of turning point can East Germans expect of Krenz? As chief of security he ordered a crackdown on dissidents in 1987.

East Germans demonstrating in the streets say they want change. A 52-year-old hard-liner has replaced a 77-year-old hard-liner. We do not think that is the kind of change they had in mind.

The Birmingham News

Birmingham AL, October 19, 1989

The rather abrupt end to Erich Honecker's iron-fisted rule of East Germany was signaled weeks ago when thousands of his countrymen let the world know what they really thought of life under the communist thumb through their mass exodus to the West.

The 77-year-old Honecker, who had been head of the Communist Party in East Germany and thus the nation's leader for 18 years, would not let the exodus move him.

He had not caved in to the reform-minded Mikhail Gorbachev and he wasn't about to let the mass escape persuade him to grant East Germans more freedom.

His party, however, seeing the dissolution of its counterpart in Hungary, decided to act for him. Honecker was stripped of his power Wednesday and replaced by Egon Krenz.

Krenz is also expected to resist pro-democracy demands. But party members apparently feel he is more reasonable than Honecker, whose entrenchment helped spur the exodus of more than 123,000 East Germans, most of them young, skilled workers.

Days before Honecker's fall was announced, party members were hinting that important changes were about to take place.

After months of declaring the perestroika and glasnost seeds Gorbachev was sowing throughout Eastern Europe were not for their citizens, the post-exodus East Germans became less strident.

By Tuesday evening, Manfred Gerlach, chairman of one of the small parties allied with the Communists, was announcing to the world that it should expect by the next day decisions "that will noticeably affect life, the living conditions of all citizens."

What does Honecker's demise mean to the Free World?

As President Bush said Wednesday, it's much too early to tell. Krenz, 52, may be younger than Honecker, but like most members of the East German Politburo he is a hard-liner.

Reports that it was Krenz's personal intervention that stopped police beatings of pro-democracy demonstrators earlier this month in East Berlin and Dresden are encouraging.

And whatever happens next, there is some pleasure just knowing that the man who ordered the infamous Berlin Wall built, Erich Honecker, no longer is in power.

Wisconsin State Journal

Madison, WI, October 19, 1989

Two days before Erich Honecker stepped down as the leader of communist East Germany, U.S. Secretary of State James Baker III made a pronouncement that many Americans found curious and that millions of Europeans no doubt found downright alarming. The reunification of Germany, Baker said, is the "legitimate right" of the German people.

The gulping sound you heard was 56 million French simultaneously choking on their wine.

Reunify Germany? The same Germany that was at the center of two world wars in this century and divided in 1945 by those who feared a third? Baker's one-Germany chat stirred old and dark memories.

Still, this is a logical time to address the long-dormant "German question," for the departure of Honecker after 18 years of iron-fisted rule is certain to accelerate the reunification movement.

For more than 40 years, East and West Germany have been separate, each championing the ideological cause of a competing superpower. West Germany is closely aligned with the United States, East Germany with the Soviet Union. Yet there are signs of wear on both sides of the border.

Honecker's East Germany has not kept pace with political changes in Mikhail Gorbachev's Soviet Union, despite Gorbachev's warning that "We have to react to the times; otherwise life will punish us." The exodus of 50,000 East Germans to the West and huge demonstrations by many of those who stayed behind are proof of his words.

Long-suppressed nationalism is on the rise in West Germany, which is already rethinking its role in the North Atlantic Treaty Organization alliance. In some ways, West Germans identify more closely with eastern and central Europe than with the West.

Gorbachev and the Bush adminstration somehow believe that a single Germany would be in their best interests. Gorbachev has stirred reunification hopes, perhaps because he hopes that a single, vibrant Germany — already, there are $7 billion worth of economic ties between East and West — would help to revive the Warsaw Pact's stagnant economy.

Baker and his boss, President Bush, believe that a unified Germany would lean to the West. In his speech last week, Baker said reunification should take place peacefully after East Germans are granted "the better life they now seek" and with the new Germany integrated into a community of democratic European nations.

Many foreign-policy observers fear the Bush administration is playing with fire. Some say a unified Germany would be neutralized to the point of instability, a thought that sends shivers up the spines of a whole generation of Europeans who suffered through World War II precisely because World War I had left behind an unstable Germany.

"I love Germany so much I am glad there are two of them," quips novelist Francois Mauriac. Before Baker and Bush fall hopelessly in love with the idea of a reunified Germany, they should know that at least one superpower suitor — and maybe both — will be jilted.

East Germany Opens Borders, Including Berlin Wall

East Germany Nov. 9, 1989 announced relaxation of restrictions on the travel and immigration of its citizens to the West. The action virtually opened the country's borders, including the Berlin Wall.

The announcement climaxed a week of monumental developments. During the period Nov. 2-8, East German leader Egon Krenz visited Moscow and Warsaw, more than half a million people staged a pro-democracy protest in East Berlin, as many as 50,000 East Germans fled to West Germany through Czechoslovakia, the East German government resigned, the Politburo of the ruling Socialist Unity (Communist) Party was purged, a reformist was named premier and the regime suggested a willingness to hold free elections. Krenz, the successor to ousted hard-line leader Erich Honecker, exhibited surprising flexibility as he struggled with rising demands for change.

The West – trying to adapt to the dizzying pace of liberalization in the U.S.S.R., Poland and Hungary – was caught off guard by the developments in East Germany, once the embodiment of uncompromising orthodox communism.

The East German government Nov. 9 lifted the restrictions that had curbed legal travel and immigration to the West. East Germans no longer required special permission from the state for private journeys or emigration. Exit visas were to be issued "immediately" to those who wanted them. "Permanent emigration is allowed across all border crossing points between East Germany and West Germany and West Berlin," the announcement said.

Some Western observers believed the East Berlin regime hoped to stem the flight to West Germany by using reverse psychology: If people knew they were free to leave, perhaps they would decide to stay.

Within hours of the announcement, thousands of jubilant East Germans and West Germans met at the Berlin Wall for an impromptu celebration that lasted into Nov. 10. Near the historic Brandenburg Gate, hundreds of youths from both countries danced atop the wall without interference from East Germany's border guards. Many curious East Berliners crossed through the wall's checkpoints simply by showing their identity cards to the sentries.

"The long-awaited day has arrived," said West Berlin Mayor Walter Momper Nov. 9. "The Berlin Wall no longer divides Berliners."

The wall had been the symbol of East-West divisions since its construction in 1961. Some people used hammers and chisels to chip pieces from the barrier, an action carried around the world in television coverage.

West German Chancellor Helmut Kohl, visiting Poland Nov. 9, welcomed the East German move: "It is hard to estimate what consequences this step will have. Our interest must be that our compatriots stay in their homeland."

U.S. President George Bush Nov. 9 hailed the development as a "dramatic happening for East Germany and, of course, for freedom." But he cautioned that it was too early to think in terms of German reunification.

Early Nov. 10, East Germany opened five other crossing points at the wall, including the Gliencke Bridge, the site of East-West spy exchanges. In addition, East Germany began issuing instant travel visas at the crossing points.

Tens of thousands of East Germans poured into West Berlin Nov. 10 on foot and by car and special shuttle buses. They were greeted by thousands of West Berliners, who offered the visitors flowers, champagne and candy at the crossing points. The sounds of ringing church bells, honking car horns and singing filled the air. A holiday atmosphere prevailed on both sides of the wall. In West Berlin, long-separated friends and relatives were reunited in tearful scenes.

The vast majority of East Germans returned to their country. West German authorities estimated that 40,000 entered West Berlin Nov. 9-10, and that 1,500 elected to stay on the western side.

West German politicians gathered on the steps of West Berlin's city hall Nov. 10 to laud the opening of the wall. Chancellor Kohl, who had rushed back from Poland, told onlookers, "I want to call out to all in the German Democratic Republic [East Germany]: We're on your side. We are and remain one nation. We belong together…Long live a free German fatherland. Long live a united Europe."

Rockford Register Star

Rockford, IL, November 12, 1989

If there is a more odious piece of real estate than the "Berlin Wall," modern minds will be hard put to name it. The Berlin Wall actually snakes its way with barbed wire and cinder block for 858 miles along the East German frontier. Now it has been breached with celebration as East Germany's borders opened last week.

But The Wall still stands. Areas of Cold War conflict still exist.

Therein lies a somber mystery.

What will the new Europe look like? And what will be its social, political and moral warp? Whether we like it or not (and some do not), a whole new pulse beat is surging through Europe with talk of unifying the two Germanys, the free and democratic West Germany with communist East Germany.

Despite the champagne reception for many East Germans as they surged into West Berlin, the fact is that a divided Germany was the premise of the peace following World War II. France still does not favor restoring its old enemy to pre-war sufficiency. Just as chary is the Soviet Union, still quaking from the loss of 20 million persons in that bloody conflict.

So, the interchange of visitors aside, the mass migration into West Germany aside, what are the stakes here?

They are, to state the obvious, immense.

Would a united Germany become one big bloc for peace? If so, at whose expense? Quite obviously, the border between East and West Germany now defines contrasting political systems and opposing war machines.

Should the unthinkable happen and unification occur (a premise that is just as viable as The Wall itself coming down some day), what happens to the NATO forces of the West, the Warsaw Pact nations of the East? Quite clearly, both the United States and Soviet Union would no longer be calling all the shots for Europe.

Would that factor pull the tooth of Soviet aggression and suspicion? Would it render the United States a nominal but not too interesting economic force?

There's a lot of nail-biting going on. The syndrome moves both ways, encompassing the powerful and the deposed, the military and the peaceniks, world trade boosters and economists of a nationalist bent.

Long range tremors of change vie with the more skittish short-range crises. What does West Germany do for instance, if it winds up with 1.2 million East Germans? Where will they be housed, how will they be fed and when, what kind of jobs will sustain them?

Where do these cascading events put the approaching summit between Soviet President Mikhail Gorbachev and United States President George Bush? How stable is Gorbachev's job, which is not delivering the consumer goods including food to his scattered millions?

Will East Germany, though communist controlled, opt for the free elections the West is demanding? Will Poles survive the economic pressures that go with the freedom they covet so arduously? Which way for Hungary and its avowed pursuit of socialism? And what about the hard liners in Czechoslovakia, Bulgaria and Romania?

Is the Cold War dead — or on ice?

Massive opposing armies still exist. Soviet support for Cuba and Nicaragua remains a nagging issue. It surely is not yet possible to declare enlightenment in our time.

Perhaps the most pertinent comment came from West German Chancellor Helmut Kohl who said, "Let us avoid the temptation to assume that a solution to the German question can be arranged in advance with a script and a calendar. History doesn't follow a schedule." He spoke with more pertinence than perhaps he knew as his views became part of that history.

JERICHO

The San Diego Union

San Diego, CA, November 8, 1989

After almost three decades, the ultimate symbol of communist tyranny, the Berlin Wall, has been effectively reduced to tatters. An estimated 170,000 East Germans have fled this year, with the pace accelerating to more than 10,000 a day since authorities eased travel restrictions to Czechoslovakia, the prime portal to the West.

In a humiliating rebuke to East Berlin's hardline regime, refugees relate accounts of half-empty factories now, with workers who are left behind forced to put in double shifts to make up for the skilled laborers and professionals who have voted with their feet or clattering Trabant automobiles. Sections of some hospitals are closing because of personnel shortages. The frenzied hemorrhage of the next generation is likely only to grow, despite the pleas and promises of East Germany's new Communist Party boss, Egon Krenz.

Opposition demands for a new government prompted the resignations yesterday of the cabinet left behind by ousted party chief Erich Honecker. The cabinet, led by Premier Willi Stoph, also issued a pitiful appeal to East Germans to remain behind the wall, asserting that "our socialist fatherland needs all and everyone."

Yet, unless Mr. Krenz is also willing to step aside soon to make way for genuinely new leadership, he may go down in history as the party chief who presided over communism's Dunkirk.

Mr. Krenz, an orthodox ruler cut from the Stalinist mold, is not trusted by his countrymen to implement Gorbachev-style reform. Even his modest pledge to relax travel restrictions to the West, allowing East Germans to leave the country for up to 30 days a year, was not accepted on faith. This fact is vividly illustrated by the hasty exodus through Czechoslovakia to West Germany by tens of thousands of asylum-seekers who prudently fear the present opportunity to escape to freedom will not last.

The lack of confidence in Mr. Krenz is well founded. As the leading protégé of Mr. Honecker, he was a staunch opponent of economic and political reform, even as Poland and Hungary implemented sweeping changes with the apparent blessing of Mikhail Gorbachev. Although eight aging members of the East German Politburo have been replaced in recent weeks, the balance of power still rests with the hidebound leadership of the Honecker era.

Even more ominous, from the standpoint of young East Germans yearning for a political voice and economic opportunity, is Mr. Krenz's fervent endorsement of China's bloodstained crackdown against pro-democracy demonstrators. Violent tactics like those used in the Tiananmen Square massacre may yet be employed by the panicky East German regime to suppress the burgeoning demands for freedom. At the very least, the country's borders could be sealed again at any hour to halt the flight to the West.

The only way to stem the waves of refugees — short of using brutal force and shoring up the Berlin Wall with more barbed wire and machine guns — is to offer East Germans legitimate cause for hope. This requires a new generation of leaders committed to free-market economics and political liberalization. Poland and Hungary already have made this leap and instilled in their citizens at least some promise for a less bleak future.

East Germany, relatively the most prosperous country in the Soviet bloc, stands to gain enormously by embracing Western-style economic and political reforms. A single change — allowing foreign investment — could spur an economic resurgence in East Germany fueled largely by West German companies. If capitalist economic policies were matched by a democratic opening, East Germany could become the envy of its neighbors rather than the global symbol of communism's wretched failings.

The Kansas City Times

Kansas City, MO,
November 11, 1989

The image of Berliners standing jubilantly on the hated wall goes into human memory along with the lone figure in front of the tanks in Tiananmen Square. Both scenes sum up momentous shifts in the history of our times. In Berlin it's as if the villagers have planted their feet on the carcass of a dragon that has swallowed them up for nearly three decades. They want to make sure the loathsome thing is dead.

This is the time for a triumphal victory holiday to honor the brave people the wall killed and maimed, and those who remembered it was there.

There will be time later to consider the long-term prospects of a unified Germany and what that can mean. Unquestionably it will reawaken genuine fears and doubts. Economic consequences may be more unsettling than any distant likelihood of a return of German militarism. Countries that for their own political purposes have been beguiling Germans with visions of unification will have to do some swift rethinking. The short-term confusion over the status of travelers and the strain the migration westward is placing on Bonn cannot be deferred very long. That is largely a German question.

At 2 o'clock in the morning of Aug. 13, 1961, units of the People's Police and National People's Army blocked boundaries between the Soviet and Western sectors. Tanks and troops lined up. No one was allowed to pass. Streets were barred off and concrete piles driven into intersections. Paving was ripped up and ditches dug. Barbed wire fences were erected. Near the Brandenburg Gate water hoses and tear-gas grenades were used against West Berliners demonstrating on their own territory.

Aug. 15 concrete slabs were laid. In a few days the ugly monument began to take shape. Aug. 29 a refugee trying to swim the Tetlow canal was shot by East guards. Many killings would follow.

Over the years much of the world became accustomed to the existence of the wall. The peace marchers and nuclear freezers seemed oblivious to the fact that life was very different on each side of the wall. Some act as if nothing has happened, and will moon over the future of "socialism," whatever that word may mean to them. East Germans know what it has meant to them. They will remember that the border guards smiling today were squinting down gun barrels yesterday. They know that the jolly rulers opening the gates this November were grinding their jackboots into helpless families a very short time ago.

The excitement will subside and Germany will turn to the sober business of working toward an orderly transition to freedom. What form the future takes concerns many people and many elements beyond the two Germanys. Some change will come quickly. Some must be deliberate.

But for now, these matters can be put aside. This is a time of celebration, a time to pay joyous homage to the endurance of the human spirit and the inextinguishable spark that yearns for liberty.

Freedom has won. Czechoslovakia is next.

MILWAUKEE SENTINEL

Milwaukee, WI, November 11, 1989

The cascade of events in East Germany, precipitated by an exodus of disenchanted citizens and public demands that a few months earlier never would have been tolerated, has culminated in the symbolically ultimate concession by the beleaguered communist government:

The opening of the Berlin Wall and the end of restrictions on emigration or travel to the West.

Only the actual destruction of this hated symbol of communist enslavement could surpass in magnitude the roller coaster of happenings that have set not only East Germany but the entire Eastern bloc on a course from which deviation now would only further rend the curtain that descended on Eastern Europe more than 40 years ago.

Communism is in full retreat on the continent.

When was it thought possible that in so short a time:

There would be free elections in the Soviet Union; Poland would install a non-Communist government; Hungary, where democracy was dealt such a cruel blow by Soviet tanks in 1956, would move toward democratic reform; East Germans, taking to the streets by the hundreds of thousands, would force a powerful Communist ruler from power and win promises of elections and freedoms of assembly, association and the press.

What the world is witnessing is nothing less than the systemic failure of a movement that after nearly half a century has brought the communist world to the brink of social and economic collapse. Things never can be the same again.

As East and West Germans bask in the sunlight of newly found liberties, the Western democracies seem to be caught off guard. Little did they know that Soviet President Mikhail S. Gorbachev's reforms would be the springboard for such a sudden and startling turn of events.

Things have moved so quickly that while they marvel at the prospect of a reunified Germany, the democracies suddenly find themselves worrying about the impact of an economically unified and revived Germany on their own economies.

There will be a role for the West sooner or later in this transformation. But for now, it is exhilarating to witness this drama of many acts, with rapidly changing scenery and a climax still to be reached.

Omaha World-Herald

Omaha, NE, November 10, 1989

The Berlin Wall has been one of the most enduring symbols of a hideous tyranny — a system so repressive that it had to build a wall to keep its inhabitants from fleeing. Now a long-held hope seems within reach. The East German government said Thursday that it will open its borders, allowing its people to emigrate.

They can even leave through the wall if they choose. What a dramatic development in what has become a year of dramatic developments in the Soviet Union and Eastern Europe.

Let the gates swing open. Better yet, let the wall come down. For years it has been an insult to decency, a tangible reminder of the fact that to live in East Germany was to be, literally, a prisoner. It has no place in the new order that may be possible if the forces of reform are allowed to operate in East Germany as they have operated in other parts of Eastern Europe. Not even as a relic of a failed philosophy.

Certainly the possibility of reform didn't come about because the government has experienced a burst of compassion. From all appearances, the country's leaders had no practical alternative when they promised free elections and open borders. With 200,000 of the best and brightest workers having fled the country and thousands of others involved in increasingly daring pro-democracy demonstrations, there can be little doubt that the patience of a good part of the population is nearly exhausted.

And calling in Soviet tanks, the remedy of the 1950s, is not a realistic option in the age of glasnost.

This isn't to suggest that opening the borders will automatically solve the problem. The industrial democracies can't absorb everyone from Eastern Europe and the Third World who wants a better life. Ultimately the solution is to improve conditions in those parts of the world — even in East Germany — to the point where it is possible to have a decent life without emigrating.

But emigration is a basic human right. A government that denies that right finds it easier to deny other rights. If reform is to occur in East Germany, the place to start is to eliminate the worst abuses, and it's hard to imagine a worse abuse than imprisoning an entire population.

President John F. Kennedy portrayed Berlin in 1963 as a place where people who were ignorant of or sympathetic toward communism could learn about the differences between the Communist world and the Free World. "Let them come to Berlin," he said.

Let them come to Berlin today and learn an additional lesson. The world of Marx and Lenin is collapsing. The Berlin Wall didn't save it. The wall stands now not only as a symbol of Communist repression but also of Communist failures.

The Evening Gazette

Worcester, MA, November 12, 1989

Events in East Germany have been unfolding with such astonishing speed that we've found it impossible to comment on them in a timely fashion. Barely has one victory for freedom been won before the next made it old news.

But if history attaches a date on which the cold war finally ended, it is apt to be Nov. 10, 1989. That was the day when the Berlin Wall that oppression built was rendered obsolete by the forces of freedom.

What few people thought possible in their lifetime seemed so simple in the end: Scores of happy Germans from the East walked or drove across checkpoints to the West to enjoy the sights and sounds of the Kurfuersterdam, one of Europe's most elegant shopping avenues.

Some crossed over from the West for a look. As bewildered East German border guards looked on, others celebrated along the hated wall.

Not since Oct. 23, 1956, when a meeting of Hungarian students grew to a massive uprising within hours, has any popular movement been so swift and overwhelming. But unlike 1956, this time there was no rancor, no threats, no shots fired — only the people's uncontrollable desire to be free.

Nothing can overshadow the joy of that day. Yet the continuing disintegration of East Germany will pose a formidable challenge to the government in Bonn, to the Soviet Union, to the United States and its European allies. The disappearance of a communist buffer state between East and West will reshape the face of Europe and international politics.

But dealing with this challenge should be a happy task compared with enduring what the past offered. For Germans, Hungarians, Poles and others, nothing matters right now but the demise of the "wall of shame" and the promise of a brighter future.

The "leading rule of the Communist Party" in a large part of Europe is being replaced by a giant victory party shared by millions of people who are celebrating a dream come true.

The Hutchinson News

Hutchinson, KS, November 9, 1989

As the Iron Curtain continues to erode brick by brick, will a new, modern wall replace the fading one?

The ease with which East Germans are flooding into West Germany should not have surprised the Bonn government, which only now is realizing the economic and social burden that is coming with the tide.

At the confluence of the acceptance of East Germans and the West German resolve to provide them sanctuary is a growing intolerance reflected by the strain in the system and the fear that is beginning to rise among West Germans that these East German refugees may eventually become competitors.

Already about 175,000 people have made the trek from east to west in search of a less restrictive life under a more flexible and less rigid government.

West Germany, with 8 percent unemployment and a housing problem of its own, cannot for long tolerate the continuing migration of new refugees. This is the pragmatic and unfortunate truth to an adventure that has inspired hope among democratic nations throughout the world.

Chancellor Helmut Kohl's West German government should have anticipated the flood of refugees. The Iron Curtain has split Germany since 1962 and has offered one half of that former unified population a repressive regime with little hope for change — until now.

If the flow continues — and there is no reason to doubt it won't — West Germans may embrace the extremes of nationalism and begin to place a new wall in the way of Germans seeking a new life in the West.

West Germans require much patience. Patience that East Germany will eventually reform sooner and not later. And that West Germany can withstand the economic and social burdens that come with being a sanctuary, as the United States has been, until reforms make life in the east more tolerable.

The resignation Tuesday of the entire 44-man East German Cabinet, bowing to pressure for reforms from East German citizens, ought to ease the concerns of worried West Germans.

But despite the swift changes taking place, it would be unfortunate if the growing tide of refugees causes West Germany to adopt restrictive policies regulating immigration, transforming itself — bit by bit — into a shape resembling the closed and oppressive regime its new refugees so recently escaped.

The Phoenix Gazette

Phoenix, AZ, November 10, 1989

They danced in the streets of West Berlin Thursday night, as 28 years of infamous history melted away under the pressure of a subjugated population that no longer would submit to its masters.

In the end, the East German rulers discovered that the only way to keep their people in was to allow them to leave. More than 200,000 East Germans have left since January — more than 50,000 in the past week — in a population drain that threatens the country's basic industries.

"We know this need of citizens to travel or leave the country," said Guenter Schabowski, a member of the Politburo who made the dramatic announcement Thursday that unleashed 28 years of emotions. The East German government acted not out of generosity of spirit but because events forced it to take a desperate gamble; they've tried everything else, why not try a little freedom?

While the euphoria of the moment will shortly fade to the reality that East Germany has many serious problems that will not evaporate, give the Germans their celebration. They have certainly earned it, enduring for four decades in a divided nation occupied by the victors of World War II.

If any instant analysis is accurate, it most certainly is that the Postwar Era ended Thursday night as the Iron Curtain was shredded. Now we move into a new era, in which German reunification is a serious proposition rather than a useful propaganda slogan. This is uncharted territory.

Another analysis is that the crumbling of the communist bloc is continuing at a dizzying pace, driven by inescapable economic realities. East Germany erected a wall 28 years ago not to keep Westerners out of its people's paradise, but to hold its people in when the economic and political freedoms of West Germany proved so much more compelling than the drab deprivation of East Germany's failed communist state.

Readers often complain that the news is so unpleasant. They ask, "Isn't there any good news?" It is hard to imagine better news than the erosion of communism throughout Eastern Europe before our very eyes, and the recognition by tyrannical regimes that basic human freedoms must be acknowledged. Today there is good news, and it is on the front pages in big, black type.

Good news? This is more than that; it is an epochal change that will be in history books for future generations to study. And East Germans will tell their grandchildren of that magical night when the gates opened and they danced in the streets of Berlin, free once again after so long.

The Globe and Mail

Toronto, Ont., November 11, 1989

Life in East Germany changed more this week than it had during the previous 40 years. The government quit, half the Communist Party leadership was fired, the borders were opened and free elections were promised. It is anybody's guess what will happen over the weekend.

As the Germans dance on the ruins of the Berlin Wall, the rest of us are left to pace the corridors of memory, wondering what kind of world is about to be born. The sound of celebrations at the Brandenburg Gate echoes throughout the nations of the East and the West, reawakening old fears.

Precisely 50 years after the world was last dragged into total war, the German question has re-emerged in yet another form. After the brutal simplicities of the Cold War era, the world has again become rich with complication and unforeseeable danger.

In the United States, many intellectuals and ideologues want to declare victory and celebrate as the collapse of communism quickens throughout Eastern Europe. "Democracy has won the political battle, the market has won the economic battle, the Cold War is finished," historian Arthur Schlesinger, a key adviser to John F. Kennedy, assured an American television audience this week.

But President George Bush has pointedly refused to crack open the champagne. "We are handling [the events in Eastern Europe] in a way where we're not trying to give anybody a hard time," he said late Thursday night.

The liberal revolution in Central Europe has tremendous implications for the Western allies. But political, economic and social developments in Poland, Hungary and now East Germany have far outrun the process of demilitarization.

Though these countries appear to be hurtling headlong toward some form of democracy, they are still bristling with tactical nuclear weapons and are host to huge numbers of Soviet and Warsaw Pact troops. The generals of the North Atlantic Treaty Organization must be asking themselves whether they have become obsolete or more vital than ever.

From Moscow, Mikhail Gorbachev congratulated the East Germans for their reform efforts and suggested that the Soviet Union could live with a non-Communist government. But Mr. Gorbachev was also careful to let the West know that he considers the reunification of the Germanys unthinkable until NATO and the Warsaw Pact are dissolved.

His caution is understandable. But the Germans may not be prepared to put their political evolution on hold for the next decade while the Warsaw Pact and NATO work out terms for dismantling the war machines built up during the past four decades.

What Mr. Gorbachev probably wants above all else right now is a breathing space during which he can seek to moderate the pace of change within the Eastern Bloc. Inside the Soviet Union, he faces potential opposition from reactionary Russians who may not be satisfied to sit idly by as their empire disintegrates. At the very least, he must preserve the illusion that he is still leading the revolutionary attempt to renew and restore socialism.

If the very conservative forces in the Red Army decide that the situation in East Germany (or any of the domestic republics) is getting out of control, Mr. Gorbachev will come under intense pressure to slow the pace of change.

When Mr. Gorbachev and Mr. Bush meet in Malta next month, they will be faced with the challenge of producing methods for coping with the creative instability of this new age. These deliberations will require courage and vision as well as the caution both have already shown.

The greater the pace of change, the greater the need for trust, lest change defeat itself by inviting disillusionment, reaction and even repression.

TULSA WORLD

Tulsa, OK, November 11, 1989

WINSTON Churchill described the Communist prison of Soviet-dominated Eastern Europe in his famous speech at Fulton, Mo. "An iron curtain has descended on the continent."

For 28 years the Berlin Wall was the concrete embodiment of the Iron Curtain. Thursday the wall, the symbol, came tumbling down, figuratively if not yet literally.

Communist authorities suddenly opened East German borders to free travel, in an effort to slow the stream of people into the West in recent weeks and to quell spontaneous demonstrations that have spread to several East German cities.

The opening touched off a euphoric celebration. Germans from East and West danced atop the wall. Others chipped off concrete souvenirs. Some embraced relatives they hadn't seen for years. Some simply drove from the East to visit the famed shopping area, the Kurfuerstendamm, in the West.

"The Wall is Gone! Berlin is Again Berlin," headlined one German newspaper. Said one young East German: "It was so simple to come over. The feeling is just indescribable."

It is difficult for most Americans to comprehend the significance of the event. The majority of Americans — those born after the end of World War II — have witnessed in recent months the greatest political upheaval to occur during their lifetime, first in China and then in East Germany and other countries in communist Europe.

The lifting of the Iron Curtain equals anything to date. Dare we hope for the actual demolition of the Wall? A re-unified Germany? Who knows?

FORT WORTH STAR-TELEGRAM

Fort Worth, TX, November 11, 1989

The opening of the Berlin Wall provides one of the bittersweet moments in history, a moment that evokes brooding reflections on the past and kindles hope for the future.

Out of the past comes a grainy picture of that gray day in 1961 when the workers came with the concrete, bricks and barbed wire that physically divided Berlin into two cities, separating families and friends, while onlookers watched in stunned disbelief.

Out of old headlines and TV footage come stories of daring escapes over, under and around the wall and of failed escape attempts that ended in tragedy.

During the 28 years of the wall's existence, almost 200 people were killed trying to flee East Germany through it.

Echoes of challenges hurled at the wall reverberate in the memories of two generations. A young U.S. president addresses a crowd of West Berliners near the monument to oppression and stirs them by shouting, "Ich bin ein Berliner."

Years later, an older U.S. president speaks to an audience in Berlin and pleads, "Mr. Gorbachev, tear down that wall."

Gorbachev took Ronald Reagan at his word. Although it was Egon Krenz, the new East German leader of less than three weeks, who opened the country's borders, Gorbachev unleashed the forces that led to that dramatic breakthrough.

One would have to be a hopeless pessimist not to see this remarkable event as a harbinger of bright promise for East and West Germany and a pivotal point in East-West relations. It is an occasion for rejoicing at the snowballing momentum gained by the forces pushing for more freedom in Eastern Europe.

It is not, however, a time for gloating, as some have chosen to do about the triumph of democracy and market-driven economic systems over Marxist systems. Much still remains to be done, and such bombast could be counterproductive.

Clearly, the United States and the Western democracies must respond creatively to rapid-fire changes that are transforming Eastern Europe and East Germany in particular. East Germany will need economic assistance from the West in order to provide the opportunities to keep its best and brightest people from leaving.

Opening its borders was the only recourse East Germany had to stop the population hemorrhage through Hungary and Czechoslovakia. Since they know they can now leave anytime they choose, East Germans will be more inclined to stay and wait to see if the government is serious about meaningful economic reforms and political democratization. That is best for the West and particularly West Germany, which would be extremely hard-pressed to take in very many more East Germans.

The prospect of a freer, more prosperous East Germany, of course, raises the issue of German reunification, which no one really wants to tackle at this time. Indeed, there is no reason to complicate matters now by grappling with that vexing question.

Although the concrete, mortar and bricks still stand, for all intents and purposes the Berlin wall is down. It is a moment for bittersweet reflection on what it stood for and dedication to keeping it down.

THE INDIANAPOLIS STAR
Indianapolis, IN,
November 11, 1989

Beyond the dancing on the Berlin Wall and all of the action breaking with dizzying rapidity, in the direction of freedom and democracy, some realities have not changed.

Some 400,000 Soviet troops are still stationed in East Germany. In the Soviet Union itself, all of the military power of the Red Army and all of the police power of the KGB is in the hands of the men at the top.

Those in command of the police, the troops, the tanks and the heavy artillery can still call the shots.

The changes are exhilarating. Hopes are high. So are the risks.

The high hopes of the French Revolution gave way to dictatorship, terror and Napoleon.

The high hopes of the Russian Revolution gave way to the Bolsheviks, terror and Stalin.

The wishes of the people in the vanguard of the great movement building and spreading in eastern Europe are clear enough. They want more freedom, free elections, more political power-sharing, more flexible economies geared to human needs, freedom of the press, guarantees of a wide range of human rights.

If their goals are to be attained peacefully, their leaders will have to join in the process of change or make way for leaders who will. In increasing degree, this is happening.

Radical changes in government can be made peacefully. America's experience of the Constitutional Convention and the creation of our new government proved that.

We hope that the changes that are taking place in eastern Europe will be guided by intelligence and good will.

The Honolulu Advertiser
Honolulu, HI, November 11, 1989

For the World War II generation and its children, the Berlin Wall's opening contradicts everything that has spelled the difference between East and West.

More than any of the other rapid-fire changes, freedom of movement for East Germans seems to foretell an excitingly unpredictable new epoch in East-West relations, with unprecedented opportunities, and maybe even a new map.

East German President Egon Krenz really had no choice but to finally accede to the demands of millions for the democratic right of free travel. Even with 400,000 Soviet troops already in East Germany, a Soviet crackdown on protests and departures was not in the cards.

Other promised reforms, including truly free, honest, multi-party elections and market economic reforms, will require more time.

What's needed to keep and bring back East German workers is to somehow balance political and economic conditions in East and West Germany, with consideration for the millions of East Germans who have accepted drab lives as a trade-off for a measure of cradle-to-grave security.

West Germany has promised to do all it can to aid the adjustment, so long as reforms continue. In anticipation of new across-the-wall business alliances, especially in construction, the Frankfurt stock exchange surged yesterday.

The rest of the West, looking on, can wonder at the implications of the changes in East Germany, and in Poland and Hungary, and perhaps brewing in Bulgaria and Czechoslovakia.

Is it still plausible to speak of a new European economic alliance of just 12 countries in 1992? What role will there be for the United States? And what of reunification of Germany, which with a combined 80 million people would be a formidable force?

The battles for political and economic readjustment have only just been joined. The fervent hope should be that this revolution ignited by Mikhail Gorbachev will continue to proceed peacefully.

The Clarion-Ledger

Jackson, MS, October 10, 1989

Not since the thousands of Chinese students amassed in Tiananmen Square last summer has the world witnessed with such awe the intensity of a people yearning for a better life than events in East Germany.

Is the Berlin Wall to finally come tumbling down? East Germany announced Thursday it was opening its borders to allow citizens to freely travel anywhere, including through the 28-year-old barrier — the premier symbol of the Cold War. It has divided Berlin and the two German nations since 1961.

With that pledge, East German leaders also promise open and free elections. This comes as thousands flee the communist country, with West German leaders estimating that as many as 1.4 million East Germans may emigrate.

How to sum this up? There's no better way than to remember the prophetic words of former President John F. Kennedy, who uttered during a Berlin visit June 26, 1963:

"There are some who say communism is the wave of the future.... Let them come to Berlin.... Freedom has many difficulties and democracy is not perfect, but we have never had to put a wall up to keep our people in, to prevent them from leaving us. ...

"All free men, wherever they may live, are citizens of Berlin, and, therefore, as a free man, I take pride in the words, 'Ich bin ein Berliner.' "

We watch our fellow seekers of freedom with joy, hope and sadness that it has taken so long for the barbed wire and fences to limit, but not crush, their human spirit. This is truly an historic event worthy of celebration.

RAPID CITY JOURNAL—

Rapid City, SD, November 10, 1989

The Berlin Wall came down on Thursday. The East German government has granted its citizens the right to travel freely outside their country.

For 28 years the wall has symbolized the denial of this most basic human right, freedom of movement, not just for East Germans but for all Eastern Europeans.

Its dismantling, if sustained, should lead to other freedoms. When citizens can vote with their feet, politicians are forced to be more responsive to their wishes. The East German government already has called for free elections.

In what might be the understatement of the year, Secretary of State James A. Baker III called free travel for East Germans a "very positive development." The Bush administration has reacted with proper caution to the tide of democracy in Eastern Europe. After all, on June 15, 1961, East German leader Walter Ulbricht said, "Niemand hat die Abischt eine Mauer zu errichten." Translation: "Nobody intends to erect a wall."

Two months later, in the predawn hours of Aug. 13, 1961, East German troops began stringing British-made barbed wire through the heart of Berlin. Five days later the first concrete blocks were laid.

Secretary Baker's wasn't the only cautious voice Thursday. In what has to be the overstatement of 1989, Soviet Foreign Ministry spokesman Gennady I. Gerasimov called the move a "renewal of socialism." Right. He also has some swampland in the Ukraine he'd like to show you.

Gerasimov's statement is reminiscent of the squads of East German Young Pioneers who serenaded the troops building the wall in the summer of 1961. One of the Pioneers' favorite songs was, "Die Partei hat immer Recht" — "The Party is Always Right" — a tune that is less on East German lips today.

In fact, it is likely some of those formerly young Pioneers are today camped out in West Germany, singing a different song. That's why Thursday's move by the East Germans is so welcome. It is not in anyone's interest to empty Eastern Europe into the west, crippling one group of nations and saddling the other with refugees.

It is in all nations' interests to expand freedom and democracy. The tumbling down of the Berlin Wall is a dramatic step in that direction.

The Seattle Times

Seattle, WA, November 12, 1989

THE Communist Party in East Germany is reacting with the nimble speed of an institution bent on survival.

As extraordinary events occur — opening of the Berlin Wall to unrestricted travel, and sweeping resignations from the Politburo -- the party leadership demonstrates a responsive, tenacious will to stay in power.

Instead of crushing protests with tanks as in China, or retreating entirely as in Hungary and Poland, new names and faces are reacting to pressure for change that has been building throughout the '80s.

Restructuring at the top levels of government is breathtaking and likely to continue.

The aging hard-liner, Erich Honecker, was replaced last month as general secretary by his protege, Egon Krenz. He may not survive a party conference next spring. The shakeup in the policymaking Politburo crowned Hans Modrow as the rising star, a genuine reformer described as East Germany's Mikhail Gorbachev.

Prime Minister Modrow and Gunter Schabowski, a survivor of the Politburo purge, are speaking to the hearts of their constituents. Schabowski told a cheering crowd: "If this Politburo proves unable to solve the problems, we are willing to step down again."

Krenz had been responsible for state security, and he might not survive the inevitable investigation that follows a blossoming of political freedom.

Viewed with Western eyes, all of Eastern Europe is the same dull, oppressive shade of gray, but significant differences exist.

East Germany enjoys the highest standard of living among its Warsaw Pact allies, and the educated population has shared a common bond through the Lutheran church.

Church basements and parish halls have been the forums for political debate and staging areas for rallies.

As early as 1981, citizen participation began to grow in city councils, local government, and academic institutions. In the past three years there has been an unofficial tolerance for political movements concerned with peace and the environment. Why, the East Germans have asked, can't we go further?

A generation of East Germans has been practicing for its own brand of democracy, but unrestricted travel and competitive local elections remained as key points of tension.

Flight from East Germany has been dramatic in the past several months, but hundreds of thousands took to the streets to affirm their commitment to stay, while demanding change.

Frustrations boiled over last May, when the same party hacks won what had been billed as free, open elections. Challenges to the government mounted.

East Germany's bloodless revolution is taking place in a country unlike its Communist neighbors. Poland and Hungary are struggling to salvage their economies by abandoning communism and turning toward capitalism.

Economic hardship in those countries has been a sobering lesson for relatively prosperous East Germans. They've found a comfort level in the security of a socialist regime.

Communist leaders in East Germany believe, as their actions have demonstrated, that they can change the party quickly enough to stay in the center of things.

Unrestricted travel is a major step. East German leaders are gambling that the exodus will slow to a trickle after a few months. Indeed, they expect that some emigrés will return with their families and job skills now that they know they can return.

The Soviet Union, consumed with troubles of its own, has made it clear that East Germany's problems are its own to solve.

In a time of dramatic changes and reversals, Gorbachev may actually be watching developments in East Germany for a model to try at home.

The TENNESSEAN

Nashville, TN, November 10, 1989

IN a stunning, obviously desperate move, the East German government has announced it is opening its borders to allow its people to travel anywhere, even through the Berlin Wall.

It was as if Mr. Egon Krenz, the new political boss, recognized that the avalanche of people fleeing to the West is virtually unstoppable and has acted to make it easier for them to go. Only days ago he was pleading for his citizens to stay.

Mr. Krenz has taken every available step to cool down demonstrations and halt the flow of East Germans to the West. He has engineered the resignations of the entire Poliburo, the country's most powerful political body, and before that the resignations of the Communist Cabinet.

Mr. Krenz has produced a blueprint for reform, including the right of travel, the formation of a constitutional court, civil service as an alternative to mandatory military service. Where he formerly stood firm against free elections, he has now retreated.

In his speech to the Central Committee, he called for a "new election law that ensures free, democratic general elections with a secret ballot." He proposed "public supervision of every stage of the balloting." Although he did not say he was urging a true multiparty system in East Germany, he did promise new laws on freedom of association, assembly and the press.

If all his promises were backed by the full party conference, scheduled for mid-December, it would amount to a virtual dismantling of the Communist Party system which has ruled East Germany for 40 years. Opening of the borders could further deplete its work force, from which more than 200,000 East Germans, mostly young, skilled or professionals, have fled.

The promise of opened borders comes after decades of fencing East Germans in to prevent their flight to the West. The Berlin Wall has divided the city and the two German nations since 1961. It is universally referred to as the "Wall of Shame." Now, if citizens are allowed to travel through it, rather than through second or third countries, it might as well be torn down. Perhaps it will be.

The question of where all this is leading seriously concerns the West, particularly West Germany which is under an intolerable burden trying to deal with the wave of refugees. And despite its low-key response, the Kremlin has to be quite worried. East Germany has been communism's buffer and Moscow's front-line defense against the Western Alliance.

The prospect of seeing communism dismantled and the inevitable pressures in the two Germanys for reunification must be rubbing the Kremlin's nerve endings rather hard these days. ∎

The Providence Journal

Providence, RI, November 11, 1989

Back in June 1987, when President Reagan visited West Berlin, he stood before the Brandenburg Gate, struck the obligatory pose of visiting American statesmen, and exhorted Mikhail Gorbachev: "If you seek peace," he declared, "if you seek prosperity for the Soviet Union and Eastern Europe, if you seek liberalization: Come here to this gate! Mr. Gorbachev, open this gate! Mr. Gorbachev, tear down this wall!"

Mr. Gorbachev, it turns out, took Mr. Reagan at his word. The Berlin Wall, built nearly 30 years ago, had come to seem an eternal fixture of the tragic divisions of postwar Europe: Between democracy and communism, freedom and tyranny, abundance and austerity, East and West. Now, practically overnight, the Wall is becoming history.

The decision of the new East German government to lift all travel restrictions for its citizens — in effect, to circumvent the Wall that symbolizes the imprisonment of those who languish behind — was an act of desperation, not inspiration, designed to ensure the survival of the regime. But we give them credit anyway. It is apparent that Egon Krenz and his colleagues have determined to travel the high road to reform, as their counterparts in Warsaw and Budapest have done. Given the choice between *perestroika* and Tiananmen Square, the East Germans saw the difference between repression and hope, and have promised to offer the ballot as well.

This is not just stunning but surprising, and encouraging as well. When President Kennedy stood before the Wall in 1963, his famous declaration — *Ich bin ein Berliner* — was understood as words hurled largely in defiance, the fighting syllables of the Cold War at its height. It should be noted that Mr. Reagan's appeal was rather different: A challenge to Mikhail Gorbachev, an invitation to put the meaning of 'reform' to the test. It is a tribute to Mr. Gorbachev's statesmanship — and, we should say, his clear recognition of the way the wind blows — that he chose to gamble on a new kind of Europe, and seems willing to dismantle the imperial barricade.

Now comes the hard part: If the repressive political system in East Germany should soon become redundant, the very reason for the state's existence is called into question. It seems evident that an end to the postwar division of Germany is in sight, and that a single democratic republic must inevitably evolve. Can this revolution, this radical redrawing of the political map of Europe, be accomplished without violence? This is the price of progress from here, and this is what the superpowers must work to guarantee.

The Wichita Eagle-Beacon

Wichita, KS, November 11, 1989

A small museum near Checkpoint Charlie tells the story of the Berlin Wall. Starting with a few strands of barbed wire in 1961, the wall eventually became a 28-mile border of concrete, land mines, surveillance cameras, armed guards, attack dogs and tank traps.

Yet the wall never stopped the quest for freedom. At least 200 East Germans died trying to get across, most of them shot down a few yards from the liberty of the West.

The Stalinist ideologues running the German Democratic Republic called it the "anti-fascist protection barrier," as if the wall were designed to keep such subversive ideas as democracy out of the Marxist paradise. But the message got through. East Germans could watch West Berlin television. They could talk to friends and relatives allowed to visit the GDR about the benefits of a market economy and political liberty. Walking along the Unter den Linden, they could see the bright lights from prosperous West Berlin reflect off the drab, colorless, delapidated buildings that line what was one of Europe's most chic boulevards before World War II.

For almost 45 years, Berlin has been the cockpit, the symbol and the reality of the Cold War. The city's dateline usually meant momentous events — the 1948 airlift, the erection of the wall in 1961, President John Kennedy's stirring *Ich bin ein Berliner* speech in 1963.

This week, Berlin was the site of perhaps the most startling turn in the course of contemporary history. The wall was opened, breached by months of peaceful protest by East Germans whose willpower proved mightier than the tyranny of their communist masters.

It is a new era. As West German Foreign Minister Hans-Dietrich Genscher said, "Nothing will be as it was before — not there, not here and nowhere in Europe."

This is not the time to worry about what happens next. True, the policymakers and the heavy thinkers must try to construct an arrangement that ensures peace and stability. Such issues as German reunification, the future shape of European politics, the role of NATO have to be addressed.

But all that will happen in due course.

It is the time for rejoicing among people who love liberty. It is time to feel the fresh winds blowing from Russia to the Baltics to Poland and through the Brandenburg Gate. It is time to remember that no wall can stop the greatest power on earth — the desire of the human spirit to breathe free.

East German Communists Choose New Leader

The ruling Socialist Unity (Communist) Party Dec. 9, 1989 restructured itself and elected a liberal lawyer, Gregor Gysi, to the new post of party chairman. He succeeded Egon Krenz as East Germany's leader.

Gysi was handed the formidable task of restoring confidence in the party in time for free elections tentatively set for May 1990. His elevation came as the party's old-guard former leadership faced criminal prosecution for alleged corruption.

A total of some 2,750 Socialist Unity delegates gathered at East Berlin's Dynamo sports complex Dec. 8-9 for an extraordinary party congress. The congress originally was to have been held in mid-December. The rescheduling had been prompted by Krenz's unexpected resignation Dec. 6 as the head of state (president) and chairman of the National Defense Council. (Krenz had resigned as the ruling party's general secretary Dec. 3 but had retained the other posts.)

Krenz had been succeeded immediately as president on an interim basis by Manfred Gerlach, the head of the Liberal Democratic Party, one of the four historic allies of the Socialist Unity Party. Gerlach was the first ever noncommunist head of state in East Germany.

The Defense Council, which controlled the armed forces, had dissolved itself Dec. 6 following Krenz's resignation.

The extraordinary party congress convened amid signs of widespread demoralization and disillusionment among the delegates. The meeting was chaired by Wolfgang Berghofer, the mayor of Dresden, who was part of a temporary working group in charge of party affairs.

Krenz was at the congress but had no active role in the proceedings. Some delegates assailed him as an unrepentant tool of the discarded regime of Erich Honecker.

The gathering lasted 17 straight hours, much of it in closed session. Gysi, 41, emerged as the party chairman in secret balloting Dec. 9. He was the only candidate for the post. (95% percent of the 2,588 delegates who voted were reported to have voted for him.)

On Dec. 8, prior to the balloting, Gysi had given a speech to the delegates accusing the Honecker regime of betraying the people through corruption and authoritarian policies. "We have to change our ways of thinking," he said.

Gysi spoke of adopting a "third way," a social-democratic path between full-scale capitalism and orthodox Marxism.

Separately, the nation's various political elements Dec. 7 agreed that free elections would be held on May 6, 1990.

An estimated 200,000 pro-democracy demonstrators in Leipzig Dec. 11 called for German reunification. The march, a weekly event in Leipzig, had begun as a celebration of the gains of the pro-democracy movement, but it turned into a mass call for reunification. "One German fatherland!" was the rallying cry.

A demonstration by 40,000 people in the city of Karl-Marx-Stadt Dec. 11 also featured calls for a united Germany.

THE INDIANAPOLIS NEWS

Indianapolis, IN, December 5, 1989

Forty years of communist rule has apparently not hindered the ability of East Germans to spot all manner of double standards, hypocrisy and corruption in their society. Kept quiet for years by Soviet oppression, the East German people seem determined to make up for lost time now that they have the chance to speak their minds.

The first targets on the list for public rebuke have been the high-living Communist Party leaders who have set up a network of exclusive restaurants, stores and neighborhoods for themselves while their people have lived in a constant state of deprivation.

Former Communist chief Erich Honecker, who was East Germany's most powerful man just a few weeks ago, has now been expelled from the party amid revelations that he squirreled away millions of dollars in private Swiss bank accounts.

Honecker's successor, Egon Krenz, resigned as party chief Sunday along with the party's 10-member ruling Politburo and its entire 163-member Central Committee. Security guards now stand outside many of the disgraced leaders' office to keep them away from documents and other evidence that may be used to prosecute them.

No measure short of a new system of governance seems to be enough for an outraged public with newly found freedom of expression. Yelled one woman at a Sunday evening rally: "We don't need any Politburo and Central Committee that is made up of criminals!"

Even more dramatic evidence of the country's new mood was a front-page editorial Monday in East Berlin's National Zeitung daily. "The truth is grim: Among those who exercised power by decree and used it despotically, criminals held key positions."

The Communisty Party has hit the fan in East Germany. Forty years of frustration are now unleashed, and woe to anyone who tries to stand against the powerful new tide.

Winnipeg Free Press

Winnipeg, Man., December 1, 1989

West German Chancellor Helmut Kohl has made his purpose abundantly clear: He aims to form East Germany and West Germany into a single state. A network of joint institutions which his government will try to establish with the government of East Germany will be intended as steps toward eventual political union.

Mr. Kohl wisely set no deadline for achieving that goal. The obstacles are enormous and the purpose may not be worth achieving. The sudden loosening of the reins in the Warsaw Pact this year has made it possible to dream new dreams and revive old ones — dreams of disarmament, world peace and universal brotherhood, dreams of unified Germany, dreams of history coming to an end. It is well that West Germany, its allies and its neighbors should be aware of each other's dreams and fears so as to know what underlies their policy.

West Germany's allies, having talked a good fight about German reunification in the 1960s, now have to respond to Chancellor Kohl's program. They have to say what part of the question is Germany's own business and what part is subject to veto by other powers.

East German leader Egon Krenz has already announced that his government is not interested in steps toward reunification. The Soviet government has also rejected the idea. While East Germany remains within the Warsaw Pact, it is close to impossible for any government of that country to follow a policy that makes the Soviets nervous. Soviet people and politicians mindful of the appalling damage their country suffered in the Second World War are highly apprehensive of a strong and united Germany. By announcing that joint institutions are a step toward unity, Mr. Kohl has ensured that joint bi-German institutions will be seen with great suspicion in the Kremlin. He has made it difficult for an East German government to take part.

Instead of proposing lunch and a movie and letting the friendship blossom, Mr. Kohl has begun by proposing marriage. The other side cannot accept any gift or joint project without seeming to agree to eventual marriage. The West German chancellor has his own domestic reasons for proceeding in that way, but it does raise the stakes in every joint undertaking.

West Germany's friends can fairly ask why the peoples of East Germany and West Germany should have a single state, for a state is a tool for accomplishing certain purposes and not an end in itself. If they wish to reunite families long divided physically by The Wall, that is being accomplished now. If they wish to unite the skills and the wealth of German labor and capital for economic growth, that is easily done through economic arrangements such as those of the European Common Market. If they wish to embark on great creative adventures of the German mind, those are easily fostered in universities and shared cultural institutions.

The German-speaking peoples of Europe are divided among several states whose borders have shifted from war to war over the decades — mainly in Switzerland, Austria, Poland and the two German states erected by the occupying powers at the end of the Second World War. Mr. Kohl's program does not contemplate a wider unification encompassing all the people of German tongue. He realistically does not challenge the existence of other borders dividing German-speaking peoples, for there is no higher law saying all Germans must live under the same government.

A state is an enduring organization which commands the military forces and collects the taxes within a defined territory. The peoples of East and West Germany have no need for a unified treasury and unified military. Any attempt to create them will arouse deep suspicion and powerful opposition from other countries anxious to preserve peace in Europe. The great constructive work that Germans have to do together needs other tools.

Chancellor Kohl has been frank and far-seeing in his program. His allies owe it to him to be equally frank in their reply. They should encourage his government to develop intra-German relations in the human, economic and cultural fields. They should tell him that the formation of a new state, a new military and fiscal entity in the most tension-ridden part of Europe, requires agreement from the other players and that he should not ask for that agreement in the near future.

"THEY SAY THAT AFTER WE'VE BEEN PROPERLY INTRODUCED WE MAY HAVE A CHAPERONED DINNER TOGETHER"

©1989 HERBLOCK

Fort Worth Star-Telegram

Fort Worth, TX, December 15, 1989

With the first opening in the Berlin Wall, the die was cast for the reunification of West and East Germany. The process began when Germans from both sides of the wall crossed over to visit and shop. It is occurring now, even as pundits speculate on when and if it will happen.

What the speculators really want to know is when the governments of West and East Germany and the governments of the United States, Great Britain, France and the Soviet Union will officially and unambiguously commit themselves for or against German reunification.

Officially and in practical terms, the prospect presents real problems for all involved. It is doubtful, therefore, that any of the major players will send ungarbled signals on the issue anytime soon. Among the issues raised by the possibility of German reunification are:

■ The fate of NATO and the Warsaw Pact, if the two central components of those counterbalancing military alliances meld into one national entity.

■ Fear that a unified Germany will emerge as the dominant military and economic power on the continent and that its imperialist tendencies will reassert themselves.

■ The economic effects of a reunified Germany on the European Community, which is completing the process of removing the remaining barriers to economic integration and will become a unified market at the end of 1992.

All of those issues will have to be addressed, but the reunification for Germany will not await the outcome of official decisions in those matters by the major players. It is pointless, therefore, for provocateurs of the Fourth Estate to attempt to pressure leaders of the involved governments into providing answers that they do not yet have to the reunification question.

The de facto reunification will precede the definitive political deed. Barring a dramatic change of leadership and reversal of foreign policy, the process will not be reversed. Although the Soviets may still have the military capacity to intervene to prevent reunification, they are not likely to exercise it even if Gorbachev is replaced.

Two Germanys only make sense in the context of the Cold War, and that era for all intents and purposes is over.

The Washington Post

Washington, DC, December 5, 1989

WHO WOULD have thought that Erich Honecker, a man with the outward aspect of a sourpuss apparatchik, would have cultivated a taste for unbridled luxury? His sauna, his satellite dishes and his deer park have all been on television—East German television, this time—along with the interesting detail that his estate required a staff of 22 people. As George Orwell put it, some animals are more equal than others.

Mr. Honecker is now out—out of office and, along with 11 other former members of the leadership, most of whom are revealed to have had similar tastes for high living, he is out of the party that he led for 18 years. Three former members of the Politburo have been arrested on charges of corruption. The whole Politburo and the Central Committee have resigned. It all represents a frantic attempt by the party to clean itself up in the hope that it might survive the judgment of the people at whose expense these sumptuous perquisites were purchased. But things seem to have gone too far for that.

The party is now collapsing. Since the party and the state are tightly woven together, the government itself is left as a kind of shell without much substance. Perhaps the Communist Party congress next week will be able to patch together enough of a transition government to keep the country going until elections sometime next year, and perhaps the elections will produce competent and trustworthy leadership. That would be the best of all possibilities.

The likeliest alternative is that East Germany, its economy paralyzed, will slide into the status of an annex to West Germany—an extralegal eastern province. That would amount to reunification in fact, but a hasty and slipshod reunification with none of the safeguards or guarantees to which Germans as well as their neighbors are entitled.

West Germans initially insisted, wisely, that any decisions about reunification would have to be made by the East Germans in free elections after they had been given time to work out a truly representative structure of government. But then West Germany's Chancellor Helmut Kohl, under pressure from his opposition, made the serious mistake of throwing the reunification issue into fast forward. Ironically, his opposition has begun to see the dangers in too much haste and, after initially applauding him, is now prudently taking its distance.

The collapse of the Communist Party and political authority in East Germany presents a peculiar exigency to the rest of Europe, not to mention the Soviet Union and the United States. Perhaps they are going to have to cooperate in keeping East Germany going until its people can, through elections, make orderly and considered decisions on their own future.

Roanoke Times & World-News

Roanoke, VA, December 5, 1989

THE RUSH to a New Order in Eastern Europe continued pell-mell over the weekend, with the resignation of the entire hierarchy of the East German Communist Party.

For party boss Egon Krenz, in power only six weeks, the attempt to project himself as a born-again reformer wasn't sufficient to withstand the pressure for change. He could not put enough distance between himself and the discredited regime of his predecessor and erstwhile patron, former party leader Erich Honecker.

Krenz resigned as the party's secretary-general, as did the nine other members of the ruling Politburo. The resignations came two days after a bumptious session of the East German parliament, the Volkskammer, which used to be no more than a rubber stamp for Honecker and the party leadership. At the session, public debate erupted over evidence of gross corruption among leaders of the Honecker regime, and the parliament overwhelmingly voted to erase a provision in the constitution that gave the Communist Party a "leading role" in society.

As of Monday, Krenz was holding on to the ceremonial post of president, but not to any real power. Several top officials of the Honecker regime had been arrested for corruption. Honecker had been stripped of his party membership. The day-to-day affairs of the state were in the hands of a committee of 25 reformists, none of whom had been members of the old Politburo. What comes next?

The committee is to run things until a party congress later this month, and power for now appears to be flowing to Premier Hans Modrow. Modrow, whose association with the party's reform wing is far longer and far deeper than Krenz's, also could be in line to succeed Krenz as secretary-general when the party congress is held.

The idea behind all the changes seems to be acceptance by the now-ascendant reform wing of the Communist Party that East Germany is headed toward some form of multiparty democracy. If so, the party must rid itself of the baggage of its old, discredited leadership.

Whether that appearance will become reality is, of course, another question. Though it removed the constitutional provision about the Communist Party's "leading role," the Volkskammer rejected a proposal to delete a passage designating East Germany as a "socialist state." Though conceding that elections might reduce the Communists to the status of "junior partner" in a future governing coalition, Modrow has said that elections should not be held until next fall — and seems not to have contemplated the prospect of an election that would remove the Communists from power entirely.

That a government with Communists in merely a junior role can be seriously contemplated in East Germany is a measure of the rapidity of change there. But the change, while welcome, should not blind us to what is still a fundamental difference between political parties of the West and even the reform-minded wings of Communist parties: the willingness of parties in the West to submit themselves to fair elections, and to yield power to the opposition if they lose.

Poland, with a government headed by non-Communists, is as far along the path to reform as any nation of Eastern Europe. Yet even in Poland, the elections that led to Solidarity's leadership of government were rigged to ensure that the Communist Party retained a role.

Perhaps in Warsaw Pact nations such as Poland and East Germany, that is the only practical route to reform. But while power-sharing and partially free elections are important steps in the right direction, they do not constitute full-fledged parliamentary democracy.

THE SAGINAW NEWS

Saginaw, MI, December 7, 1989

Even as the superpower leaders summitted, other powers, greater in their own way, were passing them by, virtually overnight.

In East Germany, a surge of public indignation cleaned out the entire Communist leadership. Party boss Egon Krenz, who lasted only seven weeks, tried hard; he deserves credit for opening the Berlin Wall. But his credibility as a reformer could not survive his long ties to a regime despised at least as much for its personal corruption as its political repression.

In Czechoslovakia, another crumbling hard-line regime with old blood on its hands stumbled toward reform. For the first time in 40 years, non-Communists joined the government. Travel restrictions were eased. But crowds returned to the streets and squares to declare that the efforts did not go nearly far enough.

How far is enough? All the way to free elections — and the demonstrators are not shy about setting deadlines.

Predicting what will happen next is foolhardy when Bush and Gorbachev themselves must catch up with current events, and the reformers don't quite know what to do with their unaccustomed freedoms.

Not so long ago, in fact, another sort of deadline might have issued quietly from the direction of the Kremlin toward Berlin and Prague: Control yourselves, or we'll do it for you with our special brand of "fraternal assistance."

Monday did, as it happens, bring a gloomy joint declaration from the Soviet Union, Bulgaria, Hungary and Poland, regarding events in Czechoslovakia.

It mentioned "unjustified actions." It spoke of "long-term negative consequences."

The target of this condemnation? The 1968 invasion by those selfsame Warsaw Pact neighbors.

Clearly, this neighborhood has changed — and we don't miss the old gang one bit.

ALBUQUERQUE JOURNAL

Albuquerque, NM, December 2, 1989

After euphoric optimism about German reunification following the breaching of the Berlin Wall, the political and institutional barriers to a quick reunification have reasserted themselves.

West German Chancellor Helmut Kohl's 10-point proposal for a "confederation" of East and West Germany as a precurser to full unification offers a viable mechanism for orderly and controlled progress toward the goal.

That proposal itself highlighted one of the biggest institutional barriers to reunification: the government of East Germany.

"A unity of Germany isn't on the agenda," said East German leader Egon Krenz, in response to the Kohl speech outlining the confederation proposal. Krenz's adamant response notwithstanding, reunification *is* on the agenda of German citizens on both sides of the border, something Kohl acknowledged when he said, "I am sure unity will come if the people in Germany want it."

Kohl cautioned that a genuinely democratic government in the east would be a necessary prerequisite to confederation, however.

The beauty of Kohl's idea is that it bypasses any necessity for Europe and the two German states to contemplate the wrenching finality of a one-step reunification. Instead, the two states could progressively reduce the barriers within the confederation framework, easing into unity at a pace and in a style to reassure all involved within and around Germany.

The Kohl confederation could even go forward without formal acceptance by the East. After all, from the breaching of the Berlin Wall on, every act of cooperation between the two German states is a step on the road to reunification.

Kohl has put a constructive first proposal on the table for the two Germanys to discuss. The next reunification move is up to Krenz — or the people.

The Miami Herald

Miami, FL, December 2, 1989

THE PREAMBLE of West Germany's constitution — which had perhaps not been taken seriously by Western Europeans until the Berlin Wall's demise — calls for the "entire German people" to vote on German unity. Extraordinary transmutations in East Germany have suddenly brought that profound longing within the realm of possibility.

West German Chancellor Helmut Kohl's proposal to create a "confederation" between the two Germanys is a helpful response to events in East Germany. Though both East German leader Egon Krenz and Soviet Premier Mikhail Gorbachev promptly rejected any thought of German reunification, events may in time make them view confederation as less menacing than they see it at first blush.

Under Mr. Kohl's plan, Bonn would immediately begin to help modernize the GDR's telephone and transportation systems. Equally important, the proposal offers concrete support to democratic reformers in the GDR, since establishing the confederation would be contingent upon free elections in East Germany. It would al-

so be contingent upon the East German Communist Party's willingness to relinquish its constitutional monopoly on power. Both conditions may occur anyway — witness this week's events in Czechoslovakia — without confederation being involved.

Like the Soviets, the British and the Italians recoil at the thought of a reunited Germany. Even deposed East German leader Erich Honecker called reunification as likely as "a marriage of fire and water." Many Jews, and other peoples victimized by Nazi barbarity, shudder at the prospect as well. Memories of World War II still frame the mental landscape of much of Europe, both East and West.

But Mr. Kohl's proposal is for confederation, which could be a precursor to — but is not in itself — reunification. In fact, if reunification is to come eventually, it would require some form of prior cooperation on mutual concerns such as those envisioned in Mr. Kohl's proposal.

Against his fears of a reunified Germany, Mr. Gorbachev must weigh his statements that peoples have a right to self-determination. He cannot be a credible advocate of choice if he denies East Germans their right to choose.

The Star-Ledger

Newark, NJ, December 15, 1989

A recent national U.S. poll asked the question: Should West and East Germany be united as one nation again? The answer was surprising. Some 67 percent, or two-thirds, of those responding answered affirmatively. Only 16 percent were fearful that a united Germany would once again try to dominate the world.

Perhaps even more surprisingly, similar polling in France and Britain produced almost identical responses. That is in sharp contrast with the attitudes of Western European leaders, who have expressed fears that the question of German unification was proceeding far too quickly.

This may be one of the times when the people are wiser than their leaders. While fears of a strong, united Germany are understandable, they are not realistic in the context of today's world. More than a half century has passed since the beginning of World War II and the Germany of today—both West and East—bears little resemblance to the Hitler era.

The fervor for reunification in Germany is really a vote of confidence in democratic institutions and free market economics. The West Germans have it, the East Germans want it and the West Germans want their compatriots in the East to have what they so dearly want.

The strongest and most meaningful opposition to the union of the two Germanies continues to come from the Soviet Union. This is only partly attributable to old resentments from World War II.

What disturbs the Soviets is that a united Germany would change the map of Europe. Such concerns neglect the fact that the mind-boggling reforms of recent weeks are going to change Europe enormously anyhow. The impact of the changes is difficult to assess at this time, but it is almost certain to be a change for the better.

For example, even if the Soviets block political German unification, the booming West German economy is likely to expand eastward anyhow, pumping huge amounts of investment capital into East Germany. That would make for economic unification, which would be a sort of de facto official unification.

The Soviets may block one Germany for now, but the feeling is that it will come, sooner or later. The coming elections of a new and probably non-Communist East German government is a further step in that direction. The sentiments expressed in the poll findings are likely to be a self-fu' filling prophesy. All that remains is the timing.

Momentum Builds for 'Neutral' Unified Germany

East German Premier Hans Modrow Feb. 1, 1990 outlined a plan for the eventual reunification of East and West Germany. The plan, which stressed that a reunited Germany should be militarily neutral, was the first from the East German premier and came two days after Modrow had met in Moscow with Soviet President Mikhail S. Gorbachev. At the talks, the Soviet leader had appeared to soften his stand against reunification.

West German Chancellor Helmut Kohl Feb. 1 rejected Modrow's proposal for a neutral Germany and said that he would negotiate a unification plan only after East German general elections, which were scheduled for March 18.

Just prior to his meeting with Modrow Jan. 30, Gorbachev made his most positive statements to date on the question of German reunification.

According to the Soviet news agency Tass, Gorbachev said the question of a reunified Germany "was not unexpected. No one casts any doubt upon it." He continued, "Time itself is having an impact on the process and lends dynamism to it. It is essential to act responsibly and not seek the solution to this important issue on the streets."

At a news conference following the talks, Modrow spoke of a "stage-by-stage" process leading to reunification and said that the Soviet leader had not ruled it out.

Gorbachev was also quoted as saying that "neo-Nazi excesses" in East Germany were among "the most dangerous obstacles" to increasing democratization there.

Kohl Jan. 31 said that Gorbachev's statements on reunification were "encouraging."

Premier Modrow, whose Communist Party had recently agreed to share power in a national unity government until the March elections, presented his plan for reunification at an East Berlin press conference Feb. 1.

The East German premier outlined four "possible" steps to unity based on neutrality. First the two German states would create an economic, currency and transport union and join their legal systems. Next, a confederation could be established with joint institutions including parliamentary and executive bodies. Later, sovereign rights of both states would be handed over to authorities of the confedration. Finally, elections in both parts of the confederation would establish a "unified German state" and lead to adoption of a constitution for a unified government.

West Germany's opposition Social Democratic Party (SPD) Jan. 29 asked Oskar Lafontaine, the state premier of Saarland, to be the party's candidate for chancellor in the federal elections scheduled for December. The offer was made by SPD leader Hans-Jochen Vogel after Lafontaine had led the SPD to a convincing state election triumph in the Saarland Jan. 28.

The charismatic Lafontaine was a former left-winger who had adopted a more populist and pragmatic tone in recent years. He asked the party for three weeks to consider the nomination to oppose two-term chancellor Kohl of the Christian Democratic Union.

The request to consider the nomination was characterized as an attempt to offset Lafontaine's image as a brash eccentric. But the choice was a weighty one given the expected strength of East Germany's Social Democrats in the March 18 general elections there, the already established ties between the two SPDs and the growing calls for German reunification.

Momentum toward the reunification of East and West Germany continued to grow in the period Feb. 10-Feb. 14. West German Chancellor Kohl Feb. 10 met with Soviet President Gorbachev and reported that the Soviets had agreed on "the right of the German people alone to decide whether to live together in one state."

After a meeting in Bonn Feb. 13, Kohl and East German Premier Hans Modrow agreed to open talks on uniting the monetary systems of the two nations under the West German deutsche mark.

FORT WORTH STAR-TELEGRAM
*Fort Worth, TX,
February 8, 1990*

Secretary of State James Baker and our NATO allies say that they support a West German proposal for a unified Germany to be part of NATO, but with no NATO troops in East Germany. Meanwhile, West German Chancellor Helmut Kohl proposes a single currency for the two Germanys.

At the same time, some Soviet officials, debating great changes in their own country, keep referring to the specter of German reunification, which remains a fearful prospect in most Russian eyes.

Reunification will happen because the Germans are one people, because the artificial ideological split in Europe that has kept the two Germanys apart is crumbling and because, given the present circumstances, a Germany divided but openly resenting that division will become an ever-greater problem.

A united Germany can also be a problem, and some facts about reunification must be recognized.

A united Germany within its present boundaries would have twice the population of any of its neighbors except France and 40 percent more people than France. Because of its sheer population advantage, its geographic location and its economic resources, a reunified Germany will dominate Europe, as unified Germanys always have. Even by itself, West Germany is Europe's dominant economic power.

Closer ties to West Germany may be the salvation of East German democratization and the key to East German economic revival, but who will provide the same boost to Poland or Czechoslovakia, both of which know the strength of a united Germany?

Present German boundaries with Poland, Czechoslovakia and France were not chosen by the Germans themselves. Already there is talk of boundary "adjustments." Is it possible to adjust those national boundaries in such a way that both Germans and their neighbors are satisfied and secure?

The best hope for reunification without explosion is in democratic institutions and strong international cooperation. German ambitions have caused several wars, but none was started by a democratic Germany or by a Germany that was part of a broad and watchful international body.

German reunification will come. The trick for the Germans and the rest of the world, in terms borrowed from nuclear physics, is to make sure that reunification is a "controlled reaction." Achieving that may be Europe's No. 1 priority for the next few decades.

The Houston Post

Houston, TX, February 1, 1990

PRESSURE FOR GERMAN reunification is building rapidly, largely because of blunders by East Germany's Communist-led government. But the timing of a new German union is still critical to European stability and East-West relations.

Soviet President Mikhail Gorbachev, meeting with East German Prime Minister Hans Modrow in Moscow this week, apparently accepted the eventual reuniting of Germany, divided after its defeat in World War II. Gorbachev warned, however, that the issue should not be decided in the streets, a reference to pro-unity demonstrations in East Germany.

Reformist Modrow's embattled Communist Party has acquiesced to the idea in principle.

The United States does not oppose reunification, long fostered by West Germany, but we don't want it to happen precipitously. After two world wars, our NATO partners and other European neighbors of a future reunited Germany are understandably nervous about it.

Growing restiveness among East Germans prompted the East Berlin government and the country's political groups last weekend to move elections, originally set for May 6, to March 18. They also formed a new Modrow-led interim ruling coalition. There were doubts that the old regime could last until March.

One mistake that soured public opinion on Modrow was his decision to form an intelligence service to fight right-wing extremist movements. East Germans, who saw this as an attempt to perpetuate the hated secret police, or *Stasis*, attacked and ransacked its headquarters. Modrow was forced to drop the idea.

The government also resisted free-market economic reforms in favor of more modest changes. That has swelled the exodus of East Germans to West Germany to more than 2,000 a day since Jan. 1. These people, most of them young, are fleeing a failed communist system.

Modrow's regime has been reversing or softening some of its unpopular policies. It has also pressed corruption charges against East Germany's ousted hard-line Communist leader, Erich Honecker, and his top lieutenants. But all this may not suffice to revive public trust.

Yet a headlong rush toward a single German state would serve nobody's interests, including those of the Germans. The Bush administration's step-by-step approach to reunification — bringing all parties along together — is still the right and prudent course.

THE SACRAMENTO BEE

Sacramento, CA, February 4, 1990

German reunification, long paid lip service in the West and adamantly opposed by the Soviet bloc, now looks inevitable – no longer a question of if but of when, and how. In recent days, Soviet President Mikhail Gorbachev seems to have accepted the prospect of German unity, without necessarily endorsing it. East Germany's Communist-led government, desperate to appease a restive populace and to avoid political and economic collapse, now proposes talks with West Germany to work out a common approach toward unification.

So quickly have Communist attitudes changed that the United States now finds itself behind the curve. Washington's longstanding support for a unified Germany "someday" has never been meant, or taken, literally. Now, the Bush administration needs to respond to fast-moving events by clarifying its position on how it should be achieved.

In East Germany, wildcat strikes, anti-Communist demonstrations, a rise in political extremism and a continuing exodus to the West have threatened public order and all but paralyzed the economy, causing many East Germans to embrace union with rich, stable West Germany as a panacea. West Germans, who've always wanted unification but hadn't expected it anytime soon, now fear that the influx of migrants from the east — 400,000 in the past year, nearly 2,000 more every day — will overwhelm social services, job and housing markets and West Germans' willingness to assume such a burden. Thus, it's reasoned, early unification might help stabilize an increasingly unstable situation.

Outside Germany, these developments raise concerns. To create an enlarged Germany out of two countries belonging to opposing military alliances before long-standing East-West security issues are resolved, and before a turbulent Eastern Europe achieves a new, democratic stability, seems risky at best. There are also fears of a newly strident, expansionist German nationalism, and of a more eastward-looking Germany weakening its commitment to Western institutions and ideas.

Some of these fears seem exaggerated. It's true that radical right-wing groups have emerged in both Germanys, but they are small; moderate new parties in East Germany with strong ties to parties in Bonn seem much likelier to do well in elections than extremists of the right or left. West Germany's democratic record is solid, and its commitments to Western institutions and to respect its existing eastern borders seem genuine.

Yet the strategic factor is perplexing. Even if President Bush's new proposal for deeper troop cuts in Central Europe is implemented, large numbers of Soviet and U.S. troops would remain on German soil. Could that work? Conceivably so, within the context of gradual unification tied to phased military disengagement. Yet that implies a neutral Germany, even though Bonn says that won't happen. If it did, how would the superpowers react? By that time, would it matter?

These are serious questions whose answers won't come easily or quickly. German unity is bound to come, but if reason prevails, only slowly and within a larger East-West context. Toward that end, the Bush administration must now commit itself to helping the process by giving equal consideration to the need for an orderly transition and to the justified impatience of millions of Europeans too long suppressed and divided by the Cold War.

THE DENVER POST

Denver, CO, February 7, 1990

MIKHAIL Gorbachev and other Soviet leaders have implicitly recognized the inevitable reunification of Germany. It's time now that political leaders in the Western alliance also accept this fact.

The real issue is *when* and *how* Germany will be reunited, not whether. But this prospect raises difficult questions for the alliance, not the least being whether the united Germany will remain in NATO.

There's also a concern of whether a newly confederated Germany will accept existing borders, since Germany historically has claimed territory in what is now modern-day Poland. Others also fear that a reunified Germany may again attempt to dominate Europe.

But if the Western allies oppose German reunification, they may be locked out of the process of molding the shape of the new nation. The most reasonable course of action is to encourage the Germans to align themselves as much as possible with Western interests.

This goal can only be done in a spirit of cooperation, through wise use of economic incentives.

In this regard, the free nations of Europe may hold the most influential position.

By 1992, most of Western Europe will belong to an unprecedented economic alliance, an outgrowth of the existing European Economic Community or Common Market.

In this new union, trade and immigration barriers will disappear, and the nations eventually will even use a common unit of currency. The new European Community's economic clout will rank just behind the United States and ahead of Japan.

West Germany would be foolish to abandon this remarkable economic union, but East Germany would have much to gain by joining it. Other Europeans should gently remind the Germans that they need to cooperate in, and not seek to dominate, this new continental confederation.

And where the united Germany's economic interests lie, there will be its military interests also.

The key to designing the new Europe lies in economic opportunities. When it comes to the question of German reunification, that reality should work to the advantage of the Western alliance.

The Miami Herald

Miami, FL,
February 6, 1990

FIRST, President Mikhail Gorbachev said that German reunification is no longer in doubt. He added, however, that the question "requires profound assessment." Then, East German Prime Minister Hans Modrow, who was visiting Moscow when Mr. Gorbachev made his remarks, presented a plan for German reunification that calls for a "neutral" German nation.

It was rightly rejected by West German Chancellor Helmut Kohl, who asserted that a unified Germany would have to be part of the Western Alliance. Mr. Kohl also said that the notion of German reunification could be discussed only with the East German government to be elected in March.

Clearly, Mr. Modrow's plan is rash and belies Mr. Gorbachev's advice regarding a "profound assessment" of the question. The Western Alliance needs to make that assessment clearly and quickly, as part of a general discussion of the character of the "new house of Europe."

To this end, the Alliance should begin by reiterating the German people's right of self-determination. Some European countries have reasonably expressed disquiet over a development that NATO has officially supported since 1954's "Germany Treaty." But whether the Alliance now supports it wholeheartedly or not, some form of unification appears to be inevitable.

Most Germans are clamoring for it. Mr. Gorbachev and the East German government have given their *imprimatur* to one variation of reunification. Strong European, Soviet, or American resistance would only boost German nationalism, a potentially dangerous force.

A unified Germany will be the most powerful nation in Europe and will alter the assumptions that guided European post-war relations. New assumptions will have to be fleshed out rather quickly so that instability does not increase in what already is a situation fraught with uncertainties. Like France, for example, Germany, could remain in NATO though all foreign troops had left its territory.

That would signal the end of NATO as we know it. But then again, Germany's reunification, following the East European tumult of 1989, would signal that Europe as we knew it will no longer exist.

THE SPECTER THAT DIVIDES GERMANY

ST. LOUIS POST-DISPATCH

St. Louis, MO, February 14, 1990

Forty-five years after the end of World War II, a peace treaty between Germany and the Allied nations has yet to be signed. As the two Germanys grapple with unification, it is now time to hold a peace conference — a meeting of top foreign ministers along the lines suggested by British Prime Minister Margaret Thatcher.

Such a meeting would have two major functions. First, the boundaries of a unified Germany would be fixed officially to the land occupied by East and West Germany. Germany would renounce all territorial claims to land now held by Poland and the Soviet Union. Second, the Allied nations of the United States, the Soviet Union, Great Britain and France would assume a formal role in determining whether a unified Germany would remain in NATO or become neutral.

A conference must be held speedily. The movement for German unification has become a mammoth snowball. Talk of a monetary union between East Germany and West Germany is already under way. And West German Foreign Minister Hans-Dietrich Genscher has proposed that plans for unification be presented to the 35-member Conference on Security and Cooperation in Europe at its meeting this fall and that these plans could be implemented by the end of the year.

As it is now stands, the central issue is whether a unified Germany would remain in NATO, the position of West German Chancellor Helmut Kohl and the Western Allies, or become a neutral, demilitarized country, the position of East German Prime Minister Hans Modrow and Soviet President Mikhail Gorbachev. If these two positions are viewed as two solutions to the same fundamental question — how to allay the legitimate security concerns of the Soviet Union and other European nations — they are not necessarily irreconcilable.

As the process of unification begins, the NATO option is better — as long as Soviet concerns are addressed. As Mr. Genscher has suggested, NATO troops would not be stationed in what is now East Germany. It would remain what it is now — a buffer for the Soviet Union.

Beyond that gesture, though, the Western allies must convince Mr. Gorbachev that a Germany tied to NATO is more controllable than a Germany free of all alliances. Indeed, the Soviets have begun to indicate that German neutrality is not a non-negotiable demand.

But the Western Allies must also prepare for the day that NATO is no longer necessary. The Warsaw Pact, for all intents and purposes, no longer exists as a fighting force; as European integration proceeds, the argument for an enduring NATO will be become less and less persuasive. The best guarantee of a stable, peaceful Germany will ultimately be a stable European house. Yet, until that house is in order, until its structure is complete, NATO will have to act as midwife to German unity.

The Birmingham News

Birmingham, AL, February 7, 1990

It is clear that sooner or later East Germany and West Germany are going to become one country again. Probably sooner.

That could happen even this year, after elections in East Germany next month that are expected to deal the struggling communists there a swift and final death blow.

Well, Hans-Dietrich Genscher, West Germany's foreign minister, has come up with a reunification plan that deserves the support of the United States and the North Atlantic Treaty Organization.

Genscher's plan, which would combine the economic, political and legal aspects of the two nations, would keep Germany a member of NATO, but without moving Western troops into what is now East Germany. His proposal also would allow Soviet troops to remain in what is now East Germany.

Genscher's proposal is just what the Bush administration has been looking for. Certainly, NATO and Warsaw Pact troops can't forever stare each other down in a united Germany.

But until negotiations to reduce troop levels on both sides are completed — and those negotiations are moving at a slower pace than the reunification movement — a shared Germany may be the only answer.

Despite the sweeping changes in Eastern Europe, the Soviet Union still has more than 390,000 troops based in East Germany. If NATO is to remain a viable defender of free Europe, Germany, because of its strategic location, must be involved.

Secretary of State James A. Baker has called Genscher's idea "pretty good," but the Bush administration should fully endorse the idea, and the U.S. should urge its NATO allies to do the same.

German reunification is going to happen. The interests of the Free World will be better served if Germany remains a partner in NATO when it does.

ARGUS-LEADER

Sioux Falls, SD, February 12, 1990

Until last November, the wall that divided the city of Berlin stood as the ultimate symbol of communist oppression.

Since then, the wall and other obstacles separating East Germany from West Germany and the rest of the free world have been crashing down.

Increasingly, the possibility of a re-unified Germany seems likely.

Reunification was probably inevitable even before the failure of socialism in East Germany because of the common ancestral ground of the two countries. The recent change in political climate has only accelerated the movement.

Experts caution, however, that re-unification will be difficult. Speculation in the United States about the pace of reunification may be unrealistic.

Lingering fears of a new Hitler rising from a unified Germany to conquer the world are unwarranted, too.

The world has changed dramatically since World War II. German people are satisfied with their borders, except for the one that continues to divide East Germany and West Germany.

West Germany is a capitalistic success story. It has risen from impoverished ruin to become a thriving leader in the world economy.

East Germany, meanwhile, has spent more than a half-century under dictatorship. Its state-controlled economy has grown stagnant. No wonder East Germans are talking seriously about reunification.

It seems like a nice fit. West Germany has money and industry; East Germany awaits as a potential labor pool.

But government experts L.H. Gann and Peter Duignan, senior fellows at the Hoover Institution at Stanford University, contend in a report published recently that restoring East Germany will be a lengthy task. They do not believe there can be true unification without a free economy and free elections in both countries.

In the meantime, Gann and Duignan urge Germans to follow an old proverb to "make haste slowly."

They do see some steps that could be taken immediately. The first one should be an agreement in which the two German states collaborate on matters such as trade, tourism and pollution.

"In the long run, the German question will be settled as part of a wider European solution in which Western and Eastern Europe will collaborate," the two scholars speculate. "But this is a task for the 21st century — not the 20th."

No matter how long it takes, the thought of a reunified Germany remains comforting.

The Chattanooga Times

Chattanooga, TN,
February 5, 1990

A reunified Germany became a virtual certainty when the East German revolution toppled the Berlin Wall. There was suddenly no rationale for denying reunion of a divided people if, given self-determination, that was what they chose once artificial barriers fell. NATO and Warsaw Pact security concerns notwithstanding, only East German communists and Soviet reluctance stood in the way.

Now, even those stumbling blocks have been swept aside by the seemingly immutable force — and persistent demonstrations — of East Germany's restive revolutionaries. Hans Modrow, East Germany's communist interim leader, must have told Soviet leader Mikhail Gorbachev as much when he went to Moscow last week. The increasingly apparent choice for both was to acknowledge the inevitability of reunion and get in a position to help shape it, or to be — again — overtaken by people power.

The message apparently took. Before Mr. Modrow's visit was up, Mr. Gorbachev appeared to give reluctant sanction to reunification — which he previously had put off. Then, Mr. Modrow, who himself had led the remnant East German communists' resistance to reunification, returned to East Berlin to announce his own reunification proposal.

As far as NATO is concerned, Mr. Modrow's cautious, phased-approach plan is a non-starter because it calls ultimately for a militarily neutral Germany. But as a beginning to European negotiations on the Germanys' fates, it is very much a key starter. It puts the question on the table and sets the other side's framework for negotiations.

In fact, some *new* form of military balance must somehow be achieved in tandem with a German reunification plan. U.S. Defense Secretary Richard Cheney predicted Thursday that Russia would withdraw all her troops from Central Europe by 1995. Presumably, that would include the 375,000 Soviet troops presently garrisoned in East Germany, Russia's key strategic outpost in Central Europe. But this is not likely to happen if the United States and NATO insist on keeping a strong contingent in Germany, where some 195,000 U.S. soldiers would remain even under President Bush's latest troop reduction proposal.

Given Germany's role in two world wars this century and the resulting apprehension with which her European neighbors regard her, a new military balance of power will not be easily found. Neither will a formula for political and economic integration between the two Germanys.

But the current situation in East Germany is clearly untenable. More than 2,000 East Germans are still fleeing daily to West Germany. Hopes for a stable East German political environment hang on elections — now moved up to March 18 — in which reformers who favor reunification are expected to triumph. If reunification seemed, in reality, unthinkable only last September, its cautious development now seems unstoppable.

East German Conservatives Win Election in First Free Vote

An alliance of conservative parties backed by West German Chancellor Helmut Kohl scored a surprising triumph in East German general elections March 18, 1990. The democratic elections came just 18 weeks after East Germany had opened its borders and installed a reformist Communist government in November 1989.

The Alliance for Germany, a conservative grouping of three parties that favored speedy reunification with West Germany, won 41.8% of the vote. Its main opponent and the early favorite in the election, the Social Democratic Party (SPD), placed second with an unexpectedly low 21.8%.

The Alliance for Germany was led by the Christian Democratic Union (CDU), the eastern counterpart to Chancellor Kohl's party of the same name. Kohl, who had campaigned prominently in East Germany, had been at the forefront of the push for a rapid reunification of the two Germanies.

The vote in East Germany (formally known as the German Democratic Republic) was the first free election there since the 1932 vote that paved the way for Adolf Hitler's Nazis to assume power in Germany the following year. The election was also the freeist election in a Warsaw Pact nation since reform began sweeping the Eastern bloc in 1989.

The Alliance for Germany March 19 asked the SPD to join it in a "grand coalition" government, but the SPD refused to join a government that included the German Social Union (DSU), one of the smaller parties in the alliance. The conservative alliance could form a majority government with the Alliance of Free Democrats, which was backed by the West German Free Democratic Party, the junior partner in Kohl's coalition government. But that combination alone would not produce the two-thirds majority in the parliament needed to make major constitutional changes.

The size of the backing for the Alliance for Germany came as a surprise. East German CDU leader Lothar de Maiziere said March 18 that he had "never expected" that his party's victory "would be as big as this."

Public opinion polls reported in February had shown the Social Democrats favored by the majority of voters, with a large number of undecided votes. The lead had been cut in the weeks preceding the elections. The swing of votes to the CDU was widely attributed to a desire on the part of East Germans for improved economic conditions. The fast pace of reunification favored by the CDU and Kohl was seen as the most promising route toward an improved economy.

The Boston Globe
Boston, MA, March 20, 1990

The East German election was a triumph for democracy and a personal victory for West German Chancellor Helmut Kohl. His vision of a quick reunification of Germany has now been ratified by the people it will affect the most.

The vote makes clear that East Germans who stayed at home share the feeling of their countrymen who emigrated to the West. They want the benefits of West German prosperity now and are willing to forgo the shabby security of a Communist state.

Left behind, with only 2.9 percent of the vote, were the courageous people who led the New Forum party, which played a pivotal role in last fall's demonstrations against the Communist regime. Their vision of a third way between capitalism and communism fell victim to the realities of everyday East German poverty.

The Social Democrats, who proposed much the same program, did more poorly than expected, gaining 22 percent, just six points better than the don't-rock-the-boat Communists.

The big surprise was the 48 percent gained by the Christian Democratic coalition. It did not matter that one party leader quit the race because he was identified as a secret police informer. The real leader of the coalition was West Germany's Kohl, who grabbed the reunification issue in November and never let it go.

While a quick reunion is not certain, Sunday's vote paves the way for an important intermediate step. Elmar Pieroth, who will become economics minister of East Germany, says monetary union will be in place by July. If that goes smoothly, political unity cannot be far behind.

The last free election in East Germany was in 1932, when Nazi brown shirts bullied their rivals in urban street fights. Like then, Germany is in a state of transition. But the trend today is toward freedom, prosperity and peace instead of tyranny, oppression and war.

The Star-Ledger
Newark, NJ, March 21, 1990

The first free elections in East Germany were more than a vote in favor of union with the West. They also provided an unexpectedly large expression of confidence for an emerging power in world politics—West German Chancellor Helmut Kohl.

In a year of enormous political surprises in the Eastern European states, Mr. Kohl's remarkable political feat ought not go unnoticed. It was a triumph that only a few months ago seemed inconceivable.

When East Germany broke from its tyrannical masters and scheduled free elections, it appeared all but certain that the Social Democrats, the chief political opponents of Mr. Kohl's Christian Democrats, would score an overwhelming victory in the East. Early polls gave the party, a minority player in the West but supposedly popular in the East, up to 80 percent of voter support.

Mr. Kohl campaigned hard in the East. While he preached the message of unity, the Social Democrats—indeed, virtually all Germans—also supported the end of the partition of their country. But Mr. Kohl convinced the East Germans and the West as well that he could get the job done better.

What really swung the tide toward Mr. Kohl and the Christian Democrats was not only unity but prosperity. The more the East Germans looked at the prosperous economic model that was flourishing in the West, the more they liked what they saw.

Chancellor Kohl managed to convince them that the way to get the good things in life that have so long been absent in East Germany was to vote for his party. Although the Christian Democrats failed to win an absolute majority and must rely on some form of coalition, they remain dominant players.

Mr. Kohl is not yet the ruler of all Germany. He faces a test in the West's parliamentary elections later this year. But the result of the voting in the East augurs well for his chances.

The prospect of a revived and unified Germany still raises considerable international concern as well as concern in West Germany over the huge costs it must bear and other problems that must be resolved in the reunification process. Despite the election victory in the East, the Bonn government now appears intent on taking a more deliberate and cautious approach to a united Germany.

Mr. Kohl, while obviously pleased with his stunning political achievement, also prudently subscribes to a slower-paced transition. At a news conference, he indicated that he did not expect an all-German election this year, nor did he indicate when unification might actually be realized. But he appears ready to become the most powerful figure in post-World War II German politics.

THE KANSAS CITY STAR
Kansas City, MO, March 21, 1990

Voters in East Germany, like people who participated in the recent Nicaraguan elections, have surprised everyone by placing themselves further to the right on the political spectrum than had been expected. Authoritarian collectivism, it turns out, is a poor way to build popular support for socialist programs.

By the time all the comrades in East Germany were finally asked to register their opinions in imported voting booths, many of them had little patience for even moderately left-wing politics. "Never again socialism," declared the Christian Democrats.

Willy Brandt, honorary chairman of the Social Democratic Party in both East and West Germany, had already begun bragging about how the party's "expected strong performance" would show that all of Europe would soon tilt to the left. Many others accepted that view.

Now the political arithmetic of German reunification is being recalculated to the advantage of the Christian Democrats and their leader, West German Chancellor Helmut Kohl. This in turn requires recalculations for the rest of Europe as it prepares to follow the lead of a united Germany.

The successors to the communists in East Germany won only 65 of the 400 seats in the People's Chamber. They were happy to do even that well.

Besides disappointing socialists and humiliating communists, the election results reflected the preference of many East Germans for quick German reunification.

During the campaign, Kohl presented himself as the champion of this approach with enthusiasm. No sooner had the election results come in, however, than Kohl and his party began backpedaling. Welcome to democracy, East Germany!

The new-found caution in Bonn reflects the growing realization in both East and West Germany that reunification will require many adjustments, precautions and at least some temporary sacrifices.

Kohl has advised the Christian Democrats in East Germany to form a coalition with all of the other democratic parties. Given the importance of the decisions to be made in the months ahead, there is much to be said for that approach.

THE BLADE
Toledo, OH, March 21, 1990

EAST Germany held a free election Sunday for the first time since 1933. But although the vote was designed to elect a 400-member parliament, in reality it amounted to a referendum on swifter reunification — which won in a stampede.

The vote will cause nervousness throughout Europe where fear of German unity is visceral. The overwhelming support for conservative-party candidates who want to push the nation as fast as possible toward reunification indicates the powerful attraction of West German-style capitalism among citizens of its eastern neighbor.

East Germans voted with their stomachs. After years of looking hungrily across the Berlin Wall — aided in recent times by television — and having seen the West German consumer society close up in recent months, there was no stopping the rush to vote for reunification-minded parties and candidates. The public chose to ignore the fact that their more protected society and culture will be largely swallowed up by West Germany.

Before the election West German Chancellor Helmut Kohl — who appears a big winner now, thanks to his vigorous campaign on behalf of his conservative party — promoted a currency reform that will help protect the savings of East Germans and promote economic good health there (even though it might spur the inflation that West Germany has labored so hard to prevent).

The shift toward a single Germany will not be as easy as East Germans might hope, of course. Growing numbers of West Germans are now aware that there will be a staggering price to be paid to establish West German-style prosperity in the east while protecting that nation's system of generous social benefits. Indeed, Chancellor Kohl may suffer in next December's scheduled election in West Germany if the public believes it will be asked to shoulder too much of that burden.

The East Germans' decision also will unsettle its neighbors, especially Poland, which are concerned about the restoration of a single Germany. The nightmare of German invasion and occupation in World War II can never be completely dispelled. The issue was underscored by Chancellor Kohl's waffling on the matter of guaranteeing Poland's postwar border with Germany.

Washington is reportedly pleased with the East German conservatives' support for NATO, and certainly the four World War II allies will have a significant voice in setting a defense policy for a reconstituted Germany, but their power to affect this region's future is no longer absolute. The United States simply isn't at this point the dominant power in Europe. However, this country may be seen more than ever as a disinterested party in resolving disputes.

A typical expression of support for the "new" Germany came from Susanna Frank, an East Berliner who told a reporter: "We should get out of this mess as soon as possible. Every day we waste not having reunification just makes matters worse."

On Sunday, a nation of voters just like Ms. Frank spoke at the ballot box — members of a society who can now feel pride that they could speak their minds and chart their future as a society in a free, uncompromised manner.

AKRON BEACON JOURNAL
Akron, OH, March 20, 1990

A COALITION of conservative parties is poised to assume control in East Germany following elections there Sunday, although the coalition will need some help to form a majority. However, the big winner was reunification.

East Germans who voted — 93 percent of those eligible to cast ballots — seemed to be saying that they want to rejoin their countrymen to the west as soon as possible. The three-party Alliance for Germany won 48.2 percent of the ballots, which will give it 193 seats in the 400-member Parliament.

West German Chancellor Helmut Kohl and his Christian Democratic Party had backed the Alliance for Germany substantially, with Kohl campaigning in East Germany before the election.

The Social Democrats, who received 21.8 percent of the vote and 87 seats, were the pre-election favorites. They advocate a slower pace toward reunification.

The Party of Democratic Socialism, which is the new version of the former Communist Party, drew 16.3 percent of the vote, which gives it 65 seats. It had campaigned on the premise that rapid unification would be harmful to those East Germans who are concerned about the retention of social services maintained under the old regime.

The Social Democrats may join the Alliance for Germany in a coalition. But the reformed communists have said they would not. It is not clear when the new government would take over.

Lothar de Maiziere, the 50-year-old East German Christian Democratic leader, appears to be in position to head the new government. A Cologne newspaper said he will seek a coalition with the centrist Union of Free Democrats. De Maiziere said he would exclude the Social Democrats from the first talks on power-sharing.

He also has raised the issue of monetary union — perhaps within months — prior to merging the two Germanys. This could be a crucial element in halting the exodus of East Germans westward.

Kohl showed his pleasure with the election results. "The German citizens have decided against every form of extremism. Most important, they want to follow a path, together with West Germany, that will lead to unification."

However, Kohl cannot be counted on to be the best judge on the conditions of reunification. He has drawn criticism for his hasty approach toward the issue, and he may be placing a higher priority on his political future than that of Germany.

THE DENVER POST

Denver, CO,
March 20, 1990

EAST AND West Germany could reunite within a year.

That's one possible result of Sunday's elections, in which East Germans supported a quick marriage with West Germany.

It was only four months ago that the Berlin Wall started tumbling — Nov. 9, 1989, to be exact. Yet only this week East Germans cast free ballots for the first time since Hitler disbanded the Weimar Republic in 1933.

The next time the East Germans vote, it could be in an all-German election, culminating in complete reunification with their Western counterparts.

When that election occurs, the old order of the now-fading Cold War will have vanished.

Many Americans are so enamoured with the euphoria of the moment that they seem blind to the difficulties that lie ahead.

The Europeans have well articulated their fears about a German reunification. But most of these concerns — rising nationalism; the ever-dangerous right wing; the specter of anti-Semitism, and the possible emergence of a new economic bully on the continent — are echos of the past.

The truly difficult struggles are those that now face the East Germans. They have seen how backward, polluted and inefficient their country is compared to West Germany. They know they may face unemployment and a loss of national identity should the two nations be rejoined.

Yet those risks didn't deter the East Germans from casting their votes for politicians who favor a merger with their Western neighbor. Perhaps their votes are a measure of how discredited and disliked the previous communist government really was.

About 90 percent of all eligible East German voters went to the polls — a remarkable show of interest, even in a country facing such a historic decision.

Maybe they know something of the value of democracy that Americans have forgotten.

The East Germans have signaled they are willing to take huge risks in order to build a more prosperous future. If they're willing to shoulder that burden, the rest of the world has no right to tell them no. All that other nations can do is encourage the Germans to keep the peace — economically as well as militarily — while they undertake the momentous task of reunification.

THE SACRAMENTO BEE

Sacramento, CA, March 20, 1990

In the end, West Germany's professional politicians had their way in East Germany's election. New Forum, the amateurs who led the popular democratic movement last autumn as Communist rule crumbled, got just 2.9 percent of the vote in a campaign dominated by conservatives financed and managed from Bonn. (The discredited Communists won 16 percent as the renamed Party of Democratic Socialism.)

On the surface, it seems the East Germans handed over their country to West Germany for the promise of a higher standard of living. Only weeks ago, the left-of-center Social Democrats, who favor gradual unification with West Germany and retention of some elements of socialism, led in public opinion polls. But the lure of a Western standard of living held out by West German Chancellor Helmut Kohl and his Christian Democrats (CDU), juxtaposed against a collapsing situation at home, proved too much for the voters to resist. The Alliance for Germany, a center-right coalition allied to the CDU in Bonn, won 48 percent of the vote and will head a new government, probably in coalition with one or more small parties among the 24 that contested Sunday's election.

Yet the fact that the conservatives fell just short of a majority and, more important, well short of the two-thirds needed to join East Germany to West Germany by a simple parliamentary vote, may help slow the rush toward unity promoted by Kohl and the CDU. It will allow the two governments to concentrate first on crucial economic and social problems, including the liberalization of a state-run economy.

Full political unity can then proceed, through negotiation, at the steady pace that serves the interests not only of Germans but of the victorious allied powers of World War II, which retain residual powers in Germany, and of Germany's European neighbors. In the best of circumstances, East-West agreement on a united Germany's role within, or between, opposing military alliances will be difficult.

How smoothly this process advances will depend on whether the exodus of East Germans abates with the promise of economic reforms, in particular an early monetary union designed to preserve East Germans' buying power, and West German funds to pay for it. To further discourage the westward flight, Bonn is likely to reduce welfare benefits for immigrants. East Germany's Social Democrats, despite getting less than 22 percent of the vote, also remain an important factor as the principal defender of the welfare state that East Germans have taken for granted.

What's vital for both German politicians and world statesmen to remember is that Germany is a society as well as a key piece on the East-West strategic chessboard. After a half-century of war, cold war and dictatorship, reshaping that society, and others in newly democratic Eastern Europe, must be done as carefully as possible so that what emerges is as stable and as democratic as possible.

The Honolulu Advertiser

Honolulu, HI, March 20, 1990

Dissecting election returns, a privilege of democracy, has now come to East Germany. But the mandate is in the eye of the beholder.

At one level, it seems simple: the Alliance for Germany, victor in the first free East German elections in decades, says the German states must move quickly to reunify.

But not so fast. The left-leaning Social Democrats won't join the alliance's coalition, saying quick reunification would wipe out the East's cradle-to-grave social services and submerge the East within the wealthy West.

The White House reads the election returns and sees a reunified Germany within NATO. West German Chancellor Helmut Kohl, godfather of the Alliance for Germany, agrees.

But many ordinary West Germans talk of a reunited, neutral nation. Moscow reads the returns and warns, again, that a united Germany in NATO would unbalance Europe.

Many ordinary West Germans, now past the euphoria brought by the fall of the Berlin Wall, see the migration from the East that strains social services. They worry that high taxes will be the price they pay for rebuilding East Germany.

Thousands of older Americans and Europeans (including Margaret Thatcher) read the returns and see grim images of Nazi soldiers, Hitler and concentration camps. They wonder about unity.

And what about the less than 3 percent vote for New Forum and other leftist groups which led the protests that breached the Wall? Lamented one leader: "The revolution has cast off its children."

One wonders whether the vote was about freedom, nationalism and a united Germany or about that most basic election issue — a fuller pocketbook.

Buffalo Evening News

Buffalo, NY, March 20, 1990

DURING THE Cold War, East Germans voted with their feet, often risking death to escape to West Germany. This week they voted freely in a national election and expressed the same sentiment — they want to be part of a reunited Germany as soon as possible.

The unexpected conservative landslide was a tribute to West German Chancellor Helmut Kohl's political savvy and a stinging repudiation of communism. East Germany existed as a separate entity for 45 years, and yet the people felt nothing but skepticism and scorn for it, rushing eagerly to vote it out of existence.

West German political leaders took an active part in the campaign, and all favored German reunification, but Kohl stood out as the one who stressed the issue, offering rapid reunification and enticing prospects of economic rewards.

Kohl wanted not only to aid his conservative counterparts in the east but to stop the flow of immigrants, who are causing economic problems for Kohl. His post-election message to East Germans was: "Stay home."

The conservative victory may simplify the negotiations that will now take place between the two parts of Germany and the World War II Allies — the United States, Britain, France and the Soviet Union — which still technically have rights in deciding the status of Germany.

Kohl's Christian Democratic Party has backed the United States in favoring continued German membership in NATO. The Soviet Union has favored a neutral Germany. As a result of the election, both German states will have similar policies.

At the heart of this issue is the future, not only of NATO and Germany, but of the new Europe, since the division of Germany symbolized the division of Europe. The Warsaw Pact foreign ministers, meeting last weekend in Prague, were divided on German neutrality, with Poland, for example, fearful that a neutral Germany might become too independently powerful.

While a Germany continuing to be anchored to NATO is reassuring to many Europeans, NATO itself seems bound to change in the years just ahead. If all Soviet troops leave Eastern Europe, there will obviously be less need for a military alliance. The Prague meeting discussed a Czech plan for an all-European security system that would replace the Warsaw Pact and NATO alliances.

NATO provides security for now, but if Europe is to be "whole and free," in President Bush's words, it can hardly have — or need — two opposing military alliances armed to the teeth.

The negotiations ahead will deal with these problems. It is only four months since the Berlin Wall was thrown open, and world leaders are still trying to catch up.

The East German election was the first free vote in that part of Germany since the ill-fated Weimar Republic was destroyed by Hitler in 1933, and the next election could well be an all-German election, possibly next year.

In the drive of East and West Germany for unity, it is fitting that the grand old man of West German politics, Willy Brandt, campaigned in the election, even though his Social Democrats came out second best.

Brandt, first as foreign minister and then as chancellor, braved the chill of the Cold War in the 1960s and 1970s to forge new ties between East and West. His vision is being realized in the new Europe.

The Dallas Morning News

Dallas, TX, March 22, 1990

The fact that the parliamentary elections in East Germany this past week were the first free elections for East Germans in almost 60 years might have had a little something to do with over 90 percent of the voters going to the polls. The fact that economics transcends all certainly had a lot to do with the overwhelming majority of them voting their pocketbooks. They gave a convincing victory to a conservative coalition backed by West Germany's chancellor, Helmut Kohl, whose appeal for quick unification of the two Germanys held out the promise of the quickest way to West German economic prosperity.

Clearly, the election result was as much a mandate for a higher standard of living as it was for German reunification.

By many accounts it was also a personal triumph for Chancellor Kohl. His vigorous campaigning for his East German allies helped deal a crushing blow to the East German Social Democrats, who were cast in the same light as the Communists for wanting to go slow on unification and rejecting the capitalist ways of the West. It is believed that this will shore up his own chances for re-election in December, and, thus for chancellor of a united Germany.

But now comes the hard part. How do the two Germanys actually unite? That has been made more difficult since the Social Democrats have refused to join the coalition government. They would be needed to constitute the two-thirds majority in parliament to make the necessary changes to the East German Constitution to join West Germany.

There is also the not-so-small matter of how to actually combine two totally different systems. East Germans will not want to lose their social safety net, while West Germans, already resentful over the increased competition for jobs and housing from the influx of thousands of East Germans who have already settled there, will be ever so reluctant to pay the price to bring East Germans up to their standards.

In the meantime, East Germans continue to flow into West Germany. Mr. Kohl's plan to have the West German mark serve as the currency for both Germanys and merge the social benefits of the Germanys by July 1, announced on Tuesday, will help some. It will be the first tangible sign of movement toward the national unity that East Germans voted for. But July 1 is also the planned date to end special benefits given East Germans who resettle in the West, and that could cause a surge before then.

Now that Chancellor Kohl is busy with the nuts and bolts of unification, there is a risk that he and his East German allies might become too absorbed in their own affairs to the exclusion of others', particularly Europeans', concerns over reunification. That makes Mr. Kohl's poor handling of the German-Polish border issue loom even larger. Therefore, it is imperative that the four World War II victors overseeing the unification process continually remind both Germanys that a united Germany must take place within the context of a united and secure Europe.

The Washington Post

Washington, DC, March 20, 1990

ALREADY ON the fast track, the movement for German unification has picked up tremendous new momentum from Sunday's election. A clear majority of East German voters swept every other consideration aside and went for the parties that promised the fastest action. Because the winning alliance in East Germany is the branch office of West Germany's dominant party, the results put the governments in both Germanys under fierce pressure to produce rapid progress.

It was a peculiar election in the sense that the East Germans were voting, through local proxies, for West German parties and politicians. They ignored the indigenous parties such as Neues Forum that courageously started the parade toward reform last year at a time when it was by no means safe to challenge the Communists. By contrast the big winners on Sunday were the East German Christian Democrats, a party with a cravenly unheroic history; it had been the docile servant of the Communists for 40 years and was still piously following them last fall when Neues Forum's people were leading protest demonstrations and getting their heads cracked by the cops. No matter. The East Germans were voting not on past records but for future hopes. The East German Christian Democrats, as they were until this year, were a good example of the kind of politics that their country desperately wants to leave behind. But they won the election because, under their present cleaned-up management, they seemed to have the best connections to the people running West Germany.

Now comes the next oddity: unification will take place under West German law, but that law leaves the initiative and timing wholly to the East Germans. West Germany will presumably have some influence over the process, chiefly through its money bags and the intricate financial arrangements that unification will require. But the Bonn government appears to feel that there's no point in dragging out the procedure.

Possibly so, but there are profound questions about both Germanys' commitments to their allies and neighbors that are nowhere near resolved. This election has fortunately put power into the hands of people who accept Germany's membership in NATO, eliminating that as an issue in unification. But Germany, and perhaps NATO as well, are going to have to find ways to reassure the Soviets and the Eastern Europeans that their legitimate interests are not going to be trampled in the rush.

The crucial thing is not whether German unification takes place—that's now foregone—but whether it takes place under terms and circumstances that increase stability and strengthen democracy throughout Europe, east and west.

DESERET NEWS

Salt Lake City, UT, March 20, 1990

The stunning election results in East Germany have increased the likelihood for a relatively swift reunification of the two Germanys — although some internal political obstacles still remain.

In an amazing voter turnout of 90 percent — showing an intense eagerness to taste democracy for the first time since the 1932 election that carried Adolph Hitler to power — East German conservatives romped to a landslide victory.

It was East Germany's first democratic election — and probably its last as a separate state. It was only five months ago that a popular uprising ousted Erich Honecker's hard-line communist government and the Berlin Wall was thrown open.

After years of unchallenged rule and sham elections, the Communists scored only 16 percent of the vote, despite their changing their name to the Party of Democratic Socialism. No one was fooled. Real democracy was the focus as voters expressed themselves without hesitation.

The Christian Democrat-led coalition won 48.2 percent of the vote, giving it 193 seats in the new 400 member Parliament, and putting it just short of the absolute majority needed to govern alone.

Lothar de Maiziere, the 50-year-old chairman of the Christian Democrats who is expected to become premier, called for a "grand coalition" to lead the country toward reunification with speed and popular support.

Such a coalition would give him the two-thirds parliamentary majority necessary to amend East Germany's constitution. With that majority, Parliament could simply declare a merger with West Germany.

Unfortunately, the Social Democrats, who garnered 22 percent of the vote and 87 seats, have indicated they will not enter a coalition. So the fast track to reunification that seemed so certain after the election may take more time than first expected.

Maiziere is also anxious to pull down the Berlin Wall as a clear sign the two Germanys are moving toward unity, and to introduce the strong West German currency into East Germany by June. Since the wall has been symbolically removed anyway, a complete physical removal would complete the Democratic transition.

Foreign observers were pleased with the absolutely democratic manner in which the elections were run, and the United States enthusiastically welcomed the results. It was a personal triumph for West German Chancellor Helmut Kohl, who has energetically campaigned for quick reunification.

Initially, the United States took a moderate approach toward reunification, although all of the major East German political parties favored it at varying speeds. In this strange new world that sometimes seems to be on a stampede toward democracy, the superpowers seem to be doing little more than trying to keep up with fast-moving events.

East German newspapers have editorialized that voters opted for what they perceived to be the quickest route to affluence — through unity with wealthy West Germany.

The desire for affluence in a country that has suffered so much economically is clearly a motivating factor, but no one should downplay the enormous drawing power of the democratic way of life that is now sweeping the world.

THE INDIANAPOLIS NEWS

Indianapolis, IN, March 21, 1990

East Germans voted Sunday in their first democratic election in 57 years. Almost 12 million voters turned out on a sunny day to cast their ballots. That is an estimated 95 percent of that nation's eligible voters.

Meanwhile, back home, the American people seem to have lost interest in this most basic act of democratic freedom. Barely half of those eligible to vote — 50.1 percent — bothered to show up at the polls in the 1988 general election.

In Indiana, 54 percent of those eligible to vote cast their ballots in the 1988 general election.

And in the 1987 election for mayor of Indianapolis, about 28 percent of eligible Marion County residents cast their ballots.

These numbers are a national, state and local disgrace. Consider:

● Well over 85 million Americans who were eligible simply didn't vote in the 1988 general election for president.

● More than 1.8 million Indiana residents could have voted in the 1988 general election but didn't.

● More than 400,000 Marion County residents who were eligible to vote in the 1987 race for mayor chose not to do so.

These irresponsible no-shows create depressing numbers such as these:

● George Bush was elected president by collecting votes from only 27 percent of U.S. adults.

● Evan Bayh was elected governor with votes from only 28 percent of Indiana adults.

● William Hudnut was elected mayor of Indianapolis with votes from less than 20 percent of Marion County adults.

East Germans are rejoicing in the right to vote in free and competitive elections. In America, the world's oldest and most prosperous democracy, half the people don't even bother to show up on Election Day. A pessimist might talk of renewal there and decline here. A pessimist might be right.

The Sun

Vancouver, B.C., March 20, 1990

NOW THAT East Germany has started the ball rolling toward reunification by electing a conservative alliance, the hard part starts: How to integrate the poor East into the booming economy of West Germany without creating an economic boomerang.

Chancellor Helmut Kohl of West Germany has promised one currency for a reunified state, and the getting from E-marks to D-marks is of great concern to both German and foreign economists.

Conversion of the East German currency at a rate of one E-mark for one D-mark, or even three for one of the robust West German marks, is being closely studied so that East Germans do not lose their purchasing power and savings.

Yet too generous a conversion rate could increase purchasing power in the reunited state by 15 per cent, some economists fear. This could lead to a boost in inflation in a couple of years from the present three per cent to five or six per cent, with an accompanying rise in interest rates.

Not just Germany would be affected. The United States, fearing a loss of investment flowing to the German union, would have to boost its rates to retain investment dollars. Ditto Canada.

Fortunately, all of the possible financial pitfalls are being studied carefully by Mr. Kohl and his numbers people. The rest of the world is counting also, hoping the cost of reunification will not be too high.

The Courier-Journal

Louisville, KY, March 20, 1990

CONCERN about the headlong reunification of the two German states is not limited to people east of the Oder-Neisse line and west of the Rhine. As the East German election approached, citizens and politicians alike expressed anxiety about being stampeded into a union with the West, all in the name of the almighty mark.

But those who favor a go-slow approach proved to be in the minority. The conservatives linked to West German Chancellor Helmut Kohl's Christian-Democratic party won a commanding plurality in the Parliament — and a mandate to move promptly toward merger.

Widespread disillusionment with socialism and a longing to share in West Germany's prosperity made it hard for the leftists to sell their view of a middle way between "materialism" and personal security. Their attempt to offer an alternative was all the more difficult because Bonn already presides over a generous welfare state.

The monetary and economic union envisioned by Mr. Kohl may be the only practical way to stanch the westward flow of workers that is draining the East's productive capacity. The next step, political unification, could follow within a year. The challenge will be to assure other Europeans, and many Germans, that *their* interests won't be trampled in the process.

The Wichita
Eagle-Beacon

Wichita, KS, March 20, 1990

They voted first with their feet. The hundreds of East Germans who started trickling west last May through newly opened gates in Hungary were the foot soldiers in one of the final battles of the Cold War. Within months, the Berlin Wall was down, the Stalinist East German government was overthrown and the country's first free election was scheduled.

On Sunday, East Germans, in effect, ended the postwar period in European history by voting for a conservative alliance that favors a quick alliance with West Germany.

The mood was summed up by Susanna Frank, a 25-year-old East Berliner: "Every day we waste not having reunification just makes matters worse."

Over the past few months, since being allowed to travel freely to the West, East Germans have discovered just how bad things are in their country. Compared with West Germany and other West European countries, East Germany is poor, polluted and spiritually depressed.

Sunday's vote was a major victory for West German Chancellor Helmut Kohl, who campaigned aggressively for parties allied with his Christian Democratic Union on a platform of a quick integration of the two Germanys. Although no timetable has been set, talks on a common currency and economic reconstruction are proceeding and many observers expect that political union will occur within the year.

The prospect of a united Germany has set off fears in Poland, France, the Soviet Union and other nations with tragic memories of 1871, 1914 and 1939. But 1990 is not an age of empire or ideology. West Germany has four decades of democracy, and the nation has none of the ambitions or resentments that led to earlier wars.

Never in history has a democratic nation started a major war against its neighbors. A single Germany will be a formidable economic power, but one that recognizes that its security depends on ensuring freedom and prosperity throughout Europe.

The Chattanooga Times

Chattanooga, TN, March 21, 1990

Considering the startling pace of recent events in East Germany, Sunday's election there seemed almost ordinary. It was not. It was a climactic demonstration of freedom the likes of which had not been seen in that land since 1933, when Hitler abolished the Weimar Republic. It was virtually unimaginable even last fall, when hard-line Communist boss Erich Honecker still reigned and plotted to use Russian tanks to suppress dissent.

After all these years of repression, however, the outcome could hardly be seen as a surprise. More than 93 percent of eligible voters, savoring the secrecy of a genuinely free election, cast their ballots in voting booths imported for the occasion from West Germany. Not surprisingly, they also largely shunned the renamed communist party. But their ringing endorsement of the Christian Democratic Union, which campaigned on a platform of quick reunion with West Germany, was a bit unexpected: Social Democrats, who favored a slower approach to unification, and maintenance of a bit more of the socialist system, had held the early campaign lead.

The West, whatever its qualms about a reunified Germany, should feel vindicated by this election. East Germans, in effect, said enough of socialism, and onward to a free-market democracy.

Leaders of the Christian Democratic Union are now looking for coalition partners to execute their agenda. They need a two-thirds majority in Parliament to change the constitution to permit reunification. Social Democrats are pouting that their slower approach was derailed by the surprisingly strong conservative express and say they won't join a coalition and make unification too easy.

No matter. Most East Germans see unification as the only way to rejuvenate their economy and secure their future. Representatives of the dozen or so smaller parties will soon respond to that mandate and help chart reunion. West German Chancellor Helmut Kohl plans to set the stage for the first step, economic and monetary union, by introducing the powerful West German mark at a one-for-one rate to individuals for their weak East marks. That hopefully will calm nervous East Germans and stem the draining rush to a West Germany now heavily burdened by new immigrants. Political union could follow within a year or two.

It would be just irony if the first free national election in East Germany is the last. But that could well be the case if the next vote is one to dissolve the state and merge with West Germany. There are, to be sure, many hurdles to be negotiated, between the Germanys, among the Big Four World War II powers that retain rights in the countries, and their European neighbors. Resolution of security and economic concerns relating to East Germany and the path to unification will not be easy, but the foundation of democratic freedom in East Germany argues for optimism for the first time in that country's bleak history.

Polish Regime, Opposition Reach Concilliation

The "round-table" talks in Poland between the regime and opposition concluded April 5, 1989 with accords on broad political and economic reform. The talks had lasted for two months. The political changes outlined in the accords placed Poland, along with Hungary, in the forefront of democratic reform in Eastern Europe. The agreements were signed in a nationally televised ceremony at the government palace in Warsaw. Gen. Czeslaw Kiszczak, the interior minister, represented the regime. Lech Walesa, founder of the outlawed Solidarity trade union, represented the opposition. Walesa called the accords "the beginning of the road for democracy and a free Poland."

Popular reaction to the accords was reported to be muted. Caution was said to result in part because of the serious economic problems faced by the nation and also from a fear of investing too much hope in the new system.

The ceremony was delayed for three hours because of a walkout by Alfred Miodowicz, the party official in charge of labor relations. The dispute centered on a compromise provision in the accords calling for workers' wages to be indexed to 80% of any rise in the cost of living. Miodowicz, backed by the OPZZ – the federation of government-supervised unions – wanted wages indexed to 100% of inflation. Miodowicz returned for the ceremony but vowed to continue fighting for full indexing.

In other major provisions:

■ *Senate and Free Elections* – The signatories agreed to a restructuring of the current unicameral national legislature into a bicameral body. The existing Sejm (parliament) would be the lower house and have 460 seats. A new Senate would be the upper house and have 100 seats.

Senators would be chosen through free elections, set for June. The Senate would have the power to veto key legislation, thus having a check on the Sejm. The ruling United Workers' (Communist) Party and its allies, the Democratic and Peasant parties, were guaranteed 65% representation in the Sejm. The remaining 35% of the seats would be filled by opposition figures and independents through free elections. The Communists and their allies, therefore, would not be guaranteed the two-thirds majority in the Sejm needed to override legislative vetoes.

■ *Strong President* – The head of state, currently a largely symbolic post, was to be elected by a joint session of the legislature for a six-year term and would have strong executive powers. He or she would have the authority to veto legislation, dissolve parliament and supervise foreign policy. Current Communist President Gen. Wojciech Jaruzelski was widely expected to be named the first president under the new system.

■ *Solidarity Legalization* – Solidarity, formally banned since 1982, was to be returned to legal status, perhaps by the end of April 1989. Two other outlawed organizations – the farmers' union Rural Solidarity and the Independent Students Association (NZS) – were also to be legalized. Mechanisms were established for the official recognition of other opposition groups.

■ *Opposition Media* – The pact provided for the creation of official opposition media outlets, including newspapers and broadcasting stations.

Poland April 5 announced agreement on a draft law that for the first time in the Soviet bloc would grant official recognition to the Roman Catholic Church. Recognition would be a step toward possible diplomatic relations between Warsaw and the Vatican. Polish church representatives had participated in the round-table talks, but the agreement was the product of separate negotiations with the regime.

THE TENNESSEAN
*Nashville, TN,
April 9, 1989*

THE agreement giving Poland its most open elections since World War II and restoring the outlawed Solidarity trade union is a history-making event.

But what may be even more significant is the approving reaction in Moscow. The Soviet government newspaper *Izvestia* praised Poland's Communist authorities and Solidarity for displaying common sense and challenged them to make the agreement work.

The agreement, reached Wednesday by Solidarity leader Lech Walesa and Gen. Czeslaw Kiszczak, Poland's interior minister, calls for the government to restore legal status to Solidarity, the farmers' union Rural Solidarity and the Independent Students Association, all of which had been banned in a martial-law crackdown eight years ago.

A new 100-member senate is to be created which would be the first fully democratically chosen legislative chamber in the East bloc. At the same time Solidarity agreed to participate in an election to be held in June to fill the 460-seat Sejm, or parliament, which guarantees the Communist party and its allies a 65% majority.

The agreement was reached after two months of round-table talks — a rare event in the Communist world. Although it doesn't provide for a complete democracy, the agreement is a step in that direction. Mr. Walesa, whose untiring efforts over many years were mainly responsible for bringing about the agreement, said the "round-table talks can become the beginning of the road to democracy and a free Poland."

Polish leader Gen. Wojciech Jaruzelski, who banned Solidarity in 1981, has been arguing for its restoration in recent months as a means of gaining public support in reviving the lagging economy.

Izvestia gave credit for the agreement to reforms carried out by the Polish Communist Party in the last eight years. But it seems the agreement owes as much to reforms in the Soviet Union as in Poland. It is unlikely that any such agreement could ever have been reached in Poland if Soviet President Mikhail Gorbachev had not led the way with his glasnost policy and begun to open up Soviet life.

In fact, the Soviets seem downright proud of the small step toward democracy in Poland, as if that might help to strengthen Mr. Gorbachev's policy at home.

The reform movements in both Poland and the Soviet Union are of historic proportions. But both have a long way to go before they can convince the world they are headed toward true democracy.

The Star-Ledger

Newark, NJ, April 7, 1989

Considering the deep-seated antagonism that triggered bloody confrontations between the Polish government and the resolute opposition of the Solidarity movement, the agreement the antagonists signed in Warsaw was achieved with astonishing ease.

The watershed agreement is the sweet fruit of mutually respectful give-and-take by negotiators who finally realized that long-irreconcilable differences would have to be compromised in order to rescue their economically imperiled country. The pact, skillfully carpentered in little more than a month, incorporates encouraging provisions that point Poland, after years of brutal denial, in the direction of democracy.

On the positive side are two major victories for Solidarity, the militant trade union formed in 1980 which has been infused with inspirational leadership by Lech Walesa, a role which won him a well-deserved Nobel Peace Prize.

Foremost, there will be a return of free elections. Second, Solidarity will regain the legal status it enjoyed briefly until it was outlawed by Gen. Wojciech Jaruzelski after he became president in 1981 and ran an iron-fisted dictatorial regime.

Democracy will take the form of a new senate to be elected by the entire citizenry, a remarkable concession that was won in a tradeoff for the establishment of a new, strong presidency. The senate, discontinued after World War II, will have the power to veto measures passed by the lower house of the Polish parliament. The president, however, will have the power to dissolve the senate.

As a consequence of the historic agreement, Poland stands uniquely apart from other countries under the Moscow-based Communist Party's stifling thumb. But the welcome result might be merely a precursor of increasing self-determination and the emergence of democracy in other Soviet satellite nations.

This heady possibility gains credence in the light of Soviet leader Mikhail Gorbachev's willingness to abandon rigid, old-line Marxist teachings in favor of a policy of openness and the substitution of flexibility in place of the Communist Party's failed political and economic dogmas.

Mr. Gorbachev has taken a pragmatic look at Marxism and has realistically concluded that there is an urgent need for sweeping reforms in a changed contemporary world.

Pittsburgh Post-Gazette

Pittsburgh, PA, April 12, 1989

The government of Communist Poland finally has had to recognize the potency of the phrase, "the consent of the governed."

In 1981, the government of Gen. Wojciech Jaruzelski banned Solidarity, the independent trade union, and declared martial law. Now, little more than seven years later, Gen. Jaruzelski's government not only has restored Solidarity but also has agreed to free elections for the Sjem, Poland's parliament.

And, unlike the recent surprising legislative elections in the Soviet Union where even "opposition" candidates were staunchly Communist, the Polish agreement will allow candidates from parties that make no bones about being against the party.

This unheard-of set of concessions on the part of a Communist government has come because the Jaruzelski government has realized its only hope of reviving the stagnant Polish economy is to restore rights to the workers and to expand some to the citizenry in general.

Such an epochal change in Poland comes against a varying background of events elsewhere in the Soviet empire. The Communist government in Hungary has just approved laws permitting political parties and allowing the formation of independent trade unions. (Leaders of other nations in the Soviet bloc — East Germany, Czechoslovakia, Romania and Bulgaria — made it immediately clear they see no need for such experimentation.)

Last week, at the same time as the Polish agreement was approved, independence reared its discomfiting head in the Soviet republic of Georgia. In a concrete example of how Mikhail Gorbachev's glasnost policy is unwittingly fanning nationalistic hopes, protesters demanded independence for Georgia. Leaders of that southern republic immediately rejected the demand. But it took tanks and troops to quell the uprising, with at least 18 killed, a grim portent of what may happen again and again in the increasingly restless Soviet empire.

Not the least anomaly of the Georgian situation is that the trouble apparently arose because the Abkhazians, a tiny minority, gathered to demand secession from Georgia and creation of a separate republic. At first, that brought clashes between the Abkhazians and Georgian activists, which then turned into a Georgian independence movement.

With more than 100 different nationalities within the Soviet Union itself, one can see why President Gorbachev may have opened a Pandora's box of woes. Among the many questions that face his government is that of how much independence he can allow in the satellite states without detonating nationalistic dynamite in his own country.

Lest we smile too much, these fast-breaking events pose a problem for American policymakers, too. If the very easing of Kremlin domination devoutly desired on the one hand results in undermining the Gorbachev reform plans, is the West a gainer or a loser? Is the "consent of the governed" irresistible against the power of tanks and guns?

Houston Chronicle

Houston, TX, April 6, 1989

A stunning thing has happened in Poland. A shipyard worker forced the Communist Party to give up its monopoly of power.

Remember in the summer of 1980 when the workers at the shipyard in Gdansk joined the nationwide strikes? The shipyard workers chose Lech Walesa as their spokesman and eventually they won the right to organize. Solidarity was formed and quickly grew 10 million strong. That was too much for the communists. Gen. Wojciech Jaruzelski declared martial law, suppressed Solidarity and arrested Walesa. The confrontation was on.

Now, nine years later, the government has approved a document that legalizes Solidarity and calls for an elected upper house of parliament with a limited right of veto. This is not a complete victory. Key posts still will be held by communist functionaries. But, in Walesa's words, it "can be the beginning of the road to democracy and a free Poland."

A combination of economic problems and unceasing public support for Solidarity forced the government to agree to talks that began in February. The Communist Party, backed by an army and by Moscow, was faced with economic chaos and civil war and made unprecedented concessions.

Walesa, the shipyard worker, prevailed.

The Burlington Free Press

Burlington, VT, April 11, 1989

Sweeping economic, political and cultural reforms adopted in Warsaw last week challenge Washington to make good on promises to help ease Poland's staggering economic woes. They also bring an opportunity for broadened U.S. influence across Eastern Europe.

Since Gen. Wojciech Jaruzelski outlawed Solidarity in 1981, the United States has emphasized that relief on Poland's $39 billion foreign debt depended on Poland restoring the trade union's legality and initiating democratic reforms.

That and more was done last week.

Aside from legal recognition, the union will get time on the state-controlled television and radio networks. The unions will also be permitted to publish a daily national newspaper and weekly regional papers.

Politically, voters will elect a parliament in June with broader and more freely chosen representation than anything seen in Eastern Europe since World War II. Economically, the government agreed to guarantee workers pay hikes at 80 percent of cost of living increases, an important economic bandaid in inflation-riddled Poland.

In response, the Bush administration quickly said it would encourage the Import-Export Bank, the International Monetary Fund and the World Bank to help ease Poland's foreign debt burden through new credits and renegotiating outstanding loans.

No amount of tinkering with the structure of Warsaw's debt, however, will make up for the decay of the nation's industries and the lack of goods in the country's shops. That is where the United States can best help Poland while gaining credibility for itself in the rest of Eastern Europe.

As the Soviet Union encourages political and economic experiments in Eastern Europe, the United States should aggressively assist agricultural and industrial modernization and reconstruction in an effort to make liberalization more successful.

The experiment launched in Poland last week will be watched for signs of failure or success by the rest of economically toubled Eastern Europe. Whatever Washington does to make Warsaw's test a success will be to Washington's benefit.

Increased American involvement in bolstering Poland's economy will also protect against broken promises. The Polish government's most dramatic previous attempt at pragmatic liberalization — legalization of Solidarity in 1980 — failed less than two years later when the union was banned, many of its leaders were jailed and broad social and economic restraints were imposed.

There is no guarantee that will not happen again. But one good bet against regression is improved Polish-American relations.

Rockford Register Star

Rockford, IL, April 10, 1989

It's safe to say that the great political changes under way in Poland would not have come about were it not for the climate of reform in the Soviet Union under Mikhail Gorbachev. Still, the people and government of Poland merit credit for their own special brand of courage in mapping a dramatic new course for their country.

The liberalization now at hand in Poland is the greatest yet in the entire Soviet bloc. Agreements signed last week will restore the legal status of the Solidarity union and several other such groups, and provide for democratic elections in June for a Parliament in which the opposition parties will hold 35 percent of the 460 seats in the lower house.

The accords also re-establish the upper house of Parliament, which was disbanded after World War II. All 100 members of this body will be chosen in free and open elections.

These reforms — almost incredible to behold in a so-called Iron Curtain country — amount to a great triumph for the Polish people, who have steadfastly maintained faith in the face of government suppression of their unions and intimidation of their Roman Catholic institutions.

The reforms also constitute an acknowledgement on the part of the government that the moribund Polish economy can be revived only with the full cooperation and participation of Solidarity and the population at large. In that sense, this political miracle is born of great necessity. But that makes it no less marvelous.

The seeds of reform that Gorbachev planted in the Soviet Union are taking root throughout the region and are producing their brightest blossoms yet in Poland. Where next in the Soviet bloc will this trend manifest itself?

Portland Press Herald

Portland, ME, April 10, 1989

Poland took a giant leap forward last week, becoming the first European Marxist state to officially embrace multiparty democracy. It has become the best example to date of the power of Mikhail Gorbachev's *perestroika*, or restructuring.

But the country still must deal with the real economic and social problems that led to the changes.

The nation's chief trade union, Solidarity, has been given formal status; non-Communist Party candidates will be allowed to compete for 40 percent of the one-house national parliament and a new 100-seat freely elected Senate will be created.

Opposition newspapers and radio and television shows will also be permitted.

The developments go beyond, but are similar to, what's been happening in other Eastern Bloc nations, including the Soviet Union itself, which recently held its first genuinely competitive elections in 70 years. In Hungary, which has practically an open border with neighboring and officially neutral Austria, what amounts to the Warsaw Pact's biggest and freest private economy operates profitably alongside the state-directed sector.

Poland is deeply in debt to foreign lenders and struggling with inflation and low productivity. The party leaders might well be bringing in a formal opposition — including Solidarity's Lech Walesa — to share some of the blame for price hikes and cutbacks that are bound to be wildly unpopular.

But, as people are more than economic units — something Marx never understood — so too does a little openness inevitably breed a desire for more. Whether further changes, which will fundamentally alter the nature of power in long-regimented societies, will succeed is still anybody's guess.

But we can wish those nations well and do what we can to help them succeed. If they prosper, so will we.

THE CHRISTIAN SCIENCE MONITOR
Boston, MA, April 10, 1989

IN announcing his approval of a new political structure for Poland, Solidarity leader Lech Walesa noted that words were no longer enough. Political restructuring may not be enough either. What the Polish people want, and have grown impatient waiting for, are tangible improvements in their daily lives.

That means economic revitalization, and that will be a long haul in a country where two years' pay for the average person equals the price of a stripped-down Fiat and where inflation hovers around 80 percent.

Still, Mr. Walesa and his interlocutors on the government side have fashioned a plan that could pave the way for real progress in Poland. The advances in political openness and pluralism are remarkable: legalization of Solidarity, free elections, substantial opposition representation in the present lower house of parliament and establishment of an upper house where all seats will be contested, freedom to form associations and political clubs, great-

er access to the mass media, an independent judiciary.

A framework for national reconciliation is thus at hand. Will the cooperative effort needed to revive the economy follow? Participants in the round-table discussions that led to the reforms agreed, also, on the need to attack inflation by lowering Poland's budget deficit. They agreed to improve living standards, cut the $38 billion foreign debt, and create freer markets. These are broad goals, which will entail, for the short term, increased austerity – a necessity no more popular in Poland than elsewhere.

The Poles will need help from abroad in enhanced trade, technology, and investment. They will need the sympathies of their major creditors in Western Europe. President Bush has said the United States stands ready to help. But US help is restricted by Washington's own budget crisis.

Everything rests on performance. The new political structure looks good on paper. But will the people who bring it to life be able

to agree on such difficult steps as removing distorting subsidies or streamlining state-run factories?

Solidarity, after all, is a union, and its instincts are to protect jobs and wages. Getting behind austerity measures will be a hard sell to its members – many of whom, particularly the young activists, are already skeptical of deals struck with the government.

Then there are the party conservatives who blanch at the political reforms, and the official unions that never wanted to see Solidarity legalized. They'll be tempted to trip up the current reconciliation process.

Poland has reached a historic crossroads and taken a turn toward democracy. Its own painful evolution, and changes wrought by Mikhail Gorbachev in the Soviet Union, have made the turn possible. Elections begin in June and implementing other reforms before then. The country's ability to stick to its new path will be a measure of its inner strength and of the strength of the democratic trend in its region.

THE SACRAMENTO BEE
Sacramento, CA, April 10, 1989

Despite all the pitfalls that lie ahead, the agreement between the Polish government and the Solidarity trade union may be truly historic. It represents a triumph of persistence by Lech Walesa and his colleagues and an acceptance of reality by the Communist regime. It's also the most hopeful sign yet that democracy and stability may be restored in a nation whose modern history has been a catalog of misfortune.

Seven years after being driven underground, Solidarity has won more than it originally sought: legal status for itself, for a peasants' union and for an independent student group; access to the mass media; and wage-indexing to combat the effects of raging inflation. Beyond that, it has won electoral reforms granting broad legislative representation for the first time in more than 40 years. In elections to be held in June, 35 percent of the seats in the Sejm, the parliament, are guaranteed to opposition candidates, although Solidarity itself will not become a political party; all 100 seats in a revived Senate will be open to all comers; the Senate, and a president with extensive powers, will have veto power over laws passed by the Sejm. The government also formally assented to free-market economic reforms, beginning with agriculture.

None of this happened because a one-party regime suddenly got democratic, capitalist religion. Poland's economic plight — shortages, stagnant production, bad management, outdated plant and equipment, a $39 billion foreign debt, sporadic strikes and 60 percent inflation — left the government with no choice but to give ground or face to-

tal collapse of the economy and public order. In these strained circumstances, the two sides were able to produce a blueprint for a new Poland that is remarkable, even compared with the changes taking place next door in the Soviet Union.

Yet the blueprint is mainly a political one. Important as that is, and even if Poles of all persuasions do their best to live up to its promise — no sure thing by any means — the odds against success will remain prohibitive. For one thing, the Polish people, so often deceived and disappointed, have reacted with deep skepticism. How will they respond when, inevitably, they are asked to make more sacrifices in the name of reform?

Those challenges will demand a positive Western response as well. Having long wanted to see democracy reborn in Eastern Europe, the United States and its European allies now have the chance to help make it happen. That means, among other things, some debt forgiveness, as much direct aid — public and private — as possible, and a willingness to treat Poland as a normal country, not as a pariah. For its part, Poland must implement the kind of free-market reforms that the government promises but that hardline Communists still regard as anathema.

The Bush administration's initial response has been positive. How that will translate into concrete steps is another matter. Consultations among Western governments and lenders, and with Polish institutions — not only the government but Solidarity and the Roman Catholic Church — must begin soon. Given the possibilities, and the potential consequences of failure, it can't happen too soon.

AKRON BEACON JOURNAL
Akron, OH, April 9, 1989

THE SOVIET Union's Communist Party newspaper, Izvestia, neatly summarized the accords in Poland: "Common sense came out on top."

What has happened is no less than a crack in the Iron Curtain. In a historic agreement last week, the Polish government reinstated the outlawed free trade union Solidarity and similar organizations, and scheduled the first free elections since the communists took over after World War II.

The reason for this "social contract" is a basic one: economic necessity. The government hopes a revived Solidarity will end labor unrest so Poland's economic reforms — to fight inflation, reduce the $39 billion foreign debt, revitalize the industrial base — can take hold.

For Solidarity, the accords are a chance to build democracy in what already is the Soviet bloc's most politically liberal country. The Communists still will control the parliament in the foreseeable future, but the agreement is a start toward freedom.

Solidarity leader Lech Walesa realizes the need to begin mobilizing for the elections. And he has offered to go to Moscow, "not to agitate or irritate, but to seek understanding for the Polish reforms."

Clearly, there is a new spirit of cooperation in Poland. But the importance of the accords goes beyond Polish borders. Poland will be pushing the boundaries of liberalism within the Eastern bloc. Moscow, and other Soviet satellites, will be watching closely the direction of reform and whether political liberalism improves the economy.

No one is claiming this is the beginning of the breakup of the Soviet bloc, but other communist countries certainly will want to test the new Soviet openness.

There also is an opportunity for the West. In Washington, for instance, recognition of Solidarity — founded in 1980, crushed 16 months later — has been a condition for economic aid, in the form of debt reduction and other measures. The United States should now take the Soviets at their word, that the Polish agreement is a positive development, and move to reinforce it.

For once, the wind of reform is blowing from the East. As Soviet leader Mikhail Gorbachev has recognized, an economy can't run on ideology alone. Each victory for reform brings a renewed sense that the Cold War is evolving into new relationships that can be nurtured, by East and West, for mutual benefit.

After decades of saber-rattling, let's hope the leaders of both sides recognize the trends and act on them, as Poland has done.

Solidarity Dominates National Elections

The Polish communist regime suffered a humiliating defeat June 4, 1989, as candidates endorsed by Solidarity, the independent trade union, all but swept the parliamentary elections. The elections left Poland in a political quandry. It was the first time in over 40 years that Poland had held open elections. The vote had been sanctioned under the "round-table" agreements signed April 5.

In the 299 majority-bloc races in the Sejm (parliament), 264 candidates ran unopposed under the banners of the ruling party and its allies, and 35 candidates ran unopposed under the banner of the so-called National list. However, nearly all of the National List candidates were senior officials of the government of the United Workers' (Communist) Party. The National List contained moderates and pro-reform officials. For that reason, Solidarity founder Lech Walesa urged Poles to vote for that bloc of candidates.

Under the election procedure, no candidate could be elected with less than 50% of the vote. Voters crossed out the names of candidates they did not wish to see elected. A candidate could be crossed out even if he or she was unopposed on the ballot.

For Solidarity, the elections were a triumph. Its candidates – running under the banner of the ad hoc Citizen's Committee – won 92% of the 100 Senate seats and 160 of the 161 seats open in the Sejm. No one received the necessary 50% of the vote in the eight Senate races and one Sejm race not won by Solidarity.

Prominent Solidarity candidates winning parliamentary seats included veteran activists Jacek Kuron and Adam Michnik and human-rights champion Wladyslaw Sila-Nowicki. Walesa did not stand for election, but actively campaigned for the union's candidates.

For the authorities, the elections were a disaster. Only five official candidates won enough votes to be elected in the Sejm, and only two of the five were on the National List. The winning National List candidates were Mikolaj Kozakiewicz, a Peasant Party activist, and Adam Zielinski, the chief judge of Poland's top administrative court. Kozakiewicz was a critic of the ruling party and Zielinski was known for his independence.

Even before the final votes were counted, the ruling party conceded that Solidarity had won a "decisive majority" in parliament. "The election had the character of a referendum," said party spokesman Jan Bisztyga. Government spokesman Zbyslaw Rykowski June 6 drew derisive laughter from the Polish press when he attempted to explain why, in his view, the elections had not been a true reflection of the will of the Polish people. Rykowski contended that the people had voted emotionally rather than rationally.

A majority of Poles appeared to be pleased by the election results. But their reaction, tempered by long-standing pessimism and the nation's crushing economic problems, was muted.

Poland's leader, Gen. Wojciech Jaruzelski, June 6 called on Solidarity to join the government in a broad coalition. The idea was rejected by the union. Solidarity spokesman Janusz Onyszkiewicz June 6 said that his organization preferred to adhere to the arrangement negotiated at the round table. "All [Solidarity] candidates for deputy and senator stated they will enter the Sejm or Senate as the opposition. That was made clear."

The elections left Poland with an unusual problem. In parliamentary democracies, the winning party had the right to form a government. But under the Polish constitution, the government was to be subservient to the United Workers' (Communist) Party. Delegations from the regime and Solidarity, headed by Interior Minister Czeslaw Kiszczak and Walesa, respectively, met in Warsaw June 7-8 to discuss the quandry. On June 8, the two sides agreed that the unfilled parliament seats (eight in the Senate and 295 in the Sejm) should be filled through run-off elections June 18. As part of the agreement, the 33 open National seats were to be fillled by competitive elections involving only candidates endorsed by the regime.

The Chattanooga Times

Chattanooga, TN, June 7, 1989

Sunday was a historic day in Poland and in the Soviet bloc: For the first time since the post-World War II communist takeover of Eastern Europe, an opposition group gained control of a freely chosen chamber of Parliament. It is a development that offers good reason for celebration.

Solidarity, the trade union that has become synonymous with political reform in Poland, won the vast majority of seats in the newly constituted upper house of Parliament and was expected to win every lower-house seat for which it offered a candidate. Moreover, it appears that most top Communist officials who ran unopposed for the lower house were denied the 50 percent majority required for election by voters who crossed their names off ballots. As a result, a government spokesman said Monday that Prime Minister Mieczyslaw Rakowski will submit his resignation and that of his Cabinet when the Parliament convenes in June.

In light of the stunning nature of the public rebuke, it is significant that communist authorities acknowledged that Solidarity had achieved "a decisive majority" in the elections even before official results were released. "It was a very important statement," Solidarity spokesman Janusz Onyszkiewicz said, "because it shows that the government and the party are committed to a peaceful transition from the present political situation to a more democratic situation."

Indeed, Polish authorities have solicited Solidarity's participation in a "grand coalition," offering a form of power-sharing previously unheard of in a Soviet bloc country. But Solidarity has apparently rejected that course, and understandably so. As Mr. Onyszkiewicz said, "All candidates for deputy and senator stated that they will enter the Sejm or Senate as the opposition." The significance of that opposition voice would be diminished if Solidarity became a junior partner in a government-led coalition.

Standing in opposition, however, does not mean that Solidarity will not exercise what a government spokesman called "co-responsibility" for the future of Poland, which is beset with economic woes. Mr. Onyszkiewicz made clear that rejection of the call for a coalition does not rule out "joint actions and joint decisions" to solve specific problems.

Solidarity has indulged in no gloating over the Communists' embarrassing defeat in the elections. It has, in fact, assured authorities that despite rejection of many Communist candidates, Solidarity considers itself bound by its agreement to give the government a majority in the lower house of Parliament. As one strategist said, "We are trying to shift the focus of power from the party to the Parliament, and for that we need these people in the Parliament." The union apparently seeks a non-threatening stability in its new relationship with the government, a course which bodes well for further political reform and needed economic change in Poland.

The Sun

Vancouver, B.C., June 8, 1989

So thoroughly has Solidarity thumped the Communists in Poland's two-thirds-free elections that the party — infinitely more truly reflective of workers' concerns than are the Marxists — is almost troubled by its success.

Representatives of both the ruling Communists and upstart Solidarity appeared on television after Sunday's elections to stress stability. The Communist leaders were talking coalition. In the West they'd be talking about cleaning out their desks and turning in their chauffeurs and limousines.

As it stands, they have lost an enormous amount of dignity but have retained power because they set up a safety net that proved indispensable.

Under the terms of the election Solidarity was allowed to seek 161 of the 460 seats in the lower house. Leading members of the ruling politburo were put on a "protected" list — uncontested by Solidarity. But to win they nevertheless had to receive more than half of the votes cast. And the voters had the option of casting negative votes by striking out their names.

There was a great deal of such striking-out. Preliminary figures indicated that not many Communist candidates attracted more than 20 per cent of the popular vote, and that eight out of 17 on the protected list failed to get the required majority — including those holding the important posts of prime minister, defence minister, and interior minister.

The devastation in the Senate, the less-powerful upper house in the Polish system, was even more complete. Solidarity won all but a handful of the 100 seats.

One fly in the semi-democratic ointment was that many Poles, given the first taste of real political choice in the East European bloc for some 40 years, elected to stay at home: only 63 per cent cast ballots.

Yes, it was no ordinary election. Solidarity leader Lech Walesa even made an election-eve plea to Poles to vote for Communist candidates who favored change in the economically chaotic nation.

But the heady victory will create unprecedented problems for his party. Solidarity has already rejected the government's hardly guileless offer to join with it in a coalition. Instead it has guardedly offered to search for joint solutions to specific problems. Mr. Walesa, not for the first time in his remarkable career, is going to have to stickhandle his way through attempts to co-opt him.

But for now a toast is in order: to democratic movements everywhere. And Poland can lay claim to having moved sharply to the forefront of them among nations where freedom has been a stranger for many years.

Toronto, Ont., June 8, 1989

For Poland's Solidarity trade union, winning was the easy part. In a sophisticated election free from any hint of skulduggery, Solidarity candidates have achieved a stunning victory.

Now comes the hard part. Although this was the freest election in Poland in 42 years, it was not fully democratic. As the price of having an election at all, Solidarity promised to keep the Communist party in office.

Under the pact with the government, Solidarity agreed not to run candidates against 35 prominent party leaders, or to contest the 299 seats reserved for Communists. The government was assured 65 per cent of the seats in the Sejm (lower house of parliament).

But Polish voters scorned the pact. Where Solidarity didn't run, voters simply crossed names off the ballot. As a result, eight powerful ministers including Prime Minister Mieczyslaw Rakowski lost. Now, there will have to be a run-off election to fill those 299 reserved Communist seats in the Sejm.

Meanwhile, Communist leaders hope to avert a constitutional crisis by inviting Solidarity's winners to join a coalition government. Understandably, Solidarity says no.

It doesn't want to accept even symbolic responsibility for the economic mess Poland is in, or for harsh measures needed to fix it. As Lech Walesa says, "We cannot replace this government, or we will become just like this government. What we want is to conduct changes together with this government."

There's a paradox here. If Poland were a true democracy, Solidarity — having won — would take office with a clear mandate to clean up the mess left by its predecessor.

Walesa and the victorious Solidarity candidates clearly can't abandon the responsibility Polish voters have thrust on them. But they have until the June 18 run-off vote to decide how they will discharge it.

RAPID CITY JOURNAL—

Rapid City, SD, June 8, 1989

For four decades the Communist Party has crushed Poland in an iron fist. When Poland's people finally were allowed one arm free this week, they delivered a stinging slap across the face of the oppressor.

Less than eight years ago tanks moved to crush the Solidarity union movement in Poland. But without Solidarity and the backing of the Polish people, the crippling economic problems afflicting Poland can not be solved. Somehow, the people had to be placated while the leaders retained their grip.

This week, the first free elections allowed in more than four decades in any Eastern Bloc nation were held in Poland. The result was supposed to be a carefully arranged loosening of the iron fingers, with the Communist Party retaining power but allowing Solidarity-backed candidates to share in government. Solidarity candidates were to be allowed to take control of the 100-seat Senate if they won a majority of seats. They were to be allowed to contest for 161 seats in the 460-seat Assembly, with the Communist and allied parties guaranteed the remaining 299 seats. Communist officials would retain 35 seats on a special "national list" of 35 unopposed Assembly candidates.

Given a chance to express themselves at the ballot box, the Polish people delivered a blow for freedom as clearly heard as the gunfire crackling across China.

The people went to the polls. At least 92 seats in the 100-seat Senate went to Solidarity. Only one of the 161 Assembly seats Solidarity was allowed to contest didn't go to a Solidarity candidate.

Most stunning, voters simply refused to vote for the 35 unopposed candidates, technically denying them election. The unopposed candidates, who included Prime Minister Mieczyslaw Rakowski, supposedly had to receive 50 percent of the vote. But voters denied a majority vote to every one of the 299 seats reserved in the Assembly for the communists, including the seats for the 35 officials supposedly guaranteed office.

In the wake of the massive repudiation of Communist Party rule, Solidarity officials and much of the free world are exultant, but cautious. Fearing nullification of the election, Solidarity officials agreed that the 35 unopposed candidates who technically can't run in a second round of voting June 18 — necessary because Assembly members must be elected by majorities — can stand again for confirmation. In that election, it will be business as usual for Communist nations — freedom to choose whomever the rulers offer.

The Communist Party, in a quandry, offered the victorious Solidarity candidates a deal — form a coalition government. Solidarity rightly spurned the offer, which would have made Solidarity accountable for Poland's economic crisis without actually giving it the power to deal with the problem.

The Communist Party took a gamble and was stunningly repudiated. Before television cameras, a party official claimed the results may not have reflected the true will of the people. He was reduced to ashen anger when the roomful of people he made the pronouncement to broke out in derisive laughter. The truth is that, given an opportunity to express themselves, the Polish people told the world the truth about Communism. After four decades of control, Communist ideology and Soviet military force have failed miserably to win converts.

Solidarity leader Lech Walesa fears repression due to the Communist humiliation, but after the election he said talks about the country's future should be reopened. He was saying, in effect, let's talk about real power sharing and not the charade of power sharing.

The world and the Poles can only wait to see how the rulers react.

DAILY ⊠ NEWS

New York, NY, June 7, 1989

IF YOU'VE BECOME DEMORALIZED by the unending stream of bad news spewing out of China and Iran, take a few minutes off to think about Poland. For the first time in 40 years, Poles were given an opportunity to vote for freedom. They exercised it to the hilt. "Landslide" isn't the word for what happened when the ballot boxes were opened. Solidarity candidates won virtually every seat they were allowed to contest. The Communist candidates didn't have a Marxist's prayer.

So far, the Polish government says it's going to play by the rules. Well in advance of the release of the final vote count, official spokesmen bit the bullet and admitted that they'd lost badly. Unbelievable? Almost. Standard operating procedure in this sort of election, as Panama's Gen. Noriega recently illustrated, is to (A) stuff the ballot boxes, (B) declare the election null and void, or (C) do both. Instead, the Polish government pulled lever (D) — and told the truth.

It isn't that simple, of course. The Polish government is perfectly capable of pulling the rug out from under Solidarity at a moment's notice. And this election, however startling, doesn't kick the Polish Communists out of power. It only gives Solidarity control of the new 100-member Polish Senate.

What it *does* do, however, is send an unbelievably loud message from the Polish people straight to the ears of Polish leader Gen. Wojciech Jaruzelski: *We've had it with your brand of "leadership." We want something better.*

That such a message could be delivered behind the Iron Curtain — and reported openly — is not the least surprising piece of news in a week full of lightning bolts.

The Burlington Free Press

Burlington, VT, June 10, 1989

Solidarity's sweeping victories in Poland's first free elections in four decades could lead to new totalitarian measures if hardline Communists feel their grip on power slipping away.

Communist Party regulars — including Prime Minister Mieczyslaw Rakowski and 32 other top officials — failed to garner enough votes to take their reserved seats in the Sejm, Poland's lower house of parliament. Their defeat posed an immediate crisis for Poland's infant democratic experiment.

As votes were still being tallied, Solidarity leader Lech Walesa met with government officials to fashion a compromise that allows the defeated Communists to try for victory again in run-off balloting on June 18.

More compromises will be essential to maintain the fragile state of cooperation between the ruling Communists and the ascending labor unionists.

While a pre-election agreement assured the Communists a 65 percent domination in the Sejm, they have no chance of prevailing in the fully-contested Senate where Solidarity will fill at least 92 of 100 seats.

Even slight Solidarity political muscle-flexing will increase pressure from reactionaries within the Communist Party to abandon democracy, prompting an inevitable chain-reaction of popular dissent and military crackdown. A return to martial law would promise renewed Western economic sanctions that would plunge Poland into a deeper economic crisis than it already suffers.

Poland's leader, Gen. Wojciech Jaruzelski will fight the hardliners. His political survival — and his place in Polish history as a leader who prevented civil war — depends on preserving the democratic process even if it ultimately means he loses power to future non-Communist electoral victories.

Solidarity's leaders will also have to resist infighting. Walesa's appeal is strong but his grip on the labor coalition is tenuous. Many hardline unionists feel the Gdansk shipyard electrician sold out their cause by agreeing to election rules that favored the Communists. Solidarity's internal differences will only grow. As more reforms evolve, craftsmen and farmers and laborers who shared a mutual desire for political freedom will have the luxury of not always agreeing.

Mikhail Gorbachev's experiment with openness in Moscow has encouraged Warsaw's leaders to redraw Poland's political landscape. The West has helped by lowering trade barriers, providing loans and mouthing supportive diplomatic rhetoric.

When President Bush visits Poland this summer, he can pack more than moral support. Improved trade status and increased loan credits should be at the top of his gift list to the Poles. With that American help, both the Communists and Solidarity will have the outside assistance they need to continue their delicate crawl toward democratic freedoms.

THE CHRONICLE-HERALD

Halifax, N.S., June 7, 1989

OVERSHADOWED by the events in China and the death of the Ayatollah Khomeini was the defeat of the Communist party Sunday in Poland's first free elections in four decades.

No one was at all surprised by the extent of the Solidarity successes in seats for which its candidates were eligible. But few had anticipated the humiliation which the Communists apparently have sustained.

Opposition candidates were allowed to run for all the seats in the 100-member Senate. They won all but a couple, where no one had a majority of votes, and these could well fall to Solidarity in runoff elections next week.

Solidarity was permitted to contest only 161 of the 460 seats in the Sejm, or lower house. It appears the labour-and-human-rights movement won every seat it contested.

By contrast, Communists ran unopposed for the remaining 299 seats, in which they were required only to win the approval rating of a majority of eligible voters. Many failed to get this nod, and that fate was not spared some 35 party and government leaders who ran unopposed for the Sejm.

The system is skewed, however, to allow government officials who are rejected to keep their posts.

What it all means is intriguing. The Senate, controlled by Solidarity members, has veto power over all legislation, though it can be overridden by a two-thirds majority in the Sejm.

However, the Communists will have only a 65-per-cent majority of the Sejm seats. An override would depend on the votes of at least 10 Solidarity members of the Sejm. Talk about a chance to dicker.

The Communist party of Poland is about to get a taste of the limited democracy it created in order to win the domestic peace necessary to reform its administration and revive the nation's pitiful economy.

Indeed, government officials have already publicly raised the possibility of a coalition with Solidarity, even to the point of giving Solidarity cabinet posts, in order to avoid damaging disputes.

There is much jubilation in Poland, but a great deal of caution as well. While the exercise has been eye-opening and instructive, it is early days for the budding democracy. Undoubtedly there are risks associated in asking for too much, too soon.

Nevertheless, very important changes are taking place in Poland. In the wake of the electoral results, one is tempted to ask: how much is too much?

Winnipeg Free Press

Winnipeg, Man., June 7, 1989

Poland's first try at a democratic election since the Soviet Union imposed totalitarian communism in 1947 sent two decisive messages about the popular will. The first was repudiation of the Communist Party. The second was overwhelming support for the extraordinary movement known as Solidarity that survived a regime attempt to crush it forever in 1981.

These striking results did not change the reality of communist control of Poland. Solidarity struck a bargain with the regime in April that guaranteed communist party control of the lower house, which gives it the power to elect the national president.

Solidarity did well in the lower house and better in the upper house but these two chambers are roughly similar in their share of legislative authority to Canada's House of Commons and Senate. Like Canada's Liberal Party, Solidarity will control the upper chamber but that control will be more symbolic than significant.

More significant is Solidarity's new role as an official opposition with broad popular support. This gives the movement the political legitimacy that the regime tried so hard to deny it, for so long.

A less resilient movement, with less support at the street level and with less of a claim to represent real resentments could not have gone through the 1981 test, when the regime sent troops, tanks and armored water cannon into the streets of Warsaw. The arrests and detention of some Solidarity leaders, the harassment of others and the murder by secret policemen of an outspoken priest who backed Solidarity's call for reforms were part of the price that had to be paid by those trying to change the hard Stalinist face of Polish communism.

It is an example that should inspire the young students of Beijing and of other university cities in the People's Republic of China. Although the massacre that the Chinese students and other citizens suffered last weekend on the orders of their regime was more horrific than what happened in Warsaw in 1981, the concept of a brutal crackdown by a change-resistant governing group was similar. The evolution in Poland to this week's election result seemed inconceivable in 1981 but it has happened.

Something similar could happen in China.

An irony of the Solidarity success is that there are grounds for concern that it could provoke a political crisis. Communist hardliners could claim that chaos exists, requiring the party to ignore the election in order to maintain stability. The regime could arrange for provocative behavior on the streets by people claiming to represent Solidarity, justifying action against an "irresponsible" organization. This, after all, is what the regime did in December, 1981.

This week, however, the regime was on its best behavior, conducting an impeccable election after a fair campaign and itself announcing that it had lost. The government spokesman's comment that Solidarity now "must take joint responsibility for the state" echoed pre-election regime suggestions of a post-election coalition. Poland's president and leader of the communist party, General Wojciech Jaruzelski, spoke about giving cabinet posts to the opposition so that a united approach might be taken to solving Poland's economic and social crisis. There was no suggestion of equality. The party would rule as before.

This presents Solidarity with a dilemma. The movement prefers to sit in opposition, offering constructive criticism, ideas and legislative support. Participating in a cabinet as a junior member could tarnish it by association, much as Canada's federal NDP suffered politically for its support of a Trudeau minority government in the early 1970s.

Political circumstances, however, may impose a decision on Solidarity to join a coalition. One such circumstance is the humiliating defeat of a group of top communist officials who ran without opposing candidates but who lost anyway because voters had the option of defeating them by scratching out their names.

One question that voters settled was the degree of dissatisfaction with Solidarity as the reform movement. The crushing defeat of Solidarity splinter factions, of a right-wing Roman Catholic party and of a nationalist party established Solidarity as the people's reform choice. Now Solidarity must display political skill in fulfilling that role.

THE LINCOLN STAR

Lincoln, NE, June 8, 1989

As change sweeps across communist nations in many parts of the world, western expectations should be tempered. The burden of victory, we should remember, is performance.

This is clear in China, the Soviet Union and Poland. At this time, Poland appears most likely to realize a peaceful and effective transition from totalitarianism to a much greater degree of freedom.

Solidarity candidates for office in Poland's parliamentary election won an overwhelming victory, totally defeating ruling communist candidates at every turn. Only where the Communist Party was guaranteed seats in Poland's lower house did it manage to maintain its political status.

Solidarity is believed to have won all 100 seats in the newly formed Senate and is expected to be the winner of all the 161 seats for which it was permitted to run in the lower house, called the Sejm. In an accord with Solidarity, the Communist Party is guaranteed 299 seats in the Sejm,

While the Communist Party and its allies will maintain a numerical superiority in the legislature, Solidarity will control the Senate. The Senate has veto power over all legislation passed and a veto override in the Sejm needs a two-thirds vote.

Solidarity has declined to accept administrative offices within the communist government but has said it will abide by the agreement giving the existing ruling party the lower house majority in parliament.

Thus, Poland is in a position to peacefully move away from its authoritarian rule to democratic reforms. This is significant because a state of chaos in Poland would not serve the country well.

Democracy is a complicated system not quickly and easily brought to fulfillment. Time and again, democratic leaders have been elected in South American countries only to find that real freedom could not be achieved.

If Poland can maintain order and move in well considered steps toward greater freedom, it may forge a democracy that can stand the test of time. A state of anarchy is not fertile soil for any kind of government.

Effective economic, political and social structures are forged over time, not provided in the course of victory at the polls. Having won election, Solidarity must now begin to build the free nation for which it has long struggled.

Calgary Herald

Calgary, Alta., June 7, 1989

Solidarity shows a keen and consistent nose for democratic principles in its refusal to formally participate in a coalition government with the Communists. It bodes well for the yearning for reform which the Communists tried time and again to stifle but to little permanent avail.

The Communist regime of General Wojciech Jaruzelski was trounced in this week's election in Poland, the freest the country has experienced since the postwar Communist takeover. Solidarity garnered the lion's share of popular confidence, humiliating the Communists, despite a pre-arranged guarantee that the government would retain a majority in Poland's parliament, the Sejm.

Although the Communists may still be in power technically, they know they have no claim to legitimacy. The moment the opportunity came, Poles transfered title to Solidarity without hesitation.

For years, Solidarity has said it would never share power with the Communists until Poland's Stalinist structure of government was torn down. An astute move it is too, for it places Solidarity in position to become the official opposition and a government-in-training, if not a government-in-waiting. Yet because of the peculiar ground rules for the election and Solidarity's overwhelming success, Poland is now in uncharted constitutional waters.

The Communists reserved 299 of the 460 Sejm seats for themselves. But included in that 299 were 35 members of the so-called national list of cabinet ministers and other prominent Communists who ran unopposed and who needed only 50 per cent of the votes to win.

Yet few if any of the 35 were elected because of the unusual system under which voters struck names off ballots. Until that critical issue is resolved, the Communists will fall just below the two-thirds majority they need in the Sejm to assure they can override legislation from the newly created Senate. There were no restrictions on the upper house and it is overwhelmingly Solidarity.

Just where Poland goes from here is anyone's guess. Ominously, the government has warned that it will not tolerate any "triumphant mood and adventurism to cause anarchy that would endanger democracy and the social order."

The upshot seems to be that neither Communists nor Solidarity can begin to tackle Poland's protracted and daunting economic problems (inflation is 80 per cent) without the other. The Communists understood that when they swallowed their Marxist rhetoric and sought a coalition. Solidarity balked, but has said that it is willing to co-operate when necessary with the Communists.

Difficult and trying months lie ahead and there seems little hope that the lot of the average Pole is about to improve simply because Solidarity has members in the Sejm.

Yet clearly Solidarity is in the driver's seat, well poised to flex its credibility and popularity. And if the movement succeeds in its goal of truly free elections in four years, an astounding and largely peaceful revolution will occur.

Four years is a long way off and many things can happen — recent events in Beijing prove that. But this election, for all its flaws, surely has demonstrated to Poles that in the end, police batons and tear gas will not better patience, conviction and resolve.

The ♣ State

Columbia, SC, June 9, 1989

ON A NORMAL news day, the staggering defeat suffered by Poland's Communist Party in Sunday's relatively free elections would have rated banner headlines around the world.

But Sunday was anything but a normal day. The Chinese army began slaughtering its own people in Beijing. The Ayatollah Khomeini, the Iranian demon who has thumbed his nose at the world for a decade, died. A major tragedy struck the Soviet Union when an explosion wrecked two passenger trains and killed hundreds.

Those momentous events knocked the Polish elections off the front pages of many newspapers, including *The State*. But in no way does that diminish the significance of the Polish people's revolt at the polls against the party that has ruled them with an iron fist for more than 40 years.

No communist government in Eastern Europe had ever risked the humiliation that befell the regime of Gen. Wojciech Jaruzelski by permitting an active opposition element to compete with it in real elections. It is a measure of Warsaw's desperation that it reached an accord in April with the Solidarity labor movement for a restructuring of the government and new elections. For the better part of a decade, Jaruzelski had tried to snuff out Solidarity, once declaring martial law and outlawing the union.

The desperation grew out of the regime's inability to cope with a restive population and a protracted economic crisis. It needed to give Solidarity a piece of the action to have a chance of gaining the support of the people for the severe austerity measures that will be needed.

Supposedly the election was rigged to prevent Solidarity from getting a large enough foothold in parliament to threaten Communist control. The April agreement set aside 65 percent of the 460 seats in the Sejm or lower house for the ruling party's candidates, permitting Solidarity to contest only for the 161 other seats. Open races were allowed for the 100 seats in the new, less influential Senate.

Poles demonstrated their disdain for the government by giving Solidarity a virtual sweep of the Senate and all but one of its allotted seats in the Sejm. It could pick up a few more in run-off elections set for June 18. This result effectively gives Solidarity the parliamentary strength to block legislation it opposes.

Most embarrassing of all for the Communists was the annihilation of the "national list" of government and party chieftains. Thirty-three of the 35 leaders on that list, including Prime Minister Mieczyslaw Rakowski, failed to get the 50 percent of the vote they needed to win seats even though they ran unopposed. Most voters simply struck their names from the ballot. While this will not necessarily cost them their government posts, they have been so thoroughly repudiated that their ability to govern is in question.

Many Communist candidates for the Sejm also did not get the requisite 50 percent and will try again in the runoff. Solidarity says it may endorse some of the more progressive of them, giving it leverage across the aisle.

In the wake of this devastation at the polls, the Communist Party is pleading with Solidarity to join it in a coalition government. Clearheaded despite the exhilarating triumph, Solidarity's Lech Walesa is resisting the pressure.

Obviously, Solidarity is not eager to join the folks who repressed it for so long and share the blame for the harsh, unpopular measures that will have to be taken to get a handle on the economy. Many of its own members, for example, have an addiction to wage and price subsidies that may have to go. But if it is to be a responsible opposition party, Solidarity will have to cooperate on essential measures to make the new order work.

And it must work if the Polish example is to have a positive impact on the rest of the Soviet bloc and even, perhaps, on Mother Russia itself. It is remarkable that Moscow has tolerated this much democracy — another sign that historic change is in the works.

But even in their hour of triumph, Poles are cautious and their situation is fragile. Said said one Solidarity leader: "Poland's geopolitical position has not changed. Neither have the people who have the apparatus of oppression in their control. We are entering a time of hope but also a time of danger. Shooting and deaths in . . . Beijing point to the kind of danger we should all avoid." Wise fellow.

TULSA WORLD

Tulsa, OK, June 7, 1989

PEOPLE will endure the most oppressive government so long as they can be convinced there is no hope for relief.

When hope breaks out, when the idea gets around that a better life is possible, tyranny trembles.

It is hard to say which is the more shocking news: the election results from Poland or the fact that a partly open election was held in the first place. It would have been unthinkable a few years ago.

The election in Poland was not a model of democracy. It was agreed in advance that the Communist Party would retain control of two-thirds of the legislative seats regardless of the voting. Even when the voters favored the opposition Solidarity Party by a possible 80-percent majority, the Solidarity leaders agreed to stick with the original agreement leaving the Communist Party as the nominal ruling force in Poland.

But even the diehards in the Communist leadership now realize that nothing is the same in Poland. Communism may endure as a word. But the idea of a permanent "dictatorship of the proletariat" as defined by Marx and Lenin is finished.

With luck, Solidarity can finesse a gradual change that will produce a quasi-democratic regime in Poland rather soon. Or an impatient public may provoke an already frightened government into some foolish response in the Beijing mold.

This week's voting leaves the future unclear. Only one thing is certain: The permament Marxist dictatorship is no longer permament.

In Poland, as in China and the Soviet Union itself, hope is on the move.

The Toronto Star

Toronto, Ont., June 8, 1989

Gales of change are gusting through Eastern Europe. Nations repressed since World War II by the Soviet bear are biting the paws that smothered their yearning for freedom.

Now look at what has happened in Poland. Be pleased, but not deluded.

The incredible Poles even unstuck a fixed election. The Communists were supposed to have been guaranteed control of the lower house, but voters massively rejected their candidates.

The most humiliating battering was reserved for the 35 Communist VIPs who ran unopposed but couldn't get the minimum 50% endorsement of voters.

That's the measure of Polish revenge on the party bosses who ruled with brute power for so long.

Old habits die hard. A government spokesman even tried to claim the defeat wasn't a true reflection of the will of the people. Polish reporters laughed.

While it was the freest election in 40 years in Eastern Europe, it doesn't yet match our brand of democracy. However, Canada and the world must be encouraged by the unprecedented results.

It's a stronger echo of a version we've just watched in the Soviet Union, where the Communist party still has the inside track with most of the seats reserved for it.

But after Poland's euphoria, there are the political and economic realities. A humiliated Communist government has called for a broad coalition, and Solidarity, flush with victory, has said no deal.

But there will have to be co-operation and concessions on both sides if Poland is to deal with the galloping inflation that is one symptom of a sick economy.

The real test of Solidarity's runaway victory will be how it deals with the pain of decisions that are in the best interests of the country but will be unpopular with union hardliners.

A political standoff can only aggravate the crisis.

We still have much to cheer as the spirit of democracy breaks the totalitarian stranglehold on Poland.

That certainly beats Tiananmen Square, and the Gulag. But it all must be kept in perspective.

The London Free Press

London, Ont., June 10, 1989

A remarkable breeze of political reform is blowing through Europe's Communist East bloc. This week it blew strongest in Poland.

It started, however, with glasnost. Soviet leader Mikhail Gorbachev's concessions to political freedoms and human rights signalled that rigid state regimentation is no longer an ideological imperative. It has encouraged reform movements elsewhere in Eastern Europe, where there is diminishing fear that attempts at political liberalization could provoke a repetition of the 1968 Soviet invasion that crushed reformist leadership in Czechoslovakia.

Though the one-party system that is the bedrock of communism has not yet yielded to multi-party politics, it has allowed political opposition an astonishingly robust voice in the Soviet Union and, more particularly, Poland and Hungary. In a stunning turnaround earlier this year, the Polish government recognized the once-banned Solidarity union, and allowed it to field candidates in last weekend's first semi-democratic election ever in the East bloc.

Though Poland's election rules were fixed to prevent the Communists from losing power, the party in effect lost the election. Not unexpectedly, the discredited Communist regime was overwhelmingly defeated wherever Solidarity candidates ran. Voters even rejected — as did Soviet voters in March — some government candidates who were running unopposed.

What is surprising, however, is the graciousness with which the Polish government has, so far at least, accepted the people's unflattering judgment — though its motives in offering Solidarity a chance to participate in a coalition government are suspect.

Andjelko Runjic, president of the parliament of Croatia, Yugoslavia's second biggest republic, says independent political groups may be allowed to compete with the ruling Communist party in parliamentary elections next May.

The loosening of restrictions is compelling evidence of a pervasive failure of communism: economic stagnation. In Poland, meat remains rationed, long lines form daily for gasoline, and toilet paper is a precious commodity. In Yugoslavia, the economic crisis is marked by 600 per cent inflation and at least 16 per cent unemployment.

Until recently, political liberalization was unimaginable, and it remains conspicuously scorned by Communist bosses in East Germany, Czechoslovakia, Bulgaria and Romania.

Freedom is addictive; a sip encourages a taste for more. How far will Communist leaders — accustomed to dictating everything, including the pace of change — be willing to let liberalization go? It would be naive in the extreme to anticipate the dismantling of communist states, even those where the spirit of reform is most evident.

It's instructive that, for all the optimism generated by Gorbachev's reforms, Soviet reaction to the massacre in Tiananmen Square has been strictly orthodox. Moscow has said only that it's an internal metter for China's Communist rulers to deal with.

leadership's mind-set, it is also a murderous reminder of the ruthlessness of authoritarian power when its rule is threatened. Eastern Europe has concerns of its own about the releasing of forces for democratic reform. In the Soviet Union and Yugoslavia, nationalistic aspirations and ethnic conflict are potential tinder boxes.

If some regimes acknowledged the supremacy of the democratic vote, what would be the response of Communist hardliners elsewhere — in East Germany, say?

The year ahead is shaping up to be a telling test of communism's readiness to respond to popular opinion and pressures for democratic reform.

Polish Parliament Elects Jaruzelski President

The National Assembly, or parliament, July 19, 1989 elected Poland's leader, Gen. Wojciech Jaruzelski, as the nation's executive-style president. Even though he ran unopposed, the general captured the post with a minimum number of the necessary votes.

Jaruzelski in June had decided against seeking the presidency, citing his unpopularity over the 1981 imposition of martial law. But officials of the ruling United Workers' (Communist) Party pressed him to run. Party hard-liners, unhappy with Poland's liberalization, were, however, less than enthusiastic in their support of Jaruzelski.

On July 14 Lech Walesa, the founder of the independent trade union Solidarity, had announced that he would support Jaruzelski or any other party figure who sought the presidency.

Jaruzelski met in private with Solidarity's parliament caucus July 17 in Warsaw and hinted that he might change his mind about running. However, he was reported to have defiantly defended martial law.

"You should not expect that I will try to create a beautiful picture of myself or flagellate myself," he was said to have told the Solidarity legislators. "I am aware that many of you here experienced painfully and directly the effects of martial law. But I don't regret the decision [to impose it]. I regret that the situation was created that led to the decision."

On July 18, Jaruzelski formally declared his candidacy for president, saying that it was his "social duty" to end the confusion over how Poland was to be governed.

Arkansas Gazette
Little Rock, AR, July 25, 1989

Poland is in the process of relearning the truths that Arkansas citizens could have confirmed on the basis of long experience: Democracy is a cumbersome process for conducting the affairs of state. Nevertheless, the Poles seem to have passed the early tests by conducting the first multiple-choice election in 40 years and then picking a president.

After four decades of communist domination, Solidarity has emerged as the new party on the scene. With a surprising show of strength in the recent election, the party headed by Lech Walesa captured about 260 of the 560 seats in the parliament where the new president would be picked. The interesting twist was that Solidarity, for all its youth, realized its limitations and had no ambition to take over the machinery of government.

A deal cut in advance was designed to assure that Gen. Wojciech Jaruzelski, the communist leader who has headed the government under the general direction and with the approval of the Soviet Union, would be elected president. Solidarity was content to remain the "loyal opposition" while the shortage-plagued economy sought to shift from the centrally planned system toward more market freedom.

Nine procedural votes were needed in parliament before Jaruzelski's election could be assured, even though no one else was seeking the office. Now at first glance it might seem that the election of an unopposed candidate should be a simple matter, but democracy is a cumbersome process. The first task was to decide how many votes Jaruzelski needed for election and the magic number was set at 270

out of the 537 legislators present. When the sheets were tallied, Jaruzelski had his 270 votes, precisely the number he needed.

The outcome of Poland's venture into democracy was promising, despite the apparent confusion. The United States has been doing this sort of thing for a couple of centuries, but it still encounters problems. This year, the Arkansas legislature could not decide how many votes it needed to approve its appropriation measures. It failed to reach a satisfactory conclusion at the regular session then came back, tried again, and failed. The matter is still undecided, and no one was able to get the case to the Supreme Court in a form that could be settled. Now the court has gone on vacation. The Poles at least matched the performance of the Arkansas legislature — and may even have moved a step ahead. At least, the parliament elected Jaruzelski and no one lost his voting key.

The very fact that Poland was able to hold its broad election, select a parliament with a sizable number of opposition members and pick a new president confirms that democracy has scored a major advance. The success lends support to President Bush's claim that the "other Europe" is changing.

"The exciting time in which we live," Bush said in the Netherlands, "gives rise to the hope that the Europe behind the wall can know the freedom the West has known."

The "other Europe" will come to realize that democracy is a cumbersome process, as Poland demonstrated. Still, no one else seems to have come up with a better system.

The State
Columbia, SC, July 26, 1989

IN THEIR maiden voyage as legislators, the moderate leaders of Poland's Solidarity movement displayed deft parliamentary skills when they maneuvered so that communist Gen. Wojciech Jaruzelski got just the number of votes he needed to win the country's new presidency.

Required for election was 50 percent of those present and voting (269), plus one. That's what he got — 270. Solidarity's moderates didn't want to vote for General Jaruzelski, who imposed martial law and banned Solidarity in 1981, but they wanted to honor an April agreement with the government to elect a communist president in return for the legalization of Solidarity and the setting of the June elections which brought the labor movement into parliament.

They calculated that there would be about 20 defections from the 299-member communist coalition. Just enough Solidarity members cast illegal ballots or took a walk to give General Jaruzelski his thin win in the face of otherwise solid Solidarity opposition.

That spared the longtime ruler from humiliation but was hardly a resounding vote of confidence. Still he will have control of defense and foreign affairs and be allowed to select a prime minister.

The election showed cracks in the coalition of the Communist Party and its five partners. Radicals in Solidarity, a collection of union activists, intellectuals, private farmers and other anti-communists, were outraged over the deal to keep a communist in power, and the party could eventually show splits in its ranks. Poland's experiment in semi-democracy may have some rough times ahead, but it is providing the most excitement and the most hope the depressed nation has seen since the heady, early days of Solidarity.

Edmonton Journal

Edmonton, Alta., July 20, 1989

The resumption of diplomatic relations between Poland and the Vatican reflects the rare spirit of realism and compromise now afoot in Poland. Astonishingly, that spirit even extends to acceptance of unpopular Gen. Wojciech Jaruzelski as the country's new president — truly a measure of Poland's desperate straits.

The need to fill Poland's political vacuum is apparent. The Communist party remains in control but doesn't enjoy the support of the people, as was demonstrated by limited democratic elections last month in which the recently-legalized Solidarity movement steamrollered the Communist party's candidates.

Those elections were agreed to by the ruling party in hopes of enlisting Poland's disenchanted masses in the monumental task of rebuilding the economy. The same motive persuaded the party in recent months to warm up to the Vatican, which has not had full relations with the heavily-Catholic country since the Communists came to power more than 40 years ago.

The church may now be an ally in the attempt to build Polish social harmony, but the dilemma facing the political parties is much more difficult to resolve — as is demonstrated by the narrowness of Jaruzelski's election as president Wednesday. The Communist and Solidarity factions bent as much as they could, but Jaruzelski still managed only one more than the required number of votes for his election. Poland, even in a mood of compromise, is far from united.

On the surface, Solidarity supporters would have virtually no reason to support Jaruzelski, because he imposed martial law in 1981 to suppress the Solidarity uprising. The union was itself outlawed. The general, recognizing his unpopularity, earlier cited resentment against the martial law declaration as the main reason for his decision not to seek the new presidency.

The Communist party and its allies, however, could not agree on another candidate. Solidarity, meanwhile, lacked the majority needed to elect its own president. Recognizing the effect of a continuing impasse on the economy, Solidarity leader Lech Walesa indicated his movement would work with Jaruzelski. The assumption is that Solidarity will come to full power when freer elections are held in four years.

The risk is that Solidarity will be tarred with the same brush as the Communist party, particularly if economic hardship continues as predicted. Jaruzelski's recent statements in defence of the declaration of martial law make Solidarity's compromise even more difficult.

U.S. President George Bush gave the Poles a modest incentive to get out of their muddled situation when he recently offered some assistance for economic initiatives. Significantly, Jaruzelski was front and centre during Bush's visit, seemingly a point of stability in the current unstable situation.

In the end, Jaruzelski perhaps became president precisely because he does represent stability to the nervous Communist party. And since Solidarity has decided the national interest requires an accommodation with the party, the unpopular general is now the reluctant president.

Omaha World-Herald

Omaha, NE, July 22, 1989

Gen. Wojciech Jaruzelski was a wise choice for president under the new semi-democratic system in Poland.

Although Jaruzelski imposed martial law and outlawed Solidarity in 1981, it is generally accepted that he did so to prevent a Soviet invasion similar to the invasion of Czechoslovakia in 1968.

Solidarity leader Lech Walesa took himself out of the race for president. Last-minute maneuvering encouraged Jaruzelski to announce his candidacy in the days just before the balloting. Walesa rightly understood that Solidarity could not meet all expectations and that the presidency should go to an acceptable Communist.

The Communist Party in Poland has taken a terrible beating in the parliamentary elections. It lost the newly created senate, 99-1, and was embarrassed in house races. If the Communists had also lost the presidency, there would have been little incentive for them to maintain the new system, especially if economic or other crises should occur. With Jaruzelski at the helm, the Communists have a stake in what happens. And their pride is somewhat restored.

Jaruzelski is one of the few authorities in Poland, other than Walesa, to be widely known beyond the country's borders. Further, he is an experienced manager and politician. For all practical purposes — first as martial law commander, then as head of the Council of State — he has been Poland's chief executive since 1981.

Jaruzelski was elected by the narrowest of margins — one vote. But his election takes some of the pressure off Solidarity, whose members have little administrative or parliamentary experience. A Solidarity president and senate would have had to bear a heavy burden of expectations. With a Communist president, the system has some balance, and Solidarity politicians will have six years to prepare for the assumption of presidential power.

The Hartford Courant

Hartford, CT, July 28, 1989

Political scientists, journalists and diplomats believe that they know a lot about the hows and whys of violent change — of the revolutions and coups that have visited the 20th century. They rightly do not claim to know much about evolution.

Generally, change on a grand scale is not managed well. In fact, the impulse toward change and toward revolt often turns to violence and chaos. In Poland, however, revolutionary change is coming about via evolution. This does not mean that the process is easier.

A multi-party democracy is growing out of a dictatorship formerly backed up by both ideology and force. The old regime had not only the Polish army behind it, but ultimately the Soviet army. The new wave is backed by an independent union that refused to die.

Amazingly, freedom won. The people wanted it and leadership came from the people. The rich Polish culture sustained it. The churches sponsored it. The Communist Party has accepted it.

But now a season of toil begins in the vineyard of liberty. The question becomes how to keep what has been gained, and how to build.

The requisites are economic and political stability. Political stability will require that Solidarity remain united. It will also require that mud not be thrown in the Soviet eye. Economic hope depends on unity, Soviet encouragement and upon maintaining expertise in the bureaucracy.

The rub is that the people, through Solidarity, have rejected the Communist Party. The leaders of Solidarity must compromise without being co-opted; they must work with the old power structure as they become the new — without turning into what they deplore.

Gen. Wojciech Jaruzelski has been elected president of Poland. He is the man who had banned Solidarity. He is also the man who has lately instituted reforms.

Solidarity helped him become president. Lech Walesa, who is not a member of the parliament but remains at the head of the union, backed the general. Poland needs stability and experience, it was argued.

Next came the same Mr. Walesa announcing that neither he nor Solidarity could work with the new government, and that until such time as the Polish government turns all power over to Solidarity the independent union would busy itself with forming a shadow government and with preparing for the inevitable day when it would rule.

This seems like a contradictory set of signals, and perhaps the confusion was strategic and intentional. Or perhaps it is a straightforward manifestation of the complexity of Solidarity's position. No handbook has been written on how to achieve revolutionary change calmly, rationally and gradually.

The Star-Ledger

Newark, NJ, July 25, 1989

At first blush, the outcome of Poland's presidential election seemed bizarre. The good Communist who resorted to ugly tactics to crush the Solidarity labor union movement, Gen. Wojciech Jaruzelski, was elected president with vital help from Solidarity legislators in the new National Assembly.

The Solidarity lawmakers owed their own election to a historic compromise agreement that gave fresh life to the labor movement after it had been officially outlawed. The accord also opened the door to limited democracy, resulted in a new two-house assembly and provided for the election of a president by the legislators.

Extremists in the Communist Party resented Gen. Jaruzelski's role in the negotiations and the concessions he extended to the trade unionists. They were unhappy with his support for reforms and demonstrated their pique by voting against the general in the presidential contest.

Some members of Solidarity who were elected to the National Assembly could not bring themselves to vote for the general. They could not forget Gen. Jaruzelski's excesses in cracking down on the labor movement, stifling its pleas for a voice in Poland's future and jailing some of its leaders.

But instead of voting against him, as so many of the disenchanted Communists did, the trade unionists abstained. These abstentions were crucial. They reduced the number of votes the general needed to win a majority among those voting, and he was able to claim victory by collecting the exact minimum required. One vote less and he would have been a loser.

Solidarity, as a result, can be expected to exert a strong influence on the policies of the Jaruzelski government, which should quickly stake claim to a broad middle-of-the-road appeal. That objective, following the cordial visit by President Bush, should assure continued cooperation between Poland and the United States.

That middle-of-the-road objective also seemed to be telegraphed by Lech Walesa, the respected leader of Solidarity, who sent congratulations in which he expressed the wish that the president would effectively lead their homeland "to freedom and democracy and to regaining Poland's proper position in Europe."

By moving toward these goals, Poland can serve as an inspiration and a model for other nations that have been yearning for independence and greater self-determination after years of stifling domination by the Soviet Union.

Houston Chronicle

Houston, TX, July 20, 1989

Surprise! Gen. Wojciech Jaruzelski, chief communist of Poland, was elected to the powerful presidency of that country Wednesday. He was the only candidate, of course, but there was a difference.

The voting in the National Assembly (freely elected earlier this year) was free and fair, and Jaruzelski could have been rejected, which was one reason he was reluctant to be a candidate.

However, Solidarity leaders had misgivings concerning the Communist Party's sincerity about sharing power and feared a premature leadership loss could mean trouble. People's republics don't change overnight.

The Augusta Chronicle
AUGUSTA HERALD

Augusta, GA, July 22, 1989

With his one-vote presidential victory in Poland's newly formed multi-party National Assembly, Gen. Wojciech Jaruzelski's remarkable transformation from the "Evil Empire's" instrument of oppression to loyal nationalist is almost complete.

In 1981, when he outlawed Solidarity and imposed martial law, the general was denounced the world over (except in Communist and fellow-traveling countries) as a traitor.

He maintained he did what he did to prevent a much bloodier crackdown by Soviet troops. But his protestations were not taken seriously. Quislings always define their betrayal as patriotism.

In this case, perhaps it's true. Once the Soviets lifted the pressure, Jaruzelski earned high marks from political observers for encouraging reforms that brought Solidarity back to life and into the legislature.

And it was Solidarity's votes on Wednesday that provided the general his razor-thin victory margin for the powerful post of president. He won it by promising more reforms, but without renouncing communism.

"My wish for you is that the time you are given to perform this office will be a stage in the history of our homeland effectively leading to freedom and democracy and to regaining Poland's proper position in Europe," Solidarity leader Lech Walesa, who chose not to run for the office himself, told Jaruzelski after the election.

Clearly, Poland's forces of freedom see the new president as a transition figure in the nation's curious, uneven odyssey from totalitarianism to democracy. History's final verdict on this Communist general will depend on how well and faithfully he performs that role.

The Salt Lake Tribune

Salt Lake City, UT, July 25, 1989

Wojciech Jaruzelski's election as president of Poland revealed how ticklish the political situation there remains.

Mr. Jaruzelski won the balloting in Parliament by the barest possible margin. A small but significant number of members in the Communist-led ruling coalition defected and either voted against the general or abstained. His victory was made possible by members of the Solidarity opposition who either invalidated their ballots or stayed home.

The voting demonstrated divisions within both the Communist and Solidarity camps. Many of the defectors from the ruling coalition were reputed to be opposed to the political reforms and power-sharing to which Mr. Jaruzelski agreed last April.

Across the aisle, Solidarity is sharply split over the strategy some members adopted to ensure the Communist chief's election. The Solidarity electors who sat out the voting or invalidated their ballots managed to put Mr. Jaruzelski in office without actually voting for him.

These realists recognized the obvious. Though Solidarity controls all but one seat in the Senate, it doesn't have anywhere near the majority of votes in the combined houses necessary to elect a president.

The deal Solidarity struck with the Communists in April was designed to produce this result. Solidarity's leader, Lech Walesa, acknowledged as much when he declined to run for the presidency himself and supported the candidacy of Mr. Jaruzelski.

Others in Solidarity suggested that as president, the general would act as guarantor of the reforms. Had Mr. Jaruzelski been defeated, the Communists presumably could have put up another candidate, but he would not be a symbol of the April reforms as the general is.

The problem, of course, is that the new president is also a symbol of repression. He guided the imposition of martial law, the outlawing of Solidarity and the imprisonment of its leaders in 1981. That was in the bad old days before the advent of a Soviet leader named Mikhail Gorbachev.

So the Polish general is a dual symbol, which explains why only one Solidarity legislator could bring himself to vote for Mr. Jaruzelski to be president.

Lacking the power to elect a president of their own, Solidarity's realists decided that putting Mr. Jaruzelski in the office was preferable to the constitutional crisis that would have been created had they blocked his election. Without a president there can be no government, since, under the new system, the president appoints the prime minister.

Some Solidarity legislators argue that their comrades who maneuvered to allow the general's election betrayed the independent labor union's cause. They say Solidarity should have voted the general down, or at least wrung concessions from the Communist coalition in exchange for electoral support. Some say the union could have won the right to appoint the prime minister or members of the cabinet in the new government.

That argument is blind to Mr. Walesa's signals, which indicate that in order to fulfill the deal made in April, Mr. Jaruzelski had to be made president. To do otherwise, or to further compromise the general's position with his own party by insisting on more concessions now, might jeopardize the whole reform process.

In short, Solidarity needs Mr. Jaruzelski. The union may have struck a bargain with the devil, but for now it's one that needs to be kept.

EVENING EXPRESS
Portland, ME, July 27, 1989

It's easy to understand why Poland's President Wojciech Jaruzelski invited Solidarity to join the Communist Party in forming a coalition government. Nor is it hard to understand why Solidarity leader Lech Walesa declined. Still, a yes might have been more helpful.

From the ruling Communist Party's perspective, a coalition would tend to mute popular criticism of government efforts to get a handle on the bankrupt nation's economy. After all, Solidarity would find it difficult to criticize the very policies it was helping to formulate.

That's one reason Walesa is reluctant to participate. Just as important, however, is the absence of a Solidarity economic platform. The fact is, Solidarity has been far more adept at creating popular support for turning Poland into an open society than it has in enunciating ways of transforming a flawed planned economy into a market-based economy.

And getting there is going to be terribly difficult. Economic reforms are likely to make the situation worse before things improve. And the natives are already restless; witness farmer opposition to a proposal to deregulate prices of some agricultural materials such as fuel and fertilizer (they would almost certainly soar) in an effort to reduce food shortages.

The trick for the Poles — and for the West as well — is to make the pain and dislocations which are inevitable in a switch to a market economy as comparatively painless as possible. Direct aid from the United States and other nations will help there. So would foreign private investment in Polish state-run industries if the government can find the will to privatize them.

The transition is going to be difficult. For now, Solidarity is largely content to stay on the sidelines and observe. Eventually, it's going to have to come out on the field. Considering its popularity and influence, Poland would likely benefit if Solidarity's participation in running the country came sooner rather than later.

The Courier-Journal
Louisville, KY, July 26, 1989

SO FAR, Mikhail Gorbachev is treating the strikes by Soviet coal miners less as a threat than an opportunity to further shake up an already shook-up Communist Party, and to remove officials whom he sees as resisting his policy of *perestroika*, or restructuring.

It's a bold move, and it may work, at least for a while. Meantime, however, the cost of trying to buy peace in the coalfields — through better pay and more consumer goods — could run as high as $8.8 billion. That's a whopping big sum for a government that finally admits that it has been running ruinous budget deficits.

And now that the miners have won expensive concessions, what's to prevent factory, railway and even farm workers from trying to get their share? If Poland's experience in 1980 is any guide, the Soviet government could be forced into retreat after retreat — until someone (by that time, perhaps not Mr. Gorbachev) cries "Enough!" and calls out the troops.

Any such attempt to return to Stalinist discipline would be socially and economically disastrous. Mr. Gorbachev knows that, and all but his most benighted critics inside the party seem to recognize it, too.

But if the government can't afford to buy more than short-term labor peace, and won't tolerate anarchy, what alternative is there to a bloody crackdown?

Mr. Gorbachev's answer is to speed up the pace of political reform — for instance, by moving up local elections scheduled for next spring to the fall. His thinking seems to run along these lines: A small dose of self-government — administered, of course, by the Communist Party — would immunize the people against the more virulent Western-style democracy, and give *perestroika* time to work.

But this assumes that Russians — and the dozens of non-Russian peoples in the Soviet empire — are fundamentally different from West Germans, Italians, Britons, Americans and others who refuse to settle for less than full democracy. And that's a risky assumption.

At some point, if the Soviet Union isn't to splinter along ethnic lines or succumb to its mounting economic ills, a leader is going to have to show more faith in the people than The Party.

Mr. Gorbachev, for all his courage and cunning, has yet to take that brave and necessary step.

Calgary Herald
Calgary, Alta., July 21, 1989

Behind the trademark pair of dark glasses is a man most Poles love to hate. Since Gen. Wojciech Jaruzelski introduced martial law in 1981, he has come to symbolize all that Poles have hated about authoritarian communism.

So what, then, has prompted the Poles to elect their reviled oppressor as their new president?

The answer is simply this — political survival.

Solidarity members of parliament have recognized the danger of letting their faltering steps toward democracy become a stampede.

Without a president acceptable to Moscow, Solidarity knows it cannot begin to institute democratic reforms.

Forty years of Communist control of the political and economic systems cannot be wiped away with one stroke.

They know Soviet President Mikhail Gorbachev will permit Poland to go its own way only if it remains secure within the Warsaw Pact. Rapid change is an invitation to trouble.

Therefore, Solidarity parliamentary members cooked the political arithmetic to insure the general's victory.

But to remind him that his past transgressions have not been forgiven, Jaruzelski was allowed to win only by a hair's breadth.

In a brief speech to the upper and lower houses of parliament after he was sworn in, the 66-year-old Communist party chief seemed chastened and acknowledged the difficulties. But he promised to work to heal Poland's deep wounds.

This will leave the minority Solidarity party where it feels more comfortable — in opposition.

The comfort level, however, is bound to deteriorate. Parliament faces an array of difficult choices that will cause hardship for the 39 million Poles.

For starters, Poland's massive foreign debt amounts to $1,000 for each citizen or $39 billion US.

Money-losing factories may be closed; consumer subsidies slashed. Jacques Delors, chairman of the European Commission who will be co-ordinating western aid to Poland, has said emergency food aid is on its way, but that further aid will be tied to tough austerity measures.

The message is clear. For western aid and investment to pour into Poland, its workers will have to show that they are willing to work hard and pay down the debt.

Are Poles up to the challenge? Christopher Young, the Moscow-based correspondent for Southam News, reports that they are keenly aware of their economic dilemma. And if self-deprecating humor is any help in rebuilding their shattered economy, they have an unlimited supply.

"The story is that Poland can be saved in one of two ways — the normal way or by a miracle," one Polish woman told Young.

"The normal way would be for a flight of angels to come down from the sky and fix all the problems overnight. The miracle would be if the Polish people got down to work."

Solidarity's Mazowiecki Confirmed as Polish Premier

Poland's Sejm, or lower house of parliament, Aug. 24, 1989 confirmed Solidarity activist Tadeusz Mazowiecki as the country's new premier. The momentous vote represented the first known democratic transfer of power away from a ruling Communist party.

Mazowiecki became Poland's first non-communist premier in four decades. The nation's first elected post-World War II government had been a coalition of the Communist Workers' Party and the allied Socialist Party, headed by Socialist Josef Cyrankiewicz. The Communists and Socialists had merged in 1948 to form the current United Workers' (Communist) Party.

Mazowiecki, 62, was a leading Catholic intellectual and a trusted adviser to Lech Walesa, the founder of the Solidarity trade union. He had been formally nominated for the post by Poland's president, Gen. Wojciech Jaruzelski, on Aug. 29, two days after the resignation of Premier Czeslaw Kiszczak.

In a statement issued Aug. 19, Jaruzelski said Mazowiecki was the best choice to form a coalition government that would be "conducive...and satisfying the needs and aspirations of the Polish people."

Mazowiecki won confirmation Aug. 24 on a vote of 378-4, with 41 abstentions. He had required 212 votes to win. After the confirmation, Mazowiecki told the Sejm: "I count on this moment becoming significant in the consciousness of my compatriots so that we can revive Poland by common effort, not because of my person, but because of the needs of Poland and the historic moment."

The Soviet Council of Ministers, or cabinet, Aug. 24 sent a congratulatory telegram to Premeir Mazowiecki. The message vowed that the "traditional relations of friendship and all-around cooperation" would continue between the two countries.

U.S. President George Bush Aug. 24 offered Washington's "strong support" to the new premier and reiterated his promise of increased U.S. aid to Poland to encourage capitalism and democracy.

ST. LOUIS POST-DISPATCH
St. Louis, MO, August 27, 1989

What an irony that when the Polish government finally broke with Cold War communism, the successor to Ronald Reagan found his own government too strapped for cash to lend much assistance at this strategic time for Eastern and Western Europe.

It's a good thing Gen. George C. Marshall, author of the imaginative Marshall Plan to rebuild Europe after World War II, isn't alive. His comments might well be critical of a government that has let a key policy tool, foreign aid, be foreclosed by a tremendous debt and the unwillingness to properly pay for the needs of the United States, one of the world's leading democracies.

According to one State Department official, "relatively modest American aid to Poland, properly tailored, could help them through the difficult transition" from a centrally controlled to free-market economy. But this administration, which is treating the amazing and rapid transformation of the Polish government with restraint and distance, is not even sure where it will find the $119 million Mr. Bush promised the Poles last month.

Because it is constrained by debts incurred by White House and congressional decisions during the eight Reagan years, the federal government has little money to take advantage of opportunities to help the Poles through the tough times ahead. Such aid need not be heavy-handed. It could be well placed and representative of a positive policy toward Poland's move to greater political and economic freedom.

The administration hasn't thrashed out its policy options yet. But it seems unlikely that Mr. Bush will go on national TV to convince voters to pay higher taxes so the United States can increase aid to a communist economy. Tadeusz Mazowiecki, the new prime minister elected by Communist and Solidarity deputies, says he wants to turn his country back "to the market economy and to a role of the state similar to that in economically developed countries."

Nothing guarantees his success, but U.S. aid could help. The administration should find a way to make such aid a priority.

The State
Columbia, SC, August 23, 1989

IN THE FALL of 1982, martial law had been declared in Poland to put a damper on unrest caused by the Solidarity free labor movement, and Solidarity's popular leader, Lech Walesa, was under house arrest.

At a Warsaw press conference with American editors, Deputy Prime Minister Mieczyslaw Rakowski was asked if he thought Poles would accept Mr. Walesa's removal from the scene. Mr. Rakowski, who had answered most questions fully and candidly, snapped, "No comment."

Later an official of the U.S. embassy who had been present explained the terse response. "Rakowski can wax eloquent on almost any subject. He's sharp and articulate and he can be witty. But he draws a blank on one subject — Walesa." He said that, as a civilian minister in a military-dominated regime, Mr. Rakowski was responsible for a number of domestic functions, including labor unions, and thus had been the government's point man in dealing with the strikes and other problems caused by Solidarity. "Now, he simply can't talk about Walesa," the American added.

This year, Mr. Rakowski was prime minister of Poland when Solidarity, legalized again after seven years as an outlaw movement, wrangled an agreement for virtually free elections from the regime and won a smashing victory at the polls in June. The prime minister, who was not elected even though he had no opposition, was forced to resign and accept the job as first secretary of the Communist Party.

Lech Walesa is, in effect, his counterpart as chief of the Solidarity party, and the two strong-willed Poles are at it again. Solidarity's candidate for prime minister is trying to put together a coalition cabinet. The Communists are expected to be offered the key defense and interior portfolios. Mr. Rakowski wants more, perhaps foreign affairs and finance too. Mr. Walesa said Monday the Communists must moderate those demands or "lose everything." Etc. Etc.

If this developing political arrangement in Warsaw does not become a marriage made in heaven, clashing personalities may be as responsible for it as clashing ideologies.

The Record

Hackensack, NJ, August 20, 1989

The agreement in Poland to form the East bloc's first non-communist government is extraordinary even when measured against the upheaval in the Soviet Union, China, and other parts of the communist world. If the accord holds, it will mark a surrender of communist power that is unmatched in more than 40 years of Soviet domination of Hungary, Czechoslovakia, and the other nations of Eastern Europe. Solidarity, which didn't even have legal status until a few months ago, will lead the coalition government. And Lech Walesa, a shipyard electrician, will have outmaneuvered the guns and tanks that have protected the Communist Party's powers.

By forming a coalition with two other parties, Solidarity last week broke the communist majority in the Polish parliament. The Communist prime minister, Gen. Czeslaw Kiszczak, resigned after unsuccessfully trying to form a government, and Polish officials said Friday that President Wojciech Jaruzelski had chosen Solidarity activist Tadeusz Mazowiecki to be the country's new prime minister.

In effect, an agreement was reached that granted Solidarity control over most day-to-day political, economic, and domestic affairs. That's an astonishing victory for a non-communist union in a nation where the government has always claimed the right to rule in the name of the workers.

As enormous as Mr. Walesa's achievements are, they have limits which help explain the Soviet Union's initial acceptance. Communist officials retain command of the army, the police, and the secret police, and will continue to set foreign policy. That ensures that Poland will remain a loyal member of the pro-Soviet Warsaw pact, and that Moscow can end Mr. Walesa's experiment as abruptly as it ended similar experiments in Hungary, Czechoslovakia, and in Poland itself.

In addition, the Communist Party must be only too glad to yield responsibility for the economy. Poland suffers form an annual inflation rate of 100 percent, a serious shortage of many consumer goods, and a foreign debt of $39 billion. In a sense, Mr. Walesa was caught. If he had declined to form a government, he would have opened himself to charges that he was little better than a complainer, unwilling to accept the responsibilities and risks that go with real power.

Commendably, he and Solidarity agreed to form a coalition capable of governing. "There are huge troubles, huge problems," Mr. Mazowiecki said Friday, speaking of the prime minister's post. But, he added, "Somebody has to try it."

No communist government has ever carried out the wrenching changes needed to introduce greater efficiency, which comes at a cost of higher prices and job layoffs. And Solidarity will have to deal with hostile and obstructive Communist Party bureaucrats who still control almost every government office.

These difficulties, however, make the Polish experiment all the more exciting. Perhaps the new government will succeed and show a new way to reform communism. They scored an enormous achievement by winning the right to try.

Los Angeles Times

Los Angeles, CA, August 18, 1989

The Communists in Poland have abdicated. The division of Europe into Communist East and democratic West has ended, at least for the Poles, and Poland's engine of change has shifted to hypersonic speed, destination unknown.

It is impossible to overstate the importance of the Communists' stepping aside in Poland. For decades American foreign policy has been predicated on the notion that Communist governments would never voluntarily relinquish power. Poland's Communist Party has done just that and the Warsaw Pact is standing by calmly, although watching closely. Western orthodoxies are crumbling as rapidly as Eastern orthodoxies.

What exactly these developments mean for Poland's future is impossible to predict. In the short run it seems that Solidarity will gain control of domestic affairs while Communist Party members will retain control of foreign affairs. This allocation was ensured by an agreement that Communists will head the defense, interior and foreign ministries. It appears to be a nice balance, bowing to the Warsaw Pact on one side and to the will of the people on the other.

But beyond this vague structure lies a swamp of questions. For one thing, Solidarity formed a coalition with two smaller parties, both of which were previously allied with the Communist Party. The United Peasants Party is descended from the communist underground supported by the Soviet Union during World War II. Both groups are unknown quantities for Solidarity and for Poland.

More fundamentally, it is unclear whether anyone in Solidarity, including its leader Lech Walesa, has any notion about how to run a country. Populists have ideas, not policies. Will Solidarity oust the current government bureaucracy? Do they have people who are able to replace the Communist bureaucrats? Or will they simply assume the top posts and try to get the bureaucracy to march to the beat of their drummer? Will they be effective ministers or will they lose public support as they abandon their placards to put on the suits and titles of the Establishment? And what if the economy gets worse or collapses? What would it take for the Communists or the military to consider a coup? In a situation so novel and so volatile, it follows that there are no answers, only questions.

Long-run predictions are no easier. George Kennan once wrote of Poland that "the jealous and intolerant eye of the Kremlin can distinguish in the end only vassals and enemies." Poland's future to a large degree depends on just how much that Kremlin view has evolved. In many ways the outcome of this change depends more on Soviet President Mikhail S. Gorbachev than on Walesa or Polish General Wojciech Jaruzelski, who declared martial law nearly 10 years ago and now seems to be running interference for one of the most stunning events in postwar Europe.

One thing that might assist a Solidarity government is foreign aid. It can not help the Polish economy—nothing short of a complete restructuring could cure its ills—but aid could gain Solidarity crucial short-term political benefits. The money might be wasted but the gesture of Western support would not be.

One thing *is* sure: Poland will be unstable for some time to come. Instability usually makes geopolitical strategists nervous. But instability is a lesser evil than coercion. For the first time since World War II, Poland has a government that is more or less self-determined. Maybe it will fail. But the freedom to take that kind of risk is one of the things that democracy is all about.

LEXINGTON HERALD-LEADER

Lexington, KY, August 23, 1989

As are others, we are filled with admiration and concern for Solidarity, the labor movement that has now, incredibly, gained political control of Poland.

The country's nominee for prime minister, Tadeusz Mazowiecki, a former weekly newspaper editor (a good sign, in our book), said it best when he commented that Poland needed "bread more than a prime minister." It will be hard enough for a new form of government to take root and grow in Poland without having to deal with what seem to be intractable economic problems.

The promise of Poland, however, lies in the nearly decade-long struggle of Solidarity. In that decade, it grew from a labor union at a single shipyard to an organization that is capable of nearly universal support among the working people of Poland. And although it may be a mistake to individualize what is a mass, democratic movement, the promise of Poland lies in the spirit of Lech Walesa.

We are continually amazed by the republican virtues of this man. Throughout the past decade, Walesa has walked the tight line between leader and supporter.

When Solidarity wanted to give too much authority to Walesa, he backed away, knowing the union needed time to develop its own leaders and a self-sufficient democratic culture. When the elected parliament had trouble forming a government, it turned again to Walesa, asking him to be Poland's new prime minister. Walesa said simply, and wisely, no.

Early in the days of this republic, there was a move to make George Washington, hero of the revolution, president for life. The formal Washington declined. He left office after two terms, knowing instinctively that a democratic culture dies if too much faith and too much power is invested in its leaders.

Lech Walesa has guided, followed and watched as Solidarity moved from a barricaded shipyard to Polish prisons to the underground to, finally, the seat of power. And as Poland met to select its new leader, Walesa, like Washington, stepped aside. From the sidelines or the seat of power, however, he seems destined to play a continuing role as the guiding spirit of the drive toward democracy in Poland — and, for that matter, throughout the world.

Richmond Times-Dispatch

Richmond, VA, August 19, 1989

The leader of Poland's communist government, Gen. Wojciech Jaruzelski, has cleared the way for the first non-communist coalition government to be formed behind the Iron Curtain. A coalition led by Lech Walesa and Solidarity including smaller parties formerly allied with the Communist Party will have a governing majority in the new Polish Parliament.

Poland's new prime minister reportedly will be Tadeusz Mazowiecki, a longtime Solidarity activist and editor of the Solidarity weekly newspaper Tygodnik Solidarnosc. Solidarity leader Lech Walesa also will play an active role. Although he said from the outset that he was not interested in being prime minister, Mr. Walesa has pledged to guide the selection of new Cabinet ministers.

It should be noted that Gen. Jaruzelski will, as president, remain commander in chief of the armed forces and will control foreign affairs. In addition, he has the power to dissolve parliament and to call elections. His power will surely temper the pace of Solidarity's remaking of the Polish government.

This new arrangement clearly has communists worried, and Mr. Walesa has sent messages intended for both Polish and Soviet consumption to reassure them that the coalition will not throw the communist scoundrels out, at least not yet. Mr. Walesa says that the Defense and Internal Affairs ministries will likely remain in the hands of communists. There is little doubt that Solidarity dare not challenge communist control of the military at this moment, but we wish Mr.

Walesa had not conceded the internal spy apparatus so quickly.

The rest of the now-communist bureaucracy will be headed by Solidarity-backed coalition ministers. And therein lies the rub. In order to refloat the foundering Polish economy, the coalition government will have little choice but to cut government bureaucracy and institute market-oriented reforms. Poles already are grumbling about temporary shortages caused by the recent decontrolling of prices, and bureaucrats whose jobs and perhaps communist-invented bureaucratic professions may be eliminated will hardly welcome the inevitable upheavals involved in creating a new economy. Solidarity itself has a dilemma on its hands: The labor union would like to retain many socialist programs with which Poles have grown comfortable, yet many of those programs must be cut back if Solidarity is to succeed on the economic front.

The more cautious among Poland watchers say that Gen. Jaruzelski and the Soviets are letting Solidarity assume the mantle of power because they believe Poland will be virtually unmanageable during the next few years, and so they are setting Solidarity up for a fall. Such caution is not unwarranted, given the sorry state of Poland's economy.

However, Mr. Walesa and Solidarity seem to have a Midas touch. The Solidarity-led coalition could succeed. If it does, we can only hope that the Soviet Union and Polish communists will not resort to Tiananmen-style force to preserve their empire.

THE DENVER POST

Denver, CO, August 25, 1989

THE CHANGES afoot in Poland are historic. The real issue, however, is whether they are permanent.

Freedom-loving peoples certainly should rejoice at recent events in the Eastern European nation. The once-outlawed Solidarity movement is now the major political force in Poland. The Communist Party has been cornered into sharing power with freely elected, non-Communist leaders. And the new prime minister openly has called for a return to capitalism.

Solidarity faces a paradoxical risk. Prime Minister Tadeusz Mazowiecki and President Wojciech Jaruzelski — the Communist official who once imprisoned Mazowiecki — must move quickly to resolve Poland's terrible economic woes. To do so, they will need the support of Solidarity chief Lech Walesa, the shipyard electrician whose uncanny leadership skills can mobilize the political passions of the Polish people.

But this unlikely trio also must be cautious, lest they threaten the old guard too much. Hard-liners in Moscow and Warsaw would welcome any chance to crush the Poles' fledgling freedom. The Soviets are more likely to react violently or unpredictably if they feel events are slipping out of their control.

Undoubtedly, the Communist hard-liners already are jittery because of the internal challenges to Moscow's iron-clad rule. For example, the peoples of Estonia, Latvia and Lithuania have staged mass protests to call world attention to their demands for independence.

These once-free Baltic countries were forced under the Soviet heel by an evil pact between Hitler and Stalin. Whether that historical wrong can be corrected is uncertain. Soviet leader Mikhail Gorbachev has encouraged greater local control throughout the Soviet Union. But it is difficult to imagine a scenario where the Baltic peoples can fully regain their liberty without terrible bloodshed.

Such thoughts must haunt President George Bush. Privately, Bush can only cheer Solidarity's achievements and the renewed Baltic spirit. Publicly, he must remain circumspect. He cannot risk provoking a Soviet crackdown.

Recent events give Eastern Europe a profound opportunity to cast off the chains of slavery and fear that have shackled these lands for a half century. But one miscalculation could cause Moscow to trample these aspirations. If recent events in Poland and the Baltic inspire hope and determination, they also should evoke caution and vigilance.

The Courier-Journal & TIMES
Louisville, KY, August 24, 1989

MIKHAIL Gorbachev broke a promise Tuesday, and for that the long-suffering Polish people and their friends in the West can be grateful.

For months, the Soviet leader has been assuring anyone who would listen that his country was finished interfering in the internal affairs of Poland and other Eastern European countries. But Tuesday he interfered — not with tanks but with the telephone.

He called Mieczyslaw Rakowski, the Communist Party boss in Warsaw, and reportedly advised him to find a way to get along with the Solidarity-led Polish government that is now in the making.

The 40-minute phone call had a dramatic effect. Mr. Rakowski immediately backed away from earlier threats that the Communists would refuse to participate in the new government. In fact, he started talking about "partnerlike cooperation" with Solidarity.

Solidarity got the message, too. Its nominee for prime minister, Tadeusz Mazowiecki, offered to give the Communists a bigger role in the government. Previously, the Communists had been promised "only" the defense and foreign ministries. These are key cabinet positions, of course, but Mr. Rakowski and other Communist leaders bridled at being shut out of everything else.

Now it appears that the Communists will get a few minor positions to assuage their hurt pride and the way is clear for Mr. Mazowiecki to assume the office — and heavy responsibilities — of prime minister. We wish him luck. Evidently, Mr. Gorbachev does, too.

The Charlotte Observer
Charlotte, NC, August 22, 1989

For the first time since what Winston Churchill called an Iron Curtain fell across Eastern Europe more than 40 years ago, a Communist Party that has ruled, when necessary, by martial law, backed by the military might of the Soviet Union, has yielded to popular will and election ballots. The Polish government now will be led by the non-Communist Solidarity trade union, which only a few months ago was outlawed by the Communist government. And without a threat or even a protest from the Soviets, who have dominated Eastern Europe through puppet governments, sometimes sustained by armed intervention, since the end of World War II.

For that last point, credit Mikhail Gorbachev — not that he wanted a non-Communist government in Poland, but because Soviet intervention would have discredited all his earnest pronouncements about openness and reform. And credit Solidarity leader Lech Walesa, who reassured the Soviets that Poland would remain in the Warsaw Pact and that Communists would be appointed to positions controlling the police and the military. By compromising instead of testing his new-found power to the limit, Mr. Walesa may have avoided a return to Soviet-backed martial law.

But even as the West celebrates this unprecedented retreat of communism and ponders what it may mean for the rest of Eastern Europe and future East-West relations, Poland remains in deep trouble. In fact, the Communists may have yielded power to Solidarity in order to let the union take the blame for the continuing deterioration of the Polish economy and standard of living. The blame for the economic mess the new government inherits rests squarely on the Communists, of course. But if Solidarity fails to bring quick improvement, it will, in the words of The Economist, "test to breaking-point the popular support that has swept it forward this far."

To break the cycle of recession and inflation (now 100% and rising) Poland will have to hold down wages and close unprofitable state enterprises, putting some people out of work. But the workers in the steelworks, mines and shipyards who are the backbone of Solidarity, whose stubborn resistance to Communist control over the years finally produced this stunning breakthrough, are demanding higher wages and job security. That is a dilemma difficult enough to doom the new government to failure.

Solidarity's hopes depend in part on economic aid from the United States. In his July visit to Poland, President Bush talked of U.S. aid in the range of about 1% of what Poland says it needs. Events since then may make Washington more generous than that.

But the burden of propping up the new government financially until it has a chance to succeed ought not lie exclusively with the United States. In fact, Western Europe has an even larger stake in the future of Poland. For the West Germans, for example, the Polish example surely stirs strong new hopes for eventual reunification of their country.

That's why President Bush may have been aiming his remarks indirectly at America's allies when he told Polish legislators last month: "Your reforms can be the foundations of stability, security and prosperity — not just here, but in all of Europe, now and into the next century."

The Chattanooga Times
Chattanooga, TN, August 18, 1989

Poland's worsening economic and political crisis appears to have finally driven the Communists from power over the nation's day-to-day life. Freedom suppressed for over four decades seems revived; President Wojciech Jaruzelski has tentatively agreed to Solidarity's historic proposal for the first opposition-led government in a Communist bloc country since World War II.

This pending deliverance is rich irony and supreme vindication for the unrelenting supporters of Solidarity — which only recently regained legal sanction -- and for the Polish people who have struggled so persistently to regain control of their nation. Yet there is little time and scant room for well-deserved celebration. Converting the opportunity still means surmounting internal Communist opposition and solving seemingly intractable problems.

The first hurdle, the Communist Party itself, now seems cleared. Communists in the lower house of Parliament, the Sejm, are now a minority since the two minor parties that had been their allies in the new government declared their willingness this week to form a majority coalition with Solidarity.

What inspired that turnaround remains unclear, but decontrolled food prices, chronic shortages of food and basic commodities and a sense of deepening public skepticism over the government's ability to deal with economic woes have exacerbated Poland's crisis. In some ways, the turmoil seems worse since the political reform in April that allowed competitive elections in the first place, perhaps because of raised expectations and freer expression.

Nevertheless, some Communists were reluctant as late as yesterday to cede control of the government to a Solidarity prime minister. With good reason, they fear loss of power and status, even though they have long since proved themselves incapable of earning the nation's support. To placate the Communists, Solidarity leader Lech Walesa promised to leave the ministries of police and army in Communist hands if President Jaruzelski approved the Solidarity-led coalition. He also pledged not to tamper with Poland's Warsaw Pact alliance. This — and Russia's tacit approval of the internal change — may have helped persuade Gen. Jaruzelski to accept the offer late Thursday.

Under the new Polish government system, President Jaruzelski must now nominate a prime minister from the coalition's slate. Mr. Walesa is an obvious choice, but there are other candidates. The new Solidarity-led coalition, with 264 of the 460 votes, could easily confer the position. President Jaruzelski would continue as commander-in-chief of the armed forces and retain authority to appoint special ministers responsible to his office, while the prime minister would lead the government's internal affairs.

If the coalition proposal holds, Solidarity's focus will be on rescuing Poland from the economic distress that finally defeated the communists. Considering the nation's debt and outmoded economic structure, it is as daunting a task for Solidarity as can be imagined. Still, it is impossible to refuse the union hope after its signal, skillful victory for Poland's political freedom.

Bush Visits Poland, Hungary; Lauds Reforms, Pledges U.S. Aid

U.S. President George Bush made his first trip to Eastern Europe as a U.S. president July 9-13, 1989 in visits to Poland and Hungary.

The stated aim of the trip was a strong show of U.S. support for the political and economic reforms in Poland and Hungary, the two countries that were pacing the Soviet bloc in liberalization. An unstated aim, according to knowledgeable Western observers, was to counter the demonstrated popularity in the Western nations of Soviet leader Mikhail S. Gorbachev.

Poland and Hungary were desperate for more Western aid to help revive their crippled economies. Both countries were heavily in debt to Western governments and financial institutions: Poland owed $39; billion Hungary, $17 billion. Hungary's foreign debt was the highest per capita in Eastern Europe.

President Bush arrived in Warsaw on the evening of July 9. He was greeted by Poland's leader, Gen. Wojciech Jaruzelski. On July 10, the president held a private discussion with Jaruzelski that lasted two hours and 15 minutes. Bush aides said that the talk was mainly of political, rather than economic, matters in Poland.

Provisions of the new Polish aid package included:
■ A $100 million "Polish-American Enterprise Fund" for investment in private Polish businesses and joint U.S.-Polish enterprises. Such a fund would have to be approved by the U.S. Congress.
■ U.S. support for a broad rescheduling of Poland's foreign debt.
■ U.S. support for $325 million in World Bank loans to help restructure Poland's industries and bolster its agricultural sector.
■ $15 million in U.S. funds for a cleanup of industrial pollution in the Krakow area. Congress would have to approve the money.
■ The establishment of cultural-information centers in each other's country.

The Bush entourage traveled to the industrial port city of Gdansk July 11. There, the president and Mrs. Bush lunched at the home of Solidarity founder Lech Walesa, and Bush made a speech at the Lenin Shipyard, the birthplace of Solidarity.

During the amiable lunch, Bush and Walesa discussed Poland's economic problems, and the union leader stressed his country's urgent need for a big infusion of Western capital. He presented the president with a copy of Solidarity's economic-recovery plan, which called for $10 billion in Western aid.

Bush later asserted that Walesa was not actually seeking $10 billion in direct aid for Poland, but rather "the potential to build through the private sector."

The presidential entourage was greeted in Budapest by Hungarian President Bruno Straub July 11. Bush was the first U.S. president ever to visit Hungary.

The president unveiled a package of aid that called for the creation of a $25 million fund for investment in Hungarian private enterprise. Like the proposed larger Polish fund, the measure would have to receive congressional approval.

Bush said that if Hungary eased its emigration policy (already the most liberal in the Soviet bloc) he would ask Congress to repeal the 1974 Johnson-Vanick amendments, which barred U.S. trade concessions to Soviet-bloc countries that restricted emigration. If Congress backed the proposal, Hungary's most-favored-nation trading status would then not come under annual review.

Other provisions of the Hungarian-aid plan included:
■ U.S. support for more Western financial aid for Hungary, including debt rescheduling.
■ The creation of an international environment center for Eastern Europe, based in Budapest. Bush said that he would ask Congress for $5 million for that purpose.

The Washington Post

Washington, DC, July 12, 1989

POLAND URGENTLY needs help from the West. But there seems to be some disappointment in Warsaw and Gdansk that President Bush spoke in terms of millions rather than billions of dollars. Even if the Western governments were prepared to finance a Marshall Plan for Eastern Europe—and there's no sign of it—a simple infusion of money would have only a temporary effect. Mr. Bush pointed Poland in a productive as well as realistic direction when he talked about trade and investment.

Poland's economy is not in trouble because it ran out of money. It's exactly the reverse. The central weakness of the economy is that it has been cut off from the world and its markets for 50 years, first by war and then by Communist autarky. Most of its factories have fallen into cranking out shoddy goods, according to the plan, with little thought for quality and less for modernization. Poles now are beginning the extraordinarily difficult process of remembering how to earn a living in a world that has developed almost beyond recognition in the years in which they were cut off from it. They have to cover the ground that the West has taken half a century to cross, as they try to catch up in technology and management.

The president's chief of staff, John Sununu, was not only offensive but wrong when he compared Poles, in their pursuit of aid, to children in a candy store who don't know when to stop. The Poles are dealing with a crisis of a complexity beyond anything—Americans must hope—that Mr. Sununu will ever face. If there is a note of desperation in their appeals, it deserves a deeply sympathetic response from the West.

The $100 million investment fund that Mr. Bush proposes is intended to lead the way for further and more substantial private investment from this country. He offers legislation to grant Polish exports better access to this country. He told the Poles that he will support international efforts to reschedule their debt payments and lighten that burden. He intends to press the other big industrial democracies, at their summit in Paris this week, to offer similar assistance.

None of these measures is dramatic, and none will transform Poland's prospects. But they are substantial and can bring Poland real benefits. The American position is not strikingly generous, but it has important advantages over the more sweeping and lavish promises that some Poles may have expected. The president's pledges are reliable and will endure beyond the present surge of emotion. They invite Poland into the economic system that has made the West rich. As the Poles approach this great transition, Mr. Bush has demonstrated that they have friends who are ready to make themselves useful.

Pittsburgh Post-Gazette

Pittsburgh, PA, July 7, 1989

President Bush's trip to Poland and Hungary next week couldn't be more timely in terms of fast-moving events there — victories for pro-democracy movements, the ceremonial reburial of a rebel leader and the real burial of his dictator successor.

Indeed, the challenge for the president will be to offer convincing support to the moves toward pluralism in those countries without unduly upsetting the Kremlin.

The president will arrive in Poland at a time when the Solidarity trade-union movement has won a crushing victory over the Communist Party in parliamentary elections but finds itself unready to take power.

The situation is such that President Wojciech Jaruzelski is balking at continuing in office, contending he is too identified with the December 1981 imposition of martial law and banning of Solidarity. But, surprisingly, even Solidarity leaders are not clamoring for him to leave, fearing a vacuum they hesitate to fill.

In Hungary, on the eve of the Bush visit, former dictator Janos Kadar died yesterday at the age of 77. That followed by three weeks the dramatic reburial of his predecessor, Imre Nagy, hanged by the Soviets and buried in a secret grave for the role he played in the 1956 Hungarian revolution that was ruthlessly crushed by 20 tank divisions of the Soviet army.

It will be interesting to see what the public response is at the funeral of Mr. Kadar. Although he was forced out of power last year by the growing liberal movement within the Hungarian Communist Party, he remained a father figure. His death should hasten all the more the rapid movement toward political pluralism that has followed in the wake of the market-system innovations Mr. Kadar inaugurated in one of the surprising twists of Eastern European history.

When Mr. Kadar was installed by the Kremlin after the Soviets had crushed the 1956 revolt, he was the most hated man in that unhappy country. But gradually during his 32 years in power, he steered Hungary in an economic direction different from any other country in the Soviet empire, with "capitalist" moves that brought increasing prosperity until the mid-1980s when the economy went into a tailspin. At that point Mr. Kadar came to be seen as a block to further reform, and he was eased out.

Clearly, Mr. Bush will arrive at a delicate time in the life of both nations. The challenge for him will be, in the words of a Heritage Foundation report, to make clear the democratic and free-market reforms that America wants to see in Eastern Europe "without frightening either Moscow or the aging Communist Party rulers into cracking down on reform as China's leaders have."

The Washington-based conservative think-tank urges President Bush to make clear to Polish and Hungarian officials that only by moving toward political and economic freedom can they enjoy the benefits of U.S. trade and economic, technological and managerial aid. He should be specific about what he means by genuine reform, such as free elections, an independent judiciary, drastic reductions in the powers of the secret police and a host of economic reforms designed to encourage private enterprise and entrepreneurship.

The Heritage Foundation report continues by urging Mr. Bush to meet openly with leaders of the democratic opposition and advocates of free-market reform and to encourage links to the private sector in the West. The report proposes that Mr. Bush avoid using the term "Eastern Europe," which connotes a connection to Russia, and instead refer to Poland and Hungary as part of Central Europe, as they were considered before World War II. The suggestion is a good one.

The Boston Globe

Boston, MA, July 9, 1989

The visits of President Bush to Poland and Hungary this week will create photo opportunities all his postwar predecessors might envy.

The president will arrive in Warsaw and Budapest as the leader of a triumphant free world. When encountering the humbled leaders of the Communist Party in Poland or the ardent reformers at the helm of the Hungarian party, Bush can play the role of the magnanimous victor in the Cold War. Lunching with Lech Walesa at the electrician's home in Gdansk, the former director of the CIA can personify America's dedication to democratic institutions and free markets.

Yet there are hidden perils in the president's mission. Poland and Hungary, like the Soviet Union, are in transition from the totalitarian past to an indefinite future. Walesa has never ceased warning against impatience or a triumphalist attitude. "The safe road is the evolutionary road," the Solidarity leader reiterated last week as he prepared for the Bush visit.

it. "We want to stay on the reform course and not provide arguments against us to those who are just waiting for them."

Walesa was alluding to communist hardliners who retain their hold on the levers of state power and who are still capable of using force to undo the political changes that have occurred so swiftly this year in Poland.

Bush will have to emulate Walesa's political tact throughout his visit. He must be careful not to imply that the dissolution of communist authority in Warsaw will enable the West to woo Poland away from the Warsaw Pact.

A more subtle danger is that the president will hold out unrealistic hopes for economic aid — both for the quantities available and the effects to be expected. The economic crises in Poland and Hungary are severe and cannot be solved by foreign aid alone. If Bush goes overboard praising the healing powers of free enterprise, he risks making capitalism the scapegoat for continued penury in both countries.

The Honolulu Advertiser

Honolulu, HI, July 15, 1989

Evaluations of President Bush's trip to Europe had best wait until after the weekend summit in Paris of the Western economic powers and Japan. That may even generate some unexpected news and differences.

But so far Bush seems to have done about as well as expected, considering the opportunities in Eastern Europe, our own economic limitations, and the ongoing byplay with Soviet President Mikhail Gorbachev.

The visits to Poland and Hungary were clearly a plus as anticipated, especially in public relations. But it left open the question of whether the United States and other Western nations are doing enough to help such former Soviet satellites bring off the reforms they are attempting.

Bush was properly careful not to provoke the Soviet Union on what is still its regional turf. Indeed, he made the point we are trying to encourage the reforms which Gorbachev has been championing. And that seems only fair because Gorbachev unleashed the forces that made the Bush visits possible.

What's going to be interesting is how the effects of Bush's trip behind the eroding Iron Curtain will play at the summit today and tomorrow.

Western economies are generally doing well. There are plenty of problems such as Third World debt that could be tackled but little extra money and political will at this time. So this is supposed to be a summit that focuses on very real environmental problems such as the greenhouse effect, holes in the ozone, ocean dumping, and Third World deforestation.

Bush also wants the summit to mobilize more economic aid for the nations of Eastern Europe. That has merit because it should be the nations of Western Europe that do most to help Eastern Europe.

The United States must do more than just provide inspirational leadership toward democracy for Eastern Europe. But we also have other economic interests and obligations in the world, including in the Asia-Pacific region.

"I THINK I'M BEGINNING TO LIKE THIS CAPITALISM ALREADY...."

Houston Chronicle

Houston, TX, July 5, 1989

George Bush has replaced Ronald Reagan since the last strategic arms control session. President Mikhail Gorbachev has made more speeches about easing East-West tensions.

But if there is anything different going on in Geneva, one has to look mighty close to find it.

President Bush has adopted the essence of the Reagan arms control policy. That has merit. Reagan in his last year in office developed a sound arms control policy that led to the agreement to bar medium-range missiles in Europe. Reagan and Gorbachev agreed to lower the ceilings on long range weapons to 6,000 nuclear warheads and 1,600 delivery vehicles each, including missiles and bombers. The Reagan proposal on the table at Geneva is a sound one.

Bush has tried to give the talks new impetus by suggesting that the subject of verification be taken up immediately. The Soviets have shown remarkable flexibility of late on that subject, so it is appropriate to determine just what they will accept. The verification issue is one that bothers Congress so much that it did not approve the last strategic arms treaty, although the terms have been observed.

Bush has also adopted the Reagan position that the Strategic Defense Initiative or "Star Wars" is a separate issue from START, and the Soviets continue to insist that SDI be part of any arms control package.

These negotiations have been going on for four years, and may last years more. If that is what it takes to achieve a verifiable, balanced and mutually beneficial arms treaty, so be it. Those quick, generalized agreements bandied about at summit meetings are worrisome and are to be avoided.

The Seattle Times

Seattle, WA, July 9, 1989

A DECADE or two ago, the worldwide language of revolution was Marxism. Today, it's democracy.

As he arrives in Eastern Europe this weekend, President Bush may not be able to say much in Polish or Hungarian, but he'll be speaking their language nonetheless.

Of all the East bloc nations, Poland and Hungary have seen the most dramatic democratic reforms in recent months.

Hungary has started tearing down the 220-mile Iron Curtain along its border with Austria — and an enterprising Hungarian firm is selling chunks of the barbed-wire fence as souvenirs.

Poland last month held the Communist world's most democratic elections in decades. The ruling Communist Party suffered a staggering defeat, losing 99 out of 100 contested seats in a reconstituted Senate to Solidarity candidates.

Now Poland's president, Gen. Wojciech Jaruzelski, has asked that his name be withdrawn from consideration for the powerful new presidency. Communist authorities are virtually begging Solidarity leader Lech Walesa — whom they once imprisoned, along with thousands of his followers — to share power in a new government.

During his visit, Bush will have lunch with Walesa and also meet with anti-Communist opposition leaders in Hungary. But what both countries need even more than encouraging words are economic aid and foreign trade.

Poland's external debt is $39 billion; Hungary's, $16 billion. The International Monetary Fund wants more austerity measures in both nations in exchange for some debt relief. Bush is expected to announced coverage of American investments by the U.S. Overseas Private Investment Corp. (OPIC), which should help considerably.

But beyond economic restructuring, these countries need more competitive political parties, freer unions, independent judiciaries, a more open press, and other democratic reforms to make real progress — and Bush should encourage those, too.

In Poland, anti-reform hard-liners are known as *betony* — literally, "cement heads." Today, the cement is cracking, but the new shoots of grass-roots democracy need careful nurturing.

The Providence Journal

Providence, RI, July 12, 1989

Things must get worse before they can get better; but sit up straight, take your medicine, and we promise that we'll help you along. That, in effect, was the message President Bush delivered to Poland this week — and from several points of view it was a welcome, as well as historic, theme.

For the Poles, who are striving to unhorse themselves from geography and history, it means that the process of political change may continue — at a price. That price, as the President declared, is economic change; for as surely as Poland has been kicked by a series of political and military jackboots in its time, it can only revive and prosper by enriching itself. The Polish economy is largely moribund, and the only hope for Polish industry and agriculture is a healthy dose of liberty and enterprise.

To that end, President Bush's package of assistance is essential. And while some, here and in Poland, may argue that the figures should be higher, the package is remarkably benevolent nonetheless. A $100 million enterprise fund, a $325 million World Bank loan, a generous rescheduling of the debt, and the promise of cultural and educational exchanges could signal the beginning of the end of Poland's agonies.

Two important points are worth remembering here. The first is that Poland is not a NATO ally but a member of the Warsaw Pact, still garrisoned by Soviet troops. Western Europe is enchanted by Mikhail Gorbachev and the promise of reduced tensions on the continent; but as even Mr. Gorbachev reminds his audiences at home, it is *perestroika* that will ultimately transform the globe, and *perestroika* which must be maintained at all costs.

In Poland, the logical consequences of *perestroika* are now falling into place: The Communist Party has been thoroughly rebuked, and is now on the run, but it is still an open question whether political reform can be fashioned and established to endure.

The second point is that the Poles recognize the critical, if inevitably limited, role the United States and its allies can play in this process. Mr. Bush has not offered Poland cheap prosperity or liberty overnight: He knows the difference between raising false expectations and encouraging genuine achievement. He has offered the wisdom of experience, and the crucial element of a helping hand. Just as Poland has learned the hard way that political and economic freedom are connected, the United States realizes that it cannot do for others what they must do for themselves.

It is time for Poland to rejoin Europe: To cease functioning as a vassal state of Russia, to resurrect the ancient energies that made Poland what it used to be, and protect the new freedoms that could make it even greater. These are exciting, very nearly disconcerting, times for the people of Eastern Europe. And it is gratifying to see that the President of the United States not only symbolizes hope, but personifies the reasons that give life to such hope.

THE TENNESSEAN

Nashville, TN, July 10, 1989

THE visit to Poland and Hungary by President Bush provides him with rare opportunity, but there are also some potential pitfalls which he must try to avoid.

Poland is in the beginning of a political transformation, in which the forces for reform are yoked with the Communist Party in the parliament. Thus Solidarity members who were once jailed by the regime are now sitting with their jailers in determining the future of the country.

It is a political experiment unknown to the Communist bloc, and its success is certainly debatable. At this juncture, however, Mr. Bush has the potential to help influence the course of events.

Poland's economy is in severe strain. Its foreign debt is huge. There has to be an enormous restructuring and that will add to privations of the public.

Polish expectations are naturally high, and in monetary terms much higher than Mr. Bush can deliver. He can do some things, in terms of trade and private investment in the Polish economy. But the array of concessions the country is looking for are far beyond U.S. abilities to meet.

Nevertheless, Mr. Bush's visit lends weight to Poland's new political experiment and helps legitimize Solidarity and its agreement with the government. This is yet a fragile arrangement that in a short time could simply collapse.

Hungary, too, is in the process of making some political reforms, but nowhere near the Polish ones. Still, it has some of the same problems of heavy foreign debt, a flagging economy and an aging infrastructure. Hungarians live better than the Poles but their problems are not minor.

The hopes of both countries for outside assistance will have to rest on some kind of consortium put together by the West, and perhaps, Japan. As a matter of fact the idea of alliance collaboration on aid to Poland and Hungary will be high on the list of the seven-nation economic summit in Paris, where Mr. Bush will go after leaving Hungary.

There, too, Mr. Bush could have substantial impact in persuading the alliance that helping Poland and Hungary now could be at far less cost than the consequences of not helping at all. This journey by Mr. Bush could well be historic. ∎

The Chattanooga Times

Chattanooga, TN, July 13, 1989

President Bush's aid package to help resuscitate Poland's economy was nowhere close to what Polish leaders desired. And the crowds surrounding Mr. Bush — at least until he went to Gdansk, the spiritual home of Solidarity — disappointed the president's aides, much as the president's somber rhetoric failed to ignite Polish passion.

But there were subtler successes and symbolic significance in Mr. Bush's trip first to Poland and then to Hungary. In these uncertain times of daring and desperate political experimentation in the reformist Warsaw Pact satellites, his journey alone ratified the importance and potential of the political changes. In Poland particularly, his presence and the offer of measured aid raised hope for the fruits of reform if Poland sustains its unity and courage through this current period of grave and potentially destabilizing economic crisis.

The changes in Poland in just the past six months are unquestionably immense and dramatic. The Polish parliament that Mr. Bush addressed in Warsaw, installed only a week earlier, was the first in a Communist satellite with deputies elected in pluralistic, contested elections. Members endorsed by the newly legitimatized Solidarity Union took 99 of the 100 seats in the parliament's senate, and all 161 seats in the lower house that were open to contest outside the Communist party.

It was only eight years ago that Solidarity was crushed, driven underground and many of its leaders jailed under martial law ordered by Gen. Wojciech Jaruzelski. But now, the general — who just a year ago still declared Solidarity dead — has declined to seek the new government's presidential post, tacitly acknowledging the shift of power.

The general's unrelenting nemesis and now his unlikely partner in a novel political experiment, Lech Walesa, is touted as a presidential candidate in 1993, when all seats are scheduled to go up for free elections. Yet just now, Mr. Walesa delicately urges caution against going too far too fast in terms of democratization and seeks aid to sustain Poland's crippled economy while reform takes deeper root.

Indeed, the common task of Polish and Hungarian reformers and President Bush is to nurture reform without provoking hardline Communists to roll out the tanks. The formula for a tolerable transition surely depends more on the carrot of economic aid and integration than on the stick of strict denial until change is complete. The Communists, after all, are only now willing to share power because of the economic collapse of the communist systems and the futility of their efforts to revive their economies without popular support. But if reformers cannot show success or attract Western relief, the possibility remains open that hardliners will retake the reins of power, brutally if necessary.

President Bush's package for Poland includes a grant of $100 million and a proposal — subject to approval at the economic summit getting underway in Paris — to reschedule debt payments, which could free around $5 billion. The latter is far more important than the miserly grant, which amounts to less than one-fifth the cost of one of the proposed 140 Stealth bombers. How much more important is Poland's reform to Western peace prospects than even one $532-million Stealth? A much smaller package is proposed for Hungary, where inflation and debt are not nearly so crushing as in Poland.

The proposals merit quick approval. More importantly, a clear promise of cooperation and continuing aid — hinged to successive political reform measures — needs to be extended. President Bush raised hopes in Poland by telling the people they "are not alone" in their quest for democratization and prosperity. His tour of the Soviet satellites symbolizes our national interest. Now, we must keep a helping hand extended for the long haul.

Pro-Democracy Movement Gains in Czechoslovakia

The pro-democracy movement in Czechoslovakia made major gains Nov. 24-30, 1989, as the nation's Communist Party leadership was replaced and the new regime hastened to make significant concessions. The opposition, led by the Civic Forum, mounted almost daily mass protests to maintain pressure on the regime. There was a nationwide two-hour strike on Nov. 27.

As the Communist Party (CP) was pushed to accept the notion of free elections, the Czechoslovak parliament Nov. 29 approved a constitutional amendment removing a provision that had guaranteed the party's "leading role" in society.

Communist Party General Secretary Milos Jakes and the other 12 members of the policy-making Presidium (politburo) resigned en masse Nov. 24 at an emergency session of the CP Central Committee. The entire Secretariat, the CP body that supervised government activities, was resigned as well.

Jakes, in power since 1987, a hard-line opponent of economic and political reform. His removal had been a key demand of the pro-democracy movement. In an address to the Central Committee following his resignation, Jakes admitted that the party had failed to understand the liberalization that was sweeping the rest of Eastern Europe.

The Central Committee Nov. 24 chose a new nine-member Presidium that included six of the resigned Presidium members. The Central Committee picked Karel Urbanek, 48, to replace Jakes as the party general secretary. Urbanek, who maintained a relatively low profile among the leadership, had no evident links to the party's hard-line faction.

The CP shake-up failed to placate the opposition, which mounted a huge demonstration in Prague Nov. 25. It was the ninth consecutive day of pro-democracy protests. The shake-up had been initially greeted with jubilation by tens of thousands of Czechoslovaks. That feeling was dampened by the realization that some hard-liners retained their seats on the Presidium.

Vaclav Havel, the dissident playwright and one of the leaders of Civic Forum, told the crowd – estimated at up to 800,000 people – that the shake-up was a "trick" to lull the movement.

In response to the continued unrest, there were more shake-ups in the regime Nov. 25. Miroslav Stepan stepped down as the Prague party chief in a round of resignations that encompassed officials nationwide.

Premier Ladislav Adamec unexpectedly announced his resignation Nov. 25, but he remained in office through Nov. 30. Adamec had been the only high-ranking official in the regime to seek concilliation with the opposition.

Former Czechoslovak leader Alexander Dubcek – the architect of the doomed 1968 "Prague Spring" reform movement – addressed a crowd of about 70,000 pro-democracy demonstrators in Bratislava Nov. 23.

Dubcek, 67, was living in official disgrace in Bratislava as a retired forestry clerk. He had previously eschewed active involvement in the dissident and human-rights circles in Czechoslovakia.

"After many years, now, I am raising my voice as a supporter of this broad-based movement," he told the cheering crowd.

On Nov. 24, Dubcek addressed about 200,000 people in a demonstration in Wenceslas Square in Prague. The protest was held the day before the announcement of the CP rally.

The Globe and Mail

Toronto, Ont., November 27, 1989

As Alexander Dubcek was saying before he was so rudely interrupted, Czechoslovakia must pursue a renewal of its society without making demands that could have tragic consequences.

The fact that 21 years of mandatory obscurity for Mr. Dubcek occurred between the original utterance and its reiteration the other day has added an almost unbearable poignancy. In Czechoslovakia today a grim joke goes the rounds. Question: What is the difference between the ideas of Mikhail Gorbachev and those of Alexander Dubcek? Answer: About 20 years.

The former leader of the Czechoslovakian Communist Party shares with Mr. Gorbachev more than sponsorship of an idea whose time has come — again. Both confronted formidable conservative reactions to their reforms, sought escape from the economic and social bondage of Stalinism and were obliged to counsel caution as the reforms moved forward. Each was a hero and a heretic.

Russian tanks are unlikely to rumble into Prague's Wenceslas Square as they did in August, 1968, when Czechoslovakia's bid for freedom was snuffed out. For the citizens who, in their hundreds of thousands, now fill the streets with nightly protest, the intoxicating breezes of the Prague Spring blow again, and this time they have toppled the hard-line Communist government headed by Milos Jakes.

There are basic changes yet to be made but this is clearly not a replay of 1968.

The Alexander Dubcek of that year ran a surprising distance before his Moscow masters tugged on the leash. The sharp lesson of how Hungary was brought back into line a dozen years earlier was still fresh enough to make reformers wary. Mr. Dubcek issued frequent verbal restraints to those who seemed dangerously enthusiastic about such things as personal liberty, a free press, freedom to travel to the West and the possibility of secret elections. He carefully injected regular proclamations of dedication to socialism into his speeches. (The Hungarians neglected to take similar precautions.)

The momentum in 1968, however, was difficult to control and, inevitably, the Kremlin became edgy. On May 6 of that fateful year, Mr. Dubcek returned from talks in Moscow to offer his people a sort of Neville Chamberlain reassurance. The Soviets, he said, "accepted with understanding" the process of democratization that he had explained to them.

It was a summer of growing uneasiness, however; of mounting pressure by Warsaw Pact allies on Czechoslovakia. Mr. Dubcek, buoyed by considerable domestic enthusiasm for his reforms, was not inclined to return to the suffocating orthodoxies of the old ways. The tanks arrived in August, and Mr. Dubcek ceased to be a person of consequence. (Given the Hungarian experience, he was lucky even to be a person.)

It took Pravda 13,000 words to explain why Czechoslovakia's reformist leader had to be removed. He had connived at counter-revolution. He and his associates were right-wing opportunists and revisionists, guilty of perfidy and treachery. Mr. Dubcek, continued Pravda, had reneged on pledges given to Russia, Poland, East Germany, Hungary and Bulgaria at two summit meetings. In Pravda's view, the elements led by Mr. Dubcek in the Czechoslovakian Communist Party were a minority. "As a result of their perfidious activities, a real threat arose to the socialist achievements of Czechoslovakia."

As Mr. Dubcek triumphantly resurfaced the other day (he is a retired forester), the question of socialist achievements is a matter of animated debate. He can still hear the old Stalinist line — diminished now, but lamentably stubborn in his own country. Mr. Dubcek, and what he stands for, is more stubborn still.

DESERET NEWS
Salt Lake City, UT, November 26, 1989

Like the other jolts that preceded it elsewhere in Eastern Europe, this week's political earthquake in Czechoslovakia constitutes another stunning setback for communism.

It also constitutes a demonstration of how quickly a regime can fall — a lesson that should be taken to heart by repressive governments around the world.

Only two weeks ago, Czechs were celebrating the anniversary of the "triumph" of the Socialist Revolution in their country.

But then, in a grass-roots uprising much like those in East Germany and Poland, hundreds of thousands of demonstrators started taking to the streets of Prague each day, demanding political reform.

The continuing pressure of the largest mass demonstrations in the country's history paid off this weekend with the resignation of the entire ruling presidium of the Czechoslovak Communist Party and the installation of a new leadership headed by Karel Urbanek, a comparative newcomer to Czech politics.

While this historic event clears the way for democratic reform, a few precautions are still in order.

First, it would be a mistake to rule out the use of force by the Czech Communist Party. True, such a step has seemed less likely ever since Moscow started indicating it would no longer intervene to prop up tottering regimes among its satellites. For this stance by the Kremlin, the world no doubt can thank the tough guerrillas who beat back the Soviet invaders of Afghanistan. Even so, it's hard to believe Czech Communists would completely relinquish power without a fight.

Second, though they certainly are an improvement over the old regime, the new rulers in Prague do not look like enthusiastic reformers. They, too, could come under pressure to step down unless substantial changes are soon forthcoming. But Western experts say there is no sign that the new Czech leaders are prepared to follow Poland and Hungary down the road to multiparty democracy.

Third, whoever rules Czechoslovakia inherits huge burdens. The country is sagging under the weight of a crippled economy, fierce air pollution and the incompetent management that comes with communism. The crisis could become even more acute if workers and students follow through on plans for a general strike.

Even so, the Free World still has ample reason to cheer the trend that has manifested itself in Czechoslovakia and to savor a sweet moment of victory. The trend in Eastern Europe is clearly in the direction of less repression and more democracy. May this long-overdue movement keep gathering more and more momentum.

The Hartford Courant
Hartford, CT, November 26, 1989

With astonishing speed, the pro-democracy movement sweeping Eastern Europe has overtaken the Stalinists in Prague. Milos Jakes, who resigned along with the rest of the Czechoslovakian Communist Party leadership Friday, became the third East bloc chieftain to fall within a month.

The thud must have unsettled the celebrants in Bucharest, who on the same day had conferred by acclamation another five-year term on Romania's strongman for 24 years, Nicolae Ceausescu. He scorns democratization and economic restructuring.

But if a new day can dawn in Czechoslovakia, it can happen in Romania. If not now, one day soon. The latest organized stirrings for freedom in Czechoslovakia began only a scant week before the party leadership gave way. "We have underestimated completely the processes taking place in Poland, Hungary and especially recently in East Germany and their effect and influence on our society," Mr. Jakes observed.

He and the other hardliners came to power after the Soviet Union invaded Czechoslovakia in August of 1968 and crushed the experiment of Alexander Dubcek and his allies, who wanted to create "socialism with a human face." Mr. Dubcek turned out to be a prophet honored in his country by the hundreds of thousands of demonstrators who chanted his name last week. No wonder: Twenty years ago he wanted to permit freedom of the press, to let dissident voices be heard, to allow a semblance of market-driven economics, greater power for the parliament and the election of party officials by secret ballot, with a limit on their tenure in office.

The Czechs got, instead, Soviet tanks and 20 years of repression.

Has there been a vindication more sweet than that enjoyed by Mr. Dubcek? He was on hand in Prague on Friday to inspire a new generation reaching for freedom: "An old wise man said, 'If there once was light, why should there be darkness again?' Let us act in such a way to bring the light back again," he told 300,000 cheering patriots in Wenceslas Square.

The Czech demonstrators have reason to celebrate, but they shouldn't rest. They must give strength to the fledgling opposition, which has to persuade the new Communist leadership to share power and permit reform. Still, their accomplishments these past few days have been remarkable — and touching.

Give credit to Soviet leader Mikhail S. Gorbachev, who has shown the way to democratization and economic restructuring in the East, and who undoubtedly used his influence for a peaceful solution in Czechoslovakia. But most of all, give credit to the Czechoslovakian students and all the other brave seekers of the light.

DAILY NEWS

New York, NY, November 25, 1989

IN 1968, SOVIET TANKS rolled into Czechoslovakia and crushed the brief movement toward democracy that flourished under the leadership of Alexander Dubcek. Now, 21 years later, the government that was installed at cannon-point has resigned in fear and frustration.

In a magnificent stroke of timing, the kind of event no fiction writer would dare create, the government's fall came just hours after Dubcek himself appeared in Wenceslas Square before a roaring crowd. He was greeted as a hero, as he deserved. After more than two decades of exile and humiliation that followed his "Prague Spring," Dubcek's vision is undimmed, his spirit unbroken. He told his audience: "An old wise man said, 'If there once was light, why should there be darkness again?' Let us act in such a way to bring the light back."

It is an open question whether that "light" of political and economic freedom will shine in Czechoslovakia. A successor to Communist chief Milos Jakes has been named. But it remains to be seen whether the new man, Karel Urbanek, represents more of same hard-line repression or is a genuine reformer.

Strangely enough, a good example of what Prague needs now can be found in Egon Krenz of East Germany: a mid-level Communist bureaucrat who is willing to keep retreating in the face of popular demands.

Czechoslovakia is similar to East Germany in at least one other respect: It was a domino whose fall virtually no one expected just hours before it happened. If Prague remains on the path of liberation, then Friday, Nov. 24, will rank right up there with the end of the Berlin Wall as one of history's finest moments.

Pittsburgh Post-Gazette

Pittsburgh, PA, November 24, 1989

Freedom fever has struck Czechoslovakia, as evidenced by the protest marches in Prague since club-wielding police dispersed a small demonstration a week ago and the meetings between Communist leaders and representatives of the opposition movement.

The surprise is that the Czechs have been quiescent so long, considering this summer's streams of East German refugees through their country, followed by the huge demonstrations in East Germany that brought a breaching of the Berlin Wall — not to mention the growing democratization of Poland and Hungary and the nascent stirrings of rebellion even in Bulgaria. After all, Czechoslovakia was one of the few true democracies among the nations created out of the old Hapsburg empire after World War I.

Obviously, the Czechs have been cowed by the memory of the failed "Prague Spring" of 1968 when the efforts of leader Alexander Dubcek to "put a human face on socialism" were squashed as Soviet Russia exerted its muscle in late August by flooding tanks and troops into its satellite country. Also, economic conditions have been better in Czechoslovakia than elsewhere in the Soviet bloc.

But even there, freedom's time has come.

The Philadelphia Inquirer

Philadelphia, PA, November 22, 1989

In 1969 a Czech student named Jan Palach burned himself to death to protest the Soviet occupation. When his grave became a shrine, the Czech government stole the body. But, years later, people still quietly dropped flowers off at the site.

This week, Czechoslovakia finally erupted in protest after police brutally beat student demonstrators and one of them was reportedly killed. His body hasn't been found either — the government denies that Martin Smid died — but this missing corpse may finally spark the demise of the hard-line Czech regime.

The Czech leaders of 1989 are nearly all the same men who welcomed the Russian invasion in 1968. But something basic has changed over the last few weeks, something that enables hundreds of thousands of Czechoslovaks to pour into the streets to protest government brutality where, previously, they dared only to leave a flower.

That something goes beyond the critical change of position by Moscow, which is no longer interested in "occupying" Prague. It goes even beyond the events in East Germany, which have had a stunning impact on a Prague regime whose leaders had counted on East Berlin hardliners backing it up.

What has changed in Prague is that people have finally lost their fear. For years in this sophisticated country, which prior to World War II was one of the world's ten industrial giants, people learned to hold their tongues. After the Prague Spring was crushed by Russian tanks in 1968, 500,000 people were purged from the Communist Party, including the country's brightest thinkers. They were fired from their jobs, condemned to menial labor. Most of their children have never been permitted to go to college.

Society turned inward. The generation of the martyred Jan Palach became silent, finding solace in family or in summer vacation cottages, as the regime provided just enough consumer goods to buy them off. Speaking out was just too risky; it meant government persecution.

But the 1968 generation's children became cynics. Too young to be frightened by memories of how much they could lose, they acted out their frustrations in illegal rock music and drugs. They made bitter jokes about the lies of public officials. They waited fifteen years for an apartment. They waited to explode.

Vaclav Havel, the distinguished playwright who heads the hastily assembled opposition coalition called Civic Forum, once explained why the Czech regime feared any small demonstration. It never knew, he said, which one could be the beginning of the end. During the years of political silence, when about 1,500 core dissidents like Havel struggled on in isolation, it seemed that this signal would never come.

But it came last week when the Czech regime sent police out to beat up its youth. At that moment the psychological balance turned. And the next day the crowds surged into the streets. Now the only way out for the band of 1968 quislings is to shoot to kill — or make way for democracy. Either way, their days are numbered, though it will take time because the political opposition is barely organized. But the mysterious Martin Smid, who may or may not have been murdered, has shown that the spirit of Jan Palach has not been stilled.

Minneapolis Star and Tribune

Minneapolis, MN, November 25, 1989

The libertarian contagion sweeping Eastern Europe claimed another victim Friday. When Hungary, Poland, East Germany and even Bulgaria have been infected so thoroughly by freedom, Czechoslovakia's lack of immunity should be no surprise. But it is.

The "Prague Spring" of 1968, when liberalizing leaders made life better for their citizens, was a sign of Czechoslovakian aspirations. Despite that evidence and despite the past week's demonstrations by hundreds of thousands, we worried that the wintry malaise imposed after a Soviet invasion later in 1968 would be too deep to dissipate quickly. So much for punditry.

To leave no doubt about the extent of Communist Party capitulation, the entire Czech Politburo resigned. The explanation by party chief Milos Jakes had none of the rationalizing you might expect from a legendary hard-liner. A sentence is worth quoting: "We have underestimated completely the processes taking place in Poland, Hungary and especially recently in East Germany and their effect and influence on our society." Jakes spoke of the need for "restructuring and democratization." The words are significant; they are the themes advocated by Soviet leader Mikhail Gorbachev.

If these drastic political overhauls are cause for any uneasiness, it is mainly that of uncertainty. Europe is being restructured so quickly that no one can predict what shape will emerge. Governments, political parties, businesses and international institutions suddenly must rethink their roles. Rapid change can be disconcerting. But it detracts not the slightest from rejoicing as the democratic fever spreads through Eastern Europe.

THE PLAIN DEALER

Cleveland, OH, November 26, 1989

A historic week in Czechoslovakia culminated in the resignation Friday of Communist Party chief Milos Jakes and the rest of the country's hard-line leadership. So were answered the demands of the citizenry, peacefully assembled on the streets, in increasing numbers day by day. Another Marxist-Leninist domino fallen, like Poland and Hungary and East Germany before it. And fittingly, just before Jakes and his crowd quit, the beloved Alexander Dubcek, proponent of "socialism with a human face," appeared in public in Prague for the first time since his ouster in 1968.

It is impossible, with events in the Soviet Bloc still fluid and the long-term impact of recent changes unpredictable, to do justice in this space to the upheaval in a world that for too long was ruled tightly from the Kremlin. Just ponder the very fact of Dubcek's return from political limbo: Was it only 21 years ago that his reform efforts were crushed by invading armies from countries that now are turning away from rigid communism?

And why is everything now going right for Dubcek's heirs and their counterparts elsewhere in the Warsaw Pact (with the lamentable exception of Stalinist Romania)? That is not difficult to explain. In spite of initial resistance in some quarters, Prague among them, the push for change begun by Soviet President Mikhail S. Gorbachev has proved too powerful to resist, especially when it has encouraged mass demonstrations that could have been put down only by a savagery that would set back Soviet Bloc progress for decades.

Gorbachev, it seems, wanted a more liberal leadership installed in Prague before his meeting with President Bush next week. According to a plausible theory, pressure from that direction, as well as from more moderate, or simply panicky, elements among the Communist elite, helped bring about Jakes' downfall.

Even if a more enlightened regime takes command of the party, the leaders will have to address themselves to popular demands for elections and for the transformation of the country into a multiparty democracy. But with workers showing an increasing willingness to join intellectuals on the front line, and the freedom movement inspired and invigorated by Dubcek's reappearance, the future suddenly looks amazingly bright.

THE SACRAMENTO BEE

Sacramento, CA, November 28, 1989

Twenty-one years after Soviet tanks crushed the Prague Spring, the dream so brutally shattered then is alive again in Czechoslovakia. Every day, the aging Stalinists who have stifled the impulse to freedom since Soviet tanks put them back in power yield a little more to the popular cry for freedom and democracy. Another Communist domino is wobbling.

It's ironic, and just, that Alexander Dubcek, the man who as the nation's leader in 1968 was 20 years ahead of his time and who suffered as a consequence, today embodies the hopes of 16 million Czechs. Because his attempt to create "socialism with a human face" went so far, the repression that followed was all the more harsh and all the more resistant to change, even in the face of stunning reform elsewhere in Eastern Europe and of the Kremlin's clear approval of this peaceful revolution.

It was the regime's brutal overreaction to a student protest on Nov. 17 that stirred the normally stoic Czechs to 10 days of massive street protests that finally have had an impact. Now, political prisoners are being released, hard-liners dropped from leadership positions, the end of censorship is promised, government officials meet with leaders of the opposition New Forum who only days ago risked being arrested for speaking out and anti-regime public rallies are not only tolerated but carried live on state television.

The battle for political pluralism is not yet won; some with so much vested in the survival of the Communist Party's 41-year monopoly of power cling to the hope of retaining it. But yesterday's two-hour general strike, in which millions of workers chanting "Dubcek to the castle!" joined in a massive rejection of the regime, makes it clear that in Czechoslovakia, as in Poland and Hungary and East Germany, the people no longer fear their masters — that indeed, the reverse is now true.

If there's to be poetic justice in this drama, Dubcek, the man who narrowly avoided execution 21 years ago, then became an obscure official in the state forestry ministry, may become the country's first democratically elected president since Eduard Benes, a patriot who was head of state during the democratic interregnum before the subjugation of Czechoslovakia by Hitler's Third Reich in 1939, and again just before the Communist coup in 1948. If anyone can heal the wounds of a nation crushed by Nazism, betrayed and abused by Czech Communists and subdued by Soviet military power, it's Dubcek. Like so many heroes, large and small, who have emerged in Eastern Europe this year, he has shown an astonishing capacity for focusing more on the need for reconciliation than on the grievous past abuses by those who promised social equality and delivered Stalinist brutality.

Nothing guarantees that such restraint will continue, that today's events will lead to a stable, democratic Czechoslovakia — nor is there any certainty of such a result in Poland, Hungary and East Germany. Yet everything that has happened in Eastern Europe these last exciting months says it must end that way, however turbulent the road just ahead. Whether that reflects the triumph of hope over experience, as skeptics still insist, remains to be seen. For now, the hope that flowered during the Prague Spring of 1968 blossoms again in the falling snow in Wenceslas Square.

MILWAUKEE SENTINEL

Milwaukee, WI, November 23, 1989

It might have been East Germany, in Leipzig or East Berlin — cities where the allure of democracy prompted thousands of marchers to pressure the government to open its borders and to move grudgingly toward revamping its institutions.

Instead, this time, it is in Prague, Czechoslovakia, where thousands are taking to the streets, demanding freedom and where an official newspaper actually published an opposition call for the ouster of top Communist leaders.

And during all this activity in one of the Eastern Bloc's most hard-line nations — a nation previously invaded by the Soviet Union to end the so-called Prague Spring of 1968 — it became clear that the guru of the Warsaw Pact's headlong plunge into freedom was sitting in Moscow, orchestrating it all.

Soviet President Mikhail S. Gorbachev publicly endorsed current demands for reform in Czechoslovakia and across Eastern Europe. It is imperative, he said, because technologically, the East lags dramatically behind the West.

At first, security forces in Prague attempted to bully the demonstrators into submission, cruelly attacking their ranks and clubbing those who would not disperse. It was a scene, within the context of the Soviet-led invasion, in character and, at the same time, out of touch

But now, things have gone too far for reformers to retreat — or for the government to restrict.

Czechoslovakia is among the last of Eastern Bloc nations to flirt with democracy. Only Romania clings to orthodoxy. It seems impossible that its hard-line leader, Nicolae Ceausescu, can resist much longer.

What started as flirtation has blossomed into full-fledged matrimony. Gorbachev has loosed upon the Communist world a revolution, at first technologically, economically and ethnically based. It has grown beyond this, however, and has launched a spirit that no tank or security bully can harness.

Czechoslovakia's Noncommunist Coalition Government

Czechoslovak President Gustav Husak Dec. 10, 1989 resigned immediately after swearing in a 21-member coalition cabinet with the Communist Party (CP) in a minority role. The party had previously reigned in Czechoslovakia for 41 years.

Czechoslovakia was the second East-bloc country, after Poland, to form a noncommunist government. However, unlike Poland, the Czechoslovak government was led by a Communist, Premier Marian Calfa. The government was to remain in place until Czechoslovakia held free parliamentary elections. No date had yet been set for the balloting.

Husak, 76, was a Communist hard-liner who had served as the Czechoslovak leader following the crushing of the 1968 "Prague Spring" reform movement. He had been Czechoslovakia's head of state since 1975. Husak's resignation had been demanded by Civic Forum, the leading umbrella opposition group.

The swearing-in came on International Human Rights Day. Civic Forum, using the threat of a nationwide general strike, had set Dec. 10 as the deadline for having a new government in place.

About 150,000 people held a joyous pro-democracy rally in Prague's Wenceslas Square Dec. 10. On Dec. 11, the day on which the threatened general strike was to have been held, millions of Czechoslovaks joined in a nationwide celebration at noon.

The Communist Party Dec. 8 in round-table talks in Prague with Civic Forum agreed to reliquish power. The discussions also included the Socialist and People's parties, once allies of the Communists, which endorsed the opposition's programs. Premier Calfa and CP ideologist Vasil Mohorita acted as the ruling party's chief representatives.

The ruling party capitulated on Civic Forum's major demands. One demand was that the new cabinet feature reform-minded noncommunists in key roles. Another demand was that the Communists support a comprehensive revision by parliament of the nation's laws to widen civil liberties and pave the way for multiparty free elections.

The new cabinet featured 11 noncommunists (seven independents and two each from the Socialist and People's parties), and 10 Communists. Opposition figures – who were in the cabinet as independents – held several important cabinet posts.

The Communists retained the key posts of premier, defense minister (Col. Gen. Miroslav Vacek), trade minister (Andrej Barcak) and deputy premier for economic planning (Vladimir Dlouhy). Dlouhy's appointment was supported by Civic Forum.

In an arrangement finalized Dec. 10, Premier Calfa placed the interior ministry – which controlled the internal-security forces – under the supervision of a cabinet-level special committee. There was no interior minister. Czechoslovakia thus became the first Soviet-bloc country with a security apparatus not under Communist control.

Dissident playwright Vaclav Havel and former Czechoslovak leader Alexander Dubcek Dec. 10 each announced his candidacy for president. Havel, one of the founders of Civic Forum, had the support of that organization and its Slovak counterpart, Public Against Violence.

By tradition, the premiership and presidency were divided between the nation's two ethnic groups, Czechs and Slovaks. As Premier Calfa was a Slovak, the next president would normally be a Czech, like Havel. Dubcek was a Slovak.

Parliament had 14 days to choose a successor to President Husak. But the selection was stalled as of Dec. 11 by a debate over a Communist proposal to have the president elected by popular vote.

The Evening Gazette

Worcester, MA, December 9, 1989

One after another, the vapid communist regimes of Eastern Europe have found themselves unable to withstand the people's relentless clamor for democracy.

The desperate holding actions in Poland, East Germany, Hungary and Czechoslovakia call to mind an image of King Canute attempting to sweep back the tide. Each set of communist officials ultimately has found it fruitless to delay the inevitable, but each in turn has tried.

Leaders of Czechoslovkia are the latest of Eastern Europe's communist elite to attempt a parliamentary sleight-of-hand to retain control while appearing to yield to the wishes of the people.

Following massive demonstrations and a general strike, the government adopted a new constitution, stripping the Communist Party of its "leading role." The ruling group then named 21 cabinet ministers, 16 of them communists — including 13 holdovers from the previous cabinet — with no representation from the largest opposition group, Civic Forum.

The people were not fooled. A throng estimated at 200,000 gathered in Wenceslas Square, scene of the massive demonstrations over the last month that brought about some historic changes.

The result has been an about-face and a government representing all segments of the political spectrum. Such a coalition can now place added responsibility on the reformers to work toward constructive changes.

The denial of reality would only place Prague's beleaguered leaders in the desperate position of King Canute.

Herald News

Fall River, MA, December 3, 1989

Eastern Europe is like a jigsaw puzzle, where the assembled design changes every day. Czechoslovakia, a long, narrow piece bounded by natural borders, has been the latest segment to be transformed.

Monochrome communist conformity has given way to a brighter spectrum: 11 days of milling throngs; the return of a national hero; last Monday's two-hour general strike; Wednesday's constitutional reform.

The ferment has been called "the polite revolution." Protestors, pleading for the young Civic Forum op-position movement, threw flowers, not rocks, and lit candles in Prague's jam-packed Wenceslas Square.

As they broke away from the communist monolith, the Czechs and Slovaks were remarkably courteous, apologizing when they jostled each other or trod on each others' toes.

Like a gentle, mythical hero, Alexander Dubcek emerged from 21 years of obscurity to address an admiring crowd. Dubcek was head of the communist party in Prague when he led an internal reform move-ment, known as the Prague Spring, in 1968. His goals then matched those of his younger comrades today: liberalization, democratization; freedom of speech, press, assembly, and religion. His ideal was "socialism with a human face."

But the reforms were suppressed by Soviet troops and tanks. Dubcek quickly fell from favor, and was ousted from the party in 1970. But the more his name and picture were outlawed, the more his mystique grew in the minds of the people. In recent years, he has been granted more freedom.

The entire Czechoslovak Politburo and its secretariat resigned, just as its hardline counterparts had in Poland, Hungary and East Germany. Party head Milos Jakes, who had been forced upon the Czechs

The Washington Post

Washington, DC, December 8, 1989

WHILE THE opposition coalition called Civic Forum is not running Czechoslovakia, neither is the Communist Party. When Prime Minister Ladislav Adamec abruptly resigned yesterday, complaining that Civic Forum was pressing him too hard, that seemed to end the Communists' last hope of controlling the course of events. Civic Forum is now talking about another general strike on Monday, simply to remind the Communists where the people stand.

The first strike, two weeks earlier, was the crucial moment in Czechoslovakia's peaceful revolution. The Communists had begun to make important concessions, but still thought of Civic Forum as merely a collection of intellectuals and students. When the workers went out in response to its strike call—millions of them, in every kind of job, in every part of the country—it was an overwhelming display of the breadth of its support. One of the strikers' purposes was to bring non-Communists into the government. Mr. Adamec responded by proposing a new cabinet that, out of 21 ministers, would have had five who were not Communists and none of them in a major job. Not good enough, said Civic Forum. That's the point at which Mr. Adamec, trained to a different kind of politics, decided to give up and walk out.

The president of Czechoslovakia has named another candidate to try to form a government, but whether he or it will take office is doubtful. The president is the same Gustav Husak who replaced Alexander Dubcek after Soviet tanks ended the previous Czechoslovak reform movement 21 years ago, and among Civic Forum's other demands, it wants Mr. Husak out of his office by Monday.

Czechoslovakia now faces the same basic political requirement as most of the rest of Eastern Europe. It needs a government with legitimacy. Shuffling the party figures around to try to find younger people who are less clearly identified with past repression won't do it. The only solution, as Civic Forum has pointed out, is to hold elections.

Civic Forum has also said that it does not want to provoke a crisis. It only wants to keep things moving in the right direction. For an organization that was founded only three weeks ago, it is moving with extraordinary skill and judgment to push its way toward democracy. It's the failure of anything similar to appear in East Germany, incidentally, that makes the situation there dangerous.

At the moment Czechoslovakia has no government and no idea when it will get one. But the country gives a strong impression of being in good hands.

in the backlash that suppressed the Prague Spring, admitted he hadn't done very well at 'restructuring,' and resigned in favor of Karel Urbanek, 48, a former railroad worker from Moravia, known as a moderate. To the reformers, he is neither inspiring nor threatening.

Dubcek, however beloved, is now somewhat subdued; he seems to call for younger leadership, which may emerge in the likes of Civic Forum leaders Valclav Havel, a playwright, and Vaclav Maly, a priest. Both epitomize the energy of a literate, industrialized society, where individuality can be supressed but not repressed.

This has been the pattern in Czechoslovakia since it was established as a "successor state" replacing part of the Austro-Hungarian Empire, at the end of World War I. It's now a federal republic, and a Soviet satellite, comprised of the Czech Socialist Republic, centered in Prague; and the Slovak Socialist Republic, in Bratislava.

Since the Prague Spring, half a million Czech reformers have been purged from the Communist party. The socialism that remains is, in Dubcek's view, a hollow shell. To him and his reformist colleagues, true socialism implies the rule of the people.

By Tuesday, the revolution went from the streets to the negotiating table. Premier Ladislav Adamec met with Civic Forum, and promised to push for a coalition government, with non-party representatives. And the constitution was revised to allow public education to veer from the Marxist-Leninist line.

Havel credited Czechoslovakian students with keeping the light of civilization alive. He said, "After 20 years with the clock stopped, they have returned to us both history and time."

The Boston Globe

Boston, MA, December 13, 1989

The "Velvet Revolution" against communist rule in Czechoslovakia seems too fantastic to be true - too peaceful, too swift, too much a triumph of ethics over force. Within a few weeks, writers and intellectuals who spent years in jail for their defense of human rights have replaced a clique of Stalinist tyrants in their nation's government.

"We must keep our peaceful revolution shining and pure," Vaclav Havel told the throng that had come to the center of Prague Sunday to celebrate the formation of a Cabinet without communist domination. "We must not let anyone throw dirt in the face of our beautiful, peaceful revolution. Truth and love and joy will win. Disbelief and hate will lose."

Other political leaders in other countries might be jeered for such a sugary discourse. But Havel and the Czech revolutionaries have earned the right to abjure the irony that they have long used as a defense against tyranny.

Their temperate uprising is an exception to the rule that might makes right. They have made a virtue of spontaneity, creating overnight a unified mass movement – in a country where there had been no political opposition other than groups monitoring the regime's violations of human rights. The leaders and the people in the streets have displayed a harmony and a discipline that defies all theories of revolution.

In the months and years to come, the velvet revolutionaries of Czechoslovakia will have to tackle hard practical problems. They will have to dismantle the entire apparatus of communist power, not only in the government but also in the secret police, the army, the factories and the media. They will have to surrender their current unity by forming political parties suited to a pluralistic future.

But for now, they deserve their moment of exultation. They are celebrating their liberation, the end of a long, unjust imprisonment. They have made a unique revolution.

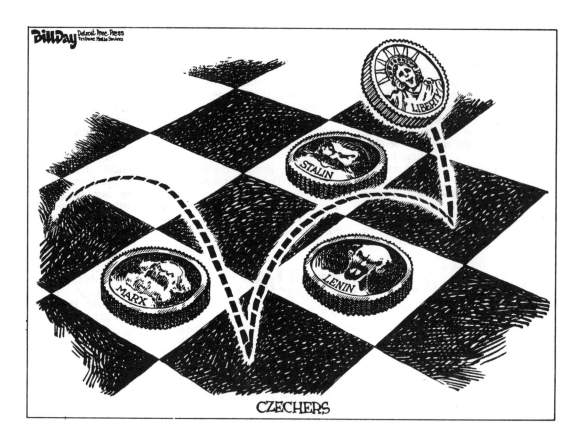

BillDay Detroit Free Press Tribune Media Services

LIBERTY

STALIN

MARX

LENIN

CZECHERS

The San Diego Union

San Diego, CA, December 8, 1989

The democratic shock waves reverberating throughout Eastern Europe have already dislocated communist governments in Hungary, Poland and East Germany. Now they are about to knock from power Czechoslovakia's Marxist rulers.

Exhausted by his inability to bridge the gap between party stalwarts and pro-democracy reformers, communist Prime Minister Ladislav Adamec resigned yesterday. President Gustav Husak, who is being pressured to resign no later than Sunday, has asked Deputy Prime Minister Marian Calfa to form a new government that can deal with the country's worsening political crisis.

Given the failure of the reform-minded Mr. Adamec to resolve the crisis, nothing short of a non-communist government will satisfy the millions of Czechs who have flooded Wenceslas Square in recent weeks.

In 1968, Czechoslovakia had a fleeting taste of freedom under

the progressive leadership of Alexander Dubcek. But his daring experiment in "socialism with a human face," which had seemed so promising, was brutally crushed by Warsaw Pact tanks. In the aftermath, Mr. Dubcek and thousands of reformers were expelled from the Communist Party and imprisoned or forced

---

... nothing short of a non-communist government will satisfy the millions of Czechs ...

---

into exile. In Mr. Dubcek's place, Moscow installed the widely despised President Husak, whose days in power are now dwindling swiftly.

Many of the same individuals arrested during the 1968 invasion are major voices in Civic Forum, the populist movement that is demanding an end to communist domination of Czech-

oslovakia. Having forced mass resignations from the ruling politburo two weeks ago, Civic Forum is now calling for the prosecution and punishment of the politicians responsible for the beating of students who demonstrated in behalf of democratic reforms. The movement also wants free elections by July 1990, the creation of free trade unions and reforms of parliament and local governments.

The embattled Czech Communist Party cannot count on another rescue mission from its East bloc allies. Earlier this week, the Soviet Union, East Germany, Poland, Hungary and

Bulgaria — the countries that mounted the invasion two decades ago — signed a joint declaration condemning the military intervention. The crushing of the Prague Spring had already been denounced by the Warsaw Pact members that did not take part — Rumania and, of course, Czechoslovakia.

If the communist government in Prague collapses, as expected, much remains to be done before Czechoslovakia makes the leap to democracy. For starters, someone of national stature has to take charge and oversee the dismantling of one-party rule and the transition to a pluralistic political system. Alexander Dubcek is a logical choice at this juncture, given his credibility with the democratic movement. Moscow already has said it would accept Mr. Dubcek's appointment as president, but he has not indicated whether he would accept the post.

During its tumultuous 70-year modern history, Czechoslovakia has been given to Hitler by Great Britain and France, raped by Stalin and brutalized by Brezhnev. Yet the country has never abandoned its democratic aspirations. If this long-repressed nation can restore its freedom, there is hope for the endurance of democratic reforms throughout Eastern Europe.

Roanoke Times & World-News

Roanoke, VA, December 14, 1989

WINTER is usually a gloomy time in Czechoslovakia, but spring can be glorious. This year, spring came to Prague in December. The democratic world joins millions of Czechs and Slovaks in hoping that this time, the political spring has come to stay. The Czechs have wrought a peaceful revolution and, for the first time since 1947, have installed a government that is not controlled by communists.

For Czechoslovakia, it has been a long, long winter. After centuries of foreign domination, the country achieved nationhood after World War I, only to see it snuffed out in 1938. There was a brief revival of democratic Czechoslovakia after World War II, but the freedom quickly sank beneath the surface of Stalin-style communism.

In 1968, Prime Minister Alexander Dubcek attempted to implement "communism with a human face." Dubcek's program called for guaranteed freedom of religion, speech, press, assembly and travel. He proposed to make the government, not the Communist Party, the last word in federal authority. He wanted independent courts. He wanted secret-ballot elections in which voters would have a choice of candidates. And he wanted to reach out for friendly relations with the West as well as the East.

This was anathema to the rulers of the Kremlin, whose leader then was Leonid Brezhnev. They sent Warsaw Pact tanks rolling into Czechoslovakia. Dubcek was drummed out of office and out of party influence. Czechoslovakia became one of the more repressive regimes in the Soviet bloc.

The Czech revolution appears to be part of the crumbling of communism in eastern and central Europe. If the country can stabilize as a democracy, it will at last have time to consolidate its nationhood.

Situated in Europe's heartland, Czechoslovakia existed for centuries mostly as provinces within larger empires. The Austrian Hapsburgs became the rulers during the 16th century. Only after World War I did the Czechs and Slovaks form a democratic federation, lead by Tomas Masaryk. It lasted until 1938, when the infamous Munich agreement gave Adolf Hitler the go-ahead to dismember the country. After the war, Eduard Benes, a Masaryk colleague, made another attempt at democracy. This time, the villain was Stalin, not Hitler. Although the communists never got more than 38 percent of the popular vote in Czechoslovakia, they were able to get into a coalition government and seize ultimate control.

It's a little ironic that the communists now are having to accept a junior role in a coalition government. The irony will be complete if the Czechs and Slovaks are finally able to eliminate them entirely as a meaningful political force.

If that happens, Czechoslovakia has a chance to become one of Europe's most prosperous countries. It has a resourceful people, well-developed industry, good farmland and deposits of iron, coal and uranium. It has been held back by communism. May it grow and prosper as a democracy.

The Wichita Eagle-Beacon

Wichita, KS, December 12, 1989

There was no general strike to paralyze Czechoslovakia Monday. Leaders of the democracy movement had planned one, but there was no need to protest. Instead, church bells rang in celebration of a peaceful revolution.

The Czechs' determined march toward freedom has paid off. For the first time in more than 40 years, Czechoslovakia is led by a government dominated by non-communists.

The joyful mood in Prague Monday came just a week after thousands of angry protestors chanted "They must go!" and "They lied to us again!" following a cynical and devious move by the government. The ruling communists and the opposition group Civic Forum had made what seemed like a democratic deal: The Communist Party would share power and a coalition government would be formed. The totalitarian rulers reneged; the "coalition" was heavily communist, with the party in charge of all key positions.

Still, the Czechoslovakian dissidents might have settled for that. They had broken the communists' monopoly on power and had won the promise of free elections next year.

They did not stop there. The taste of democracy was heady, the pressure for freedom intense. Also, many must have wondered just how free the elections would be with the Communist Party still solidly in control. The protestors ignored the party's pleas that "these things take time" and went back to the streets.

Now the victory of the democracy movement is virtually complete. President Gustav Husak, the man who led more than two decades of repression, is out. He'll probably be replaced by Civic Forum leader Vaclav Havel. Not only do Civic Forum and its allies hold a majority in the new cabinet, they also control the powerful ministries in charge of economics, labor, social welfare and foreign policy, and the police. The road to free elections appears to be free.

As the Czechoslovakian army pulls down the barbed wire fence along the border with Austria, even more pressure builds for freedom in Eastern Europe.

In Bulgaria, protestors push for swifter democratic change, demanding that the communist rulers give up their constitutional monopoly on power.

In Yugoslavia, the leaders of the second largest state, Croatia, also call for an end to the one-party communist rule. They want a multiparty system.

The leaders of the protests in Bulgaria and Yugoslavia can only be heartened by the fierce determination of the Czechoslovakian people. They can win their freedom, too, if they follow the inspiring example set by the Czechs.

The Houston Post

Houston, TX, December 13, 1989

THE DOMINO THEORY was never supposed to be like this. Now Czechoslovakia is slipping its bonds of communism, and doing so with a lot more than lip service. Tuesday, 15 hard-line Communist-dominated Parliament members — including former party chief Milos Jakes — resigned.

There is serious talk of replacing resigned President Gustav Husak, at least temporarily, with opposition leader Vaclav Havel. Havel, an often-jailed playwright who leads the Civic Forum opposition group, could theoretically be chosen by Parliament. Under the constitution, it has until Dec. 23 to elect a president.

But just as war is too important to be left to generals, many Czechoslovakians think choosing the next president is too important for politicians. There is great pressure for a popular election, and that is what Parliament is now seeking to decide. (It would take a constitutional amendment, and so far there have not been enough votes for that.) Ironically, Civic Forum itself favors having Parliament name a president, saying a referendum at this time might be too divisive.

Whoever decides, those voting would do well to choose Havel — or, as a dark horse, Alexander Dubcek, ousted in 1968 as the leader of the "Prague Spring" reforms. The mood in Czechoslovakia has not been in a more delicate balance in modern memory, and those two popular heroes probably are the only candidates who could satisfy a populace still giddy with newfound freedoms.

It is impossible to overestimate the importance of these changes. Czechoslovakia, unlike any other Soviet satellite, did not quite have communism rammed down its throat — there was an upswelling of sentiment for that system after World War II. In 1946, voters gave the Communist Party 38 percent of the total — the largest single bloc of parliamentary seats. In the end, a 1948 nonviolent coup put the country firmly in the East Bloc, but substantial support did exist. What emerged, however, was one of the fiercest Stalinist regimes of all.

What all of that means is this: Today, the only East Bloc nation outside the U.S.S.R. that even came close to *wanting* communism is saying in unmistakable terms that it is time for freedom to flower. It's hard to imagine a more convincing repudiation than that.

Hungarian Constitution Amended; Free Elections Seen 1990

The Hungarian National Assembly (parliament) Oct. 18, 1989 amended the nation's 1949 constitution to pave the way for multiparty free elections in 1990. In all, 94 changes were made in the charter.

The amended constitution was to remain in effect only the 1990 election. When the new National Assembly was seated, a new constitution was to be drafted.

Parliament translated into law an accord reached by the regime and opposition groups Sept. 19. The amendments also took into account the transformation of the ruling Socialist Workers' (Communist) Party into the social democratic Hungarian Socialist Party.

In a series of votes in the nationally televised parliamentary session, the deputies:

■ Ended the ruling party's monopoly on political power and eliminated all references in the constitution to the "leading role" of the Communist party. The amendment read: "No social organization, state organ or citizen can endeavor to seize or exercise power by force, or to possess power exclusively...No party can direct any organs of the state."

■ Provided for multiparty democracy. The amendment read: "Political parties may be freely established and may freely function."

■ Renamed the country the Republic of Hungary. The Marxist appellation "People's Republic," used since 1949, was dropped.

■ Codified civil liberties and human rights.

■ Separated the governmental functions of the executive, legislature and judicial branches.

In addition, the deputies abolished the Presidential Council, the collective state leadership, and created a single office of president with strong executive powers. President Bruno F. Straub, the chairman of the Presidential Council, stepped down. National Assembly Speaker Matyas Szuros was to be the interim president until a new head of state was elected.

Under the Sept. 19 accord, a direct presidential election was to be held in Hungary on Nov. 29. But two opposition groups that had refused to sign the agreement – the alliance of Free Democrats and the Association of Young Democrats – objected to that arrangement and were circulating petitions nationwide to have a president elected by parliament following the 1990 free elections.

The dissidents feared that the Socialist Party candidate, who was yet to be chosen, would have an organizational advantage over presidential candidates from Hungary's new political parties.

The National Assembly Oct. 18 also began debate on legislation governing the operation and finances of political parties.

Hungary marked the 33rd anniversary of the start of the 1956 uprising Oct. 23 with an official "day of national reconcilliation" at which acting President Szuros proclaimed a free republic. It was the first time that the anniversary was commemorated openly in Hungary.

The Boston Globe
Boston, MA, October 21, 1989

They said it could never happen. For the better part of a century, orthodox Leninists and Cold War conservatives believed that no communist party would ever cede its power voluntarily. Yet that is precisely what has happened in Hungary, where 80 percent of the delegates to a Communist Party congress voted their party out of existence and replaced it with a Socialist Party founded on the pluralistic principles of West European social democracy.

The implications for East-West relations are profound. The dissolution of the Hungarian Communist Party – and its successor's renunciation of such Leninist doctrines as democratic centralism and proletarian internationalism – could not have happened without approval from the Kremlin.

Mikhail Gorbachev's prompt and cordial message congratulating Rezso Nyers, the president of Hungary's new Socialist Party, was proof that he means what he says about democratic changes in the Soviet bloc. The transmutation he has tolerated in Budapest cannot be dismissed as a tactical maneuver or a face lift. The Hungarian comrades did not merely democratize the inner workings of a renamed Communist Party. They chose to become an accountable parliamentary party in a democratic polity.

In Hungary, Gorbachev has accepted the principle of political pluralism – with all its implications. It is virtually certain that next June's parliamentary elections will usher in a post-communist era in Hungary.

Not only have Hungarian communists had to yield their monopoly; they also are leaving it to the voters to decide whether the communists can retain even a share of their former power. Despite their new role as democratic socialists, they may be obliged to function in an opposition party. As members of a democratic opposition, they must prepare to be governed not merely by non-communists but also by anticommunists, who retain terrible memories of the communist era.

The Duluth News-Tribune
Duluth, MN, October 23, 1989

Unless we or our ancestors came from there, most of us likely think of Eastern Europe as several small look-alike countries.

For the past 40 years, that's been true in many ways as dour, unimaginative and dictatorial communist regimes stifled freedom and economic growth in what is really a colorful and fascinating part of the world.

But exciting signs of life have shown up lately — mostly due to the easing of communist domination in some countries and outright moves toward democracy in others.

Nowhere has this excitement been greater than in Hungary, and rulers of that nation took the biggest and best steps toward democracy last week when they shucked off the country's communist designation, renamed the Communist Party and took steps toward free elections.

A sign of the breathtaking speed of this move is that the big dispute was over when elections will be held, with current leaders ironically pushing for an earlier vote.

The nation's parliament amended its 1949 Stalinist-era constitution to provide for basic changes democracy will require. Lawmakers ended the nation's one-party system, created the office of president and provided for free elections by next summer.

Matyas Szueros, acting president until one is elected, said "a legal state is being built in Hungary on the ruins of a dictatorship of sorts."

Demands for such change have been heard, though surreptitiously, in communist countries. But seldom have they come from top leaders and never, to our knowledge, have they come from people not looking over their shoulder toward the sharp claws and teeth of the Russian bear.

Welcome change is coming to the communist bloc — and no one seems willing or able to stand in its way.

The Times-Picayune

New Orleans, LA, October 23, 1989

The trend toward democracy is sweeping so swiftly across eastern Europe that historic events draw almost casual notice. Take the latest developments in Hungary, where Soviet tanks crushed a nascent liberalization movement 30 years ago this month.

In recent months, communism has, in effect, come full circle in Hungary. The Russian Communist Party — Lenin's Bolsheviks — began as a small, radical faction of the only slightly larger Russian Social Democratic Party. In Hungary, the ruling communist party — officially the Hungarian Socialist Workers' Party — recently abolished itself and recreated itself as the Hungarian Socialist Party and adopted a platform comparable to that of today's Social Democratic parties.

Last Wednesday, with television cameras recording it all, the newly formed Hungarian Parliament changed the nation's name from the standard communist "people's republic" to simply the Republic of Hungary. Like other Soviet bloc nations, Hungary had been a "people's republic" since 1949.

Constitutional amendments adopted Wednesday end one-party rule, establish a multiparty democratic system, call for free elections by next summer and create a new office of state president.

Matyas Szueros, the speaker of Parliament who takes over as acting president until one is elected, declared that "a parliamentary democracy and a legal state is being built in Hungary on the ruins of a dictatorship of sorts."

A completely new constitution is to be drawn up and adopted by the new Parliament after the national elections. But officials considered that the 94 amendments just made to the existing constitution were necessary to make the coming elections legal.

The amendments included changes that eliminated all references to the "leading role" of the abolished communist party. "Political parties may be freely established and may freely function," said one key amendment.

The elected president will replace the 21-man collective presidency that had sweeping powers, including acting for Parliament when it was not in session and even overruling parliamentary decisions.

Like the president of the United States, Hungary's elected president will be commander-in-chief of the armed forces. He will be authorized to call national and regional elections and may initiate a referendum.

The new president can also be stripped of his office if he knowingly violates the constitution or other laws.

In a peculiar twist unfamiliar to the American system, the new president cannot be a leader of any political party.

In Poland, communists share an experimental government with members of the Solidarity labor movement and other opposition factions. It might lead to a true democracy, or it might turn back the other way, depending on events, not the least being the progress of the Polish economy.

In Hungary, change toward democratic rule appears to be occurring in one fell swoop, remarkably with hardly a murmur from Moscow. But what Moscow ultimately does may also depend on subsequent events.

Richmond Times-Dispatch

Richmond, VA, October 25, 1989

While East Germany plods stubbornly along, Hungary has virtually rewritten its constitution to allow a return to multiparty democracy. Hungary's Parliament has overwhelmingly approved more than 100 modifications to the 1949 Constitution written after Communists took over the government. Only about 10 percent of the 1949 document remains intact.

The revisions also change the country's official name, from the People's Republic of Hungary to simply the Republic of Hungary. This is more than a mere name change, but instead marks a change in how the government sees itself. Until this week, the government defined itself as a people's republic belonging to all workers and the Communist Party was the primary force. The constitutional changes include an endorsement of "the values of both bourgeois democracy and democratic socialism."

Multiparty elections are expected by mid-1990, after which the Constitution will be completely rewritten. In preparation for the elections, the changes have abolished the old presidential council, whose head is the nominal head of state, and separated the judicial, legislative and executive branches of government along traditional Western lines.

The apparent change in the government's attitude toward heeding its citizenry's wishes was evident in this week's widespread celebrations of the 1956 uprising, in which 20,000 Hungarians were killed when Soviet tanks rolled in to crush the rebellion. As recently as last year, the government moved to break up such commemorations. This week, not only were commemorations encouraged but the government participated in them. Acting President Matyas Szuros said in front of Parliament, with a portrait of 1956 rebellion leader Imre Nagy behind him, "The Hungarian Republic is going to be an independent, democratic and legal state in which the values of bourgeois democracy and democratic socialism are expressed equally."

Could Hungary, as Austria did in the 1950s, become a neutral democracy in the heart of Eastern Europe? It is possible, but in the euphoria of the moment we must note that the success of Hungary's reform efforts depends largely upon Soviet good will. If Mikhail Gorbachev stands by his promise of non-intervention in Eastern Europe, then there is a chance that Hungary can pull off its revolutionary experiment. However, we shudder to think what could result if the Soviets do not approve.

THE CHRISTIAN SCIENCE MONITOR

Boston, MA, October 26, 1989

WHILE US headlines are still dominated by the aftermath of the San Francisco earthquake, changes currently taking place beneath the political surface in the East bloc will shake those countries far into the future.

Central Europe remains the biggest international story of the year. From Szczecin on the Baltic to Trieste on the Adriatic – to borrow Churchill's phrase – restless East-bloc populations are testing the resilience of the iron curtain, and the mentality that has maintained it for the last 40 years.

Hungary is the most prominent example. This week, on the 33rd anniversary of the bloody (32,000 killed) 1956 Hungarian uprising, 100,000 marched in the streets of Budapest. The Soviet hammer-and-sickle had been ripped from the heart of the Hungarian national flag (as in the '56 uprising). The new "socialist" government (which last week broke from old Stalinist elements) proclaimed Hungary a "republic" – an "independent, democratic, and legal state" as acting head of state Matyas Szuros said – that will recognize both the socialist East and the democratic West.

What's special about Hungary is the amount of stability the system manifests. Unlike East Germany, where 300,000 people marched in Leipzig on Monday, major reforms are being accomplished in Hungary without severe unrest and tension. The Budapest leadership has stayed a step ahead of radical discontent.

Yet Budapest is not out of the woods. Open multiparty elections are scheduled for June. At the current rate of change, that is a long time to wait. To avoid an unhealthy interim power vacuum, perhaps the elections should be moved up.

As in all Eastern Europe, managing the rate of change is the major task. Talk in Hungary of neutrality – of withdrawing from the Warsaw Pact – seems precipitous. It could rally Soviet bloc conservatives and hurt Gorbachev. Democratic change should proceed apace. Economic change is the next hurdle to face. Reformers want to go fast. (As the current saying in Budapest goes, "You can't jump off a precipice twice.") As Hungary continues to be a reform model, the need is to strike a balance that all parties can live with.

The Des Moines Register

Des Moines, IA, October 25, 1989

The Soviet tanks rolled in before dawn on a November morning in 1956, and as Budapest was being pounded into submission the world heard a final radio appeal. "We don't have much time," said the voice breathlessly. "You know what is happening. Help the Hungarian nation, help its workers, its peasants, and its intellectuals. Help! Help! Help!"

Fearing a nuclear confrontation, the West did not help. In a matter of days, Hungary's brave fight for independence from Soviet domination was over. The rule of terror descended again, the freedom of the Hungarian people seemingly crushed forever.

How astonishing it is that a mere 33 years later — a very brief time as history goes — Hungary once again boldly asserts its independence. And this time Moscow smiles benignly.

In 1956, the freedom fighters retained aspects of socialism, with a communist premier and local rule by workers' councils. But the assertion of independence and attempted withdrawal from the Warsaw Pact was too much for the Kremlin. In the terror after arrival of the Soviet tanks, Premier Imre Nagy was hanged and buried face down as a traitor. Tens of thousands of others died branded as counterrevolutionaries.

In 1989, the peaceful revolution makes no pretense of retaining communism. Nagy's remains are reinterred and he's hailed as a patriot. The counterrevolution is now openly called a popular uprising. The Communist Party votes itself out of existence, modeling itself after social democratic parties of the West. The new premier declares adherence to "bourgeois democracy" as well as democratic socialism. On the anniversary of the 1956 uprising, 100,000 Hungarians hear their nation renamed the Republic of Hungary instead of the People's Republic.

It's simply breathtaking. Not long ago, any brave fool even hinting at any of these heresies would have soon felt a secret-police revolver at the base of the brain. The change is so rapid, so apparently complete, it's difficult to grasp.

Is it too good to be true? Hungarians are a stubbornly independent people whose struggles for freedom have been marked by tragedy, against the Hapsburgs in 1848, against the Soviets in 1956. Theirs is a small, landlocked nation whose freedom rests on the willingness of others to permit it.

Gyula Obersovszky, an editor whose death sentence after the 1956 uprising was commuted, reminded the crowd at the anniversary rally this week that Hungary's future depends on the still-incomplete reformation within the Soviet Union itself. As he put it: "Our freedom is an illusion until Moscow becomes free."

The Record

Hackensack, NJ, October 25, 1989

Forget talk about winds of change in the communist world. What's blowing through Moscow and Budapest, Leipzig and Warsaw, is nothing less than a tornado. Hungary proclaims itself a republic, the Soviet foreign minister says his country violated Soviet law during its nine-year occupation of Afghanistan, hundreds of thousands of East Germans march to demand democratic changes, and a non-communist government rules Poland.

It's impossible to tell how long this upheaval will continue, or how it will end, but the changes are both significant and welcome. They also pose the Bush administration with the challenge of encouraging further reform without provoking an all-too-possible counter-revolution from Moscow.

One of the proudest moments in all the months of change came Monday in Budapest. Tens of thousands of Hungarians packed into a square outside the Parliament buildings to hear acting President Matyas Szuros proclaim Hungary a republic after 41 years of communist rule. The speech had a special significance. From the same balcony exactly 33 years before, Imre Nagy addressed a crowd at the start of a 1956 revolt that ended with Mr. Nagy's execution and the deaths of 20,000 Hungarians at the hands of Russian troops. Although Hungarian leaders caution a go-slow approach on breaking ties with the Soviet Union, it's clear that Hungary is being shaken with the most important move toward freedom and democracy since 1956. "May the republic live long, and may it be happier than its predecessors," said Mr. Szuros. That's a wish in which people around the world can join.

In Moscow, Foreign Minister Eduard Shevardnadze said he understood and respected the emergence of non-communist political parties and movements in Eastern Europe. That in itself would have been extraordinary enough. But he went on to acknowledge that the Soviet Union has violated its own laws and international standards of behavior by sending troops to Afghanistan to prop up a pro-Moscow government. And Mr. Shevardnadze admitted something that the Reagan administration had long argued, that construction of a radar station near Krasnoyarsk in Siberia was a flagrant violation of the Anti-Ballistic Missile Treaty with the United States. Last month, Moscow agreed to scrap the station.

The Soviets may still, of course, crush the popular movements in Eastern Europe as they did in Czechoslovakia in 1968 or in Hungary in 1956, or as the Chinese government did this year in Beijing. Mr. Shevardnadze's admission on Krasnoyarsk gives weight to the Soviet demands that the United States not deploy the anti-missile system known as "Star Wars." But although it's important to be realistic about the changes in the communist world, it's also important not to miss what could be some valuable chances. That's why Secretary of State James Baker was right to say on Monday that new Soviet policies provide the "clearest opportunity to reduce the risk of war since the dawn of the nuclear age." Mr. Baker also said, "It would be folly indeed to miss this opportunity."

The United States can't control events in the communist world, or even predict them. But it can work to advance the kinds of changes Washington has sought for years. A failure to even try would be held against the Bush administration for years to come.

The Chattanooga Times

Chattanooga, TN, October 25, 1989

Hungary's victory was long in coming. It has been 33 years since Soviet tanks crushed the popular uprising that installed, ever so briefly, a democratic government in Budapest. Twenty thousand Hungarians died in that brutal suppression of democracy, but their countrymen's yearning for freedom, for national independence and democratic rights did not die. It lived to fuel dramatic changes in recent months and to enjoy the celebration of triumph this week, when Hungary marked the anniversary of the 1956 uprising by proclaiming itself an independent and democratic republic.

It was an intensely moving moment in history, one that provoked a deep, emotional response among Hungarians themselves and which touched the hearts of freedom-loving people around the globe. It was another thrilling climax in a gripping drama being played out in Eastern Europe. The first act was set in Moscow, with Soviet President Mikhail Gorbachev as leading man.

The Gorbachev reform program created the fertile soil in which the flower of democracy blooms again in Budapest. No wonder jubilant crowds there chanted "Gorby! Gorby!" this week. For in 1989, Moscow's reaction to Hungarian democracy is not ruthless suppression, but a pledge of non-intervention and a statement by the foreign minister that each country in the Warsaw Pact "has the right to absolute freedom of choice."

In Poland, that freedom of choice has broken the Communist Party's stranglehold on power, installing a government led by a veteran of the Solidarity freedom movement. Now in Hungary, the choice for democracy has also been made. And, as in Poland, the pace of change has been swift.

Only a year ago, a Hungarian government that still condemned the 1956 uprising as a counterrevolution ordered police to block a peaceful demonstration marking its anniversary. The government now acknowledges the October revolution as a popular uprising and has formally recognized its leaders as national heroes. In the weeks preceding this year's October anniversary, various actions heralded the profound changes under way in Hungary.

The Communist Party reorganized itself as a socialist party, changing its name and declaring its aspiration to democratic ideals. It was stripped of special privileges by the Hungarian Parliament. And the Parliament rewrote the constitution to incorporate multiparty democracy, legalizing opposition parties in preparation for free and contested parliamentary elections next year.

The emergence in Poland and Hungary of Western-style parliamentary democracies presents the United States with a historic opportunity. These countries have made the first, dramatic steps down a difficult road of political and economic transformation. They need the help of the United States. And, as surely as they represent the triumph of the ideals upon which this nation is founded, they deserve our generosity. Congress has acted wisely in working to enlarge the inadequate package of U.S. assistance offered by President Bush.

Last week, the House approved a three-year, $837.5 million aid program for Poland and Hungary. A Senate committee earlier approved $1.25 billion in assistance for the two countries. So it seems certain that whatever Congress finally authorizes will far exceed the $455.5 million program proposed by the administration, and properly so. The fledgling democracies of Eastern Europe are fragile and in need of nurturing. If we are faithful to our national heritage, we will not pinch pennies now.

LAS VEGAS REVIEW-JOURNAL

Las Vegas, NV, October 20, 1989

Time was when rumblings of democracy in the East bloc inevitably gave rise to the corresponding squeal and roar of Soviet armored divisions come to silence freedom's muse.

Now the big red stars, symbols of communist rule, have been unceremoniously removed from public buildings in Budapest, capital of the once and future democracy of Hungary. The Hungarian communist party last week committed official suicide, voting itself out of existence. This week the Hungarian Parliament radically altered the nation's constitution, paving the way for the transformation of the nation into a multiparty democracy, complete with free elections and guarantees of human and civil rights.

On Wednesday, the People's Republic of Hungary became officially, simply, the Republic of Hungary.

Yet no Soviet tanks appear on the eastern horizon.

Almost exactly 40 years have passed since the communists seized power in Hungary. Unable to win elections in (briefly) democratic postwar Hungary, the communists wrested control by stealth, subversion and force. By 1949, Hungary had become a full-blown Soviet-dominated slave state, complete with purges and executions of opposition political and religious leaders, show trials, a huge secret police force and involuntary collectivization of the peasantry.

After the death of Soviet dictator Joseph Stalin and an easing of oppression, political dissidents became emboldened. In October 1956, massive student demonstrations erupted in Budapest, with calls for a return to democracy and an end to Soviet domination. The Hungarian government, headed by reform-minded Imre Nagy, declared Hungary neutral and announced a withdrawal from the Warsaw Pact and a release of political prisoners.

Soviet armored divisions invaded, crushing the nascent democracy movement in a matter of weeks. More than 160,000 Hungarians fled the country. Ngay was hanged.

Ngay is now honored as a national hero, his body removed earlier this year from its anonymous grave and transferred to a place of honor in the capital. The Soviets raised no objections. Nor have the Soviets lifted a finger to halt Hungary's bold moves toward democracy. Indeed, Soviet leader Mikhail Gorbachev has stated, time and again, that each member of the communist bloc is free to follow its own path. Hungary is taking him at his word.

With the almost miraculous transformation of first Poland and now Hungary, can that most stalwart of communist states, East Germany, be far behind? East Germany finally has rid itself of that doctrinaire old Stalinist, Eric Honecker — creator of that hateful symbol of communist oppression, the Berlin Wall. Honecker's replacement, Egon Krenz, also has a reputation as a hard-liner, but his initial statements — including the promise of a "change of direction" and a break with Honecker's inflexible policies — are encouraging.

The world now knows beyond any doubt that the ignoble communist "experiment" has failed miserably in all respects. The subject states of the Soviet empire are struggling to reconcile themselves to this reality. Hungary and Poland — and perhaps soon the Soviet Union itself — have reached the inescapable conclusion that the only way to fix what ails communism is to trash the whole ugly mess and start over from scratch.

DIARIO LAS AMERICAS

Miami, FL, October 28, 1989

In 1949 the North Atlantic Treaty Organization (NATO) was formed with the Purpose of checking the existing imperialist invasion of the Soviet Union against the countries of the European continent. That invasion practically eliminated the sovereignty of the countries of Central Europe: Bulgaria, Czechoslovakia, East Germany, Hungary, Poland and Roumania, not to mention the Baltic countries.

Afterwards, in 1955, the Kremlin invented the Warsaw Pact with the excuse of the existence of the North Atlantic Treaty Organization. Since then they have been trying to justify this Warsaw Pact as an element to counter what NATO stands for not mentioning, of course, that NATO was a defensive reaction against the aggressions of Soviet imperialism.

The Warsaw Pact is fundamentally of a military and also ideological nature. It was created to defend the Soviet ideology —the communist ideology— as inspirer of the Kremlin's imperialist policy. Therefore, if now Hungary and Poland detach themselves from the political ideology of Soviet imperialism, it is logical that the veracity of those decisions be proved by those states denouncing the Pact which, in practical terms, means leaving it after complying with the requirements established in the corresponding international instrument.

It is senseless that Poland and, above all, Hungary, with a new juridical and political status from the institutional point of view, continue to be committed to militarily support a political philosophy which it has renounced. Normally, therefore, it is to be expected that at any minute now the new Hungarian authorities take the corresponding juridical measures to leave the Warsaw pact within the norms that the Pact probably stipulates with respect to its duration, functioning and adherence.

Logically, Moscow should not be surprised at this decision on the part of Budapest, because the most important and serious has already happened, that is, the absolute and spectacular separation of the Hungarian state from the Marxist-Leninist philosophy, proclaiming a republic with all the characteristics of rejection of communist totalitarianism. The separation from the Warsaw Pact is, simply, a logical consequence of what has happened.

DAILY NEWS

New York, NY, October 25, 1989

It's morning in Hungary. Weather report: sunny and clear. Strong breeze provided not by Nature, but by people — people waving flags and banners, 100,000 strong in the streets of Budapest, marking a marvelous day, the first in the life of the new Republic of Hungary. How much hardship endured on the road to this day! How many martyrs lost. How strong the ideal in the hearts of Hungarians. Let freedom ring!

Ex-officials Challenge Ceausescu in Romania

A group of retired senior officials had sent an open letter to President Nicolae Ceausescu criticizing the Romanian leader's iron rule, it was reported in the West March 13, 1989. The signatories, all Romanian residents, were reported to have all been arrested.

The letter appeared at a time of renewed rumors in Romania that Ceausescu, 71, was in poor health and planned to step down. The president's wife, Elena Ceausescu, seemed to be positioning herself as his successor. (Elena Ceausescu, 70, was a Politburo member and a first deputy premier. Since 1988, she had become increasingly influential in party and government decisions.)

Some Western analysts regarded the letter as the most serious challenge to the president since the 1987 worker riot in the city of Brasov. The letter accused the president of violating international human-rights agreements signed by Romania (including the 1975 Helsinki Final Act), ignoring the constitutional rights of Romanians, mismanaging the economy and alienating Romania's allies.

The signatories were particularly critical of Ceausescu's "systemization" program of destroying rural villages and forcibly relocating peasant families. The group appealed to the president to halt the program.

In a related development, the U.N. Commission on Human Rights March 9, voted, 21-7, to investigate Romania. The resolution had been offered by Western countries and co-sponsored by Hungary. It was believed to be the first time that a Soviet-bloc country had urged the U.S. to investigate an ally for rights violations.

Hungary had told the rights commission that Romania was persecuting ethnic Hungarians and other minorities in Romania through the program of rural resettlement. Hungary said that 20,000 Romanians had sought asylum in Hungary.

The Soviet Union, Bulgaria and East Germany abstained in the U.N. vote.

The leaders of the seven Warsaw Pact nations held their annual summit July 7-8 in Bucharest, the capital of Romania. The meeting came during increased signs of disunity within the Soviet bloc. Hungary, Poland and the Soviet Union were pursuing far-reaching political and economic reforms that their more conservative allies were either slow to adopt or were openly opposing. In addition, relations between Hungary and Romania continued to deteriorate.

Top-level officials of Romania and Hungary held an apparently acrimonious meeting in Bucharest July 8, during the summit. They discussed the rift between their countries over the purported persecution of ethnic Hungarians in Romania.

An estimated 20,000 ethnic Hungarians had fled into Hungary from the long-disputed Transylvania region of Romania. The region had been targeted by Romanian President Ceausescu's "systemization" program.

The Miami Herald

Miami, FL, July 21, 1989

ROMANIA'S government, which has confiscated privately owned typewriters and made it a crime for ordinary citizens to use electric appliances during the winter, now seems intent on obliterating thousands of rural villages and the life that they represent. The villagers would be uprooted and moved to massive gray blocks of flats in industrial centers.

Incredibly, Romania's rulers maintain that this wanton cultural rape is a necessary precondition to attaining modernization. Like many other policies of Romania's president-*cum*-dictator, Nicolae Ceausescu, the proposed extermination of traditional village life reflects a monstrous pattern of irrational despotism.

Most Americans may know about Romania only indirectly: This Eastern European country was the home of a medieval lord whose reputation for bloodthirstiness inspired the legend of Count Dracula. Romanians speak a Romance language that's more akin to French and Spanish than to Central Europe's principal languages.

Shortly after Stalin's death, when East Germans, Poles, and Hungarians were protesting their governments' policies, Romanians were effectively silenced by a repressive apparatus that has murdered exiled opponents in the streets of Europe. In the '60s, Romania praised the worst excesses of Mao's Cultural Revolution. President Ceausescu still aggressively denounces all Marxist "revisionism" while seeking to preserve Stalin's dark legacy of trying to "modernize" the Soviet Union by obliterating much of its rural population.

Mr. Ceausescu's dynastic Stalinism surpasses even North Korea's Kim Il Sung and Cuba's Fidel Castro in its nepotism. His wife acts the queen to his king, and he has anointed his son as his heir. The president has built grand monuments to himself in Bucharest, the capital, and the latest is his plan to destroy thousands of Romanian villages.

Whatever they think of his plan, few Romanians would dare protest lest his police swoop down on them. Their best — indeed their only — ally is worldwide protest, which has caused Mr. Ceausescu's regime to damper talk of razing the villages. Only continued protest can prevent the plan's eventual execution, so let no protest be louder than Washington's.

Omaha World-Herald

Omaha, NE, March 14, 1989

The U.N. Commission on Human Rights recently voted to investigate human rights violations in Romania. One of the nations requesting the investigation was Hungary, Romania's Communist neighbor. The spectacle of one Communist country accusing another of human rights violations symbolizes the dramatic changes that are occurring in Eastern Europe.

While the Soviet Union and some other socialist states move shakily toward a more open system, Romania's dictator, Nicolae Ceausescu, is firmly entrenched in a leadership cult that some people have referred to as Stalinist.

Stalin, like Adolf Hitler and Benito Mussolini, fancied himself a sort of social engineer. He sometimes uprooted masses of people and forced them to start new lives somewhere else, ostensibly for security reasons but often on whim.

Ceausescu, who has built massive heavy industries that now stand idle, has a plan to destroy 7,000 rural villages in his relentless — and mostly unsuccessful — drive to turn Romania into an industrial power. The forced resettlement of the people from those villages is one of the issues that has disturbed Romania's neighbor. Romania also discriminates against ethnic Hungarians, thousands of whom have sought refuge in Hungary in the past year.

Ceausescu's efforts to force Hungarian, Serbian and Saxon minorities into a Romanian cultural pattern go against long-standing principles of human dignity. In his actions, this dictator is bringing more unwanted attention to his police-state methods at a time when he is seriously out of step with his socialist neighbors, to say nothing of more enlightened countries.

It is significant that Hungary's vote was the first in 45 sessions of the U.N. Human Rights Commission in which one Communist nation voted to censure another. It was also the first time that the Soviet Union abstained when a Warsaw bloc ally was accused of such violations. Increasingly, Nicolae Ceausescu stands as a kind of dinosaur — one of the the last of the hard-line Stalinists.

THE INDIANAPOLIS NEWS

Indianapolis, IN, January 26, 1989

While other communist countries are making some moves toward freedom, Romania appears set in its unfortunate totalitarian ways.

Mikhail Gorbachev is opening up the Soviet Union in a number of ways, primarily because the alternative appears to be miserable economic stagnation. Communist China is changing, especially in the direction of free enterprise. So are Eastern European countries, especially Hungary, following the example of the Soviet Union.

But Romanian President Nicolae Ceausescu is standing firm against this tide.

Ceausescu's campaign against any glasnost, or openness, includes an emphasis on building up his own image.

"Ceausescu, Heroism, Romania, Communism," was the message on a billboard spotted by Dutch journalist Peter Bergwerff on a trip into Romania last year.

"No one in the Communist Party puts any real value on such slogans," a Hungarian-Romanian person, Eva, told Bergwerff. "Emperors feel the need to be honored."

Refugees are fleeing from the Romanian oppression, including some who even go the Soviet Union next door.

The major Soviet government newspapers, Pravda and Izvestia, can only be bought on the black market in Romania, for high prices. The Hungarian Communist Party newspaper is confiscated at the Romanian border, for being too subversive with new ideas, Bergwerff reports in Eternity magazine.

"People here are terrified," Eva commented in a visit to a village. "You can't trust anyone here. One misspoken word and it can bring serious consequences."

Economically, Ceausescu is sticking with strictly totalitarian controls, hindering economic development. Small private plots of land, though productive, are being turned over to state ownership.

"The reconstruction of the Romanian villages cannot be seen simply as an administrative measure. It is the expression of a principled political choice made by our party," commented a party official in the state press. "We are seeking to create the new man and this requires a new type of housing in which people undergo a radical change in their way of thinking, behavior, customs and practice."

In the past Romania has sought more favorable trade status with the United States and undoubtedly will be seeking such advantages in the future. Romanian officials need all the help they can get, considering the dismal performance of the economy under rigid centralized policies, in an increasingly competitive world trade environment.

American policy ought to continue to insist on fundamental changes in Romanian policy before agreeing to requests for new trade agreements.

THE INDIANAPOLIS STAR

Indianapolis, IN, April 4, 1989

Don't criticize the government in communist Romania — or else.

That is the obvious message in the case of Mircea Raceanu, who was arrested in Bucharest recently and charged by the General Prosecutor's office with having engaged in "steady, treasonable actions" since 1974 when he was, according to the secret police, recruited to spy for an unidentified country.

The maximum penalty is death. The next-highest penalty is 20 years in prison.

Since Raceanu, who was with the Romanian foreign service, served in Washington during the 1970s and most recently headed the Foreign Ministry's U.S. desk in Bucharest, it is not hard to guess what the "unidentified country" is.

What is really behind this depressing event?

Raceanu's father, Ion, was among the signers of a letter released by senior Communist Party members in January criticizing the Nicolae Ceausescu regime for making a terrible mess of things in Romania.

They attacked Ceausescu's on-going plan to destroy up to 7,000 of the country's 15,000 villages in a resettlement scheme. They criticized his policy of exporting food when Romania is suffering severe shortages.

They asked, "How are you going to improve Romania's external relations when all the leaders of the non-communist nations of Europe refuse to meet with you?"

They condemned the government's policy since the late 1970s of eavesdropping on phone calls and spying on private mail.

The letter, released to the Associated Press and news services in neighboring countries, was also signed by former Politburo members Gheorge Apostal and Alexandru Birladeanu, ex-Foreign Minister Corneliu Manescu, party veteran Constantin Pirvelscu and Silvio Brucan, a former ambassador to the United States.

Shortly after Raceanu's arrest was announced, Radio Bucharest played tapes of what it said were comments of workers in Bucharest plants. One said, "I was stupified after reading the communique in our press. Our socialist government must deal exemplary punishment to such traitors."

What is happening in Romania is one more example of what happens when a country is stuck with a bad government it cannot vote out of power.

The Providence Journal

Providence RI, July 3, 1989

For those keeping a list of the imponderables taking place in the Soviet bloc, add one more: Friday a week ago the Soviet Union criticized Romania for its record on human rights.

Granted, there has long been dissension between the two countries, with Romania regularly deviating from the Soviet course. In the past, with regard to world opinion, this often worked to Romania's advantage: Witness the warm reception the Romanian Olympic team received in Los Angeles in 1984. But world opinion of the Soviet Union has changed a bit since then, and Romania hasn't. Instead, it has increased the repression of its people — a repression which, in light of Soviet efforts toward reform, looks that much more distinct and reprehensible. For we see that it is not simply compliance with outside pressure, but the preferred policy of the home regime.

Knowing Romania's recent past, it is impossible to guess which violation of human rights the Soviets chose to condemn: The destruction of the oldest neighborhoods of Bucharest for the building of President Ceausescu's grand palaces; the proposed bulldozing of over half the country's villages; the arrest and beating of dissidents? The Soviets, speaking at a conference on human rights, actually chose one that has been little publicized in the West: The construction of a barbed-wire fence along the Hungarian border.

This is an interesting piece of news, for it means that while the Hungarians have been dismantling the fence along the western border it shares with Austria, the Romanian government, in its efforts to keep people from fleeing to Hungary, has been building a new one along the eastern border.

Does this mean that Hungary is back in the Western fold? Hardly. The Romanian regime, perhaps in response to the criticism, now appears to be taking down the fence. Nevertheless, these developments give an indication of the enormous differences now existing among the countries of the Eastern bloc. While Hungary and Poland have been at the forefront of reform, East Germany and Czechoslovakia have remained stagnant. And Romania and Bulgaria — which was also criticized at the conference, primarily for the recent expulsion of 50,000 citizens of Turkish origin — have continued, on a large and intolerable scale, the blatant abuse of their citizens' rights.

The Boston Globe

Boston, MA, July 6, 1989

An iron curtain has come down in Eastern Europe. This was not Winston Churchill's epochal distinction between the capitalist democracies of the West and the captive nations of the Soviet bloc. The barbed wire that Romanian guards dismantled last month formed a physical barrier along 450 kilometers of the border between Romania and Hungary.

The retrogressive regime of Nicolae Ceausescu (known as "the communist king") began erecting its own iron curtain a year and a half ago, to bar the flight of thousands of Romanians of Hungarian descent. The refugees were fleeing to Hungary to escape forced assimilation and Ceausescu's megalomaniacal scheme to raze traditional villages and replace them with soulless housing blocks.

These refugees are not the only Romanian peasants to be victimized by the capricious "agro-industrial complexes" that Ceausescu wants to impose. Whether of Romanian or Hungarian stock, all of Ceausescu's subjects suffer from the same impoverishment and repressiveness.

What distinguishes the Magyars in Romania is not merely the ethnic persecution they have experienced, but also the opportunity to flee to a country that was, literally and figuratively, on the other side of Ceausescu's iron curtain.

The barrier symbolized a political schism that is becoming more apparent within the Soviet bloc. Evidence of the schism was on display at a recent human rights conference in Paris; Hungary's delegate castigated Romania for its abuse of human rights, and the Soviet delegate expressed disapproval of Ceausescu's barbed wire.

This unaccustomed criticism from fraternal communist states seemed to embarrass Ceausescu into removing the barrier. Like the regimes in Czechoslovakia and East Germany, he has denounced as "revisionist" the democratic developments in Poland, Hungary and the Soviet Union. When feeling threatened, these old Stalinists revert to the maxim that good fences make good neighbors.

The Evening Gazette

Worcester, MA, March 22, 1989

Not since Pol Pot "resettled" hundreds of thousands of Cambodians during the terror rule of the Khmer Rouge has anybody attempted to perpetrate the kind of massive upheaval that Romania's Nicolae Ceausescu is now forcing upon a large segment of the population of his unfortunate country.

The supreme leader of Romania prefers to be called "The Danube of Thought" or "The Genius of the Carpathians." But most Europeans refer to him as the "Idi Amin of Communism" — and with ample reason. This ruthless dictator, who has turned a once-attractive country into an economic wasteland, must be stopped before he does more irreparable harm.

Ceausescu is the last Communist Party boss in Eastern Europe with the oppressive policies, totalitarian control and personality cult of Stalin. While Romanians go hungry, he has squandered billions on monuments to himself. Human rights are trampled, free expression is forbidden, and fear controls the government. In Romania, even typewriters must be registered with the police.

The aging despot is in the process of razing some 8,000 villages and resettling their people, mostly ethnic Hungarians, into huge "agro-industrial centers." The inhabitants of those villages, many in Transylvania, represent one of the oldest and most colorful cultures in Europe, manifested in beautiful architecture, exquisite folk art and a unique lifestyle that has endured despite much hardship and adversity.

Now Ceausescu is about to accomplish what the armies of the Tartars, Turks, Hapsburgs and Hitler were unable to do in centuries: eradicate ancient ethnic identity and replace historic population enclaves with cement concentration camps. It is a crime of historic proportions.

Many of the uprooted villagers flee to neighboring Hungary, where their plight has found national sympathy. In an unprecedented move, Hungary's government has asked the United Nations for intervention, the first communist state ever to request international sanctions against a "brother" socialist country.

Those picturesque villages are remote from other trouble spots of the world that command immediate attention. But Ceausescu's insane policies must not escape the concern of the global community. It is well within the mandate of the United Nations to step in.

The Birmingham News
Birmingham, AL, January 2, 1989

The world may be toasting Mikhail Gorbachev and his reforms which appear to be opening up the Soviet Union to more liberal ideas, but Gorbachev's glasnost program has not made an inroad into Romania. There Nicolae Ceausescu continues to rule with all the despotism one might expect of a Stalin clone.

Under the guise of a modernization program, Ceausescu plans to raze 7,000 villages. But he disavows his true intent, to remove ethnic Germans and Hungarians from their Transylvanian hamlets in a demented attempt to wash away the last vestiges of Romania's capitalist and religious past.

In a rare interview last week, with reporters for the German newspaper *Die Welt*, Ceausescu insisted that his plan to destroy about 7,000 of Romania's 13,000 villages is aimed at providing more farmland and at modernizing the agricultural industry. He said villagers will be resettled in housing complexes attached to agro-industrial centers.

"Our villages should systematically take on a new appearance," Ceausescu was quoted as saying. "Romanians in the third millennium must belong to a nation with a higher living standard enjoyed by each citizen in equal measure."

We don't believe him for a minute.

Romanian border police under Ceausescu's orders are said to have killed at least 400 Romanians, many of Hungarian or German descent, among the thousands trying to flee his repressive society and emigrate to Yugoslavia. The International Society for Human Rights in Frankfurt calls the Romanian-Yugoslavian border "the bloodiest in Europe."

The human rights group said many refugees not killed by Romanian police have drowned while trying to escape by swimming the Danube, which borders the two countries. And others who succeeded in reaching Yugoslavia were sent back to Romania, unless they somehow managed to contact United Nations authorities in Belgrade.

It should come as no surprise that in the same interview with *Die Welt*, Ceausescu rejected Gorbachev's glasnost as a model for other socialist nations. "There is no model, no stencil, for development in the socialist world," he said. It is clear that Gorbachev will not easily convince this member of the Eastern bloc to follow his lead.

The Atlanta Journal
ᴀɴᴅ
THE ATLANTA CONSTITUTION
Atlanta, GA, June 26, 1989

Any resemblance between the Berlin Wall and the not-yet-completed Great Romanian Fence is purely intentional. The functions of these two monuments to communism's failure are identical: to keep those on the inside from straying outside.

Romania's fence is especially pathetic. President Nicolae Ceausescu's raggedy regime is too resource-poor to erect a proper barrier of stone or concrete, so it has had to settle for a wire fence. Brownouts are such a integral part of Romanian life that he couldn't electrify it if he wanted to.

It's not as if Romania faced upon some glittering Emerald City of a capitalist country luring its inhabitants away from their Marxist-Leninist duties, either. The fence and its attendant ditches will separate Romania from Hungary and Yugoslavia, two communist lands not exactly famous for the abundance of their milk and honey.

Still, refuge in either country looks like heaven to most Romanians compared to the oppressive, impoverished lives they lead under the megalomanical Mr. Ceausescu, whose ludicrous poses as an empire-builder have made him the sick joke of Eastern Europe. His forlorn fence is the punch line.

Romania's Ceausescu Toppled, Executed in Uprising

Romania's president and Communist Party (CP) leader, Nicolae Ceausescu, was executed by a military firing squad Dec. 25, 1989 following a secret tiral. His wife and second in command, Elena, died along with him. They were the most prominent of thousands of casualties in a popular uprising that overthrew the Ceausescu regime Dec. 22.

President Ceausescu, 71, had been the longest-serving leader in Eastern Europe and the last to exercise absolute power. His wife had wielded more power than any other woman in the Soviet bloc.

Unlike the rest of the Soviet bloc, where the Communists rulers in 1989 had reliquished power under relatively peaceful circumstances, the Romanians fought a virtual civil war Dec. 15-31. The conflict featured the fiercest street fighting in Europe since World War II.

By Dec 26, a provisional government, calling itself the National Salvation Front, had assumed control in Romania with the aid of the army and was promising broad democratic reforms.

The revolt against the Ceausescu regime began as a large unsanctioned public demonstration Dec. 15 in Timisoara, a city of 350,000 located in the Transylvania region about 300 miles northwest of Bucharest. Army and Securitate (internal-security) troops, employing tanks and helicopters, moved in the city in force the same day and began clashing with demonstrators. Witnesses said that hundreds, perhaps thousands, of unarmed men, women and children were slain Dec. 17, when the troops fired on demonstrators in central Timisoara.

Anti-Ceausescu feelings erupted in Bucharest Dec. 21, when the president gave what was to be his last speech. Ceausescu was addressing a pro-government noontime rally from a balcony of the Royal Palace when thousands of people, many of them students, began to chant pro-democracy slogans. Romanian television coverage captured a stunned look on Ceausescu's face as his speech – promising more food and fuel for the populace – was drowned by jeers. It was apparently the first time a Ceausescu address had been interrupted by anything other than orchestrated adulation.

A Securitate car crushed two youths when the security forces attempted to break up the crowd. Securitate troops opened fire on the protesters, driving them from Palace Square (where the CP and government buildings were located) to nearby University Square, where up to 30,000 people skirmished with the security forces into the night. As many as 40 people were killed. There were more reports on continued unrest and protests in at least six other Romanian cities the same day. Also, there were reports that army units around the country had refused to join the Securitate forces in attacks on the demonstrators.

Early Dec. 22, as many as 150,000 protestors massed in University Square and began battling Securitate troops, who retreated into Palace Square.

The army, which had many thousands of soldiers in the capital, did not aid the Securitate troops and a short while later actively helped the insurgents drive the security forces out of Palace Square.

Military units parceled out automatic weapons to civilians and joined the rebels in heavy fighting in and around Palace Square. Several hundred people were killed, according to witnesses, but the Securitate forces were eventually dispersed. The Royal Palace (presidential headquarters), the CP Central Committee building, Radio Bucharest and the state television were all in the hands of the insurgents by nightfall. Joyous insurgents ransacked the Royal palace.

In the early evening, Radio Bucharest announced that a coalition of Communist former officials, intellectuals, students, dissidents and senior military officers had formed an interim ruling committee, the Council of National Salvation.

Chicago Tribune

Chicago, IL, December 24, 1989

When the first ripples of the freedom movement that had swept across Eastern Europe broke the surface in Romania, Nicolae Ceausescu, the last of the iron-fisted communist tyrants in the region, unhesitantly turned his guns on the peaceful demonstrators.

Thousands were killed, according to reports, including children arrayed outside the Timisoara cathedral as a shield of innocents to deter machine gunners.

As long-entrenched communist regimes succumbed to pro-democracy movements one after the other in Poland, Hungary, Bulgaria, East Germany and Czechoslovakia, the world watched in wonder at the low level of resistance. The Soviet Union's assurances that it would not intervene, of course, did much to encourage the peaceful if grudging changes accepted by the governments in those countries.

But everyone knew Romania would be different. Ceausescu, who had clung to the reins of power for 24 years and installed most of his family in high places with apparent dynastic designs, had been the maverick of the Soviet bloc for years.

At first, his independent ways and unpredictability made him a favorite of Western leaders. More recently, as Moscow became more agreeable, Ceausescu was viewed in the West as a dangerous eccentric who was increasingly ruling Romania with a Stalinesque paranoia, forcing his nation back to the dark ages of socialism at a time when others in the bloc were moving toward greater freedom.

So it came as no real surprise when he followed the bloody example of the aging Chinese leaders who ruthlessly crushed the student democracy movement in the Tiananmen Square massacre. What was surprising was the bold resistance provoked across Romania by Ceausescu's brutal attempts to snuff out the protests.

Unlike the docile reaction in China, where a billion people allowed the army's brutal reprisals against the peaceful students to go virtually unchallenged, the outraged spontaneous response among Romania's 23 million citizens produced an uprising across the country that within a week drove out Ceausescu.

In fairness to the Chinese democracy movement, of course, which had demonstrated some real fearlessness in the weeks leading up to the crackdown, Deng Xiaoping and his frightened communist oligarchs had control of the army and proved it by the way the massacre was carried out.

In Romania, much of the army joined the anti-Ceausescu forces to help rout the dictator. Actually, Ceausescu distrusted the military, especially after a reported coup attempt in 1984 that led to the execution of several generals. For that reason, he had kept the army weak and built up the secret police and other security forces until they greatly outnumbered the troops. Those apparently made up most of the forces that stood by him at the end.

All in all, there was a sense of *déjà vu* about the uprising. The turbulent sense of unplanned events spinning out of control to almost unimagined consequences evoked nothing so much as the stormy days of the Russian Revolution in 1917. Even the Ceausescu family's flight, with the frequent contradictory reports of its members' fate, conjured up shades of the hunted Romanoffs, the last of the Czarist regimes.

But through the turmoil, the unmatched courage of a people driven by a desperate craving for freedom was a bright and shining ornament. It should be treasured in this season, as the world prays for peace.

The Times-Picayune

New Orleans, LA, December 28, 1989

One of the most telling and uplifting reports to come out of the bloody Romanian revolution that toppled hardline dictator Nicolae Ceausescu was the news that Christmas dominated Bucharest and, for the first time in decades, the churches were filled to overflowing.

The heartening observation signaled the birth of a new order — one with a human face — as the old repressive order died a violent death.

Mr. Ceausescu, 71, and his wife, Elena, 72, were executed after a secret trial that found them guilty of "grave crimes" against Romania. The United States established diplomatic relations with the provisional government, but rightly expressed regret that Mr. Ceausescu had not been tried in public.

Many other nations were also quick to extend diplomatic recognition to the transitional ruling group led by the National Salvation Committee coalition, and there was an outpouring of support in the form of prayers, food and medical aid from around the world.

The popular uprising in Romania, unlike those of her sister nations in Eastern Europe's communist bloc, was accompanied by much bloodshed. But Mr. Ceausescu, who ruled Romania for 24 years, was a hardcase even by communist standards and refused to bow to the inevitable. His police state was a throwback to Stalinism in its ruthless suppression of dissent.

The pent-up bitterness of the people against Mr. Ceausescu, whose last-gasp effort to retain power resulted in the deaths of thousands, was summed up by a radio announcer speaking for the National Salvation Committee, who said, "The anti-Christ died on Christmas Day."

Winking at Mr. Ceausescu's tyrannical rule, the United States and other Western powers originally cultivated his relatively independent foreign policy stand within the Soviet-led Warsaw Pact. Two U.S. presidents visited Bucharest, Richard Nixon in 1969 and Gerald Ford in 1975, and President Carter held a state dinner for him in Washington in 1978.

In later years, the Romanian leader grew more dogmatic and more isolated, rejecting reforms adopted by other bloc allies such as Poland and Hungary. Earlier this year, he urged his Warsaw Pact allies to invade Poland and prevent a Solidarity-led government from taking power. He knew the Soviet army would not intervene.

Mr. Ceausescu opposed the changes in Eastern Europe and accused other Warsaw Pact countries of abandoning orthodox communism.

He invested billions of dollars in a crash industrialization program and rigidly followed a policy of domestic austerity to pay off Romania's $11 billion foreign debt. Once known as the breadbasket of the Balkans, Romania became one of Europe's poorest countries.

While Mr. Ceausescu and his family enjoyed lives of luxury, hardships became more severe for the Romanian people in the 1980s. In the end, not even the dreaded secret police or the army could keep them down.

The heroic Romanian people are going to need a lot of outside help to regain some semblance of stability while building a new government. The new freedom they purchased with their blood is a very fragile commodity whose future is uncertain.

When the dust settles in Romania and the other emerging Eastern European countries, and their revolutions give way to representative governments, their greatest need will be financial aid on the scale of the Marshall Plan that was the instrument of rebuilding Europe from the ashes of World War II.

But this time, the United States can't go it alone. The effort will require a commitment of concerted action by the world's wealthiest nations.

The Marshall Plan worked a miracle once. There's no reason to believe that a similar investment of money and talent wouldn't achieve the same result again.

The Globe and Mail

Toronto, Ont., December 27, 1989

Horror, terror, catharsis: it has taken a bloody week to bring Romania to its prospect of freedom and release. The wrenching reports of mass executions were followed, immediately it seemed, by news of the turning point of the revolution — the decision by the country's army to side with the people against the forces of Nicolae Ceausescu. Even as Romanians rejoiced to learn of the dictator's overthrow, members of his feared security network, the Securitate, fought on.

Some of them are still fighting, with advanced weapons. Yet there has been time and calm enough to discover more concretely the horrors of the Ceausescu period — to count the dead, to examine the mass graves, to confirm what had previously been rumors about the luxuries enjoyed by the dictator and those around him.

What now? In a country where the leader's spies have for years been everywhere, Romanians have some difficulty knowing whom to trust. Restoring a nation terrorized and gutted by Ceausescu and his supporters will not be easy for the provisional government, though the National Salvation Front has set the tone by promising free elections.

The immediate challenge is to avert a bloodbath of reprisal and to afford captured members of the Securitate due process. Some of the victims of the Ceausescu period will almost certainly seek vengeance against those who pillaged their country and massacred their relatives and friends. The innocent as well as the guilty may suffer unless the new system is prepared to mete out justice in more than token form.

The secret trial and quick execution of Nicolae Ceausescu and his wife should not set the standard, if the country is truly to put the horror behind it. Romania has seen too much secrecy, too much bloodshed, too much terror. It is time, with the help of its neighbors and nations around the world, to rebuild on more solid foundations.

The Oregonian

Portland, OR, December 23, 1989

Scratch another dictator, Nicolae Ceausescu, toppled from power in Romania Friday by the amazing popular earthquake that has broken the rigid old communist regimes all through Eastern Europe.

Until now Europe's Revolution of 1989 had been free of major bloodshed, but in Romania it began this week. Troops and police fired on demonstrators in several Romanian cities, and after Ceausescu fled there has been more fighting among elements of the police and army.

He leaves behind a country whose preparation for popular self-government is very much in doubt.

Romania's case is different from that of the other Eastern European countries where rapid changes have been taking place. Romania was a monarchy through World War II. Soon after the war ended the Soviet Union installed a communist system there, just as it did in Poland, Hungary, East Germany, Czechoslovakia and Bulgaria. But while until recently the regimes in those other countries have cooperated with the Soviet Union in military and economic matters, Romania has been a maverick. Historically anti-Russian, Romania expelled Soviet troops in 1959 and has been pursuing an independent course since then.

In Romania the government has not been a collective Communist Party apparatus but the highly personal dictatorship of the president, Ceausescu. He has indulged in absurd self-glorification, while imposing severe shortages of food and fuel on the Romanian people.

Adding to those grievances were the ethnic tensions that result from Romania's historically having been one of Europe's great crossroads of migrations and invasions. Romania's name and Latin-based language are leftovers from its once having been part of the Roman Empire. In the western province of Transylvania, 1.5 million ethnic Hungarians have protested that Ceausescu's programs have suppressed their culture and even their villages.

While Hungary resents the loss of Transylvania, Romania has ethnic ties across its eastern border with the people of Moldavia, which the Soviet Union absorbed in 1940 and where stirrings of independence recently have been seen.

In short, Romania is part of Europe's unfinished business. Its people deserve congratulations on their success in ridding themselves of Ceausescu, and support in replacing him with a democratic system — in a place where there is no recent tradition of it.

DAILY ■ NEWS

New York, NY, December 23, 1989

THE SURPRISES OF 1989 are continuing right down to the wire. In the absence of Soviet support, one puppet dictatorship after another has collapsed of its own weight. Now it's Romania's turn. Nicolae Ceausescu, president of Romania and one of the two last tough-guy Communist dictators left standing in Eastern Europe, has been thrown out of office. Bodily. He tried to suppress a massive wave of people power by the Romanian people. His security forces shot hundreds of protesters. It didn't work.

The situation in Romania is far different from what happened in Poland, East Germany, Czechoslovakia, Hungary and Bulgaria. This time, blood is being shed. Ceausescu and his thugs have refused to go without a fight — a brutal, savage one. It's not clear that democracy awaits. Still, the Romanian revolution makes it even clearer that Marxism's time is done.

Leaders of virtually all of Western Europe and the Bush administration were admirably quick to pledge strong support and assistance. The White House conditioned aid: It will come if Romania "moves along a path of general democratic reform."

Romania will need it. Indeed, hard times are just around the corner for all of Eastern Europe. For now, though, lift a glass to the latest country that decided it was past time to burst the shackles of tyranny.

The Morning News

Wilmington, DE, December 27, 1989

Few are shedding tears over the death by firing squad of Nicolae Ceausescu and his wife Elena.

The Ceausescus had ruled ruthlessly over their fellow countrymen for almost a quarter of a century. During that time, they had never hesitated to apply brutal force against anyone who stood in their way. The slaughter of innocent children in Timisoara earlier this month was just one recent example of the dictator's lack of respect for human life.

And as the rebellion against the Ceausescu regime grew last week, the dictator did not hesitate to call out his goon squads in response.

So it is understandable that the National Salvation Front government, which had toppled Ceausescu, was anxious to capture him and his entourage. It is also understandable that once they had the dictator in their hands, they wanted to punish him.

But why rush into a secret military trial, quickly find the accused guilty and immediately execute the dictator and his wife, who was deputy prime minister?

Would it not have been a lot wiser to hold a public trial, similar perhaps to the Nuremberg trials after World War II? No doubt, the outcome would have been the same, that is, conviction for causing the deaths of 60,000 Romanians, for packing away $1 billion in foreign banks and for ruining Romania's economy with grandiose schemes to support the Ceausescu dynasty.

Think for a moment about the global uproar if Ceausescu and his cohorts had gained the upper hand in last week's revolt and had, after a secret trial, executed the leaders of the revolt. World condemnation would have been immediate and strong. The swift justice carried out by the victors was swift indeed but hardly done in the true spirit of justice.

An open trial would have given an aura of fairness to the new Romanian government which is trying to restore peace and order. And it would have made it possible to distinguish from the outset the unacceptable dictatorial methods of Ceausescu from those of his successors who are promising a just society to their countrymen.

"THAT GOOD-WILL-TO-MEN STUFF IS BOUND TO BLOW OVER"

The Toronto Star

Toronto, Ont., December 23, 1989

The tidal wave of desire for freedom and democracy that has washed away Communist dictators throughout Eastern Europe has claimed its last, most ferocious resister.

President Nicolae Ceausescu, who ruled Romania with an iron fist for 24 years, has been forced from power by a popular uprising. He didn't go gracefully; during the fighting that preceded his downfall, hundreds of demonstrators were killed by the hated security police.

Corneliu Manescu, the former foreign minister who fell out of Ceausescu's favor and now leads a National Salvation Front, took temporary charge during the confused period immediately following the government's overthrow.

The closest Romania has had to a dissident, Manescu is also the former chief of the security forces; he may be too closely identified with the Communist regime to remain in power once the revolutionary dust has settled.

External Affairs Minister Joe Clark, meanwhile, has sensibly backtracked on an earlier decision to recall Canada's ambassador and to impose trade and economic sanctions against Romania. That decision was peculiar anyway as it put little faith in the ability of Romanians to rid themselves of an oppressor.

But with Ambassador Saul Grey staying on in Bucharest, and the other measures suspended, Canada can give Romanians a vote of confidence as they join Poland, Hungary, Czechoslovakia, East Germany and Bulgaria on the road to freedom.

The Star-Ledger

Newark, NJ, December 29, 1989

The terse announcement that Romanian President Nicolae Ceausescu and his wife, Elena, were summarily executed was reflective of the outraged reaction to the rampant violence that marked the terminal throes of this despotic regime.

Unlike the upheavals that ended Marxist regimes in Soviet satellites in Eastern and Central Europe, the Romanian uprising was a lamentably bloody affair. It was marked by mass killing of thousands of protesting, unarmed citizens—including many children—by the army and security forces that had enabled the tyrant to rule with absolute, iron-fisted power for 24 repressive years.

But fortunately, as it turned out, the ruthless Ceausescu reprisals backfired when army elements rebelled and joined the pro-democracy demonstrators in a successful counteraction that forced the dictator to flee in a futile attempt to save his life.

The reactionary Mr. Ceausescu resorted to massive military force that was grimly reminiscent of the massacre of thousands of Chinese dissidents in Tiananmen Square. But in this instance it was to no avail as Romanians spontaneously vented their long-repressed wrath against the social injustice and economic deprivation that were harshly inflicted on them by a long-entrenched, oppressive regime.

Theoretically, Mr. Ceausescu was a disciple of Marx, but he marched to his own doctrinaire, ideological beat. His flinty, authoritarian rule during the years of his regime had given Romanians many reasons to finally rebel.

In 1988, the Ceausescu government ordered the demolition of several thousand villages in a disruptive resettlement plan that was intended to victimize 50,000 ethnic Hungarians.

The moderating social and economic reforms instituted in the Soviet Union by President Mikhail Gorbachev were signs of radically changing times, but in Romania it was clearly evident that Mr. Ceausescu was intransigently committed to the old, hard-line concept of rigid Communist orthodoxy.

For Mr. Ceausescu, the only way was his way; he was not about to change, even in the face of compelling, empirical evidence of radical change in Soviet-dominated Poland, East Germany, Czechoslovakia and even stodgy Bulgaria.

And in a climactic turnaround, he discovered too late that the people had changed—and in the process brought about his overdue, fully deserved downfall—and at long last the possibility of a democratic future.

THE DENVER POST

Denver, CO, December 31, 1989

AS THE ECHO of gunfire fades from the streets of Romania, the country faces the more difficult task of creating a democracy from scratch.

The hastily concocted interim government already has promised to hold elections in April, and has discarded harsh laws restricting internal travel.

But the new leadership has been slow to institute other basic liberties. Tight restrictions remain on out-of-country travel. Freedom of speech and assembly have been claimed by the populace, but the laws have not been changed to make such actions entirely legal.

If Romania is to become truly free, the new government must move quickly to formalize fundamental human freedoms.

Among these liberties are equal and just treatment before the law; freedom of speech, religion and press; the right to assemble peacefully, and the right to form political parties.

These basic rights may require wholesale changes in Romania's constitution and laws. They certainly will require Romanians to accept disagreement and compromise as essential tools for maintaining liberty.

But already, danger signs have appeared.

The students who risked their lives for freedom by fighting Nicolae Ceausescu's supporters in the streets now demand that old-line Communists be barred from the new government. Yet interim President Ion Iliescu is a Communist and an old school chum of Soviet leader Mikhail Gorbachev.

Simply put, the next several months will be a very dangerous time for Romanians.

Revolutions that start with good intentions often turn ugly.

The French revolted to create liberty, fraternity and equality for all citizens. But the country soon deteriorated into the infamous Reign of Terror.

The Russians, too, wanted to rid themselves of an oppressive government — and wound up being brutalized even more by the iron-fisted rule of Joseph Stalin.

Even the Iranians had great hopes for their country when they ran the Shah out of power — only to find themselves subjected to the whims of Khomeini's theocratic dictatorship.

No one expects the Romanians to create an ideal democracy overnight. It may take years for these people to learn the art of self-government.

But the time for Romanians to solidify their commitment to democracy is now.

THE INDIANAPOLIS NEWS

Indianapolis, IN, December 27, 1989

At no small price, Romania has bought a ticket to self-determination, to freedom.

Great numbers of Romanians have given their lives in exchange for bringing down the tyrannical rule of Nicolae Ceausescu and his wife, Elena, who had forced their will on their subjects for 24 years. Hundreds have died in the past week and the bodies of hundreds more have been found in mass graves. Casualties of the 11-day revolution are said to run into the tens of thousands.

With the bitter taste of death came victory as the government of the Ceausescus tumbled and the National Salvation Committee claimed victory and set up a temporary government, promising an election in the spring.

Among the first acts of the new government was the trial and execution of the deposed leaders. They were held responsible for killing some 60,000 persons, abusing state power, destroying public property, undermining the national economy and bilking the country of more than $1 billion.

Romania's break from the death-grip of the hard-handed communist rule does not signal the end of bloodshed. More turmoil is expected in Romania as it now must come to terms with those who have been loyal to Ceausescu.

It is at this juncture that the United States, which has recognized the new Romanian government, should encourage Romania's leaders to set policies that will guard the human rights its people have fought and died to obtain. Instead of stalking and murdering those who have oppressed them, Romanians should seek them out and bring them to trials that are open and public.

Offering technical and polical guidance, the United States should be a force for moderation in Romania — a bridge between a bloody, painful past and a more hopeful, pacific future.

The Hutchinson News

Hutchinson, KS, December 28, 1989

The deaths of Romanian dictator Nicolae Ceausescu and his wife, Elena, at the hands of a firing squad have denied the Romanian people the public trial the Ceausescus justly deserved.

The world will never know the why and the how that resulted in the deaths of 60,000 Romanians.

In its zeal to erase the dictator from the scene, a military tribunal worked swiftly to convict the tyrant whose alleged crimes over the past 24 years of rule make other communist sins look meek by comparison. But history was not served by the quick justice the new Romanian leadership invoked.

After a popular movement toppled such an iron-fisted regime, the world and Romania's new start would have been better served had leaders merely jailed the Ceausescus until order was restored and the killing stopped. Their trial, openly conducted under the light of public scrutiny, would have been a deserved initiation for the new, democratic government Romanians seem to desire.

But Romania was premature in acting so swiftly and so decisively.

New populist governments should be formed in the public spotlight and evolve under intense scrutiny. But history ought not be banished to a dark place as new governments seek the future.

The evolutionary process depends on each step new leaders take; such steps indicate to citizens the direction in which their new government is heading.

Bloodshed is not the most desired start, regardless of what Ceausescu and his wife are thought to have done.

Los Angeles Times

Los Angeles, CA, December 23, 1989

And now Romania.

The sixth and last of the Communist governments of the Warsaw Pact to fall since August, looks to have gone down in flames and gunfire Friday. But just how many hundreds or thousands of Romanians died during the week it took to topple the government was still uncertain long hours after citizens seized the state radio and television network to proclaim themselves free. So was the question of whether Nicolae Ceausescu, dictator for nearly 25 years, and his wife, Elena, got away in a last-minute run for their lives.

Ceausescu loyalists, most likely secret police whose lives would not be worth much under a reform government, launched a counterattack late Friday, but the revolution seemed likely to prevail. Citizens emptied the jails and swarmed free through the streets. Corneliu Manescu, 75, a one-time foreign minister freed of house arrest for publicly denouncing the Romanian dictator, assembled a provisional government that he said would rule until elections could be held.

Reformers took Poland's government from the hands of the Communists without bloodshed when they elected Tadeusz Mazowiecki prime minister Aug. 24. After that, Hungary, Bulgaria, East Germany and Czechoslovakia gradually made their own changes without substantial violence. Only in Romania did the sitting government fight back, ordering troops to fire into masses of demonstrators in an act that not only failed to save the regime but undoubtedly speeded its demise.

Two scenes say much about Eastern Europe and the Soviet Union in flux. In Moscow, Parliament applauded the downfall of Ceausescu and, at Soviet President Mikhail S. Gorbachev's suggestion, adopted a resolution of "decisive support" for the Romanian people. The Associated Press reported that one member of the Soviet Parliament commented after the vote: "We are the only two dictatorships left— [Communist] Albania and the Soviet Union." What the AP called a more conservative member responded: "They are surrounding us from all sides."

In southern Transylvania, a soldier and a civilian each held Ceausescu's captured son, Nicu, by an arm, in a tableau fit for an exit line for communism in all six nations. Someone in the crowd asked the son what he had to say for himself. But the civilian captor answered for him. "Nothing," said the civilian. "The despots have spoken enough."

The Leader Post

Regina, Sask., December 23, 1989

Nicolae Ceausescu was the prototypical NIMBY practitioner. Reforms and revolutions might swirl about him, but he was resolute: "Not in my back yard."

The Romanian leader, once admired for pursuing policies independent of the Kremlin but later increasingly autocratic and tyrannical, returned to the scene of his crimes Wednesday after a convenient absence in Iran. Convenient because he missed the slaughter of possibly thousands of his countrymen.

There have been two ways to deal with reform in Soviet-bloc Europe: join it, or beat it down. Ceausescu's ruffians, obviously of the latter persuasion, decried "fascist, reactionary groups" (Ceausescu's description of them), and unleashed murderous gunfire and tanks upon protesters.

Then, suddenly, in scenes akin to the storming of the Bastille in Paris, or of the Winter Palace in Petrograd, military resolve yesterday appeared to melt into empathy with the masses of people. Oppression became liberation. Ceausescu and his wife Elena, the only other real power in Romania, were caught while trying to flee.

The nation has been kept largely sealed off from the world. This insularity, resembling that of Albania, where demonstrations also were reported this week, kept most Romanians from learning of the democratizing movements sweeping the rest of the Soviet bloc. In some areas, however, citizens could pick up Hungarian and Soviet Moldavian broadcasts, and it was in such locations that domestic unrest welled up.

For the outside world, the picture also has been unclear. A message came through of hunger and cold, but what galvanized the masses may have been pro-reform, ethnic-oriented, or simply anti-Ceausescu sentiment — or a combination of these.

If it is so diffuse, there may follow a period of continuing agony for Romanians. Simply eliminating the Ceausescus does not eradicate his supporters, who were threatening yesterday to blow up the country, or the economic problems. The nation will have to discover a new purpose and a new will to achieve it.

Given what they have lived with, that may not be too difficult.

The Dallas Morning News
Dallas, TX, December 28, 1989

Christmas in Romania will never be the same again. Not only will Romanians be free to celebrate this most holiest of days openly, as they did for the first time in decades on Monday, but they also will celebrate the liberation of their country from the reign of terror inflicted upon them by the deposed dictator Nicolae Ceausescu, who, along with his powerful wife, was executed on Monday.

The revolution that was sparked by the massacre of thousands of anti-government protesters by secret police in Timisora almost two weeks ago forced Mr. Ceausescu to flee from power, relinquishing his 24-year stranglehold on Romania. Once apprehended, the Ceausescus were quickly tried by a secret military tribunal and put to death. A statement on the proceedings by a military officer said it all: "It (the execution) was carried out exactly according to the law — the law that Mr. Ceausescu himself promulgated."

For Romanians, Mr. Ceausescu's death is the death of tyranny. They now can rightly rejoice that Romania will in fact go the way of all the rest of its Communist neighbors. Many countries, including the United States, have correctly hailed this development and moved to recognize the National Salvation Front as the "new legitimate government of Romania."

Western nations would have preferred that a public trial be held even for a ruthless dictator such as Mr. Ceausescu. That would have been right and proper. But, the new government should not judged harshly. By acting quickly and decisively, it hoped to convince well-equipped secret police forces to lay down their arms. Neutralizing these forces will be a significant factor in establishing a stable government and a must for bringing the terror to its absolute conclusion.

The National Salvation Front — a loose coalition of ex-Communist Party officials, intellectuals, students, military officers and the ethnic Hungarian priest whose threatened deportation started the revolution — already has moved to install a new government by naming a head of state. That Ion Iliescu was named as chairman of the 37-member governing council is a promising sign for the country, as he is said to be an old and close friend of Soviet President Mikhail Gorbachev's, whose support could prove positive in coming days. The government has already promised a multiparty system and free elections by April.

For the thousands of Romanians who lost loved ones in the slaughter by government forces, it was not a merry Christmas, but it was a freer Christmas. And that means the prospects for the new year are much brighter than before.

THE SACRAMENTO BEE
Sacramento, CA, December 23, 1989

Given the megalomania of Romanian dictator Nicolae Ceausescu and the brutal security apparatus he built, it seemed inevitable that his regime could be dislodged only through bloody conflict. As the grim news came in from Bucharest yesterday, it was all too clear that that was the direction events had taken. Less clear was whether Ceausescu's apparent overthrow by army units that joined in a popular uprising would withstand a fierce counterattack by secret police forces loyal to the dictator.

The worldwide response has been all but unanimous: Washington and Moscow both cheered the popular revolt, the European Community quickly pledged assistance, and relief agencies immediately dispatched doctors and badly needed medical supplies. Yet the White House's commitment to provide help only after democratic reforms are in place seems picky in the circumstances.

What's so startling about this newest Eastern European popular revolution is how quickly it spread once the regime's brutal response to a public protest in a provincial city last week became widely known. Security police shot down unarmed civilians, including children, then turned their fire on those who tried to help the wounded. By Thursday, when Ceausescu spoke defiantly to a rally in Bucharest, the cheers he apparently expected turned to jeers and calls for his ouster. Characteristically, he ordered more killing.

Within hours, army units turned on the dictator, seizing key facilities; a provisional regime was proclaimed. Ceausescu fled the capital and was later reported to have been captured.

Assuming the army succeeds in repelling pro-Ceausescu security forces, thus preserving the temporary government, Romanians, with no tradition of democracy, will face a difficult task of dismantling a police state and building an effective multiparty political system. At least as daunting are the country's economic problems. Romania is short of nearly everything, including food, medical supplies and energy, thanks to an austerity program so severe that people must go without heat for freezing apartments.

There's also serious friction between Romania and neighboring Hungary over Ceausescu's treatment of some 2 million ethnic Hungarians in Transylvania, an issue that's likely to survive Ceausescu's departure. Transylvania, a part of Romania today, was long part of Hungary. In this and in other ethnic disputes lie the potential for a revival of the nationalist tensions that have beset southeastern Europe for centuries.

For now, however, the world can only cheer the courage of Romanians in routing a dictator whose horrible treatment of his people has few parallels in modern times. Romania is well rid of of such a butcher.

FORT WORTH STAR-TELEGRAM
Fort Worth, TX,
December 27, 1989

Under the circumstances, the Romanian people can be forgiven for the swift justice meted out to their late oppressor, Nicolae Ceausescu, and his partner in repression and corruption, his wife, Elena.

In ordering his security forces and troops to massacre thousands of demonstrators protesting his repressive policies, Ceausescu piled the ultimate outrage upon a mountain of crimes perpetrated against the Romanian people during 24 years of dictatorial rule.

It was understandable, therefore, that there was no mood in Romania to be compassionate toward the Ceausescus after they were captured. Nevertheless, the execution of the Ceausescus was not just a deed dictated by aroused passions.

The primary reason for putting them before the firing squad and showing their bodies on television was to prevent further bloodshed. As long as the Ceausescus remained alive, even if in captivity, they offered some hope to the hated security police that they could regain control of the situation.

Indeed, it has been suggested that the security forces were preparing to attack the place where the Ceausescus were being held to try to free them. The security forces now know that their cause is lost and that they will have to surrender and submit themselves to the justice of the people they terrorized and brutalized for so many years.

Many are reported to be surrendering, and the sniping and blasts in the capital of Bucharest are subsiding. Food and medical supplies are pouring into Romania from neighboring countries and Western nations.

Romania has paid a terrible price for its freedom. As many as 80,000 people are believed to have been killed in more than a week of slaughter of innocent civilians and pitched battles between the army, which supported the people, and Ceausescu's security forces. Nevertheless, the pervasive mood among Romanians was one of exultation during the bloody Christmas holidays.

The Romanian revolt should send a signal to oppressors everywhere, even the tyrants of communist China, that a people who are determined to be free will face death to win their freedom. Although Soviet President Mikhail Gorbachev cannot be categorized as a tyrant, the events in Romania should send a valuable message to Gorbachev about dealing with secessionist movements in the Baltic states and other parts of the Soviet Union.

Bush Proposes Big Cutback of U.S. and Soviet Troops in Europe

U.S. President George Bush Jan. 31, 1990 proposed that the U.S. and Soviet Union reduce their conventional forces in Central Europe to 195,000 troops on each side. The proposal came in his first annual State of the Union address.

The State of the Union speech was considered an unusual forum for the unveiling of an arms-control initiative. A rumor of the proposal had circulated in Washington, but the White House had been able to keep the details mostly secret prior to the address. (Bush aides had made unheralded trips to Western Europe to discuss the plan with key allies.)

Some analysts saw the move as a response by Bush to widespread criticism that he was failing to tailor U.S. defense and arms-control policies to the recent historic changes in the Eastern bloc.

It was the president's second major proposal on reducing European forces. In May 1989, he had offered a complex plan at a summit meeting of the North Atlantic Treaty Organization. That plan was still being debated at the Conventional Forces in Europe (CFE) talks in Vienna.

Bush's newest proposal would also be presented at the CFE talks. It concerned the "central zone" of Europe, which encompassed all of Moscow's Warsaw Pact allies except Bulgaria and Romania, and all of Washington's NATO allies in Europe except Great Britain, Italy, Turkey and Greece.

The president suggested a ceiling of 225,000 on the total number of troops that the U.S. and Soviet Union could deploy in Europe, or 50,000 less than he had proposed in May 1989. Of the 225,000, each side would have no more than 195,000 in the central zone and 30,000 in European allied states outside the central zone.

The U.S. currently had about 300,000 troops in Europe, with about 260,000 in the central zone, mainly in West Germany. In contrast, the U.S.S.R. had an estimated 565,000 troops in Europe, nearly all of them deployed in the central zone. (The Soviets had about 10,000 troops in Bulgaria and none in Romania.)

Therefore, if the Bush plan went ahead, the Kremlin would have to decrease its Central Europe forces by about 195,000 compared with a U.S. reduction of about 65,000. (The figures, offered by Western military experts, were speculative.)

The president's offer was hailed by U.S. congressional leaders. Rep. Les Aspin (D, Wis.), the chairman of the Armed Services Committee of the House of Representatives, Jan. 31 said the plan brought the U.S. negotiating position more in line with "the reality of what is happening in Eastern Europe and what is likely to happen to defense budgets in the United States."

Bush had discussed the proposal by telephone with Soviet President Mikhail S. Gorbachev earlier Jan. 31. Gorbachev was reported to have welcomed the offer.

Gennadi I. Gerasimov, the chief spokesman of the foreign ministry, Feb. 1 called the proposal "a step in the right direction," but complained that Washington seemed to want to keep substantial U.S. forces in Europe "from here to eternity."

Gerasimov added, "We must continue to have as our goal no foreign troops on foreign soil."

THE DAILY OKLAHOMAN

Oklahoma City, OK, February 13, 1990

ENCOURAGING words flow from Moscow regarding Soviet troop reductions.

Kremlin leader Mikhail Gorbachev has accepted President Bush's proposal for each of the superpowers to cut troop levels in Europe lower than agreed to previously. The Soviet leadership already is engaged in troop pullout talks with Czechoslovakia and Hungary and has offered to negotiate a withdrawal from Poland.

Outside of Eastern Europe, however, Soviet military involvement is as aggressive as ever.

Last week the Senate Armed Services Committee heard testimony that the Soviets are "pouring" arms and equipment into Afghanistan at the rate of $250 million a month and that Soviet-made helicopters were delivered to Nicaragua as recently as last month.

Ethiopia's Marxist regime, heavily equipped with Soviet tanks and planes, threw an army of more than 100,000 troops against rebels in a bloody civil war. Another massive Soviet-backed military offensive threatened the defeat of anti-Communist forces in Angola.

Trimming Europe's military strength is important, but the United States also needs to turn up the heat on Gorbachev to help resolve regional conflicts in other parts of the world.

THE TAMPA TRIBUNE

Tampa, FL, February 2, 1990

President George Bush's proposal for further reduction of U.S. and Soviet troops in Central and Eastern Europe in his first State of the Union address Wednesday night got the headlines, but the more important points were to be found between the lines.

The troop withdrawal plan and the spread of democracy that he noted signify the nation's international position is the best in decades.

Yet the situation here at home is less bright than his conversational, upbeat delivery suggested. At least that was implied in his outline of what is needed so all of us may achieve the American dream:

Job creation, day care, environmental cleanup, a stronger economy, more exports, expanded opportunity, more housing, bringing the disabled into the mainstream, major improvement in education, better and less costly health care, winning the drug war, space exploration, more research and development, balancing the budget, and reducing the federal debt — "with no new taxes."

House Speaker Tom Foley, in the Democratic Party's reply, couldn't attack such a program. He could only contend Democrats could do it better.

Reaching Mr. Bush's goals without new taxes *is possible* — and he touched briefly on how: greater individual saving. The nation's pool of capital must be increased, so that industrial and business expansion can be accomplished at reasonable interest rates. With savings financing the private sector's needs, economic growth will increase tax revenues.

Mr. Bush took a cheap shot at Senator Daniel Patrick Moynihan of New York, who proposes cutting Social Security taxes, which especially penalize average workers. According to the President, "The last thing we need to do is mess around with Social Security." (The government has been borrowing from — messing around with — the Social Security Trust Fund for years.) But Moynihan would reform Social Security on impeccable grounds: Surpluses are being used to mask the size of the deficit.

The President mentioned two plans to encourage saving: capital gains tax reduction and a family savings plan. These could help, *if* they provide far more capital than have similar programs in the past. Mr. Bush made no reference to a more certain way to economic expansion: changing tax and security laws and regulations to shift the financing of economic expansion from borrowing (bond sales) to equity (stock sales).

What was also missing, although implied, is the choices we all face. We may elect to abandon the American dream the President outlined, or pursue it. If we choose to pursue it, we must also choose how to pay for it: by saving more — or accepting new taxes.

In closing, President Bush said, "And let us all remember that the State of the Union depends on each and every one of us." It would have helped if he had said specifically that what the State of the Union needs most is that we reduce consumption and transform ourselves into a more responsible, saving society.

St. Petersburg Times

St. Petersburg, FL, May 19, 1989

President Bush has taken an encouraging, albeit modest, step away from his excessively cautious approach toward improved East-West relations. In his State of the Union address Wednesday night, Mr. Bush disclosed that he had proposed that the United States and the Soviet Union cut their troop levels in Europe to 225,000 each.

For the United States, that means U.S. troops would be reduced by 80,000 instead of the 30,000 Mr. Bush had proposed earlier. American ground forces in Europe now total 305,000.

Because the Soviets have so many more troops in Europe, they would have to withdraw 340,000 in order to reduce their forces to the U.S. level, but Soviet President Mikhail Gorbachev ought to find that a welcome prospect. The Eastern European states are putting pressure on the Kremlin to get the Red Army out of their countries; the Bush offer should make it easier to acquiesce to their demands without seeming to do so directly. Second, the Kremlin desperately needs the savings that would come with a major troop withdrawal.

The United States needs to cut its military costs, too, and that was undoubtedly a consideration in Mr. Bush's offer, though the savings would not be felt soon. Beyond that, the new proposal is significant for its evidence that the president is less reluctant to come in out of the Cold War.

That he still has a way to go, however, can be seen in his refusal to modify his proposal for a 50 percent reduction in U.S. and Soviet strategic nuclear missile arsenals, and in his assertion in the State of the Union address that he wants to keep troops in Europe indefinitely. Not only that, Mr. Bush warned in his annual address to Congress against slowing down the strategic arms race. His budget includes almost $12 billion for the Stealth bomber, the MX missile and Star Wars, three programs that ought to be shelved. Thus, it is evident that the new order has not produced as much new thinking in the White House as there ought to be.

Nor, the president's address made clear, can the Bush administration be accused of fresh thinking on most other issues. Like his budget, Mr. Bush's State of the Union address was mostly a continuation of the Reagan philosophy, including tax cuts for the wealthy and spending cuts for the poor. Nevertheless, on several important issues, including education and the environment, Mr. Bush wants to do what's right. The difficulty is that he is not willing to face up to their cost. Until he does, his good intentions will be confined to rhetoric.

Edmonton Journal

Edmonton, Alta., February 2, 1990

Ever the cautious one, U.S. President George Bush has given a cautious — but welcome — push to the current troop reduction talks in Europe. The prospect is good for a substantial cut this year in troops and conventional weapons along the East-West divide.

That divide grows narrower by the day. Bush's proposal to cut the level of American and Soviet troops in Europe to 195,000 would have been a cataclysmic event even a few months ago. In the present context, it is an attempt to catch up to revolutionary times.

The Soviet Union is under pressure from several of its Warsaw Pact allies to remove troops from their soil. The Soviets, with more than 500,000 troops in Europe, are under even more pressure at home to redirect military spending to the domestic economy. In consequence, they now propose the eventual removal of all Soviet and American troops from Central Europe.

There is growing acceptance of the idea of a reunited Germany — perhaps more so in Eastern Europe than in the West, where lip service traditionally was paid to the idea. This week Soviet leader Mikhail Gorbachev stated that reunification was inevitable. The East German Communist party quickly took up the cry, adding its voice to the unity campaign in West Germany. The corollary — or perhaps the starting point — is the removal, presumably gradual, of Soviet and American troops from German soil.

By taking a cautious initiative, Bush has given a measure of support to Gorbachev, who is under pressure at home to show results for his many peace proposals. The general result is to relax tensions. At the same time, Bush reassured his NATO allies by setting a "bottom" level of 195,000 U.S. troops in Europe (275,000 are there now).

On the domestic level, Bush did his own cause some good by making a rare defence-cutting proposal. His commitment to high defence spending in budget proposals earlier this week drew protests that he was pursuing Cold War policies after the Cold War had ended. The Bush budget would cut the massive defence spending by only two per cent, frustrating those who had been looking for a "peace dividend" from the new detente. By proposing to reduce American troops overseas, Bush partly takes the sting out of those criticisms.

The White House remains committed to Ronald Reagan's destabilizing Star Wars-type research programs, to the new B-2 bomber and to new land-based nuclear missiles. Americans might well ask whether former president Dwight Eisenhower was right when he warned of the grip of military industries on the U.S. economy.

But Bush has made one concrete proposal to reduce the level of troops in Europe, adding to the optimism that surrounds the current Vienna talks on conventional forces. The proposal should speed the talks even as it reassures the Americans' nervous allies. For the rest, the world can be thankful for another step taken away from armed confrontation.

THE BLADE

Toledo, OH, February 3, 1990

FOR years the question of just how large a military presence the United States should have on the continent of Europe has remained unanswered and too often undebated. President Bush demonstrated in his State of the Union speech this week that his thinking is not encased in cement on this issue.

Mr. Bush proposed a reduction of 50,000 troops. This would be the largest reduction of U.S. armed forces in Europe since the end of World War II.

That is not to say it has been a useless enterprise. The United States' collective-security agreements with its western European allies brought about an era of peace of unprecedented length in this century. They counterbalanced the Soviet military threat and reassured Europeans who worried, and still worry, about the possible effects of German reunification.

The proposed reductions would reduce U.S. and Soviet forces in central Europe to 195,000 each, although this country also proposes, under Mr. Bush's plan, to maintain some 30,000 additional troops in Britain, Italy, Turkey, or Greece. The Soviet Union also could keep that number of troops outside the central zone of Europe — defined as West Germany, Belgium, the Netherlands, Luxembourg, Denmark, East Germany, Poland, Czechoslovakia, and Hungary.

It is difficult to imagine a more salutary development for all concerned. For the United States and the Soviet Union it would eventually mean cost savings. By one estimate the demobilization of 50,000 American servicemen under the Bush plan would mean yearly savings of $1.8 billion.

The United States now has 350,000 troops in Europe; the Soviet Union is believed to have about 565,000 troops. A land war between the two countries seems unthinkable, and in fact if there is any threat to European security, it might come from the revival of ancient communal or national rivalries or the possibility — at this point it seems a remote one — that a united Germany would succumb once more to the temptations of military expansionism.

The ultimate disposition of U.S. and Soviet forces in Europe may be out of the hands of the two countries. After all, recent events in Europe have assumed a momentum of their own, and a demilitarized Europe and a united Germany — unthinkable as recently as a year ago or even a few months ago — has become thinkable. A unified Germany certainly would not play host to two rival armies.

President Bush's troop-withdrawal initiative, while welcome, is not novel. It is also equivocal in that he also continues to press for development and deployment of costly new weapons. However, he senses the drift of events and is reacting to it. It would not be the first time a leader had to run to get in front of the people he is supposedly leading.

The Oregonian

Portland, OR, February 2, 1990

President Bush reached out and touched a Russian Wednesday, calling Soviet leader Mikhail Gorbachev for a little personal tete-a-telephone on conventional arms cuts.

What a refreshing change. When it came to picking up the phone and giving the other superpower a call, the Cold War had us all thinking hot-line. Now the warming in the Cold War is leading to more civilized if equally direct communications.

Last May Bush had proposed slashing Soviet and U.S. forces to 275,000 persons each. That was encouraging at the time, but since then a few East bloc walls and more East bloc governments have crumbled. As a senior administration official told The Associated Press' Terence Hunt, "Events were running ahead of the negotiations."

Bush has wisely responded to events. He upped (lowered?) the ante Wednesday to 195,000 troops. Further, his use of the telephone seems appropriate, given the recent pace of change in Eastern Europe. The directness is invigorating.

No doubt, the striped-pants set in the State Department and the iron-pants element in the Kremlin sniffed at this breach of standard diplomatic operating procedure. Tut, tut. The whole notion of waiting months to "table" some troop-cut proposal has grown hopelessly quaint. Such proposals might be anachronisms by the evening news.

In superpower diplomacy, the medium may be fast becoming the message.

The Philadelphia Inquirer

Philadelphia, PA, February 5, 1990

Eight months ago, last week's proposal by President Bush to cut U.S. and Soviet troops levels in Europe would have been a bombshell. Today, given the breathtaking speed of change in Europe, initiatives that might once have seemed bold now don't go far enough.

What Mr. Bush requested in his State of the Union address was a ceiling of 225,000 American and Soviet troops in Europe instead of the 275,000 he called for last May. That means bringing 80,000 American men home. (The Soviets would have to recall 345,000 soldiers, which they appear willing to undertake.)

What the President was doing was essentially playing catchup with the pell-mell developments in Europe. New leaders in the Warsaw Pact countries of Czechoslovakia, Hungary and Poland have recently demanded that the Soviets withdraw their troops from those countries, and Moscow seems inclined to oblige. That created a peculiar situation where Mr. Bush's figures might have legitimized more Soviet troops in Europe than the East Europeans or even Moscow wanted. Thus the call for new cuts.

But as the Warsaw Pact continues to crumble, and top American officials dismiss the chance of a surprise Soviet attack in Europe as nearly nil, the time has come to rethink how many American troops are needed, and what they should be doing there.

Such rethinking becomes urgent since events in Europe no longer permit the stately pace of change that seemed likely even in mid-1989. If the administration doesn't think ahead, NATO troop levels may be dictated by crowds in the streets.

To understand the urgency one need only look at events in Germany. East Germany will hold elections on March 18, and voters may well choose candidates who support unification with West Germany. After those elections, the two Germanys plan to begin negotiations on union, even as West Germany's leaders prepare for December elections.

West German voters want unification. But East German leaders and Moscow say the price must be German neutrality, a price rejected by leaders in Bonn. The chance for resolving that impasse depends on whether the West can come up with a new definition of NATO's role and further reduce troops on both sides.

Otherwise, the German drive for unification may be blocked. That could turn West German voters against NATO. So could the likelihood that the hard-pressed Soviets may make more unilateral troop cutbacks in East Europe, leaving NATO looking outmoded. And all the while, the new post-Cold War atmosphere is encouraging other NATO allies to reduce the numbers of their troops.

To turn this climate to everyone's advantage, the administration needs to tune into the European pace of change. The first challenge is to achieve Mr. Bush's proposed troop levels by completing ongoing negotiations on conventional forces in Vienna. The talks are supposed to finish this year, but have bogged down. They need a presidential push.

Then Mr. Bush must make an imaginative leap to design a leaner, more political NATO, which functions less to guard against invasion than to verify that new treaty accords are kept across an undivided Europe. The sooner that design is hatched, the better chance that a new, updated NATO will survive.

THE TORONTO SUN

Toronto, Ont., February 2, 1990

To his credit, U.S. President George Bush has upped the ante in the high-stakes game of troop reduction in Europe. And Soviet President Mikhail Gorbachev is staying in.

On both sides of the Atlantic, this is good news for everyone except the most unregenerate cold-war curmudgeons.

The Bush proposal doesn't mean the withdrawal of all U.S. and Soviet troops from Europe. Each side would still have 195,000 men in Central Europe; the U.S., in addition, would keep 30,000 already deployed in Turkey, Britain and Italy. And because the Soviets now have 565,000 troops in Europe, they would have to make the biggest cuts.

By proposing the reductions Wednesday in his annual State of the Union speech, Bush recognized the changes that have swept Eastern Europe and the Soviet Union. He called it "change so striking that it marks the beginning of a new era in the world's affairs" and transforms "a world whose fundamental features were defined in 1945."

Bush's proposal, and Gorbachev's agreement, should surely accelerate conventional arms-reduction talks in Vienna among NATO and Warsaw Pact members. When agreement is reached, even more troops — including 7,000 Canadians — may be able to go home. Then the world can truly say that the Cold War is over.

The Clarion-Ledger

Jackson, MS, February 2, 1990

Well, knock us over with a feather.

Critics have been calling for President Bush to cut troops overseas more deeply than previously indicated and he does so, offering a plan to cut each superpower's troops to 195,000.

Soviet leader Mikhail Gorbachev is reportedly delighted with the proposal, despite having to cut the most. The Soviet Union now has 565,000 troops in Central Europe, compared to 305,000 U.S. troops.

Deeper military funding cuts could be made, with the freshening of relations between the United States and the Soviet Union. But what Bush proposes is a healthy start.

ALBUQUERQUE JOURNAL

Albuquerque, NM, February 2, 1990

President Bush's proposal that U.S. and Soviet troops in Europe be limited to 195,000 each is a welcome escalation of the president's willingness to match reductions in military capability with reductions in Cold War animosities.

Even more encouraging was the Soviet response from Foreign Ministry spokesman Gennady Gerasimov that Bush's proposal didn't go deep enough.

Bush's troop plan was the biggest surprise in a State of the Union speech that was generally well received. He promised action and advocated programs from the attainable to pie in the sky.

One would hope, for example, that his promise to have American invasion troops out of Panama by the end of the month has a firmer grounding in probability than his glib assurance that his fiscal track will have the federal budget in balance by 1993. He might as sincerely have promised a colony on the moon by the Fourth of July.

But give the president his due. He is on a pinnacle of job performance approval and his State of the Union performance should do little to erode that position. The problem is that popularity points aren't exchangable for economic growth percentage points.

But despite the fluff and hyperbole, clear distinctions between the Bush agenda and that of his predecessor are beginning to emerge. Bush is elevating the Environmental Protection Agency to Cabinet rank, a priority not accorded in the Reagan years. Both Bush and Interior Secretary Manuel Lujan have already gone on record modifying or replacing Reagan-era laissez faire environmental policies.

There is overall a detail and complexity to the Bush approach that makes it better suited for negotiation and compromise with Congress. He didn't win over the other side of the aisle, to be sure — but there was more than a little "us, too" in the Democratic response by House Speaker Tom Foley.

In his first State of the Union address, George Bush has stepped out of the shadow of his predecessor.

Part III:
The People's Republic of China

If the toppling of the Berlin Wall symbolizes communism's retreat in Europe, the image of a lone, anonymous protester blocking a convoy of Chinese Army tanks in the tumult following the crackdown in Beijing's Tiananmen Square in June 1989 stands as a reminder that totalitarianism still looms over the communist world.

For a brief, uncensored moment in the spring of 1989 the pro-democracy demonstrations that erupted across China attracted the attention and sympathy of the entire world, inspiring popular uprisings from East Berlin to Bucharest. The crucial difference being that the rebellions in Eastern Europe brought down one Communist regime after another, while Chinese dissent led only to violent repression. In the months following the demonstrations, the Chinese government exerted absolute control, arresting as many as 30,000 students and workers.

China watchers point out that although the government hard-liners have faced no serious challenge to their rule since Tiananmen Square, they have reversed many of the changes that had been made in the prior five years. In stark contrast to the Soviet Union, China continues to send out a strong message that the old ways must persist. "We will surely be able to grasp the rules of history and win the final victory," China's Communist Party chief Jiang Zemin said in his 1990 New Year's address.

Symbolic calls for change by the Chinese people are not without precedent in recent history. When Mao Zedong, the architect of China's brand of Communism, died and the infamous "Gang of Four" was overthrown in 1976, the people in Beijing called for the leadership of Deng Xiaoping, a man purged twice by Mao during the Cultural Revolution and still in disgrace when Mao died. Deng, an old revolutionary who was labeled a "capitalist roader" by Mao and his followers, remained in the background of Chinese politics as people exhibited small bottles in the streets of Beijing. The bottles became a sign of popular support for Deng because in spoken Chinese, his given name, Xiaoping, means "small bottle."

By 1978 Deng had emerged from disgrace to become vice chairman of the party Central Committee and vice premier of the State Council. Although he never took the position of chairman or general secretary, Deng gradually emerged as China's paramount leader by 1981.

Shortly after his return to power, Deng masterminded what the Western media called the "second revolution." With the support and confidence of the people, Deng began to reform China's economic and political structures of the Maoist period. His reforms included the introduction of a market economy into the rigid state planned economy that had existed in China since the 1950s.

As the chief architect of the reform programs, Deng received immense credit by the end of the 1980s for greatly improving the living standard of the Chinese people as a whole. Although the problems of basic subsistence have been mostly solved since Deng took power, it should be remembered that until recently the major concern of China's rural inhabitants was sheer survival.

The strong-arm reactionary politics

that emerged following Tiananmen Sqaure have accompanied a powerful dose of economic retrenchment. While the once-stolid regimes of Eastern Europe embrace free enterprise, China is returning to the central planning of the 1950s despite Beijing's repeated claims that its reform policies remain unchanged. Instead of entrepreneurship, the official press now advocates "collective farming, collective prosperity." In a massive economic crackdown, China closed more than 2.2 million private enterprises.

In early 1990, a secret 39-point party document detailed plans to abandon the two-track price system that allowed factories to produce some goods for the free market while producing others for the state. An article in the *People's Daily*, the Communist Party newspaper, published soon afterward, took a flat-handed slap at ousted reform-minded party chief Zhao Ziyang by warning that "political regimes that are based on privatized economies breed all forms of corruption."

Making domestic changes has only been somewhat easier for the Deng government than handling foreign relations. China's dealings with the Soviets, cordial enough in 1989 to prompt the first Sino- Soviet summit in 30 years, soured in the post-Tiananmen Square chill. Beijing's criticisms of Gorbachev once again exacerbated tensions between the two Communist superpowers.

Beijing's relations with the United States have been even more complex in the months following the uprisings. Even after U.S. President George Bush dispatched national security adviser Brent Scowcroft in December 1989, some Chinese officials accused the Bush administration of excessive meddling, comparing foreign influence to that preceding the violent Boxer Rebellion of 1900. But China's increasing international isolation has placed it in an uneasy quandry in that it needs U.S. influence to secure loans from the major international lending institutions.

Though there have been signs that the hard-liners may be preparing to make gestures of capitulation, some experts on China suggest that minute policy shifts can't bring about real or lasting stability, domestically or abroad. However, the sentiment that reforms must occur is augmented by frustration and hopelessness left in the wake of Tiananmen Square.

Chinese Workers Join Students as Pro-Democracy Protests Erupt

A series of pro-democracy protests and rallies begun by Chinese students in Beijing April 15, 1989 after the death of former Communist Party leader Hu Yaobang swelled by April 27 into one of the largest popular demonstrations against the government since the Communists had come to power in 1949. The only protests of a similar scale had occurred in April 1976, when an extraordinary series of demonstrations erupted spontaneously in Beijing following the death of Premier Zhou Enlai. What distinguished the latest rallies from other recent demonstrations was not only their size but the fact that the student protesters were supported and joined by tens of thousands of workers.

The outburst of discontent was sparked by Hu's death April 15. Since being forced to resign as Communist Party general secretary in January 1987 for failing to crack down on student unrest, Hu had become something of a hero to Chinese intellectuals and liberal reformers. Within hours of his death, hundreds of students at Beijing University, the country's leading educational institution, began hanging illegal posters across the campus mourning Hu and criticizing other prominent party figures, including China's paramount leader Deng Xiaoping. Many of the posters implied that the wrong leader had died.

The first demonstrations broke out April 16, as more than 1,000 students in the city of Shanghai marched and sang national songs in honor of Hu. Like the posters, the demonstrations were illegal. Similar marches were staged April 17 in Shanghai and Beijing, where 500 students marched into Tiananmen Square, in the heart of the city, to lay wreaths in Hu's honor. The Beijing marchers also chanted slogans such as, "Long live democracy. Long Live Freedom."

The protests continued through April 20 when China's official media issued warnings that the students would be met with force if their protests continued. A statement read on the national evening news program said that "future demonstrators will be dealt with severely according to the law" and new protests would "absolutely not be allowed." A television commentator criticized the students for advocating a "China dominated by chaos." According to Western observers, the warnings marked the first time the protests had been mentioned in the news.

In defiance of the government's warning, more than 100,000 students and supporters filled Tiananmen Square April 21-22 for a pro-democracy rally timed to coincide with an official Communist Party memorial service for Hu. For the first time, students from outside Beijing and large numbers of workers joined the protests. In addition, thousands of Beijing citizens cheered marchers as they moved through the city to the central square.

The demonstrators called for numerous political reforms, including freedom of the press, speech and assembly, increased funding for education, and publication of the income and assets of top party leaders. They also demanded the formal rehabilitation of Hu's reputation.

At the official memorial service, held April 22 in the Great Hall of the People, which bordered Tiananmen Square, Communist Party leader Zhao Ziyang praised Hu as a "brave" leader who had performed "immortal deeds." No mention was made of Hu's ouster from the top party post in 1987.

The first outbreaks of violence stemming from the protests, occurred overnight April 22-23 in the provincial capital cities of Xian and Changsha, the official New China News Agency reported. The agency said a group of "lawbreakers" in Xian went on a rampage after watching a televised broadcast of Hu's memorial service. The rioters attacked the city's government complex, burning 20 buildings and 10 vehicles. About 130 policemen were injured and 18 people were arrested, the news agency said.

Tens of thousands of university students in Beijing April 24 began an indefinite boycott of classes. Western news reports said that the boycott was honored by a majority of students at institutions throughout the capital. In addition, professors and other faculty members at some schools openly supported the students.

THE PLAIN DEALER
Cleveland, OH, April 26, 1989

The funeral for Hu Yaobang is past, but student demonstrations calling for greater democratic reforms are far from over.

Instead, students are girding for a showdown that could determine whether the protests will gain wider support or die, a showdown whose outcome will indicate more than just student influence. The demonstrators have begun this latest effort by planning more organized shows of dissent—including boycotting classes—that they hope will spread from the capital of Beijing to universities across the country.

Chinese officials so far have allowed demonstrations sparked by the April 15 death of Hu Yaobang, whom many considered the champion of democratic reforms before he was forced to resign as the Communist Party's general secretary in 1987. The government has begun cracking down in the last few days, banning, for example, a newspaper that supported the demonstrators. Still, their response has been more tolerant and less violent, a strategy likely aimed at avoiding a repeat of the bloody suppression of 1976 student demonstrations. Officials also must have harbored the quiet hope that, without government fodder, the protests would peter out before May 4, the 70th anniversary of the 1919 student movement.

The current demonstrations show what Communist Party leaders dread to admit: Economic and political reforms are inescapably connected. **The loosening of some economic** restraints that allow more individual freedom in business whets the appetite for greater personal and political liberties. That hunger—or fear of it—played a part in the party's slowing the pace of economic reform.

More importantly, leaders saw the inflation and unemployment that seemed an ever-more-likely product of liberalization's fast pace. And student dissatisfaction is not nearly so threatening to the government as is unrest from frustrated urban workers who would be affected by unemployment and inflation. Worker strikes could weaken the Communist Party leadership and give the student movement the broad support it needs to continue. That realization prompted Prime Minister Li Peng to note the Chinese were "too impatient for quick results."

China also must contend with an external pressure that comes in the form of Mikhail Gorbachev's *glasnost* and *perestroika*. Chinese students have pointed to his country's political and personal reforms, an allusion that may hurt the students' cause more than help it. In a game of Communist chest-beating, the Chinese are unlikely to appear as though they're following Gorbachev's lead after years of mutual hostility by allowing embarrassing protests to occur during next month's Sino-Soviet summit. The government also is unlikely to allow pro-democracy demonstrations to persist much longer without taking actions that could stain Chinese streets with blood.

The Washington Post

Washington, DC, April 21, 1989

TO THE disquiet stirred by the pause in economic reform in China has now been added a burst of unrest over the lag in political reform. Students and others numbering in the tens of thousands seized on the occasion of the death of Hu Yaobang, the reformist Communist Party leader dismissed in disgrace two years ago, to go into the streets in Beijing waving the democratic banner and (some of them) heaving rocks. The police have escalated their responses, and beatings are now reported. The scale of the protests and the extent of the government's distress are at this point not to be exaggerated, but already these events are taking a place among the larger known outbreaks of public disorder since the Cultural Revolution convulsed China two decades ago.

Once senior leader Deng Xiaoping's heir apparent, Mr. Hu may not exactly have fully earned the rather Jeffersonian image in which the protesters have recast him. On the Chinese spectrum, nonetheless, he was unquestionably at the liberal end. Challenging the reigning reform orthodoxy, he made no secret of his view that economic reform could not succeed without political reform as well. This seems to be the fundamental point that the demonstrators are making now. In so doing, they are pressing on the most neuralgic point of the Chinese reforms: the stunted progress on the political side. Mr. Hu was ousted in a power play arising from his reluctance or failure to suppress pro-democracy student demonstrations in 1986-87. A broad historical record indicates that street protests and official responses to them are a principal medium in which politics takes place in countries that do not provide a democratic arena where different forces can legally contend.

It is often observed that the democratic spirit is sweeping the world, touching in the Soviet Union, in Eastern Europe, in Latin America and now, and not for the first time, in China. We hope it's true, but we think that what is really happening in places such as China is the collapse of an arbitrary, cruel and unworkable political order—communism. The institutions and legal procedures of democracy may not be available to those searching for a way out, but they turn as a moth to a flame to the symbols and slogans of democracy in order to establish accountability for power that has been abused. Governments under this sort of siege will be judged by whether they accept the challenge as legitimate, and meet it.

THE BLADE

Toledo, OH, April 25, 1989

ZHONGNANHAI is the name of the official compound where leaders of the Chinese government live. It is hard by the Palace Museum, the great Forbidden City of the Chinese emperors now visited by millions of tourists, and the official compound is probably about as hard to get into as the Forbidden City was in China's imperial era.

For several days protesters have marched to the vicinity of the walled compound, ostensibly to mourn the death of Hu Yaobang, and this week tens of thousands of students at Beijing's universities have gone on strike calling for human rights. Mr. Hu was responsible for much of China's recent efforts to modernize and reform its economy. He became a scapegoat after the 1986-87 student demonstrations and was forced to resign as chief of the Chinese Communist party.

This is a time of great ferment and social dissatisfaction in China. The modernization goal has at least in part gone sour because of rising living costs and the growing disparity between those who are tied to fixed wages and the new entrepreneurs who have gained considerable prosperity, especially in the countryside, because of agricultural reforms.

Visitors to China have noticed not-so-subtle changes in the attitudes of Chinese toward foreigners. In the early and mid-1980s westerners, particularly Americans, were often received with warmth and friendly curiosity. That has not changed. But increasingly foreign guest are importuned to buy paintings, works of calligraphy, and endless assortments of souvenirs, ride in black-market taxis for hard currency or the script issued to visitors who change dollars and other desired currencies, or just change money.

Mr. Hu's death cannot have meant much to the young marchers. They are increasingly aware that despite their educations and desires for material possessions, most of them will be locked into bleak living conditions and dead-end jobs. No wonder they are saying, to paraphrase a phrase of the 1960s in this country, "Hey, hey, Zhongnanhai, What have you done for us today."

These young protesters know that if they were in Japan, Taiwan, South Korea, Hong Kong, or Singapore, they would have far better career prospects. They surely cannot help but notice how well their Chinese compatriots in other Asian nations are dressed, how well they are treated in China, and how rich and diverse their career prospects are.

This presents the Chinese government with a dilemma. It cannot grant the freedoms the students demand, or at least does not think it can. Freedom of speech and the press, money for education, and abolition of regulations against street demonstrations would have a staggering impact on a society which is still grimly regimented. The government maintains tight reins on housing and jobs allocations — an extremely effective way to keep popular sentiments in check.

The Chinese government walks a tightrope between old-guard Communists and others who want to restore Maoist discipline and those who have been attracting attention in the streets of Beijing for the past several days with their demands for greater freedom. If the Communist mandarins behind the walls of Zhongnanhai ever peer out at the crowds on the street in front of their fortress, they must give serious thought to the problem of how one dismounts gracefully from a tiger.

The Honolulu Advertiser

*Honolulu, HI,
April 22, 1989*

China's most dramatic anti-government demonstrations in the communist era mark changing times and dramatize the kind of problems the regime there is facing.

Among other things, these have been the first major protests at Communist Party and government headquarters in Beijing since the 1966-76 Cultural Revolution. Then, Red Guard radical youths tried to enter the walled compound to drag out leaders they accused of capitalist crimes.

This time, in the capital and elsewhere, students have been calling for freedom and democracy and opposing corruption. They are demanding free speech and a free press, an end to bans on demonstrations, and "rehabilitation" of those arrested in past governmment anti-liberal campaigns.

The demonstrations were touched off by last Saturday's death of Hu Yaobang, who was forced out of his post as head of the Communist Party two years ago by hard-liners who felt he wasn't tough enough against student protest. The demonstrators now are saying what he did, that faster political change must come with China's market-oriented economic reforms.

China's Premier Li Peng recently rejected rapid political reforms on grounds too much democracy would lead to political instability. But students and others see what's happening in Moscow and elsewhere where the communist system is increasingly recognized as inadequate.

So now, while the outcome is still in doubt, the burden is now on China's rulers to respond with something besides a cruel crackdown.

DAYTON DAILY NEWS
Dayton, OH, May 5, 1989

Spring is China's revolutionary season for burying dead ideas and rallying in the memory of just-dead reformers. May at least a couple of flowers bloom on the grave — preferably perennials.

Seventy years ago on May 4th, Chinese students marched into Peking's Tiananmen Square. They called for "democracy and science" and for repudiation of the Versailles treaty. Their mass movement led to the end of the dominance by warlords and Confucian ideology.

Twelve years ago students demonstrated to commemorate the death of Prime Minister Zhou Enlai, who had become a liberal hero. Later that year Mao died. The regime, sensing discontent, turned on the Gang of Four. The stage was set for some loosening of the party's economic stranglehold on that huge, backward country.

This year's demonstrations of discontent became the largest faced by the 40-year-old Communist government. The April demonstrations, in which students shoved into a phalanx miles long, rallied around the death of Hu Yaobang, a liberal who had been expected to succeed Deng Xiaoping until Mr. Deng knocked him out of power to placate conservatives.

The demonstration also was fired up by dissatisfaction with a government that, since it started a half-reform in the late 1970s, had run out of ideas. Inflation and frustrated expectations had cost the regime public support. Austerity made official corruption more of an aggravation.

China has been trying to open up the economy a bit while keeping a straitjacket on expression, democracy and human rights. This makes it hard for the regime to get past the inevitable pain and chaos of restructuring a rickety economy.

The students have been better organized than they were in 1986 and 1987, and that has helped their cause. They have not called for an overthrow of the government. ("Support the correct policies of the Communist Party," said one banner.) They have been adamant, but polite, to the leadership. They have avoided turning off their public supporters, some of whom hunkered down because they got beat on by the Cultural Revolution in the 1960s. The students have formed cordons so troublemakers would not infiltrate their ranks. They are not making the mistakes that the students in South Korea have been making by taking hostages and throwing Molotov cocktails.

The leaders are at a dead end, but have one thing going for them. The students' positions are not hardened into concrete. The students aren't committed to flamingly unreasonable demands from which they cannot back off.

The students and their supporters want a system that is — somehow — more democratic and less corrupt.

So the leaders have some freedom of maneuver. But to succeed, they can only go in one direction.

The Boston Globe
Boston, MA, May 6, 1989

On May Day, the communist authorities in Beijing evinced a subtle sense of symbolism. Breaking with tradition, they chose not to display the huge portraits of Stalin, Lenin, Marx and Engels that previously had hovered over the masses assembled in Tiananmen Square for the workers' holiday.

Only those who made this decision know whether it was intended as a conciliatory gesture to the thousands of students who would arrive three days later to demonstrate for democracy, or as a practice run for the impending visit of Mikhail Gorbachev.

The old revolutionaries in the Chinese party know that the end of a regime is accompanied by the tearing down of portraits, the toppling of statues. They may have heard that on Lenin's birthday, an editorial in Pravda (the newspaper of the Soviet party's Central Committee) praised both Alexander Kerensky and Leon Trotsky. They know that Gorbachev's policy of glasnost has permitted the Soviet masses to read about Stalin's crimes in newspapers and magazines that are ebbing away from the control of party censors.

And though they have not permitted their party newspapers to report on the peaceful parades of students in Beijing, they must know what the rest of the world knows — that the students represent the desire of the Chinese people for basic freedoms.

"Down with bureaucracy! Down with corruption!" shouted the students to throngs of Beijing residents who lined their route Thursday, holding up V-for-victory signs and offering the marchers food and drink. There is nothing complicated in the demands of the marchers, no tortuous ideology. They want a free press, the right to free speech, freedom to form their own organizations.

These are the political concessions that communist rulers have begun to make to their subjects in the Soviet Union, Poland and Hungary, steps toward the democratic privileges enjoyed by China's neighbors in India, Japan, and even Taiwan. The students are politely asking the party mandarins to go the way of the May Day portraits that vanished from Tiananmen Square.

AKRON BEACON JOURNAL
Akron, OH, May 5, 1989

THE YEARNING for freedom remains strong around the globe. What has been happening within the Soviet empire and more recently in the People's Republic of China are examples of the age-old quest for liberty.

The university students in China are showing amazing courage as they seek to loosen the heavy hand of the state in that populous bastion of communism. They surely well know that similar efforts in the past have often been eventually crushed by heavy, brutal force of the government's armed might.

The uprising in China is of particular interest, since the leadership there had been gradually relaxing its iron hand and its previously rigid control of the economy. What the students are saying, dramatically and forcefully, is that freedom is not coming fast enough.

The same thing is happening in bits and pieces within the tattered claws of the Russian bear's empire: Poland, Armenia, Estonia, Latvia. Mikhail Gorbachev cannot unlock the chains of totalitarianism fast enough. *Glasnost* and *perestroika* work, and the people want more.

That has ever been the way with freedom. A rigid state can keep its people in bondage just so long, as even the white rulers of South Africa must surely know.

As Americans, we sometimes take all the freedoms we have for granted. The brave students in the streets of Beijing this week show us once again that mankind is indeed indefatigable, and that even against great odds, the dream of liberty burns bright in the human heart.

The New York Times
New York, NY, May 6, 1989

China's youth have taken to the streets in a stunning challenge to authority. They feel they are being asked to forgo the higher living standards enjoyed by non-Communist Chinese and the new freedoms enjoyed by many non-Chinese Communists. No wonder they are in open revolt.

And it's not just students. Their original demonstrations in Beijing have spread to other cities and won the support of other classes. The conservative Communist leadership that not so long ago bemoaned student apathy now needs to radically readjust its assumptions. Already it has shifted to more conciliatory language. Its ability to accommodate the student movement's ideas will help determine China's political and economic future.

Though the latest eruption has been sudden, the student movement has deep roots. The lunacies of the Cultural Revolution undermined the Communist Party's legitimacy. Inflation and corruption and nepotism accompanying the post-Mao economic reforms brought the leadership into further disrepute.

Now, two additional factors intensify the resentment. One is the growing prosperity they see in Taiwan. The other is the unwillingness of Chinese Communist authorities to emulate the reforms sweeping the Soviet Union and Eastern Europe.

Beijing's first reaction to the demonstrations was to try to intimidate and repress. Power is shared among three leaders. Deng Xiaoping, supreme leader for more than a decade, has never seen a connection between economic reform and freer politics. He is said to have ordered a crackdown on the protests. Zhao Ziyang, the party chairman, is a Deng protégé who has recently seemed in eclipse. Li Peng, the Prime Minister and a rising star, is a conservative bureaucrat.

The party leaders still seem determined to prevent the protest from going too far. But their hands are stayed by the knowledge that, for now at least, the whole world is watching. The annual meeting of the Asian Development Bank is now being held in Beijing. And on May 15, Mikhail Gorbachev arrives for a heralded summit meeting with Mr. Deng.

Mr. Gorbachev may find himself in an ambiguous position. The protesting students echo his own calls for glasnost. But he has important diplomatic business, involving Cambodia, Afghanistan and the China-Soviet border. In the past he has shown himself willing to embrace neo-Stalinists abroad, even as he attacks them at home.

Americans need feel no ambiguity. The student demands reflect deep democratic values, and our many common interests with China are not jeopardized. The movement is a hopeful portent; the students are China's future. It will be their generation that makes reforms work. China's leaders surely understand that, and it has helped stay their hands. May the world keep watching.

DESERET NEWS
Salt Lake City, UT, April 25/26, 1989

Turmoil is spreading in China as student demonstrations — the biggest since communists seized power in 1949 — call for more democracy, for human rights, for a free press and for an end to official corruption.

There may be some tendency to blame this unrest on looser controls and the free market reforms begun in China a decade ago, especially since the economy is in such bad shape. But China's problems stem from too little reform, not too much.

The market-oriented reforms actually produced an unprecedented upsurge in rural production and wealth. But along with that upsurge, there has been a growth in corruption among communist officials in cities, villages and national offices all over China.

Well-entrenched, old-party bureaucrats felt threatened by the changes begun a decade ago and have resisted them at every turn. With decentralization, local officials not only have power to resist but have grabbed the chance to enrich themselves.

As a result, some of the worst habits of the old pre-World War II China have returned. As one reformer explains, "Everything is for sale — children's places in good schools, proper medical treatment, scarce raw materials for industry," and bribery of every imaginable kind is rampant.

How extensive is the corruption? Observers say it is deeply rooted and involves not only party officials but their children and families as well. An estimated 20 percent of the national income is going into the pockets of corrupt officials. No nation can prosper in such circumstances.

The corrupt officials also have hampered existing economic reforms and kept others from being enacted.

The answer to China's problems is not a return to tight party control. In fact, at this point it may be impossible for an aging party leadership to assert that kind of absolute authority. Too much of the party apparatus is in the hands of those very same corrupt bureaucrats.

A free press, guarantees of human rights and other steps toward democracy would put pressure on corrupt officials. Such steps should be encouraged. Educated young people are either looking for ways to get to America or have taken to the streets to demand change.

The demonstrating students probably lack enough clout by themselves to bring about significant change, but if the economy gets bad enough, the turmoil could spread to other parts of the population.

China is reaching some critical crossroads. What happens in the coming months may tell if the country will be able to pull itself into economic stability in the 1990s or whether it will slowly collapse into conditions more resembling the 1920s.

Chicago Tribune
Chicago, IL, April 26, 1989

In the Soviet Union, a new policy of *glasnost* has brought long-stifled opinions into the public debate. In China, by contrast, ideological turmoil has erupted precisely because of the government's efforts to keep the nation's mind closed and locked while opening up its economy. Last week's unrest shows you can't have one without arousing hunger for the other.

The demonstrations by Beijing University students, touched off by the death of former Communist Party leader Hu Yaobang, have grown into a major challenge to the authorities. Over the weekend, the government tried to head off a mass protest in Beijing's central square, but the protesters foiled them by pouring into the square before it could be sealed off.

The protests are stimulated less by Hu's death than by widespread grievances with state policies. China's opening to the outside world has blown in new ideas that challenge the Communist system's rigid authoritarian control. The government's economic reforms have produced inflation and other dislocations, besides awakening resentment of the newly rich. They have also spawned corruption in the party leadership and bureaucracy, infuriating ordinary Chinese.

The government has retreated somewhat on its economic program. It has not retreated from its insistence on maintaining the unchallenged power of the Communist Party. China's intellectuals, like their Soviet counterparts, have chafed under this strict control, particularly since Moscow has relaxed its policy toward dissent.

The government can be expected to crack down sometime in the next few days, rather than risk letting the situation get out of hand on May 4, an important national anniversary that students have targeted for protests. It may manage to put down this expression of discontent. But China's leaders have not heard the last of demands for more fundamental reform. Sooner or later they will have to listen.

Omaha World-Herald

Omaha, NE, May 9, 1989

China's demonstrating students have, for the most part, kept their protests from crossing the line into mindless, destructive behavior. One need only look at what has happened in South Korea in recent days to admire the restraint that has been possible in China.

Like their counterparts in the Philippines and Burma who forced political changes that surprised many, the South Korean students have been instrumental in forcing a dictatorship to accept the rule of law.

Apparently not content with a history-making role in the advent of democracy in South Korea, however, the students there have expanded their demands to include quixotic or impossible goals, such as the immediate reunification of South Korea with the Communist dictatorship in North Korea.

Six South Korean policemen died in putting down recent riots in which Molotov cocktails were thrown.

Chinese students have been self-disciplined by comparison as even one of the targets of their demonstrations, Communist Party chief Zhao Ziyang, seemed to acknowledge Monday when he said that the students were acting with more reason. The official government news agency quoted him as saying: "The situation has been prevented from becoming acute because the party and government have all along adopted a very tolerant and restrained attitude and because most students have acted with increasing reason."

The students want, among other things, an independent student union — a demand not unlike the Polish demand for an independent trade union. When the Chinese government met with student representatives earlier, the representatives were from government-sponsored student unions, not from the new, spontaneously established student reform groups.

It seems that China is now learning what Hungary, Poland and the Soviet Union have also learned — that a little reform and a bit of glasnost open the door to greater and greater demands. It is to the credit of the students that they have focused on change and avoided being caught up in violence.

The Hartford Courant

Hartford, CT, May 6, 1989

Change, albeit at a slow pace, has been manifest in China for several years, since post-Mao pragmatists gained the upper hand. But nothing has been as dramatic or as hopeful as the pro-democracy rallies mounted by students in recent days.

The death on April 15 of Hu Yaobang, the Communist Party secretary who lost his job in 1986 for pressing too hard for reform, was the catalyst. What transpired was nothing short of amazing: daily marches by university students on behalf of political freedoms and bureaucratic accountability. In Beijing, 150,000 students cheered by thousands of onlookers marched through the streets last week. The student protest has grown larger since then despite government warnings against it.

But the leadership also seems to recognize that a new breeze is blowing. Major newspapers were allowed to report "the actual state of affairs." On May Day, the traditional portraits of Stalin, Marx and Engels were gone from Beijing's main square, replaced by the likeness of Sun Yat-sen, the father of Chinese nationalism.

Although police in some other Chinese cities have used clubs and gas to break up demonstrations, the authorities in Beijing have been remarkably reserved. Police guarding public buildings have stood their ground, but have not challenged the students. They yielded when the students broke through police ranks. Officials have granted some concessions and have promised to negotiate about other student demands.

Contrast that reasonable approach with the South Korean government's ordering out 20,000 riot troops to break up a planned demonstration in Seoul on Sunday and the clashes that followed the fiery deaths of policemen at the hands of radicals on Wednesday.

It would be foolish to say that democracy has come to China, but it would be blind to deny the existence of such strong new currents in Chinese political life. The students' next move might tip the government's hand.

It might be that leaders have cynically decided to stand aside in the hopes that the students' enthusiasm will fizzle, to deny them the instant legitimacy and support that repressive tactics would bring. Or perhaps the leadership's patience will be lost in the heat of continued demonstrations.

But it is just as reasonable to believe that the government — or at least the more progressive elements in it — might actually welcome this spring storm, and perhaps use it as an excuse to retire some of the remaining members of the old guard. After all, this is a government that has sent abroad thousands of students as part of its modernization program. The leaders understand that they will bring back an appetite for political reform as well as expertise in new technology.

The Kansas City Times

Kansas City, MO, May 5, 1989

The last episode of pro-democracy protests in China began in 1986 and ended with the usual crackdown. Now the crowds have returned, but this time the situation for the party leadership is more delicate. In hammering away at corruption and inflation, the students are also articulating the grievances of urban workers and peasants, and thereby winning more support than they enjoyed three years ago. With the economy stagnating and prices on the rise, resentment toward the government is at levels not seen for a decade.

These periodic outbreaks in China, and the turmoil through the communist world generally, mark the fading hold of Marxism over its adherents. Seventy years ago, communism had a certain advantage: The promise of Marx was held against the practice of capitalism; critics of the free market railed against the "robber barons" and pointed to Marx's promise of a classless society. The panics of the day underlined the doctrine of capitalism's inevitable collapse.

Today, the situation is reversed. The prosperity of the West stands out sharply against the chronic scarcity, the climate of fear, the inability of communist states to fill demand for even mundane products.

To be sure, the students in China are unclear about what they mean by democracy. They realize, however, that something has gone deeply wrong, that China is being robbed of its future. Workers, too, sense that something has come untracked, although their grievance is more basic. They spend nearly half their household budget on food and for more than a year they have watched prices outpace wages.

Workers and students have found common ground, and the only question is for how long. The situation is reminiscent of the turmoil that drove the nationalists from power 40 years ago; then as now, the key issues were corruption and inflation.

But as the dissident Fang Lizhi recently pointed out, in 1949 the alternative to the nationalists was the communists. Today, obviously, there is no opposition ready to govern. China must resolve for itself the contradictions inherent in its reigning doctrine. There is little for the United States to do in this drama, except make its sympathies clear.

TULSA WORLD

Tulsa, OK, May 1, 1989

A LITTLE bit of democracy can be a dangerous thing. And China is learning that lesson.

The Chinese government improved relations with the West and expanded personal freedom a little. It got more than it bargained for.

Last week, more than 150,000 students and workers marched through central Beijing calling for democracy. It was China's biggest march since the communists took power in 1949. The students and workers have called for sweeping democratic reforms including freedom of the press and an end to corruption.

It was, for the most part, a peaceful, 15-hour demonstration. Police had warned organizers not to march, but security forces at the scene were unarmed and showed no sign of force.

The government offered to talk with the students if they returned to their campuses and adopted a "calm and reasonable attitude." The students balked, however, saying the government will talk only with government-backed student groups. The government considers the newly formed student unions illegal.

This is especially interesting now, as we celebrate the 200th anniversary of the U.S. Constitution and the inauguration of George Washington.

Communism, which once threatened to dominate the world, seems to be losing favor in its strongholds — China and the Soviet Union.

A few more fast-food restaurants and some free enterprise could be more influential than political ideology and massive armies.

The Des Moines Register

Des Moines, IA, May 14, 1989

Glasnost fever has spread to China. In Beijing they call it *kaifang*, but it means the same thing: democratic openness.

It is too early to tell whether the student-led protests of recent

Chinese yearn for democracy.

weeks will speed China toward that democratic openness, or instead will prompt a government backlash. But it is clear that Chinese leaders can no longer ignore widespread demands for change.

Historically, student activists in China have emerged as government leaders. Mao Tse-tung, Chou Enlai and Deng Xiaoping, for example, once were student leaders, bent on overthrowing the old order and replacing it with new ideas and new practices.

Now the 84-year-old Deng is in power, and is intent on preserving the existing social order.

His desire for stability is understandable. Deng lived through the Cultural Revolution of the late 1960s, when the government was seized by a group of firebrand revolutionaries who attempted to wipe out all intellectuals by execution or imprisonment in re-education camps. Deng himself was paraded through the capital city in a dunce cap.

Now, once again, Deng and other leaders see a status quo under siege. And while the students insist they support Community Party rule, the demand for open debate would give voice to interests other than the ruling party.

Already, newspapers have backed demands for greater freedom of speech, the police have refused to fire tear-gas against demonstrators, and workers are marching arm-in-arm with students.

The peasants, who form the bulk of the Chinese population, have yet to join the marches. But they, too, are increasingly disgruntled over China's economic problems.

So far, the government has refrained from using harsh tactics to put down the protests, and has acted instead as a punching bag for the disgruntled populace.

But many fear the government will crack down with mass arrests later in the month, when there is no risk of jeopardizing the Sino-Soviet summit or spoiling the meeting of the Asian Development Bank in Beijing.

Such a course could be ruinous. Military force will not silence a peoples' desire for change, as Deng and other one-time revolutionaries must know.

There are risks involved with *kaifang*. But the dangers are far more manageable than the risk of attempting to stifle the masses who yearn for democracy.

THE BLADE

Toledo, OH, May 12, 1989

PUBLIC diplomacy, sometimes referred to as propaganda, has long been a basic tool of the American arsenal in the war of ideas, but currently it is getting a strong following in China, a country which most of the time lacks important news about itself.

The Voice of America broadcasts nine hours a day in Chinese, more than three times the volume of the British Broadcasting Corp., which has a devoted following in many parts of the world.

"Our listenership goes through the roof during protests," according to David Hess, chief of the China branch at the Voice of America in Washington. Even though the VOA is dwarfed by China's Central People's Broadcasting station, in times of turmoil, such as China is experiencing now, the Voice is eagerly listened to by Chinese to find out what is really going on in their own country.

It has been estimated that 60 million people listen to the Voice. While that is not large in terms of the total Chinese population, it represents a large urban segment in coastal areas where most of the unrest is centered.

The Voice has not been quite as important in the current wave of protests as it was in 1986, partly because the Chinese broadcasting station has been transmitting some news about the recent demonstrations to a news-starved public. Although some Chinese students have complained that the Voice is not as aggressive as it used to be, this is perhaps all to the good in the long run.

One strong element of BBC broadcasts has been the calm impartiality of its news programs. This is a valued aspect of public diplomacy, and the value of the Voice of America is enhanced to the extent that it can also maintain such a reputation.

MILWAUKEE SENTINEL

Milwaukee, WI, May 2, 1989

Whatever China's leadership might be saying in formal discussions on how to deal with anti-government demonstrations that turned out a half-million demonstrators and onlookers in Beijing last week, privately, some of its members must be looking for a scapegoat.

Conceivably, a group like the "Gang of Four," who reportedly were directing policies of the late Mao Tse-tung, could be charged with collective blame.

But it is not out of the question that Chinese leader Deng Xiaoping, who decided against carrying out a threat of a crackdown as troops gave way to the crowds, might be singled out for political opprobrium.

This would take some courage since Deng has survived two purges and has managed to control the government for years without formally holding the premiership.

More of a problem would be a response to the demonstrators who want democracy but haven't voiced much more than discontent. And there is a question as to whether their cause, when defined, would be the same as the thousands of workers who apparently supported the latest demonstration.

Conceivably, the students have been influenced by what is happening in the Soviet Union and want to share power through direct elections. To call that kind of change a reform in China would be to put it mildly.

In any case, that would require lengthy deliberations. Meantime, something must be done very soon to take pressure off the government. And the old tactic under which the leadership singles out one of its own for the focus of public discontent may yet come into play.

Rockford Register Star

Rockford, IL, May 1, 1989

What you have in China is a brand of communism that is hoist on its own petard.

On the one hand, Chinese muscle opposes any tendency toward democracy. The rule is to repress, to constrain, to quiet down student activists who have tasted change and want more. On the other hand, Chinese leaders want to inject reforms in a system that hasn't worked economically, urging private initiatives toward wealth, challenging students, scientists and entrepreneurs to expand their rewards.

What these aging rulers seem not to understand is that an appetite, once awakened, can become voracious.

The most recent show of discontent and demonstration came when Hu Yaobang died. He had been the heir apparent to Deng Xiaoping. But Deng deposed him a couple of years ago after an earlier round of student protests frightened the inner circle.

The fact that Hu Yaobang had been a revered patron of intellectual freedom made him popular with university students. He represented their future, their common bond. And now he was gone. Thus, the show of loyalty to a man fondly remembered and a rallying point for the repressed young.

Deng Xiaoping does not seem to realize the contradiction he has foisted upon his country, expecting the bright young to dare more on behalf of their country without sharing more freedom in pursuit of this role.

These could become bloody times in China. Or they may mark a turning as monumental as the China Wall. One thing is certain. The point of contention is led by the intellectual battalions of students who are China's hope, as well as its life and its blood.

Toronto, Ont., May 12, 1989

After a month of demonstrations and social ferment, China's university students are slowly returning to classes. But the country is still absorbing a dramatic lesson in democracy.

Hundreds of thousands of students poured into the streets, backed by clerks, factory workers, and even journalists. In size, these unauthorized demonstrations made history; but they borrowed from history too.

It all began when the April death of former Communist party secretary Hu Yaobang — fired for failing to suppress campus demonstrations in 1987 — triggered nationwide mourning.

Thirteen years ago, a similar outpouring of affection for another fallen leader, Zhou Enlai, had been brutally suppressed. That upheaval felled the government, and brought a reformer, Deng Xiaoping, to power.

This time, the students used Hu's death as a cloak of legitimacy for their protests, sensing that, with an eye to history, Deng wouldn't make martyrs out of mourners.

But the rallies for democracy and clean government continued long after the funeral, far surpassing the previous protests that had cost Hu his job. The students were villifying Deng, the erstwhile reformer, and targeting the weak spot in his modernization drive: a near absence of political liberalization to accompany a decade of economic reforms.

Symbolically, their rallies culminated on the 70th anniversary of the May 4 movement that replaced China's feudal regime with republican government. Clearly, the students had a shrewd sense of history — and good timing.

Now, moderate forces appear to be gaining ground. Indeed, Hu's successor as party leader, Zhao Ziyang, came close to endorsing the students' demands this week by acknowledging that political reform has lagged behind economic change. A lesson well learned.

The Star-Ledger

Newark, NJ, April 27, 1989

Time was when critics of the citadels of world capitalism and democracy, notably in the Soviet Union and equally Marxist Mainland China, rejoiced at the rioting in the streets, the confrontations between labor and management, the racial turbulence and public denunciations of the establishment by the politically disaffected.

Today the unrest is in the other camp. Satellites of the Soviet Union are making strong waves in Central Europe, the Balkans and elsewhere. And in China, tens of thousands of ordinary people have been ignoring the obvious danger associated with protest against the state to demonstrate for a more democratic way of life.

Leaders in Armenia, Lithuania, Latvia and other once-independent countries now under Soviet domination are speaking out for long-denied reforms that will give them control over their own destinies.

In China, a climactic demonstration saw 20,000 aroused students join with 100,000 workers and peasants in Beijing's Tiananmen Square to press their demands for democratic reforms.

The yearning to be free of governmental oppression is not something which simply materialized. That yearning is a natural condition of mankind. It can be suppressed by iron-fisted governments, but only temporarily.

In Moscow, Beijing, Warsaw, Prague or Riga, Buenos Aires, Pretoria, Seoul or Managua, people cherish the dream of freedom and the right to exercise a voice in their destiny. When there is not enough food to quiet the hunger pangs, when department store shelves are bare of essential clothing and household needs, unhappiness activates unrest —and eventually the demonstrations spontaneously erupt. spread and gather momentum.

At the moment, attention is focused on the drama unfolding in China, the interest heightened because of the sheer numbers of people involved and the impact that reform there could have in other repressed areas of the world.

If this particular burst of global unrest fails, there will be another and yet another—until such time as reform succeeds and governments capable of providing for basic human needs are installed.

Houston Chronicle

Houston, TX, April 19, 1989

For the first time since China's tumultuous Cultural Revolution in 1966-67, thousands of students staged a major demonstration at the headquarters of the Communist Party in Beijing.

Information about the havoc of the Cultural Revolution leaked out of China only gradually. The peaceful rally this week was reported in full. Students were quoted by name. Their signs read "Long Live Democracy."

The pace of change in China can be debated, but China is changing.

Toronto, Ont., April 25, 1989

After a week of mass demonstrations in Beijing and other major cities, the students of China are back at their colleges and universities, though not in class.

Their crusade for democratic reform continues unabated as they plaster walls and sidewalks with slogans and make speeches demanding greater human rights.

The students' demands challenge the Chinese government to go far beyond the economic reforms begun nearly 10 years ago.

By letting farmers work outside collective state farms. by fostering a free market and by inviting capitalist investment, China seemed in Western eyes to be on the verge of enlightenment. Especially when the Soviet Union was still laboring in communism's dark ages.

But now that Mikhail Gorbachev has brought the Soviets *perestroika* and *glasnost* and even relatively free elections reform in China has lost its sheen.

Unemployment is rampant, inflation nears 20 per cent, banks are inefficient and the education system isn't producing the kind of people China needs to manage a modern economy. Worse, the students are complaining about an increase of official corruption.

Small wonder that the demonstrators are demanding more information about the personal wealth of China's national leaders.

By reacting with relative calm to the student protests — so far — the Chinese government leaves the door open to political reform. That's wise. But China's leaders — Deng Xiaoping, Zhao Ziyang and Li Peng — should recognize, before it's too late, that the yearning for democracy is not a hunger easily satisfied.

Newsday

Long Island, NY, April 27, 1989

The future was in the streets this past week in China: Student demonstrations are China's harbingers of change.

Better organized than larger 1986 demonstrations, these were also more focused. Students demanded increased freedom of speech, control over student organizations and publications, more money for education, release of political prisoners and a re-evaluation of the late Communist Party general secretary Hu Yaobang, ousted in January, 1987, for being soft on the 1986 demonstrations and western liberal trends.

Those simple demands go to the heart of the problem in China's curious 10-year effort at economic reform. While successfully encouraging small private enterprise, China tripped when it tried to unharness major enterprises — energy, iron and steel, transport — from rigid government control. Along the way, the government sought to uncouple *political* change from desired economic reforms.

Students and intellectuals, more tolerant of restraints on their freedom when the government's firm hand appeared to be moving the country forward economically, have lost faith and taken to the streets.

The crackdown will come, as it always has. The government's propaganda department has already taken over one outspoken newspaper. Troops are ready to suppress the students and will certainly move before Soviet General Secretary Mikhail Gorbachev's visit on May 15. The students will go back to class, seven or eight will be sent to re-education camps, but when the next excuse presents itself, they will be in the streets again.

The Chinese could smooth their lurching stumble into democracy by realizing they can't forever divorce the rights to gather and speak out from the rights to run a factory or go to a university. When the leaders look into the streets and see masses of students — the next generation of teachers, scientists, writers and diplomats — they are seeing the future.

China, Soviet Union Normalize Relations Amidst Beijing Protests

Soviet leader Mikhail S. Gorbachev visited China May 15-18, 1989 for the first Sino-Soviet summit in 30 years. But the historic trip was eclipsed by massive pro-democracy demonstrations led by Chinese university students. At the height of the unrest during the summit, more than one million people demonstrated peacefully in Beijing May 17.

China and the Soviet Union had broken Communist Party (CP) relations in the 1960s over ideological differences followed by military confrontations along their common border. No Soviet leader had set foot on Chinese soil since Nikita S. Khrushchev in 1959.

For Gorbachev, the China visit was the culmination of a seven-year push by the Kremlin (four years with him as CP general secretary) to normalize relations. It also marked a triumph in his Asian diplomatic initiative. The Gorbachev entourage included his wife, Raisa, Soviet Foreign Minister Eduard A. Shevardnadze and Aleksandr N. Yakovlev, the Soviet CP secretary in charge of foreign relations.

At first, it appeared that the pro-democracy demonstrations would provide merely a colorful backdrop to the Sino-Soviet rapprochement. The protests, initially involving only students, had begun in mid-April in Beijing and Shanghai. While the protests had an independent impetus, they became inextricably linked to the Gorbachev visit. Gorbachev was widely admired by the dissident students for initiating the Soviet policies of *glasnost* (openness) and "democratization." (Chinese Premier Li Peng in April had explicitly rejected the notion of China adopting Soviet-style political liberalization.)

Also, Beijing was filled with foreign journalists there to cover the summit. That gave the protesters an international media stage. The state-controlled Chinese press had initially only given scant coverage to the unrest.

The bitter Sino-Soviet rift came to a formal end May 16, when Gorbachev met with Deng Xiaoping, China's paramount leader. Gorbachev also held separate discussions with Premier Li and Zhao Ziyang, the head of the Chinese Communist Party. "We can publicly announce the normalization of relations between our countries," Deng declared at the close of his meeting with Gorbachev. "We want to put the past behind us and chart a new course for the future."

Soviet foreign ministry spokesman Gennadi I. Gerasimov May 16 told reporters that Gorbachev had discussed a variety of issues with the Chinese leaders and concluded that there was a large measure of "ideological agreement" between the Communist parties of the two countries. Gerasimov said that there had been no substantial agreement on Cambodia, and that Gorbachev had proposed a "radical military detente" along the Sino-Soviet border, and had restated the Kremlin's determination to remove some Soviet troops from Mongolia.

According to Chinese officials, Gorbachev and Zhao agreed that economic liberalization did not violate Marxist-Leninist principles. But the Chinese party leader was said to have told Gorbachev that China could carry out economic reforms without "structural political reform."

Gorbachev, no longer the center of attention for most of the international media, said at a May 17 press conference at the Great Hall that he had received a letter from Chinese students praising Soviet political reforms. "I value their position," he said with apparent caution. "These processes are painful, but they are neccessary."

Gorbachev spent most of May 18 in the Chinese port of Shanghai before returning to the Soviet Union. He was carefully shielded from the thousands of people demonstrating in the city that day. Before departing China, the Soviet leader hailed the summit as a "watershed event" of "epoch-making significance."

A joint communique issued May 18 said that the two countries had agreed to "develop their relationship" on the basis of "mutual respect for sovereignty and territorial integrity, nonagression, noninterference in the internal affairs of each other, equality and mutual advantage, and peaceful coexistence."

The Star-Ledger

Newark, NJ, May 17, 1989

The Soviet Union and China have, historically, had a philosophical link—a mutual commitment to hardline Marxist principles. But it is that same ideological commitment that now finds them faced with a similar problem—a surging grassroots disenchantment with the political strictures invoked by a rigidly collectivist order.

Coincidentally, the political demonstrations in both Communist nations erupted at a time when Moscow and Beijing were moving toward a wideranging accommodation that would formally end three decades of hostile relations—a rupture marked by military confrontation, a bitterly intense rivalry and major ideological differences.

The opening of the summit meeting in Beijing this week between Soviet leader Mikhail Gorbachev and his Chinese counterpart, Deng Xiaoping, was overshadowed by a huge, pro-democracy demonstration staged by 150,000 students and workers.

Unquestionably, the mass protest was an embarrassment for the Chinese hosts, not only for its negative domestic implications but because it was partly inspired by the Gorbachev reforms.

The rapprochement between the two largest Communist states coincides with profound economic and political changes which both nations have been fitfully experiencing. The Gorbachev reforms for a more open social order have failed to allay nationalist restiveness in the Soviet regions of the Ukraine and Georgia.

But the Soviet leader's glasnost reforms have at the same time stirred political rumblings in China— a catalyst for a growing movement among Chinese intellectuals and workers to bring about similar democratic reforms in the People's Republic. The Chinese leadership has found itself struggling with how to resolve rising political dissent that more and more appears to have a broad base of support.

The Chinese demonstrations have cast a shadow over the summit meeting. But they have not diminished the importance of the potential long-range political and economic ramifications for both Communist nations. For both Communist states, there is a common need to establish a stability in the international trading community so that they can get on with addressing an urgent domestic need to begin revitalizing their lagging economies.

But at the same time, it should also be apparent that the normalization of relations between the Soviet Union and China will have a crucial bearing not only upon the future of Asia, but on the United States and its allies as well.

The LeaderPost

Regina, Sask., May 18, 1989

The strength of numbers and conviction has added almost irresistible might to the popular uprising paralysing much of central Beijing.

If Chinese leaders thought they could afford to ignore student demonstrations while concentrating on a visit by Soviet leader Mikhail Gorbachev, they were badly mistaken.

The original demonstrators, seeking new freedoms and pledging feverish patriotism, have been bolstered by open displays of support from suddenly defiant and inspired workers, writers, government employees and even soldiers.

More than one million people marched through Beijing streets yesterday, many carrying banners denouncing senior Communist officials and calling for resignations.

With near-revolutionary fervor building in the Chinese capital, the protest has now spread to other major cities, including Shanghai, Shenzhen and Guangzhou.

In the early stages, party officials tried to cope by warning students of dire consequences from further "illegal" demonstrations and by agreeing to meet with student leaders of their own choosing. Early yesterday, party chief Zhao Ziyang reluctantly moved one step further, pledging to "work out concrete measures to enhance democracy and law, oppose corruption, build an honest and clean government and expand openness".

Such talk is high in ideals, low in specifics. With student power quickly becoming people power, the time for such half-measures is gone.

It is no longer students who may face dire consequences. It is party officials, who will surely pay a price if they fail to somehow appease the (so far) peaceful demonstrators.

The London Free Press

London, Ont., May 22, 1989

When Soviet leader Mikhail Gorbachev suggested during his historic meeting in Beijing last week that "without democratizing the economy, perestroika (social and economic restructuring) will never succeed," Chinese Premier Li Peng responded that China will improve its record on freedom, democracy and human rights.

The worlds were hollow. Early Saturday, Li declared martial law in response to growing disorder steming from more than a month of student protests in support of democratic reforms.

If the historic summit between Gorbachev and Chinese leader Deng Xiaoping wasn't evidence enough of the failure of Communism as an ideological force in today's world, surely China's return to repression in putting down dissent is. The heavy-handed response provides further evidence that domestic problems in both nations prevent them from being either a military or economic threat to the West.

During the 30-year falling out between China and the U.S.S.R., the division in the Communist world was regarded as a benefit to Western stability because it forced the Soviets to divide their troops between two fronts. But now that rapproachment between the Communist giants has been achieved, there is scant concern in the West and little evidence that China is in jeopardy of falling into the arms of Russia, because in relative terms, the Soviet Union is now a much weaker world power.

Assuming Gorbachev can stave off replacement by a hardliner, the Soviet Union appears determined to continue with promised troop reductions on all fronts.

The reasons are obvious. He faces enough turmoil at home in trying to reform an inefficient and unworkable economic structure that he doesn't need foreign military adventures draining his finances.

China, too, wants to concentrate on modernizing its economy by reducing the dead weight of central controls in favor of more individual, market-driven initiative. That also requires a stable international climate and greater domestic political freedom, but the tough reaction on the weekend shows that Chinese leaders are more intent on simply clinging to power.

The Soviets as well are facing calls for more democratic reforms, but Gorbachev's biggest worry is ethnic unrest and demands for more autonomy in regions such as Lithuania, Georgia and Azerbaijan. Somehow, he has to resolve these conflicts without a return to the old style repression: It may be an impossible task and he too may find himself relying on force similar to China's.

DESERET NEWS

Salt Lake City, UT, May 19, 1989

Despite the massive student demonstrations that overshadowed this week's historic Sino-Soviet summit, Mikhail Gorbachev still left Beijing with another diplomatic triumph under his belt.

But it's a triumph that consists more of symbolism than of concrete achievements. Consequently, there are sharp limits to how much the Free World needs to worry — at least at this point — about the renewal of friendly relations between the USSR and China.

By agreeing to withdraw some Soviet troops along the border with China, Gorbachev enables both nations to devote more of their resources to civilian needs, needs that are particularly pressing in the USSR's case.

Moreover, by renouncing claims to dictate policy to the entire communist world and by initiating the first Sino-Soviet summit in 30 years, Moscow has started a process that could eventually help make the world more stable.

But the mutual antagonisms aroused during the past three decades cannot be eradicated with a single meeting at the top. The USSR and China still have deep cultural differences as well as different aims.

As the Los Angeles Times notes, "there is still no common ground (between the USSR and China) on the political future of Cambodia, while a deep awareness remains of often bitter national rivalries going back 800 years."

The student demonstrations for democratic reforms in China plus the USSR's deteriorating economy indicate that neither nation can serve as a model for the other. The USSR needs technology that China cannot provide; China needs investment capital that the USSR cannot spare. This means that both communist powers still must rely heavily on the West.

Chinese leaders politely but firmly rebuffed Gorbachev's suggestions that they join in a campaign against American nuclear forces and military bases in Asia.

While the USSR and China agreed to some unspecified military-related talks, Chinese officials are said to have made it clear that new Sino-Soviet ties would not be made at the expense of the close relations existing between Beijing and Washington.

The continuing closeness of U.S.-Chinese relations is indicated by this week's visit of three American warships to Shanghai. Moreover, Newhouse News Service reports that the United States still maintains in northwest China a secret listening post designed to monitor Soviet missile tests.

It would be a mistake to entirely rule out the possibility that the new relationship between the USSR and China could eventually turn into another aggressive partnership like the one that menaced the world in the early 1950s. But for now there's some reason to be hopeful and little reason to lose sleep over the latest Sino-Soviet developments.

"NEVER MIND THE SOVIETS – HOW DO WE NORMALIZE RELATIONS WITH THE CHINESE...?"

The Sun Reporter

San Francisco, CA, May 24, 1989

The peoples of the two greatest communist countries, the Soviet Union and the People's Republic of China, are in the process of trying peacefully to change the direction of communism in their lands, under the guise of wanting to develop more democratic rights and end corruption.

The White House, 10 Downing Street and the Quay d'Orsey are trying to assess the real meaning of this simmering teapot. Many of the unofficial spokesmen for the U.S. State Department are saying that the search for liberalism and more democratic rights for the USSR is a sign of weakness, and advisers to President Bush are silently hoping and recommending that the U.S. do nothing to ease or insure the victory of Mikhail Gorbachev in Russia, or the winning of democratic rights by the students in their struggle in Beijing.

The efforts of the Chinese students to win in their power struggle against the organized elderly elite leadership of the present Chinese government are being followed with awe by the Western world.

At this writing (Tuesday), no one can really tell how the present upheaval in China will be resolved.

We must recall the leadership of both Russia and China have called for more democratic rights, but they have said nothing about wanting to change their economic system from communism to capitalism. We must not forget that democracy is a system of governance which is not the monopoly of capitalism.

It is impressive to learn that the People's Liberation Army's top commanders have refused to order the troops to fire at their own countrymen. There is a general reluctance on the part of the USSR to contribute any rhetoric which will indicate that it is taking sides. The political experts who are advising the U.S. government must not forget that China has never been captured whole by an alien force, although Japan came close in World War II.

The history of the seizure of power by the Chinese communists in 1949 records that the communist system would feel free to rewrite the constitution every 25 years, and the system is not afraid to adopt the good features which it feels are inherent in the material success fo capitalism.

The USSR and China are attempting now, from their different cultural and economic backgrounds — the USSR having organizing the workers in 1917, and China having organized its peasants in 1949 — to revitalize their systems.

No voice from China has been heard to call for the ending of communism, while similarly there are no voices in the USSR calling for a rejection of communism.

It would be the height of folly our government to discourage the process of readjustment in the USSR and China, or to encourage the downfall of the two communist giants.

StarPhoenix

Saskatoon, Sask., May 18, 1989

The improvement in Soviet-Chinese relations cemented by this week's summit meeting in Beijing is a most welcome step toward world peace.

The meeting between Soviet president Mikhail Gorbachev and Chinese leader Deng Xiaoping marked the end of a 30-year period of strained, sometimes confrontational relations between the two powers.

The efforts to remove irritants between them prior to this summit have manifested themselves in events simultaneously applauded by the West, such as the Soviet withdrawal from Afghanistan and its current move to begin removing soldiers from Mongolia.

If the two countries could reduce the level of militarization along their 7,360-kilometre border and stop being rivals for influence in areas like Cambodia, they could both divert a great deal of manpower and money to economic revival. Again, the West has much to gain from better trading prospects and little to fear that the two major Communist powers will form an excessively close or insular alliance.

In fact, throughout Gorbachev's visit, China seemed anxious to stress the importance of improved relations with the West. Deng himself told Gorbachev relations between the U.S. and the Soviet Union have been at the centre of the world's problems and the current opportunity to turn confrontation to dialogue should be seized.

That is a remarkably different attitude than prevailed in 1959 when Chairman Mao Tse-tung took offence at the visiting Nikita Khrushchev's attempts to forge detente with the West and the 30-year rift began. The change should be profoundly refreshing for all concerned.

The Washington Times

Washington, DC, May 19, 1989

Mikhail Gorbachev flew to Beijing this week with every intention of scoring a new public relations coup. He carried along a few "unilateral" gestures, along with an offer to begin bilateral reductions of military force along the Sino-Soviet border. He had planned to unwrap these gifts in such historic places as the Great Hall of the People and the Forbidden City in Beijing.

But just as he was about to enhance his legend, the greatest political event in the communist world since 1917 stole his spot on the stage. A million students filled Tiananmen Square and demanded Democracy — not small-d, one-party, communist-hybrid democracy, but the real thing, with pluralism and free elections. Three thousand students from Beijing University went on a complete fast (no food, no water), and soon their protest spread to include workers, journalists, police, even some government officials.

Rather than engaging in the gratuitous business of prophecy, it might make sense to reflect for a moment about the causes of this startling Beijing Spring. Many people, including Mr. Gorbachev, have claimed in the past that one could democratize politically as a precursor to economic liberalization. Others, including Chinese leader Deng Xiaoping, have attempted to install economic freedom as a precursor to limited political liberty.

Both men ought to understand by now that one cannot micromanage the human thirst for freedom, and that political and economic liberty are two facets of something called "liberal democracy." A nation that has one facet of liberal democracy naturally will seek the other. The Soviets, for instance, have tried political liberalization, only to find people protesting for the right to own property. The Chinese have granted property rights, only to discover a million citizens eager for political freedom. Such discoveries aren't limited to communist countries. South Korea and Taiwan in recent years have been forced to grant political freedom to their increasingly prosperous citizens. These governments in some past age may have been able to squash the movement toward liberty. The information age changed that forever. Demonstrations in Beijing appear on television screens throughout the world, depriving Chinese leaders the option of killing a few leaders and sending the rest off to prison camp.

Political and economic liberties are messy things. They no longer can be tamed or shaped by militias; they cannot be controlled by central committees or federal agencies. Once they have taken root, a thousand blossoms bloom and a thousand leaders fall. It would be futile for one to predict what might happen in China or the Soviet Union in the months to come, but if the tide of human dreams that has covered Beijing spreads throughout China, or if the protests in isolated Soviet cities begin to ring out across the U.S.S.R., no one man, no one party, and no one army will be able to stop them.

St. Petersburg Times

St. Petersburg, FL, May 19, 1989

Mikhail Gorbachev continues to prove himself to be that rare world leader who is strong enough to admit weakness. He inherited a Soviet political and economic system that did not work. Rather than pretending otherwise, he faced up to its failures and began acting decisively to correct them.

Leaders of some other governments, such as China's and Poland's, have reacted just as decisively to seize upon the mutually beneficial opportunities that Gorbachev's fundamental reordering of Soviet priorities has presented. For example, concessions on Gorbachev's part satisfied the preconditions that China's leaders had set for the re-establishment of normal relations with the Soviet Union. For years, China had insisted upon the withdrawal of Soviet troops from Afghanistan, a cutback in Soviet forces along the Soviet-Chinese border and a reduction in Soviet support for Vietnam's military intervention in Cambodia. Gorbachev was confident enough to offer those concessions, and China's leaders were confident enough to respond in positive ways.

So far, unfortunately, top officials of the Bush administration seem to be fumbling similar opportunities. Instead, they have more often reacted with suspicion and confusion to even the most straightforward Soviet concession.

Gorbachev's clear-eyed view of the Soviet Union's political and economic failures has been the driving force behind the sweeping domestic reforms of *perestroika* and *glasnost*. His recognition of his country's economic crisis, combined with a similarly practical assessment of modern military realities, also led to his unprecedented proposals for reductions in nuclear and conventional arms. The unilateral cuts they have already made, combined with their landmark military withdrawal from Afghanistan, have demonstrably made the Soviet Union internally stronger, even as it has become less threatening externally.

In failing to understand Gorbachev's motives, the Bush administration has tended to trivialize even Gorbachev's most revolutionary domestic and foreign initiatives to the level of a public-relations contest. And as they find themselves losing even that war of public relations on their own terms, they have begun reacting peevishly.

This past week, the White House looked especially silly, mean-spirited — and yes, weak — when Marlin Fitzwater, spokesman for ersatz Texan George Bush, stooped to calling Gorbachev a "drugstore cowboy." That's the rhetorical equivalent of Andy Rooney calling Aristotle an armchair philosopher.

Rather than carping over Gorbachev's style, our government should be probing for ways in which the United States and its allies can take advantage of the opportunities implicit in the substance of Gorbachev's overtures.

Those opportunities may take many forms. The formula for significant mutual cuts in nuclear and conventional forces has already taken shape. The potential for increased economic and cultural ties is greater than ever. Even more significantly, there is a growing awareness of our mutual interest in agreements to protect the environment, to combat international terrorism, to control regional conflicts.

In each of those areas, there is a real chance to forge new international agreements that strengthen the American economy and enhance our military security. Reaching those kinds of agreements will require a recognition on the part of the Bush administration of the weakness of some of its negotiating positions, or lack of same. We will see if President Bush is strong enough to acknowledge those weaknesses and correct them.

MILWAUKEE SENTINEL

Milwaukee, WI, May 16, 1989

A few years ago, it was inconceivable that a Soviet leader would step off a plane in Beijing and take part of the blame for the cold war that divided the Soviet Union and China for 30 years.

It was even more inconceivable that the Soviet leader would leave a country bathing in the early glow of glasnost and perestroika to deplane in an ancient land where agitation for democratic reforms forced the welcoming ceremony to be moved from a central Beijing square to the airport.

But those very things have happened. And as Mikhail S. Gorbachev announced the end of three decades of ill will that sometimes erupted into armed conflict, the world must stand in awe not only of Gorbachev's whirlwind pace but also the atmosphere in which the Sino-Soviet talks are being conducted.

Tens of thousands of rebellious students remained camped out in Tiananmen Square, pressing the Chinese leadership for a more open and democratic society.

Whatever the results of the talks — normalization of relations and the inevitable economic, cultural and academic contacts — the story is not so much of those developments or the split now healed but the revolution in communist society.

While it remains for the West, where democracy is long ingrained, to view each step toward inevitable democratization in the light of communism's dark past, there seems no end to Gorbachev's surprises.

As for the student demonstrations, it's almost as if he planned those, too.

Chinese Leaders Impose Martial Law in Beijing

In what amounted to a popular uprising against the current leadership of the Chinese Communist Party, hundreds of thousands of students and workers in Beijing May 19-25, 1989 defied the imposition of martial law and continued to stage hunger strikes and massive pro-democracy protests in the heart of the capital.

The decision to declare martial law in Beijing, announced May 20 by Premier Li Peng and endorsed later the same day by President Yang Shangkun, was widely believed to have been approved by China's paramount leader, Deng Xiaoping. Although numerous military units took up positions on the outskirts of Beijing, the army refrained throughout the week from moving against the protesters. Top Chinese military commanders reportedly feared widespread bloodshed if a crackdown was attempted.

The events in the capital, and in dozens of other cities across China, were played out against a backdrop of uncertainty over the outcome of an apparent power struggle within the Communist Party between those leaders advocating a hard response toward the unrest, including Deng and Li, and a more moderate faction led by the party's general secretary, Zhao Ziyang.

Western news reports during the week cited high-level Chinese sources who said that Zhao had been forced from power by the hard-liners, but these reports were followed by others that suggested it was Li who was losing support. Li reportedly was put on the defensive after his decision to impose martial law failed to quell the protests and served instead to galvanize popular defiance against the government. Calls by the protesters for the resignation of Li and Deng became a constant refrain during the week's demonstrations. By the end of the week, however, it appeared that Li had regained the upper hand in the party, while Zhao's status remained unclear.

Li announced the imposition of martial law in the capital in a speech broadcast on national television shortly after midnight May 20. "We must adopt firm and resolute measures to end the turmoil swiftly," the premier said. "If we fail to put an end to such chaos immediately and let it go unchecked, it will very likely lead to a situation which none of us want to see."

In a separate announcement, President Yang said, "Units of the People's Liberation Army will enter Beijing to restore order." The troops sent to the capital were reported to be from the 27th Army, based in Hebei province. Western news groups May 20 quoted unidentified Chinese sources who said that the commander of China's 38th Army, based in the city of Baoding, had refused an order to move.

Li's decision to send the army into Beijing appeared to backfire May 20, as more than one million Chinese citizens poured into the streets of the capital to support the protesters. Students, workers and ordinary citizens set up roadblocks and barricades along key thoroughfares into the city to prevent troops from reaching Tiananmen Square, where the main group of some 200,000 protesters, including 3,000 hunger strikers, were encamped.

The 3,000 hunger strikers, who had been elevated to hero status among the demonstrators, May 21 ended their nine-day fast, resportedly to regain their strength for the expected confrontation with the military.

Rumors abounded among the protesters May 21 that the army was planning a nighttime assault on Tiananmen Square to crush the uprising. The rumors brought hundreds of thousands of ordinary citizens into the city to block the anticipated military action. At dawn May 22, the students and their citizen supporters broke into cheers with the realization that the army was not coming.

Chicago Tribune

Chicago, IL, May 24, 1989

Whatever the final outcome of the Chinese students' demonstrations, they've given the world a fresh reminder that even the most repressive societies cannot forever extinguish the desire for freedom.

The inspired students have held their ground for days outside the Great Hall of the People in Beijing's Tiananmen Square, standing down—with the hundreds of thousands of workers and intellectuals rallying to their cause—Premier Li Peng's futile efforts to enforce martial law. And the sense of wonder grows.

Surely, it's too soon to begin to know where their courage will lead. Even, perhaps, to greater repression. But courage it has taken. That and a collective will that came from . . . where?

At the heart of the movement that is shaking China with its fervent demands for democracy—including free speech and a free press—and for an end to corruption in the Communist Party and the government are college youths indoctrinated since childhood by the state. Many, perhaps most, are party members.

It speaks to the nature of the communication and information revolution that has swept the Earth that these youngsters have such a demonstrated sophistication about the requisites of democracy.

To hear them there in the shadow of the Great Hall quoting from Lincoln's Gettysburg Address and paraphrasing Patrick Henry's "Give-me-liberty-or-give-me-death" speech sends goosebumps down American spines. There's an awesome sense of being present at the Creation—of witnessing an instant in time that could mark an historic turning.

Of course, the "witnessing" itself may distort our sense of the import of the moment. That's the mixed blessing of this new age that's overtaken us so quickly we can't yet comprehend what it means to humankind. But we have examples of its impact. Consider the lingering effects on American political and military policy of the televised war in Vietnam.

The "global village" created by communications satellites has become a metaphorical cliche. But Li Peng sitting under the television lights in the Great Hall fuming about the students' intransigence might as well have been at an international town meeting. He was being judged by his neighbors—all of us.

When he grew wise to that and pulled the plug on foreign networks while halting live coverage of the protests at home, it was too late. The leaders of the People's Army apparently had seen enough to dampen their enthusiasm for using force to impose martial law and put down the students' protests. Soon enough, Chinese television was back on the air and the American networks were permitted to transmit again.

The media, in this newly shrunken world, have become much more than just the messengers. In this case, their treatment was closely watched for clues. The loosening of media restraints was read as evidence Communist Party leader Zhao Ziyang and his reform-minded supporters had gained the upper hand in some fierce intraparty struggle. And it was swiftly hailed by pro-democracy forces as a victory that would keep the spotlight on their cause.

Watching the churnings in Tiananmen Square with the rest of us, President Bush has been cautious in supporting the principles propounded by the students while trying not to offend the government with advice it might consider gratuitous. Given his diplomatic background and foreign-policy responsibilities, that's understandable if not very gratifying.

But you'd better believe most Americans would like to see him cut loose with cheers for those kids who want a taste of freedom so bad they've put themselves in harm's way for it. They've earned them.

The Burlington Free Press

Burlington, VT, May 27, 1989

Imagine George Bush at the Boston Tea Party:

"I would urge the government to be as forthcoming as possible in order to see more democratization and to see a peaceful resolution of this matter."

Or George Bush addressing American rebels before the Battle of Lexington:

"I don't want to be gratuitous in giving advice, but I would encourage restraint."

Hunger for democracy propelled a million Chinese into the streets. Without striking a blow, they have shaken an absolute and brutal government's authority. Even if their rebellion is crushed, they have changed the future of China. Never has the world witnessed so stunning and spontaneous an expression of popular will.

And what does the leader of the free world have to say about this? As little as possible.

President Bush is all etiquette, no passion. He doesn't have time to offer vision or a moral beacon. He's too busy following the rules of diplomacy.

The rules say don't meddle in the affairs of other countries, don't offend the government of a superpower. Bush appears to believe that any deeply felt expression of solidarity with China's masses will be read as an exhortation to the violent overthrow of Li and his gang.

Chinese students don't need the United States to tell them how to run their revolution. They deserve the enthusiastic moral support of the world's leading democracy. And surely diplomacy allows an American president to tell the Chinese government that suppression of the revolt will cool our relationship.

In the streets of Beijing, as in the voting booths of Moscow, the glacial hold of communist tyranny is beginning to break up.

George Bush's should be the most passionate voice in support of freedom as history pivots on its axis in Tiananmen Square.

The Union Leader

Manchester, NH, May 21, 1989

One million Chinese defiantly call for "democracy" in the very heart of Communist China.

Russian citizens, given the right to vote for someone other than the hand-picked Red party candidates, pick the others, even if that means voting for "none of the above."

Lithuanians demand independence from Soviet rule.

Panamanians risk life and limb to come out in the open and vote against a brutal dictator's puppet candidate.

What is going on here?

What is going on is the hope for freedom, the indomitable spirit of man, and the most eloquent and powerful testimonial yet to western ideology and American-inspired democracy and capitalism.

As Winston Churchill put it, democracy is the worst form of government imaginable, except in comparison to all other forms of government.

Let's just hope that we in America realize that what others around the world are seeking is what we have. Let's remember that it has been America's resolve and belief in that system, as renewed under Ronald Reagan, that is largely responsible for many of these incredible sights in this Surprising Spring of 1989.

President Bush, thus far, is remembering it. He has ably resisted the demands of the left, here and abroad, to make concessions to the Soviets based on empty promises by Mr. Gorbachev.

The President must be from Missouri. He is saying to Mr. Gorbachev, "Show me" before he makes concessions and grants favors.

"Promises are never enough" Mr. Bush said last week. The Soviets must earn our trust by such things as reducing their overwhelming military forces, freeing the captive nations of Eastern Europe, and ceasing their support for subversion in this hemisphere.

Columnist William Safire hailed Bush's no-nonsense strategy last week and noted remarks made earlier by the President's deputy national security adviser, Robert Gates.

"For 70 years," wrote Gates, "we repeatedly have seen a system in crisis (the Soviet Union) proclaim reform and turn to the West for help while the essential features of that system at the end of the day remain unchanged."

There is cause for hope, despite the Red Chinese government's weekend actions. The taste of freedom is most addictive. But let's not forget what has brought this about. And let us not forget how quickly and ruthlessly the Communists can ignore their promises or murder their own people.

Rockford Register Star

Rockford, IL, May 24, 1989

It started with economic problems and official corruption, but China's rulers weren't in serious trouble until millions of Chinese took to the streets to protest.

Then, when the army started balking, it became obvious that change is inevitable. Maybe not immediately. Violence may yet erupt. Maybe the present hard-line leadership will find a way to hold on for a while. But millions of Chinese have been given a heady whiff of freedom and new dreams that won't die easily.

For the leaders of China, the whole thing has been a stunning accumulation of embarrassments.

Their historic reconciliation with the Soviets occurred as Tiananmen Square teemed with student protesters, forcing Mikhail Gorbachev to relocate his schedule repeatedly.

Then Premier Li Peng ordered martial law for parts of Beijing, including Tiananmen Square. The students defied his orders. Troops brought in from outlying areas watched, but otherwise did not intrude themselves on the young protesters.

Now, seven well known military leaders — including former Defense Minister Zhang Aiping and former People's Liberation Army Chief of Staff Yang Dezhi — have written and signed a letter opposing Li's martial law order.

The letter said, "As old soldiers we have the following demands. The People's Liberation Army belongs to the people. It cannot confront the people, even more so it cannot suppress the people and it will never shoot the people. To keep the situation from worsening, the army cannot enter the city."

Meantime, the student rebellion has elicited support from Beijing's private citizens who placed themselves between the students and military postings. Likewise, in various Chinese cities, the movement against the government has spread.

Now, members of the National People's Congress, which is the legislature of China, are petitioning to protest — and to challenge — Li Peng's order of martial law.

On all fronts, there is little room left for much face-saving for China's senior leader, Deng Xiaoping. Protesters want him to resign, saying he is out of touch with mainstream China and its wishes for freedom and an end to corruption.

Obviously a new regime could emerge, perhaps soon, in China. Obviously, many persons could be at risk. It was for this reason that President George Bush chose not to electrify the situation. Wisely he counseled support for democratic goals, urged the students to "fight for what you believe in" and added:

"We revere the model of Martin Luther King in this country for his peaceful protest and so I might suggest familiarization with that for the people in China."

It is friendly advice for a cauldron that could become inflamed at any moment.

THE LINCOLN STAR

Lincoln, NE,
May 23, 1989

Massive student demonstrations will ultimately end in China but the democracy they seek to further will gain a firm footing. Such an observation must be accompanied with a degree of reservation but appears credible in the view of many.

China's communist leadership has massed a heavy concentration of military forces in and around the capital of Beijing. Martial law has been declared and a deadline fixed for the end of demonstrations.

Yet, as this was written the demonstrators had not been forced to abandon their pursuits, although the situation throughout Monday was growing more volatile. Obviously, China's leaders would much prefer that the political drama being played out in the streets simply be allowed to run its course.

That would be the path of greater promise for all concerned. Use of force to quell the students and the growing numbers of ordinary citizens who have joined them is not a weapon easily at the disposal of China's government.

This is a government whose relaxation of freedoms has encouraged students to seek a quicker realization of the promise of democracy. To use force now would set the government back in what even it realizes is essential movement toward restructuring the political and economic systems of this ancient and vast land.

It's hoped the government will not see itself pushed into a corner from which it feels it must take violent action against demonstrators. If official patience does not wear too thin too quickly and if government leaders seek a meaningful settlement of differences with students, a peaceful conclusion to the current disorder could be achieved and the modernization of China substantially advanced.

With thoughtful consideration, the students surely realize that a nation cannot move overnight from an authoritarian government to a full democracy. Events in the Soviet Union have given ample evidence of this, with Mikhail Gorbachev's glasnost (openness) and perestroika (democratization) to date having shown far more promise than results.

The student demonstrators have shown China's leadership the deep yearning of its young people and vast numbers of the entire population for a move to a more advanced political and economic system. What they have shown is that the only real hope for China's future lies with greater freedom, not with the endless failings of communism.

Omaha World-Herald

Omaha, NE, May 23, 1989

The rest of the world may never know the full extent of the courage and selflessness that have been displayed in Beijing the past few days, not only by the student demonstrators but also by generals, government officials and ordinary citizens.

A few stories have made it to the West. The Wall Street Journal told about an old woman who was instrumental in neutralizing a 50-truck convey that was on its way to Tiananmen Square. When the lead vehicle stopped to ask for directions, the woman began shouting for help. Hundreds of people surrounded the trucks and let the air out of the tires.

Other news organizations brought the stirring news of army units that refused to move against peaceful demonstrators, of citizens who approached armed troops with food and offers to talk. A hundred commanders signed a statement pledging that the People's Liberation Army would not shoot at the people. There were indications of officials high in the government, possibly including Communist Party General Secretary Zhao Ziyang, who argued passionately but unsuccessfully for a calm, humane response to the demonstrations.

A petition drive materialized among members of the National People's Congress who wanted a special session to debate the legality of Premier Li Peng's declaration of martial law.

Leaders of the demonstration, displaying a lack of respect that could have been grounds for imprisonment not too many years ago, pointedly told Premier Li that he had strayed from the subject when he talked about his family during a meeting at which they wanted to discuss their grievances.

Assertions of a willingness to die for democracy showed up frequently in the signs and badges of the demonstrators and in their comments to reporters. E. Benjamin Nelson, an Omahan who happened to be in Beijing last week, said he was struck by the purity of the "struggle for freedom."

When troops began moving toward the square Monday, thousands of Beijing citizens massed in the streets and at the blockades in a effort to keep the demonstration alive — in some cases turning back the troops.

Most Americans, lacking firsthand experience with political repression, might not feel that they know precisely what is driving the events in China. But it isn't difficult to feel pride for the thousands who have stood up for freedom in the past few says, both in the streets and in the halls of government.

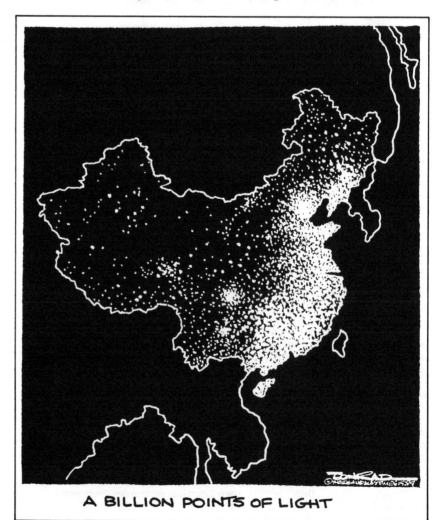

A BILLION POINTS OF LIGHT

The News and Courier
Charleston, SC, May 23, 1989

In a commencement address Sunday at Boston University, President Bush said he saw "a great irony" in the ferment that is presently sweeping through the communist world. "While an ideological earthquake is shaking asunder the very foundation of communist society," he said, "the West is being tested by complacency." Mr. Bush should know.

A full week after students demanding greater democracy in China took over Beijing's Tiananmen Square, and three days after the communist regime in China ordered a crackdown on the unprecedented demonstrations, Mr. Bush offered his first public comments on the extraordinary events. What did the president of the United States, this leader of the Free World and champion of freedom and democracy, say? He said this:

"I would encourage restraint .... I might suggest a familiarization with [the non-violent tactics of Martin Luther King Jr.] for the people of China .... I don't think it would be appropriate for the president of the United States to say ... exactly what their course of action should be."

Earlier last week, as the first Sino-Soviet summit in 30 years was totally eclipsed by the demands of Chinese for democracy and freedom, and Soviet President Mikhail S. Gorbachev was hustled in the back door of the Great Hall of the People to avoid the demonstrators, the only thing official Washington was saying was, "Thank God it was Gorbachev and not Bush."

Mr. Bush is the first president ever to have lived in Beijing, as U.S. ambassador to the People's Republic in the early 1970s. He has first-hand knowledge of the country and a special relationship with its people. He could have spoken forcefully and prudently on behalf of the students in Tiananmen Square and the cause for which they are literally putting their lives on the line. His words would have been heard and heeded behind the communist oligarchy's closed and bolted doors as well as in the square.

Instead, Mr. Bush chose the path of least resistence. He purposefully avoided saying anything even remotely inflammatory, lest the decrepit and discredited Beijing party leaders be offended. His concern for the well-being of the students is undoubtedly genuine, but they have demonstrated a courageous willingness to accept responsibility for their actions, as have the hundreds of thousands of other Chinese who have closed ranks behind them.

It was Mao Tse-tung who said, "A revolution, like an omlette, cannot be made without breaking some eggs." The Chinese students understand this, and are willing to pay the price. Is it too much to expect more encouragement from the president of the United States?

The Oregonian
Portland, OR, May 20, 1989

How can you govern a country of 1 billion people, one-fifth of the entire population of the earth?

With the greatest difficulty, with fits and starts and with many mistakes, some of them disastrous. That has been the experience of China for the past 200 years.

The imposition of what amounts to martial law could be another monumental mistake for that nation's leadership. Instead of letting the people into the political system, leaders seem bent on keeping them out.

For the past month, in Beijing and other major cities, hundreds of thousands of Chinese — college students at first, joined later by older workers — have been demonstrating with remarkable discipline and order for democratic reform.

Saturday the Chinese government called troops into Beijing to end the demonstrations. It was not immediately clear whether the government's intention was simply to keep the capital city's services operating and to clean up the central square where the demonstrators have been camping in increasing squalor, or to take harsher measures against them.

The communist leadership clearly has been divided on how tough to be and how much reform to promise. The demonstrators' demands threaten the authority of the party and the privileges of its elite.

Since Deng Xiaoping came to power in 1976, China has made remarkable gains in economic if not political matters. Reporters who accompanied the Soviet leader Mikhail S. Gorbachev on his visit to Beijing marveled at how much better the selection of food and consumer goods was there than in Moscow.

China has achieved those gains mainly by turning loose the energies of the people. The managers of state-owned enterprises have been made increasingly responsible for the success or failure of their businesses.

But with these gains has come inflation, the disease that ruined China in the 1920s. When the government tried to curb it by reimposing controls last year, it touched off a recession that has caused millions of unemployed rural Chinese to migrate to the cities in search of non-existent work.

These are real problems with which the Chinese leadership must deal while trying to pacify the students. Its best hope seems to be to find a way to allow the ordinary people a voice in the political system as they have been allowed into the economic system.

Instead, China's leadership has signaled through its troops its resistance to any opening of its political system. If that signal holds, it is a setback not only for the protesters but for those in democratic nations around the world who hoped that China could follow the Soviet Union into giving the governed more opportunity to influence the course of their nation.

Arkansas Gazette.
Little Rock, AR, May 23, 1989

Massive demonstrations centered in Beijing but now spreading throughout China are a spectacular showing of democracy's power. Regardless of the government's immediate action — brutal force or compromise of some description — China's modern history will be rewritten to reflect genuine popular change in that ancient land.

One might well argue that the protests, including hunger strikes, in Beijing's Tiananmen Square and elsewhere, grew from seeds planted when China's leaders started reopening China's windows to the world over 15 years ago, when Richard Nixon re-established relations. The light nourished movements for enhanced trade, exchanges of peoples, and some luscious buds of capitalism.

The world has been changing, as always, but the students who are the force behind demonstrations for democracy may have been inspired in part by the *perestroika* example in the Soviet Union and the loosening of government oppression on many peoples of Eastern Europe.

Indeed, irony accompanied the turnout in Beijing when Soviet leader Mikhail Gorbachev, the author of Communist liberalization and restructuring, visited last week. All of a sudden, students who had been gathering in the tens of thousands were there in the hundreds of thousands. Given the circumstances, for the students and sympathizers it must have meant the delivery of delicious embarrassment to the conservative, and dominant, wing of the Beijing government.

What lies ahead?

High military officials have been balking at using brute force to clear the public places of demonstrators and shore up the government's power. It is one matter for the government to declare martial law and quite another for the army to enforce it to the hilt. One column of soldiers was said to be forcing its way into the city yesterday, but initially at least was withholding fire.

President Bush has been circumspect, perhaps too careful, in his comments about the popular uprising, but at this stage he probably is responding appropriately.

It may well be that large-scale bloodshed can be avoided, although some amount of change in the way the government runs China will have to take place regardless. As a result of these demonstrations the Chinese people will enjoy a measure of democracy. A rough and bloody interlude may lie ahead, but yearnings for freedom and democracy, over time, are a more powerful force than guns and bullets.

Chinese Troops Crush Pro-democracy Protests

Tens of thousands of Chinese army troops, supported by tanks and armored personnel carriers, swept into downtown Beijing June 3-4, 1989 to crush the student-led pro-democracy movement that had begun in mid-April.

The bloody military crackdown, which came two weeks after the government had imposed martial law in Beijing, provoked a wave of antigovernment sentiment in the capital and numerous other Chinese cities, and was harshly condemned by nations around the world.

Although casualty figures were difficult to verify, the Western press estimated that at least several hundred and possibly as many as 5,000 people were killed in the nighttime assault and its aftermath, and that as many as 10,000 others were injured. The casualties included both protesters and soldiers, as well as civilian bystanders caught up in the disorder. Official Chinese accounts of the incident, presented variously by military and government spokesmen, were contradictory. The official statements listed death tolls ranging from zero to 300, with most of the casualties reported to be soldiers.

Shortly after midnight June 3, somewhere between 2,000 and 10,000 unarmed soldiers began a march down a central thoroughfare in the capital, headed toward Tiananmen Square. The move appeared to be an attempt to clear the vast 100-acre square of protesters without using force. The soldiers advanced to within several hundred yards of the square but then found their path blocked by tens of thousands of jeering students and workers.

The confrontation with the unarmed troops seemed to revive the pro-democracy movement. Hundreds of thousands of people in the capital poured into the streets during the morning of June 3 to show their support for the protesters. The wild celebration was short-lived, however, as new clashes broke out at midday between demonstrators and soldiers and police.

According to Western press accounts, which were sketchy and sometimes contradictory, the all-night military assault against the protesters began about midnight June 4. Dozens of tanks and armored personnel carriers and thousands of combat troops armed with automatic rifles and machine guns moved toward the central square from several points around the city. Civilians once again moved to block the army units from reaching the square but, unlike previous occasions, the troops did not back down. The confrontations, most of which took place within a 10-block radius of the square, quickly turned bloody as soldiers first fired warning shots into the air above the demonstrators' heads and then began firing directly into the crowd.

At 7:40 a.m., the local government announced that "the rebellion has been suppressed and the soldiers are now in charge" of the square.

In the days immediately following the crackdown, there were persistent reports in the Western press that rival Chinese army units were facing off against one another, sparking fears that the country was headed toward civil war. The uncertainty surrounding the loyalty of the military appeared to indicate that the ongoing leadership struggle at the top of the Communist Party – reportedly involving China's leader, Deng Xiaoping, Premier Li Peng, President Yang Shangkun and the party's general secretary, Zhao Ziyang – had yet to be resolved.

Contributing to the sense of uncertainty in China was the fact that none of the nation's top leaders had appeared in public for at least a week, leaving outside observers in the dark as to who was running the country. Rumors were widely circulated among Chinese in the capital that Deng was in the hospital or near death from cancer or had already died. Other reports asserted that Premier Li Peng had been shot by one of his guards in an attempted assassination. Western press and diplomatic sources said the rumors were impossible to confirm or discount. The reports later turned out to be false.

Chicago Tribune

Chicago, IL, June 5, 1989

To comprehend the slaughter conducted in Beijing's Tienanmen Square over the weekend, the place to begin is not in the news accounts, the thoughts of Chairman Mao or even Chinese history. The best explanation came in the nightmare vision of George Orwell's "1984": "If you want a picture of the future, imagine a boot stamping on a human face—forever."

That was the picture the world saw of Chinese communism, and a horrific picture it was: Troops firing AK-47s indiscriminately into crowds. Students lying in their tents, crushed beneath the treads of army tanks. A girl who has just heard that her brother has been killed, running toward a line of soldiers, who riddle her with bullets even after she has fallen to the ground. Many hundreds, perhaps thousands, died; many hundreds more lay wounded.

Amid the atrocities, there were inspiring acts of courage, defiance and compassion: Unarmed students seizing an abandoned tank and adorning its turrets with flags reading "Democracy" and "Freedom." A crowd facing the soldiers, chanting, "Fascists! Fascists!" Doctors, their mouths red with blood, frantically giving artificial respiration to victims.

In all the tense anticipation of how the occupation of Teinanmen Square might end, no one imagined how savage it would be. The Chinese movement for democracy had been so gentle, so reasoned, so just, that it hardly seemed possible it could be crushed.

The people cut down by the army were armed with nothing more than fire bombs and rocks, taken up only after the assault had begun; most of them weren't armed at all. The danger they presented was not of disorder and violence. It was of awakening the imaginations of their fellow Chinese.

In that the protesters triumphed. From a spontaneous march following the death of a favorite party leader in April, the demonstrations swelled with each day into one of the most authentic mass movements in Chinese history.

But flames can be snuffed, and this one may have been. The last hope of the movement was that when they were ordered to attack the protesters, the soldiers of the People's Army would refuse. But they obeyed. As long as the party and the army are united against the people, the people can be suppressed.

In responding to what has happened, the United States needs to act strongly but not recklessly. No one in China should have any doubt that our government and people are on the side of the movement for democracy. One way Washington can dramatize its feelings is to stop selling arms to the regime.

But broad economic sanctions probably would be a mistake. What brought China out of the dark ages of Mao Zedong's rule was its opening to the West. Thousands of Chinese have gone abroad as students; millions have been exposed to foreign news and foreign thinking; countless numbers have been captivated by the democracy and liberty they have heard about. The key to fostering democracy is keeping China open to commerce in goods and ideas.

By turning so violently against its own people, the regime has forfeited any pretense that it rules by popular consent. It has given vivid proof that China needs a radical change in its government. Eventually, it will have to pay for its crime.

At midnight Saturday, a 28-year-old man who supported the students, bleeding from a stomach wound, looked up at a foreign reporter and gasped, "Look at me and think." The world and the Chinese people have looked, and they cannot help but think.

ALBUQUERQUE JOURNAL

Albuquerque, NM, June 6, 1989

Sometimes it is said that a lesser value is assigned to human life in the populous nations of the Orient.

To judge by the expressions of outrage and anger filtering out of Beijing, old guard Chinese leaders are going to learn just how high a value is placed on a citizen's life. By extension, they and future generations will learn and remember how high a value those who died placed on democracy.

The conservative faction was able to purge liberal leaders from the regime; it might have been able to wait out the current heat of protest and retard the democratic tide. But, the brutal — and ultimately futile — attempt to repress the popular movement by sending troops to make war on unarmed students and their supporters in Tiananmen Square cost the government its legitimacy.

Though it may hold on to the trappings of office and channels of official communication with foreign governments, the regime will be unable to rule in the strictest sense of the term, because that requires the loyalty of citizens.

And the leadership seems incapable even of commanding the loyalty of its armies.

By some accounts the Beijing-based 38th Army balked at attacking protesters. Units responsible for the carnage Sunday and Monday appear to been brought in from outside the capital city area and misinformed about their mission and the situation. Protesters, who had been non-violent, are unable to get close enough to make personal contact.

Reports also indicate there is fighting between units of an army once held in fond esteem by civilians.

What little can be accomplished by foreign governments has been done. Beyond statements deploring the one-sided battles, and the United States' announced cut-off of military supplies that conceivably could be used against civilians, the rest of the world could only confer isolation on China's leaders while expressing support for its people.

Though this is a Chinese tragedy — at least this act — played out on a Chinese stage, it will continue to hold the critical attention of a global audience.

Wisconsin ▲ State Journal

Madison, WI, June 9, 1989

A chilling thought as communist China teeters on the edge of civil war: If hard-line forces such as the 27th Army lock horns with troops known to be more supportive of reform leaders, such as the 38th Army, will either side or both have access to nuclear weapons?

History teaches us that civil wars — once they break out — are no-holds-barred affairs. The American Civil War (1861-65) was our nation's bloodiest. In this century, the Whites vs. Reds civil war in Russia at the close of World War I; the Spanish civil war of the 1930s; the Chinese civil war that led to the ousting of the nationalists in the 1940s; and conflicts in Asia and Africa bolster the point.

When war pits countryman against countryman, no weapon is too horrible to use; no atrocity too terrible to commit.

That's why it is appropriate to speculate about what could happen if China erupts in civil war, and why the American response to that possibility is so important. The State Department is being mum on the subject, only to say, "We gather all available information; we look at every conceivable angle."

Most Americans don't know or have forgotten that China is a nuclear power. Today, China's nuclear arsenal is larger than the British and French forces combined. China tested its first atomic weapon in 1964 in the Xinjiang desert, becoming the fifth nation to join the world's nuclear club. Three years later, China startled the world when it tested a hydrogen bomb.

Over the years, China has been secretive about its nuclear capabilities, and according to the respected Arms Control Association "information on Chinese forces has been hard to come by. Chinese (missile) deployments are so hidden, in caves high in mountains and camouflaged, that Western and Soviet intelligence cannot be sure that they have located all of them."

This much is known for sure: China has short-range nuclear missiles that can be used in battlefield or "tactical" situations.

Skeptics will say, and correctly so, that it is not certain China is headed toward civil war — and it's a long shot that nuclear weapons would be used by either side, even if internal warfare broke out.

Still, it's not an outlandish leap of faith to think that hard-liners who would gun down innocent civilians in Tiananmen Square would also vaporize opposing armies in order to cement their grip on power. To communist zealots who view democratic reformers as sinful enemies, the purifying light of the mushroom cloud may have horrible appeal.

St. Louis Review

St. Louis, MO, June 9, 1989

Anyone attempting to evaluate last week's events in China faces monumental uncertainties. The thousands of student demonstrators who occupied the great square for weeks were apparently without an organized leadership to define specific goals. Uncertainties about the students were matched by similar uncertainties about Chinese governmental leadership. Who is really in charge? Who ordered the troops to attack? How much internal rebellion is occurring within the ranks of the Chinese army? These questions lead to a more important one: Does this armed suppression of the demonstrators signal the onset of a protracted civil war?

Over the past decade the Chinese leadership has allowed the introduc-

tion of capitalist economic reforms but without any accompanying political reforms within the communistic system. This week's events bear grim witness to the failure of their plans. The Russian reforms of perestroika and glasnost have been much more successful because of the Russian leadership's willingness to allow both political and economic reforms simultaneously.

The reports of the unarmed students being overwhelmed by the force of the Chinese troops and tanks has cast gloom over much of the world. When the Philippine people stood similarly unarmed before the tanks during the anti-Marcos revolt ''people-power'' won the day. What worked so well in Manila became a tragic failure in Beij-

ing. Now thousands of young Chinese lie martyred in the cause of democracy. If news of their deaths spreads to other cities in China there is some hope of success for democracy, but the Chinese Communists have had 40 years practice in suppressing their people's hope for a better life.

President Bush has acted cautiously and prudently in his measured response to the actions of the Chinese government. Oppression and persecution must always be opposed but on the international level there are many paths open when the good of so many people is at stake. The Chinese people have a long history of suffering and deprivation just as they have a long history of civilization and cultural arts. Our prayers and our assistance are both needed now.

Portland Press Herald

Portland, ME, June 6, 1989

Powerful hard-line leaders of China's Communist Party saw their country's future last weekend and, abandoning all restraint, ordered the army to destroy it.

Before a world linked by graphic television images and desperate radio voices, China's People's Liberation Army rolled in to massacre hundreds — perhaps thousands — of non-violent student protesters in Beijing's Tienanmen Square.

Among the best educated and dedicated young communists in a society which reveres its children, the protesters had peacefully confronted their government for six weeks, urging it to make modest democratic reforms. Until the government answered with tanks and guns.

Even after the ferocious bloodletting, however, the impetus for democratic reform remains. As President Bush said Monday in moving quickly to cut off military sales to China, "the depth of the feeling toward democracy is so great that you can't put the genie back into the bottle." Tragically, China's aged leaders seem determined to try.

The ruthless repression ordered by Deng Xiaoping and Premier Li Peng may well cost them their country. Already, it has brought them worldwide condemnation. (Even Switzerland abandoned its customary neutrality to condemn the "brutal" use of force.) And it has obscured forever Deng's reputation as the visionary behind China's economic modernization.

The dimensions of the Chinese tragedy are profound. At its heart are the people still being killed and injured who thought their "people's government" would listen. Ahead lie deep and abiding consequences. A regime that slaughters its own people cannot long hold a place among civilized, economically interdependent nations. To that end, Bush has pointedly reserved the right to invoke further economic and diplomatic sanctions against China "if the violence escalates."

It is a right he may well have to exercise if voices of reason cannot be found in China to prevail.

THE CHRISTIAN SCIENCE MONITOR

Boston, MA, June 7, 1989

BEYOND the shock and horror of Tiananmen Square, beyond the period of broader repression likely to follow, the Chinese people's yearning for freedom will not be put down.

China's rulers may have the guns and – for now – the loyalty of the inaptly named People's Liberation Army. But the country's recent history – the beginnings of economic liberalization and cultural openings to the West – holds seeds more potent than the discredited and in fact unnatural grip of the Communist Party and its conservative, fear-driven leaders. It wasn't just youthful and idealistic students who came forward by the thousands to witness for democracy, but a broad spectrum of Chinese. It is a story, not just political or economic, but one of the human spirit. Mary Baker Eddy, the founder of this newspaper, once wrote: "Slavery is not the legitimate state of man." It may take years. But in the end, the human spirit and legitimacy will prevail.

The recent riveting events in Beijing and throughout the country in fact indicate the weakness of Marxist-Leninism. The wrenching lessons being learned there are of supreme importance to the rest of

the communist world, especially Mikhail Gorbachev: How to keep order while providing economic reform? How to free things up economically without relinquishing one-party rule? The answer, coming now in the Soviet Union and in Poland, is that real political participation must accompany a loosening up of state economic planning and control.

Whatever the rest of the world – especially the United States – does now regarding China, the aim should be to stop the killing while keeping the lines of communication open. President Bush's immediate suspension of government military sales and commercial export of weapons to China while leaving the US ambassador in place in Beijing strikes the right balance for now. It tells the regime of Deng Xiaoping and Li Peng that the slaughter of innocents has its price. And it tells the Chinese people that the US is not turning its back on their struggle. It is tragic that Mr. Deng (whose own son was crippled in the Cultural Revolution and who survived two purges) should have moved from economic reformer to oppressor of his own people. But the true voice of China has been heard, and it will be answered.

THE BLADE

Toledo, OH, June 6, 1989

ONE of the recurring themes of China's millennia of authoritarian rule is the so-called Mandate of Heaven — the notion that the emperor or other ruling power operates by a divine sanction that can be revoked. China's Communist party, in a long weekend of carnage against its best and brightest young people, has surely lost that mandate.

That does not mean that brute force will not work for awhile. The slaughter of the students and workers in Beijing can be seen as the desperate act of a government that considered itself backed into a corner. Ironically, had the aging leaders who rule China remained patient, their apparent strategy of letting the demonstrations fizzle out might have worked.

The use of force against unarmed people has stained the reputation of the People's Liberation Army and destroyed the reputation of China's octogenarian, ailing paramount leader, Deng Xiaoping. A shrewd behind-the-scenes manipulator and a survivor, Deng now joins Mao Zedong, his former superior and persecutor, in the ranks of leaders whose accomplishments are largely blotted out by irrational and even murderous acts toward the end of their careers.

The moral bankruptcy of China's Communist party, which has given the country unified rule for 40 years and vaulted it decades forwards, is virtually complete and its future uncertain. The facade of power in China often is deceptive. The Ch'in dynasty emperor Shih Huangdi unified China in 221 B.C. and built the Great Wall and the terra cotta warriors surrounding his tomb — the two major tourist sites today in China. He appeared to be so solidly entrenched that some predicted his dynasty would last 10,000 years; it broke apart only a few years after his death.

How the United States and the American people can best respond to the tragedy unfolding in Beijing and perhaps other Chinese cities before long is uncertain. U.S. policy was based on the notion that a China moving toward economic freedom, if not political freedom, would be a stable force in the region and a counterweight to Soviet military power.

Now, as so often in China's long tangle of history, that country once again appears to be dangerously unstable. Its government is finding out, as so many other despotic regimes have, that though power appears to come out of a gun, actually it flows from the people.

Little that the United States can say or do will have much effect in this situation. The tragedy being played out in China casts in principal and supporting players those who fancied themselves as enlightened tyrants and the millions of people who have swarmed out into the streets to demonstrate for more democracy and an end to corruption.

The protests may be crushed for the moment — nobody really can say — but the stakes will be much greater in any future confrontation between the government and the people. The Economist was squarely on target when it noted last week that Marx was right in at least one respect: Political parties which cannot move with the times will find themselves sooner or later on the rubbish heap of history.

The effects of the upheaval on the vast stage of Tiananmen Square and in other parts of Beijing, as well as perhaps other cities in China, will be felt for years, perhaps decades to come. Deng, in giving his people a greater degree of economic freedom, failed to recognize what a contagious force freedom is.

BUFFALO EVENING NEWS
Buffalo, NY, June 13, 1989

THE MASSACRE of unarmed students in Beijing can now be seen, not as a wild miscalculation by an uncertain leadership, but one of a series of conscious moves to quash moves toward democracy and to restore the repressive rule of a totalitarian state.

Following a puzzling period when Chinese leaders remained out of sight, the top leadership has emerged, led by senior leader Deng Xiaoping, to congratulate the murderers of the students in Tiananmen Square, denounce any return to capitalism and call for the arrest of leaders of the democratic movement, now labeled a "counter-revolutionary rebellion."

Other ominous totalitarian measures have been taken. Employing the "big lie" technique of Nazi Germany, an army commander said on television that "not a single student was killed" in Tiananmen Square. Perhaps 300 persons were killed, the government said, but these were soldiers who had been attacked by a small group of "hooligans."

At the height of the violence last week, there were reports of fighting between army units, and this may explain a new report that 50 officers have been executed for refusing to move against the student demonstrators.

In other dictatorial moves, Western journalists have been restricted or expelled, foreign newspapers have been barred. Democratic openness has been replaced by fear. Order has been restored. The blood has been washed from the pavement of Tiananmen Square, and "normal" life goes on.

China's brutal turmoil has made its relations with the United States plunge to their lowest point since diplomatic ties were resumed a decade ago. China is now denouncing the United States for allowing a dissident leader, prominent physicist Fang Lizhi, to find haven in the U.S. Embassy in Beijing. Washington is rightly standing firm in refusing to hand him over.

Fang was the focus of an earlier confrontation last February, when President Bush, while visiting Beijing, invited him to dinner. Chinese police prevented Fang from attending.

One might have thought that Deng and Fang would have something in common, since both were victims of the Cultural Revolution, that earlier round of reactionary violence, in the 1960s. Deng was removed from power, and Fang was among those intellectuals sent to work at manual labor in the fields or coal mines.

But the two differ on a fundamental matter. Deng has been forward looking in introducing freedom into the economy, using market incentives to spur impressive economic growth. He has not, like Soviet leader Mikhail Gorbachev, allowed similar freedom in the political sphere. But as Fang has warned: "Without democratization in China, there can be no modernization."

China's ties with the United States and other Western nations have suffered a severe setback. Deng played a revolutionary role in opening up China to the world in the past decade, but now he has thrown in his lot with the old guard that opposed many of his reforms and with the army, which he used to fire on his own people.

The discredited leadership must now deal with its sizable economic problems, aggravated by the halt in Western investment and the suppressed rage of the Chinese people.

China and other communist nations have seen recurrent cycles of democratic aspiration and repression, and only now are the Soviet-bloc countries winning some elements of democracy. In China, things may get worse before they get better.

The Washington Post
Washington, DC, June 5, 1989

IN TIANANMEN Square a cynical and panicked Chinese leadership has sent tanks and indiscriminately shooting soldiers against unarmed students and workers asking for democracy. It had looked as though some other outcome might be possible, not necessarily a student triumph but a government reassertion of power by nonviolent means. The party leadership, however, evidently could not countenance any loss of face, even on terms leaving party power formally intact, especially on terms legitimizing the students' protest and cause. There was a debate behind closed doors; its result became known early Sunday. Deaths in the hundreds—according to some accounts, in the thousands—are being reported in a classic struggle of people against brute power.

China had appeared to be edging from a generally successful, party-directed economic reform into a careful and also party-directed experiment with mild political reform. This was the prospect symbolized and encouraged by Mikhail Gorbachev's visit to Beijing last month. There suddenly burst forth, however, a hunger for democracy which was unprecedented in China and which few people anywhere had anticipated—a humbling lesson in the mysteries of totalitarian rule. A wise leadership would have absorbed the impact from below and, at least to some degree, accommodated it. But the actual leadership that emerged saw the new passion as a deadly threat to party control and national stability. The measure of its misreading is on view in Tiananmen Square. For China a period of great uncertainty, tension and distraction lies ahead.

Having come to its close official connection to China by a strategic route emphasizing a common interest in containing Soviet power, the United States now is embarrassed to find the contained force, in Moscow, looking relatively enlightened, while the containing force, in Beijing, looks ugly and anachronistic. Thus really for the first time since the Cultural Revolution do Americans find themselves hard put to define a policy that expresses the new outrage as well as the factor of national interest built up laboriously over the years. This may take some time. Already, however, it is clear the American policy requires more than appeals for Chinese nonviolence and restraint. China has repudiated the hope invested in that reasonable standard and has established a new requirement for American policy to reflect the reality of a massacre by a failed party reduced to ruling by force alone.

DESERET NEWS
Salt Lake City, UT, June 4, 1989

By resorting to violence against the massive but peaceful student demonstration in Beijing, the government of China has not alleviated its international embarrassment but exacerbated it.

That embarrassment must have been acute even before Saturday's harsh assault left at least 35 persons dead and hundreds injured. Earlier forays by unarmed troops had collapsed in an undignified shambles, raising doubts about the loyalty and morale of the Chinese military.

Then came Saturday's carnage in which tanks smashed through barricades to reach Tiananmen Square. Then troops opened fire on crowds of unarmed demonstrators and bloodily beat many of them.

By stooping to bloodshed, the government demonstrated much more than just the fact that it is deaf to the protesters' complaints about official corruption and their demands for democratic reforms.

Rather, the government also showed it was unwilling or unable to even out-wait the protesters, let alone out-argue them.

Moreover, though claiming that it acted to curb chaos and insisting that foreign influence was responsible for the anti-government demonstrations, Beijing fooled no one. Chaos? Until this weekend, the standoff between the demonstrators and the government had been tense but generally peaceful. Foreign involvement? The Chinese demonstrators know better than anyone else what's wrong in China.

Like students elsewhere, the Chinese demonstrators may have been idealistic and impatient. But they merely sought dialogue and participation. Instead, they were greeted initially with stern lectures and subsequently with bullets and beatings.

Earlier, by imposing martial law restrictions that included muzzles on news coverage even tougher than the press gags in South Africa, the Chinese government merely showed the world that it had something to hide.

But it could not hide the truth that, though the vast majority of Chinese have in recent years become freer and more prosperous, the system under which they live has become corrupt. In the words of one inside observer: "Nothing, however mundane, could be accomplished without money to bribe or connections to ply. With them, rules or no rules, anything was possible. People felt powerless."

The big question now is: What's next? The demonstrators have shown a willingness to take great risks to make themselves heard. The government, however, has shown it would rather shed blood than change. The specter of this intransigence could haunt China for many years to come.

The London Free Press
London, Ont., June 5, 1989

June 1, 1989, should long live as a day of infamy in Chinese history — the day when soldiers in Beijing's Tiananmen square opened fire with tanks, machine guns and rifles on thousands of relatively unarmed civilians calling for freedom and democracy.

The world has not seen any act of political repression quite so ferocious since Soviet tanks moved through the streets of Budapest in 1956, gunning down hundreds of Hungarian freedom fighters. In the case of China, though, it's a horrible case of fratricide: Chinese soldiers killing Chinese citizens at the command of their own Chinese authorities.

Appropriately enough, External Affairs Minister Joe Clark quickly called in the Chinese ambassador on Sunday to express the outrage of Canadians and call upon the Chinese government to stop "the aggressive and senseless killing by its armed forces." Similar statements have come from U.S. President George Bush and the leaders of all the other genuine multi-party democracies. Perhaps, the tough old men commanding the troops in Beijing will pay little heed, but it's enough that the brave students who occupied Tiananmen square will hear and be encouraged.

In addition, Immigration Minister Barbara McDougall should make plain that Chinese students attending school in Canada are welcome to stay in this country so long as the current turmoil persists. Here is a clear and compelling case for a major exemption from the generally valid rule that refugee claimants must apply from outside the country.

Correspondingly, the Bush administration should also offer sanctuary to the thousands of Chinese students studying in the U.S. and immediately cut off military aid to the Beijing regime. There is no reason to fear that vigorous measures to denounce the atrocities in Beijing will force the Chinese government back into a closer embrace with the Soviet Union. Regardless of ideology, any Chinese leader will want to keep his distance from Moscow in order to protect China's independent national interests.

What will happen next in China? No one can know for sure, but it's evident that government officials have to be concerned that they have lost almost all respect among the Chinese people.

Mao Tse-tung, the first ruler of Communist China, was notorious for insisting that power came out of the barrel of a gun, but he also inspired a great many gun-toting people with a fanatical belief in Communist idealism. That faith is now dead; it remains to be seen how long his successors can cling to power by brute force alone.

Las Vegas Review-Journal
Las Vegas, NV, June 6, 1989

The geriatric leaders of the "People's" Republic of China have reared up to smite the Chinese people, and all hopes for a peaceful transition to a more democratic form of government have been brutally crushed.

Although the hopes for a peaceful transition have vanished, it is still possible that democratic-minded forces will prevail — but only after a violent upheaval that depends on elements of the army taking the side of pro-democracy protesters. Indeed, reports out of China Monday suggested internecine fighting within the army, perhaps presaging full-blown civil war or a sustained rebellion against the communist leadership. Alas, Chinese democracy is not destined to be born without a mighty struggle.

As we watch the unfolding of what promises to be one of the major historical events of the 20th century, it is essential that the United States be on the right side of that history.

The butchery in Tiananmen Square deserves America's forceful condemnation. We support the call by Nevada Sens. Harry Reid, Richard Bryan and a bipartisan collection of others in Congress to condemn the brutality and — at the very least — cut off weapons sales to the Chinese government. The United States does have a major strategic stake in maintaining good relations with China; but to avert our faces at the bloodbath in Beijing would be unconscionable.

China represents a fascinating case study in what happens when a communist nation begins to abandon the Marxist economic model. Communist rulers always have justified repression of basic human rights by arguing that other "rights" — i.e. Marxist economic "rights" — take precedence over the bourgeois rights of free speech, free assembly, etc., enjoyed in the Western democracies.

When a communist state essentially admits Marxist economic theory has failed, and when it begins to dismantle the economic superstructure of Marxism — as China has during the 1980s — it loses any "justification" for dictatorship. In essence, when a communist state abandons communist economic theory, it becomes nothing but an old-line dictatorship, no different from any other run-of-the-mill tyranny. Socialist theories are chucked into the slop bucket and all that remains to sustain the dictatorship is naked power.

Mao said: "Every communist must grasp the truth: Political power grows out of the barrel of a gun." And so the students in Tiananmen Square have learned.

Toronto, Ont., June 1, 1989

Commenting on the nature of government, Confucius once said: "The relation between superiors and inferiors is like that between the wind and the grass. The grass must bend when the wind blows across it."

Present-day Chinese Communists may no longer cite Confucius. But his metaphor remains apt to evaluate the eroding strength of the student demonstrations in Beijing.

The hero on whom the students pinned their hopes for democratic reforms, Zhao Ziyang, appears to have lost power and influence in China's ruling hierarchy. The hardline leaders, Deng Xiaoping and Li Peng, remain in control.

Almost the only official recognition of the 20-day upheaval, which has garnered support from teachers, workers, farmers and soldiers, took the form of an admonitory statement from Peng Zhen, former head of the National People's Congress.

It said, "The motives of the students are good and they are identical with what the government wants. But the methods being used are not proper and show the students are not familiar with law and lack political experience."

But grass is resilient even in a harsh wind. And so the remaining demonstrators have emphasized their demands for more democracy and less corruption by erecting a huge, white plaster-of-paris replica of the Statue of Liberty in Tiananmen Square. The statue appears to be shaking her torch at the portrait of Mao Tse-Tung that dominates the square.

It's a dramatic way to tell Deng and Li that a yearning for freedom, once kindled, isn't easily suppressed even by the 200,000 troops that ring Beijing with the threat of force.

Confucius had some words for that situation, too. "In carrying on your government, why should you use killing (the unprincipled for the good of the unprincipled) at all? Let your evinced desires be for what is good, and the people will be good."

The Sun Reporter

San Francisco, CA, June 7, 1989

The reports from China change hourly. No one really knows the true picture or the extent of the devastating and murderous army assaults on the unarmed students and civilians on Tiananmen Square.

Everyone apparently agrees that the large troop movements and the use of military hardware against the unsuspecting students on or after midnight Saturday was uncalled for and a reprehensible, frenzied action by unknown (at this time) political leaders.

The earlier reaction of the military, when martial law was decreed and they refused to use their weapons on the students, was praised and by many interpreted as the proper response of a citizens' army. However, the students themselves and apparently their allies were lulled into false security; the students' decision to continue occupying the square until the meeting of the National Central Committee of the Communist party on June 24th was the final act which created a tremendous dilemma for those in China's leadership, the authoritarians.

It seems apparent that the authorities, who accused the students of anarchy, have now themselves been caught up in anarchy.

The unprecedented use of military force in Beijing has touched off a storm of civilian resistance across urban China, spurring ordinary people to bold defiance of heavily armed troops. On the other hand, it also seems to have intensified the regional power struggle between various factions of the army as well as the political leadership.

Army units loyal to various members of the heirarchy are reported in motion, with no one quite sure who is now in command. One report which was given credence was that the troops who responded so savagely Sunday morning were forces from Western China, who spoke a different dialect, did not understand the slogans of the students, and mistook a peaceful demonstration for insurrection. The latest information seems to indicate that there are two armies, one the 28th, which refused to enforce martial law and are now preparing defensive positions, and the other the 27th, which seems prepared to carry out the oppressive orders of the Chinese heirarchy.

One thing seems certain: China will never be the same. The dreadful massacre of 1,000 to 2,000 people by members of the People's Army of China will not resolve the present conflict. Because the students were demanding freedom, democratic rights and less corruption in the ranks of government, the army (which was misjudged by the populace) and the people will now become bitter enemies.

The world leaders are presently marking time until more information is known, so that an objecive appraisal can be made of who really is in control of the world's most populous country.

It has been said that young men fight the wars, and the planning of those wars is by old men — in this case apparently old men suffering from the loss-of-face complex, so humiliated by the young students and the general population that they are unable to focus their perspective on the new realities which were born on Tiananmen Square over the past fortnight.

Arkansas Gazette
Little Rock, AR, June 6, 1989

The bloody military assault in Beijing must be deplored and condemned among all civilized peoples, as it already has been by most of Chinese society. A government so shaky that it turns guns and tanks on its own people surely cannot sustain legitimacy.

Even from the government's point of view the decision to order loyal troops against unarmed, peacefully demonstrating students in Tiananmen Square makes no sense. What support the government still had after weeks of demonstrations for democracy and freedom within the system already in place surely has greatly dissipated.

If the hard-line faction can continue to rule at all, it will be only by the force of arms, bringing more bloody confrontation and tragedy on a truly heroic scale. The calls for reform issue from the nation's young people, its future. They cannot be denied for long, although in the short term their prospects for reshaping the political, economic and social order of their homeland are bleak. More bloodshed lurks grimly in the wings.

What can the United States and other nations do? Unfortunately, not nearly as much as their emotional response to brutal slaughter tugs at them to do. In time, sharper and more dramatic steps might be in order, but for now it is hard to find fault with President Bush's initial moves. For the time being there will be no break in diplomatic relations, on the sound reasoning that in a popular struggle for freedom and democracy a continuing American presence might be helpful to those whose cause we champion.

Events could shift dramatically. China's military is known for its factions; earlier contingents sent to Tiananmen Square were reluctant to move against the students and older sympathizers.

★　★　★

In one small step, Bush yesterday suspended all military sales to China and visits to the United States by Chinese military leaders. Chinese students in the United States who wish to extend their stay here will be looked upon favorably by American officials.

These and other measures may be sufficient for the moment, but if the violence escalates and persists, American interests would be the same as those who represent China's democratic future. If the Soviet Union is as committed to sweeping, peaceful change within its own country as it seems to be, it too would be obligated to align itself with China's future.

In the meantime, America's heart must go out to those who thirst so much for democracy that they, like their fallen comrades, may have to pay a dear price in its solemn pursuit.

The Register-Guard
Eugene, OR, June 6, 1989

Deng Xiaoping blew it. He turned the last chapter of his own career from a triumph into a travesty. And he imposed on the nation he leads an appalling, utterly pointless tragedy.

The students in Tiananmen Square were a military threat to no one. They had no guns or knives. Their weapons were words and ideas — often confused, always idealistic, ideas — but still only that. The students did not deserve to be shot by soldiers and crushed by tanks as their punishment for refusing to leave a public square.

This enormously sad moment for China spoils what had been a time of hope. Deng had turned the country around economically, pushing marketplace pragmatism and abandoning many of the controls that had stifled progress in the factories and the fields. This part of the drive toward modernism had worked well, even though imperfectly.

But many had commented earlier that the old warrior/politician did not have *political* modernism in his repertoire. He could no more give up authoritarianism than stop smoking. That analysis received shocking confirmation over the weekend.

It's true, of course, that the students had attracted massive support throughout the country. That undoubtedly frightened the leaders, chiefly men who have been in charge since China's Communist revolution. Although the specific thoughts of "the people" in support of the student demonstrations were in some ways vague and unformed, there was no doubt about a strong, shared criticism of those in power.

At the same time, it was absurd for the government to try to excuse sending in armed troops on the ground that protest leaders were counterrevolutionaries plotting to overthrow the government. Some of the official government statements issued after the shooting resembled the statements Southern sheriffs and politicians used to make about "communists" and "outside agitators" secretly controlling the civil rights movement.

What will happen now? There is bound to be a national wave of revulsion against the government for the massacre of civilians. That could manifest itself in a variety of ways; widespread strikes are likely. In any case, the reaction of the people will not make governing the nation easy.

Even an authoritarian government must have a minimum level of acceptance among the governed. So ultimately, this experience will discredit China's present generation of leaders and hasten the installation of successors who can claim at least some distance from the Tiananmen Square decision-making.

In the meantime, the old men still in power face hostility at home and condemnation abroad. Against that background, the inevitable jockeying among them will add to the national instability that their misguided resort to violence has produced.

THE SAGINAW NEWS
Saginaw, MI, June 5, 1989

The people of China re-learned a hard lesson. Raw power does grow out of the barrel of a gun.

The leaders of China may yet learn another — that of an idea whose time has come.

Over the weekend, the tanks of desperation, not the times of democracy, prevailed.

"Don't shoot the people," pleaded the crowds in Tiananmen Square. The soldiers shot the people. The army listened instead to a ruling elite that failed to understand that the streets were full not of chaos, but of hope.

In a massive betrayal of the masses themselves, China's government crushed China's people. In a contradiction of the party tenets the protesters espoused — some died singing the "Internationale," the Communist hymn — the clear will of students, farmers, workers, even bureaucrats, disappeared into a storm of gas and bullets.

Few thought it would end this way. The demonstrators were peaceful, even patriotic. Armed only with the desire for a better future, they asked for nothing more than the chance to achieve it.

But something snapped in Premier Li Peng, himself the victim of atrocities during the days of Red Guard terror. And as the crowds heeded a warning that "We can't let any more blood flow," armor toppled the figure called the "goddess of democracy," modeled on the Statue of Liberty.

Statues can be brought down; not so easily can a national spirit be quelled. If the brutality augurs a new period of suppression, then a mighty nation of a billion people must wait a little longer to assert its might. These seven weeks showed, however, from every corner of China, a new mood that can be put down, but not kept down.

It was Mao who said, "To be attacked by the enemy is not a bad thing, but a good thing." At least the real enemy of the people of China has identified itself, and must stare down the barrel of a power that cannot, sooner or later, be denied.

St. Paul Pioneer Press & Dispatch

St. Paul, MN, June 13, 1989

The cosmic storm building between the United States and China over dissident Fang Lizhi promises to thunder through the human rights community with massive force. The United States must refuse to hand over Dr. Fang to the witchhunters in Beijing or risk all moral credibility.

The Chinese government on Sunday ordered the arrests of Dr. Fang, an astrophysicist, and his wife, Li Shuxian, for what authorities said were counterrevolutionary activities — that is, supporting the democracy movement. The two prominent dissidents sought refuge in the U.S. Embassy in Beijing after the unthinkable massacre happened June 4 in Tiananmen Square.

The United States has been riding a fine line well in relations with China since senior leader Deng Xiaoping and his elderly cohorts abrogated the rule of law so carefully built up over the last decade. It is wise to try to salvage what is possible for when the bloody purges and hatemongering give way to renewed reason at some imponderable time in the future.

Dr. Fang's plight, however, is real and it is happening now. The Bush administration must continue to protect him. There are no foreseeable circumstances in this tangled tale that would warrant turning the dissident over to the vengeful Chinese authorities.

In some ways the Fang case is a simplistic symbol of chaos the Chinese old guard has unleashed on its people. But it is a valid symbol, one that the world is watching.

None knows better than the prominent astrophysicist that, to borrow the Chinese idiom, there is great havoc under heaven.

Edmonton Journal

Edmonton, Ont., June 5, 1989

The Beijing Spring is over, but China's long march to democracy is not.

The weekend massacre in Tiananmen Square will in no way advance the position of China's government, or of the old guard who now appear to control it.

Indeed, it is difficult to imagine that the slaughter will do anything other than enrage and inspire the millions of Chinese who took the streets during the month of protests for democracy.

By killing the people whose trust it claims to exercise, China's government has lost its legitimacy.

It no longer has a moral or ethical basis on which to govern, it may rule only by the brute force of arms — provided it can continue to find soldiers willing to slaughter unarmed civilians.

There can be no justification, no mitigation, for the bloodshed in Tiananmen Square. The democracy movement in the square was singular for its nonviolence. In the face of past attempts by soldiers to enforce martial law, thousands of people used their bodies to block the military advance. Even then, there had been no attempt to escalate the confrontation into bloodshed.

The violence began only when an old man on his sickbed decided that enough was enough. Deng Xiaoping, supreme leader of China, suffering from cancer, reverted to the habit of a lifetime in ordering the armed assault that cleared the square — at a cost of several hundred lives.

The images of people crushed by the tanks, shot by random machine-gun fire, stand in stark contrast to the pacifism of the protesters during the month the square was occupied. Only days ago, soldiers of the People's Liberation Army joined the demonstrators, singing along with them, accepting flowers and flashing peace signs.

The soldiers who carried out Deng's order were from outside the Beijing military command. But their act has wrought a fundamental change in revolutionary China. Since 1949, the military has enjoyed a special status because its title reflected its role — the People's Liberation Army.

Now the army of liberation becomes an army of oppression, the army of the people is turned against the people. How many soldiers will accept the new situation? Only a fortnight ago, 100 senior military commanders in the Beijing region denounced martial law. How can Deng and his supporters hope to maintain the loyalty of the entire army? And without it, how can they hope to maintain control over a country of a billion people?

The propaganda line after the massacre was that the army moved in to restore order and had the support of the students and of the population at large. But in an age of mass media, this facade soon will unravel.

Having gone this far, Deng and his supporters will have no choice but to maintain an authoritarian course. They clearly have rejected any negotiations or popular reform. But the hardliners are in a hopeless position. They may maintain power for a few months or perhaps at best a few years. By ordering in the army, they have signed the death warrant of the *ancien regime*. In this, at least, the people of Tiananmen Square did not die in vain.

Calgary Herald

Calgary, Ont., June 6, 1989

Chinese students began occupying Tiananmen Square in April with but one demand — a public dialogue with China's Communist leadership to discuss political reform.

China's old guard blurted out their unequivocal answer Sunday and punctuated it with machine-gun fire in the dark.

Savagely, senselessly, China's hardliners chose to shoot blindly rather than talk with their own people. With estimates of the dead varying from several hundred to several thousand, it was a textbook display of reactionary repression.

Thomas Jefferson wrote in 1787, "The tree of liberty must be refreshed from time to time with the blood of patriots and tyrants. It is its natural manure."

China's tree of liberty was last weekend freshened only with the blood of patriots. The tyrants shed nothing. Not even crocodile tears.

The brutal arrogance of Chinese troops bears a chilling resemblance to the conduct of Soviet troops who rolled into Budapest to squelch a popular movement in 1956.

The difference, however, is that the Chinese massacre cannot be summed up neatly as a clash between capitalist and communist ideology.

Quite simply, this bloodbath was sanctioned because China's old guard leaders felt threatened. Like tin-pot dictators the world over, Deng Xiaoping chose the military solution.

No matter how reasonable, pacifist or patriotic the students actually were, they were perceived to be a threat. Deng would not deign to acknowledge one single demand. Like the emperors and warlords before him, he chose brute force over dialogue.

But should the 84-year-old live long enough, he is certain to discover that his solution is really no solution at all.

The outrage of the international community is nothing compared to the bitter seed he has planted among his own people. Feelings of wrath and betrayal are sure to dog Deng and his successors. One 36-year-old Communist party official put it this way, "We don't want to overthrow the government, but we never thought the government could be so inhumane."

Chinese yearning for a freer society and less corruption by their Communist leaders will be able to point to the Soviet model.

Mikhail Gorbachev has recognized that the Soviet Union could not achieve economic reforms without political reforms, too. Deng, who has been successful in opening up China's vast market to trade and investment, must come to the same realization.

His administration is not fighting "the dregs of society" but intelligent, articulate young people with a hankering for free thoughts and free speech.

The Chinese army has trashed the student uprising and wrecked their papier mache goddess of liberty. But like Jefferson's tree, the blood spilled has not slaked the Chinese people's thirst for reform.

Bush Responds to Chinese Massacre

U.S. President George Bush June 5, 1989 announced a package of sanctions against the Chinese government in response to the crackdown in Beijing. But in his message that day and in other statements, the president stressed that he did not want to break off the relationship with China that the U.S. had cultivated since 1972.

Bush, who had served as the head of the U.S. Liaison Mission in China from 1974 to 1975, stated at a White House news conference June 5 that he "deplored" the use of force against the pro-democracy protesters and urged the Chinese government to resume the restraint previously shown in its dealings with the demonstrators. The president emphasized, however, that the situation in China required a "reasoned, careful action" and not "an emotional response," because of the uncertainty surrounding China's political leadership.

The primary sanctions announced by Bush were the suspension of sales of military equipment to China and of all government-to-government trade. He also suspended visits between U.S. and Chinese military leaders, offered medical assistance to the injured through the Red Cross and said requests by Chinese students in the U.S. to extend their visas would be treated sympathetically.

The State Department June 6 encouraged Americans in Beijing to leave China. On the following day, June 7, the U.S. and other countries ordered the evacuation of the dependents of foreign service personnel after Chinese army troops raked the Jianguomenwai diplomatic complex in eastern Beijing with machine-gun fire.

In a prime-time television press conference June 8, Bush largely restated the themes from his message announcing the sanctions, but said that the U.S. could not have normal relations with China until the government in Beijing agreed to "recognize the validity" of the pro-democracy movement. Bush disclosed at the news conference that he had tried to call the Chinese leaders on the telephone earlier that day, but "the line was busy."

The Washington Times
Washington, DC, June 7, 1989

The press and Congress wanted George Bush to respond to China's weekend massacre of its own citizens with a series of harsh and sweeping sanctions. The president had a better idea. He ordered up a response that would improve the prospects for political liberty in China.

Specifically, Mr. Bush suspended sales of weapons from the United States to China, suspended visits between military leaders in the two nations, agreed in effect to extend the stay of all Chinese students who wish to remain in the United States, offered to assist victims of the Beijing blood bath by sending targeted aid to the International Red Cross, and promised to review options for dealing with China as events warrant.

"The process of democratization," the president noted, "will not be a smooth one." Nevertheless, his maneuvers seem designed to help our friends and hurt our foes in China. In suspending commercial and government sales of weapons to China and putting a temporary halt to military exchanges, the president has exploited the growing divisions in the Chinese military.

China's 28th Field Army, which reportedly supports ousted Communist Party leader Zhao Ziyang, and the elite 38th Army reportedly are on the verge of fighting the 27th Army, which invaded Vietnam several years ago and conducted last weekend's soulless slaughter in Beijing's streets. Mr. Bush's actions could deepen those divisions and thus aid the advantage of pro-democracy forces. A disunited military lacks the oppressive capacity of a united one.

The decision to extend visas to Chinese students and grant aid to Chinese victims sends the citizens of China a clear message that the United States really does support the enormously brave citizens who continue to stand up to the government, and that our nation will not lend support to the vicious little despots, including Deng Xiaoping, who seem to feel no remorse for slaughtering their own citizens. Consequently, he will not send students in America back to the keepers of the Beijing abattoir.

Significantly, the president did not adopt trade sanctions, which enjoy support on Capitol Hill. Nor did he put an end to cultural exchanges. Mr. Bush understands that those two activities have played an enormous role in spreading the gospel of freedom to China and allowing citizens to enjoy some of the prosperity that liberal democracy offers. Material prosperity is no substitute for real property rights, but the appearance of a few creature comforts has persuaded Chinese citizens that the roads to economic prosperity and political liberty are indivisible.

China becomes a more remarkable place with each passing day. Citizens, including members of the military, have not surrendered their courage nor their dreams of liberty. No communist country yet has seen this kind of hopeful, albeit bloody, insurrection. Mr. Bush is wise under the circumstances to remain engaged and to offer the Chinese people a workable model for a world after communism. His decision to respond to the crisis thoughtfully, instead of reacting quickly with sanctions, demonstrates that he is far more serious as a leader than his critics are as mavens of foreign policy.

The Union Leader
Manchester, NH, June 11, 1989

President Bush does himself and democracy no favors with his continued attempts to straddle the fence on the latest murders in Red China.

The wholesale slaughter of thousands of Chinese students last weekend is just the latest in a long line of barbaric acts by the Communist thugs who have run that great land for 40 years. The West should be surprised, not at the violence, but at its own continued ability to be surprised by it.

We had hoped that the President's actions last Monday — in cutting off military aid and in condemning the violence — were signals of a solid, consistent approach in dealing firmly with these butchers.

We were wrong. Instead, at his Thursday night press conference, Mr. Bush came off as well-meaning but weak. He seemed most interested in not offending any single one of the Chinese bosses.

Indeed, he came off looking like an apologist for the likes of top Red party boss Deng Xiaoping, suggesting he might not have been "involved" in the student massacre. Deng repaid that favor the next day, by showing up on Red China TV to praise the killings.

True enough, there is only so much the U.S. can do in this case. We cannot tell the Communists how to run their show. But neither can they tell us how to run our show — including with whom we deal and on what basis.

Our dealings with such bloody regimes — be they in Beijing or Moscow — should be strict and limited. They should not include trade unless it is linked with meaningful political reform — not the "economic reform" that foolish Americans are hailing.

Strengthening the Communists' economies without a change in their political creed is not only foolish, it is suicidal for the West.

George Bush knows this and he ought to be saying it, instead of referring to the murders of thousands of Chinese students as one in a series of Communist "excesses."

Minneapolis Star and Tribune

Minneapolis, MN, June 10, 1989

Those who wanted to hear President Bush talk tough about China Thursday night heard him talk tough. Those who wanted him to move cautiously saw him do that too. Trouble is, in trying to grant both wishes, Bush did justice to neither.

Bush declared that his administration would find it impossible to have normal relations with the Chinese officials responsible for the massacre of Beijing citizens last weekend. But lest those officials take too much notice of the remark, he added that it was impossible to tell just who were the culprits. "That's the Chinese system," he said.

That sounds like a president preparing to do nothing. Bush would protest that he already has done something, and we agree. He was wise to suspend military exports. He was correct to offer visa extensions for Chinese students. And he did right to shelter Chinese dissident Fang Lizhi at the U.S. Embassy in Beijing. But Thursday night's press conference was a chance for Bush to articulate Americans' abhorrence of the Chinese regime's attack on an unarmed population. Instead, he made it all sound like a policy difference.

Bush doesn't know whom to blame? Here's one: Premier Li Peng, who was filmed Thursday waving to his troops and congratulating them for their good work. Here's another: senior leader Deng Xiaoping, who reappeared Friday and also praised the army's murderous suppression of the student movement. In cynical, self-justifying overstatement, Deng said the students wanted to "overthrow communism and do away with the socialist system and the People's Republic of China and establish a capitalist republic." But they were unsuccessful, Deng said, because "our troops never forgot the people, never forgot the party, never forgot the country's interest."

Meanwhile, there are signs that the Chinese people are beginning to lose heart. Fewer of them will speak to Western reporters or show other signs of defiance to the regime. The government says it will hunt down and arrest student leaders.

Bush emphasized Thursday night that he wants to preserve the U.S. relationship with China. He is right to want to do so. But China is a country going through immense changes; the present leadership will not remain in power long. At a moment like this, the best way to serve the U.S. friendship with China is to stand more firmly with those Chinese citizens who have risked everything for the cause of democracy.

St. Petersburg Times

St. Petersburg, FL, June 13, 1989

Deng Xiaoping, Li Peng and other members of China's old-line political and military leadership came out of seclusion late last week and, with unseemly enthusiasm, claimed responsibility for the murderous suppression of their country's nascent democracy movement. They then launched a nationwide program of mass arrests, censorship, propaganda and intimidation that clearly will continue for weeks, months or even years to come.

No longer can official American policy be based on the possibility that the cold-blooded orders that have led to the deaths of thousands of unarmed protesters, as well as the unwarranted arrests and beatings of thousands more, emanated from someplace other than the solid center of the Chinese government.

The limited sanctions announced by President Bush a week ago represented a proper acknowledgement of the turmoil and uncertainty of events then taking place at the highest levels of China's political and military establishment. No such uncertainty exists today. The hardliners clearly have seized control, and they have shown themselves capable of committing almost incomprehensible barbarities to maintain it.

The time has come for the president and Congress to take much tougher actions that correspond to the Chinese hardliners' undeniable consolidation of power. Those actions should include a suspension of all normal economic ties between the U.S. and Chinese governments. We also should work to persuade other governments — particularly Japan, with whom China has developed an extensive economic relationship — to impose similar sanctions. To do less would be to betray millions of courageous Chinese citizens, as well as our own most basic democratic principles.

The immediate effects of broad economic and diplomatic sanctions will be painful for Americans and Chinese alike. At the very least, China seems certain to sacrifice most of the economic progress that had been won during a decade of reforms instituted by Deng. At the same time, our government has good reason to regret the erosion of an important bilateral relationship that had been built with painstaking care since the re-establishment of normal U.S.-Chinese relations in 1979.

However, there is little reason to believe that firm American sanctions against China will have long-term geopolitical consequences. The modern technology that China so desperately needs can be acquired only from the West. If Mikhail Gorbachev were to attempt to establish closer relations with Deng and his aging henchmen, he would immediately sacrifice the far greater prize he has won in Western Europe through his carefully developed image as an unthreatening peacemaker. The truth is that China's leaders, despite all their bluster, must either work with the West or withdraw entirely into another period of isolation.

Surely, Deng and Li had some idea of the terrible price that their country would pay for this latest plunge into repression and xenophobia, but other governments may reflect on whether firmer responses to past Chinese outrages might have helped to prevent the atrocities of recent days. The crushing of the Beijing demonstrations is different only in scale from years of brutal subjugation of the people of Tibet. Earlier this year, Chinese police and security forces massacred a group of Tibetan monks, nuns and other peaceful demonstrators in a gruesomely similar show of force. The current diplomatic standoff over the U.S. embassy's offer of sanctuary to prominent dissident Fang Lizhi also might have been avoided if American officials had risen to defend Fang during a similar dispute that arose in the course of Mr. Bush's visit to China in February.

The American people's anger over events in China has transcended partisan and ideological differences, and congressional Democrats and Republicans appear almost unanimous in their support for a much stronger presidential response. The defense of democracy often requires sacrifice, and our support for human rights in China may entail some significant short-term costs. However, hundreds of thousands of Chinese already have shown that they are prepared to make the ultimate sacrifice for the cause of freedom. They deserve the most passionate and effective support that the American government and people can offer them.

MILWAUKEE SENTINEL

Milwaukee, WI, June 6, 1989

President Bush's ban on military sales and commercial export of weapons to China won't take the guns and tanks away from Chinese army personnel who, despite spreading murder and mayhem through Tiananmen Square, have been unsuccessful in their attempts to quell a student-led democratic uprising.

It will, however, unequivocally indicate whose side the United States is on in this battle. To the extent the students get that message, Bush's support must be encouraging.

But Bush's words are just as important to that faction of China's leadership that was counseling moderation in response to student demands before being pushed out of the picture by Premier Li Peng and, no doubt, Li's mentor, Deng Xiaoping.

Supporters of former party chief Zhao Ziyang, who reportedly was placed under house arrest after the tough line against the students was initiated, now have some political leverage in the discussions that must be going on about the defiance of military action by the demonstrators.

The massacre of more than 2,000 Chinese citizens by government troops in the middle of their nation's capital reportedly has required barricades to fence off hundreds of thousands of enraged onlookers from the scene.

Obviously, the dimensions of the problem now have gone beyond the limits of gun-barrel politics, and some dialog must ensue.

Toward that end, Bush wisely rejected calls for him to withdraw the US ambassador from Beijing in addition to banning the arms sales.

"I don't want to see a total break in the relationship with China," the president said and neither should any other American who is concerned about the best interests of the valiant students.

In addition, as a former emissary to China, the president knows that the progress made since the renewal of Sino-US relations 17 years ago is too important to walk away from.

A country whose boundaries embrace one out of every four people in the world just can't be ignored.

San Francisco Chronicle

San Francisco, CA, June 6, 1989

THE ANGUISH in the battle Chinese leaders are waging against their own people extends far beyond China. French President François Mitterrand said, "A regime which is reduced to firing on its own youth to survive, when the youth it has educated rises up in freedom, has no future." But more than words and wishful thinking are needed now.

The problem is what to do before we know what the outcome of the terrible struggle will be. Official U.S. reaction is cautious, tempered by the knowledge that 10,000 Americans live in China — including an estimated 370 students in the endangered University of Beijing.

President Bush gave a minimal response. He ordered a halt to military exports and commercial arms sales to China. He said Chinese students studying in this country would be allowed to remain until peaceful conditions are restored in China, and he promised to join in international relief efforts.

BUT BUSH SAID that because it is important to avoid escalating the crisis, he would avoid severing diplomatic and commercial ties. And sure enough, at about the same time that the president was describing his position, United States exporters announced a $265 million wheat sale to China.

Congressional leaders of both parties call quite properly for a more vigorous response. We should make preparations now to receive an influx of political refugees, including much of China's intellectual leadership. We will surely see a massive increase in the flow of capital into the United States from Hong Kong, where chances for peaceful union with China look far less hopeful than they did a short time ago.

Omaha World-Herald

Omaha, NE, June 6, 1989

Congressional leaders have endorsed President Bush's measured diplomatic response to the Beijing Massacre. We hope their words of support discourage any independent effort to have Congress substitute its China policy for that of the White House and the State Department.

Henry Kissinger offered sensible advice in a Sunday interview. The former secretary of state said that U.S. leaders can't afford "emotional outbursts" and that America must beware of actions that would give the Soviet Union "a free ride" in influence in Asia.

Kissinger is right. That's why most countries have a state department or foreign office, staffed with experts who know how to convey outrage with the proper nuance to avoid long-term damage to the nation's interests.

Nuance is a tool of diplomacy; it is next to impossible to achieve in the playing-to-the-galleries atmosphere that sometimes surrounds congressional debate. Consider the comments of Rep. Mickey Edwards, R-Okla., who criticized what he called the administration's "excessively cautious" initial reaction.

Edwards said: "Diplomatic messages of disapproval are a pretty puny reaction to the murdering of innocent civilians whose only crime is to want the same freedoms we in the West take for granted."

Sen. Jesse Helms, R-N.C., and Rep. Stephen Solarz, D-N.Y., also joined in the criticism. They called for a review of U.S. policies and possible sanctions. If Bush declined to take steps that are tough enough, the congressman said Sunday, "Congress will do it for him."

But the White House is the proper place for such decisions to be made. To exhaust the diplomatic options now would leave fewer for use if the situation worsened. An overreaction at any point could push China, as Kissinger suggested, closer to the Soviet Union or otherwise permanently damage U.S. interests in Asia.

The package Bush announced Monday includes suspending the shipment of military equipment to China, ending contacts between U.S. and Chinese military officers, encouraging humanitarian aid to the victims and extending the visas of Chinese students who want to prolong their stay in the United States. Bush wisely declined to recall the U.S. ambassador — a move that Solarz had urged him to take.

Certainly a lot of Americans feel outrage over what has been happening in China. Certainly a number of troubling questions have been raised about the character of the regime with which America has cooperated for several years. Certainly a country whose heroes are Washington, Jefferson and Lincoln should side with people who are struggling for freedom and democracy.

But diplomacy isn't like professional rassling, with Congress having the option to jump in and begin pummeling the Chinese government because such people as Edwards, Helms and Solarz might not believe the executive branch is being sufficiently macho. Diplomacy is more like chess, a contest of infinite subtlety in which a seemingly insignificant mistake at one stage of the game can come back much later to cause defeat.

The president has made his move; it would be a mistake for congressmen to elbow him aside and take over the game.

St. Paul Pioneer Press & Dispatch

St. Paul, MN, June 10, 1989

It's all over in China, at least on the surface. The guys with the guns won and now they are busy scrubbing off the bloodstains, tearing down the democracy posters — and rewriting the history of this most remarkable Chinese spring.

The United States, in its desire to maintain good relations with official China, must take care not to join the history rewriters, not to slip into pretending that nothing really happened in Tiananmen Square, Beijing.

This nation will and should continue to deal with those who govern China, but it must do so now without the rose-colored glasses that filtered out official brutality in Tibet last winter and the harassment of dissidents at home more recently. Never again can it be business as usual, especially not if China's bosses follow through with threats of reprisals against the demonstrators for democracy.

President Bush has sought and hit — for now — the "proper, prudent balance" between supporting desire for democracy in China and promoting the desire for a working relationship with China in this country. He has been right in choosing limited punitive measures against China and in choosing his words. In his press conference Thursday he stressed the fundamental importance to this country of the trade and political relationship that he helped develop with China. And he stressed the need for Beijing to "recognize the validity of the students' aspirations" if normal relations are to be resumed.

Let us hope that official China was listening, and cares.

The Providence Journal

Providence, RI, June 13, 1989

The terrifying events in China this past week symbolize a number of things for Americans — not the least of which is the melancholy fact that the United States is not "the world's policeman," as our global watchdogs frequently remind us. It is natural to sympathize with those Chinese resident in the United States who feel rage and frustration about events in their homeland; but it is perilously easy to expect that this country can, by some magical process, reverse the tragic course of events now consuming the People's Republic. It can do no such thing.

It may, however, do many good things, and those are being done. Close to home, the Bush administration has offered to extend the visas of Chinese now studying in American universities — a slow-motion form of political asylum — and our embassy in Beijing can actually offer asylum to China's leading dissident, the physicist Fang Lizhi. The Voice of America must continue to broadcast that rarest of commodities, the truth, to Chinese listeners. And it should be noted that around the world the language of democratic protest is English, and that the global bulletin board is our own broadcast agency.

The administration has declared that while this country does not wish to jeopardize long-term relations between America and China, short-term understandings with the present regime are in for reassessment. That is an important point. In the wake of the massacre in Tiananmen Square, and subsequent events, it is tempting to bring our ambassador home, and declare China out of the pale. But that would accomplish little other than to stiffen the resolve of the government in Beijing, and clear the decks for a wider reign of terror. Moral superiority should not translate into self-defeating blindness: If the United States does not monitor events in China, and maintain pressure on the Deng regime, who in the world will?

For just as citizens are suffering for democracy in China, people are dying for freedom in Armenia, in Uzbekistan, in Georgia, in Afghanistan, in the Baltic republics, in Tibet, in Central and Southern Africa — and yes, in Central America as well. There is little difference between the instinct which has driven the authorities in the Soviet Union to gun down dissidents and the predictable reaction of China's ruling camp. The only real difference is a matter of focus: Our eye is trained on Beijing at the moment, and horrified by what we see. What can be done?

We can keep that eye trained closely and steadily on its target. We can institute sanctions — diplomatic, political, military, cultural — to emphasize the horror and outrage that we feel. The Chinese government is like any authoritarian breed: It understands power, and might respond to punishment. Just as the students look to America as a model and ideal, so the world looks to us for leadership now. If there is any hope for freedom in China, it may rest in our capacity to act when it matters.

THE SACRAMENTO BEE

Sacramento, CA, June 10, 1989

President Bush's press conference Thursday evening was his first formal televised news conference since coming to office and, after what the country had been subject to during the previous eight years, it was a breath of fresh air — almost always to the point, concise, intelligent.

Much of the session was, almost inevitably, devoted to China, a subject on which his two immediate predecessors might well have been tempted to engage in some heavy, and not very useful, moral breathing. And while Bush made his concern and indignation clear, he kept his focus on where this country's interests lie: why it did not make sense to recall the U.S. ambassador — who, as Bush told one questioner, has been helpful in getting Americans out — or to abrogate grain sales.

Bush pointed out the obvious — that it will be impossible to have normal relations with China under the present circumstances — but he also made it clear that he wanted to preserve relations as far as possible. It was a performance that, both in style and substance, showed a man who had not just an easy command of the facts, but who understood the complexities of diplomacy and foreign affairs and was confident about that understanding.

The general course Bush set Thursday might have been set by almost any president, but the comprehension and directness of his responses — both to the questions about China and about other subjects — generated the sense, after eight years of embarrassment, that here was a man who thought about global relationships, understood their importance and did his homework. There was no tripping over NATO missile systems, no anxious moments in the attempt to make logical connections between NATO forces, the new winds blowing from Moscow and the new challenges from the Eastern bloc.

In his days in Brussels and London during the past couple of weeks, Bush had shown, after a too-lengthy period of hibernation, that he has begun to comprehend the nature of those challenges — in what ways they require a continuation of the policies of deterrence rooted in the Cold War, and in what way they represent a new world and require new thinking. The press conference Thursday night indicated that Brussels and London were not just happy accidents.

China Reports New Arrests of Protesters

Chinese authorities June 16-21, 1989 reported arrests of more than 500 students and workers as a nationwide campaign against pro- democracy activists continued following the bloody military crackdown in Beijing two weeks earlier. The latest arrests brought to at least 1,500 the total number of people detained since the crackdown began.

At the same time, the government carried out its first public execution of protesters convicted of crimes related to the recent unrest, drawing widespread condemnation from Western nations.

Three workers in Shanghai who had been convicted of setting fire to a train that had run over a group of demonstrators were executed June 21. The executions were carried out immediately after an appeals court declined to overturn the death sentences.

Although details of the executions were not reported by the government, it was believed that the three men – Xu Guoming, Bian Hanwu and Yan Xuerong – were killed in a manner characteristic of Chinese capital punishment, with a single bullet to the back of the head. The death penalty was common in China, with hundreds of convicted criminals said to be executed each year.

Western governments, many of which had urged clemency or the three, June 21 reacted to the executions with new expressions of outrage against China. British Prime Minister Margaret Thatcher said she was "utterly appalled" by the death sentences. French Foreign Minister Roland Dumas declared, "What is happening in China is atrocious." The West German government said it was shocked by the "tragic hardening" of China's policies toward the protesters.

The reaction in the U.S. from the Bush administration was more subdued. Secretary of State James A. Baker 3rd said, "We deeply regret the fact that these executions have gone forward." President George Bush, who one day earlier had imposed new sanctions against China, declined to comment on the matter.

U.S. congressional leaders, however, were outspoken in their condemnation of the escalating crackdown. Senate Majority Leader George J. Mitchell (D, Maine) called the executions "barbarous" and urged the president to take "further steps" against the Chinese regime.

Separately, Chinese authorities June 22 reported the executions of seven people in Beijing that day and 17 others in the eastern city of Jinan. The latest executions raised to 27 the total number of people put to death since the start of the government crackdown on pro-democracy activists. The seven people executed in Beijing were among a group of eight workers convicted several days earlier of attacking military vehicles and soldiers. The fate of the eighth defendant was not reported. It was unclear for what crimes the 17 defendants in Jinan were put to death. The Chinese government June 22 announced that it had arrested 13 people it accused of being spies for Taiwan.

China's Communist Party June 24 ousted General Secretary Zhao Ziyang and several other top officials in a widely expected leadership shuffle. Zhao, who had been an outpoken proponent of economic and political liberalization, was replaced by Jiang Zemin, the party chief of Shanghai. Jiang, 62, had reportedly gained favor among China's top leaders for his tough crackdown on pro-democracy protests that spread to Shanghai from Beijing.

The shake-up was announced at the end of a secret meeting of the Communist Party's Central Committee June 23-24 in Beijing's Great Hall of the People. It appeared to herald the preeminence of the party's hard-line faction, led by leader Deng Xiaoping, Premier Li Peng and President Yang Shangkun. On June 25, the party widened its purge, calling for the removal and prosecution of all members who had supported the student movement.

In addition to Zhao, the party dismissed Hu Qili, its propaganda chief, from the Politburo's five-member standing committee. Like Zhao, Hu had been accused of supporting many of the demands of the student protesters. Hu apparently retained his posts on the full Politburo and the Central Committee.

The Kansas City Times

Kansas City, MO, June 21, 1989

America faces difficult problems with the crackdown in China. Our strategic interests have not changed: China still provides a counterweight against Soviet power. A severe break with Beijing would benefit only Moscow.

As a result, Washington must perform a difficult high-wire act in the coming months. The sanctions approved so far, including a cessation of weapons sales and yesterday's halt in high-level contacts, are appropriate. If the crackdown continues and increases in severity, we must not shrink from the consequences of more serious steps.

The Tiananmen Square massacre will go down as one of the most appallingly stupid decisions by any regime in history. With the demonstrators slowly succumbing to fatigue, time was on the side of the government. Party leaders had only to wait, yet they made no serious attempt at negotiation. In the ensuing bloodbath the Chinese Communist Party extinguished more than a decade of progress and exposed the illusions of many in the West.

The economic reforms of Deng Xiaoping amounted to yet another Chinese political campaign, not dissimilar in basic structure from those that have gone before. Like the Great Leap Forward and even the Cultural Revolution, the economic reforms had no goal or agreed-upon stopping place. Chinese society, lacking an independent court system or any institution with authority to overrule the party, remains a society without anchors. At any time, the winds may change.

Few of the economic reformers were prepared for the implications of their policies. Few understood that economic development necessarily increases pressure for political freedom. Modern growth, of the sort that China's leaders professed to seek, requires the freedom to create, to exchange ideas, to be informed about the latest developments in various fields.

The students, many of whom had studied overseas, knew this. Still, they sought not the overthrow of the government. They sought only a little more freedom and a little less repression.

The ferocity of the government's reaction has settled matters in China only temporarily. China cannot be ruled entirely by force. The question now is how long the current leadership can retain the backing of the army. In the coming months, accounts will come due.

Last year's bank runs and panic buying were only the beginning. Now the future may hold food shortages, rising inflation, factory closings, unemployment, spreading unrest. Once again, farmers will be paid with IOUs instead of cash. Once again they will hoard grain for sale in the free market where prices are higher.

Mao Zedong once said, "A single spark can start a prairie fire." When the tanks rolled toward Tiananmen Square, the tinder was laid in place. With Deng in his 80s, the incendiary spark could come at any time.

THE INDIANAPOLIS STAR

Indianapolis, IN, June 16, 1989

The original "goddess of democracy" statue stood in Tiananmen Square in Beijing.

With both arms she held a symbolic torch high as thousands of students and workers demonstrated for more freedom and a bigger role of the people in government.

The demonstration was peaceful. The goals were just.

China's Red masters acted. They gave the orders. Soldiers and tanks moved across the square. Hundreds, possibly thousands of demonstrators were gunned down and crushed. No one is certain how many died in the massacre.

The "goddess of democracy" was smashed.

Police and soldiers began rounding up leaders of the demonstration.

Totalitarianism was back to normal in China. So it seemed.

On Wednesday a new "goddess of democracy" statue was unveiled in Indiana, on the Vincennes University campus.

Chinese and American students watched the ceremony.

Enoch Poon sang at the dedication. He had fled oppression in China. He sang in mourning for the thousands who had risked death to demand democracy and freedom and the unknown numbers who had died.

A poem about the crushed statue became, in his strong voice, a defiant anthem:

"I have never known freedom . . .

". . . democracy is more than a plaster statue . . .

". . . but the memory of her will preserve the ideas she died for."

The ideas live. They live in countless brave hearts and minds. In time they will prevail.

Tyrants can kill people. They can smash statues. They cannot kill ideas.

Edmonton Journal

Edmonton, Alta., June 26, 1989

There shouldn't be much surprise that Western businesses are returning to China, only days after the bloody suppression of the pro-democracy movement.

Even as Chinese authorities step up their reign of terror, with barrages of propaganda and execution of political prisoners, some leading Western companies are making a comeback.

And it shouldn't shock people that international business is returning to China. While there may not be much new investment, there is a considerable amount of existing investment to protect.

Besides, it is a mistake to equate capitalism with liberal democracy. Look at the successful capitalist economies of Asia: South Korea, Indonesia, Hong Kong, Singapore, Taiwan. None of these countries has a democratic tradition; until recently, South Korea and Taiwan didn't even experiment with democracy.

But even if it's business as usual for the business community, it shouldn't be for Western governments.

While Canada and other Western countries are limited in the effective action they can take against China, there are a number of ways to express their revulsion for the new tyranny.

One step is to look at trade ties — China enjoys broad access to many Western markets under the status of "most favored nation." Those trade terms can be downgraded; China's access to Western countries can be on a "least favored nation" basis.

Another good measure would be to strictly limit all intergovernmental contact.

And governments should ask their own businessmen to consider whether it's wise to continue to do business in China. The "stability" in China is ephemeral, because it is enforced at the point of a gun. Once Deng Xiaoping and his generation of leaders dies, the voices of democracy may be heard once more. Businesses that were seen to be collaborating with Deng's regime might suffer. It's the argument that's applied to foreign investment in South Africa: it's profitable now, but will it be when the day of reckoning comes for the tyrants?

Canada has to show leadership in this regard, because the U.S. does not seem willing to do it. The U.S. has no plans to withdraw "most favored nation" status. There are too many U.S. business interests at stake; President George Bush's brother is among the many China traders who have emerged in the last decade.

International business is pragmatic, as is Bush. That's why the conservative right and liberal left find themselves in odd alliance in calling for the U.S. to cut ties with China. They will not get far: the U.S. government may regret the violence, but it will not go against the interests of doing business by squandering 10 years of carefully nurtured economic links. It is a favorite adage of capitalists that capital flows in the path of least resistance and there is certainly no resistance left in Beijing.

St. Louis Review

St. Louis, MO,
June 30, 1989

When Napoleon was asked about his foreign policy toward China, his response was: "Let China sleep; when she awakes the whole world will be moved."

China is no longer a sleeping giant With its population of over a billion people, vast natural resources and untold economic potential, it cannot be ignored. We can contrast the world's reaction to the protestors killed by the army and those executed by the government for their part in the revolt with the silence of all world leaders during the long, savage reign of Chariman Mao who presided over the killing of 30 million of his countrymen.

When Mao imposed his brand of communism on the Chinese people, the U.S. refused to maintain diplomatic or economic ties with China for almost two decades. The re-establishment of diplomatic relations was a significant achievement of the Nixon presidency. Those who urge that we recall our ambassador to China, invite the risk of rupturing relations between the two countries and erecting a new great wall of China.

In point of fact, it is only by remaining engaged with China, and this necessarily means with the Chinese leadership, that we can have any hope of influencing the actions of that leadership in both foreign and domestic affairs. It seems that President Bush has struck the right note in expressing displeasure over the recent events in China, while remaining engaged both diplomatically and economically with that huge country.

The events in China are further testimony to the total bankruptcy of communism. Communism is still an evil system which does not hesitate to use brute force to repress its own citizens, when all other motivations have failed.

The freedom enjoyed by people in Western countries exerts a powerful influence on the highly controlled peoples of the Eastern bloc of nations. Unfortunately, the materialism of the West is also a powerful inducement for those in communist nations to want to change their way of life. We would prefer that the spiritual values of the West play a greater part in bringing about change in the East. The materialism of the West is a more subtle form of enslavement; but, like it or not, materialism, just as communism does, makes slaves of us all.

The Houston Post

Houston, TX, June 23, 1989

THE INTELLECT and the spirit have met the gun in China, and the gun has won — for now. But as executions swell the death toll in the brutal crushing of the pro-democracy movement, President Bush is being pressed to take a tougher stance against the hard-line communist leadership in Beijing.

Some in Congress have vowed to push for strong sanctions against China to impress on its aging rulers our moral outrage at their bloody squelching of dissent. Yet the reported execution of at least 27 demonstrators in the face of clemency appeals by the president and other world leaders shows what little influence outsiders have on the course of events in China at the moment.

The steps Bush has taken, though restrained, have a better chance of eventually softening the repression than would emotion-driven economic and diplomatic retaliation. He has:

☐ Strongly condemned the June 3-4 army massacre of student demonstrators in Beijing's Tiananmen Square.

☐ Suspended U.S. military aid as well as contacts between high-ranking U.S. and Chinese officials and military officers. This has forced the cancellation of a July trip to China by Commerce Secretary Robert Mosbacher.

☐ Given sanctuary to dissident scientist Fang Lizhi and his wife, Li Shuxian, in the U.S. Embassy in Beijing.

☐ Ordered U.S. efforts to postpone approval of China's loan applications by international lending agencies. The World Bank has already suspended new loans to the troubled country.

China is heavily dependent on this money to to finance its economic development program. The architect of that program, China's 84-year-old senior leader, Deng Xiaoping, also ordered the crackdown that now jeopardizes his ambitious reforms. There is a lesson here for future Chinese governments.

President Bush has been careful, however, to avoid a rupture in relations with China. He helped in restoring those ties, first as chief of the U.S. liaison office there after President Nixon's historic 1972 rapprochement visit.

We cannot ignore 1 billion people, no matter who governs them. Only by maintaining diplomatic links do we have a chance to exert long-term leverage to moderate represssive official behavior and encourage democracy in China.

Secretary of State James Baker rightly says we must "speak with one voice" in expressing our disgust and dismay at the actions of Deng and his murderous, lying regime. But if those lawmakers who don't think we are speaking or acting tough enough try to enact more punitive measures, they could snap our already strained ties with Beijing.

Neither we nor the Chinese people would benefit if the door we have so laboriously opened is slammed shut again.

Winnipeg Free Press

Winnipeg, Man., June 19, 1989

Canadian policy towards the tragic events in the People's Republic of China so far has been sober, measured and responsible. Depriving the Chinese people of food by forbidding the sale of Canadian wheat to China would be neither humane nor responsible. The Canadian government should resist all pressure to do so.

During the developing China crisis, the department of external affairs has not seemed to put a foot wrong.

It has displayed good planning, good timing and a good grasp of the circumstances. This has been reflected in External Affairs Minister Joe Clark's surefooted performance in the Commons and in decision making.

When Beijing and other cities became uncomfortable for foreigners because of irresponsible behavior by PLA troops persecuting their own people, Mr. Clark's department, in co-operation with the Department of National Defence and civilian airlines, did an excellent job of getting out of China, mainly to Japan, any Canadian needing that help. Those wishing to move from Japan back to Canada were helped to do so.

Canada's ambassador, appropriately, has been recalled for consultations to demonstrate disapproval. It did not happen, though, until his vital task of securing the safe evacuation of Canadian citizens was done.

Chinese students at Canadian institutes of higher learning got the public reassurance they needed from Mr. Clark that they would not be sent back to the Chinese maelstrom just because their visas had expired. Such students and Chinese Canadians who wished to demonstrate peacefully in Canada to show their support for the Beijing students or their opposition to the Chinese government's actions were allowed to do so freely. Their delegations were easily able to express their concerns directly to Mr. Clark. Chinese diplomats wishing to defect are being given sympathetic consideration.

Now, some suggest that Canada is not doing enough. An exemplary performance so far is dismissed as the easy part. The hard part is supposed to be the imposition of economic sanctions to bring China to its knees and to force its Communist leaders to change their policies.

No sanctions of any kind that Canada might impose will either bring China to its knees or force a change in policy. No sanctions imposed by the whole world would have these effects. China and its one billion people have been closed to the world before and can easily be again. China can feed itself and can provide everything it needs, simply by reducing living standards to the low level which prevailed until recently.

China's leadership already has imposed international economic sanctions on itself. That most sensitive barometer, the free market, has reacted sharply to the state of violent chaos created by decisions of Deng Xiaoping and his brutal colleagues. Aircraft leaving China have been packed with foreign businessmen and technicians who came at China's invitation to establish joint ventures that would help Mr. Deng's policies of economic reform and openness to Western investment and technology.

Several Canadian companies have closed their Chinese operations for an indefinite period. Foreign investment, which is planned months and years ahead and which had only recently been coming into China in a regular, substantial fashion, now is likely to seek a more stable environment. Routine trade has been interrupted because of shippers' fears of delivery difficulties. Aid programs, such as those run by the Canadian International Development Agency, have been halted. Conditions may not soon justify their resumption.

These formidable economic penalties, caused by the decisions of the Chinese leadership, are causing knock-on effects. A Chinese deal to buy a modern steel plant in New Zealand has just fallen through because alarmed U.S. banks have withdrawn financing.

Canada's position as an international trader requires it to be a reliable supplier, a respecter of contracts and apolitical in choosing trading partners. Canada, like all major trading nations, trades with many countries whose practices do not conform to Canadian norms.

The Carter grain embargo on the Soviet Union, because of the Afghanistan invasion, provided rich earnings to Argentina's military *junta*, which cheerfully sold wheat to the Kremlin. That mistake should not be repeated. China's hungry people should not be denied bread. Canada should continue to sell wheat to China when conditions permit.

The Atlanta Journal
THE ATLANTA CONSTITUTION
Atlanta, GA, June 23, 1989

President Bush probably could be summoning up more eloquence in his appeals for reason and mercy that he has been addressing to China's vengeful hard-liners. He is not to be faulted, however, for the measured punitive steps he's taken against them — first, the suspension of military sales and contacts and, this week, the freezing of high-level diplomatic meetings and of $1.4 billion in pending loans to China.

These are appropriate measures that take dead aim at Deng Xiaoping & Co. To take stiffer action, as some in Congress have airily advocated in easy rhetorical swings at the Beijing regime and swipes at Mr. Bush, might impact adversely against ordinary Chinese or unnecessarily impede vital communications channels between Beijing and Washington.

Why is it a good idea for Mr. Bush to proceed so gingerly?

■ We don't know how long the suddenly xenophobic rulers can effectively wield power over their sullen urban population during the economic hard times that are sure to come. America needs to be in a position to monitor events, to nudge along any promising changes and, when possible, to speed the resumption of the relationship that predated this vile crackdown.

■ We want to keep electronic listening stations in China that snoop on the Soviet Union. We also want to prevent Beijing's born-again ideologues from becoming too cozy with counterparts in Moscow.

■ We need to keep talking with Beijing's testy old men because of the role China plays in conflicts nearby — to a degree in Afghanistan but more important still in Cambodia, which is scheduled to be vacated by Vietnam's forces in September.

■ Most pressing of all, we must maintain contact to try, first, to determine exactly whose finger is on China's nuclear trigger through this unsettled transition period and, second, to convey privately and firmly how unwise it would be for China to engage in any intimidation or adventuring with its nuclear arsenal.

We may have been lulled into thinking China's rulers wouldn't stoop to such a ruthless purge of their young. We know now that, when cornered, Deng Xiaoping and his cohorts will observe few restraints on their fury. We must learn precisely what those restraints are.

Richmond Times-Dispatch
Richmond, VA, June 22, 1989

It is by now quite plain that the United States has little or no leverage in China. President Bush's pleas, along with those from leaders of other Western nations, for forgiving treatment of student protesters have been answered with the first executions Wednesday of protesters in Shanghai.

Xu Guoming, Bian Hanwu and Yan Xuerong are the first three post-Tiananmen casualties of a crackdown apparently ordered by senior Communist Party leader Deng Xiaoping. The three were among a crowd that burned a train that ran over and killed protesters at the Shanghai train station during the pro-democracy uprising. In Beijing, at least eight other demonstrators await execution.

Official Washington has expressed obligatory shock and indignation at the Chinese government's latest heinous act. But no careful watchers of communist regimes should be shocked. The Chinese government is behaving exactly as a totalitarian regime should be expected: It is beheading the movement that threatens its power. At least six of the suspects named on the "most wanted" list of student leaders have been captured. An estimated 1,600 protesters are in government custody — many turned in by their own families, but some foolishly turned themselves in to authorities.

The Bush administration Tuesday turned its incremental response up a notch or two by halt-

Bush

ing all high-level government-to-government contacts and attempting to "postpone consideration" of loan applications by China before international financial institutions, such as the World Bank. The ban on contacts extends to the No. 3 level of all Cabinet agencies. It will not affect lower-ranking Ambassador James Lilley, who continues to communicate with officials in Beijing. However, a scheduled July visit to China by Commerce Secretary Robert Mosbacher has been cancelled, and a planned November visit by Treasury Secretary Nicholas Brady could also be postponed.

The administration is proceeding cautiously, in the words of Secretary of State James Baker III, "mindful of the need to preserve, to the extent that we can, what is a very, very important relationship."

But with public and congressional sentiments veering toward asking the impolite question of what's left to preserve, President Bush is running out of maneuvering room. It does not seem credible, for example, to continue normal relations with a nation whose leader refuses to answer or return calls from the president of the United States. "The pressure for much more dramatic steps is going to grow quickly," Senate Minority Leader Robert Dole warned in a floor speech Wednesday.

Most low-level protest options have been exhausted. President Bush must continue to tread carefully as U.S. actions perhaps enter the realm of long-term threats to relations. Options that would hurt the Chinese people more than the government, such as economic sanctions, should be an absolute last resort. The sad fact of the matter, however, is that whatever Washington does next is more likely to make Americans feel good than to affect events in China.

THE SAGINAW NEWS
Saginaw, MI,
June 16, 1989

The last hopes of democracy in China are falling before the power of the police state. The regime is throwing out reporters, but not before they told the appalling facts.

Neighbor is expected to inform on neighbor. People disappear from the streets. The official media build up a brazen fiction about what really happened in Tiananmen Square when the tanks rolled in. It will no doubt become the official version, no matter that the rest of the world can go to the videotape. Those who can testify to truth are subject to "severe" measures.

There is a grim reminder in this horror: Yes, civilized leaders of an ancient civilization, who smile to visitors and maybe even kiss babies, are perfectly willing to murder their own people, pretty much at random. The shoot-at-will order is out everywhere in China.

The brutality and absence of conscience of this repression deal a sad, harsh blow to idealists who think peace will come if only "we" try to "understand." What is happening in China ought to prove, once and for all, that some things are beyond either understanding or tolerance.

That some Chinese still hold out, still protest, still try to speak, attests to the indomitable spirit that rose and shone for a few brief weeks.

The watching world can do little to help, but it can do a little. A dissident who seeks refuge in the embassy, for instance, must be protected with the full diplomatic authority of the United States. No desirable relationship is worth human sacrifice. For its part, Britain could caution China that treaties such as the 1997 turnover of Hong Kong may, for good reasons, including criminal behavior, be abrogated.

The old men in Beijing cannot, really, be blamed for seeking to crush that spirit at almost any cost. Its power, given free rein, is enough to transform any society — and government.

What must truly shake the dictators is the knowledge that one day it must and will surface again. This is what is happening in almost every other corner of the globe. Try as the rulers might to drop a sharpened Bamboo Curtain over China again, too many of its people have sighted too much of a better tomorrow to forget, or to forgive.

Communists Mark
40th Anniversary

China Oct. 1, 1989 celebrated the 40th anniversary of Communist Party rule with a day of parades and fireworks in Beijing's Tiananmen Square.

The festivities, staged amid extremely tight security, were reported to be more subdued that the last big celebration, in 1984, which had marked the party's 35th anniversary in power.

Only invited guests and performers were permitted anywhere near the capital's 100-acre central square. The general public was barred from attending the celebration, apparently out of fear that dissidents might disrupt the event to protest the Chinese army's bloody suppression in June of a pro-democracy protest movement that had been based in the sqaure.

China's paramount leader, Deng Xiaoping, and other senior officials watched the celebration from a viewing stand on a balcony above the sqaure. The balcony, known as Tiananmen Rostrum, was the site on which Mao Zedong had proclaimed the founding of the People's Republic of China on Oct. 1, 1949.

Referring to the student-led protests earlier in the year, Deng told a North Korean official seated with him on the viewing stand, "What happened in Beijing not long ago was bad. But in the final analysis it is beneficial to us, because it made us more sober-minded." The comment was widely reported in the Chinese media.

The TENNESSEAN

Nashville, TN, October 3, 1989

ON Oct. 1, 1949, Mao Tse-tung stood on the rostrum in Tiananmen Square in Beijing and proclaimed the founding of the People's Republic of China.

The people were with him. Joyous crowds surged through the square celebrating what they thought would be an end to misery and oppression and the beginning of land redistribution, industrialism, health care and a better life for the masses. The future was bright.

Last Sunday, Chinese leaders, headed by 85-year-old Mr. Deng Xiaoping, stood on the same rostrum to celebrate the 40th anniversary of Communist rule. The words were similar; so were the fireworks and other outward appearances. But the mood was different. The joy and the spontaneity were gone.

The people crowding Tiananmen Square were selected party followers, not the happy workers and peasants who had gathered there 40 years before. The square last Sunday was still occupied by military forces that had been called in in June to crush student pro-democracy demonstrations at the cost of hundreds, if not thousands, of lives.

The people of the People's Republic were not welcome in Tiananmen Square Sunday. Those without proper residency permits were sent out of Beijing, and many of the city's residents were told to stay inside that day.

Much has been accomplished in China in the last 40 years. Transportation facilities were built. Industry was increased. Land redistribution did take place. Per capita income increased, and new opportunities opened up for Chinese women.

But these gains came at great cost in human life and confidence in the system. Some 700,000 people were killed in accomplishing land redistribution. The Cultural Revolution of 1966-76 resulted in the loss of many lives and great social upheaval.

Though China has taken great strides by Chinese standards, it still falls behind other countries, and that is the comparison many Chinese are making. Despite efforts to keep out democratic influences, it is not difficult for the young intellectuals of China to see that they are still being left behind by Taiwan, Hong Kong, the United States, Japan and other democratic nations.

Many of those who have greatly increased their wealth during the Communist regime in China, and many of the elderly, are grateful and remain loyal to the system. But there is a growing restlessness among the young and the intellectuals, as indicated by the bold but abortive student demonstrations last Spring.

How far the pro-democracy movement will go remains to be seen. Government security is tight, and any sign of dissent is sure to be met with brutal repression. Thus, the future could be dismal for Chinese advocates of democracy. But there will be doubt about the future of a regime that must exclude its people from the celebration of its founding. ■

The Hartford Courant

Hartford, CT, October 9, 1989

The People's Republic of China celebrated 40 years under communism last week, and it kept the people at bay. Only carefully screened party faithful could attend the somber festivities at Tienanmen Square. Tens of thousands of troops guarded against spontaneous "goddess of democracy" demonstrations.

That's a telling commentary on the lack of progress in human rights in the years since Mao Tse-tung defeated the Nationalists. That a government could not trust people to gather peacefully at the symbolic heart of China, and to savor the milestone, is an embarrassing admission of failure.

Another revealing commentary was the absence from the celebration of so many heads of state and foreign diplomats. U.S. Ambassador James R. Lilley did not appear — a deserved signal of disapproval from the Bush administration. The presence of former Secretary of State Alexander M. Haig Jr., even though he was traveling as a private citizen, was inappropriate.

The Chinese have exchanged exploitation and chaos — the old order — for cruel regimentation, and worse, the past 40 years. They have gained a large measure of stability, but the price has been the crushing of individualism, and, as the events of May and June proved, the crushing of lives.

The era of openness and economic reform ushered in by Deng Xiaoping, China's senior leader in the post-Mao era, seems but a memory today. Mr. Deng, at 85, is discredited in the eyes of much of the world and will be remembered in history as a ruthless autocrat.

Chinese leaders maintain that economic modernization will continue, that there will be no turning back, that there will be "socialist democracy" if not democracy in the Western sense. But the massacre of pro-democracy students in June spoke louder than these soothing statements.

No country can be led to economic maturity and human fulfillment at the point of a gun.

The best hope for China is the passing of this generation of leaders. When the fireworks marking national holidays are no longer seen through the octogenarian eyes of the revolutionaries who marched with Mao, perhaps the people won't have to be barred from the people's square.

Birmingham Post-Herald

Birmingham AL, October 2, 1989

Tiananmen Square, the vast plaza at the heart of Beijing, was the natural site for yesterday's ceremonies marking 40 years of communist rule over China. The square has witnessed some of the most memorable moments of this tragic chapter in China's history.

Here, Mao Zedong proclaimed the People's Republic on Oct. 1, 1949. Here, at mass meetings that one historian likens to Hitler's Nuremberg rallies, Mao staged the most extravagant pageantry of his regime.

In the summer of 1966, to launch his Great Cultural Revolution, Mao held a series of dawn rallies to inspect his young Red Guards, a million at a time. The chairman himself would appear as the sun rose, with a 1,000-piece band playing his anthem, "The East is Red."

Like his earlier attempts to transform China into an egalitarian utopia by the force of his will and the ruthlessness of his police, Mao's Cultural Revolution failed. It killed fewer people than the Great Leap Forward of 1959 — whose death toll from famine and executions is estimated at 25 million — but it embittered a new generation.

After Mao died in 1976, China seemed to change direction. A new leader, Deng Xiaoping, allowed peasants to abandon their communes and farm independently. Food production soared. The regime welcomed privately run businesses and foreign investment. A hundred thousand young Chinese streamed West to study. Average income more than doubled in a decade.

But Deng's blind spot was politics. His economic reforms shattered the regime's Marxist rationale, and public dissatisfaction grew, along with nepotism, government corruption, crime and inflation. This spring, a powerful call for democracy led by students but joined by intellectuals and workers in 80 cities was met with bloody repression.

The symbol of the democracy movement was the Goddess of Liberty statue raised by the young demonstrators on Tiananmen Square. The People's Army destroyed her. Near the spot where she stood, the party erected a statue of four ideal communists, a worker, a peasant, an intellectual and a soldier, for yesterday's carefully staged celebration.

There are no spontaneous observances in China these days. Deng rules a sullen people, who know his clampdown condemns them again to lies, poverty and fear.

Edmonton Journal

Edmonton Alta., October 3, 1989

China's "celebration" of its 40th anniversary as the People's Republic showed how little there is to celebrate.

Any such milestone in a nation's evolution should be a joyous occasion — and past anniversaries have been. But the weekend's dance-and-fireworks display in Beijing's Tienanmen Square weren't even open to the public. Participants were carefully chosen by the Communist party, ordinary citizens were made to stay away. University students had to stay indoors from Saturday onward. Unlike past years, there was no military parade, amusement park and carnival to accompany the festivities.

Yet China's supreme leader, Deng Xiaoping, was able to say that life has returned to normal in Beijing.

That might be true, if "normal" means a capital that has been in a state of siege since the crushing of the democracy movement this summer.

The Chinese government maintains that no one was massacred in Tienanmen Square when tanks and soldiers moved in against students encamped there; Chinese leaders say there were deaths, but they occurred in the sidestreets, and many of the dead were soldiers attacked by students.

The square itself tells a different story. Many of the bullet holes that have been patched up are at waist level — an indication that the army fired into the crowd to kill, not into the air to warn.

Canada and the United States say they deplore the massacre of the pro-democracy students, but want to maintain economic links with China so that it is not isolated from the outside world.

They should rethink that position in light of the 40th anniversary celebration. So far in the Communist bloc, political reforms have been a natural consequence of economic reform. In the Chinese example, political repression may foreshadow economic withdrawal. Already, the government is moving to restrict the special economic zones it had created as experiments with market economics.

The economic reform of the last 10 years, which placed emphasis on individual enterprise, might be sacrificed if the current Chinese regime feels that liberal economics might build pressure for liberal politics.

China will still want — and need — economic co-operation with the outside world. But it seems unlikely to occur on the freewheeling market-economy terms as hoped for by some Western countries.

What investors should really think about is the safety of their investments — they are not putting their money into a stable country. Repression and rigid discipline might keep Chinese society straitjacketed for years, but those will be years in which the current leadership maintains power by force rather than by consent.

In their campaign of deception, Chinese authorities say that the "counter-revolution" is crushed and that life is back to normal. Yet this is a state that cannot trust its own citizens enough to let them share in what is supposed to be a triumphal celebration of nationhood.

The London Free Press

London, Ont., October 6, 1989

In the end, the staged gala celebrations to mark the 40th anniversary of China's Communist revolution last weekend stood as a smokescreen to distract attention from the declining credibility of communism as a political and economic philosophy.

In Beijing, dragon dances, fireworks, opera singers and judo wrestlers provided entertainment in gaily decorated Tiananmen Square as China's leaders watched from a rostrum. Even the army danced. However, the uneasy memory of the Tiananmen Square massacre last June haunted the festivities. Security was tight, only the select were invited and many of the participants had been ordered to take part. So much for a spontaneous outpouring of joy.

> The party has squandered any credibility it may once have had as a force to help the common people.

The Communist party controls virtually every aspect of life in China and though it still retains the support of many Chinese, it has squandered any credibility it may once have had as a force to help the common people.

Indeed, the party's legacy is one of colossal failure. Tens of millions have died as one political experiment after another has faltered. In the '50s, for example, Mao Tse-tung encouraged shopkeepers to stay open and people to speak out. Reprisals for capitalist and counter-revolutionary behavior soon followed. Then came the Great Leap forward, a disastrous attempt to promote the economy through sheer willpower. Three years of famine came afterward. The chaos and persecution of the Cultural Revolution produced more upheaval, eased only with the overthrow of the Gang of Four and the rise of Deng Xiaoping.

Deng brought a measure of calm, though it was a false calm finally shattered by the massacre at Tiananmen Square last June. Relations were opened with the West and the early signs pointed to an economic turnaround as the standard of living doubled in a decade.

As China approaches the '90s, though, there are grounds for pessimism. After the Tiananmen crackdown, the conservatives are again in power and sending signals that Deng's famous "open door" is shut. Economic problems loom, too. China became Asia's largest borrower in the 1980s and the government has racked up a $23 billion debt with deficits in each year except 1985. Inflation hit 30 per cent last spring.

A more glaring example of the failure of Chinese Communism is the special privileges the leaders claim for themselves. A law prohibits the children of higher officials to participate in business, yet Deng's son-in-law and President Wang Zhen's son work for the largest investment company. Apparently they are above the law.

Unfortunately, the reality of 40 years of hopes has been failure. The events have been a betrayal of the objectives.

The Clarion-Ledger

Jackson, MS, October 3, 1989

In China, the people are reaching out and touching top government officials by robbing them of telephone service.

According to a report in *The Worker's Daily,* 420 miles of telephone line was stolen this year in the southern province of Hainan, with lines damaged in 18 Hainan cities.

The thieves have preyed on the exclusive lines linking government offices that are far clearer than the static-filled lines used by ordinary citizens.

Mostly peasants who sell the copper wire, thieves made off with 37 ½ miles of a 49-mile stretch between Sanya and Tongshi and 69 out of 87 ½ miles of line linking two other towns, the newspaper reported.

When the provincial government tried to hold a telephone conference with Tongshi city on Aug. 17, it found the line dead. Officials switched to a backup line that worked for only eight minutes before it was cut.

Gee, it couldn't have happened to a nicer government, as it celebrates its 40th birthday of stifling rule.

Bush Sends Tops Envoys to China

Two top Bush administration officials made a surprise visit to Beijing, China Dec. 9-10, 1989 to meet with Chinese leaders in an apparent effort to repair deteriorating U.S.-Sino relations. Ties between the two countries had been severely strained since the Chinese government's crackdown on the pro-democracy activists in June.

The U.S. mission was led by President George Bush's national security adviser, Brent Scowcroft. The deputy secretary of state, Lawrence S. Eagleburger, accompanied Scowcroft on the trip.

The two were the first senior U.S. aides to visit China since the Bush administration imposed a number of sanctions – including a ban on high-level diplomatic contacts – against the Chinese government in the wake of the June unrest.

Both Scowcroft and Eagleburger were one-time aides and business associates of former Secretary of State Henry Kissinger, who had played a leading role in opening U.S. ties to China in the early 1970s. Kissinger Dec. 13 denied any connection to the latest U.S. initiative. He had visited Beijing Nov. 7-10 for informal talks with Chinese leaders.

White House officials did not announce the surprise visit until the early morning hours of Dec. 9, after the two envoys had already arrived in Beijing. The trip had been kept secret at the request of the Chinese leadership, an administration spokesman said.

The stated purpose of the mission, according to the U.S., was to brief China on the recently concluded Malta summit between President Bush and Soviet President Mikhail S. Gorbachev. But observers said it was apparent that the 25-hour visit was focused largely on improving relations with China.

Scowcroft and Eagleburger held a total of 10 hours of talks in Beijing's Great Hall of the People Dec. 9 and 10 with key Chinese party and government leaders. Neither U.S. nor Chinese officials revealed any details of the substance of the discussions, but both sides expressed optimism after the meetings that relations between the countries would improve.

President Bush Dec. 11 defended his Beijing overture in the face of strong criticism from Democrats in Congress who accused him of "kowtowing" to the Chinese leadership.

The San Diego Union

San Diego, CA, December 13, 1989

President Bush is teetering on a narrow precipice. On one side is the prudent goal of preserving America's strategic relationship with China; on the other is the moral imperative to condemn the Beijing government's slaughter of pro-democracy demonstrators and the continuing executions of political dissidents.

Last weekend's unannounced trip to Beijing by White House National Security Adviser Brent Scowcroft and Deputy Secretary of State Lawrence Eagleburger is being denounced on Capitol Hill as "kowtowing" to China's brutal masters. (The term refers to the ancient Chinese custom of kneeling and touching the ground with the forehead to show submissive respect.) Certainly the glowing toasts delivered by the American envoys proclaiming Sino-American friendship were inappropriate only six months after the massa-- in Tiananmen Square.

But Mr. Bush is nonetheless correct to sustain a high-level dialogue between Washington and Beijing. The Scowcroft delegation's visit helped to preserve a candid working relationship. If the United States shuts off communications with China, as it did during the period of estrangement from 1950 to 1972, it will surrender its constructive role altogether.

Maintaining diplomatic contacts does not mean, however, that the administration must make concessions to appease the Chinese regime. Reports that the White House may lift some of the economic sanctions imposed after the June crackdown signal to Beijing that the United States is tacitly willing to tolerate the cruel repression imposed by the communist authorities.

Until China's aging rulers ease their crackdown, it is improper for the United States to resume "normal commercial business,"

as spokesman Marlin Fitzwater has said Mr. Bush intends to do. Allowing the shipment of three U.S.-made communications satellites for launching on Chinese rockets at the space center in Sichuan province would be an unwarranted concession at this point. The same is true of the reported lifting of American opposition to World Bank loans to Beijing.

The President was overly solicitous of Beijing's sensibilities when he pocket vetoed legislation permitting Chinese students to remain in this country after their visas have expired rather than face persecution by returning home. As he feels his way along the precipice, Mr. Bush is wise to maintain communications with Beijing. Yet he is flirting with catastrophe if he sacrifices the principles that American democracy has long stood for — most especially to the martyrs of Tiananmen Square.

FORT WORTH STAR-TELEGRAM
Fort Worth, TX,
December 12, 1989

Six months have passed since the government of the People's Republic of China saturated Beijing's Tiananmen Square with the blood of hundreds of demonstrators for democratic reforms. The Bush administration thinks that is long enough to hold a grudge.

With the weekend visit paid to China by National Security Adviser Brent Scowcroft and Deputy Secretary of State Lawrence Eagleburger, the United States has lifted the ban imposed in June on diplomatic contacts with China above the level of assistant secretary of state.

That visit signals to this country and the rest of the world that the Bush administration wants to resume business as usual with China as soon as possible, regardless of the Chinese government's human-rights policies.

Despite the long-term need to repair the damage done to Sino-American relations by the Tiananmen massacre and the ensuing arrests, executions and continuing repression, the administration is proceeding with undue haste to mend fences.

It is as though President Bush is apologizing for offending the Chinese government with the wrist-slap actions it took in response to the atrocities last summer.

Had it not been for pressure from Congress, it is doubtful that the administration would have done as much as it did. As it was, merely suspending high-level diplomatic contacts, a ban on military arms sales and limited economic sanctions amounted to gestures of little significance.

Having rescinded the most important of those prohibitions with the Scowcroft-Eagleburger visit, the administration probably will now try to scrap the remaining sanctions and resume business as usual quickly.

Congress should not allow that to happen until China shows evidence of a dramatic change in its human-rights policies internally and reins in its bloody-minded protégés — the Khmer Rouge — in Cambodia.

In the long term, it is really in the best interests of the United States to pursue a harder line on human rights with China instead of kowtowing to it.

The democratic reform movement that scared China's aging leaders into sending in the tanks was not eliminated forever. China eventually will have its version of the dramatic events that are transforming Eastern Europe. U.S. policy toward China should point toward that brighter future of freedom and hope.

The Washington Post

Washington, DC, December 11, 1989

PERHAPS THE Bush administration has a better explanation of its surprise bow to the Chinese government that just a few months back massacred hundreds of demonstrators in Beijing than that which it was offering yesterday. We truly hope it does. For what it was offering yesterday were mainly perfunctory and unconvincing statements that it of course takes human rights violations seriously—statements put in such a way as absolutely to signal their relatively low priority in the administration's hierarchy of concerns—and an utterly misleading suggestion that the only choice for the American government lay between yielding abjectly to an unrepentant Beijing and going back to a sort of pre-recognition breakdown of all relations. This of course is not the choice.

So the questions that cry out to be answered are these: Did the Chinese give something in return for what they got, which was a breach of the administration's pledge that no high-level visits would be undertaken (and presumably that no high-level professions of admiration and solidarity would be made) until the Chinese take steps to undo the damage they did in June? Or will it be a limited "show" reciprocation, such as, for example, China's relenting in its torment of a couple of famous victims, while proceeding with its remorseless search for and persecution of those who dared to demonstrate in the name of democratic freedoms?

On its face, the announcement made it look as if Mr. Bush had merely sent his emissaries to China to indicate to the people responsible for the crime that the United States is getting ready to let bygones be bygones. He appeared, in fact, to be all but apologizing to the Chinese government for the American sanctions still in place, and has surely undermined our ability to argue to friends and allies that they should keep the pressure on China. Last summer this country said that any improvement in relations would have to depend on a demonstration of greater respect for human rights in China. That is why it is so crucial to find out what if anything the Chinese did to demonstrate such respect. The alternative is to concede that after six months the administration is backing down and explaining to the Chinese that it was only kidding.

What a message this would be to send at this moment to the Soviets, and to those Communist hard-liners in Eastern Europe who still command armies and police forces and must be toying with the option of violently repressing the pro-democracy uprisings there. Until now the United States has given valuable support to the democratic movements in Eastern Europe by letting the world know that armed repression would immediately be answered by broad and exceedingly costly economic sanctions. Does the mission to China add, "but on the other hand, after a few months, maybe not"?

Incredibly, Mr. Bush's emissary, National Security Adviser Brent Scowcroft, is reported to have said to his Chinese hosts in a formal toast at a state dinner in Beijing, "In both our societies there are voices of those who seek to redirect or frustrate our cooperation. We both must take bold measures to overcome these negative forces." Just what does that mean? That the Chinese who massacred the students and the U.S. government that imposed sanctions were merely victims of a misunderstanding and of malevolent prodding from troublemakers in each of their realms? That the Bush administration and the Beijing government that perpetrated the massacre are on the same side in this matter, both having been pushed into their apparent conflict by these "negative forces" at home? In fact the statement sounded exactly like the kind of specious reasoning Gen. Scowcroft and others have rightly rejected over the years when it came to giving in to the Soviets in pressure politics and negotiations on grounds that the differences at issue were merely the handiwork of "cold warriors" on both sides.

There haven't been many massacres here, by the way, raising Chinese protests. The negative forces in China are Communist officials, bitterly anti-American and prepared to shed any amount of blood to preserve the party's power and their own families' interests.

Mr. Bush appears to be bending his policy to meet Chinese demands because the Chinese refuse to bend. The government there remains adamant in its insistence that, first of all, nothing except a politically inspired outbreak of street hooliganism happened in Beijing last June and beyond that, the way it treats its people is nobody's business but its own. The Chinese official position is accurately conveyed in a communication from Chen Defu of the Chinese Embassy, printed on the opposite page.

The president should not be making placatory concessions to a repressive and bloodstained Chinese government. Is there a better explanation than the one the public has been given so far?

The Houston Post

Houston, TX, December 13, 1989

PRESIDENT BUSH defends sending his national security adviser to meet with China's hard-line leaders last weekend with these words: "I do not want to isolate the Chinese people. I do not want to hurt the Chinese people." But it is the gang of murderous old geezers running that country that is isolating and hurting the Chinese people.

The president, a former envoy to China, made a sound decision to maintain relations with its hard-line communist regime after it brutally crushed the student-led democracy movement last June. At the same time, however, we should not give the impression that we are "kowtowing" to Beijing, as some of Bush's critics charge.

The president denies that, explaining that he sent his top security aide, Brent Scowcroft, and Deputy Secretary of State Lawrence Eagleburger to China — a trip that was not announced in advance — to brief Beijing on his summit with Soviet leader Mikhail Gorbachev.

The White House said Tuesday, however, that it may permit three U.S. communications satellites to be launched by Chinese rockets. This project was halted when Bush banned military exports after the June crackdown.

These developments follow the president's veto of a bill indefinitely waiving a U.S.-China agreement requiring Chinese students in the United State to go home after studying here. But the administration says the students won't be forced to return.

In time, all these actions might be appropriate, but not a mere six months after Americans witnessed the carnage of Tiananmen Square on their television sets. Anything we do to bolster the communist mandarins in Beijing is an affront to those Chinese who have risked and lost their lives for democracy.

Boston, MA, December 14, 1989

HOW do you best help the students and others in China who want a more democratic society?

By isolating the current regime, letting it know that the crackdown of last June did in fact sever important links to the West? Or by repairing ties to Beijing in the hope that open lines of communication will make it possible, at least, to influence future policies and actions?

If such questions didn't have a leading role in the Bush administration decision to drop its ban on high-level contacts with the Chinese government, they should have. Human rights are central to current US-China relations, not a sideshow to big-power geopolitics.

In response to critics, President Bush asserts he'll do nothing to hurt the Chinese people. He apparently believes that the diplomatic process begun by National Security Adviser Brent Scowcroft and Deputy Secretary of State Lawrence Eagleburger – like Mr. Bush, old China hands involved in the diplomatic opening of the '70s – could help prevent further crackdowns. But he hasn't adequately explained how.

Chinese authorities, meanwhile, maintain they acted last June in righteous defense of their society. They welcome, of course, Washington's move away from Tiananmen Square sanctions.

The American envoys' goal, ostensibly, was to provide a US interpretation of what happened in Malta. This is in line with the geopolitical and strategic reasoning usually invoked by the administration to justify a soft tread around China. Such reasoning makes sense to a point. But history may have taken us beyond that point.

With the Soviet Union in turmoil and the East bloc cracking before our eyes, old thinking about balancing China against Russia – playing the "China card" – is largely irrelevant.

Perhaps the very size and potential of China make resumption of closer diplomatic relations desirable. China has a hand in regional conflicts the US would like to see resolved. Will last week's trip eventually help bring about a settlement in Cambodia, for example?

All such concerns pale beside the attack on human rights and decent government unleashed by Deng Xiaoping and Company last June. And the repression continues.

Can Mr. Bush justify the Scowcroft-Eagleburger mission on the basis of what it may ultimately do to open the way for democratic expression? If he can't convincingly do so, the trip shouldn't have been taken.

Portland Press Herald
Portland, ME, December 15, 1989

The Bush administration's key adviser on human rights turns out to be Rudyard Kipling, the man who wrote, "Oh, East is East, and West is West, and never the twain shall meet. . . ."

In the West, President Bush and Secretary of State James Baker III are busy leading the applause — and raising money — for democratic reform in nations throughout the Soviet Bloc.

In the East, by contrast, Bush, National Security Adviser Brent Scowcroft and Deputy Secretary of State Lawrence S. Eagleburger have been equally busy courting Chinese leaders who ruthlessly cut down and imprisoned young people demonstrating for modest reforms in that country.

Which is it to be? Does the United States stand for human rights and support democratic reforms? Or do we merely stand, however things turn out, with the winner?

Congress can put us on record where we belong — behind human rights — by enacting a bill allowing Chinese students fearful of going home a temporary haven in this country. About 80 percent of the 43,000 Chinese studying here openly supported last spring's demonstrations in China. Many fear reprisals if, as is now the case, they could be ordered home after June 1990.

Congress wants to help. The House and Senate last session unanimously approved a measure allowing the students to remain here temporarily. Bush vetoed it, arguing his administrative action protecting Chinese students until June 1990 was adequate.

It isn't. Young people in China have been executed and thrown into miserable prisons for doing less in Tienanmen Square last June than Chinese students supporting them did here. Those afraid to go home deserve our protection.

If Bush once again vetoes the proposal, Congress should override it.

The Burlington Free Press
Burlington, VT, December 13, 1989

George Bush has a hypocrisy problem.

He treats Daniel Ortega like an international criminal for shooting back at armed rebels who are trying to overthrow the Nicaraguan government. He holds Mikhail Gorbachev at arm's length, despite four years of serious Soviet reform.

And then Mr. Bush sends his envoys off to embrace the butchers of Tienanmen Square.

Six months ago, the rulers of Beijing massacred hundreds of students seeking a more open government. The iron hand of Deng Xiaoping's hardliners has tightened its grip on China's neck. Dissent is punishable with death.

But it's not the Chinese who are trying to make amends. Instead, they insisted that Washington apologize, in essence, for American outrage at the crushing of the democracy movement. Now George Bush has dutifully sent along an American delegation that assured the Chinese they came "as friends to resume our important dialogue."

It's hard to recall a more sickening moment in American foreign policy.

"I do not want to isolate the Chinese people," Bush said, trying to justify the furtive China mission. The Chinese people already have been isolated from the world — by their government. The message Washington has sent the people of China is that the United States stands with leaders willing to slaughter a generation of student dissidents.

The reality of global politics may require the United States to deal with Beijing. But no reality forces the U.S. to kowtow, or to let China set the terms of the relationship. To hear the ruthless autocrats of Beijing described as friends offends the decency and commitment to human rights America is supposed to stand for.

The Seattle Times
Seattle, WA, December 12, 1989

PRESIDENT Bush's dark-of-night diplomatic gesture to the hard-line government in Beijing last weekend had some worthy objectives. But its more significant effect may be to further depress the hope for freedom and human rights that flickered so brightly and briefly in Tiananmen Square.

With no advance notification to key members of Congress, the White House sent a diplomatic team (headed by National Security Adviser Brent Scowcroft and Deputy Secretary of State Lawrence Eagleburger) to China to brief Chinese leaders on what had happened during the Malta summit meeting.

There was no public announcement of the trip until after the team had landed in China. Congressional leaders – including some who've been laboring to build a bipartisan foreign-policy partnership with the White House – were caught by surprise.

Secretary of State James Baker defended the mission, saying the United States doesn't want to "isolate China from the international community."

Worthy goal. But that objective could have been accomplished by using regular diplomatic channels to brief senior leader Deng Xiaoping and other Chinese officials – in a quiet way – about the Malta meeting of U.S. and Soviet leaders.

Instead, the Scowcroft-Eagleburger mission was seized and used for propaganda by the Chinese government: Across China there has been wide press coverage and TV broadcasts of the meetings. It became an extraordinary plus for China's old-guard rulers who were responsible for the tragedy at Tiananmen Square and who now seek to blot out the spirit of freedom that Tiananmen represents.

And it was a psychological blow to the Chinese students, professors and others who've demonstrated and worked so hard for freedom in China – and who look to the United States for inspiration and support.

The Bush White House needs to learn from the history of Eastern Europe in recent decades. When bloody repression occurred in Hungary and Czechoslovakia, the United States denounced it and thereafter, in dealing with the Soviets and Soviet-bloc nations, was tough and unrelenting in advocating human rights.

There were no unmixed messages. The human yearning for freedom was thus nurtured, so that it came to flower in 1989.

RAPID CITY JOURNAL
Rapid City, SD, December 12, 1989

National Security Adviser Brent Scowcroft and Deputy Secretary of State Lawrence Eagleburger met with Chinese officials in Beijing on Saturday. Senate Majority Leader George Mitchell of Maine called the trip "embarrassing kowtowing," but his criticism sounded embarrassingly partisan.

In light of recent events in Eastern Europe and the recent summit in Malta, there were plenty of good reasons for high-level, personal contact with the Chinese government. For example, hardliners in Beijing must be watching events in Prague, Berlin and Moscow with some measure of uneasiness. Voices of reason — including those of Scowcroft and Eagleburger — could ease their apprehensions and perhaps help spare the Chinese people more suffering.

The Bush administration is following a similar policy in Eastern Europe, by assuring the Soviet Union that the U.S. will not use unrest in the East Bloc to recklessly destabilize an already unstable situation. Given the thousands of nuclear weapons on both sides ready to compete with Santa for airspace over the North Pole, this policy seems prudent.

Moderation also is prudent when dealing with the Chinese government. For example, as an important aside to the Beijing trip, the two Americans received assurances the Chinese would not sell missiles in the Middle East. That alone made the mission worthwhile.

President Bush is maintaining sanctions imposed against the Chinese after the Tiananmen Square massacre, as he should. The president has agreed to give asylum to Chinese students, although less enthusiastically than one would hope. Chinese dissident Fang Lizhi still is being given sanctuary in the U.S. Embassy in Beijing.

Those measures are enough for now.

Sen. Mitchell will speak in Rapid City next Saturday. It will be interesting to hear him explain why President Bush should shun the government of the most populous nation on earth.

The Courier-Journal

Louisville, KY, December 13, 1989

PRESIDENT Bush is taking quite a beating from Democrats and even fellow Republicans for resuming high-level contacts with China's Communist bosses. That's understandable: After all, it has been only six months since the massacre in Tiananmen Square.

But even if he moved with what many see as indecent haste, Mr. Bush is right to try to put U.S.-Chinese relations back on a near-normal footing.

Both countries have much to gain from the sorts of commercial, scientific and cultural exchanges that were suspended after the massacre. And the more contact Chinese officials, scientists and students have with America, the better the chances that the pro-democracy movement so cruelly crushed in June will spring back to life.

For reasons peculiar to China,

that movement is more likely to reform than to sweep away the Communist Party. Unlike the Communist regimes in Eastern Europe, which were installed by the Red Army after World War II, Chinese Communism was homegrown. Its leaders have been responsible for horrendous crimes over the past 40 years, but the average peasant is far better off today — in terms of health, education and personal security — than his grandfather was under the warlords who ruled a politically fragmented China earlier in this century.

In any event, the United States maintains normal diplomatic and commercial relations with a number of countries with deplorable records on human rights. America's task, in every case, is to preach our basic principles while recognizing the limits of our leverage. China is no exception.

Roanoke Times & World-News

Roanoke, VA, December 14, 1989

GEORGE BUSH'S solicitude for the oppressive regime in China is remarkable. After the massacre of hundreds of students in Tiananmen Square last June, he tried to dissuade congressional leaders from imposing sanctions on that country; when Congress wanted to protect Chinese students in this country from forcible repatriation, he vetoed the bill, saying he'd take care of that himself.

Now he has sent two high-level emissaries on a secret mission to Beijing to woo China's leaders, and his administration has signaled that it will soon lift trade sanctions.

Nothing has changed in China. That government has not massacred any more of its people, but only because they know enough now not to bunch up in exposed places. The repressions, arrests, detentions and executions continue, a further lesson to those who dared demonstrate last summer for democratic reforms.

The president said: "I do not want to isolate the Chinese people." That government isolated itself with its own brutal actions. By sending national security adviser Brent Scowcroft and Deputy Secretary of State Lawrence Eagleburger to Beijing, the Bush administration maintained, it was strengthening the position of moderates there. The emissaries came late; the moderates are long gone from whatever posts they held, driven out as part of the purge that swept China after the Tiananmen Square disgrace.

Last summer, while trying to hold back sanctions, the administration insisted that relations with China could not improve unless that country showed greater respect for human rights. The president avers that the United States remains "positioned in the forefront of human-rights concerns." Actions drown out words, and the actions of the past week say plainly to Beijing: Let's not allow a little thing like murders and

repressions to stand between us.

What other country now will keep pressure on Beijing to improve its behavior? This mission not only marks an abrupt reversal of U.S. policy painfully arrived at after Tiananmen Square; it also breaks faith with the students and others who braved the Chinese government and embraced our own symbol of democracy, a goddess of liberty.

It sends a weirdly mixed message as well to the masses now breaking free of communism's bonds; what would Washington's response be if Soviet tanks suddenly began rolling again in Eastern Europe? A six-month pause, then a secret mission to Moscow?

It is all very well to point out that China has one-fifth of the world's people, is a power on this planet and cannot be ignored. Neither should gross human-rights violations be ignored. China is no longer diplomatically estranged from the United States; it is not necessary to dispatch agents under cover of night, Henry Kissinger style, to re-establish relations with a longtime adversary.

And certainly it is not necessary, once there, for them to accept a fete by China's leaders; or to lift a glass in toast, as Scowcroft reportedly did, to say: "In both our societies there are voices of those who seek to redirect or frustrate our cooperation. We both must take bold measures to overcome those negative forces." One awaits with some trepidation to learn what kind of "bold measures" are contemplated, and just who "those negative forces" are in this land of freedom.

After Bush's meeting with Mikhail Gorbachev, another voice was heard from on high in Washington, warning that the Soviet Union had not changed its spots. In the wake of this mission to Beijing, maybe it's time for Vice President Quayle to speak up again.

THE BLADE

Toledo, OH, December 15, 1989

PRESIDENT BUSH will need all his skills in diplomacy and damage control if his credentials as a proponent of global democracy are to survive his scarcely credible action in sending senior aides to China last weekend.

The most charitable light that can be shed on the visit of Brent Scowcroft, White House national security adviser, Lawrence Eagleburger, deputy secretary of state, and White House personnel director Chase Untermeyer is that Mr. Bush moved too far, too fast in his attempts to initiate a warmer relationship with China.

Mr. Bush, who was the U.S. envoy in China from 1974 to 1975, has offered several explanations for his action, claiming that he does not wish to see China remain isolated, and that his aides' visit was not a sign of a normalization of relations between the two countries.

His more disingenuous justification was that Chinese leaders offered comforting words that they would not sell missiles to the

Middle East. In fact, those missiles are still under development, and similar assurances were given earlier this year.

Further, Mr. Bush suggested that he wished to brief the Chinese on his Malta Summit with Soviet President Michail Gorbachev, and that the United States has contacts with a number of countries with abysmal records on human rights.

Such explanations hide a deeper and more disquieting notion that this country has double standards on human rights. It would be inconceivable for the United States to send a delegation to Moscow had there been a massacre in Red Square even approaching the magnitude of the tragedy in Beijing's Tiananmen Square in June.

Dispatching senior advisers to China — on the very weekend the Dalai Lama receives the Nobel Peace Prize for resisting Chinese hegemony in Tibet — sends a stark message to the rest of the world that the U.S. does not hold all countries to be equally culpable.

It is difficult to overlook the fine hand of former President Nixon who, after his return from China in October, urged Mr. Bush to restore good relations with the government in Beijing. The official response was that a change in policy would be predicated upon the Chinese government's action, but the events of last weekend have not borne that out. Indeed, the administration is now considering lifting a ban on "normal commercial exports" to China, including satellites.

Senior Democrats in Congress and Chinese dissidents are united in their outspoken criticism of this surreptitious renewal of ties with the same leaders who so recently displayed their contempt for democracy and human life.

Mr. Bush should hear their complaint. If this country is to stand for freedom and reform, it must do so unequivocally, in Asia as in Europe. It would be morally reprehensible to trade the aspirations of pro-democracy elements in China for normalization of relationships with the government in Beijing.

Must our memory be so selective, and so short?

Chinese Premier Lifts Martial Law in Beijing

Chinese Premier Li Peng Jan. 10, 1990 announced the lifting of martial law in Beijing. The decree, which took effect Jan. 11, ended nearly eight months of military rule in the capital.

Most Western diplomats and foreign observers said they considered the Chinese move to be largely a symbolic gesture aimed at international public opinion, which had been harshly critical of China in the wake of the government's crackdown on a student-led pro-democracy movement in mid-1989.

Li had imposed martial law on May 20, 1989, in an attempt to suppress widespread pro-democracy demonstrations in the center of the capital. When the move failed to stop the protests, army troops had been called in to crush the pro-democracy movement. Hundreds and perhaps thousands of students and civilians were believed to have been killed in the military crackdown.

"The lifting of the martial law imposed in parts of Beijing indicates that the situation in the capital and the country as whole has become stable, social order has returned to normal and a great victory has been won in checking the turmoil and quelling the counterrevolutionary rebellion," Li declared in a nationally televised speech.

The premier warned, however, that "hostile forces" both within China and abroad still threatened "to subvert the socialist system" in the country, an apparent reference to dissident organizations that had sprung up in the West in the wake of the crackdown.

Li also indicated that the Chinese government did not support the kind of sweeping political reforms that had recently been adopted in Eastern Europe. "No matter what may happen in the world, we shall unswervingly follow the socialist road," he said.

Foreign observers, commenting on what they said was the empty symbolism of the premier's announcement, asserted that the lifting of martial law would have little practical effect within China.

The Chinese leadership had enacted numerous restrictions since the June 1989 crackdown prohibiting any type of unauthorized political activity, including speeches, wall posters and demonstrations. In addition, most military units had already been pulled out of Beijing and replaced by police, paramilitary security forces and, reportedly, army soldiers dressed as civilian police officers. Other army units remained stationed just outside the capital in case of renewed instability, Western news reports said.

Beijing's Tiananmen Square, the geographical center of the 1989 democracy movement, was reopened to the public Jan. 11 for the first time since the military crackdown.

DESERET·NEWS

Salt Lake City, UT, January 11, 1990

The first thing to be said about China's decision this week to lift martial law is that even though it's only a cosmetic change, even a shallow improvement is better than no improvement at all. Small, insignificant changes could be followed by bigger, more meaningful steps.

The second thing is that by insisting that this move shows that President Bush's policy of snuggling up to China is starting to pay dividends, the U.S. administration is only embarrassing itself by looking too eager to claim credit.

But, in fairness to the Bush administration, it would be more instructive to pay closer attention to what it does than to just what it says about China.

One concrete move was taken earlier when the White House restored U.S. Export-Import Bank credits to China and let Beijing launch American-built satellites.

How much impact did this step have on China? Probably not nearly as much as the sharp drop in foreign earnings that China suffered when visitors stopped arriving and trade dwindled after Beijing brutally crushed the democratic reform movement in Tiananmen Square last June. This situation puts China in a painful pinch, facing the repayment of more than $40 billion in foreign debt starting this year.

Despite Washington's posturing, the White House has remained tough where it counts the most. The administration still opposes the resumption of a massive loan from the World Bank to China. Without U.S. support, China is unlikely to get this money — which is the single most important benefit Beijing lost from the West since last June's outrage.

What's more, the World Bank should keep its purse closed until China frees dissidents Fang Lishi and Li Shuxian from their confinement inside the American embassy in Beijing and calls off the continuing efforts to throttle internal dissent.

The proper reaction of the West toward China's decision to lift martial law, then, is to welcome the move but to seek more meaningful changes — many more. Such a reaction involves continued applications of both the carrot and the stick.

The Houston Post

Houston, TX, January 11, 1990

VICE PRESIDENT Dan Quayle is grasping at straws when he cites the Chinese government's decision to lift martial law as vindication of President Bush's recent diplomatic initiatives toward Beijing.

The hard-line regime that brutally crushed China's pro-democracy movement eight months ago may be pulling the troops out of the capital. But they are being replaced by heavily armed police who will enforce the repressive policies of Deng Xiaoping. Even the White House concedes that closer U.S.-China relations must await moderation of those policies, manifested by the June massacre of students in Beijing's Tiananmen Square. That slaughter was followed by large-scale arrests, executions, and an intensive communist reindoctrination drive.

Despite Quayle's assertion that the lifting of martial law is a "positive step forward for human rights," the Gang of Deng deserves no credit for withdrawing its decree after intimidating its people with a bloodbath.

In the wake of the June crackdown, President Bush sent top aides on two secret missions to Beijing. The first one, in July, was defended as an effort to impress on China's leaders the negative impact their actions had had on U.S-Chinese relations. The second, in December, was aimed at encouraging the hard-liners to ease their repressive grip. But the impression was that we were pushing too hard to warm relations with Beijing.

The president, a former U.S. envoy to China, is correct in insisting that we should maintain links with a government that speaks for a billion people. But the fate of communist regimes in Eastern Europe should prompt us to reiterate that our chief interest is in ties with the Chinese people, not their murderous rulers.

St. Paul Pioneer Press & Dispatch
St. Paul, MN, January 13, 1990

By lifting martial law this week, China has plotted another controlled move in its stylized dance to hustle legitimacy for the Tiananmen Square murderers. The move may have some small meaning on the world diplomatic stage. But not where it counts.

In the chilled Chinese streets where only raw repression covers the anger, life goes on in a nightmare for those who saw the daylight of freedom turn to bloody dusk last June. In Tibet, the regime did not even make a cosmetic change. Martial law remains in force.

President Bush, by calling the Chinese regime's action a very positive move, does nothing positive for U.S. policy. His comment amounts to just another administration round of applause for the ugly dance. Applauding creates a greater risk of encouraging continued bad behavior than pushing the regime toward better conduct on human rights.

The U.S. Congress seems headed toward an approach on China that is morally sensitive and more able to exert pressure on the dictators in Beijing.

When it reconvenes Jan. 23, Congress should pursue vigorously a package of legislation that gives Beijing a hefty whack with a stick and no carrots.

The first order should be overriding the president's veto of a bill that would prohibit the United States from sending Chinese students back home to a welcome of fear and retribution. The president says administrative remedy is enough. The Congress should be encouraged to persist by giving this act of humanitarian sanctuary the force of law.

Congress would also serve human rights by banning arms sales to China, suspending federal insurance for private investments in China and keeping a choke-hold on loans to the Chinese government.

Sanctions also have new synergy from the freedom in other former communist countries. The old dragons in China cannot dance forever if they dance virtually alone. But only continued international pushing will make them fall on their fire-breathing faces sooner rather than later.

Calgary Herald
Calgary, Alta., January 11, 1990

China's lifting of martial law in Beijing is a positive step, but all indications point to this being an end in name only.

Various arms of repression, including the security forces, are still in place.

New demands for democracy will no doubt be stamped out firmly as they were last June. After all, against armor and machine-guns, those thinking of protesting for democracy are seriously out-gunned.

The Chinese leadership's true intent was revealed in internal Communist party documents circulated Wednesday: "We must follow the principle of being outwardly relaxed while tightening internal control."

This measure, then, is aimed at placating the outside world.

By withdrawing soldiers armed with automatic rifles from Tiananmen Square, Beijing hopes to recoup some of the $1 billion lost in tourism revenues after the June massacre.

More importantly, it hopes to re-establish vital lines of aid from Japan, the United States and the World Bank.

With Communist governments going down one after another, China probably feels the need to mend fences with other sympathetic governments like the United States.

President George Bush, perhaps because of his personal familiarity with China as a former ambassador, seems only too willing to forget the uproar over China and send diplomats over there to toast the butchers.

Beijing's goodwill cannot be assessed on lifting martial law alone.

Until it begins to uphold democratic freedoms, the West should be wary of giving its blessings to China.

Los Angeles Times

Los Angeles, CA, January 11, 1990

Premier Li Peng took to China's airwaves yesterday to announce that martial law was being ended in Beijing, seven months after it was decreed in a move to crush swelling popular protests. As Li finished his 10-minute speech, the official radio began blaring a concert of triumphant martial music. The irony, however unintended, was clearly appropriate. Still fully in place, along with a heavy presence of troops in the capital, are other repressive measures that make it a crime to strike, to display political posters, to take part in anti-government demonstrations. Though martial law has been lifted, the Chinese are no freer the day after that event than they were the day before.

To be sure, not everyone sees it that way. Vice President Dan Quayle, for one, has hailed the ending of martial law as a "step forward for human rights" and a vindication of President Bush's policy of engaging in secret high-level contacts with Chinese leaders starting just a month after the June 4 massacre of hundreds, and perhaps thousands, of protesters in central Beijing. It may well

be true that National Security Adviser Brent Scowcroft, on his two unannounced visits to Beijing, urged China's leaders to ease up on repression so as to forestall further punitive responses from Congress. But it's insulting to all those who died last June or who have been imprisoned or executed since to confuse an expedient and cosmetic lifting of martial law with any genuine improvement in human rights.

Economic woes couldn't have been far from the mind of the leadership when it decided to end martial law. The World Bank is considering a $700-million loan package to China, which helps explain Li's insistence that his country is now "stable politically, economically and socially." The White House said Wednesday that it might well support the Chinese loan application. But federal law forbids endorsing loans to a country that is a "gross and consistent violator of human rights." Tragically for its people and unhappily for their economic future, China continues to fit that bleak description.

THE DAILY OKLAHOMAN

Oklahoma City, OK, January 11, 1990

LIFTING of martial law by China's Communist leaders more than seven months after the Tiananmen Square massacre no doubt is calculated to soften foreign criticism.

They will have to go much farther beyond this largely cosmetic gesture.

Despite Premier Li Peng's claims that China is stable "politically, economically and socially," the Beijing government faces problems in all three areas. Western diplomats believe the martial law order was revoked to encourage resumption of loans and high-level exchanges with other countries.

The action could provide a face-saving situation for Japan, which has promised loans worth hundreds of millions of dollars. But it may have little effect in the United States, which has influence over lending sources that suspended loans to China after troops crushed the pro-democracy demonstrations.

Vice President Dan Quayle hailed the move as "a positive step forward for human rights" and he's right, but it is only a small step. Strict laws banning dissent are still in force. Chinese leaders still oppose the release of dissident Fang Lizhi and his wife.

Restoration of normal relations must await further easing of China's hard-line policies.

ST. LOUIS POST-DISPATCH

St. Louis, MO, January 12, 1990

The Bush administration greeted the news that the Chinese government has lifted martial law in the capital by promising support for loans for certain projects before the World Bank. This, reasoned the administration, would help the Chinese people and encourage the Chinese government to continue to relax its oppressive laws. Beijing was the site of pro-democracy demonstrations and the army crackdown at great cost in human life on June 4.

Vice President Dan Quayle proclaimed eagerly that the Chinese announcement showed "dividends from the president's policy toward China." Nonsense. The facts are, given the totalitarian Chinese communist system, there is little difference between martial law and what passes for civil society.

For instance, soldiers are said to have put on police uniforms, and a new organization with people from the Public Security Ministry and the People's Armed Police has been set up to watch events in the capital. Marches and rallies that do not have government support remain banned. The press is

not free to speak an opinion different from the party line. Ordinary people must guard their words carefully, and the prisons are still full of protesters accused of being counterrevolutionaries simply because they want to exercise basic human rights.

Troubling questions remain about the timing of the administration's announcement. For instance, did the administration make a promise to Beijing to endorse the World Bank loans when two top officials visited Chinese leaders last month? Were the two announcements coordinated, as it seems, even though the administration denied that?

Congress should take a hard look at the U.S. reaction to the June 4 massacre in Tiananmen Square and general administration policy toward China. Extensive public hearings would be a good idea. Those could come right after Congress overrides Mr. Bush's inappropriate veto of a bill to allow Chinese students in this country to remain until they can safely return to their homeland.

Newsday

New York, NY, January 12, 1990

The Bush administration should stop crowing over China's decision to lift martial law in Beijing. It's a largely cosmetic move that does little to mitigate China's repressive policies. It certainly did not rate the red-carpet response it got from Washington.

Chinese authorities didn't need martial law to shoot pro-democracy demonstrators in Tiananmen Square last June. And its removal doesn't keep that from happening again — if not at the hands of soldiers, then by the reinforced police units that have replaced them.

In fact, the evidence is that China's crackdown against dissidents is continuing unabated. Hundreds of arrests and trials for

"counterrevolutionary activities" have taken place recently on Beijing university campuses. Laws remain on the books banning rallies, strikes, wall posters and anything else that smacks of dissent. So the U.S. talk of restoring China's eligibility for World Bank loans is grossly disproportionate. Since the beginning of the crackdown in June, loans and other favors have been on hold — and that's where they still belong.

The administration has been too anxious to believe that China is easing the crackdown. It's too eager to claim vindication for national security adviser Brent Scowcroft's unjustified mission to Beijing. For treating Beijing

more gingerly than it would other governments that brutalize peaceful protesters, it has reaped the meagerest of rewards — while undermining its own human rights commitments and undercutting the pro-democracy students who represent China's future.

It's a mistake to view China, as the administration does, through the optics of the 1970s. The China card has been devalued: The Soviet Union is hardly the adversary it was 15 years ago, and the road to Moscow doesn't run through Beijing anymore. China needs us more than we need China. If there ever was cause for sacrificing American principles to curry favor with China, there isn't any more.

The State

Columbia, SC, January 12, 1990

THE CHINESE government's decision to end martial law in Beijing this week was more show than substance, since tough prohibitions against popular dissent remain in force. The United States should not rush to restore normal relations with the Communist regime until democratic reforms become a reality.

Wednesday, Premier Li Peng announced that "China is now stable politically, economically and socially.... A great victory has been won in checking the turmoil and quelling the counter-revolutionary rebellion."

What he did not say was that the "victory" was won by slaughtering hundreds of unarmed demonstrators in Tiananmen Square and elsewhere last June and by mass arrests and wholesale repression of citizens' human rights since then.

Thus, the lifting of martial law must be viewed by democratic nations as but a small step away from the Chinese Communists' hardline policies and as a public relations ploy to deflect foreign criticism and encourage resumption of foreign loans and diplomatic exchanges.

Vice President Dan Quayle was quick to point out that the move proves President Bush's much-criticized China policy — which included secret missions to Beijing by National Security Advisor Brent Scowcroft — is paying dividends.

But apparently the Bush administration also recognizes that those dividends are still very meager: *The Los Angeles Times* reported that the President opposes the resumption of a $700-million World Bank loan program to China until the Communist overlords relax their anti-democratic stance. And, of course, the U.S. embassy in Beijing continues to give sanctuary to Fang Lizhi, a Chinese astrophysicist and dissident, and his wife.

Some members of Congress are taking an even tougher line. Rep. Nancy Pelosi, D-Calif., whose bill to ease visa restrictions for Chinese students in this country was vetoed by Mr. Bush last year, characterized the lifting of martial law as an "empty gesture" and said she would push for a congressional override of similar visa legislation this year.

For the most part, even the Chinese people have been unimpressed with Premier Li's announcement. "It won't have any effect on most people's lives," one young woman told the Associated Press. "Of course they may feel more light-hearted to know that martial law is gone. But that's all."

Indeed, Chinese security forces still have power, under a law passed last November, to ban strikes, political posters and all but pro-government demonstrations. And large numbers of soldiers remain in the capital to enforce order.

Nevertheless, there is hope that the Chinese government will follow up with further reforms and that its initial caution may be designed to prevent a repeat of the Tiananmen Square debacle. But the United States and other free nations must not resume business as usual with Beijing until the freedom-loving Chinese people have a real victory to celebrate.

Lincoln Journal

Lincoln, NE, January 12, 1990

For our money, President Bush was too enthusiastic praising the lifting of martial law in China this week after almost eight months of hard rule by the gun. One very modest cheer would have been ample.

It was way back last June 3-4 that the brutal autocrats in Beijing ordered troops to smash pro-democracy demonstrators gathered in Tiananmen Square, and elsewhere. Thousands of unarmed people were slain. Iron military control was imposed.

If it has taken until now for the rulers to feel comfortable again without martial law, the screws must have been very tightly applied in the intervening months.

"Very positive" move, the president said of China officially ending martial law; "...a very sound step."

On what "normalcy" might be in the People's Republic of China, given its intricate system of cultural and governmental controls driving people toward conformity and compliance, we aren't competent to discuss at length. But normalcy in the PRC today clearly means a somewhat greater level of police and security force presence, especially in Beijing and perhaps Shanghai, and a quick reliance by authorities on surveillance and punitive laws against expressions critical of the government.

That strikes us as more a description of a minimum security prison than a society once more on the move for expanding human rights.

The Atlanta Journal AND THE ATLANTA CONSTITUTION

Atlanta, GA, January 14, 1990

President Bush is quite wrong to label this supposed relaxation of Beijing's harsh line as "a positive step forward." It by no means vindicates his unfathomable forgive-and-forget response to June's atrocities committed under orders of pals of his from his days as ambassador to China.

For Beijing's "subjects" still yearning for some small measure of control over their own lives, nothing of substance has changed. They still dare not strike, gather in a rally, carry about "subversive" posters or otherwise publicly display dissent. Oh, they wouldn't be carted off by soldiers any more; but they'd be arrested just the same.

Premier Li Peng's announcement of the end of martial law should have been a tip-off for the White House. Not once did he express remorse for last June's massacre or the slightest merciful inclination toward dissident leaders still being hunted and/or persecuted. Instead he hailed the regime's vicious, ongoing crackdown as a triumph and vowed unceasing vigilance against democratic heresies. It was a speech that Nicolae Ceausescu would have gladly delivered.

And the timing for Beijing's gesture was so propitious, too. Just as the World Bank is mulling over China's application for a hefty loan. Just as Congress is about to reconvene and is of a mind to take legislative action against Beijing's unrepentant butchers.

Mr. Bush took months to accept Mikhail Gorbachev's peaceful tenders at face value and still totally mistrusts the likes of Nicaragua's Daniel Ortega; yet he swallows China's lure hook, line and sinker. He should know better.

For sheer cynicism and phoniness, it's hard to choose between a) China's meaningless restoration of civil law last week and b) the Bush administration's gushing, self-congratulatory acceptance of same as a fact.

U.S. Congress Reconvenes; Bush China Veto Upheld

The 101st Congress reconvened Jan. 23, 1990 to confront a host of legislation that was still pending from 1989.

President George Bush won a major political victory at the start of the new session when the Senate voted Jan. 25 to uphold his veto of a bill that would have barred the deportation of Chinese exchange students from the U.S. The House had voted overwhelmingly Jan. 24 to override the veto.

The action came one day after the house had voted by a wide margin to override the president's veto, and it followed earlier head-counts indicating that the Senate would vote to override as well. A two-thirds vote was needed in both houses of Congress to overturn a presidential veto.

The final vote in the Senate, 62 to 37 in favor of an override, fell four short of the necessary two-thirds majority. Eight GOP senators joined 54 Democrats in support of an override, but Bush was able to win over 37 Republicans – including many who had expressed doubts about the administration's China policy – in what was widely portrayed as a test of the president's political strength at the start of the new congressional session.

The House Jan. 24 had voted, 390-25, to override Bush's veto. A total of 145 Republicans joined with 245 Democrats in favor of the override. All 25 lawmakers who supported the president were Republicans.

The legislation in question had been approved by Congress in November 1989 in response to the Chinese government's crackdown on a student-led democracy movement in Beijing earlier in the year. In vetoing the bill, Bush argued that he had already signed an executive order that would protect those Chinese students who feared persecution if forced to return to their homeland when their visas expired.

Much of the debate in both the House and Senate prior to the override votes had focused on the president's controversial policy toward China.

Democrats repeatedly criticized Bush for secretly sending a pair of envoys to Beijing in July and December 1989 after publicly announcing a ban on high-level contacts between U.S. and Chinese officials. The trips came to light after Congress had recessed for the holidays in December 1989.

"On the issue of China, the president has lost credibility," Rep. Stephen J. Solarz (D, N.Y.) said Jan. 24.

The sponsor of the original legislation, Rep. Nancy Pelosi (D, Calif.), declared the same day, "Congress must send a very clear signal to the butchers of Beijing."

At a White House news conference Jan. 24, after the House vote, Bush had again called the congressional legislation "totally unnecessary" and predicted that China would cut off all student exchange programs with the U.S. if his veto was overridden in the Senate.

Rockford Register Star

Rockford, IL, January 29, 1990

George Bush's stance on China now prevails. It is a sad case of kowtowing.

Bush will say, with some elan, that he has now won all 11 of his veto tests. This last one is nothing to brag about.

Does he really wonder why the United States House voted a spirited 390-25 to cancel the message that Bush is sending? Does he ponder why the Senate mustered 62-37 votes to do the same —failing by just four votes the needed two-thirds for an override? Let him rest any doubts.

Those who parted company with the president were reflecting the vast sentiment of the American people who are outraged at the aging, communist rulers in Beijing and the butchery that cut down unarmed youthful protesters last June in Tiananmen Square. Against these young marchers, Deng Xiaping loosed the People's Liberation Army and ended its myth of benign heroism and protection.

The snort of machine guns, the burst of automatic rifles, were not the only perils students and workers incurred. Some fell beneath the treads of advancing tanks. Arrests and executions followed.

Lest they be forced home to face similar atrocities, more than 30,000 Chinese students here welcomed what they thought would be a U.S. law giving them a guaranteed four-year respite from being forced to return to China as their visas and passports expire.

Bush's veto effectively cancels any such guarantee.

He must now rely on the federal bureaucracy and hope that no bonafide Chinese student gets his marching papers simply because some paper technicality intervenes.

Midway in the congressional voting, after the House had made its stand and the Senate was about to, China's foreign ministry took to the airwaves calling Washington's action reprehensible meddling in its internal affairs. A veto override would dampen future relations with China, the ministry said.

Bush said the same.

He said something else. He said the House vote represented "crass politics." What were his lobbying calls to Republican senators if they were not "crass politics"? When he sent National Security Adviser Brent Scowcroft to China, once secretly before the blood had been washed from Tiananmen Square, again publicly to sit with Deng Xiaping, fraternize with him and toast the Chinese despot, what was that if not "crass politics"?

George Bush even had the help of another ally in his Senate strong-arming, none other but that unindicted co-conspirator from the Watergate days, Richard Nixon, an old China hand now asking five senators to side with the president. They did. Some spectacle!

It will not go away.

It will not recede, because Americans have long memories. They know patriots when they see them, especially when they are young and dead in Tiananmen Square, the same place where they had erected, but could not sustain, their own model of our Statue of Liberty.

Bush's veto tells China its policies are on course. That is the tragedy.

MILWAUKEE SENTINEL

Milwaukee, WI, January 27, 1990

Although President Bush came within four votes of being overridden on his veto of a controversial bill involving Chinese students in this country, staving off the onslaught on his power to make foreign policy was a major victory.

In winning this battle, Bush had to cope with two problems:

One was a Democratic majority, jealous of the president's high standing in the polls.

The other was a concern by many Republicans that they would be looked upon as virtual Simon Legrees if they did not support the bill allowing the students to stay in the United States after their visas expired.

Bush was not blind to this widely circulated impression that he is uncaring. At issue, however, was a matter of principle involving the president's right to conduct policy and Congress' well-documented ability to botch it up.

It has been easy for supporters of the bill in Congress to pontificate about the plight of the poor students if, in fact, they would be sent back to China.

But it also was convenient for these Chicken Littles to dismiss the president's pledge that his executive authority would protect any affected student from being sent back to China.

And let's suppose the veto had been sustained. What would have been the advice of Bush's opponents as to the next step in our relations with Beijing? What could Congress itself do? There's no word that the Chinese savings and loan industry needs any help.

If the lawmakers are so filled with compassion for emigres, why don't they put forth a policy proposal urging that the US take in all or at least some of the Vietnamese boat people who face forcible repatriation by Britain from Hong Kong?

Just because they weren't able to testify at a congressional hearing is no reason they should be ignored.

AKRON BEACON JOURNAL

Akron, OH, January 28, 1990

PRESIDENT BUSH is claiming a victory for his policy on China.

His veto of a bill protecting Chinese students from deportation stands despite an override attempt by Congress.

However, the facts simply do not support Bush's victory claim. And those facts — the political reality — are to be found within the president's own Republican Party.

Virtually none of the GOP senators who remained undecided on the morning of the Senate vote and finally were persuaded to take the president's position said they were swayed to support Bush by his conduct in handling relations with China. The vote was 62 to 37 to override, which was four votes short of the two-thirds majority needed.

The Republican senators who fell into line said they did so because Bush promised no student would be sent home by his action; he convinced them their political support was needed; and they believed the president, not Congress, should make foreign policy.

Adding the Senate vote to that of the House the day before, the totals show only 62 members of Congress supported the president, while 452, including 145 House Republicans and eight GOP senators, said "no."

The bill would have given 40,000 students studying in the United States four more years to apply for new visas or permanent residence, and would have waived the requirement that they return to China first. It would have permitted any students whose visas expire to remain in the United States as long as danger exists at home, and would allow them to work while in this country.

When Bush vetoed the bill Nov. 30 he said he had ordered the Immigration and Naturalization Service to adopt measures giving Chinese who want to remain in the United States exactly the same protection.

The president also said the Beijing government had taken steps justifying his policy, citing the lifting of martial law in the capital; the release of jailed demonstrators; a promise not to sell medium-range missiles to Syria; acceptance of Peace Corps volunteers, Fulbright scholars and a Voice of America correspondent; and muting of anti-U.S. propaganda.

But many who supported the bill passed by Congress wanted the force of law behind them, rather than a less formidable executive order, which could be subject more readily to court challenges or be reversed by the stroke of a pen.

The president would be making a grievous error of judgment if he failed to realize the depth of opposition to his handling of relations with China. Many of those critical have been offended by secret diplomatic initiatives mounted by Bush after the slaughter of peaceful protesters in Beijing last spring. Indeed, the secret missions tend to erode Bush's credibility when he says he will guarantee the safety of Chinese students.

THE ⬚ SUN

Baltimore, OH, January 25, 1990

What does the bloody fall of Nicolae Ceausescu have to do with the repudiation of President Bush's China policy on Capitol Hill? More than a glimpse at the map would indicate.

The overthrow of the authoritarian Romanian dictator in December must have struck Peking's hardliners as a fate they avoided by massacring students in Tiananmen Square on June 4. They had seen less iron-willed Communist regimes fall to a democratic tide in Eastern Europe. And they had embraced Mr. Ceausescu as a brother in arms and ideology just weeks before he was executed.

So while Chinese dissidents took heart from Eastern Europe and continued their passive resistance, the Chinese regime continued its crackdown. Oh yes, the authorities lifted martial law as a cosmetic gesture. They let a Voice of America reporter back into the country (even while threatening foreign correspondents with censorship and worse). They accepted Peace Corps volunteers. They released a few hundred political prisoners.

How depressing it was to hear President Bush rattle off these supposed gains from his China policy at yesterday's press conference. For he knows China well, has a feel for its nuances. But his overtures smacked of Nixonian geo-politics, not Wilsonian idealism at a time when moralism (cynical or otherwise) is good coinage on the Hill. So what made good sense when he twice dispatched his security adviser to Peking to promote liberalization has turned into a nightmare.

The administration's first miscalculation, wholly its own doing, was to try to keep its diplomatic initiatives secret, thus inflaming sentiment here that the policy move was premature and overly conciliatory. The second miscalculation, utterly out of Washington's hands, was the Romanian revolution and the reaction it set off in Peking.

Given these events, Mr. Bush's decisions to veto a bill guaranteeing Chinese students in this country four more years of residence and then to fight the override by Congress are myopic. The president says Congress will have "only itself to blame" if China retaliates. Yet in the next breath he says his own administrative actions will keep the students as safe from forced repatriation as anything Congress can enact. If this is literally true why would Peking "retaliate" against congressional but not presidential action?

According to the president, retaliation could take the form of denying students now in China an opportunity to study in the United States. This logic is also suspect. After the Cultural Revolution, China sought a jump-start on the technology and science its students had missed by sending legions to this country. This remains a national imperative for China as it strives to catch up economically. So if China retaliates, the regime would only be hurting itself and hastening the day when the pro-democracy movement revives.

The Washington Post

Washington, DC, January 26, 1990

PRESIDENT BUSH fought hard and won a notable political victory yesterday when the Senate fell four Republican votes short—all the Democrats went against him— of overriding his veto of the Chinese student bill. But the China policy thus confirmed is no better for the wear, and may be the worse. An extra burden falls on the president to show the Beijing authorities he is not playing the part they seem to have assigned him in their cynical effort to suppress the shoots of democracy in China.

Before the vote, Mr. Bush had met objections that he was offering inadequate visa protections to Chinese students who were fearful of going home. He did so by taking administrative steps and by offering personal assurances extending protections beyond the terms of the bill Congress wished to make law. That eased most legislators' worries that democracy-minded students might be sent home against their will to a vengeful Chinese government. It allowed senators to turn to the two other grounds on which they were being asked to sustain their president's veto: either that they approved his accommodating approach to China or, if they did not, at least that they accepted his claim as chief executive to take the lead in conducting foreign policy.

In fact, something happened in midstream that surely provided cause for sober reflection. On Wednesday an aroused House voted to override, by a vote of 390 to 25. The Chinese responded with a blunt threat to the Senate not to follow suit, warning of "serious harm" to relations and in particular of danger to exchanges. Here was China, in the middle of an American debate, threatening more harshness and reacting to a step that Congress had proposed in order to protect the choices and rights of Chinese students in this country, with a step that would limit the choices and rights of Chinese students at home. And yet the Senate went along.

The basic cause for dismay about Mr. Bush's China policy has been that for ill-considered strategic reasons he was acquiescing to repugnant Chinese deeds and that Chinese officials and people alike would in their respective ways mistake his solicitude for tolerance for repression. This risk is aggravated by a visa-bill result that may be read by the authorities in Beijing as a signal that the president has bested his opposition on this issue. Will the Chinese now feel they are free to crack down as they please? Or is President Bush going to be able to show that the course he has chosen, and that Congress has now upheld, will produce greater respect for democracy and human rights?

The Courier-Journal
Louisville, KY, January 27, 1990

PRESIDENT Bush got a lot of undeserved criticism after it was discovered that he had sent secret envoys to China last year, not long after the Tiananmen Square massacre. But the President deserves all the criticism he has been receiving for vetoing a bill that would have barred deportation of Chinese students in this country.

And the 37 Republican senators — including Kentucky's Mitch McConnell — who voted Thursday to sustain Mr. Bush's veto were just as wrong as he was.

There's a big difference between maintaining contacts with the Chinese government, as Mr. Bush tried to do by sending special emissaries, and letting that government meddle in America's legal and political affairs.

That's what the veto was all about. The bill passed by Congress was both an attempt to protect Chinese students from repression if they were sent back home and an expression of Congress's outrage at that repression. It was not interference in China's internal affairs; the students are *here*, not in China.

In vetoing the bill, President Bush said the legislation was unnecessary because he had no intention of sending any students home against their will. He also argued that the bill interfered with his prerogative, as president, to make and execute foreign policy.

Sen. McConnell and 36 of his GOP colleagues bought that argument — or succumbed to appeals for party loyalty. Whatever their motives, they've sent the wrong signals to the bosses in Beijing.

Roanoke Times & World-News
Roanoke, VA, January 29, 1990

PRUDENCE seems the hallmark of George Bush's foreign policy — preferable, certainly, to rash adventurism.

The president has applauded the moves toward democracy in Eastern Europe, but he has not made commitments that America cannot keep.

He has voiced hope that Mikhail Gorbachev's policies of *glasnost* and *perestroika* can continue to progress in the Soviet Union, but he has not engaged in a futile effort to tell Soviet reformers how to go about it.

In some ways, even the invasion of Panama was an exercise in prudence. It came only after the failure of months of struggle to oust Manuel Noriega via diplomatic means, and only after Noriega himself virtually invited American intervention by force.

But when it comes to China, reasonable prudence seems to give way to an all-absorbing desire to get right with Deng. Never mind Tiananmen Square, it seems; never mind the ruthless suppression of dissent by Deng Xiaoping's government. Regardless of who China's rulers are or what they do, it seems, America should be good buddies with them.

In late November, Congress passed a bill to extend by four years the visas of Chinese students residing in the United States. Bush vetoed it, and last week used all his powers of presidential persuasion to muster enough Senate votes to sustain the veto. He succeeded, by four votes.

Taken in isolation, the flap was a tempest in a pot of oolong. A presidential proclamation already has done what the bill would have done; no student, Bush has pledged, will be forced to return to China so long as he is president.

Why, then, should Congress make such a big thing of it? And why should Bush expend so much political capital on preventing a veto override?

The answer: The flap cannot be taken in isolation. There is a context.

Not content to deal through the American ambassador to China, Bush since Tiananmen has sent high-level covert missions to Beijing to try to smooth things with the old men who run China.

Economic sanctions imposed after Tiananmen, sanctions Bush was reluctant to impose in the first place, are being lifted gradually. Apparently in deference to Chinese sensibilities, the United States continues to treat Cambodia and Vietnam as pariah nations — even though the communist regimes there (especially Cambodia's) are proving more receptive to reform these days than are China's communist rulers.

The difference between visa extensions based on a presidential proclamation and visa extensions set firmly in the law was not lost on the 40,000 Chinese students in America, who lobbied Congress hard to override the veto. Nor is the difference being lost on Deng and his cronies, who condemned the House of Representatives when it voted overwhelmingly to override the veto.

Why so soft a spot for China in the president's heart? Perhaps there's an empathy with the Chinese leadership that dates to the president's days as U.S. ambassador in Beijing. Perhaps Bush's soft spot derives from fond memories of the days of Sino-American *rapprochement* under Richard Nixon and Henry Kissinger. Or perhaps the explanation goes deeper: Perhaps Bush's attitude stems from a longstanding American myth that there's one heckuva market over there to tap, if only we could find the key. The key has never been found, because the market doesn't exist — and won't as long as China remains so poor a nation.

But whatever the explanation, the result is a quirky U.S. foreign policy. Prudence often compels restraint, and American judgment can be flawed. Still, America seeks in most of the world to promote human rights and democratic freedoms. Why then with China does America's goal seem to be to give succor to the forces of suppression?

OLD CHINA HANDS

The Hartford Courant

Hartford, CT, January 27, 1990

The Senate's failure to override President Bush's veto of a bill to protect Chinese students from deportation sends all the wrong signals.

It tells the president to continue his ill-conceived policy of premature reconciliation with China — a policy that has failed utterly to convey the outrage of the American people over the Chinese government's massacre of pro-democracy demonstrators in Tiananmen Square in June.

It tells the old men in Beijing that their blustering pays off. The House of Representatives voted by a huge margin to override Mr. Bush's veto, and the Chinese autocrats promptly threatened to retaliate. On the next day, the Senate caved in; 37 Republicans, including many who supported the student-protection bill when it passed before Christmas, voted to sustain the president. The veto-override attempt failed by four votes. Deng Xiaoping roars and the U.S. government quakes.

What are the pro-democratic Chinese to think? Those brave people stood before a portrait of Mao Tse-tung in Beijing's central square and quoted Jefferson and Lincoln. They erected a statue, the "Goddess of Democracy," that was the image of the Statue of Liberty. It was no secret that part of their inspiration came from these shores.

The demonstrators at home were supported by many, perhaps most, of the 40,000 Chinese studying in the United States. Beijing's persecution of dissenters in the wake of the spring rallies puts the students at risk.

This is how Washington responded to the massacre and to ongoing repression of the pro-democracy movement: Mr. Bush publicly canceled high-level contacts with the Chinese, but secretly sent his representatives to meet with the tyrants. Minor economic sanctions were imposed, but transfers of high technology to the Chinese have been resumed and the Bush administration may again approve bank loans to Beijing. Congress overwhelmingly passed a bill to protect the students from deportation, but Mr. Bush vetoed it. And now, faced with the president's appeal for party unity and the government of China's displeasure, the Senate collapses and Mr. Bush's veto stands.

It makes no difference that the president has done by executive order most of what the bill required. The executive order can be scrapped in a moment, whenever Mr. Bush feels a further concession to Beijing is in his best interest. Mr. Bush says that no Chinese student will be sent home involuntarily while he is president. But he also said that he had canceled high-level contacts when he had not.

The Bush administration believes its policy to be pragmatic and in the country's best interest. But its policy is pursued at the expense of America's most cherished values.

The Philadelphia Inquirer

Philadelphia, PA,
January 29, 1990

President Bush won a victory in the Senate last week, one that should gladden the hearts of the Chinese leaders who ordered the massacre in Tiananmen Square.

Those leaders threatened the United States with "grave consequences" if Congress overrode the President's veto of a bill protecting Chinese students in America from deportation. The House of Representatives voted against the President 390-25. But enough Senate Republicans (including Sens. John Heinz and Arlen Specter of Pennsylvania and William V. Roth Jr. of Delaware) voted with the President to ensure that the Senate fell four votes short of the two-thirds margin necessary to override the veto.

It is true that the President has promised that he will ensure by administrative action that no Chinese student who wants to stay is sent home. But Chinese students find it hard to trust a President who has sent out secret and public missions to glad-hand with a Chinese leadership that continues to hold thousands of pro-democracy demonstrators in prison.

Mr. Bush's secret policy has also undercut trust of his judgment on China in Congress. Republican senators who supported him were said to be swayed not by that policy, but by the argument that a veto override would be a serious political blow to the President.

Thus when Mr. Bush told a press conference that he believed that the Senate vote — 62-37 against him — represented "a trust factor in the administration," he showed that he still does not understand the mood of Congress over how he has dealt with Chinese leaders who have made a mockery of human rights. On China policy, it seems that the only leaders who trust Mr. Bush are his allies in Beijing.

China Unveils Budget, Economic Plans

China's vice president Yao Yilin and finance minister Wang Bingqian March 21, 1989 unveiled the government's economic plans and budget for 1989. Yao, head of the state planning commission, announced the imposition of a number of austerity measures that had been proposed by Premier Li Peng.

Yao told the People's Congress that the government would sharply reduce capital spending and cancel or delay virtually all new construction projects until at least the end of July. Other provisions included restricting investment loans to privately and collectively owned businesses to reduce growth; closing down companies that produced poor quality goods or used excessive amounts of energy or raw materials; and establishing a new income tax system to "gradually narrow the wide gap" between the nation's rich and poor.

The 1989 state budget, which included a deficit for the third year in a row, was presented to the congress by Finance Minister Wang. Revenues were expected to increase by about 10% over the previous year, to $76.75 billion, Wang said. Expenditures were expected to rise at nearly the same rate, to $78.74 billion. The resulting deficit would be $1.99 billion, down from $2.16 billion in 1988, the finance minister reported.

The largest expenditures in the proposed budget were government subsidies for state industries and consumers. Payments to industry were to total $14 billion in 1989, up 17% from the previous year. Subsidies for consumers were expected to reach $11 billion, an increase of 29% from 1988.

In an attempt to offset the effects of inflation in urban areas, where prices had been rising considerably faster than in the country as a whole, the government was planning to raise the wages of city workers, Wang said.

He also announced that a new 10% surcharge would be levied on the after-tax profits of private and collective enterprises.

The Washington Post

Washington, DC, April 30, 1989

SURPRISE UPON surprise in China, where for nearly two weeks students have been pressing a largely peaceful campaign for democracy. Upward of 100,000 demonstrators, defying official warnings of academic reprisal, marched through Beijing on Thursday, enveloping and dissolving the police formations sent to contain them and drawing support from workers and others usually thought immune to the appeals of the young. Senior leader Deng Xiaoping, seeing this demonstration as precisely the onslaught on one-party Communist rule that it is, reportedly urged repression "whatever the cost." But the government thought better, backing off and agreeing to the "dialogue" students had sought. A negotiation of sorts is now going on over its terms.

Worker sympathy is the key new element of this protest. The students seem to have been alert to opportunities to use the unemployment and inflation resulting from China's economic reform, and the corruption resulting from China's lack of political reform, as issues with which to draw in the larger constituency. It's early to say a permanent, strong and new coalition is forming. But there is a name for the collective that might be created from students, intellectuals and workers: a political party. This is what troubles the Communist Party. But it has had its chance—40 competition-free years—to show it truly represents the people in whose name it rules. Some of the police, fraternizing with students they were dispatched to control, seem to have gotten the point.

It is an important advance that the government refrained from using force and committed itself to meet protest with talk. But what might now come from a "dialogue" between students and the authorities is another matter. In the Soviet Union political change is coming from the top of the party, but in China it comes from the streets and has at best uncertain party sponsorship. In the Soviet Union, moreover, political reform is producing a measure of turbulence that is bound to feed into the incipient debate on whether to pursue political reform in China. As it happens, Mikhail Gorbachev, who has just conducted a spectacular purge of some of his party opposition, arrives in Beijing next month for the first Sino-Soviet summit in 30 years. Already at the center of a Soviet storm, he could find himself at the center of a Chinese storm too.

THE KANSAS CITY STAR

Kansas City, MO, April 19, 1989

The Soviet Union and China may share an outward devotion to Marx and Lenin, but they are opposites in at least one respect. Russians yearn for the economic reforms that have improved Chinese living standards, while Chinese yearn for glasnost.

Yet in China political reform remains out of the question, and now rising inflation is slowing the drive toward economic modernization as well. The most striking sign of disaffection is the growing unpopularity of Deng Xiaoping, the man who was instrumental in launching the reform movement a decade ago. He has received the credit for China's recent progress, and now he is getting the blame for its attendant problems.

Public criticism of the Chinese leader remains off limits, but clear signs of impatience are appearing. When former party leader Hu Yaobang died recently, anti-Deng posters appeared at Beijing University with biting slogans such as "The wrong person died." Hu was strongly associated with the reform movement. He was forced out in 1987 for tolerating dissidents and moving too fast toward a market economy.

Until recently, reform was popular in China because most people had seen some improvement in their lives. Real per capita income doubled in a decade. Last year, industrial output was up by nearly 18 percent. But inflation was up too, and in the cities prices are rising by 50 percent a year by unofficial estimates.

Price reform remains the key to China's modernization, but Chinese socialism, like most non-market economic systems, carries an inherent dilemma. Decontrolling prices—allowing them to properly signal scarcity and value—would mean a huge run-up in inflation because the country's factories, mines and farms are inadequate to meet demand.

Yet productive capacity cannot be expanded without the incentive of higher prices for scarce products (coupled, of course, with freer capital markets). This is not the first time China's leaders have confronted this dilemma. Until prices are allowed to do their job of sending signals to buyers and sellers, it won't be the last

THE ARIZONA REPUBLIC

Phoenix, AZ, March 22, 1989

THE love affair with economic and political reform has not worked out as well as some Chinese officials had hoped it would. So, having flirted with economic change for nearly a decade, China has decided to break off the engagement.

Premier Li Peng spelled out the government's intentions this week at the opening session of the National People's Congress. Beijing, he told members of China's rubber-stamp legislature, would rely more on central planning and less on market economics.

Deng Xiaoping, China's senior ruler and for more than a decade the leading advocate of economic reforms, was conspicuous by his absence. Chinese officials said he had "asked for leave," which suggests that he may not have been keen to observe his reforms being publicly repudiated.

The new guidelines are an extension of an austerity program initiated last fall that had resulted in sharp cutbacks in construction, banking activity and spending. Officials had put on the brakes in an effort to slow inflation, which had reached an annual rate of 36 percent — a postwar record.

Beijing wasted little time in putting the new policies into practice. The screw-tightening includes new controls and taxes on private businesses, collective enterprises and free-market farming, with consequences for production that are yet to be seen.

In the normal course of events, the development of a largely undeveloped country is economically healthy. China, however, is still hampered by socialist economics, which creates inevitable dislocations. Last year's 20 percent industrial growth rate, for example, overtaxed China's energy supply and transport network, with the result that many factories have been forced to cut production schedules in half.

China will not turn its back on market-oriented changes, such as the development of stock markets, Mr. Li said. The plan is to put most restructuring on hold — probably for two years at least — so that the government can, during this period of retrenchment, regain control of the economy.

But behind these economic tussles lies concern over the loss of power by the central government. Among China's Marxist rulers, the fear is that without a strong helmsman at the rudder, China will drift deeper into economic chaos and social unrest.

China is on a tightrope, precariously balanced between an old world characterized by strict regimentation and a new world geared to free markets. Though fearful of a return to the Maoist past, when millions starved, China's rulers are unwilling to embrace capitalism either. In groping their way forward, they are reaching for a hybrid socialism that would include a little of both worlds — a hybrid that is nowhere known to exist.

Roanoke Times & World-News

Roanoke, VA, March 26, 1989

THE TRANSITION from a command economy to a market economy isn't easy, as the mainland Chinese are learning. The Beijing government is turning to wage controls, import controls and other measures to slow down an economy that has become overheated.

For a number of years now, China has been encouraging private enterprise, especially in rural areas, where the population was growing faster than the economy. The strategy worked. The Chinese economy grew at a rate of 10 percent a year and young people were able to stay on the farms instead of flooding into the cities.

But even a market economy needs a certain amount of governmental regulation. In the West, this is usually accomplished through "macro-economics" — by manipulating interest rates and money supply and by government borrowing and spending.

The Chinese have little experience in macro-economics. They still lack the institutions to make indirect controls effective. Their banking system is primitive. Until a few years ago, they didn't even have a central bank.

Nevertheless, the Chinese people understand the profit motive. When beer and fish became more profitable than wheat and rice, they began selling their grain to breweries and dredging their rice paddies into fish ponds. Now there's a grain shortage in China. Beijing has responded to conditions with the tools most familiar to a communist state: direct controls.

Two years ago, Edwin Lim, head of the Chinese mission of the World Bank in Beijing, told visiting editors that the Chinese challenge "is to control inflation without going back on reforms; to control through macro-economics rather than central controls. It's a delicate transitional state that China is in."

In that transitional state, the Chinese still have to revert to some of their old methods. But private enterprise in China is not dead. It's just been fitted with a halter until the central government is sure the economy has been stabilized.

The New York Times

New York, NY, April 11, 1989

After more than a decade of reform, China has slipped into unmistakable retreat. The telltale signal came when Prime Minister Li Peng told the recent session of the National People's Congress that his Government plans to reimpose a measure of centralized economic control.

Until now, China has been more willing than any other Communist country to introduce free-market techniques, achieving changes, especially in agriculture, that Mikhail Gorbachev still only talks about.

This retreat is regrettable. Yet it's important for Westerners to grasp two points. One is that Beijing hasn't retreated significantly from post-Mao foreign policy. Relations with the U.S. remain good. The other is that recent Chinese history has left an entire generation of Communist Party leaders fearful of rapid political changes like those with which Mr. Gorbachev has fired Soviet imaginations.

•

During the Cultural Revolution, many Chinese now in power were pilloried by rampaging Maoist Red Guards. It's not surprising that they now reflexively retreat into a defensive posture whenever it seems that uncontrolled passions might be unleashed from below. Indeed, the most reform-minded among them have been politically hurt by their perceived failure to contain protest and disorder. Two years ago, Hu Yaobang lost his job as party leader after student protests. Now, it appears, his successor, Zhao Ziyang, has been politically weakened by economic unrest.

The results are now on display: the growing ascendancy of Prime Minister Li Peng, a cautious bureaucrat; the rebuffs to domestic and foreign pleas for greater political liberty; the move back toward centralized economic control. Alarmed by inflation, violence in Tibet and growing interest among intellectuals in expanding democratic rights, Beijing's leadership has decided on at least a temporary retreat to orthodoxy.

There have been several previous attempts to pull in the reins since Deng Xiaoping launched China's reform program in 1978, but this time, the elderly Mr. Deng appears less able to protect his reformist protégés than in the past.

Unfortunately, the effort to maintain some control over the pace of reform could actually worsen the very imbalances China now cites as a reason for pulling back. For example, under the incompletely reformed pricing system, the same goods command different prices depending on whether they are exchanged in state or private markets. That almost guarantees bottlenecks, shortages and inflation.

Matters are also complicated by the uneasy coexistence of wide-open, thriving special economic zones and more traditionally regulated regions. Given such fragmentation, it is reasonable to wonder whether recentralization is even possible, let alone a practical remedy for troublesome distortions.

China's economic reform policies have done so much to liberate the energies of the population, especially in the countryside, that there probably can't be any real return to the stifling old ways. The more realistic danger is that fear of taking further political risks will leave China in limbo, with one foot mired in the past. Beijing's friends can only hope its leaders will come to understand that those risks are justified by the promise of a more prosperous, freer future.

The Washington Times

Washington, DC, April 11, 1989

As part of its one-family, one-child population policy, the government of China forbids expectant parents who already have a child to bear any more. If the parents don't obey, the government hauls the mother into a "hospital," kills the baby and then sterilizes the mother. It's called family planning.

Beijing doesn't hesitate to extend its policies to the United States. Chinese nationals temporarily living here have received some very straightforward letters from their government, leaving no doubt about the stiff penalties that await them on their return. "Fix your problem," Dr. and Mrs. Quan Bang Li were ordered. "If you have trouble obtaining an abortion in the United States, you should return to China immediately for the operation. ... Second children are banned. You know the policy." To an unfortunate lady named Ping Hong the government wrote, "punishment for this kind of violation [having a second child] is very severe. ... There is nothing ambiguous about our order! Make up your mind immediately!"

Many couples in this situation want to stay in the United States because they have a "well-founded fear of persecution." Former Attorney General Edwin Meese agreed, noting that resistance to the family planning policy amounted to "political dissent." In one of his last official acts, he granted the Lis and two other couples asylum in a memorandum to the Immigration and Naturalization Service.

But now the INS has appealed a judge's order granting asylum to another dissenting couple who fled China after the population minister's family planners did away with the woman's unborn child. In another case in New York, where the INS is opposing the appeal of a man denied asylum after fleeing China the day before he was scheduled for a

forced sterilization, the argument has been further refined. "Those persons subject to the sterilization operations are not being singled out," the INS argues. "Every family which has more than one child is being sought by the Chinese officials to submit to a sterilization operation." In Orwellian terms, since everyone is persecuted, no one is.

Abortion with the consent of the parents is one thing; forced killing of fetuses and punishment of parents who resist is another. Attorney General Richard Thornburgh needs to reaffirm Mr. Meese's order and make sure the INS is on the same wavelength as most people when they talk about what persecution really means.

The News and Courier

Charleston, SC, April 10, 1989

Lenin once described the advance of communism as two steps forward, one step back. His celebrated maxim might well be applied, ironically, to the cause of diluting communism in that other totalitarian giant, China.

A decade ago, China's post-Mao leadership amazed the world, especially the communist world, by abandoning that icon of Marxism-Leninism, collective agriculture. In place of community farming came the "responsibility system," a euphemism for the return to family farming. As a result, farm income in China tripled and food production rose by more than 40 percent.

But Beijing has found it much more difficult to extend these capitalist-style reforms to the urban and industrial sectors of its economy. Real reform requires that the communist government surrender more power over the economy, and that is anathema to the party leaders — not to mention their legions of bureaucrats and functionaries honeycombed throughout the land.

China's struggle with salvaging its econ-

omy is played out against the backdrop of the continuing struggle to determine who will succeed 84-year-old Deng Xiaoping as principal leader. The contenders at present are Premier Li Peng and the party's general secretary, Zhao Ziyang. Broadly speaking, Mr. Li is the more orthodox communist, Mr. Zhao the more liberal reformer.

Regrettably for China, recent events suggest that Mr. Li and the hard-line communists he represents are gaining the upper hand. At the recent opening of the National People's Congress, China's rubber-stamp parliament, Mr. Li announced the government would increase centralized planning and controls as part of an austerity program lasting several years.

In economic terms, this retrenchment will mean less reliance on market forces, fewer reforms and, of course, less growth for China's economy. In political terms, it casts into doubt the presumption that a communist state can accomplish the most essential reform of all: an end to the communist party's monopoly of power.

THE CHRISTIAN SCIENCE MONITOR

Boston, MA, March 29, 1989

WHILE political reform has unleashed the unknown in the Soviet Union, economic experimentation has stirred things in China. Too much, according to the Party powers that be.

Speaking before the National People's Congress in Beijing, meeting last week and this, Prime Minister Li Peng decried the mistakes that have allowed China's economy to lurch into the uncharted regions of inflation, bank runs, and panic buying. He warned of at least two more years of austerity, marked by higher taxes and tightened controls on investments and loans.

It was a sharpened turn away from the decentralization of economic control that has been the hallmark of Chinese reform. Austerity surfaced last September, prodded by inflation, which climbed to 30 percent in many urban areas.

But the leadership's swing back toward centralized planning doesn't mean quick changes in the way many Chinese are doing business. The economic engines puffing away all over China – in rural cooperatives, collective industries, and small family-run businesses – aren't going to draw off the steam simply because Beijing has so proclaimed. As with the urge for political autonomy in a number of Soviet republics, the entrepreneurial energy in China's provinces won't easily be confined again. Profitmaking can be exhilarating – and the Chinese, in contrast to their Russian counterparts, are good at it.

Li Peng and others have good reason to rein things in. Inflation is causing hardship, and income disparities are widening. People in the inland regions resent the prosperity of the coastal areas, which have received the lion's share of development help from the government. Corruption is said to be widespread.

An overheating economy triggers alarms in any country, on whatever side of the ideological divide. The Chinese, however, have junked many of their old "command" means of economic adjustment, and new tools, like a strong central bank and monetary controls, aren't yet in place.

Some Western observers think the current austerity measures won't reach the root causes of inflation and are likely to simply breed "stagflation" – stifled growth but continuing price rises.

On the political side, meanwhile, Beijing has been inclined to tighten up on dissent even as it tries to tighten the economic controls. All in the name of social stability.

Though the Chinese try hard to mask differences among their leaders, it's clear that the current difficulties are causing a rift between those who counsel caution and those, led by party leader Zhao Ziyang, who have pushed for radical change.

For the men of both Beijing and Moscow, the goal is to get from here to the prosperity and dynamism way down there. The passage involves risks – including the possible evolutions of their systems into something an old-line Marxist might not recognize. Stability may prove inadequate as a governing value.

The Washington Post

Washington, DC, March 27, 1989

WITH THE GENIE of economic reform half out of the bottle, China's leadership is looking anxiously for a way to slow the process down. Gathering momentum over the past 10 years, reform has visibly raised the standard of living in China. The country's growth rate last year was a phenomenal 11 percent. But with that has come a scorching inflation that, in a country unaccustomed to it, is generating widespread strikes and demonstrations. Fearful of rising social turmoil, the government announced last week an attempt to reimpose central control over some sectors previously allowed to run more or less free.

All of the Communist countries are now struggling with the same dilemma. They are all confronted by the extreme difficulty—not to say danger—of trying run an economy partly ruled by the free market and partly by the old bureaucracies. Throughout China, the Soviet Union and Eastern Europe, people urgently want to live better, and they know that, under different economic rules, they can. They demonstrably want more political freedom, and the two go together.

But for 40 years or more, these people have been living under regimes in which even the most inefficient factory never went bankrupt, and the most careless employee was never—except for political reasons—fired. Prices of most goods were held down by subsidies and controls. That meant endemic shortages, but people learned to live with them. The idea of markets in which prices rise with demand is a new one and, to many Chinese, evidently frightening: the public reaction to inflation has been fierce, and the Chinese leadership has been signaling since last summer that it is not prepared to let things go much farther. The leadership knows how to run the old kind of economy, and it thinks that it knows how to run the new kind. But it is getting from one place to the other and taking a billion people with it that is the tricky part.

China lacks a federal reserve board to raise interest rates as a brake when inflation accelerates. As a matter of policy, China holds its interest rates low because an increase would force thousands of inefficient factories to fail, throwing their employees out of work. With rates frozen, it's hard in any country to keep inflation under control.

But the key to reform, in China and everywhere else, is the pricing system. China now finds itself with a dual system, in which some prices move with the market and some are controlled. That creates enormous corruption and confusion, since some sectors are profitable and some are not. But no Communist country is yet ready to leave the prices of basic foodstuffs and shelter to the market.

The Chinese leadership has slowed down the process of reform a couple of times before, and the present retreat may well turn out to be only temporary. But there is no doubt that this half-completed transformation is creating enormous perplexities, not of mere ideology but of practical management. Presumably, no one is watching China's progress more closely than Mikhail Gorbachev.

THE ⬛ SUN

Baltimore, MD, March 22, 1989

The campaign of austerity, renewed central planning and retrenchment on reform proclaimed by government leaders to China's formal legislature this week actually began last October. Central controls were reimposed on bank credit at that time, investment was curtailed, state trading monopolies reinstated on metal products and, in general, the hot economy was cooled off and central authority reimposed.

What the National People's Congress, or rubber stamp legislature, has been hearing now suggests that last October's measures were not emergency stoppers but the first round of a deeply thought-out plan to stabilize China and curtail without rolling back the movement toward market economics. Austerity is never popular, and that is what the billion Chinese people have just been promised for a few years.

Premier Li Peng criticized past optimism and decentralization. He called for more "guidance" and "resolute measures to curb inflation." He preached more of the austerity that began last October. His Monday speech may have been the 60-year-old Moscow-trained bureaucrat's shot across the bow of his predecessor and current party chairman, Zhao Ziyang, 70, for succession to the leadership exercised by Deng Xiaoping, 84.

China is a decade ahead of the Soviet Union in *perestroika*. Nothing done this week suggests it doesn't work. It has worked. Since 1981, China has been running a 10 percent growth rate, the greatest of any major country. But it is also out of control. Private enterprise was begun in rural areas, to encourage people to stay put and not migrate to cities. But as a byproduct, agriculture shrank and the grain shortage is getting worse. And so the new curbs hurt most the new rural industry. Inflation is running at 36 percent, making anyone who has not been getting richer, poorer. The cities are hit by hoarding and bank runs. That's what needs to be cooled off.

Combatting growth run amok does not mean that China's version of Yegor K. Ligachev is in charge or that China's *perestroika* will be repealed. Construction is cut back, but private enterprise still hums and foreign investment is still sought. The measures do mean that Communist central authorities believe in central control and are struggling to regain it over the market forces they unleashed. It also means that China's economic growth will slow down for the near future. Whether China's next leaders go into a new round of reforms will probably depend on how well they stabilize the gains from the last round.

THE CHRISTIAN SCIENCE MONITOR

Boston, MA, January 10, 1989

EVENTS in China are tarnishing its image as a liberalizing society. Brakes have been applied to the celebrated push toward "capitalism." Africans studying in Chinese universities have become the targets of racial hatred and rioting. Physicist and human-rights advocate Feng Lizhi was denied the right to travel abroad.

Clearly, liberalization has its obstacles in China. But it also has momentum. Capitalistic approaches to management, marketing, and ownership have transformed much of the Chinese economy over the past decade. Incentives, private property, and a still primitive stock exchange have become part of the nation's commerce. Home-grown entrepreneurs, sniffing profits, have turned small manufacturing concerns and productive vegetable plots into money-makers. The Chinese, Westerners assumed, were discovering what makes an economy hum.

They were also discovering the ills of an overheating market economy. Inflation, in particular, shocked the Chinese. It grew at a rate of 17 percent for the first 10 months of 1988. The government, lacking the kind of central bank that counters inflation in the US, has had few levers to pull in its newly decentralized economy.

China's leaders decided, accordingly, to slow things down. Some centralized controls have been reapplied, and long talked about price reforms, considered the key test of Chinese commitment to reform, have been delayed.

But it's well to remember that China's leaders, though bent on reform, have never forsaken socialism. Zhao Ziyang, the Communist Party chief and leading reformer, is determined to make that system work within the context of a world that increasingly runs on high technology and instant information.

The present slow-down is a course correction, not a change of course. And the course, in China, includes continued tight party control over political life. This in the name of stability – a value that inevitably collides with liberalizing impulses on the economic side.

That explains why a respected intellectual like Feng Lizhi isn't allowed to take his dissident views abroad, and why average Chinese can no longer banner their views on wall posters.

It doesn't explain, of course, why mobs raged against African students who had attended a dance with Chinese dates.

Part of the explanation is resentment against the privileges widely accorded foreigners in China. But that occurrence is also rooted in a long history of isolation and xenophobia. Those habits of thought, every bit as much as ingrained authoritarian tendencies, are going to have to give way before China can truly merge into the mainstream of a world dependent on global markets and a global outlook.

Omaha World-Herald

Omaha, NE,
January 16, 1989

Mao Tse-tung must be turning in his grave. Three top economists in China, all members of the Communist Party, have suggested that the government give up state ownership of certain industries and allow individuals and institutions to own shares.

State ownership of the means of production has been the key to socialism, marxist and non-marxist. One of the chief ideas in Karl Marx's view of revolutionary socialism was that the state would seize factories and run them on behalf of the workers. Vladimir Lenin added a non-democratic government to the formula, and Josef Stalin added collectivism and totalitarian methods. None of it worked.

From the Soviet Union and Romania in Europe to China in Asia to Angola in Africa and Cuba in the Western Hemisphere, state socialism hasn't worked. In democratic countries such as Great Britain, government ownership is being successfully dismantled, to the good of economic development.

The obvious is beginning to be acknowledged in the Kremlin and throughout the Communist world. Still, a high-level call for privatization seems remarkable in a country such as China, where the Communist Party has closely guarded its power and influence.

If government disinvestment became a fact of life, it would be the final rejection of the economic ideas of Karl Marx. In China, it would mean the end of the socialist era, which would make it a history-making event.

S.T. HSU, Taiwan's Minister of the Interior

THE TAMPA TRIBUNE

Tampa, FL, February 15, 1989

In public as in private matters, there are times when problems seem beyond solution even when they aren't. Human perspective is such that what may only require patience and fortitude often appears forever hopeless.

This fact came to mind the other day when we read the first paragraph of a front-page story in the New York Times:

"In a bold proposal for change, three influential Chinese economists with close ties to the Government have called for China to abandon state ownership of industry."

Now that is something. During the four decades of Communist rule in China, the idea of totally denationalizing industry in that country has been absent from Western speculations. For many years, to mention it even as a possibility, absent a revolution, was to invite the contempt of all.

But the Times story makes clear that this most extraordinary departure from the Marxist canon is indeed being considered in Beijing. There are several reasons why China's leaders would choose to hear out the three economists, and they include everything from Milton Friedman's lectures there to the proximity of Japan, which, although perilously short of natural resources and elbow room, has used capitalist tools to build the second-largest economy in the world.

Still, what inspired China's new train of thought may be less important than the lesson of its unexpectedness. Circumstances change, and when they do, so do minds. Weariness wears down commitment. New comparisons are made. People and institutions reshuffle priorities. Opportunities, previously invisible, assume shape and color.

The Soviet Union has gotten most of the publicity for making some tentative efforts at economic reform. So far, however, those efforts have been dithering. But the Chinese, a business-oriented people if there ever was one, began 10 years ago to re-examine the Marxist ideology that was causing them to fall ever further behind the booming capitalist societies of the Pacific Rim.

Moscow, for its part, doesn't appear to know what to do. Unlike the Chinese, the Russian people have never been expert at domestic or foreign commerce. And after the 1917 revolution, they were denied all chance of learning. How then can the Kremlin motivate men and women to succeed in the marketplace? Indeed, how can the Kremlin afford to replace collectivism with even modified capitalism without running political risks unacceptable to the party hierarchy?

China's situation is different. Its population is cohesive, unlike the Soviet Union's patchwork of frequently antagonistic nationalities and creeds. And though China has its own cautious bureaucracy, that bureaucracy is not nearly so stuck in concrete as the Russian model. Too, the unfolding economic revolution in China is unlikely to threaten the country's political stability. The Chinese for centuries have cherished the freedom to do business. The who and how of lawmaking, while interesting and important to them, are not so interesting and important as the opportunity to make money. This, we realize, is a large generalization but it is supported by history. It is also supported by the experience of the Taiwan Chinese, who manage to combine economic freedom with political rigidity.

What the future holds for the Soviet Union is altogether unknowable, and that itself is cause enough for concern. But in Western capitals there is growing confidence that China is on its way toward becoming a major participant in the world's business.

And that's important to the United States, because a China pushing its way back to a free-market economy, while a perplexity to Moscow, is unlikely to cause major problems for the world. The profound changes in China, which is still very poor, partly explain why the Soviets are suddenly so anxious to improve relations with the potential powerhouse on their southeastern border — and why it's urgently important for Washington to strengthen Sino-American ties.

Nothing lasts, it's true. But that lament occasionally has its bright side, which is why optimism doesn't necessarily signify foolishness.

The Seattle Times

Seattle, WA, January 16, 1989

THE People's Republic of China has undergone dramatic changes in modern times, but one of the most extraordinary transformations of all was recently proposed.

Three influential Chinese government economists, all Communist Party members, have called for an end to state ownership of industry and the selling of shares in companies to individuals, universities, and local governments.

China has experimented with limited forms of capitalism and free enterprise in the 1980s, but this far-reaching proposal would shake that nation to its very foundation.

People's Daily, the Communist Party newspaper, did not directly endorse the idea, but said the three economists had "courageously pointed out that public ownership no longer is the premise of socialism." Such a comment would have been unthinkable only a few years ago.

The leader of the "Gang of Three" economists, according to The New York Times, is Hua Sheng, 36, the Oxford-educated head of the microeconomics department at the Chinese Academy of Social Sciences' Institute of Economics. He and his colleagues also are behind such previous innovations as allowing prices of certain goods to float freely, and auctioning off to the highest bidder the right to manage some companies.

However, this notion goes far beyond those experiments. It also envisions eventual far-reaching changes in the political system. Hua said a new definition of socialism was needed, focusing on social justice and equality of opportunity rather than public ownership of industry.

Having shareholders and boards of directors run companies would make them more efficient and productive than being owned and managed by the government, Hua said.

It's highly unlikely that the idea will be adopted overnight. Opposition from government bureaucrats at national and local levels is expected to be considerable.

Still, the fact that this remarkable proposal has surfaced at all, with at least semi-official sanction, is astonishing. Chairman Mao and Karl Marx are no doubt rolling over in their graves.

Rioting Erupts in Tibet; Martial Law Imposed

At least 12 people were killed March 5-7, 1989 in clashes between anti-Chinese demonstrators and police in the Tibetan capital city, Lhasa, the Chinese government reported. Four other people died later of injuries suffered in the unrest, raising the official death toll to 16. Tibetan sources claimed that the actual number of casualties was much higher.

The rioting broke out exactly one year after 18 Buddhist monks had died in a similar protest rally in Lhasa, and marked the fourth time in less than a year and half that a pro-independence demonstration in the Tibetan capital had erupted in violence.

The unrest also came only days before the 30th anniversary of a bloody Tibetan uprising against Chinese occupation forces that left an estimated 87,000 Tibetans dead and forced the Dalai Lama, Tibet's spiritual leader, to flee into exile. Western observers said the latest disturbances represented the most serious challenge to Chinese rule in the disputed region since the 1959 revolt.

According to reports by the official New China News Agency, the confrontation began midday March 5, when 13 Buddhist monks and nuns began an illegal march to demand independence for Tibet. The marchers were soon joined by some 600 other protesters, who began throwing stones at police, and looting and burning local shops, restaurants and hotels.

Official accounts of the violence could not be confirmed independently because foreign journalists were barred from traveling to Tibet. However, Western tourists speaking by telephone from Lhasa quoted Tibetans who said that between 30 an 100 people had been killed in the three days of unrest.

In response to the rioting, the Chinese government March 7 imposed martial law in Lhasa for the first time since the 1959 uprising.

The Record

Hackensack, NJ, March 10, 1989

Human rights is a tricky business. The United States leans on the Soviet Union, Chile, and South Africa, but all but ignores other abusers. China stands out. New killings and arrests by Chinese forces in Tibet show again that the Chinese can be as brutal and heavy-handed as other notorious human rights violators, and that they deserve the same condemnation. Washington has gone easy on China ever since the heady days of U.S.-Chinese friendship that started in 1972. It's time to stop looking the other way.

Imagine that events in Lhasa, the Tibetan capital deep in the Himalayas, had taken place in Moscow or Santiago or Warsaw. Demonstrations break out against the government. Troops and police respond with volleys of gunfire. The United States would be outraged.

Official Chinese accounts report 16 deaths, but Tibetans put the toll far higher. They say Chinese troops fired indiscriminately on crowds. Foreign travelers report seeing Chinese police drag Tibetans from their homes and haul them away in trucks. To put an end to such reports, the Chinese yesterday expelled all foreigners. "Tibetan affairs are China's internal affairs which brook no interference by a foreign government, organization or individual," says Li Zhaoxing, spokesman for the Chinese Foreign Ministry.

Sure. Just like uprisings in Afghanistan were internal affairs of the Soviet Union. Tibetans have their own culture, their own language, their own religion, and their own ingrained traditions — none of which have anything to do with China. The Chinese rule Tibet for one reason — they invaded and "annexed" the country in 1951, ending decades of independence. The Chinese had ruled Tibet during the 19th century and much of the 18th century, but that was a relatively brief interlude in long centuries of independence or control by the Mongols and other outside powers.

The Chinese have attempted nothing less than the destruction of Tibetan culture. A wave of murders and violence followed the initial invasion. Recently disclosed Chinese documents show that 87,000 Tibetans were killed after anti-Chinese demonstrations in 1959. During China's Cultural Revolution, as many as 3,500 Tibetan monasteries were destroyed.

In response to the latest violence, the Bush administration has expressed regrets, but softly. "While we recognize the right of a government to maintain order, we object to the unwarranted use of lethal force," a State Department spokesman said. That's only a shade better than the carefully balanced statements the State Department has issued in the past. Mr. Bush, to his credit, invited Chinese human rights activists to a state dinner on his recent visit to Beijing, but the affair was badly handled. Dissident Fang Lizhi, who is as well-known in China as Andrei Sakharov is in the Soviet Union, wound up being barred by Chinese authorities. Mr. Bush, according to his spokesmen, never mentioned human rights during his discussions with Chinese leaders, and the Bush administration statements on human rights in China were vague.

There's nothing confusing about the present reports from Tibet. "People begged us repeatedly over the last few days — 'tell the world, help us please,'" an American traveler in Lhasa told a reporter. A West German visitor had a similar story: "They grab your hand and say, 'help us,' and they cry.'" Washington can help. It can condemn in the strongest possible terms the suffering that the Chinese inflict on Tibet, and bring the same pressures to bear on China that it routinely does on other nations. Freedom is freedom, and the administration should nourish it in Lhasa as carefully as in Pretoria or Moscow.

THE DENVER POST

Denver, CO, March 15, 1989

IN THE shadow of the Himalayas, the people of Tibet are agitating for freedom. Protesters want to end China's 30-year rule of their country, and to restore their spiritual leader, the Dalai Lama, to secular power.

Last week, a dozen or more people died in renewed rioting. Chinese police imposed martial law on the capital of Lhasa and ordered foreigners out of the city.

Witnesses said Chinese police broke into homes, tossed hundreds of terrified civilians into military trucks and hauled them away to an unknown place. The world does not know what conditions these captives now endure.

China is a developing nation seriously in need of Western technology and trade. Since the mid-1970s, Chinese leaders have courted American favor. They eagerly invited foreign tourists to visit Tibet's magnificent Himalayas.

Yet the Chinese now willfully ignore global revulsion at the violent repression occurring in Tibet. Having flung open its doors, China now wants to slam them shut. But if China truly wants to become a full-fledged member of the community of nations, it must submit to the court of world opinion.

Unfortunately, the U.S. government has not forcefully objected to China's mistreatment of the Tibetans. But oddly, the Boulder City Council has articulated America's ethical obligation. The council sent a strong but diplomatic letter to the Chinese-backed government in Lhasa, calling for restoration of basic human rights in Tibet.

The Boulder City Council, obviously, does not set foreign policy. But in this situation, it was appropriate for the council to express its collective concern.

Boulder and Lhasa have been sister cities for several years, undertaking exchanges of medical personnel and art-restoration programs. As a result, Boulder's council members have credibility with their counterparts in Tibet.

Boulder's letter won't convince China to give Tibet its independence. But it might make the Chinese aware that the world knows of China's reprehensible actions.

The Pittsburgh
PRESS

Pittsburgh, PA, March 16, 1989

If the KGB were to gun down peaceful demonstrators in Estonia or Lithuania, even super-salesman Mikhail Gorbachev would have trouble persuading Washington to continue improving relations. But Gorbachev's counterparts in Beijing evidently think they can murder Buddhist protesters in Tibet without suffering damage in their ties with the West.

The Chinese communists seized Tibet in 1950, a decade after the Soviet Union overran the Baltic republics. Both Moscow and Beijing used mass terror to suppress cultural and political traditions; both suppressed religions.

The latest clashes began when a small group of Buddhist monks and nuns began a protest march in Lhasa, Tibet's capital. The government-controlled media claim Chinese police opened fire to stop armed rioters, but American tourists said they did not see any demonstrators with guns. In any case, at least a dozen Tibetans were killed.

When President Bush failed to raise the issue of human rights during his recent meeting with China's rulers, they may have concluded that for the next four years they can ignore him on that issue.

The Washington Post

Washington, DC, March 12, 1989

THE CURRENT demonstrations in Tibet are described as the most serious challenge to Chinese rule since the Communist government put down a major uprising that began there 30 years ago. Whether this is so is hard to confirm, given the means Beijing has available to spare the territory outside scrutiny. But it is plain that, although Chinese policy over the years has resulted in the death of hundreds of thousands of Tibetans, relentless attacks on Tibetan culture and religion, continued human rights violations and the staged influx of Han Chinese people into areas where many Tibetans live, Tibet retains a deep sense of its own identity and a commitment to live a life of its own. In this sense, China's attempt to build a smoothly integrated multinational state has failed.

For years after the initial "rape of Tibet," as it was fairly called, the exiled leader, the Dalai Lamai, was the focus of a movement for the independence of Tibet. The Chinese, denying that Tibet ever had any claim to independence (at no time has any government ever recognized such a claim), set up a "Tibetan autonomous region" even as the decimation of real Tibetan autonomy

proceeded. In the past few years, the Dalai Lama, who is now 53, has asserted a more modest claim for a "middle way, not complete independence," asking for an "association" with China that would ensure the autonomy it has long espoused. He has sought a dialogue with Beijing on the status and future of Tibet. The Chinese, who contend that the status is already settled, have been sparring with him over the ground rules.

President Bush's recent visit to China left a certain sour impression that he had failed to press the matter of Chinese human rights violations with sufficient personal vigor. The question of Tibet was not glowing hot at the precise moment he was in Beijing, but that question certainly falls into the category of human rights issues that require sharp American attention. In the first instance, Americans cannot fail to protest against official acts of repression in Tibet. In a broader context, the United States is right to use its diplomacy to nudge China and the Dalai Lama toward the direct talks that they seemed to be moving toward before the latest cycle of Tibetan protest and Chinese violence. Chinese respect for its pledges to Tibet is essential to build American respect for China.

THE SUN

Baltimore, MD, March 9, 1989

There are only two million Tibetans in the undeveloped Himalayan vastness. It is a tribute to the tenacity of their identity that nationalism flares anew. This is 39 years after Chinese Communist troops destroyed Tibet's priestly regime and 30 years since their spiritual-national leader, the Dalai Lama, fled to India following the suppression of a popular uprising.

Chinese authorities say a dozen people have died in the capital of Lhasa since this bout of unrest began Sunday; Tibetans say 75. China imposed martial law. One result is to keep Tibetans in their houses for fear of being shot and another is to keep out tourists and embassy travelers, who are the West's only source of news.

Tibetan riots against ethnic Chinese shops are not surprising. During the Cultural Revolution in the 1960s and '70s, Chinese poured into Tibet in hope of swamping Tibetan ethnicity. In 1980, Beijing pulled back and appointed a number of Tibetan officials to run things. But despite the destruction of monasteries, Buddhist monks kept nationalism alive; demonstrations have now broken out in each of the last three years.

China's suzerainty over Tibet is undisputed. But Tibet lived in autonomy that was virtual inde-

pendence until 1950. China's invasion that year was so much a national rather than ideological matter that the rival Republic of China government on Taiwan endorsed it. Although the Dalai Lama has been circumspect in his sanctuary in India, his preservation of the torch of national identity is one of the friction points in the difficult relationship between India and China that keeps India friendly with the Soviet Union.

The Chinese occupiers had a collaborator in the second-ranking spiritual leader, the Panchen Lama, but he died in January. The Dalai Lama has proposed Tibetan home rule with Chinese troops based in Tibet for national defense and Chinese responsibility for foreign policy. Beijing has rejected this idea, but ought to take it up.

In the course of its economic liberalization, the regime of Deng Xiaoping is cracking down on dissent that goes beyond a line of his drawing. Beijing is ready to tell the world, as it so brusquely told President Bush, that what goes on inside its borders, including Tibet, is no one else's business.

But Tibetan nationalism will not die. It is no threat to China. Beijing would have no Tibet problem if it would send its troops to border barracks, its officials home and let the Dalai Lama return.

The Evening Gazette

Worcester, MA, March 15, 1989

China's brutal oppression of Tibet is both deplorable and rich in irony. As part of its communist policy, the People's Republic of China has supported movements of national liberation and assisted the struggle against "imperialist oppression" — as long as the "imperialists" were the United States, the Soviet Union or Vietnam. Yet China's occupation of Tibet is a classic example of oppressive colonial rule.

Beijing claims Tibet has been part of China since the 13th century. But Tibetans are a distinct people with their own language, culture and religion. Many say Tibet should be independent under the political, as well as religious, leadership of the Dalai Lama.

Since 1950, when Chinese troops invaded the land of the snows in the Himalayas, there has been unrest. After an aborted uprising in 1959, the Dalai Lama was sent into exile. China's increasing brutality prompted violent demonstrations by Tibetans both in Beijing and in Lhasa, Tibet's capital. Last week China declared martial law in Tibet, prompting the Dalai Lama to call international attention to his people's suffering.

The United States has routinely criticized heavy-handed Chinese actions and recently deplored the use of weapons against pro-independence protesters. Washington, which has common interests with Beijing, has been pragmatic enough to know that any call for Tibet's autonomy would be bitterly rejected by Beijing. Indeed, full independence may not be a realistic goal at this time; not even the Dalai Lama is seeking it.

But the United States could do more than issue occasional objections. It could intensify the pressure to stop the brutality, acknowledge that the Dalai Lama has political standing and support his request for cultural and religious freedoms.

Bringing about reconciliation would also be in China's interest. After all, even the Soviet Union has resolved to acknowledge the mistakes of the Stalin era and pledges democratic reforms. The "new" China could hardly count on full recognition within the world community if it continues to insist on the discredited policies of Mao Tse-tung.

ST. LOUIS POST-DISPATCH

St. Louis, MO,
March 10, 1989

The people of the Tibet Autonomous Region, under the direct control of China since 1951, have begun to take the meaning of their "autonomous" relations with Beijing seriously. In what may be a classic example of a revolution of rising expectations, Tibetans have been protesting in the streets of Lhasa, the capital, for an end to Chinese repression and the rights to more political and religious freedom.

Human rights champions such as the United States and Western European countries should speak out forcefully against individual and collective human rights violations by Beijing. The Chinese leaders will not like that, but there is no reason China should not be held to the same standards as the Soviet Union, Vietnam and the Eastern Bloc countries. The danger, as shown during President Bush's recent visit to China, is that nothing at all will be said; good bilateral relations with China seem to overshadow obvious human rights violations.

Tibet is one of the forgotten tragedies of Asia; ignoring the plight of its people as Chinese soldiers kill dozens in the streets to enforce martial law will be nothing new. When the Chinese communist government invaded in 1950, the United Nations refused to take action. Aid promised by Britain and India failed to materialize. Tibet was taken over by China and in the nearly four decades since, a traditional Buddhist way of life has been virtually wiped out while the world said nothing.

During the late 1970s, Chinese repression was relaxed after the horrors of the Cultural Revolution left hundreds of temples and monasteries in ruins. More freedoms were granted in 1984 as China added certain democratic features. Now Tibetans want greater independence and religious freedom. They deserve the outspoken support of the democratic nations.

The News and Courier

Charleston, SC, March 15, 1989

Under Mao Tse-tung, China could hide its dirty little secrets from the world. But as China opens itself up to economic development, its authorities will have to realize that freedom is indivisible. Freedom of the market place must extend to respect for basic human rights.

Ridding China of all remnants of Mao's tyranny is not high on the list of reforms introduced under leader Deng Xiaoping, as was made clear during President Bush's recent visit to Beijing. The president invited a leading dissident to dinner at the U.S. Embassy but police prevented him from attending.

It was an insult to the president and everything the United States stands for. It should serve as a warning that despite the remarkable changes ushered in by Deng, Washington and Beijing operate under totally different standards.

The simmering revolt in Tibet is another of China's areas of darkness. This month marks a series of anniversaries that will remind the world that the communist regime continues its repression of a once free people. March 17 is the 30th anniversary of the day the Dalai Lama fled for India. On March 19 and 20, 1959, Tibetans will remember the brutal force used by the Chinese army to suppress the uprising against totalitarian rule from Beijing.

Although Beijing claims that Tibet has been part of China since the 13th century, the Tibetans in fact enjoyed the freedom granted by isolation. It was not until 1950 that China forcibly annexed Tibet. Since then the state on the roof of the world has been in rebellion. Chinese efforts to wipe out Tibetan religion and culture have failed, despite the ferocity of the occupation. While China, and Tibet, remained closed to the outside world, the Chinese communists could, and did, apply genocidal policies to discourage normal population growth among the Tibetans, while encouraging Chinese to settle in the area.

Today, if Deng's agenda of economic reform and modernization is to be successful, the Chinese authorities must grant the Tibetans self determination. The Dalai Lama has offered to recognize China's right to decide foreign policy and security matters. In return, Beijing could offer Tibet some sort of "one country, two systems" arrangement similar to plans for Hong Kong.

It is not merely a question of telling the communist rulers in Beijing that the democratic nations will not work with them if Tibet continues to be a jail. They must also be made to understand that China itself will not work unless a degree of autonomy is granted to those of its people who are not ethnic Chinese.

DESERET NEWS

Salt Lake City, UT, March 11, 1989

Thirty years after crushing a bloody Tibetan uprising, the government of China has resorted to force once more to secure its rule on this isolated region. But world voices protesting this brutal suppression are curiously absent.

Despite pleas by Tibetans to foreigners, "Tell the world . . . help us, please," there is unlikely to be any help. Foreigners were promptly evacuated from Tibet by the Chinese.

Hundreds of Tibetans took to the streets of the capital city of Lhasa last week demanding Tibetan independence. Although police chose not to intervene the first day, blood was subsequently spilled as police fired automatic rifles at demonstrators — killing at least a dozen and injuring more than a hundred others.

Martial law was subsequently imposed. Soldiers flooded the city as part of a massive crackdown with orders to take "any measures necessary to restore order."

These latest developments have the Chinese in a quandary. Although China eased controls on Tibet in the 1980s, allowing a few monasteries to re-emerge and recently agreeing to discuss anything short of independence, the flames of freedom continue to burn brightly in the Himalayas.

But the Chinese continue to resist any efforts to undermine their control of the region, claiming Tibet has been part of China for centuries — despite the extreme cultural differences.

Beijing, however, suffered a recent setback in its efforts to quell the Tibetan independence movement with the death of the Panchen Lama — Tibet's second-holiest religious figure.

Western diplomats say the Panchen Lama's death has left a power vacuum among top leadership assigned to safeguard China's Tibetan interests. It has also strengthened the political position of the exiled Dalai Lama — the holiest figure in Tibetan Buddhism and former political leader of the region. His flight to India to avoid an alleged Chinese kidnapping plot 30 years ago led to the first Tibetan uprising.

The Dalai Lama has issued repeated appeals to world leaders to pressure the Chinese to halt their oppression, but so far his requests have fallen on deaf ears.

Unfortunately, perhaps the best chance for a solution in Tibet — the Dalai Lama and Beijing have agreed in principle to hold talks — is on indefinite hold as the two sides cannot agree on who the participants should be.

However to think that simply gathering people around a negotiating table will resolve the Tibetan situation is to forget the past 30 years. The real problem in Tibet runs as deep as the people's hunger for independence.

The Register

San Francisco, CA, March 12, 1989

The Communist Chinese continue to kill Tibetans working to gain independence for their mountainous land. Protests and rioting last week have led to the deaths of at least 30 Tibetans, and some reports put the toll as high as 60. The deaths are the most since the bloody protests of 1959.

A Tibetan woman said by phone to the Associated Press correspondent in Beijing, "Soldiers are all over the place and they're grabbing everyone." She said the roundups involved "many people. It is many more than when the foreigners were here. I can't speak to you; we are all afraid." Communist authorities have ordered foreigners out of the country.

Things probably will get even worse. Hu Jintao, the Tibetan Communist Party boss imposed by the Communist regime in Beijing, told occupation police who had been injured: "The party and the government thank you for not fearing sacrifice or hardship to complete your tasks. You must maintain vigilance against separatists now that martial law has been declared, and you must take even sterner measures against those who stubbornly resist."

Previous "stern" measures included firing into crowds of protesters. The Dalai Lama, Tibet's religous and political leader now living in exile in India, said Thursday he feared the Chinese Communists might turn Lhasa into a slaughterhouse. He praised his countrymen for working for independence.

Mass murder would not be a new experience for Tibetans. After the Chinese Communists annexed the country in the early 1950s, they slaughtered tens of thousands of people, and shut down and demolished almost all the country's Buddhist monasteries. It was an act of cultural barbarity ruthless even for this century of totalitarian destruction and mass murder.

In preparation for the expected new oppression, the Chinese Communists continue expelling foreigners from Tibet. Like Stalin, Hitler, and Mao before them, they don't want witnesses to genocide. And pictures of blood flowing in the streets wouldn't help the good PR image Beijing is trying to portray of the "new" People's Republic of China. Said the Dalai Lama: "Now no foreigners. That means no witnesses, so the Chinese now feel completely free to do whatever they want."

During his visit to Communist China last month, President Bush encouraged new ties with the Beijing regime. He should use that new relationship to insist that Beijing stop violating Tibetans' human rights, and give the people independence. He should tell Beijing that the eyes of the world are watching, and that any oppression will become known in the end, even if all foreigners are expelled. The Communist slaughter and repression of the 1950s and 1960s is now well known, despite the absence of westerners in Tibet at the time.

An American from New Orleans who was recently expelled from Tibet said: "People begged us repeatedly over the last few days — 'Tell the world, help us, please'."

St. Petersburg Times

St. Petersburg, FL, March 10, 1989

Imagine the legitimate outrage that the U.S. government would publicly express if South African troops were to begin shooting at Archbishop Desmond Tutu and other unarmed clerics staging a protest against apartheid, or if Soviet forces were to open fire on Christian, Jewish and Moslem religious leaders peacefully demanding full freedom of worship throughout the Soviet Union. Such acts of brazen brutality clearly would have drastic effects on the nature of American relations with the offending governments.

Now try to imagine what possible justification the Bush administration can claim for its feeble response to the Chinese government's decision to allow its occupation police and security forces to massacre Tibetan monks, nuns and other unarmed demonstrators opposing the continued Chinese repression of their homeland.

The State Department belatedly managed to "deplore" the violence, but the official U.S. response went to considerable linguistic contortions to avoid apportioning blame for the dozens of deaths and injuries. Is the Bush administration so concerned with the Chinese government's delicate sensibilities that it feels the need to imply that the spiritual leaders of Tibet must share responsibility for the violence directed against them by the agents of their military conquerors?

After President Bush became aware of the broad criticism of his public failure to broach the subject of human rights during his brief trip to China last month, he suddenly remembered that he and other members of his traveling party had raised the issue during private conversations with Chinese leaders. If his revised version of events is accurate, his private criticism of Chinese human-rights abuses was about as persuasive as his private criticism of the plan to sell arms to Iran. Less than a week after Mr. Bush's visit, China launched the most brutal campaign against Tibetan dissidents in 30 years. The timing of the imposition of martial law in Tibet, like the detention of dissident Fang Lizhi during the president's visit to Peking, amounts to a direct affront to the government of the United States.

China's leaders have come to believe, with good reason, that the United States is so eager to improve and expand U.S.-Chinese relations that it will overlook blatant acts of violence and irresponsibility that would never be tolerated on the part of other presumably civilized nations. Until told otherwise in the most forceful possible terms, China will assume that it can act with impunity to use whatever force is necessary to maintain its four decades of illegitimate control over Tibet.

In its failure to hold China accountable for its own human-rights abuses and its military support of other terrorist states, the United States and other world powers are allowing China to claim ever greater international influence without committing itself to the responsible conduct that goes with that enhanced status. Each passing day of silence and inaction makes the eventual day of reckoning between the United States and China that much more delicate and dangerous.

Dalai Lama Announced as Nobel Peace Prize Winner

The 1989 Nobel prizes were announced in Stockholm, Sweden and Oslo, Norway in October. The Norweigian Nobel Committee announced the winner of the Nobel Peace Prize Oct. 5, 1989.

The Dalai Lama, the exiled religious and political leader of Tibet, received the peace prize for his efforts to free his homeland from Chinese rule using nonviolent means.

The 54-year-old Tibetan leader, whose given name was Tenzin Gyatso, had become enthroned in 1940, at age five, as the 14th Dalai Lama – the spiritual reincarnation of Buddha and political leader of Tibet.

In 1950, however, China had invaded Tibet, and seized power from the Dalai Lama. He attempted to mediate between the Chinese government and the Tibetans, but increasing Chinese repression sparked an unsuccessful revolt in 1959. The failure of the revolt led him and 100,000 other Tibetans to flee to India, where they received asylum.

Since that time, the Dalai Lama had settled in the town of Dharmsala in the Himalayas, where he continued to call for an end to Chinese control over Tibet and to advocate nonviolent protest.

The peace prize award to the Dalai Lama sparked controversy after Chinese leaders Oct. 6 accused the Nobel committee of "interference in China's internal affairs."

"Tibet's affairs are wholly and purely China's own business," said Wang Guisheng, a counselor to the Chinese embassy in Oslo. "The Dalai Lama is not simply a religious leader but also a political figure...who aims to divide the mother country and undermine political unity."

The timing of the award was widely regarded as politically significant. Although the Dalai Lama had been a top Nobel contender for several years, the prize was awarded five months after the violent suppression of pro-democracy student demonstrations in China, as well as the crushing of independence protests in Tibet.

The San Diego Union

San Diego, CA, October 9, 1989

After receiving the world's highest tribute as a promoter of peace, the Dalai Lama downplayed his contribution and reminded the world: "I am a simple Buddhist monk — no more, no less."

For a man renowned for compassion, gentleness, wisdom and honesty, it was no surprise that Tibet's exiled religious and political leader would acknowledge the Nobel Peace Prize with such humility. Yet he is clearly much more than a simple Buddhist monk.

He was born to a peasant family about the time the 13th Dalai Lama died. At age 3, the precocious youngster was singled out by religious leaders when he spied prayer beads that had belonged to the late Dalai Lama and claimed them as his own. A year later he was brought to the capital of Lhasa to begin the rigorous religious training that would prepare him to lead his people spiritually and politically.

Ever since the Chinese invaded Tibet in 1950, the Dalai Lama has been waging a nonviolent campaign to end China's domination of his homeland. He and a group of 100,000 faithful followers fled to Dharmsala, India, in 1959 after attacks on monks and monastaries became increasingly brutal and an uprising was crushed by the Chinese.

While Tibetan exiles began a three-day celebration marking the Nobel award, Chinese leaders saw it as a slap in the face. They are right to take it as a searing indictment of China's repressive occupation of Tibet.

The Dalai Lama had been nominated for the prize in three previous years; but the continuing crackdown in China, coupled with the quashing of pro-independence demonstrations in Tibet earlier this year, made the religious leader a very attractive candidate among this year's 101 nominees. While the Norwegian Nobel Committee asserts the award is not political, its focus in recent years has

been on human rights. The award is, in fact, as much a denunciation of China's repressive actions as it is a recognition of the Dalai Lama's heroic pacifism.

Until the bloodbath in Beijing, the Dalai Lama had held indirect talks with the Chinese. Just 16 months ago he refused an offer to return to Tibet in exchange for renouncing independence. He is holding out for a middle solution — allowing Chinese troops to remain if a self-governing democratic body is established. Without this step toward freedom, his three decades in exile will continue.

Always a proponent of solving conflict through "understanding not fighting," the Dalai Lama has repeatedly resisted pleas by his followers to take a more violent path, insisting that patience and tolerance are necessary. For Tibetans, the Nobel Peace Prize is a moral victory and a signal that the world has not forgotten their long struggle for freedom.

The LeaderPost

Regina, Sask., October 6, 1989

By awarding its 1989 peace prize to the Dalai Lama, the Norwegian Nobel Committee appears to have found a way to extend a congratulatory hand to the Tibetan spiritual leader while landing a diplomatic slap on the Chinese.

Exiled for 30 years from his native Tibet as a result of the country's takeover by Chinese communists in 1959, the Buddhist god-king persistently has sought non-violent means of ending the Chinese occupation in his homeland.

The Tiananmen Square massacre in June was preceded earlier this year by Beijing imposing martial law in Tibet in the wake of rioting against the Chinese presence.

Questioned whether the award could be seen as encouraging the pro-democracy movement in China, Nobel committee chairman Egil Aarvik said, "The committee would not have anything against them interpreting it like that." And he added: "If I was a Chinese student, I would be fully in support of the decision."

In Norway itself, the award also is seen as somewhat of a rebuke of Norwegian officials who last year refused to meet with the Dalai Lama, fearing such a meeting would annoy the Chinese.

Meanwhile, the Chinese have reacted to the award by calling the Dalai Lama a political figure intent on "splitting the fatherland".

The award is a fitting recognition of the Tibetan leader's continuing efforts on behalf of his land and his people. If the Nobel prize causes discomfort to the powers that be in Beijing, so much the better.

The Evening Gazette

Worcester, MA, October 11, 1989

The 1989 Nobel Peace Prize, awarded to the exiled Dalai Lama of Tibet, recognizes his powerful embodiment of moral force and uncompromising ideals against violent oppression by the Chinese.

Indirectly, the prize also is a condemnation of China's brutal crackdown on dissent that began with the massacre of students in Beijing's Tiananmen Square. The message was not lost on the Chinese leadership, who called the award an insult and interference in their internal affairs.

The Dalai Lama, revered by the faithful as the reincarnated God-king of Tibet, has earned his people's adulation and the world's respect for his enduring, non-violent effort to liberate Tibet from Chinese rule imposed violently in 1950.

The Dalai Lama fled Tibet after an unsuccessful uprising in 1959, taking thousands of his people with him. In India, he established Tibetan schools and industries and maintained a national identity outside the physical boundaries of his homeland.

Although he might have returned to a comfortable life — under terms set by the Chinese — this ruler-in-exile has refused steadfastly to give in.

Directing such a peaceful resistance movement from afar seems odd to some in the West. Yet, the actions are fitting for the spiritual leader of the people of this Buddhist nation.

The Dalai Lama stands among excellent company in non-violent opposition to oppression. Mohandas K. Gandhi, India's great leader, showed the British that passive resistance could overcome any force. Martin Luther King led American blacks in civil disobedience during sit-ins and marches against unjust segregation laws.

The Dalai Lama *is* Tibet. The Chinese have long oppressed the fiercely independent people under their control, but so long as the Dalai Lama remains free, independent and morally strong, hope remains alive for this ancient land — and for oppressed people everywhere.

The Register-Guard

Eugene, OR, October 7, 1989

Several recent Nobel Peace Prizes have been awarded in a fashion that seems calculated to create discomfort among abusers of power. Thus, Poland's military authorities were put on the spot when Solidarity leader Lech Walesa won the prize in 1983, and South Africa's apartheid regime was embarrassed when the award went to then-Bishop Desmond Tutu a year later. Now it's China's turn: The Norwegian Nobel Committee has given the 1989 prize to the Dalai Lama of Tibet.

The choice was somewhat surprising — a pair of Czech dissidents had been considered the leading candidates. But the Dalai Lama is a deserving recipient, and the timing could not have been better. The world needs to be reminded of Tibet's long effort to gain cultural and political autonomy, which has reached an important juncture in recent months. And after the events of last June, China's leaders deserve the slap that comes when the coveted prize goes to an opposition figure.

China has controlled Tibet for most of its history, but only since 1950 have the Chinese rulers attempted to uproot Tibet's ancient indigenous culture. The Dalai Lama has played an important part in Tibet's efforts to resist forcible integration with Chinese society. He refused China's request for assistance in suppressing tribal revolts in 1959 and soon after fled to exile in India. Since then he has acted as head of a government-in-exile as well as leader of the most important Tibetan Buddhist sect.

The Nobel committee praised the Dalai Lama's non-violent approach to dealings with the Chinese. His pacifism, however, is born of pragmatism. "Non-violence is not a question of holiness," The New York Times quotes him as saying. With a billion Chinese and only 6 million Tibetans, non-violence "is a question of reality."

Yet the Dalai Lama will not yield on vital issues. Last year China invited him to return from exile, provided that he renounce the goal of independence. He refused. Later he said he would accept Chinese control of Tibet's defense and foreign policy, but insisted on Tibetan self-government. China's current leadership is not inclined to accept such a compromise.

The Dalai Lama's position is entirely reasonable and deserves world support. Granting internal self-government to Tibet would cost China nothing, either economically or in terms of security. Indeed, it would relieve China of the cost of policing a resentful people and would improve the government's battered international image.

The Dalai Lama's Nobel Peace Prize should focus attention on the situation in Tibet, resulting in greater pressure for a resolution to this long-neglected problem. As the spiritual and temporal leader of his people, the Dalai Lama's prize will thus benefit all of Tibet.

Los Angeles Times

Los Angeles, CA, October 6, 1989

Since it was first awarded 88 years ago, the Nobel Peace Prize has sometimes gone to honor measurable contributions to achieving or preserving peace, while at other times its purpose has been to emphasize a political or moral point. This year's award to the exiled spiritual leader of Tibet, the Dalai Lama, most reflects the latter aim. The Dalai Lama, who fled Tibet 30 years ago after a failed popular revolt against China's occupying army, was cited for advocating "peaceful solutions based upon tolerance and mutual respect in order to preserve the historical and cultural heritage of his people." Whether this commitment to nonviolence would have won such generous recognition now had it not been for last June's bloody events in Beijing's Tian An Men Square is a fair question.

Certainly the Chinese government sees the award as implicit criticism of its behavior, as do some Tibetans close to the Dalai Lama. In that regard this year's award follows a creditable precedent. It does not detract from the considerable accomplishments of such recent Peace Prize winners as Bishop Desmond Tutu of South Africa, Lech Walesa of Poland, or Andrei Sakharov of the Soviet Union to note that the activities for which they were honored had more to do with their courageous resistance to oppression than with any concrete advancement of the cause of peace.

The award to the Dalai Lama should, at a minimum, refocus international attention on the plight of Tibet, which enjoyed less than 40 years of independence before it was invaded and occupied by China in 1950, and which has been under martial law since anti-Chinese demonstrations there earlier this year. China says that what happens in Tibet is its internal affair and not the rest of the world's business. The Nobel Peace Prize committee is saying, in effect—and not for the first time—that when human rights are abused and freedom is denied the world has a moral responsibility to pay attention. The Peace Prize is an acceptable vehicle for furthering that aim.

Chicago Tribune

Chicago, IL, October 9, 1989

The ferocious crackdown on the student democracy movement in June was a reminder, for a world that had forgotten, of the fundamental brutality of Chinese communism. Tibetans never needed reminding. They suffered their own Tiananmen Square in 1950, when the tiny country was invaded and occupied by Mao's army, which has never left.

Throughout that bitter period, Tibetans and others have been inspired by the resolve and patriotism of the Dalai Lama, the country's exiled spiritual leader and symbol of resistance to Chinese rule. Last week his devotion to nonviolence and to Tibet's independence was honored when he was named the winner of the 1989 Nobel Peace Prize. The committee praised his work for "peaceful solutions based upon tolerance and mutual respect in order to preserve the historical and cultural heritage of his people."

The Chinese government responded with characteristic disdain. The Nobel committee's decision, it said, "is interference in China's internal affairs. It has hurt the Chinese people's feelings." It accused the Dalai Lama of trying to "divide the mother country and undermine national unity."

What Beijing stubbornly ignores is that Tibetans regard China as a captor, not a parent. If Tibetan nationalism undermines China's national unity, it is because Tibetans never wanted union with China in the first place. Tibet, an independent country for decades before the invasion, is to the Chinese communist regime what the Baltic republics are to the Kremlin: the victim of unprovoked aggression.

The Dalai Lama, a Buddhist monk who escaped Tibet in 1959 as the Chinese were savagely crushing a popular uprising, has never returned to his country, refusing Beijing's offers to let him back if he abandons his campaign for Tibetan independence.

The day when he will be allowed to return to an independent Tibet may be no closer. But the Dalai Lama's peaceful efforts to liberate his country from an alien tyranny deserve the world's admiration and help.

The Washington Post

Washington, DC, October 12, 1989

F. W. DE KLERK, South Africa's new president, continues his experimental ways. Fresh from permitting open anti-apartheid protests, he has stepped up the pace of releasing political prisoners. The latest eight include Walter Sisulu and other African National Congress figures convicted of treason and sent up for life in 1964. Their release leaves confined, among long-term prisoners, only senior ANC leader Nelson Mandela. Unlike some of those earlier released, the eight are not barred from taking part in the still tightly limited political activity permitted to blacks. By the way they act and by the way the public responds to them, the government will determine whether to let Mr. Mandela go. Mr. de Klerk wants progress in bringing blacks into negotiations on a new racial dispensation, but peaceful progress. He wants peace not as the result of government guns but as the result of black commitment to a shared future.

The first impact of the freeing of the Sisulu group may be in the realm of black politics. Mr. Sisulu, 77, represents an older generation revered in legend but unpracticed in contemporary political conditions. Younger and more activist and radical leaders have come along, reflecting the frustrations of an additional quarter-century of apartheid. Tribal and class divisions add to the mix. The strategy of apartheid has been to divide blacks from each other, the better to avoid facing their common political demands. Mr. de Klerk is testing a strategy built more on black unity, the better to have an interlocutor who can speak to and for his community. But blacks will have to generate their own unity.

As inadequate as leading South African blacks yet find Mr. de Klerk's initiatives, many South African whites find them imprudent verging on reckless. He is showing, however, a firm hand. It is widely observed that one of his purposes is to head off a threat of further economic sanctions—a purpose he hesitates to acknowledge lest pro-sanctions forces raise the ante. Whatever the purpose, what he is doing in starting to allow political expression to the black majority is a striking departure. It leaves spokesmen of the two races far apart on eventual goals: the African National Congress seeks a transfer of power to the black majority, the de Klerk government speaks of providing blacks representation in their own governance. In the very composing of an authentic black voice, however, and in the shaping of a white response lie possibilities for reconciliation that South Africa has not known.

The Courier-Journal

Louisville, KY, October 8, 1989

THE Nobel Peace Prize honors men and women who have worked effectively for international harmony. But the decision by a Norwegian committee often conveys a political message, sometimes to the discomfiture of rulers and governments. Recently, the committee has shown an appropriate bias in favor of nominees who confound oppressors and promote human rights.

The unexpected choice of the Dalai Lama, who calls himself a "simple Buddhist Monk" and is believed by his followers to be a reincarnation of the Lord of Infinite Compassion, is very much in that tradition. His tireless advocacy of harmony among people and with nature makes him a worthy addition to a list that includes Dr. Martin Luther King Jr., Andrei Sakharov and the Rev. Desmond Tutu.

The announcement in Oslo stirred no joy in Beijing, which has ruled Tibet, the Dalai Lama's former homeland, since its seizure by Communist forces in 1950. The award draws world attention not only to the extinction of Tibetan independence, but also to the trampling of human rights in China after the butchery at Tiananmen Square. "It has hurt the Chinese people's feelings," grumped a government spokesman.

The exiled Tibetan leader preaches a "middle way" to restoring Tibet's nationhood that is both nonviolent and pragmatic. While reminding followers who are eager to engage the Chinese in guerrilla combat that they are hopelessly outnumbered, he urges Beijing to accept an arrangement that allows Tibet to be a "self-governing political entity," but subject to China's foreign policy decisions.

The Dalai Lama's approach requires patience, which he has in abundance, along with a mischievous sense of humor. But his nonviolent perseverance shames Tibet's oppressors in a way armed combat never can. International tensions that seemed intractable have recently, and surprisingly, become susceptible to peaceful resolution. Along with the right circumstances and a bit of luck, the attention that comes with the prize may help speed his way back to Lhasa.

The Honolulu Advertiser

Honolulu, HI, October 6, 1989

Awarding the 1989 Nobel Peace Prize to the Dalai Lama sends a calculated message to the Chinese.

Although it's hoped the award may eventually give the Dalai Lama greater bargaining power to gain autonomy for Tibet, for now the Chinese government is predictably insulted and angry.

Since he fled Tibet in disguise during a failed uprising against China 30 years ago, the Dalai Lama has lived in India. From there he travels the world, calling for freedom for the 6 million people to whom he was both political and religious leader.

Fifteen months ago, he dropped demands for full independence, publicly proposing that China continue to control Tibet's defense and foreign policy in exchange for greater Tibetan autonomy.

Beijing has rejected even that more moderate plan. The official line is that, in order to modernize what all agree is a poor and backward country, it was necessary to attack feudal religious customs and the theocracy that enforced them.

But Tibetans say that beyond persecuting their religion, Beijing is importing Han Chinese to destroy the distinctive Tibetan people and culture by intermarriage and immigration.

Though he preaches non-violence, the Dalai Lama's followers have had bloody clashes with Chinese authorities in the last two years. Lhasa remains under martial law and travel by foreign reporters to Tibet is forbidden.

The Dalai Lama has been nominated for the peace prize before, but he wins this year in the aftermath of the Chinese government's brutal suppression of the pro-democracy movement in Tiananmen Square and elsewhere last June.

The Norwegian Nobel committee is sending a clear message of support to that movement, just as in the past prizes have encouraged other human rights activists and supported peace efforts.

Whether the prize will have a positive political effect, it's too early to tell. But it serves notice that the world is concerned about human and political rights in China, and watching its dealings with Tibet, Hong Kong, Taiwan and its own people.

The Burlington Free Press

Burlington, VT, October 9, 1989

Say "Tibet," and many Westerners think not of the Dalai Lama, this year's winner of the Nobel Peace Prize, but of Chinese soldiers killing monks.

The Dalai Lama, a spiritual leader in exile from his people, stands not for international peace, but for non-violent struggle against oppression.

The Chinese swallowed Tibet in 1950. A million Tibetans are believed to have died of starvation during forced collectivization in the 1960s. The Chinese have destroyed thousands of Buddhist monasteries, killed dissidents and, through immigration, turned Tibetans into a minority in their own country.

Beijing instantly recognized the peace prize as the indictment it is. The prize, complained a Chinese diplomat in Norway, is "interference in China's internal affairs. ... Tibet's affairs are wholly and purely China's own business."

So the Polish government might have responded to Lech Walesa's peace prize in 1983 and the apartheid government of South Africa to Bishop Desmond Tutu's prize in 1984.

In an era of relative global harmony, the Nobel committee uses the award as a moral force, focusing world attention on violations of human rights. The Dalai Lama could have been a candidate for the peace prize any time during the past 30 years. It was surely no coincidence that his selection came just four months after the massacre of pro-democracy students in Tianamen Square.

By singling out a victim of Beijing's terror, the Nobel committee says, again, that persecution and oppression can never be "wholly and purely" the internal business of any country.

The Salt Lake Tribune

Salt Lake City, UT, October 13, 1989

British Prime Minister Margaret Thatcher calls the South African government's release of eight leading black political prisoners, most notably Walter Sisulu, a "major step in the right direction." She sees the release of Sisulu, the former secretary-general of the African National Congress who was sentenced in 1964 to life imprisonment for plotting to topple the white minority, and the other seven as precursory to the release of Nelson Mandela, the ANC leader who went to prison with Sisulu.

More cynical, but more realistic, is the view that South African President F W de Klerk's action came in anticipation of the 48-nation British Commonwealth meeting that begins Oct. 18 in Malaysia.

Mrs Thatcher, after all, stands virtually alone among the Commonwealth leaders in her steadfast refusal to impose sanctions against South Africa as a means to force an end to apartheid.

These prisoner releases can reasonably be regarded as Pretoria's ploy to strengthen the resolve of the prime minister. Continued absence of British sanctions would be a boon to South Africa, which has been economically trampled by the sanctions of other countries, including the United States.

Cynicism aside, the release of Sisulu and the other seven has its positive aspects, including indications that the new South African leadership is moving toward a more conciliatory beckoning to its black constituency.

It probably brought one step closer official recognition of the ANC, the black guerrilla organization that has been banned since Mandela, Sisulu and their cohorts went to prison.

Strengthening this supposition are reports that Mandela, although still a prisoner residing in a bungalow at a prison farm in the wine-growing region of Paarl near Cape Town, played an active role in negotiating the details of his comrades' liberation.

If so, and presently there is no overwhelming reason to question the reports, the de Klerk government is demonstrating far more political pragmatism than did its predecessor, which promised much but delivered little.

Such a sensible modification of attitude can't help but have a quieting effect on black agitation. Granted, it doesn't lessen the frightful restrictions under which South Africa's blacks live, conditions which the eight released prisoners must also endure outside of prison.

This is the point made by the Rev. Allan Boesak, president of the World Alliance of Reformed Churches, when he asks, "What is the use of releasing them [the prisoners] when we still have a state of emergency and when our organizations are still banned?"

Still, despite all the honest but negative interpretations that can be placed on the release of Sisulu and the others, the fact remains they were released. Nelson Mandela had a significant role in arranging their release and the de Klerk regime is moving progressively with an alacrity never witnessed during the tenure of former President P.W. Botha.

These optimistic elements have to be viewed, for the moment anyway, as presaging a loosening of the social, political and economic shackles repressively clamped on South Africa's 25 million black citizens by the country's five million whites. That is probably how — in bits and pieces — progress will come to South Africa.

Edmonton Journal

Edmonton, Alta., October 8, 1989

As many as a million people may have been killed in Tibet in the last 14 years; a genocide in a population of six million.

Of the monasteries that serve as its leading scholastic, religious and cultural institutions, some six thousand have been destroyed.

For all intents and purposes, the world turns a blind eye to Tibet, and if it cares at all, shrugs and says it is China's internal affair.

Yet Tibet is perhaps the saddest of the world's nearly lost causes: a Buddhist country rooted in the spiritual values of the pre-industrial age, once a kingdom of God, swallowed up by Mao Tse-tung's armies in 1950. Unlike other remote countries oppressed by an alien invader, Tibet has no outspoken defenders in the world at large.

That's why it's particularly welcome that the 1989 Nobel Prize for Peace has gone to Tenzin Gyatso, the 14th Dalai Lama of Tibet and spiritual leader of Tibetan Buddhists.

The award may do little, in practical terms, to improve the life of the Tibetan people. But it affirms the right of Tibetans to a life of justice and dignity, and it will have considerable value in drawing the world's attention to the systematic destruction of an old and important culture.

Ideally, the Nobel Prize would prod democratic countries to recognize the legitimate aspirations of Tibetans, and to put diplomatic pressure on China to end the mass repression.

But that ideal is lacking. The Western world has long accepted Chinese domination of Tibet. Canada does not question China's territorial control. The one friend Tibet had for years was India, the home in exile to the Dalai Lama and some of his followers. But that trust has been betrayed by Indian Prime Minister Rajiv Gandhi: India wanted to improve relations with China, and Gandhi declared Tibet's aspirations as an internal Chinese concern.

Canada and India are full of self-congratulatory rhetoric at every Commonwealth meeting, as they hail each other's efforts to bring South Africa to sanity. But when it comes to Tibet, they are strangely silent — all the more strange because the Chinese destruction of Tibetan civilization and culture is incredibly thorough.

Over the years, Tibetans have been moved from productive agricultural land to marginal land in the foothills and mountains; they have been forced to change the crops they grow. Their holy places and repositories of culture have been destroyed. The country's medieval architecture is being supplanted by modern housing built for the Han Chinese colonizers. Tibet is cut off from the world as far as possible.

If the Nobel Prize does nothing more than stir the world's conscience, it will have been of help.

There is a more subtle message in the award: it is a protest against the repression practised by the current Chinese regime in the wake of the failed democracy movement. It is a reminder that the brutality of China is visited not just upon Tibet, but upon its own citizens.

The citation of the Nobel Prize, hailing the Dalai Lama's advocacy of non-violence and peace in the face of terror, should be required reading for every apologist who speaks of the importance of keeping good relations with the Chinese government.

INDEX

G

GENSCHER, Hans-Dietrich
German unification momentum
88–91
GEORGIA (Georgian Soviet Socialist Republic)
Gorbachev presidential win 8–11
National unrest 50–53
GERASIMOV, Anatoly
1989 Soviet elections 4–7
GERASIMOV, Gennadi I.
1989 Soviet elections 4–7
GERLACH, Manfred
East German Communist Party shakeup 84–87
GERMAN Democratic Republic (East)
Austria-Hungary border fence removal 60–63
Berlin Wall opening 76–83
Communist Party shakeup 84–87
Election results 92–97
Honecker ouster 72–75
Mass exodus 64–71
Unification momentum 88–91
GERMAN Social Union (DSU)
Election results 92–97
GERMANY, Federal Republic of (West)
Berlin Wall opening 76–83
China nationwide crackdown 176–179
East German elections 92–97
East German leader's ouster 72–75
Unification momentum 88–91
GORBACHEV, Mikhail Sergeyevich (Soviet Communist Party general secretary)
   Baltic Republics
Hitler-Stalin pact revelations 30–33
Lithuania confrontation 38–41
Lithuania CP break 34–37
Lithuania independence declaration 42–45
Lithuania military occupation 46–49
   China
Bush envoys secret visit 182–185
Visit amid protests 156–159
   Eastern Europe
Bush European troop cutback proposal 142–145
Bush visit 116–119

German unification momentum 88–91
   Government
CP monopoly revocation 16–19
CP one-party rule disavowal 20–25
Presidential win 8–11
1989 Soviet elections 4–7
   Labor & Employment
Coal miners strike 26–29
   Transcaucasian Republics
Azerbaijan ethnic unrest 54–57
GREAT Britain & Northern Ireland, United Kingdom of (UK)
Bush European troop cutback proposal 142–145
China nationwide crackdown 176–179
GREECE
Bush European troop cutback proposal 142–145
GYATSO, Tenzin—*See DALAI Lama*
GYSI, Gregor (East German head of state)
Communist Party shakeup 84–87

H

HAVEL, Vaclav
Czechoslovakia noncommunist government 124–127
Czechoslovakia pro-democracy movement 120–123
HITLER, Adolf (1889-1945)
East German elections 92–97
1939 Stalin Baltic pact revelations 30–33
HONECKER, Erich (East German head of state; ousted Oct. 18, 1989)
Berlin Wall opening 76–83
Communist Party shakeup 84–87
Ouster 72–75
HUMAN Rights
China martial law declaration 160–163
Czechoslovakia noncommunist government 124–127
Czechoslovakia pro-democracy movement 120–123
Dalai Lama Nobel Peace Prize 200–203
Hungary constitutional amendments 128–131
Polish parliamentary election results 102–107

Romania UN probe 132–135
HUNGARY (Hungarian People's Republic)
Austria border fence removal 60–63
Bush East Europe visit 116–119
Constitutional amendments 128–131
HU Qili
China nationwide crackdown 176–179
HUSAK, Gustav (Czechoslovak president; resigned Dec. 10, 1989)
Noncommunist government 124–127
HU Yaobang (1916-89)
Pro-democracy protests 148–155

I

IMMIGRATION & Refugees
Austria-Hungary border fence removal 60–63
Berlin Wall opening 76–83
East German mass exodus 64–71
INDEPENDENCE Movements
Gorbachev Lithuanian confrontation 38–41
1939 Hitler-Stalin Baltic pact revelations 30–33
Lithuanian CP break 34–37
Lithuanian declaration 42–45
Soviet Georgia unrest 50–53
Soviet Lithuanian troop occupation 46–49
INDIA, Republic of
Dalai Lama Nobel Peace Prize 200–203
ISLAM
Azerbaijan ethnic unrest 54–57
Soviet Georgia unrest 50–53
ITALY
Bush European troop cutback proposal 142–145

J

JAKES, Milos (Czechoslovak Communist Party general secretary; resigned Nov. 24, 1989)
Pro-democracy movement 120–123

German unification momentum
88–91

P

PATIASHVILI, Dzhumber
Soviet Georgia unrest 50–53

PELOSI, Rep. Nancy (D, Calif.)
Bush China student veto victory
190–193

PERESTROIKA (restructuring)
Gorbachev presidential win 8–11
Soviet coal miners strike 26–29
Soviet CP monopoly revocation
16–19

POLAND (Polish People's Republic)
Bush East Europe visit 116–119
East German mass exodus 64–71
Jaruzelski presidential election
108–111
Noncommunist government
112–115
Parliamentary election results
102–107
Political conciliation 98–101

POLITICS
China
Bush envoys secret visit 182–185
Bush student veto victory 190–193
Martial law declaration 160–163
Nationwide arrests, crackdown
176–179
Eastern Europe
Czechoslovakia pro-democracy
movement 120–123
East German elections 92–97
East Germany Communist Party
shakeup 84–87
German unification momentum
88–91
Hungarian constitutional
amendments 128–131
Polish noncommunist
government 112–115
Polish parliamentary election
results 102–107
Polish political conciliation
98–101
Polish presidential election
108–111
Romania challenge 132–135
Romanian revolution/Ceausescu
execution 136–141
USSR
CP monopoly revocation 16–19
CP one-party rule disavowal
20–25
1989 elections 4–7

Gorbachev Lithuanian
confrontation 38–41
Gorbachev presidential win 8–11
Lithuanian CP break 34–37
Lithuanian independence
declaration 42–45

POLLUTION—*See
ENVIRONMENT & Pollution*

POPOV, Gavril K.
Gorbachev presidential win 8–11

**PRAVDA (Soviet Communist
Party newspaper)**
Communist Party one-party rule
disavowal 20–25
1989 elections 4–7
Georgia political unrest 50–53
Gorbachev presidential win 8–11
1939 Hitler-Stalin Baltic pact
revelations 30–33

PROKOFYEV, Yuri
1989 Soviet elections 4–7

R

RELIGION—*See also specific
denominations*
Azerbaijan ethnic unrest 54–57
Dalai Lama Nobel Peace Prize
200–203
Polish political conciliation
98–101
Soviet Georgia unrest 50–53
Tibetan violence 200–203

ROMAN Catholic Church
Polish political conciliation
98–101

**ROMANIA, Socialist Republic
of**
Austria-Hungary border fence
removal 60–63
Bush European troop cutback
proposal 142–145
Revolution/Ceausescu execution
132–141

RUSSIA—*See UNION of Soviet
Socialist Republics*

RYZHKOV, Nikolai I.
Gorbachev presidential win 8–11

S

SAIKIN, Valery
1989 Soviet elections 4–7

SCOWCROFT, Brent
Bush envoys secret China visit
182–185

**SECESSIONIST
Movements**—*See
INDEPENDENCE Movements*

SHANGHAI, China
China nationwide crackdown
176–179

**SHEVARDNADZE, Eduard
Amvrosiyevich**
Gorbachev China visit amid
protests 156–159
Soviet Georgia unrest 50–53

SIBERIA
Soviet coal miners strike 26–29

**SOCIAL Democratic Party (SPD)
(East/West Germany)**
East German election results
92–97
German unification momentum
88–91

**SOCIALIST Unity Party (East
Germany)**
Communist Party shakeup 84–87
Honecker ouster 72–75

**SOCIALIST Worker Party
(Hungary)**
Constitutional amendments
128–131

**SOLARZ, Rep. Stephen J. (D,
N.Y.)**
Bush China student veto victory
190–193

**SOLIDARITY (Polish Labor
Movement)**
Bush East Europe visit 116–119
Noncommunist government
112–115
Parliamentary election results
102–107
Polish political conciliation
98–101
Presidential election 108–111

SOLOVYEV, Yuri
1989 Soviet elections 4–7

SOVIET Bloc—*See EASTERN
Europe*

SOVIET Union—*See UNION of
Soviet Socialist Republics*

SPD—*See SOCIAL Democratic
Party*

**STALIN, Joseph (Joseph
Vissarionovich Dzhugashvili)
(1879-1953)**
1939 Hitler Baltic pact revelations
30–33